Visio® 2000 Bible

Visio® 2000 Bible

Mark H. Walker

Hungry Minds™

HUNGRY MINDS, INC.

New York, NY ◆ Cleveland, OH ◆ Indianapolis, IN

Visio® 2000 Bible

Published by
Hungry Minds, Inc.
909 Third Avenue
New York, NY 10022
www.hungryminds.com

Copyright © 2000 Hungry Minds, Inc. All rights reserved. No part of this book, including interior design, cover design, and icons, may be reproduced or transmitted in any form, by any means (electronic, photocopying, recording, or otherwise) without the prior written permission of the publisher.

ISBN: 0-7645-3457-2

Printed in the United States of America

10 9 8 7 6 5 4 3 2

1O/QV/RY/QR/FC

Distributed in the United States by Hungry Minds, Inc.

Distributed by CDG Books Canada Inc. for Canada; by Transworld Publishers Limited in the United Kingdom; by IDG Norge Books for Norway; by IDG Sweden Books for Sweden; by IDG Books Australia Publishing Corporation Pty. Ltd. for Australia and New Zealand; by TransQuest Publishers Pte Ltd. for Singapore, Malaysia, Thailand, Indonesia, and Hong Kong; by Gotop Information Inc. for Taiwan; by ICG Muse, Inc. for Japan; by Intersoft for South Africa; by Eyrolles for France; by International Thomson Publishing for Germany, Austria and Switzerland; by Distribuidora Cuspide for Argentina; by LR International for Brazil; by Galileo Libros for Chile; by Ediciones ZETA S.C.R. Ltda. for Peru; by WS Computer Publishing Corporation, Inc., for the Philippines; by Contemporanea de Ediciones for Venezuela; by Express Computer Distributors for the Caribbean and West Indies; by Micronesia Media Distributor, Inc. for Micronesia; by Chips Computadoras S.A. de C.V. for Mexico; by Editorial Norma de Panama S.A. for Panama; by American Bookshops for Finland.

For general information on Hungry Minds' products and services please contact our Customer Care Department within the U.S. at 800-762-2974, outside the U.S. at 317-572-3993 or fax 317-572-4002.

For sales inquiries and reseller information, including discounts, premium and bulk quantity sales, and foreign-language translations, please contact our Customer Care Department at 800-434-3422, fax 317-572-4002, or write to Hungry Minds, Inc., Attn: Customer Care Department, 10475 Crosspoint Boulevard, Indianapolis, IN 46256.

For information on licensing foreign or domestic rights, please contact our Sub-Rights Customer Care Department at 212-884-5000.

For information on using Hungry Minds' products and services in the classroom or for ordering examination copies, please contact our Educational Sales Department at 800-434-2086 or fax 317-572-4005.

Please contact our Public Relations Department at 212-884-5163 for press review copies or 212-884-5000 for author interviews and other publicity information or fax 212-884-5400.

For authorization to photocopy items for corporate, personal, or educational use, please contact Copyright Clearance Center, 222 Rosewood Drive, Danvers, MA 01923, or fax 978-750-4470.

Library of Congress Cataloging-in-Publication Data

Walker, Mark (Mark H.)
  Visio 2000 Bible/Mark H.Walker.
      p.   cm.
  Includes index.
  ISBN: 0-7645-3457-2 (alk. paper)
  1. Mechanical drawing.2. Visio. I. Title.
T353.W2335   2000
604.2'0285'5369--dc21   00-026772

Hungry Minds˜ is a trademark of Hungry Minds, Inc.

About the Author

Mark H. Walker is a former naval officer and explosive ordnance disposal diver. He has been writing professionally since 1992. During that time he has written hundreds of magazine articles on computer technology, computer gaming, and auto racing for major publications such as *Visio Smart Pages, Autoweek, Alaska Airlines Magazine, Playboy, Computer Games Strategy Plus, Sierra Interaction, Computer Gaming World, The Science Fiction Weekly, Civil War,* and popular Websites such as *Visio's, Gamecenter, The Daily Radar, Incite Games,* and *Gamepower*. Additionally, he has authored 28 books, user manuals, and corporate studies including *How to Use the Internet,* and numerous major gaming guides.

In his spare time he writes military science fiction and modern military adventures. His most recent piece of long fiction — "Total Victory" — will be published in the military adventure anthology *Alternate Wars* later this year.

Mark recently escaped from the hectic city life of San Diego, CA. to rural Virginia. He now lives ten miles from the closest fast food restaurant with his wife Janice, and their three daughters: Denver, Jessica, and Ayron.

Credits

Acquisitions Editor
Laura Moss

Project Editor
Sharon Eames

Technical Editor
Kristen Tod

Copy Editors
Lane Barnholtz
Laura Hester
Ami Knox
Amy Eoff

Project Coordinator
Linda Marousek
Marcos Vergara

Graphics and Production Specialists
Robert Bihlmayer
Jude Levinson
Michael Lewis
Ramses Ramirez
Victor Pérez-Varela
Dina F Quan

Illustrators
Mary Jo Richards
Brian Drumm

Proofreading and Indexing
York Production Services

Cover Design
Evan Deerfield

This book is dedicated to Little Debbie Shortcake Rolls

Preface

Welcome to the *Visio 2000 Bible*, a guide to using the most popular business drawing software in the world today. This book extensively covers Visio 2000, starting with program fundamentals and building on these features with more complex functions and applications. Overall, examples, tips, and walkthroughs are geared to take readers from an introductory level to that of a lower advanced user.

The *Visio 2000 Bible* discusses and demonstrates the software's newest additions, as well as standard features. The latest Visio software series is more dynamic and easier to use than its award-winning predecessors. Visio 2000, for example, features tighter Microsoft Windows and Office integration, more SmartShapes, new ShapeSheet editing features, and a customized toolbar. Such aspects promise to continue revolutionizing the way businesses communicate. This book is designed to help business professionals explore and use Visio 2000's latest innovations, along with basics like stencils and templates.

Visio has demonstrated that visual communication is a critical element in relaying information through today's fast-paced business world. The people who have worked on this IDG guide are committed to that same idea. That's one of the reasons this book presents Visio 2000 in an easy-to-use-and-find format with numerous tables and visual aids. I believe the end result is the most thorough and user-friendly Visio 2000 guide available today on the market. Accordingly, readers can use the book for tutorial sessions or as a reference guide. Step-by-step examples are also presented to help you gain insights and ideas for creating your own projects.

Is this Book for You?

All kinds of Visio 2000 users can benefit from this book. Absolute beginners will find information presented in a straightforward style, less intimidating and more colloquial than those found in most software guides. Intermediate users can apply numerous tips and examples for taking their business drawing skills to more sophisticated levels. Highly advanced users of Visio 5.0 will learn about some of the newest features and applications offered in Visio 2000 — the latest prerequisites for taking over the world!

Time-pressed business people, ranging from IT analysts to advertising consultants, will, no doubt, find the information (and the way it's presented here) quite helpful. Visio 2000 software is an extensive business drawing series that consists of several products (e.g. *Technical*, *Professional*, and *Enterprise*), many that cater to the demands of specific business sectors. Nonetheless, the fundamental basis of these products is *Visio 2000 Standard*. The chief difference among the various editions lies primarily in the types of shapes and templates available, not in features. Accordingly, this book focuses on *Visio 2000 Standard*, while only touching upon the various nuances and applications found in the other 2000 versions.

No matter what your profession, this book will show you how to compose business drawings in a knowledgeable and efficient manner. I think that this guide covers *Visio 2000* in greater detail than any other you can currently buy. I hope you think so, too, finding the information and techniques here helpful for later assimilating your own visual documents with greater ease and efficiency.

Conventions Used in This Book

To make instructions easy to follow and less wordy, certain conventions are employed in the *Visio 2000 Bible*. These are as follows:

✦ I make a distinction between left- and right-clicking the mouse buttons. Clicking the left mouse button is indicated simply by the word "click." If you must click on the right mouse button, I tell you instead to "right-click."

✦ Throughout the book, I use the word "select" or "choose" in reference to implementing a menu command or toolbar buttons. You can select menu commands by using the keyboard or clicking the left mouse button. However, you can only access toolbar buttons by using your mouse.

✦ Arrow symbols, ⇨ , are inserted between a menu selection process. For instance, to print a document from the menu bar, you must select Print from the File drop-down menu. File ⇨ Print, thus, indicates the same selection process in a more simple and direct manner.

✦ Keyboard combinations require that you press several keys at the same time. Such combinations are indicated in tables by plus signs that are placed between keys. For example, Shift + F1, indicates that you need to hold down both the Shift and F1 keys to implement a particular function. As popular convention goes, the plus sign, thus, is not indicative that you must hold down the + key along with Shift and F1.

Icons and Alerts

Several graphic symbols, typically used in the IDG Bible series, are featured consistently throughout the book. These icons, which are placed in the margins, indicate that information in the adjacent area is of special interest. You will find the following icons in this book:

Note   This icon alerts you to noteworthy details concerning subject matter in the preceding paragraph(s).

Tip   This icon highlights hints that may help save you time or trouble.

This icon warns that certain functions and methods can result in technical problems if not used carefully.

 This icon indicates that more information on a specific topic is located in other chapters.

 This icon calls attention to new features introduced in Visio 2000.

How This Book is Organized

The *Visio 2000 Bible* contains 37 chapters, which are divided into eight parts, along with three appendixes.

Part I: Getting Acquainted with Visio 2000

Part I familiarizes readers with the latest version of Visio business drawing software. To keep things simple for beginners, it contains only two chapters. The first chapter explains some of the most basic aspects of Visio 2000, along with some of its new features and the types of projects towards which it's used. The chapter also mentions a few of the major corporations associated with Visio software, gives a brief history of the Visio Corp., and lists contact information. Chapter 2 takes you on a tour of the *Visio 2000* environment, discussing basic functions found on the start-up window. Chapter 3 walks you through your first drawing.

Part II: Starting Your Project

Two chapters comprise Part II. This section is designed to give readers a comprehensive look at more Visio fundamentals, including an in-depth discussion on the program's Standard Toolbar buttons and Menu bar commands. You also learn two more ways for creating a drawing from scratch: templates and wizards. In Chapter 4, a summary, accompanying a list of stencils, explains how each template is generally used to create projects. Chapter 5 then discusses the purpose and applications involving the Page Layout Wizard.

Part III: Drawing with Visio 2000

Part III's nine chapters offer a detailed approach to more drawing basics. For example, Chapter 6 explains how to create and format lines and shapes with key Standard, Format, and Format Shape Toolbar buttons. Chapter 7 explains how you can delete selections and apply the undo and redo features. Learn methods to format pages and set page parameters in Chapter 8. In Chapter 9, I explain ways to use window and viewing functions. Chapter 10 concerns manipulating rulers, grids, guide lines, and the snap and glue. Chapter 11 helps readers understand how to view and modify file properties. Information regarding saving documents is located in Chapter 12. Chapter 13 discusses methods to open both Visio and non-Visio documents. Chapter 14 closes the section by teaching you to use the print and print preview features.

Part IV: Using and Manipulating Shapes

This section contains information on various methods you can use to create and format shapes. Creating and editing masters, stencils, and templates is the subject of Chapter 15. Chapter 16 explains how you can size, reposition, and duplicate shapes. Chapter 17 discusses connecting shapes to one another. Chapter 18 details formatting methods involving the Color Palette and Format Painter. In Chapter 19, I cover methods to align, distribute, and array shapes. Understanding what layers are and how they work is the subject matter of Chapter 20. Chapter 21 turns your attention back to connectors, specifically layout and routing functions. Chapter 22 discusses methods for modifying shape behavior. Chapter 23 explains ways to edit and customize shape properties and fields. Chapter 24 covers group-related functions. Chapter 25 finishes up Part III with exercises and examples on shape operations.

Part V: Mastering Visio 2000 Tool Option and Macros Features

Part V contains three chapters that cover tool options and standard Visio 2000 macros. Chapter 26 details general, drawing, and advanced features on the options dialog box. Topics include manipulating user settings, enabling screen tips, and setting text options. Chapter 27 covers some of the macros found in Visio 2000. Then in Chapter 28, you learn how to create projects with database related wizards, including ways to incorporate information from Microsoft Excel files into Visio.

Part VI: Creating and Manipulating Text

Visio 2000 is not just about shapes. Part VI takes readers on an in-depth tour of the program's many text features. For example, Chapter 29 covers a multitude of basic text functions, such as positioning and rotating text and adjusting text styles. Chapter 30 focuses on ways to align and format text, including methods for creating paragraphs and adjusting margins. Finally, Chapter 31 helps you utilize spelling check features.

Part VII: Inserting and Exporting Drawings

Refer to the two chapters in Part VII for information on importing objects into Visio files and exporting Visio documents into a number of other formats. Chapter 32 covers methods for inserting comments and objects into Visio 2000. You also learn how to edit objects and work with linked objects. Chapter 33 then informs readers on ways to export their drawings into various file formats, including GIFs, JPEGs, and TIFFs.

Part VIII: Applying Visio's Extensive Business Capabilities

Visio 2000, as you will learn in this section, caters to a diverse range of business drawing applications. ShapeSheets, discussed in Chapter 34, are a pivotal means to directly editing shape numerical and function data. Chapter 35 concerns the use of hyperlinks and HTML files in your business drawings. Chapter 36 explains how engineers can incorporate AutoCAD drawings with Visio 2000. Chapter 38 closes by briefly enumerating a few more fields for which Visio software is usually found useful.

Appendixes

This book contains three appendixes. Appendix A includes information on installing and running Visio 2000. Appendix B features keyboard shortcut combinations for various drop-down menu and toolbar button functions. For quick access, these are listed in tables arranged by category. Appendix C helps users apply numerous integrated aspects of Visio 2000 through various exercises and examples.

Acknowledgments

First off I'd like to thank my wife, Janice, and my daughters: Denver, Jessica, and Ayron. They are my life.

Thanks to Sharon Eames at IDG Books Worldwide. I've written 28 or so books, and she is the best editor that I've worked with. Thanks to IDG Books' Laura Moss for both the work and her patience. Thanks also to copy editors Lane Barnholtz, Laura Hester, Ami Knox, and Amy Eoff. Thanks to Mike Emberson, David Busch, Robert Thompson, Avigail Frij, and Greg Blaha for their help with the text. Thanks to Kristen Tod for her excellent technical edit.

Thanks also to Rob Thomas, Matchbox 20, and their *Real World*, the thought of Angelina Jolie as Lara Croft, the breeze through the trees on the ridge behind my house, a go-cart in a full 20° drift, and Little Al's success in the IRL. I'd like to acknowledge the following inspirations: a good joke, Porsche 911s, mini-skirts, ice cold beer, my children's laughter, my wife's smile, Farscape, Michael Schmidt, Kurt Warner, Def Leppard, my Lola T-342, Gerry Layer, Tom Coughlin, and Greg Michel.

Finally, I'd like to ask everyone to turn off the news, their radio (you can leave on the rock stations), and computer. Go outside with your children and run through the sprinkler. You don't have to grow up. It's a myth.

Contents at a Glance

Contents

Part V: Mastering Visio 2000 Tool Option and Macro Features   419

Part VI: Creating and Manipulating Text   511

Chapter 29: Basic Text Functions 513

Chapter 30: Formatting and Aligning Text 529

Getting Acquainted with Visio 2000

Part I is an introduction to *Visio 2000*. Besides learning about the program's capabilities and newest features, you are acquainted with some of the business drawing tasks for which professionals use Visio. Also included is a brief history on the company and its software series, along with a tour of *Visio 2000* start-up window functions.

Understanding Visio 2000

Visio is a software line of drawing programs designed
especially for business professionals. However, because
the software is so convenient for creating diagrams and visual
presentations, a variety of people use them for a multitude of
purposes. After all, the visualization process is necessary in
many circumstances. Whether planning a landscaping project
around the house or working on a database-structure model at
the office, Visio drawing software helps people get the job
done with precision and ease.

Visio's Revolutionary SmartShapes System

The key to the programs' success lies in their patented
drag-and-drop SmartShapes system, a technology that makes
drawings quick, simple, and professional looking. You don't
have to be an artist to use Visio. Find the appropriate symbol
or shape and drag it onto the page. Next, just manipulate the
object's properties to suit your purposes. For instance, the
example in Figure 1-1 required only several clicks of the
mouse. Designs are impressive because thousands of shapes
are available in ready-made stencils. However, you also have
the option of creating your own shapes.

SmartShapes technology is an indispensable tool for constructing
a multitude of diagrams, from organization charts to maps. Visio
stencil shapes are much more than just clip art, though. Unlike
the latter, they do not distort when resizing. Visio also provides
users the option of connecting shapes and placing text over them
to form new objects. Furthermore, SmartShapes are compatible
with imported documents from Autodesk AutoCAD and Microsoft
Word, among many other programs. It's truly an innovative idea.

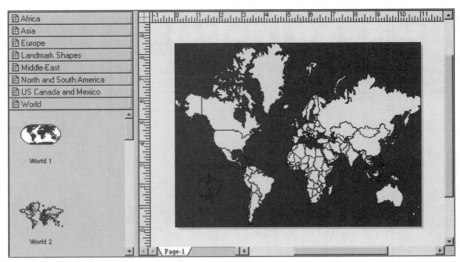

Figure 1-1: SmartShapes make "drawing" easy.

A Brief History of the Visio Corporation

Business markets have changed quite a bit over the past 15 years. With the mass proliferation of the desktop computer, larger corporations, and the emergence of the Internet, new ways of thinking have become crucial for all companies' present and future. The Visio Corporation has responded to these changes by creating and utilizing efficient tools in the fields of electronic and visual communication. This is a crucial step in saving businesses time and money when discussing and implementing new ideas.

In 1990, several developers from Aldus Corporation (the producers, at the time, of the desktop publishing software PageMaker) founded Shapeware Corporation (which would later change its name to Visio in 1995). The Seattle-based company released Visio 1.0 in 1992. The program was an instant success, becoming the launching pad for versions 2.0, 3.0, 4.0, and 5.0. Accommodating the business world's diverse needs, Visio soon released, along with the Visio Standard software line, Visio Technical and Visio Professional. Today, several million people around the world use Visio products.

In 1999 Microsoft acquired Visio Corporation around the same time that the company released its Visio 2000 software products. The merger is not that surprising, and, in fact, is ideal for several reasons. First, Visio has become a major player in business utility software, an area that Microsoft has dominated and perfected over the past fifteen years. Secondly, previous Visio products have integrated Microsoft technology for some time. Furthermore, before the acquisition, Visio had announced Visio 2000 support for Microsoft Office 2000 and Microsoft Visual Basics Applications. If anything, this deal will likely strengthen Visio's hold on the drawing software market.

Who Uses Visio?

As the top-selling business drawing software in the world, Visio has become a daunting international force with numerous operating branches overseas. In fact, Visio Corporation's growth is at an all-time high. Visio program users have doubled to three million worldwide since 1997, the company's products are available in more than 45 countries, and its drawing program software is translated into 12 different languages. Now with Microsoft at the helm, you can expect this growth to continue.

Companies and careers involving Visio technology

Numerous corporations and organizations, both large and small, either already use and/or are affiliated somehow with Visio technology. For example, BMW, Motorola, and the U.S. State Department hold Visio accounts. Triaster, a software services company, has utilized Visio technology for helping clients such as British Airways, Hewlett-Packard, Nokia, and Philips. Technical engineers even used Visio programs for orchestrating the 71st Annual Academy Awards.

In essence, Visio drawing programs are designed for business professionals in all walks of life. Software designers, business managers, marketing executives, architects, Internet specialists, security systems experts, industrial engineers, and members of various medical and environmental facilities rely on Visio products. This list, of course, is hardly exhaustive. More and more people are realizing that Visio tools are indispensable for planning and setting forth strategies in today's competitive global market.

Choosing the right Visio program for your needs

Visio has developed several drawing program packages for use at home and in the workplace. Visio 2000 Standard is, of course, the most basic program. It's designed for general office use and is an essential tool for creating financial reports, business process designs, and corporate presentations similar to the one in Figure 1-2. Most professionals find that Visio 2000 Standard caters to their needs. Others, specifically those working in information-technology- and engineering-related fields, may find it inadequate at times.

Figure 1-2: Visio is ideal for corporate presentations.

That's why Visio created three other drawing packages. Visio 2000 Professional (which comes with Visio 2000 Standard) provides support for tasks such as software design and systems analysis. Visio 2000 Technical (which also comes with Visio 2000 Standard) works best for engineering solutions involving such things as plant designs and assembly drawings. The third software package, Visio 2000 Enterprise, includes that drawing program as well as Visio 2000 Standard and Professional.

Visio 2000 Standard

A favorite of the general business community, Visio 2000 Standard makes learning Visio easier than ever before. Pop-up SmartShape tips, nudge tools, customizable toolbars, and larger drawing capabilities ensure that the latest standard is *the* drawing program for human resources, sales, and marketing departments. It's also not a bad idea for users to keep a copy at home.

Visio 2000 Professional

The Visio 2000 Professional edition contains improved network shapes and directory services programming. Software designers, Webmasters, and data systems analysts often find that this drawing program makes networking solutions easy and manageable. It's especially designed for creating IT diagrams and conducting data systems analysis. Specifically, software developers and system analysts will find the Unified Modeling Language solution ideal for handling various programming languages, from Java to Visual C++.

Visio 2000 Technical

The latest installment of Visio Technical is one of the most sophisticated 2D technical drawing programs on the market. Visio 2000 Technical offers more than 4,000 SmartShapes along with Autodesk AutoCAD, IntelliCAD, and Bentley Systems Microstation compatibility. With the program's network drafting capabilities, you can link complex amounts of information from spreadsheets and databases to your diagrams. The program is truly an engineer's dream.

Visio 2000 Enterprise

Visio 2000 Enterprise builds on the Professional edition, enabling IT professionals to efficiently document and modify data systems. The program includes more than 18,000 manufacturer-specific Visio Network Equipment Shapes. Its AutoDiscovery technology supports switched, frame relay, and IP network environments. Users also have the ability to import directory structures from Microsoft Active Directory, Novell Directory Services, and LDAP-based directories into Visio 2000 Enterprise.

Looking for Visio support?

Additional information about Visio can be located at their homepage (visio.com) and in the company's magazine, *Visio SmartPages* (as shown in Figure 1-3). Numerous companies have joined Visio's Partnering program for additional assistance and ideas. Members have access to consulting groups, support, and a multitude of other services. Some developers in the Partnering program also produce commercial software applications integrated with Visio technology. Two of the company's most successful groups are the Visio Registered Developer Network (VRDN) and the Visio Business Partner Program.

A variety of opportunities exist for those seeking support from Visio programs. For example, Visio Business Partner Program members are kept up-to-date with Visio technology. Companies can also receive white papers, patches, and Beta Visio software. Members, though, must pay a prorated annual $500 fee and maintain and/or reach several requirements to join.

Developers, however, can join the VRDN for free. The organization currently contains over 1,300 platform developers, including BankAmerica, Boeing, Xerox, and Bell Atlantic. Members have access to online development training, interactive broadcasts, product discounts, and Visio news. Learn more about the VRDN and the Visio Business Partner Program at visio.com.

Figure 1-3: *Visio SmartPages* keeps users up-to-date with the latest information.

What Can Visio Do?

Whether your career involves creating electrical schematics, process designs, Web site diagrams, or just simple office layouts, Visio can provide the tools you need. Many companies have found a wide variety of uses for Visio technology. Some tasks entail elaborate information system models; others involve customary documents such as five-step process charts and marketing. The choice depends on you and your company's needs.

Of course, different situations require different solutions. BSC Consulting, a British firm of consulting engineers, used Visio drawing programs for mapping clients' information databases, an instrumental procedure in quickly and efficiently identifying company Y2K compliance problems. Some hospitals, on the other hand, have employed Visio products for a multitude of day-to-day concerns, such as constructing diagrams to correlate patient needs with proper staffing. The software's versatility lends itself to the user's imagination.

Visio's drawing programs are renowned for their flexibility. Did you know that, for instance, Visio 2000 Standard can do the following?

✦ Create office and boardroom blueprints

✦ Design a map of your local street

✦ Create fax cover sheets, business cards, and calendars from Visio templates

✦ Orchestrate detailed project timelines

✦ Use data from Microsoft Excel files to create marketing charts

✦ Aid you in creating Web pages

✦ Edit AutoCAD drawings

Standard SmartShape Stencils

Visio Standard stencils place many of the SmartShapes you need at your fingertips. These consist of several thousand shapes, many of which are mentioned below. If those aren't enough, Visio's Solutions Library series probably has what you need. Current Solutions include stencils for legal professionals (Crime Scenes), IT professionals (Visio Network Equipment), network administers (Visio Frame Relay Pack), and business people who require an extended use of maps in their line of work (Visio Maps).

First, though, before considering stencils in Visio's Solutions Library or in other Visio 2000 programs, examine the quality and selection in the Visio 2000 Standard edition. You have access to several general-category stencil folders, including Block Diagrams, Flowcharts, Maps, Office Layout, and Project Schedules. Many of the SmartShapes in these stencils are sufficient for general business needs.

Block Diagrams

This stencil folder contains basic shapes like arrows, circles, diamonds, stars, crosses, and, of course, blocks. Depending on the category, you can choose from basic two-dimensional and three-dimensional SmartShapes. The differences in each are subtle. Take for example Blocks Raised and Blocks with Perspective. Raised blocks are three-dimensional but lack the single-point-perspective realism of the latter category. Figure 1-4 demonstrates how the Blocks with Perspective work. Many shapes in this folder are essential for Visio drawings.

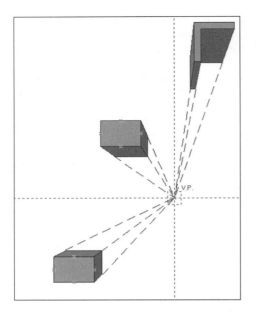

Figure 1-4: Notice how Blocks with Perspective converge at a single viewpoint.

Flowcharts

Flowcharts are an integral way of visually explaining processes. Some of the more common stencils here are used to detail data systems procedures, business department interactions, and employee motivational factors. The folder offers a multitude of categories, including Work Flow Diagrams, Audit Diagram Shapes, Data Flow Diagrams, and Mind Mapping Diagrams. Figure 1-5 is a good example of how a flowchart represents a typical business process.

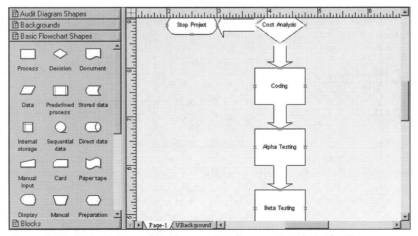

Figure 1-5: Steps in generic software development and production

Forms and Charts

Marketing executives will find these stencils useful for many day-to-day tasks. Users can modify shapes involving graphs and grids according to data-specific statistics. For example, the number of items represented in a chart as well as each figure's correlating amounts depend on your input. Various charts are available, including Bar Graphs, Line Graphs, and Pie Charts. There's even a template for creating FAX covers and Business cards (as shown in Figure 1-6).

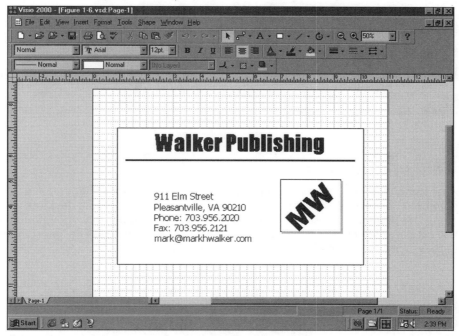

Figure 1-6: Design your own business cards with Visio.

Maps

You will find all kinds of shapes in the Maps section for travel-related diagrams. Stencils include crucial public signs like those in Transportation Shapes (Stop, No Parking, and One Way) and Recreation Shapes (common health club and park insignias). Of course, you can build maps of locations both small and large with Road Shapes and numerous shapes of continents and individual nations. There's even a Flags category representing over sixty different countries. Figure 1-7 demonstrates how you can coordinate some of these features into an impressive local map.

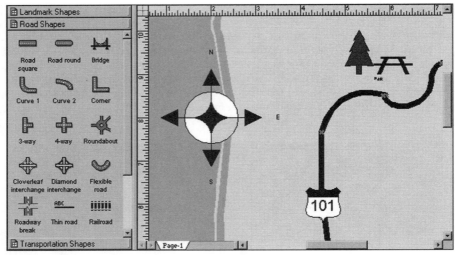

Figure 1-7: A map of the beach

Network Diagrams

This stencil folder contains three categories of Basic Network Shapes, each comprised of various technological devices. One can choose from desktop computer items (as shown in Figure 1-8) to an array of other network equipment like satellites, communication towers, telephones, and servers. The SmartShapes in these categories are ideal for explaining network setups.

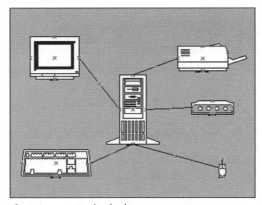

Figure 1-8: Basic desktop computer system

Office Layout

Although architects, carpenters, and interior designers will love this stencil, just about everyone else will, too. The Office Layout SmartShapes helps executives and managers plan for changes in office space coordination. It can be use for the most simple of tasks, as illustrated in Figure 1-9, from rearranging the furniture (including plants) to figuring out how much of your current furniture you can move into your new office. It also is beneficial for installing electrical outlets and phone jacks in the most strategic places for employee productivity.

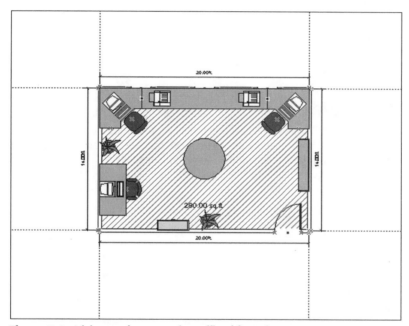

Figure 1-9: Visio excels at creating office blueprints.

Organization Charts

Plan and develop your company's hierarchy with this SmartShapes category, as shown in Figure 1-10. These stencils will aid you in filling upcoming vacancies, making promotions, and creating new positions. You can customize charts according to names and titles. Whether your company is a large corporation or a small five-person operation, templates exist for all types of hierarchical structures.

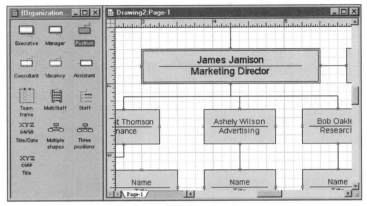

Figure 1-10: A company organization chart

Project Schedules

Never miss another deadline. With Visio's four Project Schedules stencils, you can design office calendars, create corporate presentations with both Gantt and PERT Chart Shapes, as well as develop a timeline to accommodate goals outlined in your business reports (see Figure 1-11). In the end, impress your colleagues at businesses meetings and guide company projects with utmost efficiency.

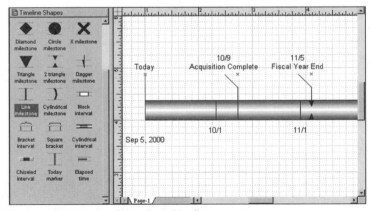

Figure 1-11: A simple project timeline

Visio Extras

This stencil folder contains much of the material you would commonly associate with electronic clip art selections. In fact, it even holds a stencil of shapes entitled Clip Art, some of which are used in Figure 1-12. These pictures consist of transportation illustrations, computers, and "cute" objects like a Money Tree and a clock with wings (Time Flies). This folder also contains Background, Border, and Symbol stencils. The latter includes meteorological figures and familiar things such as a No Smoking sign.

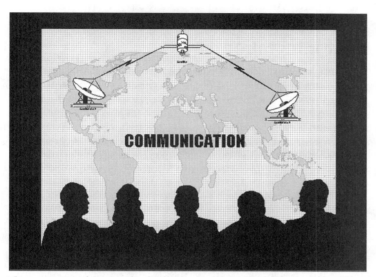

Figure 1-12: This simple drawing uses a World Background, Clip Art, and Connectors.

Why Is Visio 2000 Special?

Visio is a name within the business world synonymous with quality. Therefore, it's no surprise that Visio 2000 has outdone its competition and predecessors. The product's versatility makes it a favorite for business people of all walks of life. Visio not only supports such diverse clientele as engineers and marketing executives, but also caters with its richness to both beginners and experienced alike. Visio 2000 has bridged the gap between these people with its "smartest" designs to date.

Easy to use

Visio 2000 is not only the best business drawing program on the planet, but also the easiest to use. As with previous versions, its interface has many similarities to those found in Microsoft programs. For instance, there are the typical buttons like Cut, Paste, Save, and Format Painter. Visio toolbars also operate in the same manner as those in Microsoft Office products. Users' familiarity with such features makes the transition from the usual business software fare to Visio products easier than that in other drawing programs.

Beginners love Visio. Stencil tips are available for helping drawing program novices select the right shapes for their projects. Besides, many functions can be activated from several different areas within the program. For instance, the Help button contains an index that enables users to search for specific shapes. One can also use the Shape Explorer to conduct the same task as well as look for stencils and templates. Easy-to-find shapes and functions are essential elements in Visio's popularity.

Tight Microsoft integration

Visio's 2000 software line supports a multitude of Microsoft technologies. The programs, for example, run on a variety of Windows versions (Microsoft Windows 2000, Windows 98, Windows 95, and Windows NT 4.0). Visio 2000 products are compatible with Microsoft Office 2000, as well as Office 95 and 97. They also support Microsoft's Visual Basic for Applications 6.0. Furthermore, Visio wizards are capable of creating organization charts from data in Microsoft Access, Excel, and Exchange Server. With Microsoft's recent acquisition of Visio Corporation, expect an even stronger compatibility with future Microsoft products.

More capabilities

The latest installment of Visio products offers the business professional quicker designs, larger drawings, and an extended number of SmartShapes. Templates and various wizards make importing information into charts and diagrams easier than ever before. Visio has also added more color schemes, backgrounds, and styles for their users. All this work has resulted in the best Visio product line to date.

Cost-efficient upgrades

See if you qualify for a Visio 2000 Upgrade. Many people who own a Visio 5.0 product can upgrade to Visio 2000 at a fraction of what it would cost to buy the other software. Visio Corporation has also made the process simple and easy. All you need to do is visit the Visio 2000 Upgrade Center at visio.com/upgrade or call 1-877-NEW-VISIO to purchase the latest upgrade.

Summary

Visio 2000 offers professionals and laypersons extensive diagramming capabilities, making it the premiere business drawing program on the market. The program is truly a state-of-the art necessity for today's business world. In this chapter, you learned the following:

✦ Visio products are used as aids in the visualization process, a necessary component of business affairs.

✦ Visio's patented drag-and-drop SmartShapes technology makes drawing easy for even the most artistically challenged.

✦ The first Visio program, Visio 1.0, was released in 1992. Other versions include 2.0, 3.0, 4.0, 5.0, and the latest, the 2000 series.

✦ Microsoft acquired Visio Corporation in 1999.

✦ Visio 2000 comes in four flavors: Standard, Professional, Technical, and Enterprise, each geared for a particular segment of the business market.

✦ Visio 2000 offers a variety of solutions, including templates and stencils in the following categories: Block Diagrams, Flowcharts, Forms and Charts, Maps, and Project Schedules.

✦ Visio's latest series is noted for its user-friendliness, its tight Microsoft integration, and more efficient and extensive capabilities.

The next chapter introduces you to Visio 2000's start-up window along with the program's most basic functions and buttons.

✦   ✦   ✦

Exploring the Visio 2000 Project Environment

Learning Visio 2000 is easier after taking a guided tour through the everyday project environment. This chapter is designed to help you accomplish this in an efficient, step-by-step process. The focus is not on creating drawings, but on becoming accustomed to those aspects necessary for developing an initial understanding of the program. Overall, sifting through Visio's basic applications and windows provides the best foundation from which to build.

At this stage of the learning process, don't worry about anything other than orienting yourself towards the program. I try to make this as easy as possible. During a brief excursion of the Visio landscape, I point out the locations and functions of individual features and buttons as you come to them. This section therefore is presented strictly by interface features and not by topics. Such a format usually makes program tours simpler to follow and learning much easier to grasp for beginners.

Operating the Welcome to Visio 2000 Window

After installing a copy of Visio 2000 on your computer, access the program by double- clicking on its desktop icon. If you did not install an icon on your desktop, access the program icon from the Microsoft Windows Start menu. Either action pulls up the Visio 2000 window. Once you start the program you should notice a smaller window entitled "Welcome to Visio 2000" that accompanies the main screen. Users can create new drawings or open existing files from this window. Notice the two selection options available for these tasks.

Using these features is easy. Guide your mouse next to either of the options on the Welcome to Visio 2000 window and then click. This should place a black dot next to the selection of your choice (as shown in Figure 2-1). Next, highlight the file or stencil under the option by clicking on it. Wait first before clicking on the OK button at the bottom of the window. This action results in taking you to a blank page with stencils, something that I want to discuss in just a second.

Figure 2-1: Click the circular box next to the appropriate option to access the files in the box below it.

Note   After selecting an operation from the Welcome to Visio 2000 window, you can only reach the window again by closing and reopening the program.

Preparing a new drawing

Only four templates are listed under the "Create new drawing" area. There are many more at your fingertips, though. Click the first listing, "Choose drawing type," and then click OK. This takes you to a new window (as shown in Figure 2-2) containing a Solutions tab that gives you instant access to the available templates in your Visio 2000 edition. These are listed in the left-hand half of the window under the Category title.

The Create New Drawing window contains two boxes, one for Category and the other for Drawing type. I will discuss these in just a minute. First, though, observe the four buttons located at the bottom of the window. The button to your left has a question mark on it. It's the Help button, which gives users access to a multitude of program help features. The Cancel button closes the window, and the OK button is used for finalizing a selection. These three buttons are located on most Visio windows and dialog boxes. The Browse Templates button enables users to search for templates within the Visio 2000 program and their computer. I relay more information about that feature in Chapter 4.

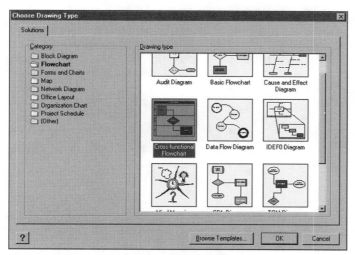

Figure 2-2: The Choose Drawing type window

For now, click the Category (solution folder) to find the subcategories (templates) within each. Notice that by selecting each, a different pictorial display appears in the right half of the window. These pictures represent a drawing type or template within that folder. For example, if you click Map under the Category side in Visio 2000 Standard, two pictures appear under the Drawing Type box. The first is called Directional Map, illustrated with trees, a building, and a pond. The second picture is of the African continent, and it represents Geographic Maps. These are shown below in Figure 2-3.

To choose a drawing type (template), click the picture and then click the OK button. This brings up a blank drawing page and the appropriate stencil windows to the document's left. Just click one of the stencil title bars to view its contents. For example, if you choose the Directional Map template, SmartShapes stencils appear for Landmark Shapes, Metro Shapes, Recreation Shapes, Road Shapes, and Transportation Shapes. Click the Landmark Shapes title bar and the SmartShapes within that stencil expand into view, as shown in Figure 2-4. Right-clicking on a stencil title bar enables you to close the stencil or modify its properties.

Cross-Reference　I discuss more stencil features in Chapter 15.

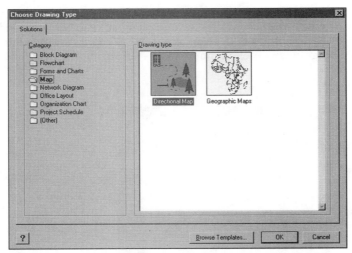

Figure 2-3: The Category and Drawing type are presented on the Solutions tab.

Note   A stencil is a single green window of shapes, a template holds one or more stencils, and a solution is a folder containing one or more templates. This hierarchical relationship is easy to remember. Take Landmark Shapes for example. It's one stencil among a group of stencils, in this case a constituent of the Directional Map template. And that specific template is part of the Map Solution folder's contents.

Before exiting this document, notice that two sets of three common Windows icons are situated at the top right corner of your screen. The first set — the ones at the very top — control the Visio program; the second set is for adjusting your document. In order from left to right: The first button minimizes the program, the second reduces/increases the program screen size, while the third one closes Visio. The bottom set operates in the same fashion except that it only minimizes, adjusts, and closes documents. You can click any of the buttons in the second set without affecting the program. The top set, though, actually closes or adjusts the program viewing area. For now, close the program by clicking on the small X-like button in the farthest right-hand corner.

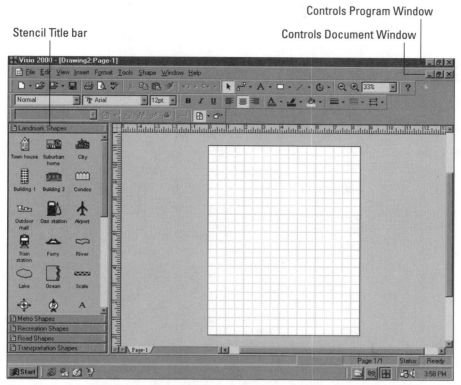

Figure 2-4: By default, stencil windows are located to the left of the screen. Click each to view its contents. The Windows icons for the program and, under them, the icons for the document, are located in the upper right-hand corner of the screen.

Preparing to open existing files

Open the Visio program once again. The second box on the Welcome to Visio 2000 window is entitled "Open existing file." Up to four titles of saved drawings can appear there. Left-click the "Browse existing files" line and then the Open button to retrieve more documents. Clicking on the Cancel button closes the window. There's little need to worry about opening files yet. I will discuss that later in the book, once you have a firmer grasp on the drawing process.

For more information on opening documents, see Chapter 13.

Closing the Welcome to Visio 2000 window leaves you with the program's basic Visio 2000 window (as shown in Figure 2-5). Three drop-down menus and five icon buttons are located in the upper left-hand corner. They operate the same way as those in many Microsoft programs do. Click the drop-down menu titles and scroll to access the features listed below. Next, click the listed feature. Regarding the icon buttons, just click each to implement the desired operation.

Figure 2-5: The basic Visio 2000 Window

Basic Drop-down Menus

Three drop-down menus are present on the basic Visio 2000 page's menu bar: File, Tool, and Help. Some of the functions within these features overlap those found in the Welcome to Visio 2000 window and in the icon buttons. For example, you can open previous drawings via the File drop-down menu, the Open button, or the Welcome to Visio 2000 window. You will find in ensuing chapters that many features throughout the program overlap in similar manners. This aspect makes accessing Visio program elements quick and easy.

File drop-down menu

Click the File drop-down menu and scroll through the list below. Notice that two items within this list, New and Stencils, have black arrows to their right. Resting your cursor on either arrow causes another list to emerge to the right (as shown in Figure 2-6). Move your cursor to that list and click the option of your choice. This is how you select the operation that you need. Such features, of course, work exactly the same as in any other Microsoft product.

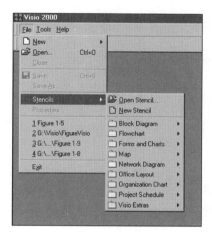

Figure 2-6: Drop-down menus behave like those in any typical Microsoft program.

File ➪ New functions

A number of options exist under the New function. You can select File ➪ New ➪ Choosing Drawing Type, which brings you to the same dialog box that can be accessed from the Welcome to Visio 2000 window. Here you can choose the Category and Drawing Type appropriate for your needs. The option of browsing templates is also available.

Choosing File ➪ New ➪ New Drawing takes you to a Visio window with a blank document and the Standard and Format Toolbars (as demonstrated in Figure 2-7). You can achieve the same result by selecting the Blank Drawing template at the bottom of the list. Selecting a Solution such as Map or Office Layout and a Drawing Type to the side of the Solution results in opening a blank page with the appropriate stencils.

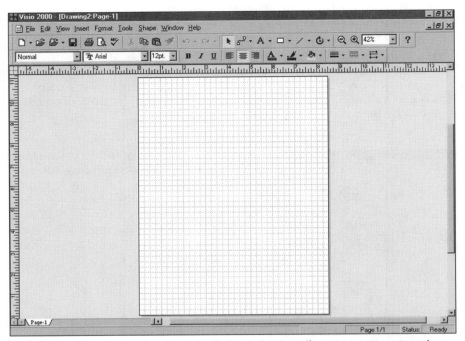

Figure 2-7: A blank document appears after selecting File ⇨ New ⇨ New Drawing.

File ⇨ Open, File ⇨ Save, and File ⇨ Save As functions

The Open function enables users to browse their computer for saved documents. This works similar to those functions in other Microsoft Windows products, just as the Save and Save As functions do. Because opening documents is something further along the path to learning Visio, I have included more information on this feature — along with saving documents — in later chapters.

Cross-Reference   Learn more about saving files in Chapter 12.

File ⇨ Close and File ⇨ Exit functions

Use the Close function to close your document, whereas the Exit function closes the Visio program. Activate these features by clicking them, as with all drop-down menu functions.

File ⇨ Stencils functions

Open existing stencils or customize your own with the File ⇨ Stencils features. File ⇨ Stencils ⇨ Open Stencil pulls up a window with the Solution folders and their stencils. For example, double-click the Block Diagram folder. When it appears in the "Look in" box, its contents are revealed in the large white box below (as shown in Figure 2-8). Just double-click one of its files to bring up those stencils applicable to that Drawing Type. You can also open files by clicking once on them and then clicking on the Open button.

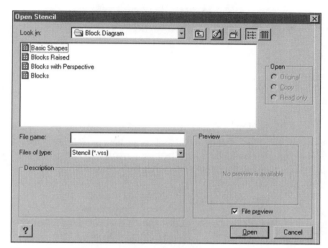

Figure 2-8: The Open Stencil window enables users to search for and open stencils.

You can access the same Drawing Type stencils by scrolling on the folders listed below the New Stencil function. For example, rest the cursor on the Block Diagram folder (File ➪ Stencil ➪ Block Diagram). Four Drawing Types appear to the right. Click one to bring up stencils contained in that subcategory.

Note   No blank drawing page appears in these instances. You must select File ➪ New ➪ New Drawing to bring a drawing medium to your window.

The File ➪ Stencils ➪ New Stencil feature pulls up a blank stencil window handy for placing those SmartShapes you use frequently from other stencils. You can also create and/or modify stencils and place them into a new stencil, too. This feature is one of the most commonly used aspects in Visio products.

Cross-Reference   For more information on creating and modifying stencils, read Chapter 15.

File ➪ Properties functions

You can access the File ➪ Properties functions once you've pulled up a drawing page. Clicking on this feature brings up a dialog box with several tabs. They are as follows:

✦ **General.** Lists the file's size, type, and location.

✦ **Summary.** User can insert such things as the author's name, title, and subject matter.

✦ **Contents.** Lists document contents.

✦ **Output Format.** Enables user to format contents for printing, Microsoft PowerPoint, and HTML or GIF output.

These functions enable users to format a variety of file properties. You will learn more about these later in the book.

Cross-Reference

See Chapter 11 for more information on file properties.

Recently used files

As with Microsoft programs like Word and Excel, Visio 2000 lists the four most recent files you've saved and/or opened within its program. These four are numbered from most to least recent. The listing is located in a box between the Exit and Properties functions in the File list as shown in Figure 2-9. You can open recently used files by simply clicking on one of those documents' titles.

Figure 2-9: The four most recent files saved and/or opened within Visio appear in the File drop-down menu.

Tools drop-down menu

There are many more functions that appear under the Tools drop-down menu when working with a page as opposed to the basic Visio 2000 window. The Visio 2000 window only lists two categories: Macros and Options. I'm just going to discuss these two features briefly at this point because they aren't applicable at this stage of the learning process. It's necessary right now to just be aware that these functions exist.

The Tools ⇨ Macros functions

The Tools ⇨ Macros section includes the following:

✦ **Macros.** External modules with Visio capabilities.

✦ **Visual Basic Editor.** Useful for building Visual Basic for Applications programs.

✦ **Custom Properties Editor.** A popular wizard program essential for modifying the properties of numerous shapes at one time.

✦ **Shape Explorer.** A search tool that hunts specifically for certain shapes, stencils, templates, and wizards.

✦ **Numerous Wizards and Converters.** These programs help users quickly assimilate data into diagrams and charts.

Note The Visio 2000 Wizards and Converters can be found by selecting Tools ➪ Macros ➪ Visio Extras.

Cross-Reference I discuss aspects of Visio's numerous wizard features in Chapters 5 and 28. I take up Macros in Chapter 27. And the Custom Properties Editor is discussed in Chapters 23 and 27.

Tools ➪ Options function

Selecting the Options function results in pulling up a dialog box with six different tabs:

✦ **General** includes User Options, Color Settings, and Enable Screen Tips.

✦ **Drawing** includes Text Options, Drawing Options, and Freeform Drawing settings.

✦ **File Paths** includes path listings for Drawings, Templates, Stencils, Help, Add-Ons, Start-Up and Filters.

✦ **Regional Settings** includes Default Units and Asian Options.

✦ **Spelling** includes Search and User Dictionaries options.

✦ **Advanced** includes User Settings, Developer Settings, and Stencil Spacing options.

These functions are used for various aspects of the drawing process. I will discuss these when applicable to particular exercises in later chapters.

Help drop-down menu

In the early stages of learning Visio, the Help drop-down menu is of great benefit. Due to its importance, I will discuss this feature in detail here. The Visio 2000 Help features are so abundant and substantial that going through them is useful even for users acquainted with previous Visio versions. In fact, you can learn more about all of Visio's new enhancements in the latest build from this section.

Help ➪ Visio Help function

Clicking on the Help drop-down menu calls forth a list of Help features. The first is Visio Help. Select it and a large dialog box appears. The right half of that box lists a chart that contains basic tips for using shapes, dialog boxes, and other features.

Table 2-1 is a copy of that chart. The File ➪ Visio Help section even includes information on new Visio 2000 features for developers.

Table 2-1 The Visio Help Chart	
For Help On	*Do This*
Concepts, Terms, Features	Click the Search button on the Help toolbar, and then type your question to use the Visio intelligent search capability.
Shapes	Do one of the following:
	Pause your pointer over the shape in the stencil window until a tip appears.
	Type the name in the Index, and then click Display.
	Right-click a shape on the page or stencil, and then choose Help.
Dialog boxes	Do one of the following:
	Click the Help button in the dialog box.
	Type the name in the Index, and then click Display.

The left half of the Visio Help dialog box (shown in Figure 2-10) contains three tabs essential for searching for more in-depth tips and instructions: Contents, Index, and Favorites. You can hide this half of the dialog box by clicking on the Hide button at the top of the screen. Once hidden, you can reveal the hidden half again by pressing the Show button. The Contents tab divides subject matter into four key topics: Visio Solutions, Visio Basics, Keyword Shortcuts, and Service, Support, and Licensing. The Index tab contains a keyword search feature for finding help for a wide variety of things, including particular shapes. The Favorites tab enables you to add topics in an easy-to-find retrieval location there.

First, look at the Contents tab. Notice that each icon (a purple book) has a plus sign (+) to its left. Click the plus sign to see the contents of that category. For example, clicking on Visio Basics reveals eight subtopics beneath the heading (as shown in Figure 2-11). Each of the eight icons has a plus sign next to it. Clicking on a particular subtopic reveals more topics beneath it. Continue with this process until you reach a topic with a question-mark icon. Click the icon that's appropriate to your question, in this case Visio Basics, and information and help steps appear on the right half of the screen. Click and hold the mouse button to move the scroll bar to read all of the contents of that help file.

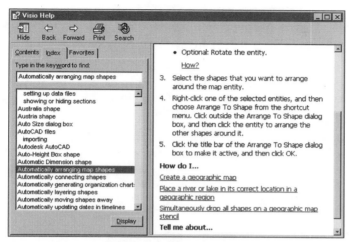

Figure 2-10: The Visio Help dialog box

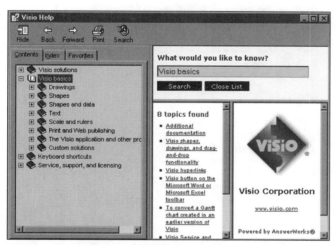

Figure 2-11: Clicking on the plus sign (+) next to each Contents topic icon reveals more subtopics.

Tip

You can print Help contents by simply right-clicking the question-mark icon of a particular topic and selecting Print. You can also do this by right-clicking on the tips displayed in the right half of the dialog box and then choosing Print. Or just click the Print button at the top of the window.

Two methods exist for closing the tips. First, you can click the minus sign (–) next to the purple books to close each individual topic. Secondly, you can right-click the icon and select Close All. This is the quickest way to close all the icons under a given topic at once.

Note   Right-clicking on an icon and selecting Open All will open *all* topics marked with a question-mark icon. Because this method can seem somewhat chaotic for beginners, it's advised that only persons familiar with the help topics use this method.

The Index tab is usually the quickest way for finding helpful tips. Just type in the subject with which you need help. For example, type **Connection points**. This instantly pulls up that topic along with several related subtopics (see Figure 2-12). Click any of these and click the Display button to reveal information on that subject in the right half of the window. Click the green crosses for more details.

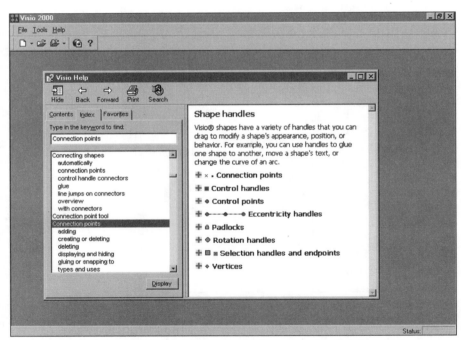

Figure 2-12: You can search for Help topics on the Index tab. Click the Display button to reveal the available information on the right half of the window.

The Search button at the top of the Visio Help dialog box enables users to search for helpful hints regarding a particular issue. Just click the related topics listed below for a detailed display in the box to your right. Use the scroll bar to read all of the information listed.

Note Click the Back and Forward buttons to navigate through already-viewed contents. This is simple and works the same way a Web browser does.

If you thought the Index tab and Search button made things easy, well the Favorites tab makes them even easier. After selecting an interesting topic in the Index section, just click the Favorites tab. The topic should appear in a dialog box towards the bottom of the window (as shown in Figure 2-13). Click the Add button to add the topic to your Favorites list. Notice that the newly added topic appears in the Topics box. Just click the Display button to refresh yourself on the information. When you feel that the information is not necessary any more, remove the topic from the list by highlighting it and then hitting the Remove button.

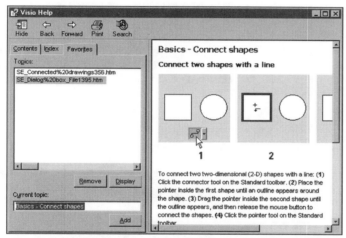

Figure 2-13: The Favorites tab is ideal for adding interesting topics to a personalized list.

Help ⇨ Search, Help ⇨ Shape Basics, and Help ⇨ Developer Reference functions

Click the Help drop-down menu again and scroll the list. Notice that three topics exist in a section below the Visio Help function. A similar icon, a small purple book with a yellow question mark, characterizes each. All three operations even pull up similar windows. While the right side of each window display is different, the left half is the same, presenting a Contents, Index, and Favorites tab along with standard Help buttons at the top of the window like Hide, Back, Forward, Search, and Print.

The Help ⇨ Search function is the same as that discussed earlier when clicking on the Search button present on the Visio Help dialog box. Type in a particular topic you need help with and hit enter. Related topics are displayed below for you to access. Click them and view their contents in the box to your right.

The Help ➪ Shape Basics function pulls up a window with nine helpful tips on SmartShapes features. These are as follows:

Select a shape	Add or change shape text
Move a shape	Change shape size
Change how a shape looks	Connect shapes
Rotate a shape	Use the shortcut menu
Time-saving tips	

Select a topic by clicking on it. Instructions appear in the dialog box to your right. Don't forget that you can use the Back and Forward buttons to navigate through this material.

Clicking Visio's Help ➪ Developer's Reference function presents a useful chart on developer tools and features. See Table 2-2 for a copy of that chart. Several topics are listed below the chart in the program. Just click each for more information. Some of those listed in the Visio 2000 Standard edition are as follows:

✦ New functions in Visio 2000

✦ New objects in Visio 2000

✦ New properties, methods, and events in Visio 2000

✦ New sections, rows, and cells in Visio 2000

✦ Properties and methods with a universal name equivalent

Table 2-2
What's new in Visio 2000 for developers?

Feature or tool	Description
More complex drawing support	Create drawings that contain a larger number of shapes and more complex formulas.
Improved Undo capabilities	Take advantage of seamless integration between the add-ons and external programs you develop and the Visio Undo manager.
Richer window model	Host windows inside the Visio frame with your add-on or external program.
Support for Microsoft Visual Basic for Applications (VBA) 6.0	Use the same version of VBA as Microsoft Office 2000 for easier coding and better interapplication development support. VBA 6.0 offers new features such as support for modeless forms and language parity with Microsoft Visual Basic 6.0.
Customizable toolbars	Create more customized solutions by tailoring the appearance and behavior of toolbars and menus to your needs.

Feature or tool	Description
Live dynamics	Drag a shape, and the document is updated as the shape is manipulated. This feature provides more immediate feedback as drawings are modified.
Richer and leaner geometry	Make your solutions more efficient by using new geometry types, such as nonuniform rational B-splines (NURBSs), ellipses, and infinite lines, and representing other geometry types, such as polylines, more compactly. In addition, shape instances now can inherit geometry from masters.
Document properties	Maintain and refer to document-wide properties in cells associated with a document.
Master shortcuts	Add shortcuts to masters on stencils to save file space and time maintaining masters. Shortcuts also can have drop actions that let instances of each shortcut behave or appear differently from the master.
Cross-container references	Reference any cell in a document from another cell in the document. A shape can base its behavior on properties of its document or on properties of any other shape, page, master, or style in the document.
Increased object uniformity	Rotate any shape—bitmaps, metafiles, and OLE objects. Add text or geometry to any shape, including guides and groups.
Enhanced group capabilities	Add geometry directly to groups, and choose among three distinct group select modes (group first, member first, group only).
Improved localization support	Assign universal names to objects and alternate names to documents so that they can be used by solutions regardless of the language in which they are running.
In-place cell editing	Click a cell in the ShapeSheet window and type directly in the cell rather than the formula bar. And, resize columns in the ShapeSheet window to view long formulas.

Help ⇨ Visio on the Web function

If you need to check Visio's Web site for an assortment of information including upgrades, news, and new Visio tools, click this function. You are prompted to connect to the Internet. Once completed, you are taken to the "Visio on the Web" page. This Web site contains headings such as Visio Product Information and Events. You can also register your copy of Visio here as well as research developer resources.

Help ⇨ About Visio 2000 function

The About Visio 2000 function opens a page (see Figure 2-14) that primarily features licensing and copyright information on Visio 2000. This page is also useful for locating your Product ID number and system information. Access the latter by clicking on the button in the window's bottom right-hand corner. Learn more about Hardware Resources, Components, and the Software Environment simply by clicking on them. Information is revealed in the box to your right.

Figure 2-14: The Help ⇨ About Visio 2000 function presents users with licensing, copyright, and system information.

Note   The System Information page works in the same manner as the Contents tab on many of the Help dialog boxes. For example, clicking on the plus sign (+) enables users to view the contents under each heading. Clicking on a minus sign (–) closes the contents.

Basic Toolbar Buttons

The basic Visio 2000 window contains five icon buttons. These functions give users quick access to what they need and use most. Three of those buttons, the New Drawing, Open, and Open Stencil functions, are standard buttons present on the drawing Visio windows uses when working with stencils, templates, and drawing pages.

New Drawing button

Selecting the New Drawing button pulls up a blank drawing page. However, if you desire to incorporate several templates with the page, scroll down the New Drawing button list for templates. For example, click the arrow next to the icon and scroll to Project Schedule. This reveals four templates: Calendar, Gantt Chart, PERT Chart, and Timeline. Click Calendar and then click the template stencil, and a blank drawing page appears (as shown in Figure 2-15).

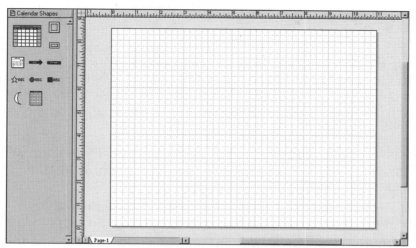

Figure 2-15: You can pull up a blank drawing page and stencils by clicking on the arrow adjacent to the New Drawing button. Just select the desired template and you are ready to go.

Open button

Clicking on the Open button enables users to look in various folders for both Visio files and other graphic documents that you can import into the Visio 2000 program. Just click the file you wish to open and then click the Open button. This window has other features that I will discuss later in the book. The most important thing is that you know how to access the window.

Open Stencil button

The Open Stencil button enables users to search for stencils within their computer. Simply clicking on the button takes you to a window with a dialog box built for searching available stencils. To pull up the stencil of your choice, select it and then click Open.

Note   You can only open stencils from this window. The file type dialog box does not permit you to look for templates (.vst) or drawings (.vsd).

You can also pull up stencils by clicking on the arrow next to the Open Stencil button. Scroll down the list to view the stencils available within each Solution folder. Click the template to view it in the Visio main window.

Visio on the Web and Help buttons

Clicking on the Visio on the Web button results in the same action as clicking on Help ➪ Visio on the Web. If your computer has Internet capabilities, you can connect to visio.com for the latest information. The Help button pulls up the Visio Help dialog box, which can also be accessed by pressing F1 or by selecting Help ➪ Visio Help.

Summary

This chapter took you on a brief tour of some common Visio 2000 features. You've discovered the locations and functions of the tools necessary for developing hands-on activities throughout the rest of the book. You're also now familiar with some of the different ways to begin a Visio document from the Welcome to Visio 2000 window.

In this chapter walkthrough I covered the following points:

✦ You can create new drawings from a number of starting points.

✦ You know how to use many of the drop-down menus, icon buttons, and functions on the primary Visio 2000 window.

✦ A hierarchical relationship exists between stencils, templates, and solution folders.

✦ You can select stencils and templates from folders for creating Visio drawings.

✦ Visio 2000 offers many new development features.

✦ A variety of Help functions are at your disposal.

In the next chapter, you can learn about the many toolbars available in the Visio 2000 Drawing window.

✦   ✦   ✦

Your First Steps: Getting Acquainted with a Visio Project

Visio 2000 offers a variety of templates from which to begin your project. Whether you are interested in an office layout, a flowchart, or landscaping your home, there is a Visio template that will get you up and running. Many, however, prefer to start with a clean sheet of paper, and that is where I prefer to start this book.

Not only will this chapter explain how to start a "clean sheet" project, but also it will show the multitude of modifications that you can make to that project. So, follow along as I explain how to begin your first Visio project.

Starting Out

As discussed in Chapter 2, once you have booted the program, click the Create New Drawing radio button, and then highlight Choose Drawing Type and click OK. This displays the Choose Drawing Type window. Under Category, click Other. This pops Blank Drawing in the Drawing Type window (as shown in Figure 3-1).

Note　The Welcome window displays the last four files (or file types) that you have opened.

Figure 3-1: Highlight Blank Drawing in the Drawing Type window and click OK.

These actions place a graph-like piece of paper on your screen. Let's take a look at how we can manipulate and alter that blank sheet of paper.

Understanding the Standard Toolbar buttons

Across the top of the screen are a series of drop-down menus. These menus (File, Edit, View, and so on) — aggregately called the menu bar — will be discussed in later chapters. Below the drop-down menus are the various Visio 2000 toolbars. By default, Visio 2000 displays the Standard Toolbar (as shown in Figure 3-2). These are the most basic tools with which you may work on your document.

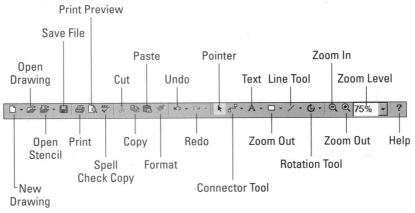

Figure 3-2: The Standard Toolbar with descriptions

New Drawing

Clicking on the New Drawing icon (at the far left of the standard toolbar) opens a new Visio document. Clicking on the arrow to the right of the New Drawing icon drops a menu displaying the various Visio solution folders that house templates. You may click a template to select it.

Open

Selecting the Open folder pops up a dialog box that enables you to choose what document you wish to open. Note that you can browse to other folders using standard Windows 9X navigation procedures.

Tip   The button to the right of the Up One Level icon in the Visio Open Drawing window lets you instantaneously browse your desktop.

Open Stencil

The Open Stencil button, which rests to the right of the Open folder, enables you to choose a stencil to use with your blank drawing. Note that although stencils are assigned to templates, which in turn are grouped by solution folders, any stencil may be used with a drawing.

Cross-Reference   To learn more about opening and using stencils, see Chapter 15.

Save

The Save button saves your work. If you have previously assigned a filename and location to your drawing, clicking the Save button saves your work under that file name and location. If you have not yet assigned a name, clicking the Save button displays the Save As window. From this window you may choose the name and location to which you wish to save the file. For more details see Chapter 12.

Print Page

The Print Page button does just that. Note that the orientation of your drawing must match the orientation of your printed page or you will receive an error.

Cross-Reference   Chapter 14 goes into further details on printing.

Note   More often than not, you'll want to work with 8.5-x-11-inch paper. Check the File ⇨ Page Setup ⇨ Print Setup Tab ⇨ Paper Size to ensure you have the proper dimensions set.

Print Preview

The Print Preview button displays the Print Preview screen. This screen shows you what your drawing looks like on paper.

Tip   Go to View ⇨ Actual size to see exactly what the document will look like on paper.

Spelling

The Spelling button checks the spelling of every word of text on the page. Frequently business applications and procedures have a dialog unique to the particular business. Visio's spellchecker may not recognize words common to this dialog. You may, however, add words to the dictionary and hence check their spelling in future documents.

Tip   You may create a custom dictionary that incorporates words for a particular document. To do so choose Tools ⇨ Options and then click the Spelling Tab. Under User Dictionaries, click Add. Under the File Name, enter a dictionary name, click Open, and then click OK.

Cut, Copy, and Paste

To the right of the Spelling button are the Cut, Copy, and Paste buttons. These work identically to other Windows applications' Cut, Copy, and Paste functions. First you select the shape, text, or whatever, and then you choose whether you wish to copy or cut your selection. Finally, move your cursor to where you wish to paste the selection. Clicking on a Visio drawing only selects the shapes in the current layer. If your selection doesn't include everything that you expected, you may need to either group your objects or switch the active layer.

Cross-Reference   See Chapters 15 and 20 for additional details on the cut, copy, and paste functions.

Painter Tool

The Painter Tool is the next button, and a very useful function. The Painter Tool can copy a shape's color and place it in another shape. To do so, select the shape whose color you wish to copy. Click the Painter Tool and then click the shape to which you wish to impart the properties.

Note   By double-clicking the Painter Tool you can click on an infinite number of shapes, imparting the initial shape's colors to each. Also note that after clicking the initial shape, you may select numerous additional shapes (Shift+click) and then click the Painter Tool, imparting the initial shape's color into each of the subsequently selected shapes.

Undo and Redo

Next on the Standard Toolbar agenda are the Undo and Redo buttons. Again, these work like Undo and Redo buttons in most Windows applications. If you make a mistake you may click the Undo buttons. Each stores the previous ten actions in its memory. You may undo more than one action by highlighting the actions you wish to change in the drop-down menu adjacent to the Undo or Redo buttons, and then left-clicking.

Pointer Tool

The Pointer Tool is the next button. The pointer is normally black. The pointer turns white when passed over a selectable shape, text, or any other object that may be selected or deselected. The pointer has a number of other shapes; each will be explained in the appropriate sections of this book.

Connector Tool

Moving right we find the Connector Tool. Click the tool and select a shape or a shape's connector point (marked with an x). Then drag the connector pointer to another shape's connector point to form a static connection, or the interior of another shape to form a dynamic connection. Static connections remain hooked by the initial connector points despite subsequent rearranging of the connected shapes. Dynamic connections always move to connect the shapes by the shortest route.

See Chapter 17 for more details on connecting shapes

Text Tool

To the right of the Connector Tool is the Text Tool. Once you select the Text Tool you may click any shape and begin typing. If the selected shape is small, Visio will automatically magnify the shape so that you may see what you are typing.

See Chapter 29 for additional information on basic text functions.

Ellipse and Rectangle Tool

The Ellipse and Rectangle Tool is to the right of the Text Tool. To access the Ellipse Tool, activate the drop-down menu to the right of the Rectangle Tool. Use these tools to design different rectangular and elliptical shapes. Click once where you wish to plant the shape and then drag your mouse until the shape is properly formed.

Rotation Tool

The Rotation Tool can pivot your shapes and text boxes. Simply click the Rotation Tool and click the box that you wish to pivot. This changes the view of the selected shape to one similar to that shown in Figure 3-3. The shape may be rotated by moving the cursor over any of the circular attachment points.

Chapter 16 explains in detail how to size, position, and duplicate shapes.

The shape pivots about the pivot point that is initially displayed as a small circle centered in the shape. You may, however, hook the pivot point with your cursor and move it (even placing the point outside of the shape).

Cursor

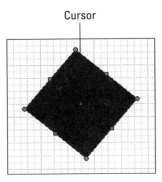

Figure 3-3: A Rotation-Tool-selected shape looks like this. Note the position and appearance of the cursor. This means that the selected shape can be rotated from this point.

Zoom

The final controls are the Zoom controls. Clicking on the magnifying glass with the plus sign (+) in the middle increases the magnification of your page. Clicking on the magnifying glass with the minus sign (–) in the middle decreases the magnification of your page. Alternately, you may set the magnification by either selecting a value from the pull-down menu or by highlighting the current magnification window, typing in the magnification that you desire, and tapping enter on the keyboard.

A glimpse of the remaining toolbars

Now that you have familiarized yourself with the Standard Toolbar, there are a number of other toolbars that you can use to customize your project. You may view these toolbars by either right-clicking anywhere on a toolbar or by selecting View ⇨ Toolbars.

Format Toolbar

The Format Toolbar provides formatting tools for a variety of functions. Included are the text and line formatting buttons in addition to Fill Color button.

Tip   You may choose how you wish to end your lines under the Line Ends icon. First select your desired ending and then select the Line Tool on the Standard Toolbar. Each line that you subsequently draw will end with the selected ending type.

Format Text Toolbar

The Format Text Toolbar houses the icons for more advanced text formatting. From this toolbar you may adjust your font sizes, space and align paragraphs, generate bulleted lists, or type in small caps, superscript, and subscript.

Each increase or decrease in text size "steps" the text to the next size. In other words, tapping the Increase Font icon increases 10-point text to 12-point text. Note that right-clicking in a text box pops up a menu with the same options as found in the Format Text Toolbar.

Format Shape Toolbar

The Format Shape Toolbar provides the basic icons for formatting shapes. This includes setting shape fill patterns, how corners will be rounded, the Shadow icon, and a layer selection menu.

The Corner Rounding Tool is a powerful device. The squares pictured in Figure 3-4 are the same basic shape, but each square's corners (as viewed from left to right) are progressively more rounded. You can use this feature to create a unique appearance to your Visio drawings.

Figure 3-4: Each square (when viewed from left to right) has progressively more rounded corners.

Action Toolbar

You'll use the Action Toolbar and the tools that it contains as much, if not more, as any other toolbar in Visio 2000. Included on this useful row of icons are the majority of the positioning tools used in Visio drawings. From this toolbar you may align and distribute your shapes, automatically lay them out on the page, quickly rotate and flip shapes (as well as text boxes), group/ungroup shapes, and change their layer position.

Tip
You may select several shapes that you wish to connect (by holding Shift as you click) and then click the Connect Shapes icon to connect them all.

Cross-Reference
Part IV covers how to use and manipulate shapes.

Snap and Glue Toolbar

This toolbar contains a variety of essential tools. The toolbar is divided into two sections. The left-hand section consists of four icons, the right-hand section consists of ten. I'll cover the Snap and Glue Toolbar in depth within Chapter 11, but for now you need to know the following.

When the Snap icon (the first icon on the left) is depressed, shapes will snap to (or align themselves with) the objects — such as Ruler Subdivisions and Shape Geometry — that are selected in the right-hand toolbar. By the same token, when the Glue icon (the second icon on the left) is depressed, shapes will glue themselves to the objects selected in the right-hand toolbar.

To learn more about the Snap and Glue Toolbar, as well as the ruler and grid, go to Chapter 11.

Layout and Routing Toolbar

The Layout and Routing Toolbar enables you to determine how you would like to route the connectors in your Visio drawing. The toolbar includes options to determine how your connector will "jump" connectors that it intersects, when the connector will be rerouted, and how to handle shapes dropped on the page subsequent to connector routing.

 The Routing Style indicator (the left-hand icon of the toolbar) may be used to globally change how the connectors interact with the shapes in a Visio drawing. Some of the options include connecting the shapes center-to-center or using a tree-like flowchart.

 For more information see Chapter 21.

View Toolbar

The View Toolbar holds the various icons needed to dictate what Visio displays on your screen. It is here that you may toggle whether Rulers, Guides, Grids, and Connection Points will be displayed. You may also display the Size and Position window, which shows the size and position of the currently selected shape.

The Pan & Zoom Tool (shown in Figure 3-5) is a handy device for navigating your drawing. Clicking on the icon pops up a small window. Dragging the small, red-trimmed rectangle in the Pan & Zoom box repositions the main viewing area. It's a convenient way to navigate a drawing.

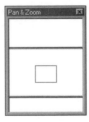

Figure 3-5: The Pan & Zoom window displays a box that you can move to reveal different sections of the drawing.

Web Toolbar

The Web Toolbar displays an Insert Hyperlink icon, Forward and Back icons, and a Visio on the Web icon. If you have an active Internet connection, clicking the Visio on the Web icon displays the Visio home page in your browser. The Forward and Back icons navigate between previously visited links.

The Insert Hyperlink Icon turns any Visio shape into a hot link to the Internet, to a file on your hard drive, or to another page of the same Visio document. To do so follow these steps:

1. Select the shape you wish to transform into a hyperlink. If you select nothing before proceeding to the next step, the entire drawing page will become a hotlink.

2. Click the Insert Hyperlink icon. This displays the Hyperlinks dialog box as shown in Figure 3-6. If you know the Web/file address you wish to link, you may type it into the Address field. Otherwise press the Browse button and browse to the location.

3. If you are browsing to an Internet address, copy the address (Ctrl+C) and then paste it (Crtl+V) in the Address field. If you are browsing to a local file, click Open once you have found the file.

Note   You may link to another page in the Visio document. Click the Browse button adjacent to the Sub-Address field, and then choose the document and page to which you wish to link.

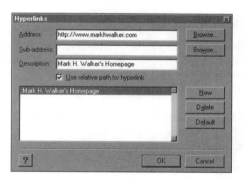

Figure 3-6: Insert the desired hyperlink addresses into the Hyperlinks dialog box.

Cross-Reference   For more information on objects and hyperlinks, see Chapters 32 and 35.

Developer Toolbar

The Developer Toolbar includes tools for running macros, displaying the ShapeSheet window, opening Microsoft Visual Basic for Applications (VBA), inserting controls that govern how a shape interacts with other shapes, and switching to design mode while working in VBA.

The Design mode enables several developer-user interface functions. For example, if checked, the Show ShapeSheet command is added to a shape's shortcut (right-click) menu.

Cross-Reference   For more information see Chapters 26 and 27.

Stencil Toolbar

The Stencil Toolbar includes tools for opening new stencils, opening a stencil that includes the shapes currently in your document, or selecting how you would like to display the stencil shapes.

The first icon on the left opens a new stencil; you may then add shapes to the stencil by dragging them off your drawing onto the stencil. Immediately to the right of the New Stencil icon is the Show Document Stencil Icon. Clicking on this displays all the shapes currently used in the document.

Tip   You may change each instance of shape in a document by editing the Master Shape in the Document Stencil. Simply right-click the Master Shape in the Document Stencil, select Edit Master, and then edit the shape. Close the Shape Editing screen and tell Visio to update all instances of the shape found in the document.

Cross-Reference   For more information on stencils see Chapter 15.

Customize Toolbar

You may customize the toolbars and menus by either right-clicking on a toolbar and choosing Customize or selecting View ➪ Toolbars ➪ Customize. This displays the Customize dialog box as shown in Figure 3-7.

Figure 3-7: The Customize dialog box enables you to modify your toolbar and menu settings.

The default tab is the Toolbars tab. Select which toolbars you wish to display from this screen. The Commands tab enables you to edit Visio's menus. To do so follow these steps.

1. Select the menu (from the Categories list) that includes the command that you want to add (to another menu).

2. Drag a command from the Commands list to the menu on the menu bar into which you wish to insert the command. Insert the command.

3. By selecting the command that you inserted from the Customize Window, you may click the Modify Selection button and choose how the command will be displayed in the drop-down menu.

Options is the final tab on the Customize Window. From here you may alter the appearance of menu animations, and when and how screen tips are displayed.

A New Client—Your First Visio Drawing

Imagine, if you will, that you need to show a new client the way to your office. Previous commitments prevent you from meeting the client at the airport and the client is unfamiliar with your city. You could overnight a city map and hope for the best, or—using your recently acquired Visio knowledge—design a personalized route in a Visio drawing and e-mail it to your client. Here's how.

1. Open a new Visio Drawing and select the Road Shapes stencil (as shown in Figure 3-8).

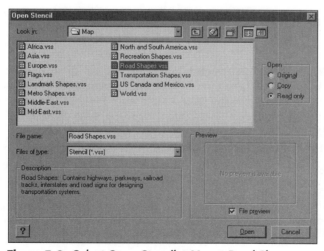

Figure 3-8: Select Open Stencil ⇨ Map ⇨ Road Shapes.

2. Drag the appropriate road shapes onto your map (as shown in Figure 3-9). To rotate the road segments you may either right-click them, select Shape, and click the appropriate rotation, or click the Rotation Tool and pivot the shape with the tool.

Note If the rotation tool is selected you may still drag shapes from the stencil to the drawing. Once you place the shape, you may immediately rotate it.

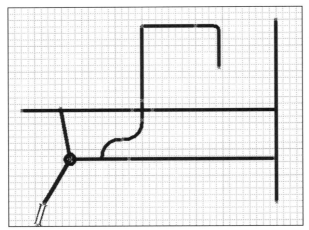

Figure 3-9: Our map with the initial roads placed.

Note You may also set the thickness of the road by right-clicking the section of road and choosing the desired thickness.

3. Select Map ⇨ Landmark Shapes and then place the building pertinent to your directions on the drawing. You may name each shape by double-clicking on the shape. This zooms in on the map and enables you to type whatever name you wish. Right-clicking on the text box displays the text-formatting options. You may also name streets by double-clicking on them.

4. Finally, select Project Schedule ⇨ Calendar Shapes and drag the yellow star/text box to every road junction where you wish to give directions. A portion of what your finished map should look like is shown in Figure 3-10.

Note The Project Schedule can be found under the File menu under Stencils. On the other hand, you can also access the Project Schedule by activating the drop-down menu next to the Stencil button on the Standard Toolbar.

5. Use the File ⇨ Save As command to save your file. You may now attach the file to an e-mail and send it to your client. Little fuss, and no muss.

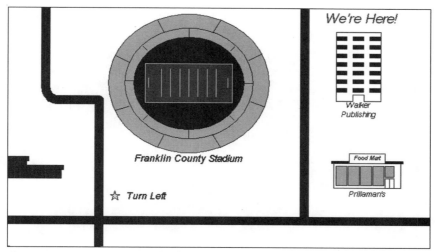

We're Here!

Walker
Publishing

Franklin County Stadium

Food Mart

Prillaman's

☆ Turn Left

Figure 3-10: Our map with the buildings placed.

Summary

In this chapter you learned about the basics of Visio's toolbars and how to create a simple Visio Drawing. We discussed these points:

✦ The Visio Standard Toolbar and its uses.

✦ How to make your first Visio drawing.

✦ A brief summary of the other Visio toolbars.

The next chapter will cover how to make a Visio drawing from a template.

✦   ✦   ✦

Starting Your Project

P A R T

✦ ✦ ✦ ✦

In This Part

Chapter 4
Creating a New
Project from a
Template

Chapter 5
Creating a New
Project from the Page
Layout Wizard

✦ ✦ ✦ ✦

Knowing how eager you are to create a drawing, Part II is designed to help you get "your feet wet." In this section I discuss two ways in which you can start a new project from scratch: templates and wizards. You are further acquainted with toolbar features, a detailed list of *Visio 2000 Standard* templates and stencils, and a step-by-step guide to the Page Layout Wizard.

Creating a New Project from a Template

A template is a collection of one or more stencils, distinguished by a distinct set of characteristics and parameters. For example, stencils in the Office Layout template open with a landscape-styled drawing page and rulers measured in feet. The Cause and Effect Diagram template contains a drawing page with a ready-made fishbone diagram. Others vary. These two, however, offer some of the more noticeable differences for people first acquainting themselves with Visio 2000. In short, templates are useful for two reasons: 1) organizing stencil themes and 2) preventing redundant formatting. They are therefore the basis for creating many of your day-to-day projects.

Starting with a Template Drawing

Now that you have an idea what a template is, let me show you how to access them. Beginning from the primary Visio 2000 page, click the File drop-down menu. Scroll to New and then to the pop-out menu to your right. The solution folders are arranged alphabetically in the Visio 2000 Standard edition from Block Diagram to Project Schedule. Each folder contains one or more templates.

Tip You can also access templates from the primary Visio 2000 window by clicking on the arrow next to the New Drawing button and scrolling the drop-down menu. A less convenient way involves accessing templates with the Open function or Open button.

Scan through each of the folders to run through the variety of templates at your disposal. Do this by dragging your pointer over each solution and its contents. Notice that a template is represented by a small white square icon (containing four tiny green squares) with a yellow top. Stencil icons, on the other hand, are small green squares that contain four tiny white squares (see Figure 4-1). To select a template, click that template's title or icon. This action pulls up the appropriate stencils and a drawing page. You probably will want to choose each template as I discuss it in this chapter. Exercises are designed for introductory purposes.

Note   Accessing a template automatically pulls up an accompanying drawing page. This is not the case, however, when opening a stencil. Notice that the Blank Page template only pulls up a drawing page (minus any stencils), though. You must then choose the stencils you need by selecting the Open Stencil button.

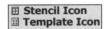

Figure 4-1: The Template icon (left) and the Stencil icon.

Templates in the Block Diagram Folder

The first solution you will come to is the Block Diagram folder, which contains three templates: Basic Diagram, Block Diagram with Perspective, and Block Diagram. Because these templates are standard fare in many professional fields, they are used in a wide assortment of drawings, from proposal visuals and figure displays to product modeling and accident reports.

Basic Diagram

This template is ideal for everyday presentations, creating personal diagrams, or just streamlining or coordinating some ideas into a rough draft. An assortment of masters exists in the Basic Shapes stencil, including essentials like connectors and arrows. Stencils available in the Basic Diagram template include the following:

Backgrounds

Basic Shapes

Borders and Titles

Note   Shapes within a stencil window are called *masters*. Once they have been dragged onto a drawing page they are called *instances*. In both cases, however, they are still sometimes referred to simply as *shapes*.

Click Basic Diagram. Notice the stencils docked to your left. You can access each by clicking on its title bar. For instance, clicking on Backgrounds will expand that stencil window, compressing the others to the bottom of the page. Click and drag one of the background masters to the drawing page. A dialog box appears next, asking if you want this background on the page (as shown in Figure 4-2). Click the Yes button. Here's a simple demonstration involving connecting two shapes.

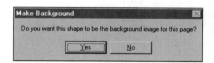

Figure 4-2: The Make Background dialog box.

1. Click the Basic Shapes title bar. The window should expand, revealing the masters in that stencil.

2. Click the triangle in the upper left-hand corner of the stencil and then drag it near the top of the page.

3. Click the square and then drag it near the bottom of the page.

4. Scroll down the Basic Shapes stencil. Click the dynamic connector. Drag it towards the square, connecting one of its ends to a connection point (blue x) on the square.

5. Click the connector's open end, dragging it to a connection point on the triangle. The result should look something like that in Figure 4-3.

6. Close the document, clicking the No button when asked whether you want to save your changes.

Cross-Reference Learn how to adjust the stencil windows and further manipulate stencil masters in Chapter 15. See Chapter 17 for more information on linking shapes.

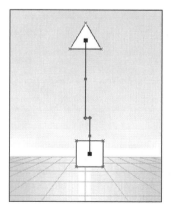

Figure 4-3: Connect the two Basic Shapes masters like this.

Block Diagram with Perspective

Add more pizzazz and depth to your charts with this template. The Blocks with Perspective stencil contains an adjustable vanishing point. This feature creates a three-dimensional effect by controlling the angles at which the shapes appear to the eye. In short, a shape's perspective lines converge at the established vanishing point. You have access to the following stencils when using the Block Diagram with Perspective template:

> Backgrounds
>
> Blocks with Perspective
>
> Borders and Titles

The adjustable vanishing point makes this template an eye-catcher. The following is a brief exercise illustrating how it works:

1. Click the Block master. Drag the shape near the top of the drawing page.

2. Select another block and situate it near the bottom of the page.

3. Notice how the gray sides on each block "point" towards the vanishing point (see Figure 4-4).

4. Click the vanishing point, dragging it to the center of the page. Notice how the gray sides reorient themselves towards it. This happens each time that you move the vanishing point.

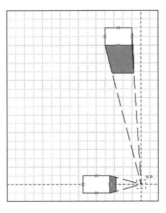

Figure 4-4: Shapes in the Blocks with Perspective template orient themselves towards the vanishing point.

Note   Although you can place more than one vanishing point in a drawing, only the oldest of the existing points is active. The others will have no effect on the shapes.

Block Diagram

This template offers Visio users a little bit of everything. The Blocks stencil contains an assortment of arrows (both one- and two-dimensional), auto-size boxes that automatically size to fit the text inside them, partial and concentric layers, and tree diagramming figures, among other shapes. Although masters within the Blocks Raised stencil lack an adjustable vanishing point, they still provide three-dimensional depth to presentations. The Block Diagram template's stencils are as follows:

Backgrounds   Blocks Raised

Blocks   Borders and Titles

Note   Running your pointer over a master shape causes a small white box with information to appear. The information tells you how to use the master.

Raised blocks in this template are three-dimensional, but they do not have a vanishing point. Complete the simple exercise below, and you will see the difference between this template and the previous one.

1. Pull several shapes out of the Blocks Raised stencil onto the drawing page. It doesn't matter which masters you choose.

2. Notice that all the shapes' gray sides "point" in a similar direction, just as they are represented in the stencil. However, Figure 4-5 reveals that they are not pointing towards one point like shapes in the Blocks with Perspective template.

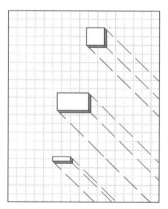

Figure 4-5: Shapes in the Raised Block stencil are three-dimensional but do not have a vanishing point. Notice that the imaginary lines drawn along the shapes' sides are parallel and do not converge towards a single point.

Templates in the Flowchart Folder

Flowcharts are one of the most common ways in the business world to illustrate processes, whether they be diagramming information flow or analyzing operation methods. Often, these charts are critical for improving department relationships, planning projects, and, overall, just facilitating improved approaches to handling business affairs more efficiently.

Audit Diagram

This template contains stencils useful for financial management purposes. The Audit Diagram Shapes, specifically, are geared for diagramming tasks like fiscal information tracking with masters representing disk storage, lined documents, and data transmission. The template uses these stencils:

Audit Diagram Shapes

Backgrounds

Borders and Titles

Basic Flowchart

The Basic Flowchart template is a useful tool for designing generic flowcharts, common for tasks ranging from creating typical business top-down drawings to diagramming the processes of a software project. Here is a list of the stencils that comprise the Basic Flowchart template:

Backgrounds

Basic Flowchart Shapes

Borders and Titles

One of the keys to designing flowcharts involves labeling each step in the process. The following exercise reveals how you do this.

1. Drag the Process shape onto the drawing page.

2. Double-click inside the shape. This action results in a close-up view of the instance (100%) with a blinking cursor inside its boundaries. See Figure 4-6.

3. Type the word **process** inside the shape.

4. Click outside of the instance to deactivate the text block.

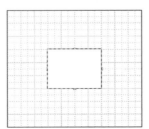

Figure 4-6: Double-clicking on a shape zooms your view so that you can type text within the shape.

See Chapter 29 for details on how to use and manipulate text.

Cause and Effect Diagram

Templates like the Cause and Effect Diagram are ideal for diagramming problem-solving solutions. The Cause and Effect Diagram automatically inserts a fishbone diagram on the drawing page, which users can modify with primary and secondary cause arrows, category shapes, and even a fish frame. Stencils in this template consist of the following:

Backgrounds

Borders and Titles

Cause and Effect Diagram Shapes

Primary and secondary causes are critical elements in designing a cause and effect diagram. Learn how to use the cause arrows with the following activity.

1. Double-click the box in the upper left-hand corner of the page.

2. Drag a Primary cause arrow to the arrow connecting the box you just double-clicked. Connect the instance towards the midsection of the arrow. Watch as one of the connected endpoints changes to red.

3. Notice the green selection rectangle at the end of the instance. Type the words **primary cause**. Do not click or double-click the green selection rectangle; just start typing. After you finish, double-click outside of the instance.

4. Drag a Secondary cause arrow to the primary cause arrow. Type the words **secondary cause** in the instance's selection rectangle. Double-click outside the shape. You should now have something similar to the illustration in Figure 4-7.

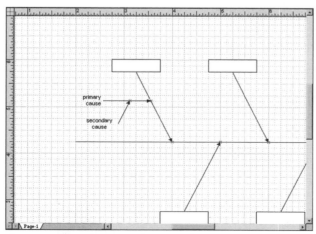

Figure 4-7: Setting up a cause and effect diagram

Cross-Functional Flowchart

Cross-Functional flowcharts are usually the most ideal flowchart format for illustrating process relationships between a number of units, such as departments, organizations, and corporate subsidiaries. This template lets you choose the number of bands and their orientation, and then it maps the drawing page accordingly. Only two stencils are part of the Cross-Functional Flowchart. They are:

> Basic Flowchart Shapes
>
> Cross-Functional Flowchart Shapes

Working with dialog boxes is a major part of setting up a cross-functional flowchart. Here's how to get started with this template:

1. Select the Cross-Functional Flowchart template. A blank drawing page, some stencils, and a dialog box will appear on your screen.

2. The Cross-functional Flowchart dialog box (as shown in Figure 4-8) enables you to choose three things: band orientation, number of bands, and whether or not you want a title bar. Choose the horizontal orientation, 5 bands, and a title bar.

3. Simply click the title bar and each band's function title area to type in the titles of your choice.

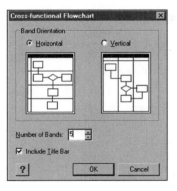

Figure 4-8: The Cross-functional Flowchart dialog box.

Data Flow Diagram

This template is designed for diagramming data processes. Data store and Data process shapes (loops and ovals) are some of the unique masters found in the Data Flow Diagram Shapes stencil. The Data Flow Diagram contains the following stencils:

> Backgrounds
>
> Borders and Titles
>
> Data Flow Diagram Shapes

The following method is a quick way to connect two shapes in a data flow diagram:

1. Drag the Start state master onto the drawing page.

2. Drag the Data process master onto the drawing page. Notice that a broken line runs through the center of both instances. This is the snap feature.

3. Drag one of the Center-to-center connectors onto the drawing page, linking one of its green connector points (green point with a small plus sign) to the center of the Data process instance. It's connected once the point turns red.

4. Click and drag the other Center-to-center shape's connector point (it's green and marked with a small *x*) towards the center of the Start state instance, as shown in Figure 4-9.

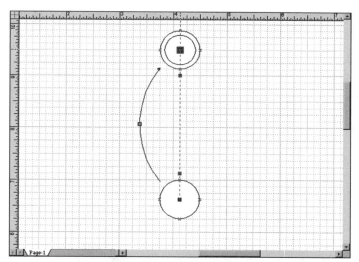

Figure 4-9: Drag the Center-to-center shape's connector point to the center of the next shape.

To learn more about the snap feature, refer to Chapter 10.

IDEFO Diagram

The IDEFO Diagram template offers shapes to users who need to create hierarchical charting models in their field of work. The IDEFO Diagram Shapes stencil contains several connectors, a diagram node, an activity box, and a label, among other masters. The IDEFO Diagram template uses only one stencil—IDEFO Diagram Shapes.

Mind Mapping Diagram

Mind mapping is a technique pioneered by Tony Buzan nearly two decades ago to facilitate increases in memory and creativity. The shapes found in the Mind Mapping Diagram Shapes stencil are intended to help users create graphical presentations (see Figure 4-10) that coordinate both right and left brain characteristics. This template's stencils include the following:

Backgrounds

Borders and Titles

Mind Mapping Diagram Shapes

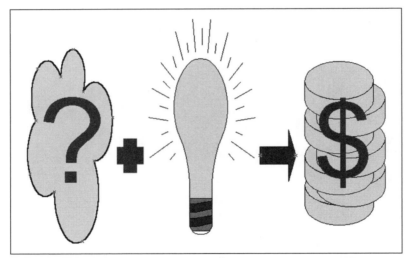

Figure 4-10: A simple mind-mapping diagram on the relationship between brainstorming and productivity

SDL Diagram

The Specification and Description Language (SDL) Diagram template provides a means for analyzing network and communication systems. The following stencils are part of the SDL Diagram template:

Backgrounds

Borders and Titles

SDL Diagram Shapes

TQM Diagram

Total Quality Management (TQM) Diagrams are utilized by the business world for identifying operation problems and, thus, improving the overall business process. The TQM Diagram template contains the following stencils:

Backgrounds

Borders and Titles

TQM Diagram Shapes

Work Flow Diagram

This template is designed to help executives document steps and methods in various departments, including production and distribution (See Figure 4-11). The following stencils comprise the Work Flow Diagram template:

Backgrounds

Borders and Titles

Work Flow Diagram Shapes

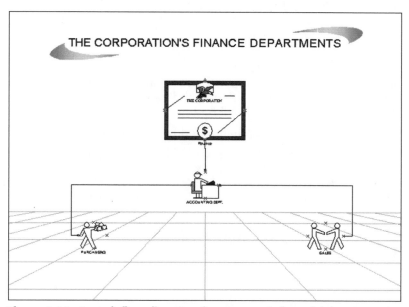

Figure 4-11: A work-flow diagram of a company's financial departments.

Templates in the Forms and Charts Folder

Human resources, public relations, finance, and marketing professionals often find that the Forms and Charts solution folder holds many of the templates they're looking for. Users can create various kinds of graphs, customize business cards and fax coversheets, and design an assortment of clip-art-related visuals.

Charts and Graphs

This template helps business professionals illustrate statistical data in easy-to-read graphs. Furthermore, designing many of these charts is simple. For instance, you choose the chart characteristics you desire by clicking on the master and filling out the ensuing Custom Properties dialog box with your data. There's no need to actually draw the charts. Even a stencil of clip art is included in this template, too. The following is a list of stencils in the Charts and Graphs template:

Backgrounds	Charting Shapes
Borders and Titles	Marketing Clip Art

Because many of the graphs and grids in this template differ, setting an instance's characteristics in the Custom Properties dialog box is often a little different. The following exercise demonstrates one of the easiest ways for customizing a pie chart for your needs:

1. Drag the Pie chart shape onto the drawing page.

2. Custom Properties dialog box appears, prompting you to enter the number of slices you would like in your pie chart. Scrolling down the arrow at the end of the white box, select 5. Click the OK button.

3. Right-click on the pie chart. A pop-up window appears. Select "Set slice sizes."

4. Another Custom Properties dialog box appears as shown in Figure 4-12. Manipulate each of the numbers in the white boxes so that they total 100 but are not divided equally (not five 20s, for example). I chose the following numbers for input: 11, 24, 30, 15, and 20. Click the OK button.

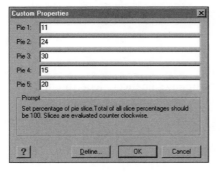

Figure 4-12: Insert the sizes of slices you need for a pie chart.

Tip   You can always reformat a graph by simply right-clicking on it, choosing the function necessary, and then changing the data in the specific Custom Properties dialog box.

Form Design

Visio's Form Design is one of the few templates that contains only one stencil. Human resources and public relations employees find many of the masters beneficial in creating and editing company forms, letters, and business cards. The Form Design template contains a single stencil — Forms Shapes.

You can create a nice-looking business card in no time with this Visio template. Here's how:

1. Select the Business card shape and place it on the drawing page.

2. Double-click *Company Name* and then delete the text by pressing Delete. Click outside the business card instance.

3. Drag the Reversed text master where *Company Name* used to be. Stretch the shape from one end of the card to the other by dragging the green handles.

4. Double-click the reversed text instance. This highlights the word *text* within it.

5. Move your pointer to the Font Size box (on the Format toolbar). Adjust the size from 10 pt. to 18 pt. and then click the Align Center button on that same toolbar. Feel free to modify the font as well.

6. Type your company's name in the reversed text instance.

7. Click the card and then click on each text box within it. Type in the appropriate information, adjusting the text size if necessary. You should end up with something like the example in Figure 4-13.

Figure 4-13: Create business cards in a few simple steps.

Note   You can also add clip art from other Visio stencils or place your company's logo on a business card.

Marketing Charts and Diagrams

Marketing Charts and Diagrams contains all the stencils in the Charts and Graphs template along with an additional Marketing Diagrams stencil. Thus, the Marketing Charts and Diagrams template is the most ideal template for building marketing charts. It enables marketing professionals to create pricing matrices, step charts, and Venn diagrams as well as things like bar graphs and clip art documents. Here's a group of the available stencils in Marketing Charts and Diagrams:

Backgrounds	Marketing Clip Art
Borders and Titles	Marketing Diagrams
Charting Shapes	

Templates in the Map Folder

The map folder features templates for building maps — local, national, and global. Choose from signs and landmark masters, among other shapes, to take your drawings to the next level.

Directional Map

Visio has truly thought of everything. The Directional Map template is a tool for urban planning, accident reports, metro diagrams, transportation department projects, and designing visual directions to conferences and seminars. It also offers a plethora of signs and map-building figures. The Directional Map template, in fact, features the following:

Landmark Shapes	Road Shapes
Metro Shapes	Transportation Shapes
Recreation Shapes	

The Directional Map template is easy to use. It's handy for navigating your clients from the airport to your corporate headquarters. Just use a strategy similar to the following:

1. Click the Zoom-In button (on the Standard toolbar) one or two times. Shapes from these templates will appear extremely small if you don't.

2. Drag a road shape from the Road Shapes stencil onto the drawing page.

3. Drag several more road shapes onto the page, connecting the ends of the roads.

4. Next, place buildings, signs, and landmarks onto the page. You should end up with a map similar to the one being developed in Figure 4-14.

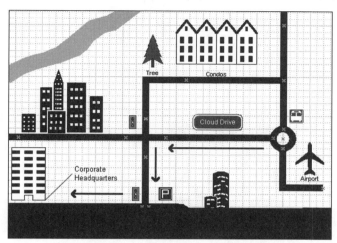

Figure 4-14: Build a map to guide your clientele from the airport to company headquarters.

Geographic Maps

Many corporations today have offices around the globe. The Geographic Maps template is one of Visio's answers to handling affairs overseas. The template enables users to construct professional-looking maps (see Figure 4-15) for presentations involving the international scene. An assortment of countries as well as all seven continents are at your fingertips, including the following stencils:

Africa	North and South America
Asia	US Canada and Mexico
Europe	World
Middle-East	

Note The Flag stencil is not available in any of the templates. You must pull it up individually: Open Stencil⇨Solutions⇨Map⇨Flags.

Tip Don't needlessly waste time connecting separate country shapes together. The World stencil features the continents with national boundaries.

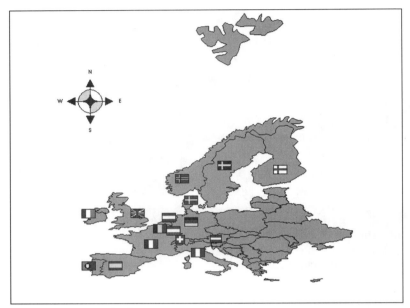

Figure 4-15: A map of western Europe

Templates in the Network Diagram Folder

Sometimes you can confuse an audience with lots of technical jargon. The Basic Network template enables you to break through this confusion with clear and precise network system diagrams.

Basic Network

The stencils in the Basic Network template enable you to create network diagrams, from office computer equipment to satellite/communication tower facilities (See Figure 4-16). The following stencils are located in this template:

Backgrounds   Basic Network Shapes 3D

Basic Network Shapes   Borders and Titles

Basic Network Shapes 2

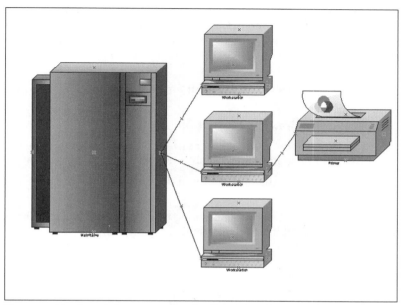

Figure 4-16: A mainframe-workstation hook-up diagrammed with the Basic Network template

Templates in the Office Layout Folder

Office professionals, architects, electricians, and telephone-installation service providers often find Visio's office layout capabilities helpful in their line of work. The template's ability to produce scaled drawings and a number of layout masters makes it ideal for organizing offices.

Office Layout

The Office Layout template is useful for diagramming offices. You can include a number of features in layouts, from chairs, desks, and filing cabinets to windows, computers, and plants. Whether buying new furniture, adding office space, or installing additional telephone jacks, this template helps you complete those tasks with utmost efficiency and planning. The Office Layout template consists of the following stencil — Office Layout Shapes.

Designing an office is easy with Visio 2000. In just a matter of minutes you can produce a professional-looking "blueprint" like the example in Figure 4-17. The following walkthrough will show you just how simple it is:

   1. Drag the rectangular Room master onto the drawing page.

2. Notice that the area represents 100 square feet. Perhaps your office is 120 square feet, though. No problem. Click the guide (blue dotted line) located to your far left. Once it's highlighted in green, drag the guide two grid spaces to the left. Next, click the room space (the area with diagonal lines) and pull it to the wall. Now the room is the right size.

3. Select the furniture you want and place it inside the room. Use the Rotation Tool to orient objects:

    a. Simply click the Rotation Tool button.

    b. Move the pointer over one of the corner connection points on the selection rectangle until an icon with two circular arrows appears.

    c. Orient the object in the direction you desire by pulling the object at that connection point.

Tip　　Use the dimension line master as "measuring tape," placing it along desks, files, and tables to help you get their size just right.

Figure 4-17: Map your office space.

Templates in the Organization Chart Folder

The Organization Chart Wizard and Organization Chart templates enable companies to represent a number of working relationships with visual diagrams. You can create hierarchical charts of staff positions, design teams, and business departments. Overall, it's an essential tool for project coordination and organizational development.

Organization Chart Wizard

The Organization Chart Wizard provides the means to incorporate data from a text file, Microsoft Excel file, or Microsoft Exchange Server directory into an organization chart. This wizard offers users the following stencils:

Backgrounds

Borders and Titles

Organization Chart Shapes

Note Before accessing the template's stencils, the user is presented with a wizard dialog box. The box gives you the option of either using data from a file or database or, instead, inserting information via the wizard.

Cross-Reference For more information on the Organization Chart Wizard, see Chapter 5.

Organization Chart

The Organization Chart template enables you to create a structured diagram of the people and positions within your company. It contains the same stencils as the Organization Chart Wizard; these are as follows:

Backgrounds

Borders and Titles

Organization Chart Shapes

Like most things in Visio 2000, drawing an organization chart from scratch only takes a few steps. Remember these simple rules when putting together a diagram:

✦ Drop a superior shape (executive, manager, and so on) first on the drawing page.

✦ To create the next level of people within the company's hierarchy, drop the corresponding shapes on top of the their immediate supervisor/superior. The template then places them accordingly.

✦ Adjust the shapes in other fashions by using the five buttons on the Organization Chart window (as shown on Figure 4-18). Click the supervisor/superior shape and then click one of the buttons. The instances you create under the superior shape are then arranged in a corresponding order. See the example in Figure 4-19.

✦ Double-click each box to type in the names and positions.

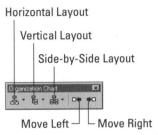

Horizontal Layout

Vertical Layout

Side-by-Side Layout

Move Left — — Move Right

Figure 4-18: The Organization
Chart toolbar

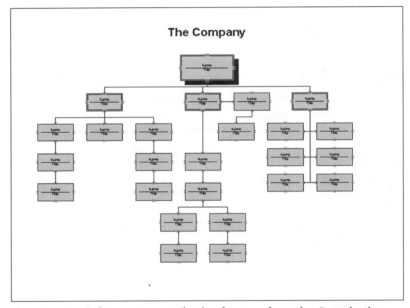

Figure 4-19: A chart constructed using features from the Organization
Chart toolbar buttons

Templates in the Project Schedule Folder

The Project Schedule solution folder contains four templates tailored for
documenting and planning company timetables and milestones. Depending on your
style and needs, Visio offers templates for creating calendars, Gantt charts, PERT
charts, and timelines.

Calendar

Visio 2000 gives you the option of customizing both monthly and annual calendars for your use, emphasizing notes and project timelines. Furthermore, you can format annual calendars on one page or instead proportion each month per page. You can do all this with just a single stencil—Calendar Shapes.

There's no need to purchase a calendar again when you can produce calendars like the one below (see Figure 4-20). The program enables users to personalize their calendars, which makes being on time both convenient and fun. The following activity involves creating a monthly calendar.

1. Select the Large month master and center it upon the drawing page.

2. A Custom Properties dialog box appears, prompting you to enter the month, the year, the day to begin each week, and whether you would like weekends shaded and the weeks numbered. Type in your choices.

3. Drag shapes designating significant dates. Use frames and labels for a single day and timelines and arrows for several days. To enter your text, simply double-click each item.

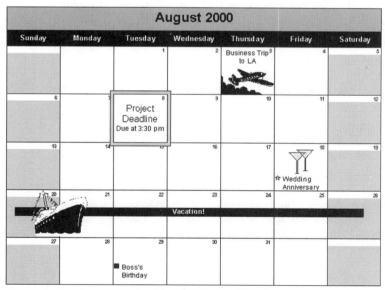

Figure 4-20: Set up a calendar like this in just minutes.

Tip

Don't forget to customize your calendar with clip art from the Visio Extras solution folder.

Gantt Chart

Gantt charts permit professionals to document tasks and statistics in a timetable. The Visio template's interrelated sections and task buttons enable users to modify the data and visuals in these charts quickly. The Gantt Chart template consists of three stencils:

Backgrounds

Borders and Titles

Gantt Chart Shapes

By selecting the Gantt Chart template, a dialog box entitled Gantt Chart Options appears on the screen. The box contains two tabs for adjusting settings: Date and Format. The first is divided into four different sections:

✦ **Task Options.** Select the number of tasks in your project

✦ **Duration Options.** Select the time format for measuring each task's duration

✦ **Time Units.** Select the major and minor units of time for graphically rendering each task's duration

✦ **Timescale Range.** Choose the project's beginning and end dates

The Format tab is divided into three sections where you can choose the graphic format for each of the following:

Task Bars

Milestones

Summary Bars

Once you've chosen what you need, you can complete the timetable with masters from the Gantt Chart Shapes and the Gantt Chart toolbar buttons. Due to the number of steps involved in completing a Gantt chart, I discuss that information later in this book.

Cross-Reference

See Chapter 37 for a detailed look at constructing Gantt charts. They are discussed along with several other solutions for managing projects.

PERT Chart

The Program Evaluation and Review Technique (PERT) Chart is the best template in the Project Schedule folder for diagramming step-by-step goals in your project agenda. The following is a list of stencils in the PERT Chart template:

Backgrounds

Borders and Titles

PERT Chart Shapes

Putting a PERT chart together like the one in Figure 4-21 is not complicated. Just remember these basic steps when constructing these kinds of diagrams:

1. Use the PERT 1 or PERT 2 masters for each task, including information like the starting and finishing dates.

2. Connect the task boxes with connectors or arrows to designate their chronological order.

3. Use the legend master to include things like the current date, the company's name, and the author or project director.

 Tip

Using arrows instead of connectors is sometimes ideal for expressing the order of tasks in a PERT chart.

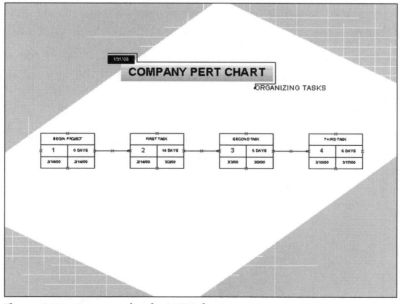

Figure 4-21: An example of a PERT chart

Timeline

The Timeline template offers a linear model for presenting annual report plans and significant points in a project's development. Choose from several different timeline, interval, and milestone masters. The Timeline template features the following:

Backgrounds

Borders and Titles

Timeline Shapes

Summary

Although this chapter covered all of the templates in Visio 2000 Standard, you can find more information about these tools throughout the book. Chapter 15 discusses how to create new templates, personalized for company use. Chapter 37 details ways you can use templates for a multitude of business-related goals. I covered the following points in this chapter:

✦ Templates consist of at least one drawing page and a collection of one or more stencils.

✦ Templates exhibit distinct sets of characteristics and parameters that are specially designed for certain tasks.

✦ The icon representing templates looks different than the one for stencils.

✦ The Blank Drawing template does not contain any stencils.

✦ A shape's vanishing point affects the orientation of its three-dimensional sides.

✦ Certain stencils are included in 26 of the Visio 2000 Standard templates.

✦ The Flags stencil is not located in any of the Visio 2000 Standard templates.

✦ You learned how to construct a number of charts from different templates, including a business card, a personal calendar, and an office "blueprint."

The next chapter introduces you to the wizards available in Visio 2000 Standard, along with several exercises and examples to get you started on working a little magic of your own.

✦   ✦   ✦

Creating a New Project from the Page Layout Wizard

✦ ✦ ✦ ✦

In This Chapter

Learning how the Page Layout Wizard works and how to use it to start a project

Generating a title block for your drawing

Inserting a company logo into the title block

✦ ✦ ✦ ✦

The Page Layout Wizard can set up the pages in your drawing. Using this wizard makes sure you don't miss any of the configurable options. You can use the Page Layout Wizard to help you set up a new drawing or adjust the layout options for an existing drawing. Follow the wizard screens to set the size of the printed page, the page orientation, the number of pages, and the drawing scale. You can also designate if the drawing pages will have a title block and a border. Additionally, you can insert a company logo into the title block. The configurable features of the Page Layout Wizard — the kind of drawing scale and the type of title block and border — are especially useful for technical or architectural drawings. Let's take a look at this handy tool.

Starting with the Page Layout Wizard

The steps are the same whether you are using the Page Layout Wizard for creating a new drawing or adjusting an existing drawing.

Tip   Do not use the Page Layout Wizard more than once on a drawing after you've run the wizard and saved changes. If you are not happy with your results and want to change an option, such as the placement of the title block, do not save the changes you've made. Reopen the drawing and run the Page Layout Wizard again.

Accessing the Page Layout Wizard

To access the Page Layout Wizard, click Tools ➪ Macros ➪ Visio Extras ➪ Page Layout Wizard. The wizard's opening screen appears, as shown in Figure 5-1. It gives you an opening description of the wizard. Click Next to continue.

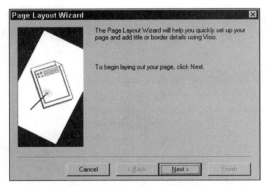

Figure 5-1: The Page Layout Wizard's opening screen

The Page Layout Wizard lets you create a new drawing or work with the current existing one. If you have already opened a new drawing to configure, choose the second option (see Figure 5-2). Click Next to continue.

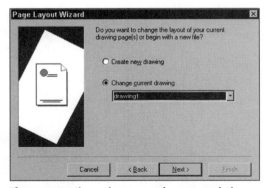

Figure 5-2: I'm going to work on an existing drawing.

The next screen enables you to set the size of the page and the number of pages. The page size drop-down list consists of pre-defined page size formats. Also indicate how many pages you expect the drawing to have. Click Next to continue.

Cross-Reference Learn more about Pre-Defined Size Drawing Page Formats in Chapter 8. See Tables 8-1 and 8-2.

The next screen enables you to set the page orientation to portrait or landscape. Click Next to continue.

The next step, shown in Figure 5-3, is choosing whether to create a drawing scale or not. Click Next to continue.

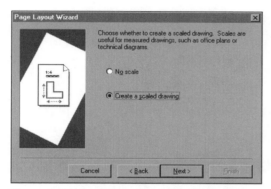

Figure 5-3: The fifth screen of the Page Layout Wizard enables you to use a scaled drawing.

If you want to create a drawing scale, the next screen offers you a selection of standard drawing scale types. They are Architectural, Mechanical Engineering, Civil Engineering or Metric. Depending on which of these options you choose, the drawing scale changes according to your selection in the drop-down list on the bottom of the screen. Choose a drawing scale from the drop-down list. Click Next to continue.

 Cross-Reference Learn more about drawing scales in Chapter 8.

The next layout feature to set is whether to include a title block in your drawing. You have four standard choices: No Title, Title across the top, Title across the bottom and Title in the lower right corner. Click Next to continue.

Then you set the information you want to appear in your title block. You can set it to appear automatically on all the pages (for standard information that usually appears on similar drawings). As you can see in Figure 5-4, your options are: company logo; drawing title; creator, company; date, time, and page numbers; filename; and drawing scale.

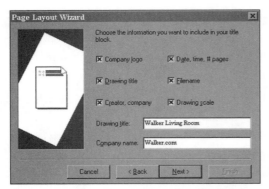

Figure 5-4: The Page Layout Wizard's eighth screen provides options for your title block.

Then you designate if the title block should appear on all the pages of your drawing or just on the first page or just on the last page (see Figure 5-5).

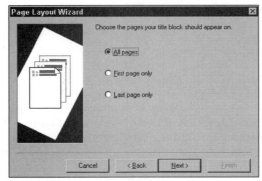

Figure 5-5: Choose which pages you want the title block to appear on.

The final setting is what type of border (if any) the drawing will have. The options are: No border, Classic style border, Single line border, or Multi line border. When you select one of the border options, the screen shows the border's appearance. The Classic style border is two lines with the outer one in bold. The Single line border is one line bordering the drawing. The Multi line border is three lines bordering the drawing.

On the last screen, click Finish. The wizard sets up the drawing pages according to the settings you chose.

The title block

If you designate a title block when configuring the options in the wizard, a title block appears in your drawing. Figure 5-6 shows an example of a title block.

Figure 5-6: A title block with company logo

Notice that the title block has information filled in. It is generated by the wizard from the options you choose. The file name is taken from the actual name of the file. The Creator of the drawing is taken from the Author field of the Properties of the file.

Tip   When you save a new drawing, the name you give it is automatically updated in the title block. Similarly, if you change other information such as the drawing scale, for instance, the information is updated in the title block.

You can also change the Creator's name by changing the information in the Author field of the Properties of the file. To access the file's Properties, Click File ⇨ Properties.

Modifying the title block and border

You can modify the information in the title block or make changes to the appearance of the title block and border.

To modify the information in the title block

1. Select the Layout Background tab on the bottom of the Visio screen. You can now access the background page that holds the title block.

2. Select the title block shape and ungroup it.

3. Click each of the ungrouped parts of the title block that you want to modify. Modify the text as you would with other shapes.

To make changes to the appearance of the title block and border, treat the lines as you would when formatting lines of other shapes.

Inserting a company logo

In Figure 5-6, the title block includes a company logo. When the title block is generated, a logo placeholder shape is placed in the title block, indicating that you should place your logo there. In order to insert your company logo, you have to access the title-block shapes that are on the Layout Background page of your drawing. Follow these steps:

1. On the bottom of the Visio screen, select the Layout Background tab. You can now access the background page that holds the title block.

2. Click the logo placeholder shape. Delete it.

3. Insert an image file with your logo by selecting Insert ➪ Picture. A dialog box opens for you to choose the logo's image file.

4. Select the file and click Open. The image appears on the background page.

5. Resize the logo image to fit the space provided.

Summary

Although this chapter covered the Page Layout Wizard, you can find more information about page layout settings in Chapter 8. I covered the following points in this chapter:

✦ The Page Layout Wizard helps you configure all the page layout options.

✦ You can configure a title block for your drawing.

✦ You can insert a company logo into the title block.

Part III delves into the comprehensive list of Visio basics including Visio's fundamental drawing tools, basic actions, and more details about setting up pages.

✦　　✦　　✦

Drawing with Visio 2000

Part III's nine chapters offer a detailed approach to more drawing basics, including opening, saving, and printing documents. This section, in particular, presents walkthroughs, tips, and exercises on editing a shape's lines, fill color, and drop shadows with the Standard, Format, and Format Shape Toolbars. I also discuss ways to set page parameters, manipulate rulers and grids, and adjust views.

Using the Fundamental Drawing Tools

The previous chapters acquainted you with many of Visio 2000 Standard's basic features, such as solution folders, templates, stencils, and wizards. However, as you learned in Chapter 3, there's more to drawing than simply using stencil masters. This chapter details Visio's fundamental drawing tools — those included in the toolbar buttons and Menu Bar functions.

Key Buttons for Drawing Lines

The Standard Toolbar contains a variety of icon buttons, many of which are standard Microsoft Windows tools (for example, the Save, Cut, Paste, Format Painter, and Undo buttons). These buttons, for the most part, are located on the left side of the Visio Standard Toolbar. The right side of the toolbar contains buttons designed specifically for dragging, connecting, and drawing.

Only two of those buttons are necessary for our discussion at this moment: the Pointer Tool and the Line Tool (as shown in Figure 6-1). The first is useful for selecting, placing, and sizing shapes. You will use it quite often in Visio. The second is important for constructing lines in a drawing. Notice that the Line Tool button has a small down arrow to its right. If you click the arrow, a drop-down menu appears revealing four more icons (see Figure 6-2), one being identical to the Line Tool icon visible on the Standard Toolbar. Clicking each icon formats your line accordingly.

Pointer Tool

Line Tool

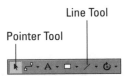

Figure 6-1: The Pointer Tool and Line Tool are located on the Standard Toolbar.

Figure 6-2: Access the Line Tool, Arc Tool, Freeform Tool, and Pencil Tool by clicking on the arrow.

Note By default, Visio 2000 Standard opens drawing pages accompanied with the Standard and Format Toolbars.

Tip Highlighted buttons on the toolbars indicate that the feature is active.

Using the Line Tool

Two icons represent the Line Tool on a newly opened Visio drawing window. Clicking on either results in the same action. Select the Line Tool and move your cursor to the drawing page. Notice that a crosshairs cursor appears with the Line Tool symbol as your new drawing instrument. This indicates that the Line Tool is active. The highlighted Line Tool button on the Standard Toolbar also reveals this.

The Line Tool is used specifically for drawing straight lines, many of which you can form into a closed shape. On the other hand, Visio drawing aids make the process even easier. Here's an example of how to create a right triangle using Visio drawing aids.

1. To ensure that you have activated drawing aids, select View ➪ Toolbars ➪ Snap & Glue and then click the Drawing Aids button (fourth button from the left on the Snap & Glue Toolbar) if it is not highlighted.

2. Click the cursor on the drawing page and, holding the right mouse button, drag the cursor to form a small horizontal line. Simply release the mouse button where you want to end the line.

3. Create a new line from the previous segment's endpoint by dragging the mouse from that segment's endpoint. Notice while dragging the cursor that broken lines appear at 45-degree increments from the point where you last clicked. These broken lines are drawing aids. Form a 45-degree angle between the previous line and the one you're drawing. Release the mouse button when your line coincides with the appropriate drawing-aid line (see Figure 6-3).

4. After drawing the second line, notice that the endpoints on the first segment have changed into vertices (green diamond-shaped handles). Vertices enable you to create two-dimensional objects from line segments. If this did not happen, then you clicked one too many times after completing a segment.

5. Extend another line connecting the two segments into a right triangle.

Tip Hold Shift as you drag a line to avoid having to manually place the segment you're drawing upon a drawing aid line. This action positions the line you're making in 45-degree intervals. This only works, however, if the Drawing Aids function is active.

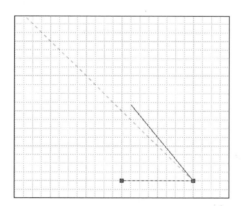

Figure 6-3: Using the Line Tool with the Drawing Aids

Placing lines with the Line Tool is only a matter of clicking and dragging the mouse. To move a line or shape, simply click and then drag it to the desired location. You should be able to drag the right triangle you've just created anywhere on the page. If you are only able to move one line at a time, you've clicked the cursor an extra time somewhere during the process. This deactivates the lines, preventing the endpoints from morphing into vertices.

Tip Make sure that you simply drag each endpoint when adding another segment to a previous one. Clicking more than once to end a line deactivates it and prevents endpoints from transforming later into vertices.

Using the Arc Tool

Click the down arrow next to the Line Tool button. Select the Arc Tool from the drop-down menu. Notice, again, that your cursor consists of a crosshairs symbol but this time also features an Arc Tool sign. Draw an arc in the same manner as you would a line; just click the page and drag until finished.

Once you've drawn your arc, you may later find that you have to alter certain characteristics. This is when the Pointer Tool comes in handy. Click and drag various parts of the segment to create desired effects. In fact, there are three different methods to format an arc with the Pointer Tool. These are as follows:

✦ To move an arc to another place, simply click and drag it with the Pointer Tool.

✦ To extend the length of an arc, click its endpoint and drag as needed.

✦ To increase or decrease the extent of the arc's bow, click the control point (round green handle in the center of a line) and drag accordingly. You can even drag the control point directly between the arc's endpoints to create a line.

You can manipulate lines drawn with the Line Tool, Freeform Tool, and Pencil Tool in a similar way. The key lies in dragging the endpoints and/or control points.

Using the Freeform Tool

The Freeform Tool offers more precision and control than the other line-drawing functions. For instance, you can create a multitude of curvy lines (such as arcs and splines) with the Freeform Tool by clicking once and dragging. The Arc Tool, however, requires you to draw one curve at a time, clicking on the previous line's endpoint to continue. Furthermore, most freeform lines contain a multitude of control points, convenient for tugging certain sections of the line, rather than the entire line itself. This section-by-section manipulation is not possible with the other tools unless they've created lines that contain vertices.

Taking your time is the key to effectively drawing with the Freeform Tool. Gradually dragging the cursor onto a certain path — steadily and slowly — enables the line to "stick" in that region. Here's a simple exercise involving precision and manipulation. Follow these steps to draw an *M*.

Tip   The slower you drag the Freeform Tool cursor when drawing, the more control you have over the line you're creating.

1. Click the Freeform Tool and then click the drawing page.

2. Drag the cursor in an M-like shape. Do this slowly.

3. Release the mouse button when you finish the *M*. You should end up with something similar to the drawing in Figure 6-4.

4. Notice the various control points (green circles marked with *X*s) located on the lines. Move the cursor to one of these points. Click, holding down the left mouse button, and then drag the points.

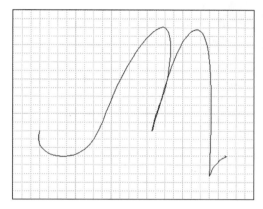

Figure 6-4: You can draw letters with the Freeform Tool.

Drawing is fairly easy with the Freeform Tool, if you take your time. With enough practice, you can even learn to write you name.

If you're having problems drawing with the Freeform Tool, you have several options at your disposal. Visio 2000 enables users to set a freeform line's precision and smoothness. This can be done by adjusting features on the Options dialog box. Simply choose Tools ➪ Options from the Menu Bar. The Options dialog box appears. Select the Drawing tab.

The Freeform drawing section is located at the bottom of the Drawing tab page (see Figure 6-5). There are two features that you can adjust on a scale from zero to ten (tight to loose):

✦ **Precision** affects user's drawing control.

✦ **Smoothing** affects smoothness of lines.

The combination of these two features control the number of control points on a line and whether lines have a tendency to arc or appear sketchy-looking.

Tip

For smoother lines, disable the Snap function. Do this by choosing Tools ➪ Snap & Glue. A Snap & Glue dialog box appears with two tabs. Under the General tab, uncheck the Snap feature (in the "currently active" section) by clicking on the small white box.

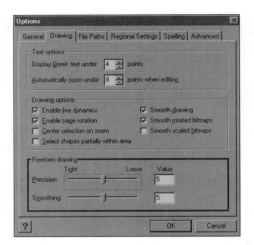

Figure 6-5: The Options dialog box contains a section where you can adjust Freeform drawing features.

Using the Pencil Tool

You can draw both straight lines and arcs with the Pencil Tool. To morph the Pencil symbol next to the plus sign (+) cursor into the Line Tool symbol, simply click and drag your cursor straight. Sweep your cursor in a curve-like manner and the Pencil symbol changes into the Arc Tool symbol. Under Pencil Tool mode, the Arc Tool has more flexibility, enabling it to create almost circular-like arcs (as shown in Figure 6-6).

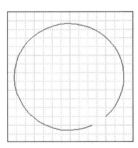

Figure 6-6: The Pencil Tool provides greater freedom in creating arcs.

Note   Clicking on a shape with the Pencil Tool reveals the shape's vertices.

Formatting Lines

There are five ways to format a line. You can alter its weight, pattern, color, ends, and style. These features are accessible on the Format and Format Shape Toolbars and from the Define Styles dialog box (Format ➪ Define Styles).

Altering line style

The Line Style box is situated on the far left of the Format Shape Toolbar. View the available styles from the feature's drop-down menu. Choose from Guide, No Style, None, Normal, and Text Only. The two most common formats are the None and Normal selections. The former is useful for erasing the black lines around colored shapes. Normal is the standard line style.

Caution   Changing a shape's line style to Text Only and No Style erases the shape's fill color.

Tip   You can also adjust line styles by selecting Format ➪ Style.

Altering line color

Add more color to your drawings with the Line Color button. Scroll down the drop-down menu and select the color of your choice. If you don't see the color you're looking for, click the More Line Colors button. This pulls up the Line dialog box where you can select 24 standard colors. Select the Custom button at the end of the list to view the Edit Color dialog box (as shown in Figure 6-7).

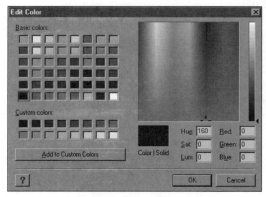

Figure 6-7: The Edit Color dialog box

You can choose colors from the Basic colors and Custom colors sections. If you still find the selection limited, click a color within the large Color Selector palette. The color bar to the right of the palette contains various shades of the color you've selected. Click the hue you want. If the correct color appears in the Color/Solid block then click the OK button. Whatever lines you construct on the drawing page will be of this color until you change it.

Tip   Each color you select and Add to Custom Colors appears in the Line dialog box's color list and in the Edit Colors' Custom colors category.

Altering line weight

A line's weight refers to its thickness. The more weight a line has, the thicker it is. Like the Line Color button, the Line Weight button is situated on the Format Toolbar. Select a weight from the button's drop-down menu or choose the More Line Weights button. Doing the latter pulls up the Line dialog box.

Scroll through the available weights in the Weight box. If you select Custom from the list of choices, the Custom Line Weight dialog box appears (as shown in Figure 6-8). Insert the thickness you need in either inches or points. Figures not specified as one or the other are interpreted as inches. Use the Preview window to see the changes before applying them.

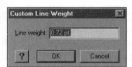

Figure 6-8: The Custom Line Weight dialog box

Tip   An inch is the equivalent of 72 points.

Altering line patterns

Line patterns consist of a vast array of dotted and broken lines. Choose these selections from the Line Pattern button. Choosing More Line Patterns brings up the Line dialog box. Although you cannot customize your own line pattern, you'll find 23 different line pattern varieties there.

Altering line ends

The Line Ends Pattern button enables Visio users to place ornamentation on the endpoints of each line. Choosing More Line Ends from the button's drop-down menu pulls up the Line dialog box. Select from the variables available in the Line ends section (as shown in Figure 6-9). Here you can choose from 45 different line ends and seven sizes. You can even opt for two different line ends (and weights) for the same line.

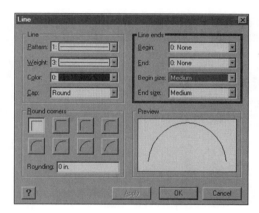

Figure 6-9: The Line ends section of the Line dialog box

Altering line caps

Although there is a Line Caps button on the toolbar, you can also adjust line caps from the Line dialog box. Besides navigating to the box from other line-drawing icon buttons, you can reach the Caps function from the Format drop-down menu. Here are the steps:

1. Select Format ➪ Define Styles and the Define Styles dialog box appears.

2. Click the Line button, which calls up the Line dialog box.

3. Select Cap and then choose either the squared or rounded-off line ends.

Tip Choosing Format ➪ Line also permits access to the Line dialog box.

Note You can't see how the Cap function affects line ends unless the line is fairly thick. Adjusting the drawing page view, however, does make this more noticeable.

Creating and Formatting Basic Shapes

You now know how to draw an assortment of lines, some of which are illustrated in Figure 6-10. It's time to add drawing shapes to your repertoire. Visio contains features that make some of the most ordinary shapes look quite impressive. With functions for rounding corners, applying fill colors and patterns, and placing shadows, even the novice can put together a quality document in just minutes.

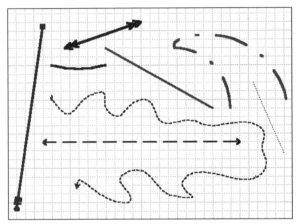

Figure 6-10: A variety of line types

Using the Rectangle and Ellipse Tools

Visio tools on the Standard Toolbar enable users to draw four different shapes: rectangles, squares, ovals, and circles. The Rectangle Tool is used to draw the first two and the Ellipse Tool is used to draw the others.

Click the Rectangle tool. Notice that the Rectangle symbol accompanies your cursor to the drawing page. Follow these brief steps for drawing both a rectangle and a square:

1. Click the drawing page, holding the left mouse button. This places one of the polygon's corners at the location where you first clicked, while dragging the cursor tugs at the opposite corner, increasing the shape's size. When you finish dragging the cursor, release the mouse button to place the object onto the page.

2. Did you notice that as you were dragging the rectangle, drawing aid lines appeared? By placing the corner of the polygon onto a drawing aid line, you can create a square.

Click the arrow next to the Rectangle tool. The drop-down menu contains the Ellipse tool. Select it. Use the following exercise to draw circles and ovals:

1. Click upon the drawing page again, holding the left mouse button. Drag the ellipse cursor in the same way you did the rectangle cursor. Form an oval.

2. Use the drawing aid lines to create a circle. Do this simply by placing the cursor crosshairs anywhere on a drawing aid line (as shown Figure 6-11).

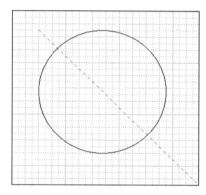

Figure 6-11: Use the drawing aids to draw a circle.

Rounding corners

Four primary ways exist for rounding shape corners:

✦ Choose Format ➪ Line to open the Line dialog box, and then open the Corners dialog box.

✦ Choose Format ➪ Corner to open the Corners dialog box.

✦ Choose Format ➪ Define Styles to open the Define Styles dialog box, and then open the Line dialog box.

✦ Use the Corner Rounding button on the Format Shape Toolbar.

From the Corners dialog box (as shown in Figure 6-12) and Line dialog box you can select eight different corners or customize a size in the small Rounding box. To use any of the formatting drop-down menu methods, first click the shape, and then choose the corner type.

Using the Corner Rounding button is the easiest way to format shape corners. Simply click the arrow next to the button and choose the cornering that's right for you. Clicking on the More Corners button in this menu pulls up the Corner dialog box in which you can use the Rounding box. Here, set the corner size you think necessary.

Figure 6-12: The Corners dialog box

Note   Regarding the Rounding box, any corner sizes adjusted to 0.55 inches or higher result in a circle. The closer your corner sizes approach 0.00 inches, the more that circle becomes square-like.

Applying fill colors

Spice up your drawings with a little color. Three primary ways exist for applying fill colors to shapes:

✦ Choose Format ➪ Fill to open the Fill dialog box.

✦ Choose Format ➪ Define Styles to open the Define Styles dialog box, and then open the Fill dialog box.

✦ Use the Fill Color button on the Format Toolbar.

The first two methods involve scrolling down the Format drop-down menu and attaining the Fill dialog box. Choose from the variety of colors in the fill color box. You can even select Custom and then pick a color from the Edit Color dialog box. The easiest way to color shapes, though, is with the Fill Color button. No matter which method you use, you should end up with results like those in Figure 6-13.

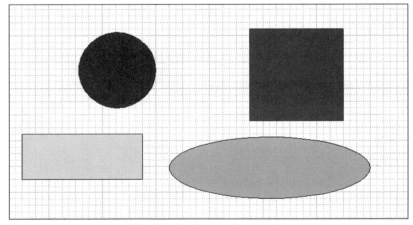

Figure 6-13: Use a multitude of colors to jazz up shapes.

Tip There are two ways to use the Fill Color button. 1) Click the shape and then choose the color you want from the button, or 2) click the Fill Color button first and then click the shape. Either method colors shapes.

Altering fill style

Fill Style settings affect the color and substance of a shape, at times making it appear solid, at other times transparent. Fill Style is available in two places:

✦ The Format Shape Toolbar (to the right of the Line Style box)

✦ The Style dialog box (choose Format ➪ Style)

Normal, which is solid white, is the default fill style for Visio shapes. The No Style and Basic styles are similar to the Normal style. The Text Only style prevents you from seeing any shape other than the text inside of it. However, clicking reveals a field in place of the shape. Simply dragging this field drags the text. The Guide style reveals the page's grid and guide lines in place of the shape's segments.

 Caution Using any of the Fill Styles upon a shape with a fill color (other than white) replaces that fill with the current style.

Applying fill patterns

Fill patterns are another way to shade shapes for colorful presentations. There are three primary ways for adding and modifying fill patterns:

✦ Choose Format ➪ Fill to open the Fill dialog box

✦ Choose Format ➪ Define Styles... to open the Define Styles dialog box. Click on the Fill button to open the Fill dialog box

✦ Use the Fill Pattern button on the Format Shape Toolbar

The arrow next to the Fill Pattern button provides users with seven different fill patterns. You can attain more patterns by clicking on the More Fill Patterns button. The Fill dialog box contains 40 different patterns. Their variety is illustrated in Figure 6-14. You can even manipulate the color of the pattern you choose. For example, choosing fill pattern 4 and then selecting pattern color 2 changes the gridlines from black to red.

 Note A combination of the Pattern Color and Color are both used in the Pattern.

 Tip The way a pattern displays itself in a shape is difficult to judge from the Fill Pattern box. The Preview box is a far better gauge.

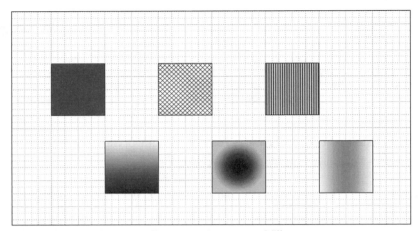

Figure 6-14: Visio 2000 offers an assortment of fill patterns.

Creating shadows

Although in operation they work the same way as fill color and patterns, shadows are still somewhat different. As the name implies, they function primarily behind a shape. In essence, by forming a backdrop to an object, they add more dimension to a shape. Visio 2000 offers three different ways to apply shadows:

✦ Choose Format ➪ Fill to open the Fill dialog box.

✦ Choose Format ➪ Shadow to open the Shadow dialog box.

✦ Use the Shadow Color button on the Format Shape Toolbar.

The Fill dialog box contains a section for shadow manipulation similar in nature to the one for fill (see Figure 6-15). The names of the small boxes, the variety of patterns, and the ability to interact shadow color and pattern color are all basically the same. The only difference is that these functions do not directly control the shape, only its shadow.

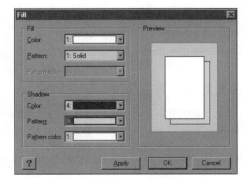

Figure 6-15: The Fill, Shadow, and Preview sections on the Fill dialog box

Tip

Shadows are not a second layer, but actually are part of the shape they're shadowing. Thus, resizing a shape (accompanied by a shadow) automatically adjusts the shadow as well.

Using Keyboard Shortcuts

Table 6-1 provides keyboard combinations for many of the most basic Visio drawing tools. Press the given keys together to implement the chosen function rather than selecting it from the icon buttons. Once committed to memory, these steps will save you lots of time.

Cross-Reference

See Appendix B for more keyboard shortcuts.

Table 6-1	
Basic Drawing Keyboard Shortcuts	
Function	*Keyboard Shortcut*
Arc	Ctrl+7
Ellipse	Ctrl+9
Fill	F3
Freeform	Ctrl+5
Line	Ctrl+6
Pencil	Ctrl+4
Pointer	Ctrl+1
Rectangle	Ctrl+8

Summary

Visio is much more than stencil shapes. Complemented by an easy-to-use interface, Visio 2000 provides users with state-of-the-art drawing tools. This chapter covered many of these fundamentals, including the following points:

✦ You can use the drawing aids to help design squares and circles.

✦ Connecting several lines into segments enables the user to move the connected lines together as one shape.

✦ Dragging an arc's control point between its endpoints transforms the arc into a straight line.

✦ The Pencil Tool draws both straight lines and arcs.

✦ Clicking on a shape with the Pencil Tool reveals the shape's vertices.

✦ Line Weight refers to a line's thickness.

✦ Visio 2000 Standard offers over 20 different line patterns and over 40 different line ends.

✦ Line Caps involve the squaring and/or rounding off of a line's ends.

✦ Any square's corner-size rounded to 0.55 inches or higher results in creating a circle.

✦ The Edit Color dialog box is a key tool for adjusting line color, fill color, fill patterns, and shadows.

In the next chapter, you learn to undo, redo, and delete actions.

✦   ✦   ✦

Undoing/Redoing Actions and Deleting Objects

Visio 2000 offers a variety of ways to undo or correct actions. These undo/redo actions enable you to correct mistakes and experiment with your layout and drawings. The basic functions I will discuss in this chapter are *Undo, Redo,* and *Delete*.

Visio 2000 enables you to do multiple layers of Undo and Redo. Setting the number of Undos and Redos is the first thing on our agenda.

Setting Undo/Redo Layers: How Many Layers Are Enough?

Let's discuss the number of layers of Undo and Redo commands you can set in the program. The more you plan to experiment or the more complicated the drawing, the more layers of Undo/Redo you will want. It's usually best to have more, rather than less. Although simple drawings (such as projects in which the entire structure is preplanned) may appear to need minimal layers, last-minute changes frequently necessitate as many as 10 layers or more of Undos. Accordingly, I normally recommend a minimum of 15 layers of Undo/Redo.

For more complicated drawings and for experimental layouts, I suggest 20 layers of Undo/Redo. It is possible to set 99 layers, but you'll probably find that you may have trouble remembering 99 layers of work.

To set your Undo/Redo layers, go to your menu bar and open Tools. Scroll to the bottom and select Options. In the Options dialog box, select the General tab. The Undo levels input box resides in the bottom-left corner of the User Options section (as shown in Figure 7-1). It normally displays the default level of 10. Either use the scroll arrows to change the value or click in the box and type the number of layers you want. The maximum is 99; the minimum is 0. When you are done, click the OK button to save. This setting applies to the current and all future drawings.

Note If you change to a low number of levels while currently in a project, the program 'forgets' the extra layers of actions already performed and will not remember them if you reset to a high number of levels.

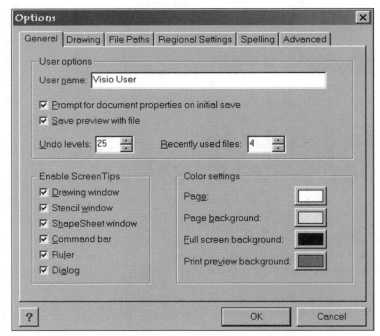

Figure 7-1: Set the number of Undo levels in User Options and click OK.

Now with your Undo levels set to at least 15, you are ready to start a project. In the next section I'll explain how to undo and redo actions.

Using the Undo Commands

There are three main ways to undo an action.

The first way is from the Menu Bar: Choose and click Edit. The first choice on the drop-down menu is Undo (name of last action). Clicking it undoes the action named. If there is no action to be undone, Undo is grayed out.

The Edit ⇨ Undo command names the last type of action taken. This can be useful if you were distracted and unsure of what the action was. For example, if your children picked that instant to demand a snack, or if a coworker dropped by.

The second Undo method is tapping the Undo command button located near the middle of the Standard Toolbar. It is a bent arrow that curves up and around to the left (as shown in Figure 7-2). Click it to undo your last action. This will be grayed out if there is no action to be undone. If there is more than one action that can be undone, there will be a small down-arrow on the right side. I will discuss the down-arrow's use during the following example.

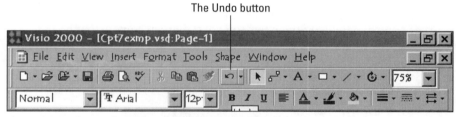

Figure 7-2: The Undo Button on the Standard Toolbar

The third Undo method is the shortcut keyboard command. To Undo, hold down Ctrl and press Z (Ctrl+Z). Obviously, this only works if there is an action to be undone. In other words, if it ain't broke, Visio won't fix it. Now let's set up an example to see these different methods in action.

Creating an example

Start with a new page. From the File menu, choose New. Scroll down and choose Office Layout Solution ⇨ Office Layout Template from the folder. Now make an office cubicle by dragging the square room shape from the template to the page. Zoom in by clicking twice on the Zoom In button (magnifying glass with plus sign) on the Standard Toolbar. Now Drag a Door from the shapes stencil and place it on the top wall at the right (as shown in Figure 7-3). We will work with this basic cubicle in this chapter. Now drag a Sofa from the stencil and place it above the cubicle. Drag a Desk Chair and place it outside the cubicle on the right side. Drag a Chair over from the stencil and place it outside the cubicle to the left (as shown in Figure 7-3).

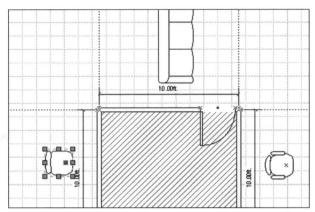

Figure 7-3: Cubicle with furniture outside

Select the chair on the left side and drag it in to the center of the cubicle. Now grab a corner control handle on the chair (one of the green squares on the corners) and drag it out a small distance to change the size of the chair (as shown in Figure 7-4).

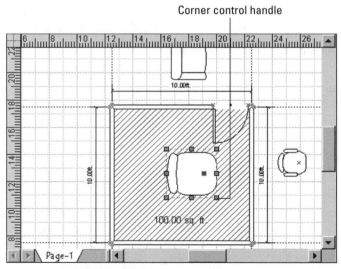

Figure 7-4: Cubicle with resized chair inside

Using the Edit ➪ Undo method

Now we will undo a bit of our work. From the Menu Toolbar click Edit. The Undo command on the drop-down menu says "Undo Size Object" (as shown in Figure 7-5). The last action taken was changing the chair's size, so that is the first action you may undo. Click Undo Size Object and the chair returns to its previous size.

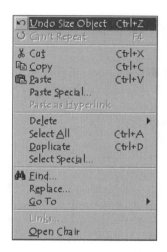

Figure 7-5: The Edit ➪ Undo menu names the last action taken.

Again click Edit from the Menu toolbar. The Undo command says "Undo Move Object." Click it to return the chair to the outside of the cubicle. Click Edit again and you will see that the Undo command now says "Undo Drop On Page." This of course refers to the action where you dragged the chair onto the page from the stencil. Go ahead and click Undo Drop On Page to remove the Chair from the page.

As you can see, the Edit/Undo command is useful not only to undo your previous action rapidly, but also to remind you what that action was. However, because it only undoes one action at a time, the next method has a distinct advantage if you need multiple actions undone.

Using the Standard Toolbar Undo control

Click the down-arrow to the right of the Standard Toolbar's Undo button to display the Undo drop-down menu. Currently the top undo option is Drop On Page (as shown in Figure 7-6). The top option is automatically selected. Selecting any item below the top item will undo *all* the actions from the top item to the selected action. You cannot select an action out of order to undo. The bottom of the drop-down menu shows how many items are selected for undo. With the drop-down menu open, draw your mouse pointer over the Drop On Page item that is immediately below the top selected item. The bottom of the drop-down box should now say "Undo 2 Actions." Click the second action to undo both the top and second action.

Figure 7-6: The Undo drop-down menu on the Standard Toolbar

Using the keyboard Undo command

Now with the furniture gone we'll use the door to demonstrate the keyboard Undo command. Hold down Ctrl and press *Z*. The door disappears. Keep the page you've been using open; we will use it to show the Redo Commands.

Using the Redo Commands

There are three ways to redo an action. The first is from the Menu Bar; choose and click Edit. The second choice on the Edit drop-down menu is Redo (name of last action undone). Clicking Redo will redo the action named. This will be grayed out if there is no action to be redone. The Edit ➪ Redo command names the type of action that was last undone, as did the Edit ➪ Undo command.

Using the Redo button on the Standard Toolbar is the second way to Redo. The Redo button is located near the middle of the Standard Toolbar, just to the right of the Undo button. It is a bent arrow that curves up and around to the right (as shown in Figure 7-7). Click it to redo your last undone action. This will be grayed out if there is no action to be redone. If there is more than one action that can be redone, there will be a small down-arrow on the right side. Clicking the down-arrow shows all the actions that can be redone. I will discuss that further in the following example.

The Redo button

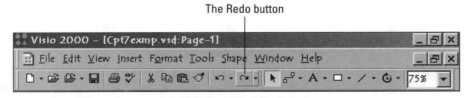

Figure 7-7: The Redo Button on the Standard Toolbar

The third way to Redo is by keyboard command. To Redo an action, press Ctrl+Y. If there is no action to be redone, nothing will happen. Now let's go back to our example to see demonstrations of these different methods in heart-stopping action.

Using the Edit ⇨ Redo method

Go back to your Office Layout page. From the Menu Toolbar click Edit. The Redo command on the drop-down menu says "Redo Drop On Page" (as shown in Figure 7-8). The last undone action was the gratuitous removal of the door, so that is the first action you may redo. Click Redo Drop On Page and the door returns to its residence on the cubicle wall.

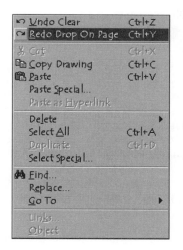

Figure 7-8: The Edit ⇨ Redo menu names the last action undone.

Using the Standard Toolbar Redo control

Now, for a multiple redo. Click the down-arrow to the right of the Standard Toolbar's Redo button to display the Redo drop-down menu. The drop-down menu shows the top redo option, Drop On Page (as shown in Figure 7-9). The top option is automatically selected. Selecting any item below the top item will select *all* the actions from the top item to the one you select. As with the Undo drop-down menu, you cannot select an item out of order to redo. The bottom of the scroll down menu shows the number of items selected for redo. With the drop-down menu open, draw your mouse pointer down the list to Move Object. The bottom of the drop-down box should say "Redo 4 Actions." Click the fourth item to redo all the items.

Figure 7-9: Redo drop-down menu on the Standard Toolbar

Using the keyboard Undo command

Use the keyboard command to redo the last undone action. Press Ctrl+Y. The Chair in the office is now re-enlarged to its previous ballooned size.

Save your example for use in the next section.

Deleting Objects

Removing an object from your page is often necessary long after you've added many other objects or taken actions that you do not want to undo. In such cases Deletions are your weapon of choice to remove unwanted objects from your page.

There are many methods to delete an object from your page. First I'll show you how to remove individual objects from the page. Later we will deal with removing an object from a set group of objects.

Note   Objects can be permanently deleted or they can be removed to the clipboard. Objects on the clipboard may be pasted anywhere within your document or — in most cases — another document.

Methods to delete an object

There are three methods to delete an object.

For the first method, select the object and then choose Edit from the Menu Toolbar. Then on the Edit drop-down menu select Delete. From the Delete submenu, select Selection.

Note   The Help file tells you to select Clear from the Edit menu. There is no Clear on the Edit menu. Hey, even the folks at Visio aren't perfect.

For the second method, select the object and then press Delete on your keyboard.

The third method uses the Drawing Explorer. I recommend this method for advanced users only. From the Menu Toolbar, select View. From the View drop-down menu, select Windows. From the Windows pop-out menu, select Drawing Explorer (as shown in Figure 7-10). In the Drawing Explorer dialog box, open the Foreground Pages folder. From the pages in the folder, open the page with which you wish to work. Then open the Shapes folder on the page. Find the shape you want to delete. Right-click the shape and select Delete. When using this method you must be very careful not to select the wrong shape.

For the vast majority of users, the select-object-and-click-the-delete-key system works best; it's direct, it's quick, and it's easy.

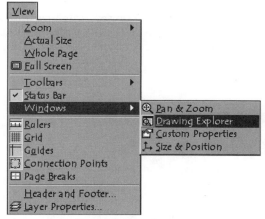

Figure 7-10: Drawing Explorer option in the View ➪ Windows submenu

Let's use the first two methods in our example. On the page, select the Sofa object. Select Edit from the Menu Toolbar. Scroll down and select Delete. From the Delete submenu, select Selection. The sofa is history.

Select the oversized chair inside the cubicle. Hit the Delete key on your keyboard. The chair vanishes. Easy, simple, quick.

Now I'll show you how to use the Drawing Explorer to delete an object. Undo your last Delete to return the oversized chair to the cubicle. Select View ➪ Windows ➪ Drawing Explorer. The Drawing Explorer dialog box appears in the top left corner of your working page. In Drawing Explorer open the Foreground Pages folder. Inside should be one page—probably labeled Page 1. Click the plus sign (+) to open Page 1. Two folders are inside. Open the Shapes folder. Inside are all the objects on your page. Take a moment to look at the list. Some of the items you may not understand or recognize. For now you can ignore them. Look for the object named Chair. Right-click Chair and select Delete Object. Chair disappears from the folder and the page.

Close Drawing Explorer by clicking the small *x* at the top right of the Drawing Explorer box. Now let's go to the next section on how to delete an object from the page while keeping it in memory for later use.

Methods to delete an object and save it in memory

There are three methods for deleting an object from the page while keeping it in memory for later use. Let's look at all three.

The first method is to cut the object using the Edit Menu. Here's how: Select the object and choose Edit from the Menu Toolbar. Select Cut from the Edit submenu. The object is now removed from the page and placed on the clipboard.

The second method is to cut the item using the Cut icon on the Standard Toolbar. To do so, select the item and then click the Cut button on the Standard Toolbar. The Cut button is represented by the pair of scissors (as shown in Figure 7-11).

Figure 7-11: The Cut button on the Standard Toolbar

The third method is to select the object and then cut it using the keyboard shortcut. To do so, select the item and then press Ctrl+X.

From our example page, select the desk chair. Then select Edit from the Menu Toolbar. Select Cut from the Edit submenu. The Desk Chair disappears and is stored in memory. Undo the action to return the chair to the page. Now with the Desk Chair still selected, click the Cut button from the Standard Toolbar. Undo to return the chair. Now with the Desk Chair selected, press Ctrl+X. Leave the chair in memory; we have plans for it.

Copying the deleted object in memory back to the page

There are three methods, which correspond with the previously described Cut methods, to paste an object residing on the clipboard onto a page.

Note   Pasted objects appear near the middle of the page. You may then drag them where you want. If you paste multiple copies of an object onto your page, they stack in the same place. Just keep dragging the top one off to access the other objects.

The first method is to select Edit from the Menu Toolbar. Then select Paste from the Edit submenu.

The second method is to select the Paste button on the Standard Toolbar. The Paste button is the second button to the right of the Cut button. It looks like a clipboard (as shown in Figure 7-12).

Figure 7-12: The Paste Button on the Standard Toolbar

The third method is to press Ctrl+V.

Let's use the paste methods to create three desk chairs for your cubicle. First press Ctrl+V. The desk chair should appear near the middle of your page. Now click the Paste button on the Standard Toolbar. It looks like nothing has happened. Don't worry. You'll see the chair in a minute. Now select Edit from the Menu Toolbar. Click Paste in the Edit submenu. It still looks like you have only one chair. Click it and drag it to another part of the cubicle. You see that another chair was under it. Click that chair and drag it to another part of the cubicle. You can now see all three desk chairs created with the three paste methods.

Methods to delete an object in a group

Visio 2000 gives the user the ability to define several objects as a single group for easy handling and altering. Occasionally you will need to remove an object from a group of objects.

Cross-Reference   For more detailed information on groups and removing objects from groups see Chapter 24.

To remove an object from a user-defined group of objects, first select the group. Then click the object in the group you want to delete. Then you may use either of the following two methods. 1) To remove the object totally, press Delete. 2) To remove the object but keep it in memory, press Ctrl+X. You may then return the object to the page but not as part of the group by pressing Ctrl+Y.

Note   You may also use the Menu Bar or Standard Toolbar commands once the object is selected.

Deleting Text

Most of same methods applied to deleting objects may be used for deleting text. Select the text to be deleted and press the Delete key. Or you may use the Edit ⇨ Delete or Standard Toolbar functions. Cut and Paste methods work as well. Drawing Explorer may also be used but is recommended for advanced users only.

For more information on Deleting and Replacing Text see Chapter 29.

Deleting Pages

There are times when you may need to remove a page from a multipage project. There are two methods for deleting a page from your project.

Deleting a page with Edit ⇨ Delete

There is no need to preselect the page. Go to the Menu bar and select Edit. From the Edit menu select Delete. From the Delete menu select Pages. A dialog box appears listing all the pages connected with the currently open project (as shown in Figure 7-13). Select the page name you wish to delete and click the OK button. If you accidentally selected the wrong page, you can resurrect it using the Undo command.

Figure 7-13: The Delete Pages dialog box lists all pages in the current project.

Deleting a page with Drawing Explorer

Select View ⇨ Windows ⇨ Drawing Explorer. In the Drawing Explorer dialog box, select either the Foreground Pages folder or the Background Pages folder, depending on the type of page you are deleting. In the folder, right-click the page you wish to delete and select Delete Page from the pop-up menu. Again, if you accidentally selected the wrong page you may use Undo to return it.

Summary

In this chapter we covered the basics of setting Undo layers, undoing actions, and different methods of basic editing commands. We covered keyboard shortcuts, menu commands, Standard Toolbar commands, and special methods available for

✦ Undoing and redoing actions

✦ Deleting objects, objects in groups, text, and pages

✦ Cutting and pasting objects, objects in groups, and text

With these powerful and commonly used commands you can now easily make changes in your pages and projects. In the next chapter we will go into detail on how to set up your pages and page options.

✦   ✦   ✦

Setting Up Pages

I've discussed four of the five fundamental elements of Visio 2000: stencils, templates, wizards, and drawing tools. I now want to turn your attention to another key ingredient — the drawing pages. In Visio, pages are more than just a medium to place shapes. Sure, you can set page parameters concerning margins, size, and orientation, but Visio also enables users to create background pages and set drawing scales for architectural and engineering precision. This chapter discusses the numerous advantages of Visio page layout.

Creating a New Page

Before learning how to set page parameters, I want to discuss inserting pages into a project. Visio 2000 Standard lets users create pages in three different ways. Ultimately, however, the Page Setup dialog box must be opened to complete the process. The difference lies in how each set of actions begins. The following example demonstrates how to create a new page by using the page tab.

1. Right-click the page tab. Visio, by default, calls the initial page *Page-1* in new drawings. The page tab is located in the lower left-hand corner of your screen (see Figure 8-1).

2. Choose Insert Page from the pop-up menu. This pulls up the Page Setup dialog box.

3. Select the Page Properties tab on the dialog box. In the Page properties section a new name appears (as shown in Figure 8-2). Visio numbers these generically (for example, Page-2, Page-3, and so on). You can change the name. Click the OK button when finished.

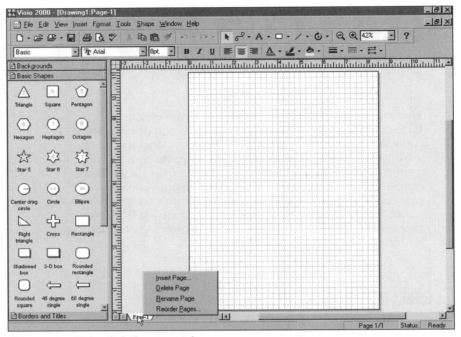

Figure 8-1: Right-click the page tab.

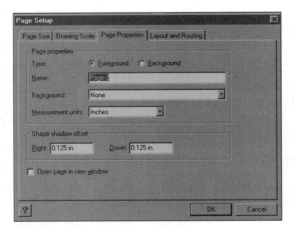

Figure 8-2: Inserting a new page

Note   Inserted pages, by default, exhibit the same features and settings as the page in the drawing window.

You may also insert a page via the menu bar. Simply click Insert and then select Page. This action pulls up the same Page Setup dialog box as in the previous exercise. Change the name if necessary and then click OK. You can also insert pages from the Drawing Explorer, as the following step-by-step exercise indicates:

1. Select View ➪ Windows ➪ Drawing Explorer.

2. Right-click the Foreground folder and then click Insert Page.

3. The Page Setup dialog box appears. Choose the name you want for the new page and then select OK.

Note The Page Setup dialog box accessed in these instances is slightly different than the one found from File ➪ Page Setup. The latter also contains a Print Setup tab.

Renaming Pages

There are several ways to rename pages. First, you can select File ➪ Page Setup to pull up the Page Setup dialog box. Next, choose the Page Properties tab and then change the name on that page. Click OK and the new page name appears on the tab in the lower-left corner of the screen.

The menu-bar method is fine, but it can be time-consuming. Rather than using a drop-down menu, simply edit the page tab. The following exercise demonstrates one of the ways to do this:

1. Double-click the page tab. This highlights the page's name within that tab.

2. Type in the new name in place of the highlighted text. Press Enter or click outside the tabbed area.

Note You can also right-click a page tab and select Rename Page. This action highlights the page's name within that tab. Type in the appropriate name and then press Enter.

Going to Another Page

It's easy to navigate between pages. The Go To function is one of several methods, shown in the following procedure:

1. Select Edit ➪ Go To.

2. A pop-out listing of the current pages appears. Choose the page that you want to see.

Tip You can navigate from page to page by simply clicking on the tab of the page you need. This action places the page of the selected tab on the drawing screen.

Reordering Pages

As you've probably learned by now, Visio provides users with several different ways to accomplish the same task. This is also true when reordering pages. There are two primary ways to reorganize drawing pages: by dragging and dropping or with the Drawing Explorer. The drag-and-drop method is as follows:

1. Click the tab of the page you want to move.

2. Hold the left mouse button and drag the page to its new position in the page tabs (as shown in Figure 8-3).

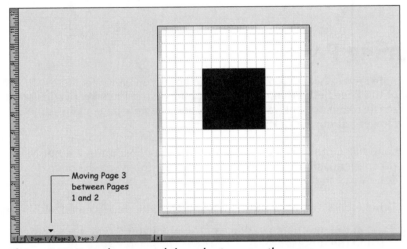

Moving Page 3
between Pages
1 and 2

Figure 8-3: Drag the page tab in order to move the page.

Tip   Notice that a page icon appears with the cursor along with a shifting black pointer along the tabs. Line up the icon with the pointer to ensure that the pages (and tabs) are reordered.

Note   Visio 2000 renumbers the default names (for example, Page-1, Page-2, and so on) when rearranging pages with the drag-and-drop method.

You can also rearrange pages with the Drawing Explorer:

1. Choose View ➪ Windows ➪ Drawing Explorer.

2. Right-click one of the page folders and then select Reorder Pages.

3. The Reorder Pages dialog box appears, revealing the Page Order. Highlight (click) the name of the page that you want to move.

4. Use the Move Up and Move Down buttons to place the page where you want it.

Check the Update Page Names box when using Visio default names. By doing so you enable the program to rename the pages accordingly.

You can also access the Reorder Pages dialog box by right-clicking on a page tab and then selecting Reorder Pages from the pop-up menu.

Deleting Pages

Delete pages as follows:

1. Select Edit ➪ Delete ➪ Pages.

2. The Delete Pages dialog box (as shown in Figure 8-4) contains all of the current pages. Highlight the page you wish to delete by clicking on it. Selecting OK deletes the page.

Figure 8-4: The Delete Pages dialog box.

On the other hand, you may right-click the appropriate page tab and select the Delete Page function from the pop-up menu, as demonstrated in the following:

1. Right-click the tab of the page that you would like to delete.

2. Select Delete Page.

Both of these functions remove pages from your projects. Remember that if you accidentally delete a page, you can retrieve it by using the Undo button.

Rotating Pages

Visio provides several different methods for viewing drawings; many are discussed in the next chapter. Rotating pages is among these ways. However, unlike other viewing aids, this feature is more than just a viewing mechanism. Page rotation provides a quick means for placing numerous shapes at a particular angle. It is especially helpful when working with maps and office layouts.

Enabling the Page Rotation feature

Before tilting pages, you need to activate the page rotation feature. Follow these three steps to do so:

1. Select Tools ➪ Options.

2. Choose the Drawing tab on the Options dialog box.

3. Check the Enable Page Rotation box within the Drawing Options section and then click the OK button.

Using the Rotation Tool

In cases where you must place several shapes at a certain angle, rotating the drawing page is easier than manipulating individual shapes. Not only do grids remain fixed when rotating a page, but also the angle of rotation is listed on the screen. These two aspects of the rotation page feature make placing particular shapes (for example, roads, rivers, and office furniture) quick and simple. The following activity demonstrates how to tilt a page so that you can place a shape at a particular angle:

1. Select the Rotation Tool from the Standard Toolbar.

2. Place your cursor over the drawing page's top-right corner.

3. Once the cursor changes into the circular arrows symbol, drag the corner to the right. The angle of rotation is displayed in the lower left-hand corner of the screen. This is determined by the way the page pivots from the corner with a gray dot. Place the page at –30° (see Figure 8-5). Shapes turned up to 180° counterclockwise are represented by negative numbers, whereas those turned up to 180° clockwise are positive.

4. Open a stencil and drag one of its shapes onto the page.

5. Rotate the drawing page back to its original position. The shape remains at a –30° angle.

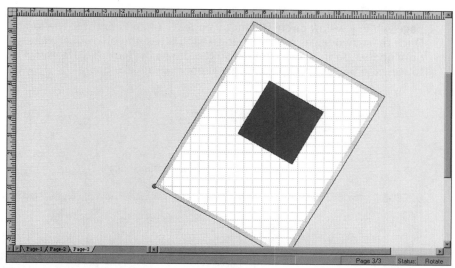

Figure 8-5: Rotating a drawing page

 The intersection of the two rulers' zero points is the pivot point for rotating a page. See Chapter 10 for more information about zero points.

 Rotating a page does not affect its printing settings. Therefore, a project set at portrait orientation prints at that setting even when the drawing is tilted 180°.

Objects on a rotated page do not respond to the Distribute Shapes function.

Working with Foregrounds and Backgrounds

One or more foreground pages constitute a Visio drawing. For instance, a drawing may contain the default pages Page-1 and Page-2. Both of these items are foreground pages within the drawing file. Background pages are positioned behind foreground pages. When a foreground and background page merge, the foreground acts somewhat like a transparency. In short, shapes on the background page appear when viewing the foreground page.

For example, a blue square is located in the lower right-hand corner of a background page, while a yellow circle sits in the upper left-hand corner of the foreground page. Once these two pages are assigned to each other, the blue square and yellow circle both appear on the foreground page (as shown in Figure 8-6). However, if you choose to view the background page, you will only see a blue square.

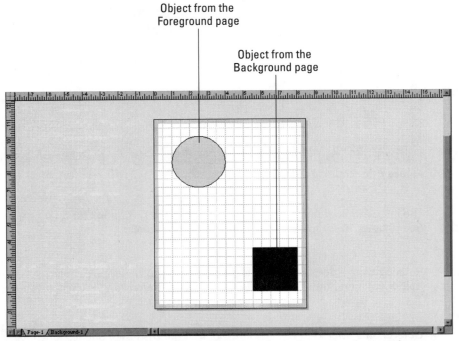

Figure 8-6: When a background page is assigned to a foreground page, shapes on both can be viewed from the foreground page.

Note You cannot make changes to shapes in the foreground page that are part of the background page. You can only do this by directly editing from the background page. Bring up the background page by clicking on its tab.

The background page is a convenient tool; it enables users to attach the same figures to different drawings. This feature comes in handy for a number of practices, in particular, placing a company or organization's logo on all its related charts and diagrams. It's one of the many time-saving aspects of using Visio software.

Creating a background page

You must assign a background page to a foreground page in order to simultaneously view both. First, here's how to create a background page:

1. Right-click a page tab and then choose Insert Page from the pop-up menu. If you prefer starting at the menu bar, choose Insert ➪ Page.

2. Select the Page Properties tab on the Page Setup dialog box.

3. In the Page Properties section of the dialog box, click Background. Name it accordingly and then click OK.

Assigning a background to a foreground page

Once you've created a background page you may assign the page to a foreground. This relationship enables the two to interact as one drawing page. The following are instructions for assigning a background page to a foreground page:

1. Click the tab of the page to which you'd like to assign a background page.

2. Select File ➪ Page Setup. A Page Setup dialog box appears on the screen.

3. Click the Page Properties tab.

4. In the small box designated by the word *Background*, choose from the list of backgrounds available (as shown in Figure 8-7).

5. Once you're pleased with the selection, click OK.

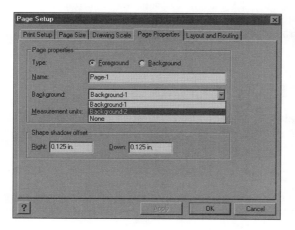

Figure 8-7: Assigning a background page to a foreground page

Some projects may require you to use shapes from several backgrounds in one foreground page. This is possible although you cannot assign more than one background to a foreground page. For example, you have Page-1, Background-1, Background-2, and Background-3. Assign Background-1 to Page-1. Next, assign Background-2 as a background to Background-1. Finally, assign Background-3 as the background to Background-2. This process enables you to view shapes on all four pages from the foreground page (in this case, Page-1).

You can place your company logo on a background page and save it in a new template. Learn more about this in Chapter 15.

Canceling a foreground-background page assignment

If you later change your mind about a foreground-background page assignment, Visio lets users cancel the relationship. Here's how:

1. Click the Foreground page tab.
2. Select File ➪ Page Setup.
3. Choose the Page Properties tab on the Page Setup dialog box.
4. Choose None in the Background box and then click the OK button.
5. Once you complete these steps, the background page is prevented from interacting with the foreground page. Now editing the former will not affect the latter, and you may delete the background page without any restrictions.

You cannot delete a background page once it's assigned to a foreground page. Thus, you must cancel the assignment between the two pages before you can delete the background. Foreground pages, however, can be deleted when still assigned to a background.

Setting Page Parameters

You can modify a number of Visio page characteristics, including color, size, orientation, and drawing scales. Set these variables to suit your drawing.

Adjusting page color

The Options dialog box enables users to manipulate color settings for pages, the page background, the full-screen background, and the print-preview background. To set these features, follow these steps:

1. Select Tools ➪ Options. This pulls up the Options dialog box.
2. On the page with the General tab, look to the lower right-hand corner for an area entitled *Color Settings*. Here you can adjust four color blocks.

3. Click the color block adjacent to the area's name to modify the color. Selecting one of the blocks takes you to the Edit Color dialog box.

4. The Edit Color dialog box enables you to choose the color you want. Click one of the Basic or Custom Colors and then select OK. However, if you still find the selection limited, click a color within the large Color Selector palette. The color bar to the right of the palette contains various shades of the color you've selected. Click the desired hue. Click OK when the correct color appears in the Color/Solid block.

To view your changes, go to the appropriate location. Page and Page Background are viewed on the Visio 2000 window (see Figure 8-8). You must select View ➪ Full Screen to view the Full Screen Background and File ➪ Print Preview to see the Print Preview Background.

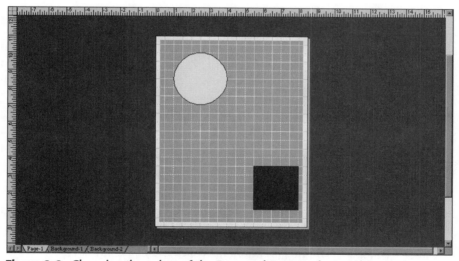

Figure 8-8: Changing the colors of the Page and Page Background

Removing grids, rulers, and connection points from pages

Visio drawing aids make constructing diagrams easy and precise. In fact, they are often essential for connecting, measuring, and aligning shapes. You may, however, find that in some stages of the drawing process these aids become cumbersome. In such instances it's best to follow Mark Twain's advice, "When it doubt, take it out."

Note   Grids, rulers, and connection points do not appear on the Full-Screen view. They also are not represented in printouts of a Visio drawing.

Removing grids, rulers, and connection points from a drawing page (as shown in Figure 8-9) is simple. From the View drop-down menu, choose the element in the list that you desire to remove. For instance, selecting View ➪ Grid disables the Grid drawing aid from appearing on the page. Notice that light-colored buttons represent activated selections on the drop-down menu. For example, after selecting View ➪ Grid, Grid in the drop-down menu is no longer highlighted. By default, all Visio 2000 Standard drawing-aid elements are activated, except the Page Breaks.

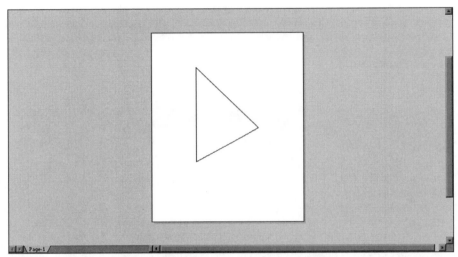

Figure 8-9: A drawing page without grids, rulers, guides, or connection points

Reactivate a drawing-aid element the same way you disabled it. For instance, simply select View ➪ Grid again to restore the lines upon the drawing page. The same applies to Rulers, Guides, Connection Points, and Page Breaks. This one-step process takes care of adding and removing these drawing aids. No fuss, no muss.

See Chapter 10 for more information on setting rulers, grids, and guide lines.

Setting page margins

Page margins are the areas around a page in which you choose not to print material. The following exercise shows how to adjust and view page margins:

1. Select File ➪ Page Setup to bring up the Page Setup dialog box.

2. Choose the Print Setup tab on the Page Setup dialog box and then click the Setup button.

3. Insert the settings you want in the Margins (Inches) section and then click OK.

Note You may set the unit of measurement that is used on a page by accessing File ➭ Page Setup ➭ Page Properties.

4. Click OK on the Page Setup dialog box.

5. Go to View ➭ Page Breaks to view the page's new margins (represented in gray).

 Note Visio 2000, by default, sets the page margins at 0.25 inch.

Adjusting page size and orientation

Select File ➭ Page Setup. Choose the Page Size tab on the Page Setup dialog box. You have several options for page sizes. Check the preview window to the right to see how your choice corresponds to the printing settings (as shown in Figure 8-10). For instance, clicking on "Same as printer paper size" sets the drawing page to the same size as the printing page.

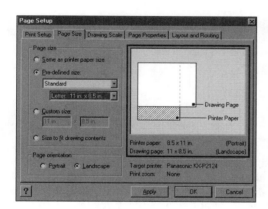

Figure 8-10: The preview window indicates that this drawing size is too large for the current print configuration.

The other drawing-page sizes may require you to update the printing settings. The Pre-Defined size enables users to select from Standard, Metric (ISO), ANSI Engineering, and ANSI Architectural standards (see Tables 8-1 and 8-2 for detailed lists of those formats). Custom size gives you the option of creating your own page sizes. "Size to fit drawing contents" adjusts the drawing page's size to fit the shapes on it.

 Note Modifications in a drawing page's settings are not automatically reflected in the printing settings, which remain the same. Therefore, check to make sure that settings on the Page Setup dialog box's Page Size and Print Setup tabs correspond with each other before printing.

Table 8-1
Pre-Defined Size Drawing Page Formats (Standard and Metric)

Standard	Metric (ISO)
Letter: 8.5 × 11 inches	A5: 148 × 210 millimeters
Folio: 8.5 × 13 inches	A4: 210 × 297 millimeters
Legal: 8.5 × 14 inches	A3: 297 × 420 millimeters
Tabloid: 11 × 17 inches	A2: 420 × 594 millimeters
	A1: 594 × 841 millimeters
	A0: 841 × 1189 millimeters

Table 8-2
Pre-Defined Size Drawing Page Formats (ANSI)

ANSI Engineering	ANSI Architectural
A: 8.5 × 11 inches	9 × 12 inches
B: 11 × 17 inches	12 × 18 inches
C: 17 × 22 inches	18 × 24 inches
D: 22 × 34 inches	24 × 36 inches
E: 34 × 44 inches	30 × 42 inches

Once you decide on the drawing page's dimensions, set the orientation. Selecting Portrait places the page in a vertically elongated manner, while Landscape orients the page in a horizontally elongated manner. Note that if you've selected "Same as printer paper size," orientation features are not accessible. Click OK when you've finished your selections on the Page Size tab.

Adjusting drawing scales

Certain charts involving architectural layouts and maps need realistic drawing scales. To do this, select File ➪ Page Setup. Choose the Drawing Scale tab on the Page Setup dialog box. There are three different ways to set drawing scales:

✦ **No Scale.** Click this if you are not working on a scaled drawing.

✦ **Pre-Defined Scale.** This includes formatted dimensions available for Architectural, Civil Engineering, Metric, and Mechanical engineering drawings (See Table 8-3).

✦ **Custom Scale.** If you cannot find the dimensions you're looking for in the Pre-Defined Scale category, create your own here.

Tip

Page Size (In Measurement Units) reveals the representational size of your project. For instance, a drawing on an 8½ × 11-inch sheet of drawing paper (actual size of project) scaled as ½ inches = 1 foot results in a representational size of 17 × 22 feet.

Cross-Reference

See Chapter 10 for more information on setting measurement units.

Table 8-3
Pre-Defined Drawing Scales

Architectural	*Civil Engineering*	*Mechanical Engineering*	*Metric*
In Imperial Measurements	**In Imperial Measurements**	**In Imperial Measurements**	**In Metric Standard Scales**
³⁄₃₂" = 1'0"	1" = 10'0"	¹⁄₃₂:1	1:1000
⅛" = 1'0"	1" = 20'0"	¹⁄₁₆:1	1:500
³⁄₁₆" = 1'0"	1" = 30'0"	⅛:1	1:200
¼" = 1'0"	1" = 40'0"	¼:1	1:100
⅜" = 1'0"	1" = 50'0"	½:1	1:50
½" = 1'0"	1" = 60'0"	2:1	1:25
¾" = 1'0"	1" = 70'0"	4:1	1:20
1" = 1'0"	1" = 80'0"	6:1	1:10
1 ½" = 1'0"	1" = 90'0"	8:1	1:5
3" = 1'0"	1" = 100'0"	10:1	1:2.5
			1:2
			10:1
			20:1
			50:1

Tip

You can adjust the unit of measurement for pages from the Options dialog box. Under the Regional Settings tab, select the appropriate default unit (inches, yards, miles, meters, days, and so on) for your projects.

Adding headers and footers

Ascribe dates, page numbers, and file names to a document with the Header and Footer function. You can also place other text along the top or bottom of a page. Here's a step-by-step look at this feature:

1. Go to View ⇨ Header and Footer to reach the Header and Footer dialog box.

2. Type in the text you want to appear in the left, center, and right portions of the header and footer. You can alter the margins for the header and footer as well.

3. Modify font-related aspects with the Choose Font button, which pulls up a Choose Font dialog box where you can choose among fonts, font styles, sizes, effects, color, and script.

4. Click OK to close the dialog boxes.

Tip You must either select Print Preview or print the drawing to view the header and footer. They do not appear on the drawing page.

Print a variety of elements as your header and/or footer. By clicking on the arrows to the right of the header and footer boxes, you have the option of selecting several elements the program can fill in for you. For instance, if you want the date, you only need to select Current Date (Long). There's no need to type in the day, month, and year yourself; the program takes care of that for you. See Table 8-4 for a list of header and footer elements.

Table 8-4
Header/Footer Elements and Shortcuts

Element	Shortcut
Page Number	&p
Page Name	&n
Total Printed Pages	&P
Current Time	&t
Current Date (Short)	&d
Current Date (Long)	&D
File Name	&f
File Extension	&e
File Name and Extension	&f&e

Summary

In this chapter, you learned numerous ways to create and modify pages. You created, renamed, reordered, and deleted pages. I taught you the difference between background and foreground pages and how they interact. You also learned to manipulate a variety of Visio page parameters. Overall, this chapter explained the following points:

✦ The easiest way to create a new page is by right-clicking on that page's tab and then choosing Insert Page.

✦ You can also right-click the page tab to rename or delete the page.

✦ Navigate between pages by clicking on the tab of the page you want to view.

✦ Reorder pages by sorting the page tabs with your mouse.

✦ Page rotation is ideal for placing a number of shapes at a specific angle.

✦ Shapes on a background page appear on the foreground page when the two pages are assigned to each other.

✦ Adjust page color by accessing the Options dialog box.

✦ Use the View drop-down menu to remove rulers, guides, grids, and connection points from drawing pages.

✦ Manipulate page size, orientation, margins, and drawing scales from the Page Setup dialog box.

✦ Modifications in a drawing page's settings are not reflected in the printing settings.

✦ You can customize your own drawing scales or use predefined scales such as those for available for architectural and mechanical engineering purposes.

✦ The Header and Footer dialog box enables you to print things such as the time, date, and page number on each page of a drawing.

In the next chapter, you learn how to adjust views.

✦   ✦   ✦

Adjusting Views

Bifocals are the bane of middle-aged existence. I'm
constantly tilting my head to see this or magnify that.
Luckily, life with Visio 2000 is much simpler. With its windows
and zoom and pan features you may look at your work
however you like . . . without getting a cramp in your neck.

Zooming and Panning

The zooming and panning features are important tools for
any project of moderate or reasonable complexity. Everyone
knows that drawings sometimes require concentration on
minute details or an overhead view of an entire drawing.
Visio 2000 gives you a couple of ways to zoom in and out
of drawings.

With the panning tools, you can quickly and easily move from
one area of your drawing to another for editing. Some of the
commands and buttons may be familiar from other programs,
many of which have similar functions. However, a few
commands may be new to you. This chapter will review
all of the zooming and panning features in Visio 2000.

Standard Toolbar zoom buttons and the Zoom List button

The Zoom Out, Zoom In, and Zoom List buttons are located
on the far right side of the Standard Toolbar. The only button
further to the right is the Help Button, which is denoted with a
standard question mark. The Zoom Out button has a magnifying glass with a minus sign in it. The Zoom In button has a
magnifying glass with a plus sign inside it. And the Zoom List
button has a list box that shows a percentage, as well as a
down arrow button to the right of the list box (as shown in
Figure 9-1).

Note If you are using a low resolution setting on your monitor, such as 640 × 480, you may not be able to see all of the buttons that are on your Standard Toolbar. Visio 2000 shows as many buttons on the toolbar as space allows. If there are more buttons than can be shown, then some will be cropped off the display. Unfortunately, the Zoom In and Zoom Out buttons are among the first to go. To get access to these buttons, you will need to either reset your video display to a higher resolution or remove other toolbar buttons.

Cross-Reference For more information on how to modify the toolbar, see Chapter 3.

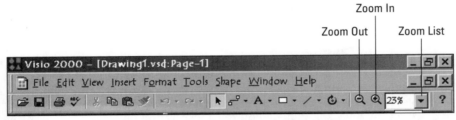

Figure 9-1: The Zoom Out, Zoom In, and the Zoom List buttons on the Standard Toolbar

Using the Zoom Out and the Zoom In buttons

Let's try using the Zoom Out and Zoom In buttons on some maps. From the menu, choose File ➪ New. Scroll down to the Maps folder and choose Geographical Maps. This opens several stencils on your left. The US Canada and Mexico stencil should be on the list. Click Alaska and drag it to the center of the drawing sheet. (I've chosen Alaska because it offers some nice coastline detail for this example.)

Click the Zoom Out button (the magnifying glass with the minus sign) a few times until the drawing stops shrinking. 10% should appear in the Zoom List box beside the Zoom buttons. 10% is the minimum zoom out allowed when using the Zoom buttons. Pay attention to the percentage in the Zoom List box as you click the Zoom In button (the other magnification glass with the plus sign). Keep clicking it until the percentage stops changing. You will see that the percentage rises in preset steps until you reach the limit, usually somewhere between 2000% and 3500%.

Note The type of video card installed in your computer can affect the limits of your magnification settings.

Using the Zoom List feature

The Zoom List feature has options that are not available when just using the Zoom Out and Zoom In buttons. A short drop-down menu appears (as shown in Figure 9-2) by clicking the Zoom List button. Six preset magnification percentages are listed: 50%, 75%, 100%, 200%, and 400%. Simply scroll down the menu and click the setting that's best for you.

Tip Selecting View ➪ Zoom pulls up a pop-up menu with features similar to those in the Zoom List box. In fact, you'll find that the Last Zoom and Page Width options offer the same six preset magnification percentages as the Zoom List box.

Notice that three options lie below the six magnifications: Last, Width, and Page. Selecting Last will return the drawing to its previous magnification. For example, if you changed your viewing perspective from 75% to 100%, then choosing Last would return you to 75%. Unfortunately, the feature doesn't work like the Back function on a Web browser. It only brings you back to the previous setting, not a connected string of previous settings.

Choosing Width will set the page magnification so that the width of the drawing page fills most of the available width of the working space. This varies according to several factors, such as the monitor's resolution, the page size and layout, and the size already set for the working space.. Therefore, a set percentage does not exist for Width.

Page is similar in not having a set percentage. It will be in whatever size is necessary in order to fit the entire drawing page into your available working space.

100% ▼
400%
200%
150%
100%
75%
50%
Last
Width
Page

Figure 9-2: The Zoom List drop-down menu options

Like the Zoom List box in many Windows products, the Zoom List can be manipulated by typing in specific numerical figures. For instance, you can enter any percentage directly into the list box. Try it. Click the number in the list box. Enter any percentage that you want and press Enter. The program will set your drawing to the specified magnification. You do not even need to put in the % symbol; Visio 2000 will do that for you.

Try entering 1%. I know; that's probably smaller than you will ever use, but the option is there if you need it. If you enter anything smaller than 1%, the figure will automatically round up to 1%. Once you reach your magnification limits (usually affected by your computer's video card), any percentage over the limit will be reduced to that limit. Thus, you can focus in on a particular Alaskan island or view the state as a whole.

Note   It is possible to enter decimal fractions into the Zoom List box. Visio 2000 will show the drawing at that magnification. However, it will round off the number in the Zoom List box to the nearest whole number. For example, if you enter 20.5% in the Zoom List box, the drawing will go to a magnification of 20.5%. The percentage shown in the Zoom List box will be 21%. Try it by entering 1%, 1.5%, and 2%. Watch the different sizes that the page will take for each request.

Zoom dialog box

Using the Zoom dialog box is another method for changing a drawing's magnification. Its options are similar to those in the Zoom List box — with a few slight differences. I will discuss those later in the chapter. But first, let's go over how to open the Zoom dialog box.

Opening the Zoom dialog box

Two methods exist for opening the Zoom dialog box. The first (and harder) method involves the Menu Toolbar. Click View ➪ Zoom. Go to the bottom of the Zoom menu and click Zoom. . . (see Figure 9-3). This opens the Zoom dialog box. Click Cancel at the bottom of the box, and we'll open it again, but now with the second method.

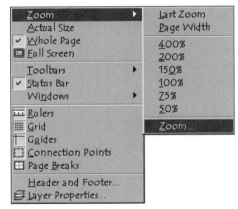

Figure 9-3: Accessing the Zoom dialog box from the Menu Toolbar

The other method used for accessing the Zoom dialog box is a cake job. Simply press the F6 key. This action directly brings up the dialog box. This is a prime example of how beneficial shortcut keys are. Don't close the Zoom dialog box just yet, though. Keep it open, so I can discuss some of its options.

Zoom dialog box options

The Zoom dialog box (as shown in Figure 9-4) contains nine magnification options. The top six are preset magnification factors, ranging between 50% and 400%, the same as the Zoom List options. It also has Page Width and Whole Page Magnification options, which work the same as the Width and Page options that were discussed in the "Using the Zoom List feature" section. The Zoom dialog box's default setting is 400%. To select another magnification, click the radio button beside the desired magnification and choose OK.

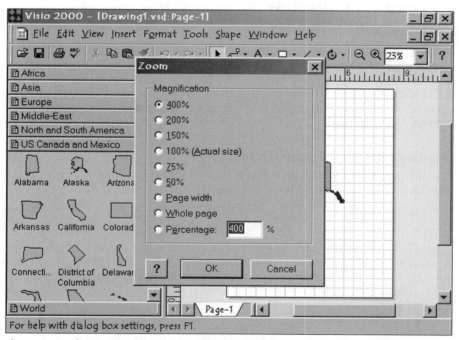

Figure 9-4: The Zoom dialog box with default settings

The Percentage box is the final feature on the Zoom dialog box. Reopen the Zoom dialog box. The list box beside Percentage will be highlighted, but the radio button beside 400% will also be selected (as shown in Figure 9-4). Typing in the magnification percentage that you want is the simplest way to use Percentage. The program will automatically switch the radio-button selection to Percentage. Next, click OK at the bottom of the box.

The Zoom dialog box is a little different from the Zoom List box. For instance, you can only input whole numbers. The Zoom dialog box will not accept decimal fractions. Instead of rounding to the nearest acceptable value, as the Zoom List box does, the Zoom dialog box returns an error message if it does not accept a value. In this way, it is not as flexible as the Zoom List box. The Zoom Dialog Box also does not have a Last option. So, if you need to switch back and forth between two magnifications, you will want to use the Zoom List box's Last option.

The next section deals with zooming — without all that worry about magnification percentages. Before starting some examples, though, reset the magnification of your drawing page to 100%.

The Pan & Zoom functions, and the Pan & Zoom window

Zooming is fine, but sometimes the area that you want to bring up isn't in the center of the drawing. Perhaps you may be working at a high magnification, and you want to find certain details without switching to a different magnification. The Pan & Zoom window enables you to select the area that you want to zoom in on. I'll cover another method in the section "Setting Center selection on zoom." But in this section, I will discuss the Pan & Zoom window, its chief functions, and how to use it.

Opening the Pan & Zoom window

The best way to learn about the Pan & Zoom window is to use it. To open it from your Menu Toolbar, select View ➪ Windows ➪ Pan & Zoom (as shown in Figure 9-5).

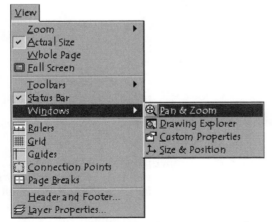

Figure 9-5: Accessing the Pan & Zoom window from the Menu Toolbar

The Pan & Zoom window will appear in the upper right corner of your workspace (as shown in Figure 9-6). The whole drawing window is represented in the Pan & Zoom window in proportion to the size of the page in which you're working and the whole of the page. As a result, part of the page won't be cropped off, and therefore, out of sight. You will probably see a red square enclosing Alaska. This is your active workspace. It, too, is proportional to the size of the page and will remain so if its size changes.

Note If your viewing perspective is fairly low, such as 33%, the red box will not be visible. This is because your active workspace is larger than the workspace revealed in the Pan & Zoom box.

Figure 9-6: The Pan & Zoom window

Resizing the Pan & Zoom window

You may want to enlarge or shrink the Pan & Zoom window in order to increase drawing efficiency. To change the window's size, move your cursor to the window's edge. The cursor becomes a two-headed arrow, indicating that it's ready for resizing (as shown in Figure 9-6). Click and drag the window's edge down a little. You will see that the width of the window changes in proportion with any change in the height of the window.

Hiding the Pan & Zoom window

Of course, having this window open prevents you from, at times, seeing a good bit of your drawing page. Don't fret; a couple solutions are available. You could activate the window's Autohide feature. To do this, right-click anywhere within the Pan & Zoom window. A menu will appear with three options: Close, Float Window, and AutoHide (as shown in Figure 9-7). Click AutoHide. Now, move your cursor out of the Pan & Zoom window. It will scroll itself out of your way, leaving only a small title bar.

Tip   The AutoHide feature will not work while the Pan & Zoom window is in float mode. You must first anchor the window in order to "hide" it.

What if you need the window back? Just place your cursor over the title bar and the window will automatically scroll back out for you. Now you have quick access to the Pan & Zoom window, without it blocking the view of the working drawing. To turn off the AutoHide feature, right-click anywhere on the Pan & Zoom window, and then click AutoHide in the pop-up menu in order to deselect it.

Figure 9-7: Right-click to get the Pan & Zoom window control menu.

Moving the Pan & Zoom Window

So, you want to move the window somewhere else? No problem. Right-click anywhere on the Pan & Zoom window, and select Float Window from the pop-up menu. Notice that the Pan & Zoom window changes again. You can now move the window by clicking and holding on the title bar and then dragging the window anywhere you want — even out of the workspace window and over the stencils.

AutoHide feature doesn't work in Float Window mode. In order to retrieve the AutoHide feature, you will need to anchor the Pan & Zoom window. Do this by right-clicking anywhere on the Pan & Zoom window. Notice that the Float Window option on the pop-up menu has been replaced with the Anchor Window (as shown in Figure 9-8). Click the Anchor Window. The Pan & Zoom window then attaches itself to the nearest corner or side in the working window of the drawing.

If you want to place the Pan & Zoom window in a particular corner, at a particular spot along one of the sides, or at the top or bottom of the window, just float the window and slowly drag it to the spot. When it comes into contact with the side or corner, the window will automatically switch out of float mode, reverting to anchored mode.

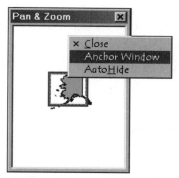

Figure 9-8: Menu options while window is in Float mode

Closing the Pan & Zoom window

To get rid of the Pan & Zoom window, simply close it. Do this by clicking the "X" in the title bar or by right-clicking the Pan & Zoom window and then selecting Close from the menu. Poof! The Pan & Zoom window is no more.

Well, now that you know how to control the window, it's time to begin using the window for panning and zooming.

Panning with the Pan & Zoom window

If you have closed the Pan & Zoom window, reopen it. Place your cursor to the center of the red square in the window; your cursor sports a four-directional arrow (as shown in Figure 9-9). This lets you know that you can adjust the viewing area (the red square). To do this, click and hold with the four-arrowed cursor in the red square, and then drag the square to where you want it. This is panning. Try taking the cursor completely off of Alaska. Now, pan back to Alaska by using the scroll bar that is located to the far right of the Visio drawing screen. Notice that once again, the red square encloses Alaska.

Figure 9-9: The four-arrowed panning cursor

Zooming with the Pan & Zoom window

You know how to pan with the window; let me show you how easy it is to zoom in and out with this handy-dandy tool. Make sure Alaska is approximately centered in the red box. Next, move your cursor until it's over a side or corner of the red box. The cursor will change into the two-headed resizing arrow, with which you're already familiar. Click and drag from the center of the box. All four sides of the red square will increase in size. Notice, however, that the side opposite from the one in which you're directly moving does not jut out like the others.

> **Note** The viewing box always maintains proportion with the active drawing area in the program.

When you make the red box larger, you zoom out. When you make the red box smaller, you zoom in. It's that simple, and you don't have to keep up with the magnification percentages. Now, with the ability to move and hide the Pan & Zoom window, you can easily and quickly move from detail to detail in your drawings.

Setting Center selection on zoom

There may be times when you are using zoom features that you will want a specific detail in the center of your drawing. This section tells you how to change the default zoom point from the center of the page to any point your little heart desires.

Activating the Center selection option

To activate the Center selection option, select Tools ➭ Options. This brings up the Options dialog box. Select the Drawing Tab. You'll see the Drawings option section in the middle of the window (as shown in Figure 9-10). The third option on the left side of the section is the Center selection on zoom option. Check the box to activate the option. Next, click the OK button.

Using the Center selection on zoom

Center selection on zoom focuses the zoom on whatever shape in the drawing is selected. If no shape is selected, then the center of the working space will remain the center when zoom is initiated. If you have a drawing that has several shapes in it — and none are selected — zooming will keep the center of the workspace as the center. If, however, you select a shape that is, say, off in the left bottom corner, then the program will center the selected object in the workspace when you zoom. To make this clear, let's try it out.

Using Center selection on zoom

In order to show how Center selection on zoom works, more than one drawing element must be available for the program to choose from. So, add a couple more states to our drawing. First, zoom out, allowing yourself more room for adding states. Next, drag California to the right of Alaska. Drag Colorado, placing it directly under Alaska. Now you have three shapes that the program can center on.

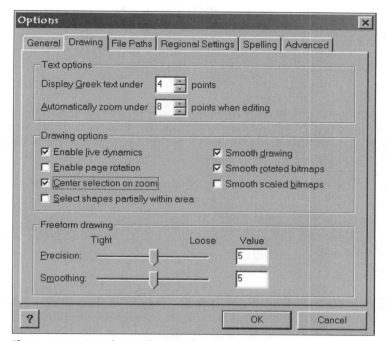

Figure 9-10: Drawing options in the Options box

Click California to select it, and then go to the Standard Toolbar and click the Zoom In button. California is now in the center of the workspace. Click a blank section of the page to deselect California. Zoom out and back in. California still remains in the center because it was centered to begin with. Now, click one of the other states and zoom out. That state is now in the center. Leave it selected and use the Pan & Zoom window to move away from the selected state. Now, zoom again. Your selected state will return to the center. Keep your example running so you can use it for the next section "Viewing Windows."

Note   Center selection on zoom does not effect the Pan & Zoom window function. When you use the Pan & Zoom window, the selected object will not automatically be centered. Center selection on zoom does, however, function with all other methods of zooming that already have been described in this chapter.

Other Pan & Zoom methods

I'd like to briefly discuss two more methods for panning and zooming. The first applies to all users, and the second applies only to those who own a Microsoft IntelliMouse.

Keyboard shortcuts

As you learned earlier, keyboard shortcuts can save you much time. However, these Pan & Zoom methods involve more than just keys; they require the use of a mouse. So, "keyboard shortcuts" is a bit of a misnomer. But, I'm sure you get the drift.

Zooming

To zoom in, simultaneously hold down the Control and Shift keys, and left-click your mouse. To zoom out, simultaneously hold down the Control and Shift keys, and right-click your mouse. Keep in mind that if the spot you click is not centered, the drawing may shift position in order to keep that spot within the working space.

If you want to zoom in on a particular area of your drawing, simultaneously hold down the Control and Shift keys, and hold down the mouse button. Drag it so that it draws a rectangle around the area that you want to zoom in on. Keep in mind that the rectangle you draw will not be kept proportional to the workspace. If you draw a long thin rectangle, the program will zoom in only as far as it has to in order to fit the longest side of the rectangle within the workspace.

Panning

To pan, simultaneously hold down the Control and Shift keys along with the right mouse button. As you drag the mouse, a hand icon replaces the magnification symbol and the drawing moves wherever you drag it. You can continue dragging even when your cursor leaves the workspace. Thus, you're not limited by the size of the workspace when moving the drawing this way.

Microsoft IntelliMouse shortcuts

These shortcuts use the IntelliMouse's wheel — that small, rubber device situated between the right and left mouse buttons. Two methods exist for panning. You can use each for moving either horizontally or vertically. There is only one shortcut method, however, for zooming in or out.

Panning up or down

The first method involves rolling the mouse's wheel. The direction that you roll the wheel depends upon your mouse's setup options. The second method is to press on the wheel and move the mouse. Either technique will pan the drawing area up or down.

Panning side to side

Panning from side to side is easy, too. Hold down the Shift key and roll the mouse's wheel. The direction that you roll the wheel depends upon your mouse's setup options. In the second technique, simply press on the wheel and move the mouse.

Zooming

To zoom, hold down the Control key and roll the mouse wheel. The direction to roll the wheel for zooming in or out depends upon the mouse's setup options.

Viewing Windows

Sometimes you will need to compare different parts of a drawing. This can be difficult if the parts are small and placed some distance from each other on the page. Tougher still, you may need to switch between different drawings. But there's no need to get tangled in a knot; the Viewing options on the Windows menu offer quite a bit of flexibility. Let's study each of the three commands.

New Window

This command gives you a new workspace window with the currently selected drawing page in it. This way you can have multiple windows with the same drawing in them. You can access the drawings from the bottom area of the Window drop-down menu.

Opening a New Window

Select Window ➪ New Window. This opens a new window that has the same drawing in it that the previous window had (as shown in Figure 9-11). The new window appears to the right of the old window. However, the program does not duplicate the stencils in the new window. The program also distinguishes the new window from the old by adding "-2" to the title of the second drawing.

Open another window. You will see that the stencils have been pushed out of the way in order to make room for the third drawing. The display of each drawing side by side is called tiling. By default, Visio 2000 tiles new windows.

Reinstating your original view

What if you need to grab something off your stencil and add it to the drawing? No problem. To bring your first, or any other window, to full size, just Maximize it. Go to your first window, which is the one on the far left. Click the Maximize button in that window's title bar, which is the middle of the three buttons with the square in it. Now your view is like it was before we created the new windows. But what happened to the other windows? They're still there. We will now see how to tile them on command, and then we'll look at another way to arrange them.

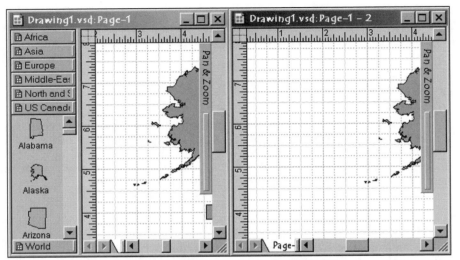

Figure 9-11: The new window adds a second workspace with a copy of the drawing in it.

Tiles

Visio 2000 tiles new windows by default. However, if you have changed your view and want to return to a tiled view, a simple command will do this.

Tiling windows

To tile your windows, simply select Window from the Menu Toolbar. In the Window menu select Tile. All the open drawing windows will now appear side by side. If there are more than three windows, they will arrange themselves in both columns and rows.

Using tiled windows

Keep in mind that the controls and commands only work in the active window. So, if you want to move from one window to another, you must click the new workspace or the new title bar before using any commands.

If you still have three tiled windows open, try this in order to see this function's versatility. First, if the Pan & Zoom window is not on in each of the windows, open them by selecting the windows and turning them on by following the instructions given earlier in this chapter. Also, turn on the AutoHide feature for the Pan & Zoom Window, which was also described earlier in the chapter. AutoHide is necessary in order for this example to work.

Now, center and zoom each of the states in a different window. You need not worry about selecting the window first in order to use the Pan & Zoom window. It will activate as soon as your cursor opens up the AutoHide Pan & Zoom window and you first click it. Now, you have three different shapes out of different areas of a drawing at different levels of magnification at your easy perusal (as shown in Figure 9-12). Neat!

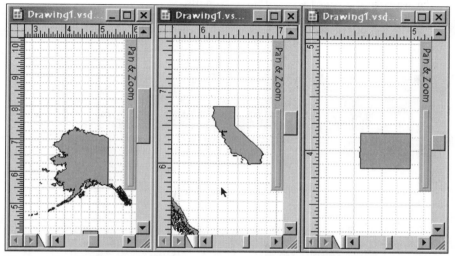

Figure 9-12: Tiled windows allows a user to simultaneously concentrate on different areas.

But what if you want to open even more windows? The workspaces for each window can become too cramped for use. How can you switch back and forth among bigger workspaces? One word — cascade.

Cascade

Cascading windows allows you to use a bigger workspace while still being able to center on a different area of a drawing in each window. It can also allow you to switch between different drawings with ease and efficiency. First, you will learn how to cascade windows, and then we will look at how to use cascade.

Cascading windows

From the Menu Toolbar select Window. From the Window menu select Cascade. All the open windows will now be stacked on top of each other with their toolbars showing (as shown in Figure 9-13). The order in which they appear will be determined by which window was selected when they were cascaded. As with tiled windows, only the original drawings will keep a set of stencils with it. If you have different drawings with different stencil sets, the original for each will keep its stencil set with it. Copies will not have stencils.

Note   When cascading, the currently selected window will be placed in front.

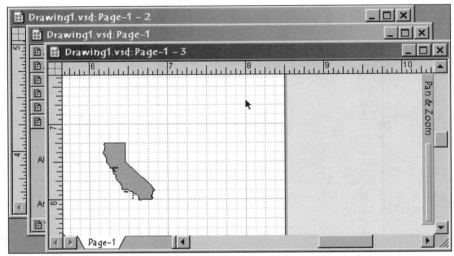

Figure 9-13: Cascade mode gives a user larger working spaces and retains quick access to other windows.

Switching between windows

To retrieve one of the hidden windows, simply click a part of a hidden window that is sticking out from underneath the top window. Be careful, though, not to click the Close Window button in the title bar, or you will lose that window. The Close Window button is in the top right corner of each window, and it has an "X" in it.

Try clicking the middle window's title bar in order to bring it on top. If you want, retrieve the bottom window by clicking its title bar. Not a bad way to maneuver between windows. Try bringing up the window that is now on the bottom of the stack by clicking the bit of that window which sticks out at the bottom. Now we have a bit of a problem. The bottom window has only two small bits that are visible: the Close Window button at the top right, which you don't want to click, and the small corner at the bottom left (as shown in Figure 9-14). You can retrieve the bottom window by clicking the small bit on the bottom left. However, if more than three windows are open, you may have a hard time telling which corners belong to which windows. So, we will now look at another way to bring windows out of the stack.

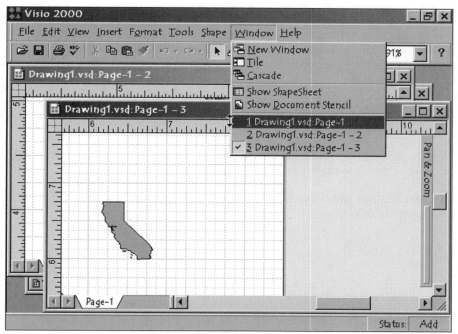

Figure 9-14: A buried window needs to be brought out to the top of the stack.

Another way to switch between windows is to go to the Menu Toolbar and select Window. At the bottom of the Window menu you will see a list of all open windows with their titles (as shown in Figure 9-14). Clicking any window in the list will bring it to the top of the stack.

Summary

The first part of this chapter covered many methods for zooming in and out of a drawing, panning to different areas of a drawing, and how to set options for some zooming and panning controls. The following tools were discussed:

✦ Using the Toolbar icon button controls for Zooming, the Zoom List box, the Zoom dialog box, the Pan & Zoom window, Keyboard shortcuts, and Microsoft IntelliMouse shortcuts

✦ Panning with the Pan & Zoom window, Keyboard shortcuts, and Microsoft IntelliMouse shortcuts

✦ Setting the Center selection on zoom option

The second part of this chapter covered how to create new windows when a user is simultaneously working on different parts of a drawing. This part of the chapter also discussed two methods for managing multiple open windows of the same or different drawings:

✦ Tiling windows

✦ Cascading windows

With these methods, you can easily manage and edit different parts of a single drawing or multiple drawings at any magnification.

The next chapter will cover how to set up rulers and guides that will help place and scale parts in drawings.

✦   ✦   ✦

Working with Rulers, Grids, and Guides

CHAPTER

10

This chapter discusses two principle aspects of shape arrangement: manipulating visual positioning aids, such as rulers, grids and guides; and using the snap and glue features. Understanding these tools is essential in order to perform many of the chapter exercises in Part IV of this book, "Using and Manipulating Shapes." This chapter covers the most basic methods for measuring, positioning, attaching, and gluing objects.

Setting Ruler Measurements

Rulers are an integral tool used for arranging shapes symmetrically, scaling objects in maps and architectural drawings, and matching an instance's size with that of another instance. Visio 2000 enables users to manipulate measurement units, unit subdivisions, and ruler zero points. Such enhancements accommodate a variety of circumstances, including cross-referencing standard building plan measurements with those in the international metric system.

Note   Lines appearing on both the vertical and horizontal rulers correlate with the cursor's location on the drawing page. The status bar also reveals this information in the lower left-hand corner as the X and Y coordinates. The status bar, however, lists shapes' coordinates by their height and width.

Selecting units of measurement

Certain drawings demand — or at least request in a stern voice — changes in unit measurement. In conjunction with other scale drawing features, you can convert rulers for additional convenience. Adjust the Visio 2000 rulers according to the measurement unit of your choice, using the following steps:

1. Select File ➪ Page Setup, which pulls up the Page Setup dialog box.
2. Click the Page Properties tab.
3. Choose the unit in the box next to Measurement units and then click the OK button.

The following measurement units are available:

Inches	Millimeters	Didots
Feet & Inches	Centimeters	Weeks
Yards	Meters	Days
Miles	Kilometers	Hours
Inches (decimal)	Picas	Minutes
Feet (decimal)	Points	Seconds
Miles (decimal)	Ciceros	

Pick the unit of measurement necessary for your diagram. Visio 2000 contains a variety of both spatial and temporal measuring features.

Note   Applying a Pre-defined Scale on the Drawing Scale tab (Page Setup dialog box) can change the measurement units you've set on the Page Properties tab.

Applying various unit subdivisions

Ruler subdivisions are formed by the small marks listed between each major unit of measurement. For instance, the 1/4 marking of an inch is a 1/4 subdivision of one inch. You can govern the amount of detail provided by subdivisions with three settings: Fine offers the most detail, Normal an intermediate amount, and Coarse supplies the least.

In order to see the difference in detail, leave the vertical ruler at the Fine setting and adjust the horizontal ruler to Coarse. At 100% viewing, the horizontal ruler is divided into eighths (8 markings per inch), while the vertical ruler is separated into 32 markings per inch (as shown in Figure 10-1).

Note   The level of detail is relative to both the subdivision and viewing settings. For example, a ruler viewed at 100% reveals more detail than when viewed at 50%. However, the finer the subdivisions, the more detail permitted per viewing perspective.

The following exercise illustrates how subdivision settings work and how they're also affected by viewer settings:

1. Set the magnification on 100% and then select Tools ⇨ Ruler & Grid to call forth the Ruler & Grid dialog box.

2. In the Rulers section, select Fine as the subdivision form for the horizontal ruler and Coarse for the vertical ruler.

3. Click the OK button to activate the new settings.

4. Adjust the Zoom box on the Standard Toolbar to 50%. Notice the difference in detail caused by the new ruler and viewing settings.

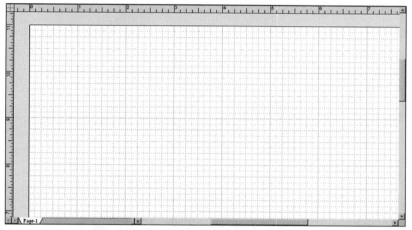

Figure 10-1: The horizontal and vertical rulers have different subdivision settings.

Now that you have a grasp on how they work, keep in mind two important points about subdivisions. First, do not confuse unit subdivisions with the rulers you see on the Visio 2000 drawing window. Those markings on the rulers are merely a method for measuring unit subdivisions. For instance, you can place a 1/4 of an inch line anywhere on the drawing page, not just at the ruler marking listed at 1/4 of an inch from the ruler's zero marking. Second, the number of subdivisions that you move a shape is indicated on the ruler. Working with ruler subdivisions can be quite easy if you remember these two things.

Placing ruler zero points

Ruler measurements are listed in both negative and positive numbers. The zero point on each ruler is located so that only positive numbers are adjacent to the drawing page. As Figure 10-2 demonstrates, the zero point is shown on the horizontal ruler at the drawing page's top-left corner, and the vertical ruler's zero point is listed near the drawing page's bottom-left corner. These are the default settings.

Keep in mind that two types of zero points exist in Visio 2000. The status bar lists the X-Y points (0,0) for the bottom-left corner of the page. These are not the ruler zero points, but instead are considered the page-position zero points. Note, however, that both point types are directly related to one another. For example, imagine that a horizontal axis runs from the vertical-ruler zero point down the left edge of the drawing page. Also imagine that an imaginary vertical axis runs down the bottom of the drawing page from the horizontal-ruler zero point. These axes converge at the X-Y page-position zero points.

 Tip   You may choose to move ruler zero points in order to focus in on a particular shape or room.

You can adjust each ruler's zero points from the Ruler & Grid dialog box, using the following steps:

1. Select Tools ➪ Ruler & Grid to access the Ruler & Grid dialog box.

2. Set the zero points in the horizontal and vertical boxes under Ruler zero. See Tables 10-1 and 10-2 for descriptions on how to work the settings.

3. Click the OK button.

Table 10-1
Horizontal Ruler Zero Point Configurations

Setting	Result
Type in a positive number	Shifts ruler zero point to the right
Type in zero	Ruler zero point in top-left page corner
Type in a negative number	Shifts ruler zero point to the left

Table 10-2
Vertical Ruler Zero Point Configurations

Setting	Result
Type in a positive number	Shifts ruler zero point upward
Type in zero	Ruler zero point in bottom-left page corner
Type in a negative number	Shifts ruler zero point downward

You can also use the Control key and mouse to adjust the rulers to your liking. For instance, place the cursor on the horizontal ruler. Press the Control key and drag the cursor onto the page background. A small black line appears on the screen.

The vertical ruler's zero point is determined by that line's placement. Likewise, the horizontal ruler's zero point is determined by where you place the vertical line. Simply drag the line, using the ruler to visualize the setting of the new ruler zero point.

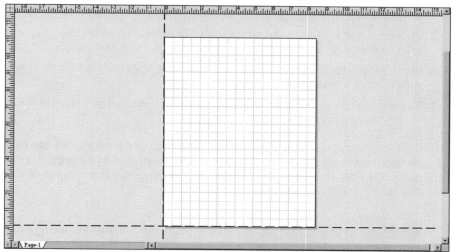

Figure 10-2: The default zero point settings

Tip You can reset the zero points to their default positions in one quick step. Simply place the cursor where the two rulers intersect and double-click. This action restores the program's initial zero point configurations.

Using Grids

Grids are the net-like lines that appear on drawing pages. Like lines on graph paper, these horizontal and vertical grids enable users to plot two- and three-dimensional shapes with a high degree of precision. Use the grids in conjunction with rulers and guides to facilitate accurate drawing.

Setting grid spacing

Unlike with ruler subdivision settings, Visio 2000 offers more than just Fine, Normal, and Coarse adjustments for grids. You can select Fixed grids, line markings that remain stationary regardless of whether you zoom in or out. The other three settings are considered variable grids because (like the ruler unit subdivisions) the viewing perspective affects how they are presented on the drawing page.

The appearance of variable grids is relative to the grid setting and the zoom-in percentage. For example, grids viewed at 75% reveal more detail than when viewed at 25%. However, as with subdivisions, the finer the grid the more detail permitted per viewing perspective. The following activity illustrates these points:

1. Select Tools ⇨ Ruler & Grid to call up the Ruler & Grid dialog box (as shown in Figure 10-3).

2. Choose a grid format in the boxes under Horizontal and Vertical. In this case, select Coarse for the horizontal grid and Fine for the vertical grid.

3. Click OK. Notice that fewer grid lines intersect with the vertical ruler than with the horizontal ruler.

4. To see how the viewing perspective affects variable grids, select another viewer setting in the Zoom box.

Note   Variable settings correlate only with the number of grid lines that intersect with a particular ruler. For example, choosing a coarse vertical grid affects the number of horizontal lines that intersect with the vertical ruler—not the number of vertical grid lines present on a page.

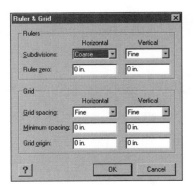

Figure 10-3: The Ruler & Grid dialog box

Fixed grids—lines best thought of as cemented to the drawing page—are important for projects requiring precision, such as architectural layouts. Unlike with other settings, magnification does not affect these grids. Complete the following exercise to understand better how Fixed grids work:

1. Select Tools ⇨ Ruler & Grid.

2. Choose Fixed in the Horizontal and Vertical grid spacing sections.

3. Type **1 inch** in both Minimum spacing boxes.

4. Click the OK button.

5. Adjust the viewer settings. Notice that the distance between the grid lines does not change.

Note

Unlike the variable-grid spacing settings, Fixed-grid settings require a minimum spacing number higher or lower than zero.

Setting minimum spacing for grid lines

Minimum spacing settings are used primarily in conjunction with Fixed-grid spacing. In those instances, the number of units specified indicates how many units of space are accorded between each grid line. For instance, a minimum spacing of 2 inches means that 2 inches of space are placed between every grid, as the exercise below demonstrates:

1. Access the Ruler & Grid dialog box by choosing Tools ➪ Ruler & Grid.

2. Insert **2 inches** as the minimum spacing for both horizontal and vertical grids and then click OK.

3. Adjust the viewing perspective. Notice that that 2 inches separate each line no matter what the magnification.

Setting grid origins

Imagine the old X-Y diagrams you used in algebra and geometry classes. The X-axis and Y-axis intersected exactly where both coordinates were set as zero. Visio 2000 grid origins work in a similar manner, with the origins corresponding somewhat to those X-Y/(0,0) axes. However, there are two chief differences. First, the grid origins are not highlighted or darkened and, thus, look the same as the rest of the grid. Second, the grid origin's numbers do not always correspond to the X-Y listing in the Size & Position window. X-Y listings in Visio 2000 match the ruler settings. Other than these differences, though, grid origins are similar to those axes popular in high school and college math.

1. Choose Tools ➪ Ruler & Grid in order to pull up the Ruler & Grid dialog box.

2. Insert **Fixed** (grid spacing) and **2 inches** (minimum spacing) for both the horizontal and vertical grids.

3. Type in a horizontal grid origin of **3 1/2 inches** and then click OK.

4. Notice that although 2 inches separate each grid line, a vertical grid intersects the horizontal ruler's 3 1/2-inch mark (see Figure 10-4). This is one of the grid origins.

Tip You must coordinate the grid origin's numbers with the zero ruler points in order for the Size & Position window's X-Y listings to match the location of the grid origins. Otherwise, these listings will only correspond to the ruler zero points.

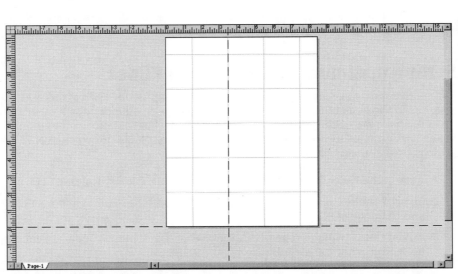

Figure 10-4: The horizontal grid origin (3 1/2 inches) and the vertical grid origin (0) are shown as a broken line for illustration purposes. You cannot darken them in the program.

Using the Dynamic Grid

Using rulers and grids is not always necessary. The Dynamic Grid helps Visio 2000 users place shapes with precision and speed by suggesting locations for plotting masters. The suggestions are derived from where you have previously placed instances. Using the locations of other shapes, the Dynamic Grid enables you to position shapes in a more aesthetic manner. The following exercise demonstrates how it works:

1. To activate the Dynamic Grid, first select Tools ➪ Snap & Glue. Under the General tab, check the box labeled Dynamic Grid. Click OK.

2. Using the Rectangle Tool, place a polygon in the page's upper-right corner.

3. Draw another polygon in the page's bottom-right corner.

4. Drag the shape clockwise from the page's bottom-right corner to the upper left corner. Notice the dashed lines that appear during this movement. The idea behind the Dynamic Grid is to place the center of your shape along either one of the single Dynamic Grid lines or where both lines intersect (as shown in Figure 10-5).

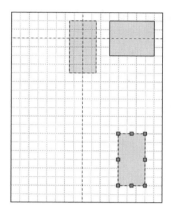

Figure 10-5: The Dynamic Grid helps you place a shape onto the drawing page.

Placing Guides and Guide Points

Used in conjunction with rulers and grids, guides and guide points enable Visio users to place shapes onto a page with almost effortless precision. In fact, guides are often employed for aligning shapes, while guide points are helpful in centering multiple shapes upon each other.

Setting guides

Guides are lines that help you position text and objects on a page. In order to see a guide, place your mouse on a ruler, and then drag the mouse. A blue dotted line, parallel with that ruler, appears. Drag the guide to the page. You can select as many guides as you want from each ruler. For example, use three horizontal guides to divide a drawing page into quarters. Perhaps you need to mark a critical point on the page with two intersecting guides; this is also possible with Visio 2000.

Figure 10-6 illustrates a number of guides, some rotated and intersecting. You can move guides (and shapes attached to them) by dragging and dropping the guide to a new location. Unlike grids and rulers, guides move with a rotated page. You can also rotate guides without moving the page. Just use the Rotation Tool to click a guide's rotation handle (large green circle) then pivot. You can also delete guides by clicking the guide and then pressing the Delete key.

Tip   Guides do not print unless you first uncheck the Non-printing Shape feature on the Behavior dialog box. Select Format ➪ Behavior and then look on the Behavior tab (under the Miscellaneous section) for the feature.

Cross-Reference   See Chapter 19 for more information on aligning shapes.

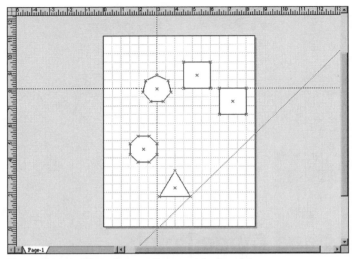

Figure 10-6: Align shapes along guides

Setting guide points

Guide points operate in a similar manner to two intersecting guides, except that rather than stretching over an entire page, they form a small blue, crosshair object on the page. Whereas guides are used for aligning instances, guide points are particularly helpful in centering a multitude of shapes.

To use a guide point, place your cursor in the area where the two rulers intersect, press the left mouse button and drag. Two guides will emerge, one from each ruler. Drag the lines onto the drawing page. Drop the guides, and a guide point will appear where the two lines intersected (as shown in Figure 10-7).

Note   Guide points enable you to move shapes attached to the guide point by simply dragging and dropping the guide point.

Applying the Snap and Glue

The snap and glue features often play an important role in placing objects onto a drawing page, especially when working with a multitude of shapes. The snap feature acts somewhat like a magnet, tugging shapes to a variety of objects, including rulers and guides. The glue feature holds objects together. Together, they are useful for aligning instances and simultaneously moving numerous shapes.

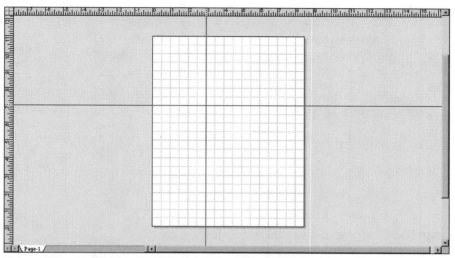

Figure 10-7: Positioning a guide point onto the drawing page

There are two ways to activate and set snap and glue. First, you can use the Snap & Glue Toolbar buttons (as shown in Figure 10-8), or you can select Tools ➪ Snap & Glue to adjust settings in the Snap & Glue dialog box. The Snap & Glue Toolbar button and dialog box are interrelated, so a change in one also is recorded in the other. The following exercise demonstrates the relationship:

1. Pull up the Snap & Glue Toolbar. Do this by right-clicking the Menu Toolbar and then checking the appropriate listing. Notice that the button farthest to the left (activates the snap) is highlighted.

2. Select Tools ➪ Snap & Glue to access the Snap & Glue dialog box.

3. Uncheck the Snap box in the "currently active" section of the General tab and then click OK.

4. The Snap button on the Snap & Glue Toolbar is no longer highlighted, indicating that the feature is now deactivated.

Both the toolbar and dialog box enable you to do many of the same tasks. The toolbar obviously cuts a few steps, so I highly recommend it. Once you're acquainted with the buttons on the Snap & Glue Toolbar, it will keep you from flipping through numerous drop-down menus and check boxes.

New Feature

Unlike Visio 5.0, Visio 2000's Snap & Glue dialog box contains shape extension options (Advanced tab). The Snap & Glue Toolbar also contains a button that offers these features.

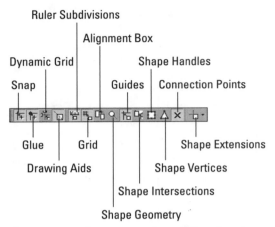

Figure 10-8: The Snap & Glue Toolbar buttons

Keep one key fact in mind when using the Snap & Glue Toolbar: The activation of a Snap & Glue toolbar button is ultimately determined by two buttons — the Snap button and the Glue button. The other buttons are merely ancillary to these features. For instance, clicking the Shape Vertices button when the snap and glue features are activated enables both functions to affect vertices. On the other hand, clicking the Shape Vertices button when only the Snap button is activated enables just the snap function to affect vertices. This, in essence, is how the Snap & Glue Toolbar works.

Using the snap

The snap feature is primarily used for aligning instances and placing shapes together. By activating certain Visio features, shapes have a tendency to "snap" into line with guides, ruler subdivisions, and other features. Overall, this quickens the drawing process. Furthermore, you have ten choices from which to snap shapes:

✦ **Alignment Box**. Dotted green box that appears around shapes when moving them

✦ **Connection Points**. Small blue, X-like objects on shapes

✦ **Grid**. Nonprinting lines on pages

✦ **Guides**. Blue dotted lines that you can drag from the rulers

✦ **Ruler Subdivisions**. Measurements indicated by small markings on rulers

✦ **Shape Extensions**. Features that apply to the drawing tools on the Standard Toolbar

✦ **Shape Geometry**. A shape's outermost lines

✦ **Shape Handles**. Green square-like objects on shapes

✦ **Shape Intersections**. Involves intersecting shapes, shape extensions, and grids

✦ **Shape Vertices**. Green diamond-like objects on shapes

All of these features can be activated from the Snap & Glue Toolbar or the Snap & Glue dialog box (Tools ➪ Snap & Glue). For the most part, you will use the snap feature for lining shapes in a row, a task often involving guides.

If you find that the snap is not exerting enough pull on objects, you can increase its strength. Go to the Advanced tab on the Snap & Glue dialog box and adjust the snap's pixel range for Rulers, the Grid, Guides, and Points. Once finished, click OK.

At times, the snap feature's strength is very noticeable. For example, activate the guides for the snap feature and adjust the guides' snap strength to 30. Drag a guide onto the drawing page. Place a shape about two inches from it. Drag the instance toward the guide, getting relatively close to the dotted blue line. Notice that the shape's alignment box skips a few grid blocks and snaps onto the guide (see Figure 10-9). Thus, you don't have to place shapes precisely onto a guide; the snap feature takes care of that for you.

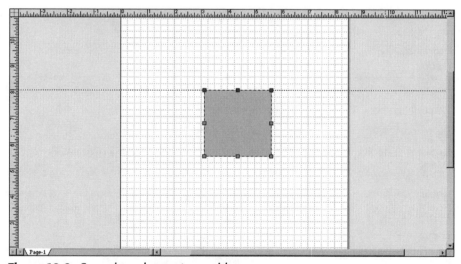

Figure 10-9: Snapping a box onto a guide

Note   Snap pixel settings range from 1 to 30, with 1 being the weakest and 30 the strongest.

Tip   To get the feel of what a pixel is, select a shape and then simultaneously press Shift and one of the arrow keys. This allows the shape to "jump" one pixel in the direction of the chosen arrow key.

Shape extensions are drawing aids that can snap lines. As the name implies, these aids — in the form of dashed lines — "extend" or appear on a shape in order to help you form 1 of 13 different looks (see Table 10-3). Shape extensions work with connectors and any of the drawing tools on the Standard Toolbars, such as the Line, Arc, Ellipse, and Rectangle buttons. You can set options in two ways:

✦ Go to Tools ➪ Snap & Glue. Select Shape Extensions in the "Snap to" section, located under the General tab. Next, choose a specific shape extension on the Advanced tab page.

✦ Click the Shape Extensions button on the Snap & Glue Toolbar. Click the arrow button next to the Shape Extensions button. Choose the shape extensions snap-on aids that you want.

Selected extension aids appear either when constructing lines, or moving a shape or line with your cursor. Notice that the Center Alignment Axes and Linear Extension options are activated by default. It's best not to run more than two or three options at a time in order to prevent a barrage of distracting aids from inundating the page. Basically, just use the ones that you need at the time.

Table 10-3
Shape Extension Options

Option	Purpose
Alignment Box Extension	Lining up shapes by their edges
Center Alignment Axes	Lining up shapes by their centers
Curve Interior Tangent	Creating tangents to arcs
Segment Endpoint	Connecting a shape or line with a segment's endpoints
Segment Midpoint	Placing a line directly through the middle of a segment
Linear Extension	Illustrating the path of a line if the line were to be extended
Curved Extension	Connecting two arcs into an ellipse
Endpoint Perpendicular	Creating two right angles with two lines
Midpoint Perpendicular	Creating four right angles with two lines
Horizontal Line at Endpoint	Placing a horizontal line upon another line's endpoint
Vertical Line at Endpoint	Placing a vertical line upon another line's endpoint
Ellipse Center Point	Connecting lines precisely to an ellipse's center
Isometric Angle Lines	Forming isometric angles

Note

To use the Isometric Angle Lines option, you must type in the angles that you wish to use in the Isometric Angles box (Advanced tab of Snap & Glue dialog box). Place a comma between each specified angle. The feature allows extensions for up to ten angles.

Tip

When dealing with shape extensions, it's best to strengthen the snap feature for points and grid. This is especially true when using the Curved Extension option, making drawing an ellipse with the Pencil Tool much easier.

Using the glue

Think of the glue feature as the engine behind a "shape train." Whereas the snap feature is critical for lining up shapes, the glue feature makes transporting a group of instances possible. In essence, the snap feature helps plot objects and the glue feature keeps them in place. Once the shapes are fastened to a guide, you can simply move the guide, and the instances glued on to the guide will move with it. This enables you, with just one action, to make changes involving several shapes.

Glue features can be selected from the Snap & Glue Toolbar (when the Glue button is activated) or from the Snap & Glue dialog box (General tab). You can fasten lines, shapes, and guides together with the glue feature. Connectors, however, do not require glue; they are already programmed to fasten to other shapes. As shown on the General tab, you can use glue with the following:

✦ **Shape Geometry**. A shape's outermost lines

✦ **Guides**. Blue dotted lines that you can drag from the rulers

✦ **Shape Handles**. Green square-like objects on shapes

✦ **Shape Vertices**. Green diamond-like objects on shapes

✦ **Connection Points**. Small, blue, X-like objects on shapes

Cross-Reference

Chapter 17 contains tips on connecting shapes, involving information concerning static and dynamic glue.

Transporting shapes with the glue feature is easy, as the following exercise demonstrates:

1. Activate Glue for Shape Handles and Guides.

2. Drag a guide from the horizontal ruler onto the page.

3. Draw three rectangles below the guide using the Rectangle Tool.

4. Place each rectangle upon the guide. A red square appears on either the center or outside of the alignment box. Once glued to the guide, the shape handles turn red.

5. Click the guide and then drag it anywhere along the page. The shapes will shift to the new position.

Guides are a convenient means for moving objects, especially for office layouts. For example, transferring a wall of furniture from one side of the room to another side is a piece of cake. Place a guide through the objects and apply the glue. Rotate the guide accordingly and move the furniture to another wall (as shown in Figure 10-10). Don't you wish moving the actual furnishings could be this easy?

Learn more about rotating, flipping, and centering shapes in Chapter 16.

You do not need guides to drag a collection of instances. If the are shapes glued to each other, you can move an entire group by just dragging one of the shapes.

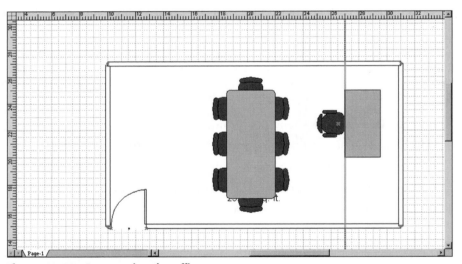

Figure 10-10: Rearranging the office

Summary

In this chapter, you learned how to use several shape-positioning aids in conjunction with the snap and glue features. Practice exercises introduced you to some key tools. Understanding how to operate these tools will benefit you in Part IV of this book. This chapter covered the following aspects of shape arrangement:

✦ You can accommodate rulers with 20 different measurement units, including feet, miles, points, picas, and hours.

✦ Unit subdivisions are not actually the rulers that you see on the Visio 2000 drawing window. Those small markings are merely a method for measuring unit subdivisions.

✦ Pressing the Control key and dragging your mouse from a ruler enables you to set the zero point for the opposite ruler.

✦ Use grids in the same fashion as you would a piece of graph paper.

✦ The Dynamic Grid feature, found on the Snap & Glue Toolbar, helps you line up both stencil shapes and figures drawn with Standard Toolbar buttons.

✦ Unlike grids and rulers, guides move with a rotated page. You can also rotate guides without moving the page.

✦ Guide points are usually used to individually center several shapes that have been placed upon each other.

✦ You can adjust snap strengths for rulers, guides, points, and the grid.

✦ Shape-extension options are drawing aids equipped for the snap function.

✦ The glue feature enables you to attach shapes, lines, and guides to each other. With glue you can transport a collection of objects by simply dragging and dropping one of the shapes.

The next chapter contains information on accessing file properties and setting file paths.

✦　　✦　　✦

Understanding File Properties

You've learned a great deal about Visio 2000 drawing
fundamentals. Now it's time to briefly direct your
attention toward file properties. Before taking a look at saving
and opening documents, this chapter will introduce you to
some basic aspects necessary for accessing and manipulating
file characteristics and descriptions. In fact, certain elements
in this chapter, such as modifying read-only documents and
resetting default file paths, will come in particularly handy for
opening and saving drawings.

Viewing File Properties

Several popular methods exist for viewing file properties,
from either within or outside Visio 2000. You can use typical
Windows procedures to view a document's properties without
having Visio 2000 open. Simply right-click a Visio file icon.
Select Properties on the drop-down menu. In Windows 98,
this action will retrieve the Test Properties dialog box, which
contains five tabs: General, Summary, Statistics, Contents,
and Custom. Click each tab in order to view file-property
data. Windows 95 displays a similar properties box. However,
Window's 95's box only offers General, Summary, and
Statistics tabs.

Note   Several of the tabs on the Windows Test Properties dialog
box correspond closely to those on the Visio Properties
dialog box. For example, the General page on both contains information such as the file's name, type, location,
and size.

Tip
You can also view file properties with Quick View, a feature within Microsoft Windows. To learn more about it, select Help from the Windows Start bar menu.

From within Visio 2000, you can view a file's properties by selecting File ➪ Properties. The Properties dialog box then emerges, enabling you to view several tabbed pages of information. A good deal of this data also appears within Microsoft Windows' Test Properties dialog box. Therefore, no matter which route you take, you're bound to find what you're looking for.

Accessing File Properties

"Look but don't touch," or so the saying goes. A practical program, such as Visio 2000, however, is for more than just the eyes. The file properties listings are a prime example of this. Not only can you view vital information; you can manipulate it, as well. Choosing File ➪ Properties is the primary way to access and modify file properties. Choosing File ➪ Properties retrieves the Properties dialog box, which contains four tabs: the General, Summary, Contents, and Output Format categories. You can also access the dialog box by clicking the drawing icon in the Drawing Explorer window and then choosing Properties from the drop-down menu.

Cross-Reference
See Chapter 15 for additional information on the Drawing Explorer window.

The General tab

Click the General tab in order to view its contents. This section contains the most basic file information, such as a document's name, format, and location. The tab (as shown in Figure 11-1) separates data into the following categories:

✦ **Type**. Reveals the file's format (for example, Visio Drawing File)

✦ **Location**. Refers to the folder path where the document is saved (for example, C:\My Documents\Visio Drawings)

✦ **Size**. The amount of space required in bytes for the file's storage

✦ **Based On**. Indicates which template was used to compose the document (for example, C:\Solutions\Maps\Geographic Maps)

Note
Data in the General tab categories cannot be edited from the Properties dialog box area.

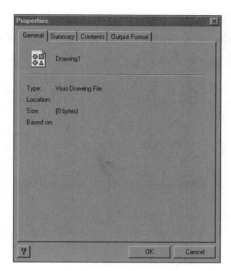

Figure 11-1: The General tab on the Properties dialog box

The Summary tab

Think of information in the Summary tab as a document's fingerprint. However, unlike with a fingerprint, you must format most of the data yourself. However, this isn't a drawback because you can customize a page so that it better suits your needs. For instance, this area enables users to include information that identifies clients, the drawing type, and your company's name. The following categories are listed in this section:

✦ **Title**. The name of the document

✦ **Subject**. A description of the document's contents

✦ **Author**. The name of the person who composed the document

✦ **Manager**. The name of the person heading and/or coordinating the project

✦ **Company**. Labels the organization responsible for creating the document

✦ **Category**. Includes the drawing type (for example, PERT chart, computer network diagram, business cards)

✦ **Keywords**. Words relevant to the project and/or client

✦ **Description**. Further details that the author may want to include concerning the project

✦ **Hyperlink Base**. Paths for relative hyperlinks

✦ **Preview**. Enables the user to view document pages from the Open dialog box

✦ **Quality**. Sets the preview quality to either Draft or Detailed

Try entering information that you would like to accompany a file. For an example, see Figure 11-2, which contains a Summary page and corresponding information. These categories, for the most part, "summarize" aspects critical for finding files. For instance, you may have drawn several diagrams relating to a particular project over the past year. Rather than sifting through a confusing amount of similar titles and subject matter, you can try to locate that document by checking the Summary tab contents. Information in the Category, Keywords, and Description areas is especially useful for this task.

Cross-Reference Learn more about hyperlinks in Chapter 32 and Chapter 37.

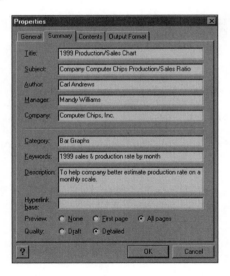

Figure 11-2: The Summary tab on the Properties dialog box

A few parts on the Summary tab are geared for previewing drawings. The Preview area allows you to click one of three previewing formats. You can save pages without previews (None), with only a preview of the first page (First Page Only), or with previews of all pages (All pages). Furthermore, you can dictate the quality of these previews. Choosing Draft in the Quality area reveals only Visio shapes. Selecting Detailed, however, enables users to view previews that contain all objects, including text and embedded shapes.

Note Previews are available in the bottom right-hand corner of the Open dialog box, though the File Preview box must be checked in order for you to be able to view the previews.

Tip You can prevent others from setting preview formats by disabling the feature in the Protection Document dialog box.

The Contents tab

The Contents tab lists each page and the names of the masters that appear on it. The document contents provide a quick and simple way to locate all of the names of the masters used in a particular document. This beats having to cross-reference each instance with its template master!

The Output Format tab

Visio 2000 gives users three primary ways to present diagrams and charts. Whether you're e-mailing a document to corporate associates or preparing a slide show presentation for the monthly department conference, Visio has you covered. The Output Format tab (see Figure 11-3) allows users to format drawings for the following:

✦ Printing

✦ Microsoft PowerPoint slide show

✦ HTML or GIF output

The Printing format is the default setting. The two other formats are intended for onscreen display. Accordingly, the PowerPoint format is best suited for slide show demonstration quality, while the HTML/GIF format works best for Web-based presentations. Simply click the format that you desire for a particular project and then select OK.

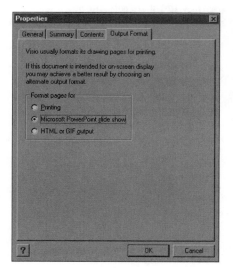

Figure 11-3: The Output Format tab on the Properties dialog box

Protecting Files

Suppose you have created an important chart for an upcoming presentation. You're about to leave the office, but several other coworkers still have access to the computer network. Obviously, you don't need some nimble-brained employee tampering with the file. Well, preventing someone from invoking Murphy's Law is no problem for Visio 2000. The program offers password protection for a variety of drawing elements. In fact, you can prevent coworkers from editing a document's shapes, styles, and masters.

File protection and protection dialog boxes

The Protect Document dialog box is the key to this "lock" feature. To access it, retrieve the Drawing Explorer window. Do this by selecting View ➪ Windows ➪ Drawing Explorer. You can then pull up the Protect Document dialog box by right-clicking the drawing icon in the Drawing Explorer window. Next, select Protect Document from the drop-down menu. This action calls forth the Protect Document dialog box, as shown in Figure 11-4.

You can prevent others from making inadvertent changes to specific aspects of your drawing by checking the appropriate box, typing in a password, and then clicking OK. If someone else right-clicks the drawing icon in the Drawing Explorer window, he or she will need the password in order to enable the Unprotect Document feature. Only then can that person edit your drawing.

Note   Although a person cannot edit specific elements within a password-protected document (depending on the features chosen), they can still add instances to the drawing.

Caution   Don't forget your password. Instead, always write it down and store it in a safe place. If, by chance, you've lost track of the password, contact Visio Support and Services.

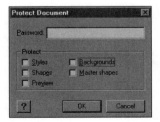

Figure 11-4: The Protect Document dialog box

The Protect Document Dialog box offers the following five protection areas:

✦ **Styles**. Prevents others from creating and editing text, line, fill, and shape styles

✦ **Shapes**. Prevents others from tampering with shapes when used in conjunction with the Protection dialog features (see Figure 11-5)

✦ **Preview**. Prevents others from viewing the document preview within the Open dialog box

✦ **Backgrounds**. Prevents others from editing and deleting background pages

✦ **Master Shapes**. Prevents others from creating, editing, or deleting masters within a file's templates

Tip　You cannot view the original version of a password-protected file. However, copying the file enables you to view the copy's preview.

When you or another person tries to edit a protected element, the program informs the user that the command cannot be completed. Editing specific features is possible only by setting the Unprotect Document dialog box. Access this box by right-clicking the drawing icon within the Drawing Explorer window. Next, click the Unprotect Document feature in the drop-down menu. Type in the password in order to disable the protection feature; only then can the document be edited.

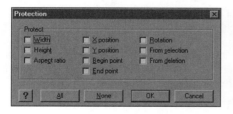

Figure 11-5: Use the Protection dialog features to prevent people from selecting or deleting specific shapes. Access this by clicking View ➪ Windows ➪ Drawing Explorer, right-clicking the Drawing Icon and selecting Protect Document.

Cross-Reference　Learn more about Protection dialog box features in Chapter 18.

Caution　Checking the Shapes box will not keep others from tampering with instances and shapes that you have already drawn. You must also set specific protection features in the Protection dialog box. Do this by selecting Format ➪ Protection and then checking the applicable boxes; otherwise, shapes you've drawn may be deleted or changed.

Read-only protection

One of the easiest ways to prevent coworkers from editing an important document is to convert the documents into read-only files. This is really easy. Exit Visio 2000 and then right-click the file that you want to convert into read-only format. Select Properties on the drop-down menu. Next, click the General tab and choose the read-only format for that document.

Other people can open your read-only files. They can even make changes when they open that document. The catch is that the person cannot save those changes to the same file name as your read-only record. Therefore, others can only make a copy of your work. So, let them edit to their little heart is content — as long as it's not your drawing.

Caution   Read-only files, like those using password-protection, can be deleted. As always, don't forget to make copies of important documents on a disk.

Setting File Paths

Before moving on to the next chapter, there's just one more thing you might like to know about file properties — how to set default folder paths for your documents. If you create designated file paths, they will be real timesavers when you save drawings, templates, stencils, and other similar items. Rather than searching through directories in the Save As dialog box, you can get everything up to snuff in one try. The same holds true for the Open dialog box.

So, where do you set file paths? The Options dialog box contains a File Paths tab (as shown in Figure 11-6) that allows users to modify default paths. This is your one-stop, take-care-of-business area for creating default file directories. Follow these steps in order to access this section:

1. Select Tools ➪ Options.

2. When the Option dialog box appears, click the File Paths tab.

3. Edit the appropriate areas within the tabbed area. Simply type in the folder or directory path of your choice.

The File Paths area contains seven sections in which you can edit. Each lists the default location for that specific element. For instance, the My Documents folder listed next to Drawings means that every time you go to the Opens or Save As dialog box, the My Documents folder will be the first location in which the program looks. Visio 2000 has already assigned each element its own default paths (as shown in Table 11-1). These, of course, can be changed. For the most part, though, you only will modify file paths for drawings, templates, and stencils.

Note You cannot create folders in the File Path tab area; therefore, you must type a valid directory (one that's already been created) inside the File Path tab boxes. Otherwise, the program will not recognize it.

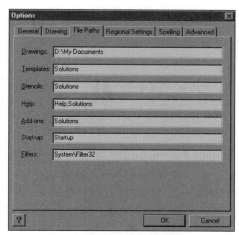

Figure 11-6: The File Paths tab

Table 11-1
Default File Paths

File	Folder Location	
Drawings	My Documents	
Templates	Solutions	
Stencils	Solutions	
Help	Help; Solutions	
Add-Ons	Solutions	
Start-Up	Startup	
Filters	System\Filter 32	

Change file paths by deleting the default listing and inserting a new one. You can also do this by using a directory listing. For instance, perhaps you want to save your drawings in a newly created folder inside the Solutions folder. Simply type **Solutions\My Drawings** inside the Drawings box, and click OK. Once the program updates the directory cache, you can save your documents in this folder without making changes in the Save As dialog box.

Note   The Help file contains two default locations. Multiple paths can be inserted in each box by placing a semicolon between each folder and/or directory listing.

Summary

In this chapter you learned how to access and modify a number of features pertaining to Visio 2000 file properties. This section covered the following aspects:

✦ You can view Visio file properties from within or outside the Visio 2000 program.

✦ The Summary tab on the Properties dialog box is used to create an ID of sorts for each file.

✦ A Visio file's output can be formatted for your printer, slide shows, e-mail attachments, and Web sites.

✦ You cannot view the original version of a password-protected file. However, copying the file enables you to view the copy's preview.

✦ Features on the Protect Document dialog box are ideal for preventing other network users from editing important drawings.

✦ Read-only file format is another way to prevent other users from editing your work.

✦ The Options dialog box contains a tabbed page where you can edit the default file paths of drawings, templates, stencils, and other similar items.

The next chapter will cover one of the most common procedures: saving files.

✦   ✦   ✦

Saving Files

Hey, you can't work all the time. Sooner or later you'll
have to push away the keyboard, get up, and go home.
You might want to make sure your work is waiting when you
return. That's what this chapter is all about — making sure
that your work is there when you go back to work.

This chapter covers every conceivable manner to save your
drawing. Whether it be Save As or Print to File, this chapter
will explain how to store your data.

Save Options

There are several methods for saving work. Which method
you use is a matter of personal preference and dependent
upon when you want to save your work. Let's briefly take a
look at the options before we move on.

+ The File drop-down menu includes both the Save and
  Save As icons. The Save As icon is used either for a
  drawing's first save or if you wish to save a document
  using something other than Visio's default .VSD file.
  The Save icon is used in all other cases. See "The File
  drop-down menu and the Save As window" section for
  further explanation.

+ The Save Button in the Standard Toolbar functions
  identically to File ⇨ Save.

Tip

It's a good idea to save often. From power surges to kids,
there are numerous unforeseen problems and interrup-
tions that can cause you to lose a hard day's work. Make it
a habit to click Ctrl+S every few minutes.

+ The Print to File window saves files using methods similar
  to the methods of the Save and Save As functions. Because
  Print to File saves files as Post Script files, the files may be
  opened by other programs, such as Corel Draw or Adobe
  Distiller.

The File drop-down menu and the Save As window

Clicking on File in the menu bar drops a menu with both Save and Save As commands. The first time you wish to save your drawing (or if you wish to save using a format other than the default .VSD format), select Save As from this menu. This displays the Save As window, as shown in Figure 12-1.

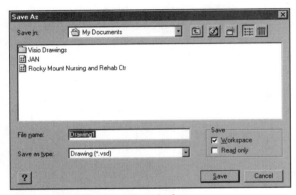

Figure 12-1: The Save As window

Note Clicking Save in the File drop-down menu will also open the Save As window on your screen if it is the first time that you have saved the drawing.

Following are explanations of the options offered in the Save As window:

✦ **Save In**. Shows the currently selected folder. Your document will be saved in this folder.

✦ **Up One Level**. Clicking this icon enables you to view or save work in the preceding folder in the folder hierarchy.

✦ **Create New Folder**. Clicking the Create New Folder icon enables you to create a new folder.

✦ **List**. The List button displays the files and folders in the selected folder (or area) as a simple list. This list only displays the name of the file or folder.

✦ **Detailed List**. This button retrieves a detailed list of the files and folders in the selected area. This list includes the file's name, size, type, and the date that it was last modified.

✦ **Viewing Window**. The large window located within the Save As window. It functions like other open folders in Windows. You may choose how to view or arrange the presented files. You can also decide how to create new folders, shortcuts, Briefcases, and so on. You can decide how to examine the window's properties, as well.

✦ **Naming Window**. The Naming Window sits below the viewing window. Type the file's name here.

Note

As with all Windows 95/98 programs, Visio 2000 does not limit the name that you choose to eight characters. The name may include as many letters as you desire, as well as spaces, dashes, and just about anything except slashes or periods.

✦ **Save As Type Window**. In this window you choose the type of file your drawing will be saved as. Visio 2000 supports 25 files, from the standard VSD files to several types of graphic files. You may save your drawing as a stencil or template, or even as an HTML web page. Note that Visio Standard does not save in AutoCAD formats (.dwg, .dxf, .dgn), but Visio Technical does.

Tip

When saved as a stencil, each shape in a drawing is available when the newly saved stencil is reopened. This is helpful when a drawing uses multiple stencils. You can save the drawing as a stencil and then create similar drawings utilizing the previously saved stencil.

Saving your drawing as a graphic file, such as BMP or PCX, brings forth an options window, as shown in Figure 12-2. This window's options are specific to the file type chosen. For example, saving a file as a .pcx file pops a dialogue box that asks at what resolution and color level (i.e. 16 or 256 color) you wish to save the file. On the other hand, saving as a .bmp also allows you to choose 24 bit color, in addition to several other options.

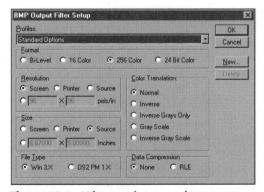

Figure 12-2: When saving your document as a graphics file, the BMP Output Filter Setup box appears.

✦ **Workspace Feature**. Saves the position of your work's windows, in addition to the data contained in the file. In other words, each stencil that was opened, as well as the work's last window size and position, will be restored when you reopen the work.

✦ **Read Only Feature**. Files that are saved as read-only files cannot be modified, and subsequently, cannot be saved to the same file name.

Once you have chosen the applicable options, click Save in order to save your work. If you change your mind, you may click Cancel in order to exit the Save As dialog box.

The Properties dialog box

After a file has been initially saved, the Properties dialog box, shown in Figure 12-3, appears onscreen. In the dialog box users are able to modify properties of the file, provide a detailed description, and several other useful functions.

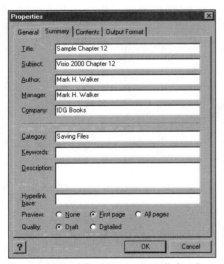

Figure 12-3: The Properties dialog box

You may also retrieve the Properties dialog box through the File drop-down menu. To do so, select File ➪ Properties.

See Chapter 11 for a complete description of the file properties.

Subsequent saves

You may save a previously saved file by clicking the Save Icon in the Standard Toolbar or by selecting File ⇨ Save. Either method quickly saves the file with its current name in the previously selected location.

You may save previously saved files using the Save As feature. This retrieves the Save As window. This is useful when you wish to save a file as a different file type or if you wish to rename the file.

You may also rename a file without starting Visio 2000. From Windows Explorer, highlight the file that you wish to name and then click it. Backspace to eliminate the current text and then type the new name (See Figure 12-4).

You may also rename a file by right-clicking on the file. Chose Rename from the file's drop down menu and then type in the new name.

Caution

If you attempt to rename a file's suffix, Windows will display a warning. Such actions may make the file unusable.

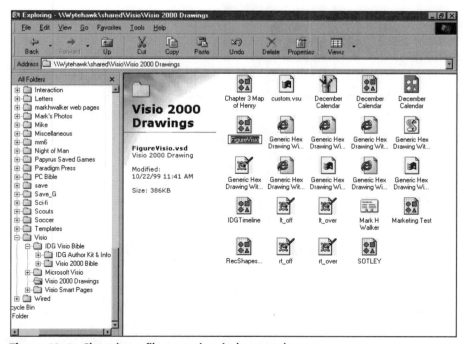

Figure 12-4: Changing a file name in windows explorer

Print to File

The Print to File feature functions like a save file feature. A file saved using Print to File becomes a Post Script file and may be opened by other programs, such as Corel Draw or Adobe Distiller, and subsequently printed. Therefore, it is helpful to use the Print to File feature on Visio 2000 drawings that you would like to send to associates who don't own Visio 2000. To print a drawing with the Print to File feature, select File ➭ Print. The Print Dialog box will appear, as shown in Figure 12-5. Select the Print to file box and click OK. This retrieves the Print to File window.

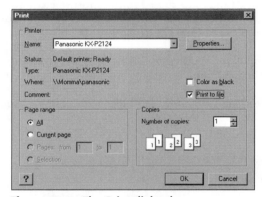

Figure 12-5: The Print dialog box

Details of the Print dialog box are discussed in Chapter 14.

The Print to File window (as shown in Figure 12-6) is similar to the Save As window. Following are its most useful features:

✦ **Save In**. Shows the currently selected folder. Your document will be saved in this folder.

✦ **Up One Level**. Clicking this icon enables you to view or save work in the preceding folder in the folder hierarchy.

✦ **Create New Folder**. Clicking the Create New Folder icon enables you to create a new folder.

✦ **List**. The List button displays the files and folders in the selected folder (or area) as a simple list. This list only displays the name of the file or folder.

✦ **Detailed List**. This icon retrieves a detailed list of the files and folders in the selected are. This list includes the file's name, size, type, and the date that it was last modified.

✦ **Viewing Window**. The large window located within the Print to File window. It functions like other open folders in Windows. You may choose how to view or arrange the presented files. You can also decide how to create new folders, shortcuts, Briefcases, and so on. You can decide how to examine the window's properties, as well.

✦ **Naming Window**. The Naming Window sits below the Viewing Window. Type the file's name here.

✦ **Save As Type Window**. Print to File may only be saved as a generic *.* file.

Once you choose the applicable options to print to file, click Save. If you change your mind, you may click Cancel instead of Save in order to exit the Print to File dialog box.

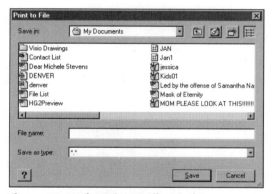

Figure 12-6: The Print To File window.

Summary

In this chapter you learned how to save files with Standard Toolbar icons or with drop-down menus. Following are the major points covered in this chapter:

✦ Using the Save As window for a file's initial save

✦ The File Properties dialog box

✦ Saving a previously saved file

✦ The Print to File feature

In the next chapter, I'll discuss how to open drawings. See you there.

✦　　✦　　✦

Opening Drawings

In previous chapters, you learned how to open new Visio drawing files (Chapter 2) and how to use the Open command in menus and toolbars (Chapter 3). This section will cover how to open existing Visio and non-Visio files.

Opening Existing Visio Drawings

There are three ways to open an existing Visio Drawing. One way is through the Visio startup screen, and the other two can be used when Visio is already running.

Opening an existing file at startup

When you open Visio 2000, click the button beside Open Existing File in the Welcome to Visio 2000 dialog box. This highlights the Browse Existing Files option, which displays a list of the last four files that you have opened in Visio 2000. If the file that you want is among them, select it and click OK. Otherwise, select Browse Existing Files and click OK to bring up the Open file dialog box. Select the folder and file that you need.

Opening an existing file after startup

Once you get past the Visio Welcome screen, you have two more choices for opening an already existing file.

To use the first method, select File from the menu bar. Then select Open. The Open file dialog box appears (as shown in Figure 13-1). Locate the folder and file name that you want and select the file to highlight it. Then click the Open button at the bottom of the page.

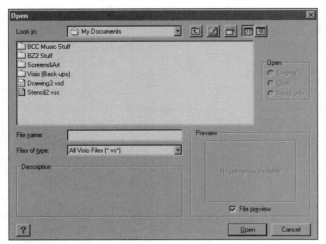

Figure 13-1: The Open file dialog box enables you to find and open existing files.

To use the second method, click the Open File icon in the Standard Toolbar (it looks like an open yellow folder) in order to bring up the Open file dialog box. From there, select the folder and file name that you want. Then click the Open button at the bottom of the page.

Open file dialog box options

The Open file dialog box has a few options, most of which affect files that you've already selected. But you should consider one option *before* selecting a file.

File Types

When you first retrieve the Open file dialog box, the File Types option automatically sets to All Visio Files (*.vs*). You'll view Visio files in the Available Files box under the open folder, including stencils, templates, workspace files, and drawings. In a folder with a large assortment of Visio files, you may want to select the arrow at the right end of the File Types input box. A pop-up menu will appear. Select Drawing (*.vsd) from the pop-up menu in order to limit the available files shown to only Visio drawing files. (We'll discuss opening other file types later in this chapter.)

When you select the Visio drawing file that you wish to open, several options become active.

Description

When you select a Visio file, the Description box displays the description that was entered in that file's Properties area. Such descriptions can be invaluable for organizing and placing drawings properly. If a drawing lacks a description (or has a bad one), consider opening file properties (File ⇨ Properties) and placing a description there. This will save you time later and help your coworkers on shared projects.

Preview

The Preview area of the Open file dialog box displays a File Preview check box. Click it in order to place a check mark there. With the Preview option enabled, you can view a thumbnail of each file in a folder before you open it — invaluable when you're unsure of a file's name.

Note Description and Preview work only with Visio file types.

Open options

Visio 2000 offers three options in the Open file dialog box for opening files. The default option is Original. To select the Copy or Read only options, simply click their radio buttons in the Open box, located on the right side of the Open file dialog box. Following are explanations of the three options:

✦ **Original**. Opens a file in the workspace. Any change that you make to a file in the workspace will also appear in the saved file. This is how most files are opened.

✦ **Copy**. When you want to keep a file unaltered while making changes to a copy of the file, open the file using the Copy option. When you open a file with the Copy option, a copy of the file with a new file name (for example, "Drawing3.vsd") appears in your workspace. Use Save As for changing the file name to something more relevant to your project. The original file will keep its original name and will be unaffected by changes that you make to the copy.

Tip I strongly recommend opening most files with the Copy option. Murphy's Law dictates that on the last day of a project — just before deadline and right after you've opened the original file, but before you've had a chance to save it — a power surge will get past your $1,000 surge protector and scramble your file!

✦ **Read only**. The Read only option opens the file in your workspace but allows no changes. This option is useful in shared projects, where others may need to view a file but should make no changes to it. This is also good for those of us (myself included) that may be distracted by the boss or a coworker, and may try to make a change to a master file before realizing it. Also, this option is the only way that you can open Read only files.

Note A Read only file, when opened, will have "Read-only" enclosed in brackets on the title bar, to the right of the name of the document.

After you select a file and select the way that it will open, click the Open button at the bottom of the Open file dialog box.

An example

Let's practice. First, click File on the menu bar, and then click Open. Now find the Samples folder and open it. Open the Visio Extras folder. Because File Types is set to All Visio File Types, you should see seven files here. Let's trim that down.

Click the down arrow, located to the right of the File Types text box. From the pop-up menu, select Drawing (*.vsd) from under All Visio Files (*.vs*). Only four files now appear.

Make sure the box beside File Preview is checked.

Click Sample Database Airplane Seating.vsd. A description will appear in the Description area and a thumbnail in the Preview area. Original is selected in the Open options area on the upper right. Select Copy instead. Now, click Open at the bottom of the dialog box in the preview area.

Notice that the file now has a different name in the title bar: — Drawing x: Page y (x and y will vary according to how many earlier drawings and projects you have opened this way).

Now try opening a file as Read only. Click the Open file button on the task bar. The Open file dialog box will appear in the same folder as before, but File Types has reverted to All File Types (*.vs*). Click Sample Database Network Layout.vsd. Click beside Read only in the Open options area. Then click Open at the bottom of the page.

Visio 2000 may take a little longer to open the file in Read only mode. The name of a file opened this way displays with brackets in the Title Bar. You may make any changes you like to the file, but when you try to close and/or save it, you must do so under a new file name. The original file will remain unchanged.

Shortcut

To open one of the four most recently opened files, click File on the menu bar. At the bottom of the drop-down menu, you'll see a list of the last four files that you opened in Visio 2000. Double-click the file name that you want to open as an Original file; Copy and Read only options are unavailable using this shortcut (unless the file was earlier saved as a Read only file).

Opening files from earlier versions of Visio

All versions of Visio 2000 — Standard, Professional, Technical, and Enterprise — can open all versions of Visio files, from Visio 1.0 to Visio 5.x. Open them as you would a Visio 2000 file.

Note

If you are working with people who have Visio 5.0 (or earlier) they will not be able to open Visio 2000 files. If such is the case, be sure to save your files as Visio 5.0 files.

Cross-Reference

See Chapter 12 for more information on saving as a specific file type.

Previewing and Opening Files Using Microsoft's Quick View

If the Quick View viewer wasn't installed with your Windows system, install it before you continue. Go to your Windows Start Menu and select Settings, and then Control Panel. In Control Panel, select Add/Remove Programs and then Windows Setup. Locate Quick View under Accessories. Select Quick View and click OK. Follow the instructions in order to finish the installation. If you're on a network, the network administrator may have to install Quick View for you. However, once it's installed, you can use the Quick View viewer to preview and open Visio files from Windows Explorer.

Previewing and opening Visio files

You can preview and open Visio files even if Visio 2000 is not running. To do so, open Windows Explorer, and browse until you find the file that you want to preview or open. Right-click the file name, and a menu will appear. Select Quick View (as shown in Figure 13-2). This opens the file in the Quick View window (as shown in Figure 13-3) in a reduced view, so some detail may be missing. To open the file with a normal view, either click the Visio 2000 icon on the Quick View viewer taskbar; or select File from the menu commands, and then select Open In Visio. Visio 2000 will open with this file in the workspace.

Note

Quick View can't open all file types. Those that it can will open in their respective programs. Visio files open in Visio 2000; text files open in your text editing program. You can't use Quick View to open non-Visio files in Visio 2000.

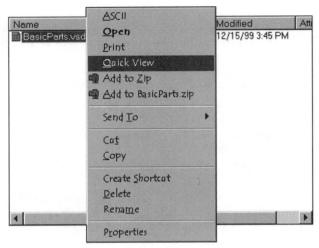

Figure 13-2: Right-click the file name in order to bring up the File Options menu with the Quick View option.

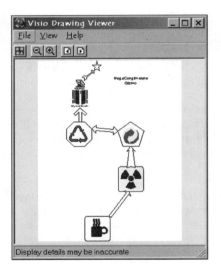

Figure 13-3: The Quick View viewer shows a reduced version of the Visio file.

Example

Let's try an example. Minimize Visio 2000, and then open Windows Explorer. Find and open the Visio folder. Open the Samples folder in Visio. Now open the Block Diagram folder. Right-click Block Diagram.vsd. Select Quick View from the pop-up menu. The file is now open in the viewer for your preview. From the viewer's menu, click File. Select Open in Visio. Now the program bar is highlighted in your taskbar, where Visio is in minimized mode. Click it to bring it back up. The file that you selected is open.

What about the file that was there before? It's still open. Click Window in the Menu bar, and select Cascade. Now you can access all files currently open in Visio, including the one that was open before you opened Block Diagram.vsd. Close these files if you like.

Opening Non-Visio Files

Visio 2000 can open many non-Visio files and convert them into Visio drawings. Graphic formats, CAD formats, and text formats all can be opened as a Visio drawing. This ability makes Visio 2000 one of the most versatile and useful programs on the market.

Try opening a non-Visio file as you would a Visio file by either clicking the Open icon in the standard toolbar or selecting File ⇨ Open to view the Open file dialog box. Next, select the folder containing the non-Visio file that you want. Click the arrow to the right of the File Types text box. From the list, choose the file's type. The Available Files area will display all files of that type in the open folder. Select the file name and click Open.

When you open a non-Visio file, Visio 2000 creates a bitmap or metafile of it, depending on the file format. You can treat that bitmap or metafile as you would any Visio shape, using resize, move, connect, copy, or cut-and-paste functions.

Note

Metafiles have limitations. If you won't need to rotate a metafile, choose Windows Metafile Format (WMF) in the file's Conversion dialog box. If you will need to rotate it, choose Enhanced Metafile Format (EMF).

When cropping a metafile, do not rotate it. If you do, its handles will gray and disallow cropping. Also, never rotate Metafiles when grouping them

These limitations don't apply to bitmap files

File Conversion Options

When you click Open to open a non-Visio file, a Conversion Options box appears. Given that there are so many file types, option boxes for different file types differ greatly, as Figures 13-4, 13-5, and 13-6 show. If you're unfamiliar with the options for the file type that you're converting, refer to the manual for that program. Or, if you're lucky enough to know a graphic artist, ask for help. You can't beat a professional opinion when dealing with these types of details.

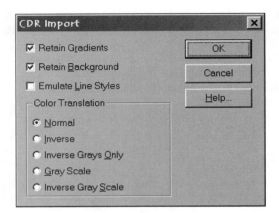

Figure 13-4: The File Conversion options box for a CorelDRAW! drawing offers several choices.

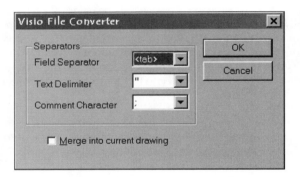

Figure 13-5: A text file File Conversion options box offers fewer choices, but they may be unfamiliar ones.

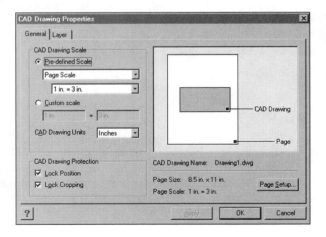

Figure 13-6: The File Conversion options box for a CAD drawing displays so many choices that they must be organized using tabs.

How the file opens

When you open a non-Visio file in Visio 2000, it will open as a new drawing with a generic file name (Drawing 5: Page 1, for example). The new drawing is separate from the drawing that displayed in the workspace when you opened the new drawing. To place it in another drawing, cut and paste it from its original page to the page that you're working on. To open a file as a shape in the drawing that currently is in your workspace, you must import it.

For information on how to directly import a non-Visio graphics file, such as a shape, onto a page in progress, refer to Chapter 32.

You can open 27 file types in Visio 2000.

ABC FlowCharter; versions 2.0, 3.0, 4.0: (.af2, .af3)

Adobe Illustrator: (.ai)

AutoCAD Drawings: (.dwg, .dxf)

Bently Microstation Drawing: (.dgn)

Computer Graphics Metafile: (.cgm)

Corel Clipart: (.cmx)

CorelDRAW! Drawings; versions 3.0, 4.0, 5.0, 6.0, and 7.0: (.cdr)

CorelFlow 2.0: (.cfl)

Encapsulated PostScript: (.eps)

Enhanced Metafile: (.emf)

Graphics Interchange Format: (.gif)

Initial Graphics Exchange Specification: (.igs)

Joint Photographic Experts Group: (.jpg)

Macintosh Picture: (.pct)

Micrografx Designer Version 3.1: (.drw)

Micrografx Designer Version 6.0: (.dsf)

Portable Network Graphics: (.png)

PostScript: (.ps)

Tag Image: (.tif)

Text / Comma Separated Values text: (.txt) / (.csv)

Windows Bitmap: (.bmp and .dib)

Windows Metafile: (.wmf)

Zsoft PC PaintBrush Bitmap: (.pcx)

Because these programs and Visio 2000 share the same basic shape formats, Visio 2000 converts the drawings into Visio 2000 smart shapes. There may be slight differences, so you may need to adjust a drawing after conversion.

Experiment with this on your own. Find and open other file types on your computer. Open and close a file repeatedly, choosing different conversion options each time, and note the differences (if any).

Summary

This chapter explained how to open Visio files by using the startup Welcome box, the File menu, the standard toolbar Open icon, and the Windows Quick View viewer. The chapter also explained how to preview a Visio file before opening it by using the Quick View viewer and the Open file dialog box.

It also covered many options that you will encounter as you convert various file formats into Visio drawings. Because of their scope and complexity, it often is a good idea to get advice from a professional graphic artist concerning available options for a particular project.

Proceed to Chapter 14 to learn about previewing and printing drawings.

✦　　✦　　✦

Previewing and Printing Drawings

Let me help you put your ideas on paper. Having created, saved, opened, and modified documents, it's time to take that critical step toward mastering the final element in the creation of a basic Visio 2000 drawing—printing documents. Printing in itself, of course, is easy. There's much more, however, to optimizing results than just clicking the Print Page button. This chapter contains everything you ever wanted to know (and perhaps some stuff you didn't) about printing, from editing with the Print Preview window to setting up print properties.

Using the Print Preview Window

The Print Preview window (as shown in Figure 14-1) is useful for viewing exactly how your document would look after it is printed. There are two ways to retrieve the Print Preview window. You can use the Print Preview button or select File ➪ Print Preview in order to call up the window (See Figure 14-2). On the other hand, there are three methods for exiting the Print Preview window. You can click the bottom "X" in the top right-hand corner, click the Close button, or select File ➪ Print Preview. All three actions take you from the Print Preview window back to the Visio Drawing window.

Click File then Print Preview
to close the window

Click to close the Print
Preview window

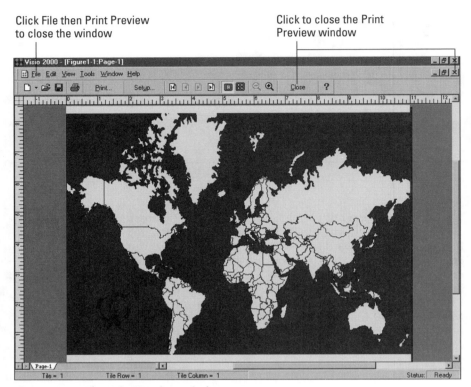

Figure 14-1: The Print Preview window

Figure 14-2: Accessing Print Preview

Print Preview buttons

There are several buttons within the Print Preview window that are probably familiar, such as New Drawing, Save, and Zoom. These buttons work the same as their counterparts in the Visio Drawing window. Six buttons, specific to the Print Preview window, are situated along the top center of the window. These features, as shown in Figure 14-3, are useful for viewing both drawing pages and print pages (tiles). They cannot, however, be used to view unassigned background pages.

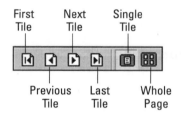

Figure 14-3: Six key Print Preview buttons

Before taking a look at these buttons, let me answer this chapter's burning (at least smoldering) question: What's the difference between drawing pages and print pages? Drawing pages, as you learned in Chapters 2 and 3, are blank pages within the Visio Drawing window on which you place shapes. Print pages — with the exception of tiled drawing pages that are revealed in Whole Page mode — are pages in the Print Preview window.

Sometimes the dimensions of a drawing page exceed the limits set for your printer. This can be the result of different orientation or measurement settings. When a drawing page's dimensions extend farther than the printing page dimensions, a drawing is divided into separate print pages or, as they're often called, tiles.

When the subject matter on a drawing page cannot fit onto one printable page, it is then divided into tiles.

See Chapter 8 for information on adjusting page dimensions and orientation.

The special Print Preview buttons are designed specifically for viewing tiles. They can help you coordinate your drawings with the printer settings and are quite useful for handling oversize drawings — flowcharts, timelines, and diagrams with extensive documentation. Following are the six handy features:

First Tile. Click in order to view the first print page or tile in a document.

Previous Tile. Click in order to view the print page or tile that you previously saw.

Next Tile. Click in order to view the next print page or tile.

Last Tile. Click in order to view the final print page or tile in a document.

Single Tile. Click in order to view a single tile or drawing page.

Whole Page. Click in order to view one drawing page that consists of two or more tiles.

Note Many of the same features can be found in the View drop-down menu, including Whole Page, Single Tile, Previous Tile, and Next Tile.

Use the first four features to scan over numerous tiles. The Single Tile button will remain highlighted when using these buttons. Click the Whole Page button in order to view all of the drawing-page tiles. Placing the Print Preview screen in Whole Page mode, however, does not force the printer to print a multitiled image on one page. Make those changes in the Page Setup dialog box.

Note The Whole Page function refers specifically to the drawing page and all tiles as a whole. However, gray markings (indicative of page breaks) sometimes appear on the drawing page. These illustrate how the pages will be divided when printed.

Other Print Preview navigation features

You can navigate through various pages by using the View and Edit drop-down menus. Many of the buttons have their equivalents on the View drop-down menu. In the Edit drop-down menu, the Undo and Go To Page functions can take you back through various pages. Selecting Edit ➪ Go To pulls up a pop-up menu that lets you choose which page you want to see. You can even view background pages with this method. As with the Drawing window, users can also view different pages by simply clicking the appropriate tab in the bottom left-hand section of the window.

Simultaneously viewing the Print Preview and Drawing windows

You can edit a drawing from the Drawing window while viewing how those changes will look in a printed copy. Although it's a feature you won't use often, it has its advantages, especially when dealing with multitiled work. Here's how to get started:

1. Go to the Print Preview window.

2. Select Window ➪ New Window. This takes you to a copy of your Drawing window.

3. Select Window ➪ Tile from the Drawing window menu bar. Both the Drawing and Print Preview windows should appear on your screen (see Figure 14-4). You can edit the file by using the available toolbars.

Due to limited screen space, this method can be quite cumbersome. It is best used when working with multiple tiles; otherwise, just stick with the Drawing window for edits.

Tip Use the Page Break function to view the nonprintable print-page area within the Visio Drawing window. Simply select View ➪ Page Breaks to enact this feature. The gray edges indicate where the nonprintable margins are located.

Drawing window   Print Preview window

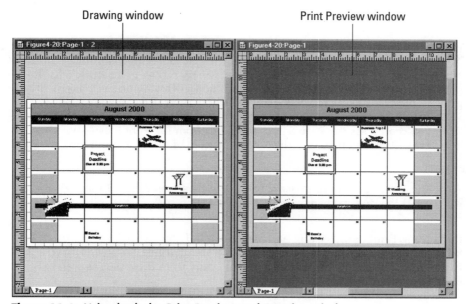

Figure 14-4: Using both the Print Preview and Drawing windows

Printing Documents

Once you're finished using the Print Preview window, it's finally time to send your drawings to a printer. The following three dialog boxes can help you do just this:

Page Setup dialog box (Print Setup tab)

Print Setup dialog box

Print dialog box

And what would printing be without Print buttons? They're discussed in this section, as well, along with a simple walkthrough for printing ShapeSheets.

Setting up a print job

Preparing for your usual printing is fairly easy. The following steps take you through the basic print job setup:

1. Select File ➪ Page Setup from either the Visio Drawing or Print Preview window.

2. Choose the Page Setup dialog box's Print Setup tab.

3. Adjust the paper size and orientation to fit your printer's format.

4. Click the OK button.

Of course, you have other options. You can set the Print Zoom features using the Adjust To and Fit To boxes. Enlarge a drawing by selecting a setting greater than 100 percent. Decrease the drawing page's size by typing in a setting less than 100 percent. Use the Fit To boxes in order to place a drawing on several pages of printer paper. This gives users more control over how their drawings are tiled.

Tip   You can access the Page Setup dialog box from the Print Preview window. Select File ➪ Page Setup, or click the Setup button in order to call forth the dialog box.

Note   The Print Setup tab's preview window shows how Adjust To and Fit To settings affect the drawing-page print-page relationship.

Pull up the Print Setup dialog box (as shown in Figure 14-5) in order to make adjustments concerning the printer source and margins (in inches). You can center small drawings horizontally or vertically from this spot, as well as making other adjustments.

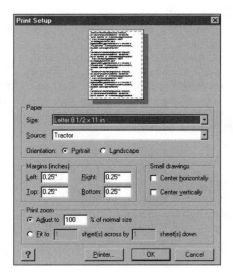

Figure 14-5: The Print Setup dialog box

Printing drawings

You're almost ready to print your drawings. Select File ➪ Properties, and then click the Output Format tab of the Properties dialog box. Make sure that the document is formatted for printing output. Next, select File ➪ Print on either the Visio Drawing or Print Preview windows. This calls forth the Print dialog box (as shown in Figure 14-6).

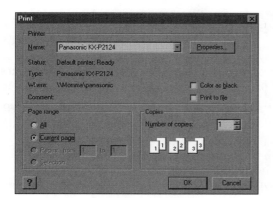

Figure 14-6: The Print dialog box

The Print dialog box not only includes information about the printer's type, status, and location, but enables users to adjust a number of features, including page range and ink color. Choosing Current Page prints the page displayed on your screen. Collate (found by clicking the Properties button and then clicking the Paper Tab), used to organize multiple copies, arranges one drawing copy per set (as shown in Figure 14-7). Color as black renders all colors in black ink. Once everything is set the way that you want, click the OK button. Presto! The document will then print.

Figure 14-7: Collated copies versus non-collated copies.

Print Page buttons are popular alternatives to dialog boxes. To use them, select the Print Page buttons on either the Drawing or the Print Preview windows in order to print the selected drawing page. This method bypasses all dialog boxes and automatically instructs the printer to print the page whose tab is highlighted.

Note You can access the Print dialog box and its Properties button from both the Visio Drawing and Print Preview windows.

Tip

Select the Properties button in order to make printer-specific adjustments. The type of dialog box that appears depends upon your printer brand and type. Consult your printer's instruction booklet for details.

Printing ShapeSheets

Each object in Visio has its own ShapeSheet, spreadsheets that contain data relating to a specific shape. ShapeSheets are discussed in more detail later in the book. However, for those interested, I've included the following steps for printing ShapeSheet data:

1. For information concerning a particular shape, click that shape. The instance is now activated, so data found on the ShapeSheet applies strictly to that object.

2. Select Tools ➪ Macros ➪ Visio Extras ➪ Print ShapeSheet in order to pull up the Print ShapeSheet dialog box.

3. If you need data for more than one shape, choose the data that you need, such as Page, Styles, or All Shapes, in the Sheet Type section. Select the Print To area if needed. For the most part, you will probably be working with a printer, the default source.

4. Choose which data types you need by clicking the appropriate boxes in the Print Sections area.

5. Click OK to print the information.

Cross-Reference

See Chapter 34 for an in-depth look at ShapeSheets.

Summary

This chapter discussed numerous aspects related to printing Visio documents, such as how to access and use the Print Preview window, and how to create and adjust printing properties. The chapter covered the following points in detail:

✦ Drawings that cannot fit on one printable page are divided into tiles.

✦ Six buttons, specific to the Print Preview window, are designed for viewing tiles and drawing pages.

✦ The Whole Page button allows you to view an entire drawing, including all of its tiles.

✦ Use features on the Window drop-down menu to simultaneously view the Print Preview and Visio Drawing windows.

✦ The Print Setup and Print dialog boxes are important features for modifying and setting print properties.

✦ The Tools drop-down menu must be used to print ShapeSheets.

Chapter 14 completes this part of *Visio 2000 Bible*. In the next chapter, you'll learn more about stencils and templates, and the next section will further instruct you on how to use and manipulate shapes.

✦   ✦   ✦

Using and Manipulating Shapes

Part IV contains information on various methods used to create and format shapes. You will learn, specifically, how to size, connect, align, layer, and group shapes. Included, as well, are ways to create and edit master shapes, stencils, and templates.

Stencil and Template Applications

Part I introduced you to the stencils and templates found in Visio 2000 Standard. Exercises demonstrated how to place masters on drawing pages. Here I take you to the next level, creating and manipulating your own masters, stencils, and templates.

Opening a Stencil

As you learned in Chapters 2 and 3, opening stencils is easy. Simply click the Open Stencil button or the down arrow next to it. The manner you use to open the stencil is a little different, but the result is the same. The two following examples show how the processes differ. If you already remember how to do this, skip to the section on creating stencil files; otherwise, enjoy the brief refresher course.

Clicking on the Stencil button

Perhaps you're looking for the Flags stencil. You can't access it from the any of the Maps templates, so you need the stencil. You can use the following steps to find and open it:

1. Click the Stencil button to call up the Open Stencil dialog box.

2. By default, the program looks first in the Visio Solutions folder. Look in that folder's contents for the subfolder that contains the stencil you want. In this case, it would be the Maps subfolder. Double-click it.

3. The Maps subfolder contents are revealed. Either click once on the Flags stencil and then click the OK button, or double-click the Flags stencil. Both actions open the selected stencil.

Selecting File ➪ Stencils ➪ Open Stencil pulls up the same dialog box.

Clicking on the Stencil arrow button

Take a slightly different approach. This time open the Flag stencil by using the down arrow beside the Stencil button. Here's how:

1. Click the Stencil arrow button. A drop-down menu listing solution folders (for example, Block Diagram, Flowchart, Forms and Charts, and so on) appears.

2. Scroll down the menu until you find the Maps folder. By resting your cursor on it, a pop-up menu emerges to the side.

3. Click the stencil labeled Flags. This opens the stencil.

Selecting File ➪ Stencils pulls up a section within its pop-up menu similar to that here. Just scroll to the folder and then click the stencil.

Creating Stencil Files

Visio 2000 offers an incredible number of stencils for various tasks. However, each business will still naturally find it convenient to modify those files and even create its own. Furthermore, the program enables users to do just that. You can design new masters and place them within a new stencil file, or simply edit masters from Visio stencils, plopping them in a stencil of your own.

The New Stencil feature is essential for creating stencils. Click the New Stencil button on the Stencil toolbar or choose File ➪ Stencils ➪ New Stencil. Both actions pull up a blank stencil window (see Figure 15-1). The new stencil title bar contains a generic name such as *Stencil2*.

With a blank stencil window on your screen, all you need to do is place shapes on it. There are two ways: You can create new masters for the stencil, or you can copy existing masters onto the new stencil. The choice is yours.

A red asterisk, located in the left part of the title bar, always appears in new stencils. This lets users know that a stencil is currently in edit mode. You must, however, select edit mode to edit existing Visio stencils.

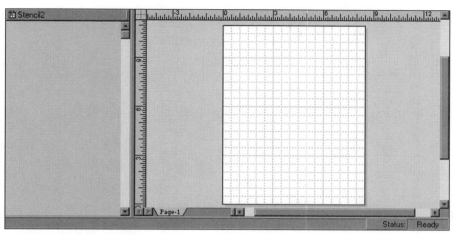

Figure 15-1: A new stencil

Creating new masters

The following steps take you through the process of adding new masters to a new stencil:

1. Right-click the green section of the stencil window. A pop-up menu appears.

2. Select New Master. This pulls up the New Master dialog box (as shown in Figure 15-2). Fill in the name, prompt, icon size, and name alignment for the shape. Once finished with the properties, click the OK button. A generic block shape appears in the stencil window.

Note   The Prompt feature on the New Master dialog box refers to those tips that appear when you move your cursor over a specific master icon.

3. Right-click the generic block shape, pulling up the pop-up menu again. This time, select Edit Master.

4. The Edit Master drawing window, which fills the screen except for the toolbars, contains a drawing page on a green background. Draw the shape you want or insert clip art or pictures on the drawing page. You can even place shapes from other stencils on the page.

5. Close the Edit Master drawing window. A dialog box appears asking whether you want to update that master. Click Yes. Presto! The new master appears in your stencil.

6. Save the stencil by right-clicking on its title bar and choosing Save As. You know the rest of the drill.

Figure 15-2: The New Master dialog box enables users to modify a master's properties and behavior.

Note   You can select the New Master feature from the Drawing Explorer.

Placing existing masters in a new stencil

New stencils make ideal homes for new masters. However, they also work well for storing frequently used and modified shapes. All it takes is a little copying and pasting. The following steps are a useful guide:

1. Create a new stencil and then open an existing stencil.

2. Right-click a shape icon in the existing stencil and choose Copy from the pop-up menu. You can also just click the object and then click the Copy button.

3. Click the title bar of the new stencil to bring up its contents — or, in this case, the place for its contents. Right-click the green contents holder and then choose Paste from the pop-up menu. You can also click the area and then select the Paste button.

Tip   You may simultaneously select several shapes by holding Shift as you select subsequent shapes. You may even select all the shapes in a stencil by right-clicking on the stencil's green field and choosing Select All from the menu.

4. Right-click again on the new master. Select Master Properties from the pop-up menu. Give the shape the name, prompt, icon size, and name alignment you want.

5. Save the stencil by right-clicking on the title bar and choosing Save As.

Tip   Click the Save icon inside the stencil title bar to save your work after you've used the Save As function once.

Note You can also copy shapes from a drawing—instead of an existing stencil—into a new stencil file. Simply drag the shape from the drawing page to the stencil title bar.

Perhaps you are modifying an existing master and placing it in a new stencil, but you want the old master to reflect the changes of its modified version. For an example, drag the sofa from the Office Layout Shapes, but enlarge it and color it blue. Next, check the Match Master by Name on Drop feature for both the *blue sofa* and the original *sofa*. Save the changes and close the Office Layout Shapes stencil and the new stencil. Now when you place the sofa shape from the Office Layout Shapes stencil onto a drawing page, it will appear as the updated version in the new stencil—as a large, blue sofa. Do not check the Match Master by Name on Drop feature if you do not want your modifications to show up in the derivative master-instance process.

Placing a master in multiple stencils

As you are learning, editing stencils is a breeze. Visio 2000 even enables users to insert a master into more than one stencil — easily. The master shortcut feature is designed specifically for this purpose. Here's how it works:

1. Open a stencil with a master that you want to also insert in another stencil.

2. Open this other stencil, the one to which you would like to add the master.

3. Right-click the title bars on both stencils. Select Edit from their menus. These actions enable you to edit both stencils, in other words create the master shortcut.

4. Drag the master icon from one stencil towards the title bar of the other stencil to which you want to add the master. Do this by holding down the Control and Shift keys when dragging.

5. Save your changes by clicking on the Save icon within the title bar. Now this stencil contains a master shortcut.

6. Take the stencils out of Edit mode.

The stencil's new master icon appears as a shortcut of the original. Thus, you can access the master from both stencils, rather than from just one. Simply, drag the icon on to the drawing page. The master shortcut appears on the page just as the original would. How about that!

New Feature The Master Shortcut feature is one of the new conveniences found in the Visio 2000 series.

Note You can adjust the master shortcut's properties by right-clicking on the shortcut's icon then selecting *Master Shortcut Properties...* from the pop-up menu. From there, users can edit features such as the shortcut's name, prompt, and icon size.

Setting Stencil File Properties

If you don't want a generic title like *Stencil2* for your new stencil, you can name your stencil files appropriately using the Properties dialog box. Right-click the stencil's title bar and then choose Properties on the pop-up menu. This action pulls up the Properties dialog box.

Tip   You must place the stencil in edit mode to access the Properties dialog box.

Cross-Reference   See Chapter 11 for an in-depth look at file properties.

The Properties dialog box is organized in the same manner for stencil files as it is for all other files. Four tabs are located on the dialog box: General, Summary, Contents, and Output Format. Click the Summary tab to change the title. You can also add information such as the subject matter, the author's name, keywords, your company's name, and so on.

Using Document Stencils

Document Stencils are exactly what the name implies. They are stencils that accompany your documents. Of course, they're not automatically visible; select the Show Document Stencil feature either by clicking the button on the Stencil toolbar or by choosing Window ➪ Show Document Stencil. You can also access the Document Stencil through the Drawing Explorer window. The stencil contains masters of all the shapes used in that current document. For example, if you have placed a square, triangle, and octagon on your drawing page, all three polygons will appear in the document stencil (as shown in Figure 15-3).

Unlike other stencils, document stencils are only available in a read-only format. The document stencil itself will not allow you to change its properties; however, you can modify the properties of objects within the stencil. For example, add masters to a document stencil by right-clicking on the contents area and selecting New Master from the pop-up menu. Modify masters by using Edit Master. You can even delete objects. In fact, many of the right-click features are identical to those found in other stencils. You just can't save a document stencil as an entity by itself; it is bound to the document.

The most unique characteristic of document stencils lies in their ability to edit instances. You can right-click a shape and then stretch its boundaries in the Edit Master drawing window. Simply updating the master automatically updates all of the instances within that drawing. For example, if you stretch a square to twice its original size, those changes—when updated—are implemented on all squares within the document. Changes such as those involving an existing Visio master's fill, shadows, and rotation, however, cannot be made to Visio masters. Only sizes can be adjusted.

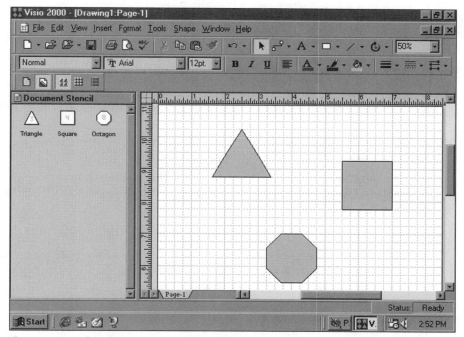

Figure 15-3: The document stencil contains masters of shapes used in that particular drawing.

Note Unlike existing Visio stencil masters, shapes drawn by the drawing tools (for example, the Ellipse icon tool and Line icon tool) are not automatically added to document stencils.

Editing a Stencil File

Time and the course of your business will affect the evolution of your stencil files. No sweat, Visio 2000 makes enacting these changes easy. Besides later adding masters to a stencil, you may choose to modify the existing masters or even rename the file. Whatever your demands, this program has you covered.

Editing masters

You know how to create masters, but what about editing them? No problem. Right-click the master icon to access the multipurpose pop-up menu. The pop-up menu contains numerous options, including those for modifying, duplicating, and deleting masters. The following is a quick rundown on how to get started with the editing process:

1. Open the stencil you would like to change.

2. Right-click the stencil window's title bar. Select Edit on the pop-up menu to convert the stencil from read-only to edit mode. Right-click the green area and choose Select All to highlight all the masters within that stencil; this option works well for copying or deleting multiple masters.

3. Right-click the master that you want to edit. Another pop-up menu appears; select Edit Master.

4. Make the appropriate changes in the Edit Master drawing window (see Figure 15-4). Close the window and then update the changes by clicking Yes on the dialog box.

5. Click the Save icon in the stencil title bar to save your changes.

 Do not save changes to an existing Visio stencil unless you're absolutely certain that you no longer need the original. In most cases, it's best to work with copies.

 To erase a master from a stencil, right-click the shape and then select Delete from the pop-up menu.

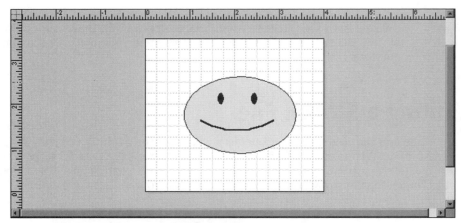

Figure 15-4: The Edit Master drawing window.

Note You can arrange masters in any particular order by dragging them.

Tip Modify an existing master and still keep the one you have—without using the Copy feature. Right-clicking on the shape and then selecting Duplicate from the pop-up menu is one of the easiest ways to do this. A copy of the original master will then appear in the stencil. You can edit the copy while keeping the original in pristine condition.

Editing icons

The small visual representations of masters in each stencil are called icons. Sometimes, after creating a new master, you'll find that its icon is indiscernible. This is often due to the level of detail present in the master as well as the icon's small size. The master's title is usually helpful enough in these cases. Changing the icon, in certain circumstances, may be the best alternative.

For example, if your company has several masters that resemble one another and are of a similar subject matter, modifying their icons is your best bet. Why waste time dragging shapes onto a drawing page just to see what they are? There's no need to do this in Visio 2000. Just change the icons. Here's how:

1. Open the stencil that contains the indiscernible icon.

2. Right-click the stencil title bar and then select Edit from the pop-up menu.

3. Right-click the icon in question and then choose Edit Icon from the pop-up menu.

4. The Edit Icon drawing window (shown in Figure 15-5) appears to the right of your screen. Use the Edit Icon drawing toolbar to manipulate the icon. Notice that all changes appear simultaneously in the stencil and Edit Icon drawing windows.

5. Close the Edit Icon window by clicking the X.

6. Close the Stencil window by right-clicking on the title bar and choosing Close. A dialog box then appears asking you if you want to save the changes. Choose Yes. Now the new icon is part of the stencil.

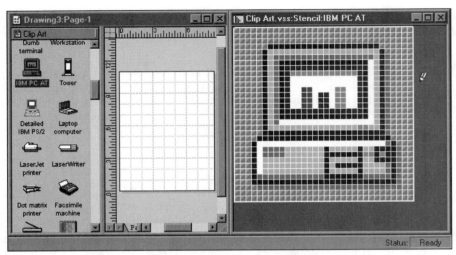

Figure 15-5: Editing an icon from the Edit Icon drawing window

Unlike the Edit Master drawing window, the Edit Icon window contains a unique toolbar (as shown in Figure 15-6). The toolbar consists of a palette of sixteen different colors, the transparent stencil background color, and four drawing buttons. The two blocks labeled *Left Color* and *Right Color* signify which colors are allotted to the respective mouse buttons. Change these by clicking on a color. The drawing tools are used to either color, select, or move the icon blocks. They include the following:

✦ **Pencil Tool.** Used to paint each individual block.

✦ **Bucket Tool.** Used to paint an entire area.

✦ **Lasso Tool.** Used to select an irregular shape of colored blocks and then place it elsewhere within the icon.

✦ **Selection Net Tool.** Used to select a rectangular group of colored blocks and then place it elsewhere within the icon.

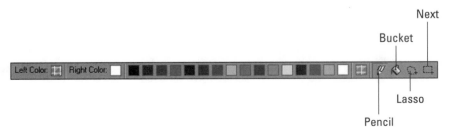

Figure 15-6: The Edit Icon toolbar

Keep two things in mind when modifying an icon: alter it enough so that it is recognizable from similar icons, but refrain from making changes that are totally out of line with the master's title and subject matter. For instance, don't make a habit of constructing smiley faces for icons representing your department. As a rule, edit icons only when you or others have a hard time telling them from each other.

Tip Uncheck the Generate Icon Automatically From Shape Data feature (located on New Master and Master Properties dialog boxes) to prevent the master's icon from resembling the actual master.

Renaming a stencil file

Modifying numerous masters may require you to re-title the stencil. For example, after adding a couple logos from your corporate subsidiaries to the mother company's clip-art stencil, it best to reflect those changes in the title. This is hardly a problem, though. Just follow these steps and your stencils are back up to date:

1. Open the stencil that you would like to rename.

2. Right-click the stencil title bar and choose Edit from the pop-up menu.

3. Right-click again on the stencil title bar, this time selecting Properties.

4. The Properties dialog box contains four tabs. Click the one titled Summary. Change the stencil's name in the title box. Reformat any other boxes (subject, author, keywords, description, and so on) as necessary.

5. Click the OK button.

Adjusting Stencil Windows

Like other Visio windows, you can adjust stencil windows for your viewing pleasure. Read on to learn more about closing and positioning stencils as well as viewing stencil contents.

Viewing stencil contents

Everyone has their own way of doing things. The people at Visio know this. As one would expect from a company that has revolutionized how the business world visually presents ideas, Visio has put the same amount of expertise to work within their program. The various viewing formats are a prime example of this same genius at work. Visio 2000 offers three different methods for viewing stencils:

✦ **Icons and Names.** Individual icons accompany each master's title.

✦ **Icons Only.** Only individual icons appear in the stencil.

✦ **Names Only.** Each master's title is adjacent to a generic block.

Figure 15-7 contains pictures of all three representations. These can be adjusted from buttons on the Stencil toolbar, or by right-clicking on a stencil's title bar and then choosing one of the views from the pop-up menu.

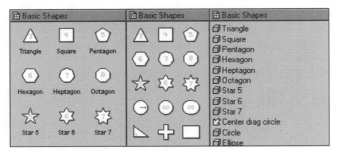

Figure 15-7: Visio 2000 offers three different ways to view a stencil's contents.

Positioning stencil windows

For a moment, think of each stencil as a vessel in the sea. Like ships, Visio stencils are portable; you can dock them onto the drawing window or leave them floating about on the screen. This means that you can place a stencil window in the location most comfortable for you. Simply right-click the stencil's title bar, and then select Position. From there, choose from five different stencil positions:

✦ **Docked to Left.** Places stencil window to the drawing window's left.

✦ **Docked to Right.** Places stencil window to the drawing window's right.

✦ **Docked to Top.** Places stencil window to the drawing window's top.

✦ **Docked to Bottom.** Places stencil window to the drawing window's bottom.

✦ **Floating.** You can move the stencil window across the drawing window.

Docking a stencil window to the top or bottom positions the window in an elongated horizontal fashion, while stencil windows docked to the right or left appear in a thicker vertical format. The orientation of a floating stencil depends on its previous position. Therefore, floating stencil windows can appear both vertically and horizontally on the screen.

New Feature   Visio 5.0 only lets users dock stencil windows on the drawing page's right and left. However, with Visio 2000's new docking formats, you can now position stencil windows to the top and bottom of the drawing window as well as to the window's right and left.

Note Unlike some Visio 2000 windows (for example, the Drawing Explorer and Custom Properties windows), stencil windows do not possess an AutoHide feature.

Closing stencil windows

To close a stencil window, right-click the title bar and select Close from the pop-up menu. If you have opened a stencil window without the drawing page, you can close it by selecting File ➪ Close. Of course, closing the file will close all of the document's contents, including stencil windows.

Using Templates

Visio templates can contain one or more stencils in addition to several background and foreground pages. As I mentioned in Chapter 4, templates are useful for two reasons: they provide a basis for organizing stencil themes and prevent time-sapping, redundant formatting.

Creating and Modifying Templates

As you learned in Chapter 4, Visio 2000 Standard offers over 25 different templates. You can refashion these files to fit your needs or make your own utilizing one of two means:

✦ Designing new masters and stencils and saving them as template files

✦ Making changes within an original Visio 2000 template and then saving it as a new template file

In both cases, you must save your work as a new template file. (Remember that templates have a file extension of .vst.) Don't save over an original Visio template unless you're absolutely certain that you'll never use it again. You can name or rename your template when saving it. Also, select File ➪ Properties to add the document's title, subject matter, keywords, and author's name.

Caution When modifying a Visio standard template, work on a copy and save the new template under a different name to avoid losing the original template. Do this within the Open dialog box by opening a template as a *copy* instead of an *original*.

Cross-Reference Chapters 11–13 contain detailed information on file properties, saving documents, and opening drawings.

Walking through a template example

Suppose that you work as a public relations professional for a fictional computer hardware company called Techno Savvy Systems. You need to create a template containing a stencil of company clip art. To keep things simple, we'll place a logo and two pictures of computers within a new stencil.

First, open a blank drawing page and then the stencil entitled "Basic Network Shapes 3D." Use the New Drawing and Open Stencil buttons on the Standard toolbar. Next, create a new stencil. You can do this by either selecting File ⇨ Stencils ⇨ New Stencil or clicking the New Stencil button on the Stencil toolbar. Now you're ready to start cooking—or, drawing, that is.

Tip   Place the appropriate stencils with each newly formed template you send to coworkers, especially if you've customized the applicable stencils on your computer. Colleagues working from a disk or network may not have access to those stencils.

Place two computer masters into the new stencil by copying two stencil icons from the Basic Network Shapes 3D. I chose the ones called Personal Computer and Laptop. To do so, right-click a computer master and then select Copy from the pop-up menu. Next, right-click anywhere within the green part of the blank stencil, and then choose Paste from the menu. Do this again for the next icon. You're almost there.

Tip   You may also drag the master onto your new stencil. Little fuss, no muss.

Create a company icon by right-clicking on the new stencil and choosing New Master. Type in the stencil name and prompt message in the New Master dialog box and then click OK. Next, right-click the new icon, selecting Edit Master from the pop-up window. Create a logo in the Edit Master drawing window using the Text, Line, Ellipse, and Rectangle icon tools.

Tip   You may also import images and use them as your logo. To do so, copy the image, right-click the Edit Master drawing window, and select Paste.

Once you've finished creating the company logo, close the window and click Yes to update the icon. Now you have three masters on your new stencil (see Figure 15-8). Close the Basic Network Shapes 3D stencil window and then save (and rename) your new stencil. Next, save the new template as Techno Savvy by selecting File ⇨ Save As from the menu bar.

Note   When working with a template, remember to save new or modified stencil(s). Just placing masters in a template is not enough. Stencil changes are not reflected in a template unless you save both the stencils and the template individually.

Figure 15-8: The new Techno Savvy Systems template.

Using the Drawing Explorer

Select View ➪ Windows ➪ Drawing Explorer to access the Drawing Explorer window. The Visio 2000 Drawing Explorer helps users approach drawings in a more analytical fashion. In fact, it enables you to break down a document into a vast hierarchy of elements, providing a quick look at every single component within that drawing. This sometimes makes editing a document easier. Basic document elements included in the Drawing Explorer are the following:

Foreground Pages	Fill Patterns
Background Pages	Line Patterns
Styles	Line Ends
Masters	

A folder represents each of these elements. All features added within a drawing are labeled in one of these folders. For example, each master placed on a drawing page is documented under the Masters folder. Click the adjacent plus signs to view the accompanying contents (see Figure 15-9). Accordingly, click the minus signs to retract the contents from your viewing area.

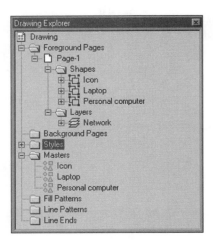

Figure 15-9: The Drawing Explorer window documents all features present within a drawing.

Right-click a folder or one of its components to modify it. Delete and edit features with this method. For example, by right-clicking on the drawing icon, access the Properties, Print Setup, Header and Footer, Color Palette, Protect Document, and Show ShapeSheet features. Table 15-1 reveals some of the options available by right-clicking on an element's respective folder.

Table 15-1
Drawing Explorer Element Modification Features

Folder	*Right-click Pop-up Menu*
Page Folder	Page Setup Ruler & Grid Delete Page Show ShapeSheet
Style	Define Styles Delete Style Show ShapeSheet
Master	New Master Show Document Stencil

New Feature The Drawing Explorer is a tool unique to the Visio 2000 series.

See Chapter 8 for information on inserting and reordering pages with the Drawing Explorer, Chapter 11 for information on file properties (especially password-protected files), Chapter 14 for information on print previews, Chapter 18 for information on the color palette, and Chapter 34 for information on ShapeSheets.

Adjusting the Drawing Explorer window

Like the other peripheral windows, the Drawing Explorer can at times be a hindrance. Luckily, you can manipulate the window's size and position to make things easier. The Drawing Explorer window operates the same way as the Pan & Zoom window, which I discussed earlier in the book. Adjust the Drawing Explorer window accordingly:

- ✦ **Resize window.** Place the cursor on the edge of the window. When the double-headed arrows appear, drag the edge to manipulate the window's proportions.

- ✦ **Dock window.** Drag the Drawing Explorer window onto the edge of the drawing window.

- ✦ **Float window.** Right-click the Drawing Explorer window and then choose Float Window from the pop-up menu.

- ✦ **AutoHide window.** Right-click anywhere on the window's edges and then select AutoHide from the pop-up menu. Remember that the AutoHide features only work when the window is docked.

- ✦ **Hide window.** Right-click the floating window's title bar and then select Hide from the pop-up menu.

- ✦ **Move window.** Drag the window by the title bar. You can also right-click the title bar when in Float mode and select Move. Place the four-pronged arrow over the window title bar and drag the Drawing Explorer.

See Chapter 9 for similar information on adjusting the Pan & Zoom window.

Defining styles and patterns with the Drawing Explorer

You can define styles (see Figure 15-10) for elements like guides and text by right-clicking on each listing under the Styles folder. Click the Text, Line, and Fill buttons to access each component's dialog box. Also, use the Fill Patterns, Line Patterns, and Line Ends folders. Right-click each and then select New Pattern from the pop-up menu to access the New Pattern dialog box (as shown in Figure 15-11). From there you can name the master and edit its behavior. For instance, Visio enables users to manipulate the angle at which an arrow attaches itself to a line.

Afterwards, an icon representing those insertions and changes will appear in the Drawing Explorer window.

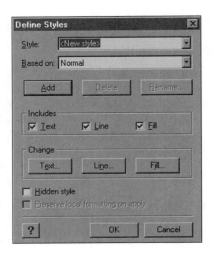

Figure 15-10: The Define Styles dialog box

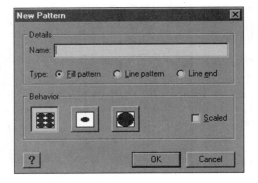

Figure 15-11: The New Pattern dialog box

Using the Shape Explorer

Perhaps you're looking for a specific shape. Rather than scour every stencil, use the Visio Shape Explorer. The Shape Explorer is a popular macro within the Visio 2000 series that enables users to search the program for specific masters, stencils, templates, and wizards. Furthermore, you can even create a personalized database within the macro.

Select Tools ➪ Macros ➪ Shape Explorer to open the Shape Explorer. The Shape Explorer window (as shown in Figure 15-12) contains a menu bar, two tabs, and an area for viewing a list of items. Close the macro by simply clicking on the X in the upper right-hand corner of the window or by selecting File ➪ Exit from the Shape Explorer menu bar.

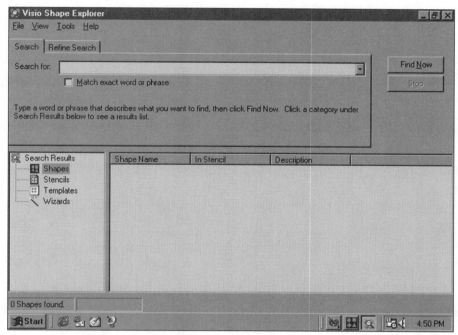

Figure 15-12: The Shape Explorer window

Searching

Finding what you want is easy. Type in a name or brief description of the item you seek on the Search tab. For example, type in the word **network**. Click the Find Now button to the right. A list of items related to your search appears below. The Your Search Found section reveals the item types. In this case, 14 shapes, 6 stencils, and 2 templates were found related to the search for network. Click each of the item types in the Your Search Found section to view a detailed list in the viewing window panel.

Tip   Select View ➪ Details to obtain a list of the items' names, locations, and descriptions in the viewing window panel. Choose View ➪ List for just the objects' names and file extensions.

You can refine your search in several ways. First, check the box (entitled "Match exact word or phrase") under your search terms. The Search Explorer then only searches for items containing that word. For example, if you type in *star* without checking the box, a number of items emerge. Many of the objects may not contain the word *star*—instead they use *start* in the description, or other words with the s-t-a-r combination in them. However, you can avoid this problem by checking the Match exact word or phrase box. In this case, the feature restricts your search so that only items with the word *star* appear.

Once you refine your terms you can refine your search locations. Click the Refine Search tab. Notice the four categories under the Search Categories section: Shapes, Stencils, Templates, and Wizards. The Shape Explorer, by default, conducts searches for all these categories. Uncheck the appropriate boxes to restrict the search (see Figure 15-13). For example, uncheck the Shapes, Stencils, and Wizards boxes; then the Shape Explorer will only search for templates. Type in the word **network** once again and click the Find Now button. Only templates appear in the viewing window.

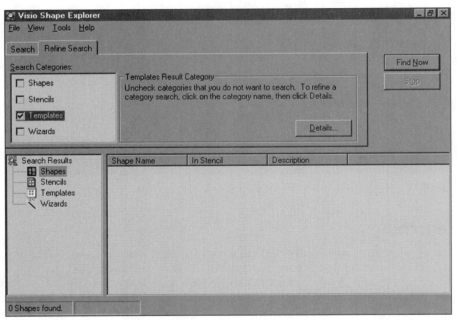

Figure 15-13: Uncheck the Refine Search tab boxes to restrict the search categories.

These two search methods are ideal for finding specific items. However, when looking for generic objects, you probably want to search throughout all of Visio's formats and items. You may also consider using some of the database search options mentioned at the end of this chapter.

Using items from the Shape Explorer

So you think you've found the shape you've been looking for. Well, use the preview to get a better look. If it's the right one, *Visio 2000* helps you place that item onto or near your drawing window. You don't have to memorize the directory or any of that stuff; just click.

Previewing a shape

After compiling your search for a specific master, you can preview each shape from the viewing window's list. Simply right-click one of the items and then select Properties from the pop-up menu. Alternatively, you can double-click the item. Click the Show Preview button on the Properties dialog box; the small window then displays the shape (as shown in Figure 15-14). Click the OK button to return to the Shape Explorer window.

Note   Previews for stencils and templates are not available. Selecting Properties for those items reveals only a description of the components found within them.

Tip   Use the Preview feature to read the entire description listed within the viewing window panel.

Figure 15-14: Previewing a shape with the Shape Explorer's Properties dialog box

Adding items to the drawing window

Add shapes, stencils, and templates that you find in the Shape Explorer to either your drawing page or the drawing window. Simply right-click the chosen item and then select the appropriate feature. The lists below detail these right-mouse-button features, along with others.

Right-clicking a shape will yield the following features:

✦ **Add to Drawing.** Places the shape on the drawing page

✦ **Open Containing Stencil.** Opens the stencil that contains the selected shape

✦ **Create New Stencil.** Creates a new stencil that contains the selected shape

✦ **Properties.** Shape description and preview

The following are features obtained when right-clicking a stencil:

✦ **Open Stencil.** Opens the stencil inside the drawing window

✦ **Open Containing Template.** Opens the template that contains the selected stencil

✦ **Create New Drawing.** Creates a new drawing page accompanied by the selected stencil

✦ **Properties.** Stencil contents description

These are your options when you right-click a template:

✦ **Open Template.** Opens the selected template

✦ **Properties.** Template contents description

Right-clicking a wizard will yield one feature:

✦ **Run Wizard.** Operates the selected wizard

New Feature   Unlike in *Visio 5.0*, *Visio 2000* enables you to add shapes found in the Shape Explorer to your drawing.

Creating a personalized database

Visio's Shape Explorer can create shape databases. Using the Create User Database and Add Files dialog boxes, you can design personalized database files (.mdb). Here's how:

1. Select File ➪ Create User Database from the Shape Explorer menu bar.

2. In the Create User Database dialog box (as shown in Figure 15-15), type the name of the database you wish to create. Don't forget to indicate the location where you want to save this file; choose a folder from the "Save Database In" section. When finished, click the OK button.

3. A second dialog box asks if you would like to add files to the new database. Select OK to view the Add Files dialog box. If you choose Cancel, you can still add files later by selecting Tools ➪ Add Files.

4. The Current User Database section includes the directory path of the new database file. You can select whether you'd like to include files or folders in your file. Click the appropriate box and then select the Browse button.

Depending on your choice, you can select components via the Select a Visio File dialog box or the Select Folder dialog box. Click OK on the Add Files dialog box and the ensuing dialog box to add the selected components.

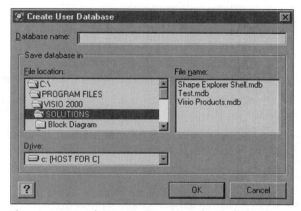

Figure 15-15: The Create User Database dialog box

Tip   When in the Add Files dialog box, check the Subfolders box to include the chosen folder's subfolders within the new database.

Note   Click the Remove button (Add Files dialog box) to remove the selected file from the database.

More database options

The Database Options dialog box enables you to include databases within your searches. You can add and browse files within the Visio Shape Explorer database or your own personalized database. Select Tools ➪ Database Options to access the Database Options dialog box. Check the two "Include in Search" boxes to extend your search to database files. The Location section reveals the directory of the file. You can change this by either using the Browse button or by typing in the directory of the file you want to find. The Visio Shape Explorer enables you to include Visio database files like Visio Products.mdb and Shape Explorer Shell.mdb in searches. Use the User Database section to incorporate personalized database files in your searches.

Summary

This concludes my discussion on stencil and template applications. Now you know how to create and manipulate stencils and templates using a variety of methods and features. Specifically, I covered the following points:

✦ Several different ways exist for opening stencil files.

✦ Use the New Stencil feature to create stencils.

✦ You can design your own masters or copy existing masters into a new stencil.

✦ The Show Document Stencil feature contains master icons of all shapes used in that current document.

✦ Modifying a master from the Document Stencil enables you to instantly change all of that master's instances in the drawing.

✦ If a master's icon is indiscernible, modify the icon using the Edit Icon drawing window.

✦ Three different options exist for viewing a stencil's contents.

✦ Visio 2000 enables you to customize the location of your stencils.

✦ Two primary ways exist for creating new templates.

✦ When editing, work with stencil and template copies to avoid losing the original file.

✦ You can create a personalized template for your company.

✦ The Drawing Explorer enables you to break down a document into a vast hierarchy of elements, providing a quick look at every single component within that drawing.

✦ The Shape Explorer enables you to refine your search methods.

In the next chapter, you master more techniques concerning sizing, positioning, and duplicating shapes.

✦   ✦   ✦

Sizing, Positioning, and Duplicating Shapes

Without the expertise to manipulate shapes, working on projects can be downright tedious. Don't sweat; by the time you finish this chapter you'll be a shape-shifting guru. Using a variety of methods, including functions involving flipping, rotating, sizing, and stretching objects, you will be well on your way to mastering the Visio 2000 environment.

Using the Size & Position Window

Hey, it's a precise kind of world. We all need to know exactly what time it is, precisely how much we will be paid, and the accurate distance to the nearest McDonald's. The folks at Visio understand our need for exactness and provide the tools to make it happen. Perhaps the primary tool for determining and altering exact shape location is aptly named the Size & Position window as shown in Figure 16-1.

Size & Position - Heptagon	
X	3.5 in.
Y	5.8359 in.
Width	1.5 in.
Height	1.5 in.
Angle	0 deg.
Pin Pos	

Figure 16-1: The Size & Position window

As with all elements of Visio 2000, the Size & Position window is a multifunction display. It not only provides accurate data on the selected shape, but also enables you to modify the shape by altering the values in the window. Let's take a look at the window's features and walk through an example of how to use it.

Examining the Size & Position window

Select View ➪ Windows ➪ Size & Position to place the Size & Position window on your screen. Included in the window are the following features.

Tip   You may also open the Size & Position window via the toolbar. Right-click any toolbar to display the drop-down tool bar menu. Check View to display the View toolbar. On the View toolbar, tap the Size & Position window icon to display the window.

Note   To display these features you must first select a shape on an active drawing.

✦ **X.** The first field is simply titled *X.* This is the shape's location on the X or horizontal gridline. The larger the number, the closer the shape is to the right edge of the screen. This field not only indicates the shape's location, but also may be used to move the shape. To do so, highlight the field, press Backspace to delete the current entry, and type the location desired.

Note   You may change the unit of measurement used in either the X- or Y-axis. Select File ➪ Page Setup and then click the Page Properties tab. Select the measurement units you wish by highlighting the units in the drop-down menu adjacent to the Measurement Units field.

✦ **Y.** This is the shape's location on the Y or vertical gridline. The larger the number, the closer the shape is to the top edge of the screen. This field not only indicates the shape's location, but also may be used to move the shape. To do so, highlight the field, press Backspace to delete the current entry, and type the location desired.

✦ **Width.** This is the shape's width measured in the same unit of measurement utilized on the X- and Y-axis. As with the other fields, this not only provides information, but may be used to alter the shape. To do so, highlight the field, press Backspace to delete the current entry, and type the desired size.

✦ **Height.** This is the shape's height measured in the same unit of measurement utilized on the X- and Y-axis. As with the other fields, this not only provides information, but also may be used to alter the shape. To do so, highlight the field, press Backspace to delete the current entry, and type the desired size.

✦ **Angle.** This is the shape's angle relative to the bottom of the page. To set a desired angle, highlight the field, press Backspace to delete the current entry, and type the desired angle.

✦ **Pin Pos.** This is the shape's pin position. The pin is the point from which the X,Y coordinates are derived. The default location is the center of the shape, but you may also place the pin elsewhere. To see the effect, drag a square onto a new drawing as shown in Figure 16-2. Select the square and then open the Size & Position window (View ➪ Windows ➪ Size & Position). Highlight Pin Pos and display the scrolling menu. Select Top Left. You'll notice that although the X,Y coordinates do not change, the window shifts down and to the right as shown in Figure 16-3. That is because the X, Y coordinates now refer to a point in the upper left-hand corner of the square.

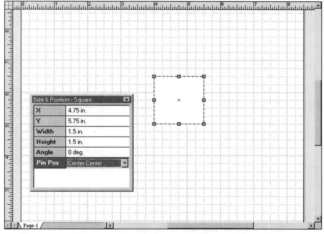

Figure 16-2: The square with its original centered pin position

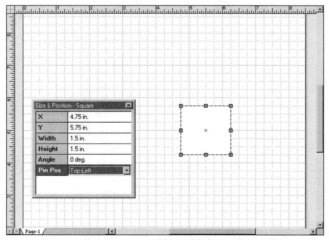

Figure 16-3: The square with a top left pin position. Notice that the X, Y coordinates stay the same.

A Size & Position window example

Open a new drawing. Place two triangles onto the page in the approximate positions shown in Figure 16-4. Select the top triangle and move its pin position to Bottom Right. Select the bottom triangle and move its pin position to Bottom Left. Now copy the X, Y coordinates from the top triangle to the bottom triangle. If done correctly, your drawing will look like Figure 16-5.

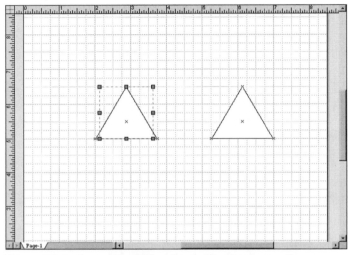

Figure 16-4: A couple of triangles waiting for instructions

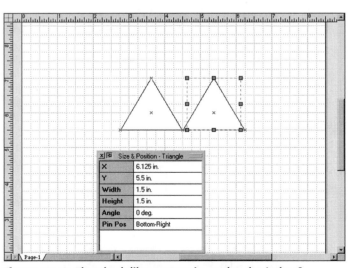

Figure 16-5: They look like mountain peaks, don't they?

Tip

You don't have to type the coordinates from the top triangle into the fields in the bottom triangle—that's so 1970. Highlight the X field in the top shape and press Ctrl+C to copy the field's contents. Highlight the X field in the bottom triangle, press Backspace to delete its contents, and then press Ctrl+V to paste the contents of the top triangle's X field into the bottom triangle's X field. Rinse and repeat with the Y field.

Now its time to modify the twin peaks. Select the right-hand triangle; delete the contents of the Angle field and type in 180. Voilà! You have—as shown in Figure 16-6—a diamond; not quite as lustrous as those at a jeweler, but a heck of a lot cheaper.

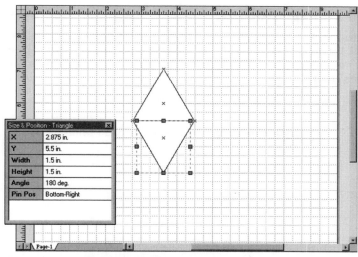

Figure 16-6: A homemade diamond

Positioning the Size & Position window

As with nearly all Visio windows, you can place the Size & Position window wherever you like—as long as it's still on the Visio window. To do so, right-click the window and select Float Window. You may now drag the window about.

Note

The window automatically locks onto the side of the Visio drawing window even when Float Window is selected. To unlock it, simply drag the window away from the abutting border.

When the Size & Position window is positioned on the edge of a Visio drawing page, right-clicking on the window and selecting AutoHide normally collapses the window when the mouse cursor leaves the Size & Position window. The window expands when the cursor passes over the window's title bar.

Tip Depressing the PushPin icon in the top left of the Size & Position window freezes the window in the open position. This is a useful feature when you're spending a lot of time in the window.

Sizing Shapes

Unlike airline life jackets, one size does not fit all in the world of Visio shapes. Fortunately, modifying a shape's size is both easy and quick. Let's discuss the multitude of shape-sizing options available in Visio 2000.

The click and drag method

The simplest method for changing shapes is to click and drag. Open a new Visio drawing. Choose the Block Diagram ➪ Basic Shapes stencil. Drag a circle onto your drawing. Click the circle to select it. Notice that passing your cursor over any of the green "handles" morphs the cursor into a double-arrow cursor as shown in Figure 16-7.

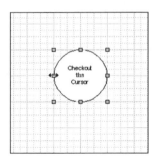

Figure 16-7: As if by magic the cursor morphs into a double-headed arrow cursor.

Click and drag to expand or shrink the circle. Releasing the mouse fixes the size of the circle.

Remember, however, that it's not a round world. Well, actually it is, but all the shapes that we use aren't. Shapes thrown onto a drawing from a stencil retain their relative proportions when expanded or shrunk. In other words, a square is a square no matter how small. On the other hand, rectangles and ellipses drawn using the Rectangle and Ellipses tool owe no allegiance to uniform geometry. You can, however, bend their form to your will by utilizing Visio's drawing aids. Here's how.

Right-click the Standard toolbar and select the Snap & Glue toolbar from the drop down menu. On the Snap & Glue toolbar, click the Drawing Aids button as shown in Figure 16-8.

Click here to activate the Drawing Aids tool

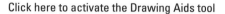

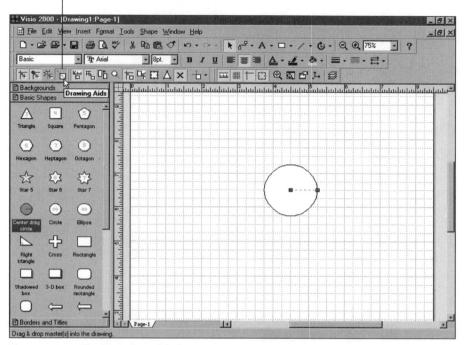

Figure 16-8: The Drawing Aids button

Now, using the Rectangle tool, create a rectangle on the drawing. Note that as you start to drag the cursor to define the rectangle, a dotted line originates at the rectangle's initial placement point and continues away from the point at a 45-degree angle as shown in Figure 16-9. If you release the mouse button anywhere on this line you form a perfect square. You can form circles in a similar manner.

Note

You can choose how shapes resize when part of a larger group. Select a shape, right-click it, and then choose Format ⇨ Behavior. Click the Behavior tab in the Behavior dialog box. There are three options under Resize Behavior: Scale with group, Reposition only, and Use Group's setting. For our purposes Scale with group and Use Group's settings are identical. Both resize the individual shape's size when the shape group is resized. On the other hand, Reposition only retains the individual shape's size yet repositions the shape in relation to the other shapes in the group so as to keep their general spatial relationships.

The Drawing Aids line

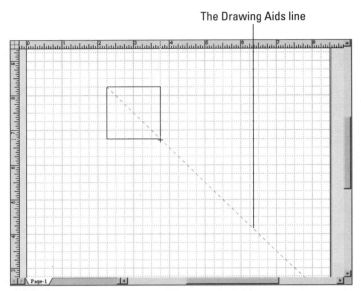

Figure 16-9: The Drawing Aids line enables you to create a perfect square.

Sizing by the numbers

The click and drag method is an easy way to size shapes, but not always the most exact method. Sometimes you'll need to draw shapes of an exact size. Although we briefly touched on this capability in the descriptions, let's review the method.

Drag a hexagon onto a blank drawing. Select the hexagon and bring up the Size & Position box. Enter the size you desire in the Width and Height fields and press Enter.

Tip   Perhaps you wish to draw a circle with a specific radius. You may select a circle, open the Size & Position window and set a width twice the length of the desired radius. On the other hand, you can also drag a Center Drag Circle shape onto the drawing. Select the shape and call up the Size & Position window. You'll notice that the window includes a radius field. Put in the radius you desire and you're off to the races.

Scaling Shapes

Shape scale isn't always an issue. After all, whenever you are diagramming the chain of command for your organization the scale doesn't matter — as long as you make sure that the boss has the biggest shape!

There are, however, instances when the scale is a primal concern. Examples are your office layout, a landscaping diagram, or architectural drawings. When working with a scaled drawing, such as an office layout, Visio automatically scales your shapes to fit the drawing. To do so select File ➪ Page Setup and then choose the Drawing Scale tab as shown in Figure 16-10.

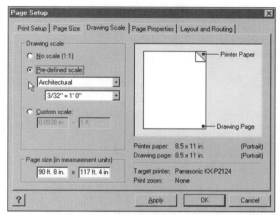

Figure 16-10: The Drawing Scale tab on the Page Setup dialog box

There are four pre-defined scales: Architectural, Civil Engineering, Metric, and Mechanical Engineering. Each has different scales from which you may choose. Additionally, you may select Custom Scale and define your own scale.

The Pre-defined scales for Architectural, Civil Engineering, and Mechanical Engineering are in Imperial Measurements. For a complete listing of these scales and the metric pre-defined scales, refer to Table 8-3.

Cross-Reference

Chapter 8 has more information on the four pre-defined scales.

Choose a scale and click Apply and subsequently click OK. The new scale will be applied to the current page. The larger the number on the left of the scale equation, the larger the shape will appear on the page. The chair and table in Figure 16-11 were drawn using the Architectural scale of ¼" equals 1'. The page is zoomed 75%. The chair and table in Figure 16-12 were drawn using the Architectural scale of 1" equals 1'. The page is zoomed 75%. The chair and table in Figure 16-12 appear much larger although they are identical to the ones shown in Figure 16-11.

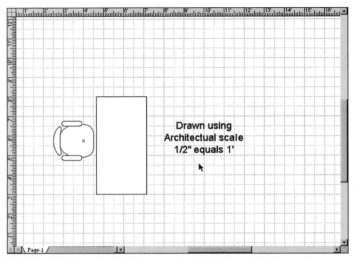

Figure 16-11: The chair and table on a scale of 1/2" = 1'

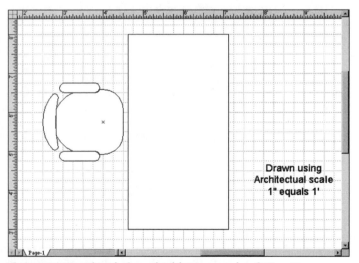

Figure 16-12: The chair and table on a scale of 1" = 1'

Moving Shapes

Nothing is ever exactly where we want it. That's why we rearrange furniture in the spring and why Visio provides a jillion tools that enable us to move our shapes. In this section I'll show you how to use those tools to do some springtime rearranging.

Rotating shapes

There are four methods to rotate shapes in Visio 2000: the Shape menu, the Action toolbar's Rotate Icons, the Rotation Tool, or the Size & Position window. Let's place first things first and lead off our discussion with the initial method.

Rotating Shapes with the Shape menu

Rotating shapes with the Shape menu is easy. Select the shape that requires rotation. Next choose Shape ⇨ Rotate Left/Right. This rotates the selected shape 90 degrees in the direction selected.

Rotating Shapes with the Action toolbar rotate buttons

Just as simple as rotating shapes with the Shape menu is the toolbar rotation technique. Right-click the Standard toolbar and select the Action toolbar. Select the shape that you wish to rotate and click the rotation buttons as shown in Figure 16-13.

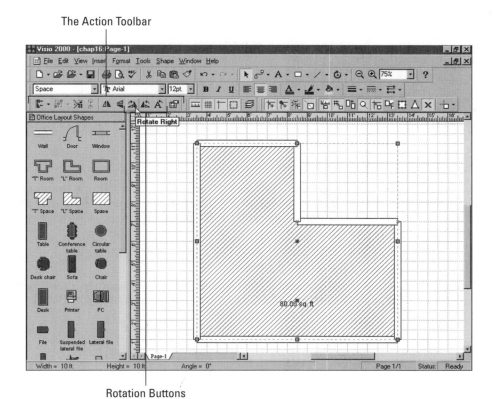

Figure 16-13: Clicking View ⇨ Toolbars ⇨ Action also makes the Action toolbar available on your screen.

Note   Shapes are not the only objects you can rotate. Lines, or nearly anything else you plop on the page, may be selected and rotated.

You may also right-click the shape and then select Shape from the pop-up menu. This in turn displays an Action pop-up menu. Clicking on the Rotate icons will rotate the shape.

Rotating Shapes with the Rotation tool

Rotating shapes with the Rotation tool is another straightforward process. Select the object that you wish to rotate and click the Rotation tool icon. You'll notice that several points on the object — denoted with green circles — become rotational handles. Passing the Rotation tool cursor over these handles morphs the cursor into a pair of tail-chasing arrows. You may now click and drag the shape to change its rotational attitude without changing its latitude (it's an old Jimmy Buffett joke).

Note that the rotated shape has a unique rotation handle in the center. This is called the rotation pin. The rotation pin is the center (or focus) of the shape's rotation. You may move this pin and hence change the focus of the shape's rotation.

Rotating Shapes with the Size & Position window

The Size & Position window is the weapon of choice when rotating shapes a precise amount. Here's how to do it. Select the shape and then open the Size & Position window (View ➪ Windows ➪ Size & Position). Enter the degrees from horizontal that you wish to rotate the shape. Positive values rotate the shape clockwise. Negative values rotate the shape counterclockwise.

Flipping shapes

A subset of shape rotation is flipping shapes. Visio makes it as simple as the rotation. There are three ways (four if you count physically upending your monitor): the Shape menu, the Action toolbar Rotate Icons, and the Shape menu that pops up after right-clicking a shape. Let's look at each.

Flipping shapes with the Shape menu

Flipping shapes with the Shape menu is easy. Select the shape that requires flipping. Next choose Shape ➪ Flip Vertical or Flip Horizontal (as shown in Figure 16-14).

Figure 16-14: The Shape menu

Flipping Shapes with the Action toolbar flip buttons

Just as simple as flipping shapes with the Shape menu is the toolbar technique. Right-click the Standard toolbar and select the Action toolbar. Select the shape that you wish to flip and click the Flip Vertical or Horizontal buttons as shown in Figure 16-15.

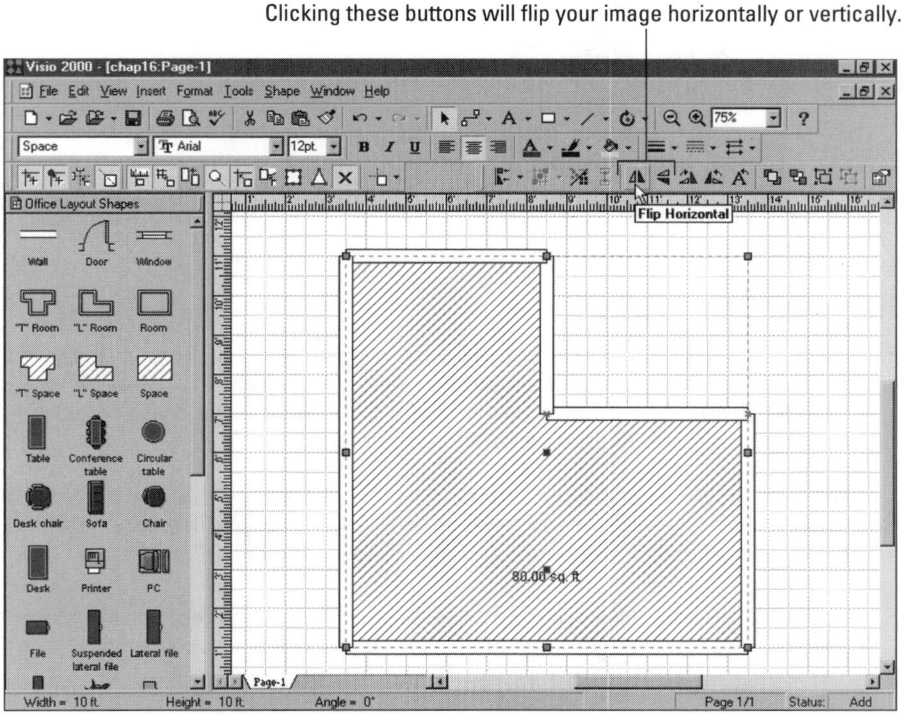

Clicking these buttons will flip your image horizontally or vertically.

Figure 16-15: The Flipping buttons on the Action toolbar

Flipping shapes with the shape pop-up menu

The final way (discounting monitor rotation) to flip a shape is with the shape pop-up menu. Right-click the shape to be rotated. This opens the shape pop-up menu as shown in Figure 16-16. Select Shape ➪ Flip Vertical or Flip Horizontal.

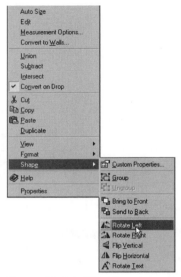

Figure 16-16: The Shape pop-up menu

Dragging shapes

Dragging is perhaps the easiest method of moving shapes from one place to another. To do so select the shape, and then left-click and hold anywhere within the shape. Drag the shape to its new position while continuing to press the left mouse button. Release the mouse button when you are finished.

Tip   You may drag several shapes at once. Select subsequent shapes by pressing Shift as you select them. Once you have selected all the shapes, left-click and hold in the interior of any of the shapes and drag them to their new home.

Note   Do not click the handles (the little green boxes). Pulling on them will not move the shape, but rather change its dimensions as described previously.

Working with overlapping shapes

Shapes are placed on the page in the order you bring them into the drawing. The most recent shapes are placed on top of previous shapes. More often than not this isn't a problem. Sometimes, however, we need to rearrange this order. There are several way to do so.

The Shape drop-down menu

You may change a shape's relative position on a drawing by using the Shape drop-down menu. There are four options available:

✦ **Bring Forward** brings the selected shape forward one layer.

✦ **Bring to Front** moves the selected shape in front of all the other shapes.

✦ **Send Backward** moves the selected shape back one layer

✦ **Send to Back** moves the selected shape behind all the other shapes.

The Action toolbar

The Action toolbar includes two of the preceding options: Bring to Front and Send to Back. They function identically to the commands found on the Shape drop-down menu.

Tip You may also access the Bring to Front and Send to Back commands from the shape itself. Right-click the shape and then choose the command you wish to invoke.

Overlapping shapes: an exercise

Let's take a look at how to work with overlapping shapes. Open a new drawing and the Office Layout Shapes stencil. Drag a PC, Desk, and Chair (in that order) onto the drawing. The jumble should look something like Figure 16-17. The PC is on the bottom, the Desk above it, and the Chair on top. That will never do; let's do a bit of rearranging.

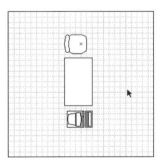

Figure 16-17: The jumbled office equipment

Select the chair and from the Standard menu choose Shapes ➪ Send Backward. This puts the chair back where it belongs. Okay, now we have the chair under the table, but so is the PC.

Right-click the PC and choose Bring to Front. This places the PC on the table. Unfortunately it's facing the wrong way. Center the PC in front of the chair, right-click the PC, and choose Flip Horizontal. Aha! Everything — as demonstrated in Figure 16-18 — is once again right with the world.

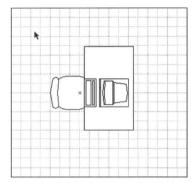

Figure 16-18: Once again, all is right with the world.

Duplicating Shapes

Duplicating work in the real world is a waste of time. Doing the same within a computer program is an essential key to computing efficiency. In any computer program, be it Microsoft Word 97 or Paint Shop Pro, you must be able to copy phrases or objects and paste them elsewhere. Visio 2000 is no different. It may take a few minutes to resize and color a shape, so after the work is done you'll want to copy the shape in order to reuse it.

Note   Duplicating a shape is not always the most efficient way to reuse it. If you intend to repeatedly employ the instance you may want to make it part of a new stencil. See Chapter 15 for details.

There are several ways to duplicate shapes: You may stamp them, select and copy them, or copy all the shapes on a layer. Let's examine each in turn.

Duplication by stamping

The Stamp tool is a simple method for duplicating masters from the stencil. Here's how.

1. Select the Stamp tool (it's in the Connector-tool drop-down menu).

2. Select a master on your currently selected master.

3. On the drawing click where you wish to duplicate the master, as many times as you like.

Duplication by selection

Select the shape that you wish to duplicate. Click the Copy icon on the Standard toolbar or press Ctrl+C. Press the Paste icon on the Standard toolbar or press Ctrl+V to paste the object onto the center of the page. You may now reposition the object where you like.

Tip

You may simultaneously select more than one shape by holding Shift as you select subsequent shapes. Each subsequent shape will have blue handles instead of green.

Duplication by layer selection

You may rapidly select all the shapes on a layer. To do so choose Edit ➪ Select Special. This displays the Select Special dialog box as shown in Figure 16-19.

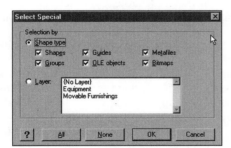

Figure 16-19: The Select Special dialog box

To choose all the shapes on a layer, select Layer and then choose the layer you desire from the list. To choose shapes not assigned to a specific layer, choose No Layer. You may also choose multiple layers by pressing Ctrl as you select subsequent layers.

Note The Select Special dialog box also lets you further narrow your choice by limiting what objects within the layer are chosen. You may choose Shapes, Groups, Guides, OLE Objects, Metafiles, or Bitmaps.

Tip Visio 2000 Technical Edition offers a unique way to duplicate shapes . . . sort of. The end result isn't an exact duplication but may be useful for a variety of tasks. In Visio 2000 Technical Edition, select Tools ⇨ Array Shapes. This opens the Array Shapes dialog box as shown in Figure 16-20. This dialog box controls how many copies are made and where they will be positioned. You may choose the number of columns and rows, the spacing between the columns and rows, and whether the spacing is measured from the shape's center or edge.

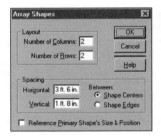

Figure 16-20: The Array Shapes dialog box, available in Visio 2000 Technical Edition

Creating stackable and extendable shapes with the Chart Shape Wizard

The Chart Shape Wizard helps you create your own stackable and extendable shapes. You can use stackable and extendable shapes to create special effects in charts and graphs. Stackable shapes are shapes that, when stretched, stack horizontally or vertically. In other words, they duplicate themselves; therefore we cover them here.

You can use stackable and extendable shapes to create special effects in charts and graphs. While Visio provides you with a few stackable and extendable shapes, the Chart Shape Wizard is a terrific tool to take any shape and convert it to a stackable or extendable shape. You can convert a Visio shape, a clip-art drawing, or a shape you draw.

Before we get into how the Chart Shape Wizard works, lets take a look at exactly what Stackable and Extendable Shapes are and how you can use them in a chart.

Stackable shapes

Visio provides you with stackable shapes, such as the Stretchable Dollar,which (in addition to being stackable(can expand like a middle-aged man's waste, the Stretchable Pound, and the People shapes in the Marketing Clip Art stencil. For example, you can represent growth in profits by using the stackable dollar as shown in Figure 16-21.

Figure 16-21: The Stackable Dollar shape

Creating a stackable shape

Drag a shape or clip art from one of the stencils onto the drawing page, or insert a clip-art picture to be converted into a stackable shape. To insert a clip-art picture, click Insert ➪ Clip art from the menu bar. The wizard will produce a new shape consisting of duplicates of the shape that you insert.

Access the Chart Shape Wizard from the menu bar: Tools ➪ Macros ➪ Forms And Charts ➪ Chart Shape Wizard. The first wizard screen introduces you to the Chart Shape Wizard. Click Next. On the second screen, choose Stackable Shape as shown in Figure 16-22, and then click Next.

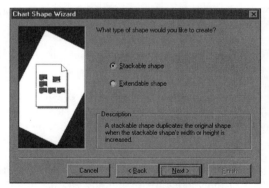

Figure 16-22: Choose Stackable shape.

On the third screen, you designate a number of variables as shown in Figure 16-23. The first variable governs if the shape is going to be a smart or fixed shape.

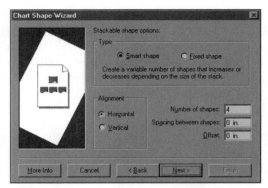

Figure 16-23: Screen #3: Choose if the shape is going to be a smart shape or a fixed shape and other variables.

A smart shape can represent a percentage of growth by manipulating the shape on the right side. Actually, a portion of the shape is hidden from view so that only a part of the duplicate shapes show. In the fixed shape option, the created shape consists of the duplicate shapes that may not be manipulated.

Next, choose the duplicated shape's alignment — good or evil (just kidding). Horizontal duplicates shapes to the side of the original. Vertical stacks the duplicated shapes vertically.

Next, set the following numbers: Number of shapes, Spacing between shapes, and Offset.

Tip   Set the spacing in a decimal format, such as 0.05 inches, for example. Also, the Offset option determines the vertical offset of subsequent shapes.

After you have set all the options, click Next to continue. The next screen asks you to pick a shape from the page. Click the shape you want to convert. (Remember, the shape has to be already on the page.) Click Finish and the Stackable shape is created.

Note   You can modify a stackable shape anytime after you've created it. Just right-click the shape and choose Configure. You can change the height and width, the offset, or the stack's background color.

For example, imagine that you want to create a diagram that shows the growth of families in your city. To do so you may make a stackable shape from the parents.wmf clip-art shape.

Then, in a Visio chart, you can represent family growth horizontally by stacking the shape as shown in Figure 16-24.

Figure 16-24: Showing family growth from the parents.wmf clip-art shape

Extendable shapes

Extendable shapes are shapes that can be stretched. The shape appears to grow without distortion. The shapes are useful for graphically demonstrating growth.

The extendable shape is made up of two or three parts. Only one of the parts extends. Depending on how it is built, the left part, the middle part (if it is has three parts) or the bottom part expands, making the shape appear as if it stretched without losing proportion. Visio provides you with extendable shapes, such as the Pencil, Growing Flower and Extend-O-Hand in the Marketing Clip Art stencil. Each is a valuable tool in your graphical repertoire. For example, you can indicate market growth over a period of time by using the extendable Growing Flower shape as shown in Figure 16-25.

Figure 16-25: The Growing Flower extendable shape

Creating an extendable shape

Drag a shape or clip art from one of the stencils onto the drawing page, or insert a clip-art picture to be converted into an extendable shape. To insert a clip-art picture, click Insert ⇨ Clip art from the menu bar.

Now make copies of the shape. Copy the shape. For pasting the copies, select Edit ➪ Paste Special from the menu bar. The Paste Special dialog box appears as shown in Figure 16-26.

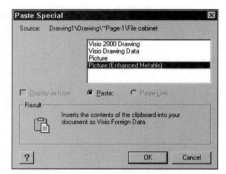

Figure 16-26: The Paste Special dialog box

Select the Picture (Enhanced Metafile) option and click OK to paste the shape. Repeat the Paste Special step if you are making a three-part extendable shape.

The next step is to adjust one of the shapes using the crop tool. From the Rotation icon on the toolbar, access the drop-down choice and select the crop tool as shown in 16-27.

    Figure 16-27: Accessing the crop tool from the Rotation icon.

Crop each copy until it looks like one-half or one-third of the extendable shape. Now we are ready to finish our shape with the Chart Shape Wizard. Access the wizard from the menu bar: Tools ➪ Macros ➪ Forms And Charts ➪ Chart Shape Wizard.

The first wizard screen introduces you to the Chart Shape Wizard. Click Next.

On the second screen, choose Extendable shape as shown in Figure 16-28, and then click Next.

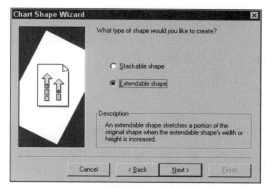

Figure 16-28: For this exercise, choose Extendable shape.

On the third screen, designate a number of variables as shown in Figure 16-29. The first variable is if the extendable shape is made up of two pieces or three pieces.

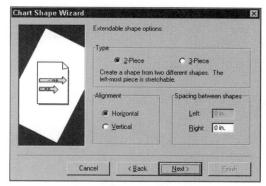

Figure 16-29: Set the attributes of the extendable shape.

Next, choose the duplicated shape's alignment. Horizontal extends the shape to the right. Vertical extends the shape upward. Make sure to set the Spacing between shapes.

For a two-piece horizontal shape, the left piece extends. For a two-piece vertical shape, the bottom piece extends. For a three-piece shape of any kind, the middle piece extends. Choose the setting you want and click Next.

If you chose a two-part extendable shape, two dialog boxes ask you to indicate which shapes will be the top and bottom shapes if you chose vertical, or which shapes will be the right and left if you chose horizontal. If you chose a three-part extendable shape, a series of three dialog boxes asks you to indicate the shape's positioning: top, middle, and bottom shape for vertical; or right, middle, and left for horizontal.

Click Finish and the wizard produces the extendable shape.

> **Tip**
>
> You can modify an extendable shape at any time. Right-click the shape you want to modify and then select Configure to change the height, width, or spacing between the parts.

Summary

Okay, now you're a shape-shifting guru. From the Size & Position window to extendable shapes, you've learned how to bend, drag, and morph shapes to suit your every whim. Specifically we discussed the following:

✦ Using the Size & Position window

✦ Sizing, scaling, and stretching shapes

✦ Rotating and moving shapes, including the ability to move shapes forward and backward on the page

✦ Duplicating shapes

✦ Using the Chart Shape Wizard

In the next chapter, I cover ways to connect shapes.

✦   ✦   ✦

Connecting Shapes

Connectors are among Visio 2000's most important and powerful features. These elements represent logical flow (as in a computer programming diagram), hierarchical relationships (as in a corporate management chart), physical and virtual connections (as in electrical and computer network diagrams), and almost any form of relationship between any two objects that can be shown as shapes in a drawing. When you connect any two shapes on a drawing page using a Visio 2000 connector, they stay connected even when you move one or both, which prevents you from accidentally losing the original relationships between shapes — enormously helpful when you add or revise later on. Connecting two shapes is simple, but keeping in mind which options to use while doing it is a little more complicated. Fortunately, it becomes easier with practice.

Before you try connecting any shapes, look over the following information.

Visio's Shapes and Connectors

Shapes in Visio can be open or closed and one- or two-dimensional. Open shapes include line arrows, zigzags, arcs — any shape that encloses no area. Closed shapes can be rectangles, circles, or any shape where an outline encloses an area. Connectors are usually *open* shapes. The shapes they connect can be open or closed.

Connectors are 1D shapes. They behave like lines; when selected, they show endpoints (where they connect to shapes). These can best be thought of as the classic line-arrow connecting one object at its tail point to another object at its head point. Connectors may be two-headed or headless (simple line), and can even be arcs. When you select a connector, red boxes denote its endpoints. The beginning-point box shows an *x* and the ending-point box shows a plus sign (+).

Note Not all connectors appear as 1D objects, but all are *treated* as 1D objects. An enclosed arrow outline used in stencils is still a connector and has endpoints. It may have control handles to adjust its width, as well. Look for the endpoints to determine whether an object is a connector or a shape.

Up to this point, you've used mostly 2D shapes. Most stencil shapes are 2D. Virtually every drawing you create or import into Visio will be 2D. When you select a 2D object, a rectangle with selection handles surrounds it. A closed object — a drawing of a state, for example — obviously is 2D. But Visio handles an open object, such as a sales graph line, as 2D, as well. Just remember that when you select 2D shapes they are enclosed in a box, and 1D connectors show endpoints.

Finally, Visio 2000 handles 3D shapes as 2D. The third dimension is an illusion created by the use of perspective. The drawing of the shape itself exists in two dimensions on the page and is treated as such.

Connection Points, the Connector Tool, and Static Glue

Some shapes have connection points — that is, points where the program "glues" a connector's endpoint. You can glue a connector to a shape *dynamically* or *statically*. I will cover dynamic glue in greater depth later in this chapter. For now, just keep in mind that what you do with connection points in this section uses *static* glue.

When you use a static-glue connection, the connector always stays connected at the original point, no matter where you move the shape on the page. Static glue is the default option for connections.

Using connection points with static glue

Connection points show up as blue x's when you turn on the Connector Tool on the Standard Toolbar, as shown in Figure 17-1. With the Connector Tool on, a small red box appears around the point when you drag your cursor over a connection point on a shape. This tells you it's a valid connection point.

Not all the connection points are on the perimeters of the shapes. Each of the four shapes shown in Figure 17-1 has a connection point at its center. You can create connection points wherever you want them — within an object or outside it. Let's experiment with creating connection points, connecting some, and then moving the shapes around.

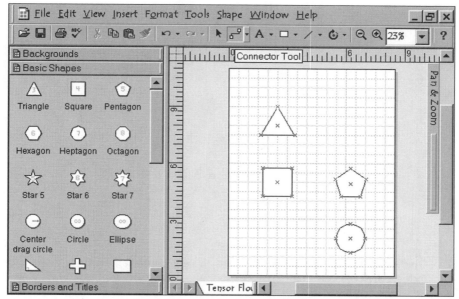

Figure 17-1: The Connector Tool on the Standard Toolbar and shapes with connector points

An example using a static glue connection

Open Visio 2000 (if it's not open already) and start a new drawing. For type, choose the Basic Diagram option from Block Diagram. From the Basic Shapes stencil, drag a triangle, a square, a pentagon, and a circle onto the page and arrange them, as shown in Figure 17-1. Click the Connector Tool in the Standard Toolbar to turn it on. Move your cursor to the lower-left corner of the triangle. As your cursor passes over the connection point at the corner, a small red box appears around the point. Click that connector, hold, and drag your mouse until the cursor is over the upper corner of the pentagon. When the red box appears around the connection point at the top of the pentagon, release the mouse button.

Now a Connector line connects the lower-left corner of the triangle to the upper corner of the pentagon (see Figure 17-2). While the connector is selected, you see red blocks at the endpoints where it connects the two shapes. The x in the red block on the triangle indicates that that's where the connector started from. The plus sign in the red block on the pentagon indicates where the connector ends. When direction of flow is important, this feature can help you determine where it starts and ends.

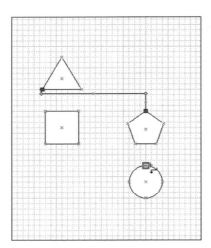

Figure 17-2: The triangle and pentagon are connected.

 Note   The *x* and the plus sign may be hard to see, particularly with a low-resolution screen. Try adjusting color balances to make them more visible. You may need to reset your monitor to a higher resolution.

Now let's see what happens when you move one of the connected shapes. Select the Pointer Tool (the button with the cursor arrow) from the Standard Toolbar. This deselects the Connector Tool. Select the pentagon shape and move it straight up until it's even with the triangle, as shown in Figure 17-3. The connector keeps the two selected shapes connected at the original points. Notice that the connecting line changed its path to keep the shortest distance between the two endpoints.

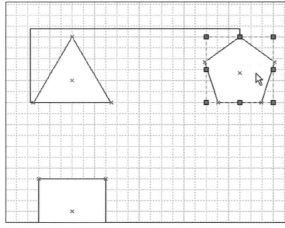

Figure 17-3: The connector moves to keep the shapes connected at the selected points.

Save and keep the example open. You'll use it next to add connection points to a shape.

Some objects lack connection points. Those with connection points may not have enough for your needs, or may have them in the wrong places. Visio 2000 enables you to add connection points to a shape wherever you need them.

I cover the different types of connection points in greater detail later. In this section you'll be working with an Inward connection point, which is probably the most common. To add an Inward connection point, use the Connection Point Tool.

Connection Point Tool

The Connection Point Tool is in a submenu under the Connector Tool; click the down arrow on the right side of the Connector Tool to bring up the submenu, as shown in Figure 17-4. The Connection Point Tool is the second button from the top, with the blue *x* on it. Click it to activate it.

Note   Be sure you select the object to which you want to add connection points *before* you activate the Connection Point Tool.

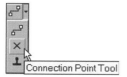

Figure 17-4: Connection Tool submenu containing the Connection Point Tool

The Connection Point Tool icon replaces the Connection Tool icon on the Standard Toolbar. To switch back, access the submenu again and select the Connection Tool.

With the Connection Point Tool active, you can add a connection point to a shape; hold Ctrl and click the left mouse button. This adds an *Inward* connector. (Again, this is covered later in the chapter.) You can add the connector anywhere on the perimeter of the shape, anywhere within the shape, anywhere on the page outside the shape — in other words, anywhere! Visio 2000 will associate that point with the selected shape automatically no matter where they are in relation to each other. When you move the shape, the connection point moves, too, maintaining the same distance and direction from or on the shape. Because you can place a connection point outside its associated shape, it's critical to select the correct shape before you add a connection point.

Practice using the following examples.

An example of adding connection points

Open the example from earlier and select the square. Now select the down arrow just to the right of the Connector Tool on the Standard Toolbar. Select the Connection Point Tool (the blue x) from the submenu. The dotted green lines around the square tell you it's the selected object while the Connection Point Tool is on. Bring your cursor arrow down and place the point midway on the top line of the square. Now hold Ctrl and click the left mouse key. A small purple x appears at the midpoint of the square's top line. It will turn blue when you take another action.

Now add another point outside the square. On the right side of the square, place another point out to the right of the square, about halfway up the side and half the square's width away (as shown in Figure 17-5). Remember to hold Ctrl before you click the mouse button.

Note   A shape must be selected in order to add a connection point anywhere on the drawing page.

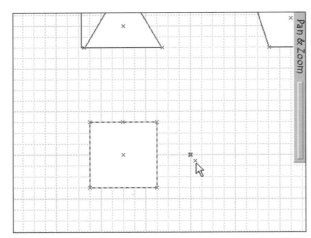

Figure 17-5: Adding a connection point outside a shape

An example of moving connection points

If you're dissatisfied with where you've placed a point, you can move it! Move your cursor over the point you just created. (It becomes a four-directional arrow.) Click and hold the left mouse button and move up to align the cursor with the top of the square. When you release the mouse button, the connection point disappears from its original place and reappears at the new location.

Now use your new connection points. With the square selected, open the Connector Tool submenu in the Standard Toolbar. Select the Connector Tool from the submenu. Move your cursor over the connection point you put at the midpoint atop the square. When the red box appears around the point, click and drag it to a point in the center of the triangle. Release the mouse and the connection line passes through the side of the triangle to connect the center point.

Now move your cursor over the point you placed outside the square. Click and drag it to the lower-left corner of the pentagon, as shown in Figure 17-6. Now watch what happens to this line when you move the square.

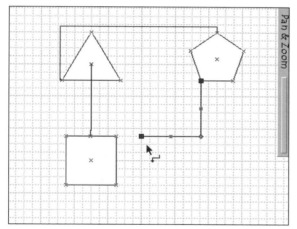

Figure 17-6: Connection lines go from point to point even outside a shape.

Select the Pointer Tool from the Standard Toolbar. Click the square and drag it to the right until it lies directly under the pentagon. The point outside the square moved *with* the square (see Figure 17-7). Save and keep the example at hand.

Note   The two sets of connecting lines overlap each other now. I address this problem later in this chapter.

An example of deleting connection points

Whether you placed the connection points yourself or they were established already via the stencil, you may remove them at will. To delete a connection point, first make sure the correct shape is selected. Then select the point you want to delete. Press Delete (or use other delete-command options) and *voilà!* It's gone.

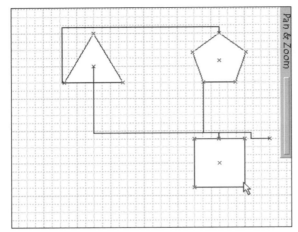

Figure 17-7: A connection point created outside a shape moves with the shape.

In this example, get rid of the point you made outside the square first. With the Pointer Tool active, click the connection line to the connection point outside the square. Press Delete to eliminate the connection line. Now click the square to select it (unnecessary when deleting points, but a good habit). Select the Connection Point Tool from the Standard Toolbar (in the Connector Tool submenu). Now click the connection point outside the square. It turns purple. Press Delete and it's history!

Now delete a point you didn't create. Move your cursor over the square's lower-right corner and click the connection point there to turn it purple. Press Delete. The connection point should disappear, leaving the corner empty.

If you still want to make a connection point, you could do so, but you're probably wondering if you need to do so for all shapes that don't have connection points. There's another way — you can specify for the connectors to connect to other points on a shape. Save your example for the next demonstration.

Other usable connecting points: glue options

Connection Points aren't the only points to which you can glue a connector, but they're the default, along with guides as seen in Chapter 10. To activate other points you must set your options for them.

From the menu bar, select Tools. From the Tools menu select Snap & Glue. The Snap & Glue dialog box appears. It has two tabs; you want the General tab. There are five "Glue to" options on the General tab. By default, Guides and Connection points are selected (as shown in Figure 17-8). You should be familiar with Guides from Chapter 10, and Connection Points from earlier in this chapter, so this section covers the remaining three options.

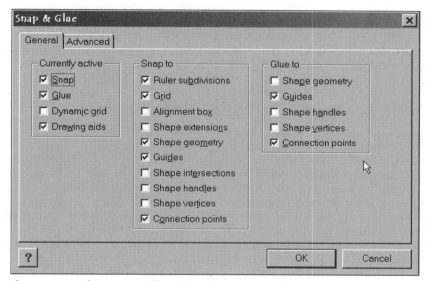

Figure 17-8: The Snap & Glue dialog box showing the default Glue to options selected

Shape geometry

When you activate Shape geometry under the "Glue to" options, the connectors can connect to any point on the perimeter of a shape. You can connect any point on the perimeter where a small red box appears under the cursor. Not all shapes allow this, however. When you try to connect to a shape that doesn't allow Shape geometry connection or you try to connect to a part of the drawing other than the allowed perimeter, a red box will appear around the *entire* shape, signifying that you cannot do a static glue to a particular point on that shape. Visio 2000 enables you to dynamically glue to the object instead. Dynamic glue is covered a little later in this chapter.

Shape handles

When you activate Shape handles under the "Glue to" options, the connectors can connect to the control handles around the shape, which is particularly useful when you need to connect very irregularly shaped objects. When connecting shape handles, you don't see the handles if the shape isn't selected, but Visio 2000 still highlights the invisible handle with a red box when your cursor crosses over it, making it fairly simple to find the handles.

Shape vertices

When you activate Shape vertices under the "Glue to" options, the connectors can connect to any point in the shape where two lines meet, which is most useful for regularly shaped objects. Because Visio 2000 represents most curves by a number of very short lines, this option enables you to connect to a curved portion of a shape most of the time. The best way to find out if you can connect on a curved area is to try it and look for the small red box that denotes a valid point. If Shape vertices don't work on a curve, then use Shape geometry to connect to a curved section of a shape.

Example using other points in connections

Go back to your example project. On the menu bar, click Tools. From the Tools menu, click Snap & Glue. The Snap & Glue dialog box appears. In the "Glue to" section under the General tab, click Shape vertices to turn it on. Click OK to return to the workspace. Make sure your Connector Tool is activated, and remember that you deleted the connection point at the bottom-right of the square. Move your cursor over that corner, and a small, red box appears — because the program now includes vertices along with defined connection points. Click and drag your mouse down to the circle. While still holding the mouse button, move your cursor around the circumference of the circle. The small, red, connection-point box appears only over the points where a defined connection point exists, because this is a true circle, not one made up of tiny little lines. Drag your cursor over to the right side of the circle and release it over the connection point there. You now have a connector running from a vertex to a connection point.

Open the Snap & Glue dialog box again. In the "Glue to" section, activate Shape handles. Click OK. Now open the Standard Toolbar and click your Pointer Tool. Click the circle on the page to select it — its shape handles appear as green blocks outside it. Turn on the Connector Tool. Move the cursor over the upper-left-corner shape-handle of the circle. When the red box appears, click and drag up to the middle of the bottom of the square. Even though there's no connection point or vertices in the middle of the bottom of the square, a red box appears (as shown in Figure 17-9). That is where a shape handle for the square is, and that's where you should connect.

Open the Snap & Glue dialog box. Deselect Shape handles and Shape vertices, select Shape geometry, and click OK. Note that the previous connections made with handles and vertices did not disappear when you deselected the options. Once on the page they stay until deleted.

Now move your cursor over various places in the drawing. Everywhere your cursor moves over a line, a red box appears, regardless if the line is around a shape or is part of a connector — using Shape geometry you can even connect connectors to each other. Move your cursor to the connector about midway between the triangle and the pentagon. Click and drag straight down until you get to the connector between the triangle and the square (as shown in Figure 17-10). Connect the connectors!

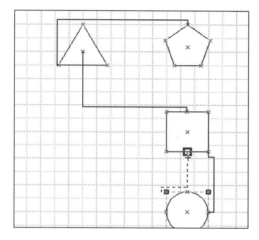

Figure 17-9: A red box appears around a shape handle even when the shape isn't selected.

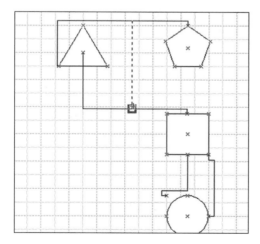

Figure 17-10: Connections between connectors, shape vertices, andshape handles

The Three Types of Connection Points

Up until this point we have been using a particular type of connection point called an Inward connection point. This section goes into even more detail about Inward connection points and covers the other two types of connection points: Outward points, and Inward & Outward points.

Inward connection points

Inward connection points are denoted by a blue x, and are used for most applications. They connect to Inward & Outward connection points and to Outward connection points (e.g. found in Electrical Outlet shapes). An Inward connection point does not connect to another Inward connection point. For example, if you dragged the square in our example over the triangle until the corner Inward connectors overlapped, they wouldn't glue together — you'd need to change one of the points into either an Outward or an Inward & Outward connection point.

Inward connections are used mostly for connecting two-dimensional shapes to one-dimensional shapes in a flowchart. To create an Inward connection point, select a shape. Turn on the Connection Point Tool. Hold Ctrl and click the mouse cursor over the spot where you want to add the point.

Outward connection points

Outward connection points are denoted by a dark-blue dot, and are used in particular shapes and applications where a shape will be glued to a certain set of points. These points usually have an Inward connection point where the Outward point needs to be glued. An example of this can be found in wiring diagram shapes. Electrical Outlet shapes have an Outward connection point already included in them. A wall or wire drawing with Inward connection points can easily be used to glue the outlets in their correct spots.

Outward connection points can connect to Inward points, Inward & Outward points, and to Geometry points when the Shape-geometry glue option is on. Outward connection points do not connect to other Outward points or to one-dimensional objects like connectors.

To create an Outward connection point, select the shape. Turn on the Connection Point Tool. Hold down Alt and Ctrl and click the mouse cursor over the spot you want to add the point.

Inward & Outward connection points

When you aren't sure which type of connection point to use, use the Inward & Outward connection point. Inward & Outward connection points are denoted by a blue x with a dark-blue dot in the center, and combine the abilities of both Inward and Outward points as their name and symbol imply. They connect to one-dimensional shapes, Inward connection points, Outward connection points, Inward & Outward connection points, and Geometry points. In other words, they connect to everything, making them the most versatile of the three types.

To create an Inward & Outward connection point, start by creating either an Inward or an Outward point. Right-click the point and select Inward & Outward from the submenu.

If you're unsure about which type of connection points connect to what connection points, look at Table 17-1. The column on the left is the type of connection point being used. The top row lists the type of points to which each point can be connected.

Table 17-1				
Valid Connections for Connection Points				
	Inward connection points	*Outward connection points*	*Inward & Outward connection points*	*Geometry points*	*1D shapes*
Inward connection point	No	Yes	Yes	No	Yes
Outward connection point	Yes	No	Yes	Yes	No
Inward & Outward connection point	Yes	Yes	Yes	Yes	Yes

An example using Outward and Inward & Outward connection points

Lets go back to the example we've been using. Drag a five-pointed star into the open area on the bottom left of the page. Turn on the Connection Point Tool. On the star, right-click the upper-right arm's connection point. Select Outward from the submenu to convert the point to an Outward connection point. Now go to the connection point on the bottom-right arm of the star and right-click. Select Inward

& Outward from the submenu. The star now has all three types of connection points on it.

Go to the Standard Toolbar and turn on the Connector Tool. Access the Snap & Glue dialog box under the Tools menu in the menu bar. Deselect the Shape geometry "Glue to" option. Click OK. Move your cursor over the top point, the upper-right point, and the bottom-right point of the star. A red box appears around the top point and the bottom-right point, but not the upper-right point. This is because connectors are 1D objects. The upper-right point is an Outward connection point that doesn't connect to 1D objects, so no red box appears there. However, the Outward connection point will glue to an Inward connection point. We will use this to glue two shapes together.

Select the Pointer Tool from the Standard Toolbar. Drag the star over to the square until the upper-right point of the star is over the lower-left corner of the square. When they line up, a red box appears around them (as shown in Figure 17-11). Release the star. It is now glued to the square. The side control handles have changed from green to red, indicating that the star shape is glued to another shape. Click the square. Its handles are all still green because the star was glued to the square, not the square to the star. Visio 2000 keeps close tabs on the hierarchy of connections.

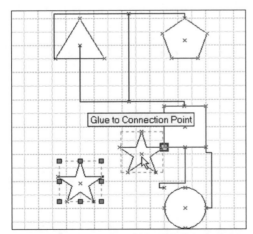

Figure 17-11: Two shapes with different connection-point types can be glued together.

For our next trick we will move the combined star/square shapes. Select the square and move it left to the middle of the page. The star and the connectors all move with it. Now select the star and move it down — it disconnects from the square because the star was the object that was glued onto the other object; it can be unglued and moved away from the square. You can disconnect connectors in the same way. If you want the objects to stay together permanently you need to define them as a group.

What you have used up to now are examples of static glue—the points you connect to stay the same no matter how you move the shapes around. Dynamic glue is a different animal, and is covered in the next section. Save your example, because you'll be using it soon.

Dynamic Glue

When you connect two shapes using dynamic glue, the connections don't stay at the same point when you move the shapes. When one of two (or more) connected shapes using dynamic glue are moved, the connector ends move around the perimeter of the shapes to keep the shortest distance between them. This is useful for times when you expect to make major revisions during a project.

How to use dynamic glue

There are different ways to use dynamic glue on shapes. The first is when you create a connector.

Dynamic glue on a new connector—duel dynamic ends

With the Connector Tool active you can create a dynamic glue connection when you create the connection. Hold Ctrl when you move the cursor over the first shape you wish to connect. A large red box appears around the entire shape. Click and drag the connector to the shape you're connecting to. When a large red box appears around the entire shape you can let go of the mouse button. The connector automatically takes the shortest distance between the two points, no matter where the shapes are moved on the page. Both ends of this type of connection are dynamic.

Note   The shortest distance may not always be the *shortest* depending on the snap-to options selected in the Snap & Glue dialog box. If the snap-to options are active, the connector may go to the nearest of those points rather than the point mathematically closest. If the shape is moved so another snap-to point is closest, then the connection will move to that point.

Another way to apply dynamic glue is very similar to static gluing. Activate the Connector tool and move your cursor over the first shape you're connecting. Keep moving it over the shape until you find a spot that makes a large red square appear around the entire shape. Click and drag to the second shape. Keep moving your cursor around over the second shape until you find a spot that makes a large red square appear around the entire shape. Release the mouse button. Both ends are dynamic.

Note   Not all shapes have a natural dynamic-glue spot inside them. Should you find a shape without a natural dynamic-glue spot, you need to use the preceding method to dynamically glue it.

Note   Not all shapes allow dynamic gluing. Shapes with predefined connectors built in, such as electronic component shapes, can only be statically glued.

Dynamic glue on a new connector – one static and one dynamic end

The Connector Tool must be activated. To start with a dynamic connection and end with a static connection, move the cursor over the first shape until you find a spot that makes a large red box appear around it. Click and drag to the second shape. Move the cursor over the spot you wish to statically glue to. When the small red box appears around the spot, release the mouse button.

To start with a static connection and end with a dynamic connection, move the cursor over the spot on the first shape until a small red box appears around the point you want to statically glue. Click and drag to the second shape. Move the cursor over the second shape until you find a spot that makes a large red box appear around it. Release the mouse button.

Dynamic glue on an existing connector

To make one end of a static connection dynamic, select the connector. Click and drag the endpoint off of the shape. Hold Ctrl and click and drag the connector end back to the shape. When a large red box appears around the shape, release the mouse button.

To make both ends dynamic, repeat the procedure on the other end of the connector.

When to use dynamic glue

The primary use of dynamic glue is in flowcharts where the exact point of connection to a shape isn't important. At other times you may want to use dynamic glue where you expect to make heavy revisions during the project. When you get close to the final form, switch the connections back to static glue to show proper connection points.

An example using dynamic glue

Going back to the example, we will add a connector from the star to the square that is static on the star and dynamic on the square.

On the Standard Toolbar, make sure the Connector Tool is activated. Move the cursor over the bottom-right corner of the star. When the little red box appears there, click and drag the connector over to the square. Drag into the square and move around until a large red box appears around the square. Release the mouse button.

From the Standard Toolbar select the Pointer Tool. Click and drag the star up and down the page. You may notice that the connection on the square moves, but only between vertices or connection points. This is because of the snap-to options you selected.

On your own, experiment with what snap-to options you need to turn off to get the connector to move up and down the side of the square instead of jumping between vertices and connectors.

When dynamic gluing is automatic

There are two situations where dynamic glue is applied automatically to shape connections: when you connect shapes while dragging from the stencil and when you connect multiple shapes automatically. I cover both situations in their own sections later in this chapter. First, though, it's time to introduce you to a tool you'll use to set up a new example to show those techniques.

Using the Stamp Tool

The Stamp Tool enables you to make multiple copies of a shape on a page without having to drag the shape out over and over again — a real time-saver even over copy and paste methods. The Stamp Tool is located in the Connector Tool submenu.

To use the Stamp Tool you must first activate it. Select the Connector Tool submenu by clicking on the down arrow beside the Connector Tool. Select the bottom item in the submenu — the Stamp Tool (as shown in Figure 17-12). Click a shape in the stencil. Move the pointer to the spot on the page where you want the shape and left-click the mouse. Keep moving and clicking until you have all the copies you want. Now let's try it.

Figure 17-12: The Stamp Tool in the Connector Tool submenu

Because our other example page is getting pretty full, let's start a new page for this example and add it to the project. From the menu bar, select Insert. From the Insert menu, select Page. Name the page anything you want and click OK. Now from the Standard Toolbar click the down arrow on the right side of the Connector Tool to open its submenu. Click the Stamp Tool icon at the bottom of the submenu. Go over to the Basic Shapes stencil and click the hexagon shape to select it. Do *not* drag. Move the mouse pointer over to the upper-right portion of the page. Left-click the mouse. Move straight down and left-click again. Move down again and left-click. You should now have three shapes straight up and down on the right side of the page (as shown in Figure 17-13). Save the page for use in a later section.

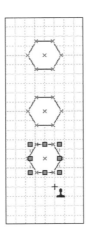

Figure 17-13: Multiple shapes are easily made using the Stamp Tool.

Other Connector Shapes

Due to the enormous amount of interconnected information and options in this chapter, I have intentionally held back information about some options to give you a chance to absorb the more basic principles involved. At this point you should be familiar enough with the basics for me to introduce some more options. Up until now we have been using only one type of connector between shapes: the dynamic connector shape.

Dynamic connector shape

Don't confuse the *dynamic* in dynamic connector shape with the *dynamic* of dynamic glue. The *dynamic* in dynamic connector shape refers to the connector's ability to automatically route itself around shapes to get from one point to another. If a shape is directly between two connected shapes, the dynamic connector routes itself around the obstacle instead of going through it.

The dynamic connector shape is the default connector, and is used when no other connector is selected. In some situations, like automatically connecting while dragging a shape from the stencil, it is the only option that can be used. It is also one of the two basic connectors.

There is a group of advanced connector shapes on the Basic Shapes stencil, which I discuss in the next sections.

Line-curve connector

The line-curve connector is similar to the dynamic connector in appearance but not in behavior. When the line-curve connector is selected from the Basic Shapes stencil and used to make a connection, the connector goes through other shapes rather than around them. It has a control handle near the middle of the line. When you move the control handle, the connector line curves in relation to the amount and direction you move the control handle. Thus the line-curve connector can curve around obstacles. It can also be used when you want a curved connector rather than a straight-line connector.

Shaped connectors

There is a group of connectors that are made of 2D shapes. Even though they are 2D they behave mostly like the regular 1D connectors. They have endpoints and connect 2D shapes. The two main differences between shaped connectors and 1D connectors are that shaped connectors may have control handles that can be used to adjust their width or other features, and they cannot dynamically reroute themselves around obstacles. They always go straight from their beginning point to their endpoint over any intervening obstacles.

To use shaped connectors, simply select the one you want from the Basic Shapes stencil before turning on the Connector Tool, and then make your connections the same way you would using the dynamic connector shape. This process applies to both dynamic gluing methods and static gluing methods.

There are several shaped connectors on the Basic Shapes stencil, all of which are variants on the arrow shape. They are: Flexi-arrow 1, Flexi-arrow 2, Flexi-arrow 3,

Double Flexi-arrow, 45 degree tail, 45 degree double, 45 degree single, 60 degree tail, 60 degree double, 60 degree single, and Fancy arrow.

I use the Fancy arrow in an example in the next section.

Connecting Multiple Shapes Automatically

When you have several items that need to be connected together in order you can do so rather easily. Simply select the first shape to be connected, and then hold Shift and select the remaining shapes in the order you want to connect them. Once they're selected, choose the type of connector you want to use. To use the dynamic connector, click the green background of the stencil to make sure no other shape is selected. To use another connector, click it in the stencil, and then use one of the following two methods to connect the shapes:

✦ From the menu bar select Tools. From the Tools menu select Connect Shapes.

✦ Click the Connect Shapes button on the Action Toolbar. To bring up the Action Toolbar, click View in the menu bar. Scroll down the View menu to Toolbars. From the Toolbars menu select Action to bring up the Action Toolbar.

Let's use the first method to connect shapes in the following example.

Return to the new page we created on our example project with the three hexagons. From the standard Toolbar select the Pointer Tool. Click the bottom hexagon to select it. Hold Shift and click the middle hexagon and then the top hexagon. Notice that the first shape selected has green shape handles while the following shapes have light-blue shape handles. This helps you keep track of which shape you first selected. Move over to the Basic Shapes stencil and click the Fancy arrow icon. From the menu bar select Tools. From the Tools menu select Connect Shapes (as shown in Figure 17-14).

The hexagons are now connected by arrows going from bottom to top. These connections are dynamically glued. To make these static glue connections you would have to disconnect the connector ends from the shapes and reconnect them using static glue methods, which is why connecting multiple shapes isn't always a useful tool. It would be easier to create a series of static glue connectors one at a time if that's what is needed.

Connecting multiple shapes with shape connectors is useful for creating flowcharts where dynamic glue connections are common.

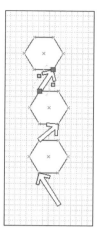

Figure 17-14: The Connect Shapes option in the Tools menu connects the selected shapes.

Connecting Shapes while Dragging

Another way you can automatically connect shapes is while dragging a shape from the stencil onto the page. There are restrictions on the type of connections that can be made this way; the connection is automatically glued using the dynamic connector shape, and the connector must start from a shape on the page and end at the shape being dragged to the page from the stencil. Unless you're sure you will be dragging the shapes onto the page in the correct order *and* you want to use dynamic glue *and* use the dynamic connector shape, this method won't be much use.

For those few situations where it might be useful, this is how you do it: Make sure the shape you will be connecting from is selected. (Click it with the Pointer Tool if it isn't.) Activate the Connector Tool in the Standard Toolbar. Select the shape in the stencil you want to connect to. Drag the shape out and place it on the page where you want it. The shape you just placed on the page is now the selected shape. Drag out another shape and it will connect from the last shape to the new shape.

Click the Pointer Tool in the Standard Toolbar. Click the top hexagon to select it. Click the Connector Tool on the Standard Toolbar to activate it, and then from the Basic Shapes stencil click and drag a rectangle over to the left of the top hexagon. Release it. The rectangle is now the selected object. Go back to the stencil. Click and drag a shadowed box out and place it near the bottom-left of the page. The top hexagon is connected to the rectangle, and the rectangle is connected to the shadowed box with dynamic connectors. If the connectors didn't appear when you dragged the new shape onto the page, either there wasn't a shape selected on the page or the Connector Tool wasn't activated. Save the example; there are a few more things to do with it before the end of this chapter.

Activating the Snap & Glue Toolbar

One of the advantages of Visio 2000 is that it often gives you many ways to accomplish a task. This can also be a disadvantage when you are learning how to do something, because the variety of choices can be confusing. This is why I've waited until now to tell you about the Snap & Glue Toolbar.

From the menu bar, select View. Scroll down the View menu to Toolbars. From the Toolbars menu select Snap & Glue. The Snap & Glue Toolbar appears under the Standard Toolbar (as shown in Figure 17-15).

The Snap & Glue Toolbar

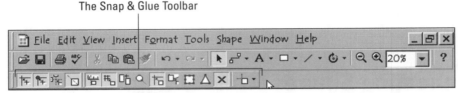

Figure 17-15: The Snap & Glue Toolbar appears under the Standard Toolbar.

Make sure your screen tips are activated. (If they are, skip to the next paragraph.) From the menu bar, select Tools. From the Tools menu, select Options. When the Options dialog box appears, the General Tab is foremost. On its lower-left side is the Screen Tips area. Click in any empty boxes there to check them, and then click OK at the bottom.

From left to right on the Snap & Glue Toolbar are the following buttons (unless they've been customized by the user): Snap, Glue, Dynamic Grid, Drawing Aids, Ruler Subdivisions, Grid, Alignment Box, Shape Geometry, Guides, Shape Intersections, Shape Handles, Shape Vertices, Connection Points, and Shape Extensions with a submenu. For now I'll only cover those buttons we use in this chapter:

✦ **Glue.** This button turns the glue ability on and off. When it is off you cannot glue a connector to a shape.

Note   Leave the Glue button turned on almost all the time.

✦ **Shape Geometry.** This is the Glue to option found in the Snap & Glue dialog box. When it is selected you can glue a connector to any point on the perimeter of a shape.

✦ **Guides.** This is the Glue to option found in the Snap & Glue dialog box. When it is selected you can glue a shape to a guide or grid. This is one of the default options.

✦ **Shape Handles.** This is the Glue to option found in the Snap & Glue dialog box. When it is selected you can glue a connector to the shape handle of any shape.

✦ **Shape Vertices.** This is the Glue to option found in the Snap & Glue dialog box. When it is selected you can glue a connector to any point where two lines meet on the perimeter of a shape.

✦ **Connection Points.** This is the Glue to option found in the Snap & Glue dialog box. When it is selected you can glue a connector to any defined connection point on the perimeter of a shape, within the shape, or outside the shape. This is one of the default options.

In general, unless you will be changing your Glue to options frequently in a project, the glue controls in the Snap & Glue Toolbar won't be of great use. You're usually better off accessing the options through the other toolbars and having the extra workspace available to view your page.

Line Jumps and Routing

You may have noticed in earlier examples that lines sometimes cross or lie on top of each other, making it difficult to tell which lines go where. The developers of Visio 2000 didn't overlook this problem.

Line jumps and Routing options apply only to the dynamic connector shape. All other connectors simply cross or lie on top of each other in the order they were laid out. *Line jumps* are ways to keep crossing lines from being confused with each other. There are several different styles for doing line jumps: Arcs (as shown in Figure 17-16), Gaps, Squares, and multi-sided jumps ranging in size from two-sided to seven-sided. You can also adjust the size of the jump to make it bigger or smaller.

You cannot, however, mix styles and sizes on a single page. The options set for a page apply to the entire page but not to other pages in the project file. In other words, all the jumps on one page will be the same type and size. If you change the options, all the jumps on that page change to the new options. Changing the style option on one page does not change the option on other pages, so if you need to keep the same style throughout, remember to change all the pages, not just the one you're working on at the time. This applies to routing options as well.

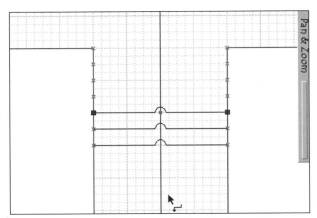

Figure 17-16: Arc Line jumps on the horizontal lines

Routing options help keep lines from overlapping and set how they route themselves around obstacles. They can maintain set spacing between lines and shapes.

To access Line jumps and Routing options, click File in the menu bar and select Page Setup. The Page Setup dialog box appears. Select the Layout and Routing tab. You now have access to the Line jumps and Routing options (as shown in Figure 17-17). At the top are the Routing options. On the lower-right is a view box that shows an example of the current Routing Style. On the lower-left are the Line jumps options. Near the bottom-left is a button that says Spacing, which accesses the Layout and Routing Spacing dialog box. This dialog box enables you to set spacing between lines and shapes (as shown in Figure 17-18).

To go over all the different options for line jumps, routing, and spacing in an example would be a chapter in of itself! Instead I suggest you do some experimentation on your own. Go back to the first page of the example we've been using in this chapter, the one with all the different shapes and dynamic connections. Add a couple of shapes to either side of an existing connection line and make a dynamic connection between them that crosses over the existing line. Now open the Page Setup dialog box and make changes on the options under the Layout and Routing tab. Look to see what changes this makes to the drawing. Do this several times, changing different options back and forth. Keep making changes until you feel comfortable with using these options. A lot of the look and feel of you projects will come from your skill with these options.

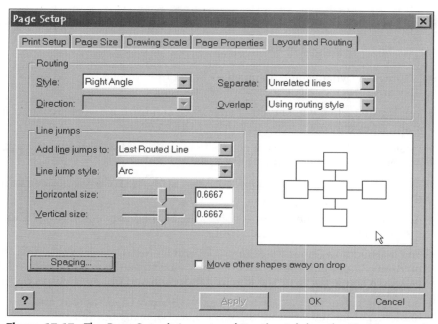

Figure 17-17: The Page Setup's Layout and Routing tab has the Line jump and Routing options.

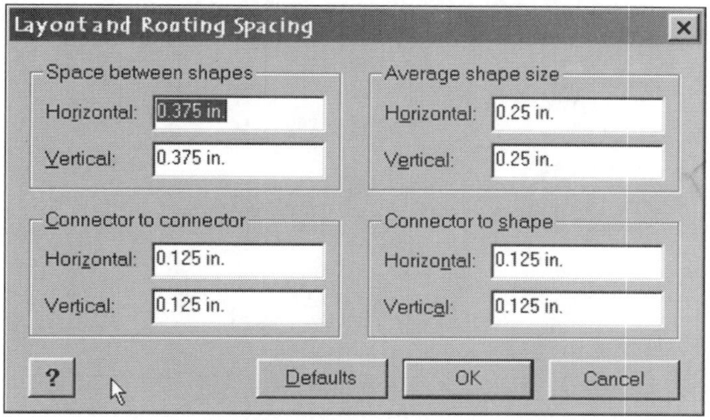

Figure 17-18: Layout and Routing Spacing dialog box

Summary

We covered a lot of ground in this chapter:

✦ I discussed Dynamic and Static glues: when they should be used and when they are automatically chosen by the program.

✦ You learned when you should change back and forth between dynamic and static glues and when you can't change the glue type.

✦ I went over the three types of connection points and what they connect to, and how to move and delete them.

✦ Two basic connector shapes exist in Visio 2000: the Dynamic connector and the Line-curve connector.

✦ A third connector shape type involves the Shaped connector group. I also discussed using the Connector Tool.

✦ You learned how about the Stamp Tool and its restrictions, connecting multiple shapes and the restrictions on doing so, and connecting automatically to a shape being dragged in from a stencil and the restrictions on that.

✦ You were instructed on how to access the Snap & Glue Toolbar, and implement Line jumps, Routing options, and Spacing options.

✦ You can have a connector with dynamic glue on one end and static glue on the other!

Whew! Fortunately, the next chapter isn't quite so heavy. Next you will learn how to format shapes quickly, but you might want to take a break first. I know I will!

✦   ✦   ✦

Quickly Formatting Shapes

Chapter 6 covered drawing fundamentals, including basics involving the Format Shape buttons. This chapter discusses more sophisticated formatting techniques, especially those that make drawing easier and more efficient. In fact, several of the features in this chapter enable users to simultaneously format multiple shapes. This may sound hard to believe, but it's true. After you've finished reading this chapter, you'll know how to modify several instances — not in a few minutes — but in an instant.

Quickly Formatting Shapes

Selecting a group of shapes is an essential step for concurrently formatting multiple objects. Whether you're modifying or deleting shapes, or just adjusting shape styles, you won't get far without some of the following basic techniques under your belt.

Selecting specific shapes on a drawing page

Visio 2000 offers users two methods for selecting specific shapes. Imagine that you need to format three of five squares on a drawing page. First of all, using the popular Windows feature to select the shapes is not a bad idea. Simply click the first square and then simultaneously click and press the Shift key when moving your cursor over each of the other two shapes. Notice that the first square, the primary shape, is represented with green selection handles, while the secondary shapes have light blue selection handles. To deselect these shapes, just click a blank portion of the drawing page.

The second method is easier but more restrictive. You can use the drag-net technique—minus Joe Friday—to lasso your shapes. Just click and hold down the left mouse button, and then drag; a rectangular dotted line called the *net* appears. Drag the net over the shapes that you wish to format (as shown in Figure 18-1). As with the other method, deselect the shapes by clicking a blank portion of the drawing page. Obviously, you can only lasso the shapes that you need when they're not separated by shapes that you don't want. After all, any shapes that fall completely within the selection net will be highlighted. This problem can be avoided by using the Shift-click technique, which was described in the preceding paragraph.

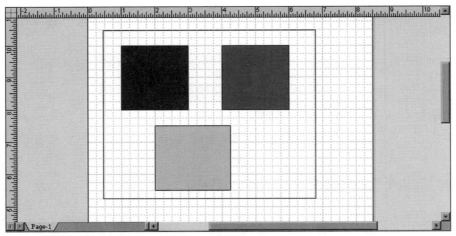

Figure 18-1: Select shapes with the drag-net technique.

Note   To select shapes that fall partially within the boundaries of the drag-net, check the Select Shapes Partially Within Area box on the Drawing tab of the Options dialog box.

Selecting all of the shapes on a drawing page

Visio 2000 offers three methods for selecting all of the shapes on a drawing page. The two discussed in the "Selecting specific shapes on a drawing page" section work fine, although they can take a few moments. Selecting Edit ➪ Select All is the third and quickest way. This action, by default, selects all objects within the drawing window, including shapes, guides, and guide points. Furthermore, you can modify which objects the Select All function selects by designating the objects in the Select Special dialog box.

Access the Select Special dialog box by choosing Edit ➪ Select Special. Each checked box indicates a category of objects that will be selected when using the Select All function. At this point, you only need to worry about three shape types: shapes, guides, and groups (two or more shapes that operate as a single instance). I'll discuss OLE (object linking and embedding) objects, metafiles, bitmaps, and layers later in the book. For now, check the categories that you would like, and then select OK. When you click the Select All feature, the applicable shapes will be highlighted on the drawing page.

Note   The Select Special dialog box's All button selects all of the above items; the None button deselects these items.

Cross-Reference   For more details on the Select Special features, see Chapter 22.

Using and Editing the Color Palette

The Color Palette formats lines and shapes. Access the feature by selecting Tools ➪ Color Palette. The Color Palette dialog box (as shown in Figure 18-2) contains 24 colors (numbered 0 to 23), a Copy Colors From section, and several buttons. Each of these features enables users to edit colors within a given drawing.

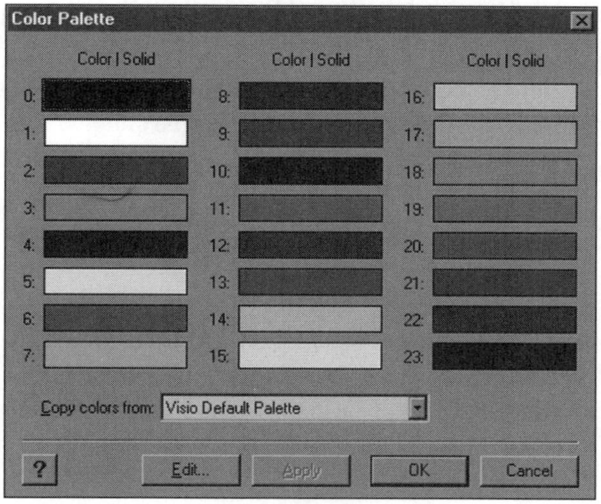

Figure 18-2: The Color Palette dialog box

See Chapter 6 for more information on using line colors, fill colors, and color patterns.

The Color Palette, as mentioned previously, contains more than 20 colors. The first 16 colors can be accessed from the arrows next to the Font Color, Line Color, and Fill Color buttons. For example, if you click the Fill Color button's arrow, you'll find color blocks representing colors 0 through 15. However, you can access all 24 colors in the Text, Line, Fill, and Shadow dialog boxes, which all are located in the menu bar's Format drop-down menu. Visio 2000 enables users to edit these colors and, subsequently, the objects that contain these colors.

As was discussed in Chapter 6, the Edit Color dialog box is essential for modifying palette colors. Click any color within the Color Palette that you wish to change, and then select the Edit button in order to access the Edit Color dialog box. You can also achieve the same result by simply double-clicking a particular color. For instance, double-click color #11. The Edit Color dialog box reveals that color's location on both the Color Selector palette and the color bar to its right on the dialog box. Once you have selected a color, you can choose to modify it in one of three ways in the Edit Color dialog box:

✦ Click a color from the Color Selector palette, refining the selection with the color bar.

✦ Choose a color block within the Basic Colors section.

✦ Select a color block within the Custom Colors section.

The selected color is presented in the Color/Solid box, which is located below the Color Selector palette. Simply click the OK button and the newly selected color will appear in the Color Palette's #11 block. Click the OK button on the Color Palette dialog box in order to finalize your decision. Any shapes, lines, shadows, or patterns using the previous #11 color will now reveal the new #11 color. This method is one of the quickest and most uniform ways to modify colors for multiple shapes.

You can also use the Copy Colors From section in order to edit colors. This feature enables you to use color palettes from other drawings and programs. For instance, you can copy a palette from one drawing to another by following these steps:

1. Open both drawings. Select Tools ➪ Color Palette.

2. Scroll down the list in the Copy Colors From section and then choose the other drawing's color palette.

3. Click the OK button. Now all color changes will be reflected in the new drawing.

The Copy Colors From section also allows you to return to the Visio default palette, as well as access program formats, such as the Excel chart color palette. Just scroll the section's list for options. In general, this method is great for reformatting a multitude of shape colors in a minimum of time.

Applying the Format Painter

The Format Painter is an excellent tool for modifying multiple objects in a similar fashion. In fact, the feature allows you to copy or fill text characteristics to other shapes. It can also be used on lines. Frequent applications involving the Format Painter include quickly adding rounded edges, shadows, and fill patterns to numerous shapes.

Note You cannot copy shapes with the Format Painter, only the shape's attributes. Use the Copy and Paste buttons in order to copy and paste a shape in its entirety. To save a step, you can also right-click the shape that you want to copy and then select Duplicate from the pop-up menu.

Formatting shapes with the format painter

Hindsight is 20/20, or so the saying goes. Your artist's eye is still developing, so you might have discovered that the shapes that you've drawn are missing something. Most likely they need a more uniform look. In these cases, you realize that you'd like to use the same fill or pattern on two or more shapes. The problem is that you've already drawn the shapes, each with different formatting. Well, that's not really much of a problem — not with the Format Painter button. Just follow these steps, and your hindsight will not become oversight:

1. Click the shape whose color characteristics you wish to copy to other shapes.

2. Click the Format Painter button in order to copy characteristics to just one shape. Double-click the Format Painter button in order to copy characteristics to a multitude of shapes.

3. Click the shape or shapes that you wish to format (see Figure 18-3).

4. Click a blank portion of the drawing page in order to finalize the process, unhighlighting the formatted shape or shapes.

Format Painter tool

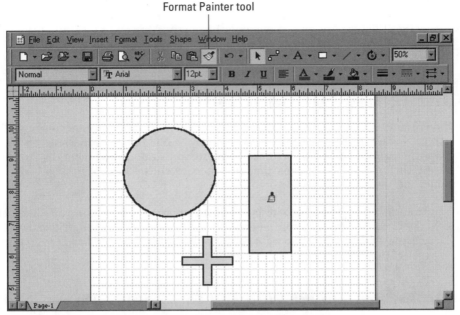

Figure 18-3: Apply the Format Painter to several shapes.

Formatting text within a shape by using the format painter

The text style within a shape is malleable, too. In fact, you can also format a shape's text with the Format Painter button by following these steps:

1. Double-click the shape that has the text characteristics that you'd like to copy to other shapes.

2. Click the Format Painter button in order to copy characteristics to a shape. Double-clicking the Format Painter icon in this instance will not allow you to format more than one shape's text.

3. Double-click the shape or shapes whose text you want to format.

4. Type in the text of your choice. The font, including its style, color and size, is formatted in the same manner as the font of the first shape.

5. Click a blank portion of the drawing page in order to finalize the process, unhighlighting the formatted shape and its text.

Note

You can only format one shape at a time when using the Format Painter feature with text.

See Chapter 30 for more details on formatting text.

Reestablishing a Shape's Original Style

After you've made modifications to your original shapes, you may decide that you preferred the original shapes over the modified shapes. In these cases, use the Style dialog box in order to return a shape's characteristics to their default settings. Select Format ➪ Style from the menu bar, or from the pop-up menu that appears by right-clicking a particular shape. Either action calls up the Style dialog box (as shown in Figure 18-4).

If the shape that you're working with is a Visio stencil master, set all of the style boxes back to Use Master's Format. If the shape was created from *a* drawing tool (for instance, *the* Line icon tool *or the* Ellipse icon tool , select Normal from the Text, Line, and Style box lists. Do this even if these boxes already have a Normal setting. Once you're finished, click the OK button. The shape should return to its original features.

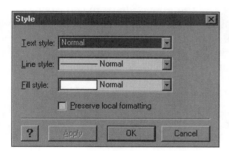

Figure 18-4: Adjust the settings in the Style dialog box in order to set a shape's default features.

You can also edit a shape by making the appropriate changes within the All Styles box, a feature on the Format toolbar. The All Styles Box is located above the Line Style box (Format Shape toolbar).

Defining New Shape Styles

Visio 2000 enables users to create and to edit new shape styles with the Define Styles dialog box. Access the feature by selecting Format ➪ Define Styles. With this dialog box, you can create, change, and delete styles.

Creating a style

You can create new styles for your stencils, templates, and drawings by utilizing features on the Define Styles dialog box. The following steps will help you get started:

1. Create a shape with certain fill and line characteristics. For example, draw a rounded polygon with red fill. Next, select the shape.

2. Select Format ➪ Define Styles from the menu bar.

3. Choose <New Style> from the Style listings. Highlight the setting and then type in a name, for example, "Round-Red."

4. Use fundamentals from other styles by choosing from the listing in the Based On area. A good shape style derivative is Normal.

5. In the Includes section, check the boxes that you want this new style to accommodate. For instance, check the Line and Fill boxes.

6. Click OK.

Now every time that you want to format a shape with the same characteristics, just click that shape and then choose the name of the new style from the New Fill or New Line boxes on the Format Shape toolbar. In this situation, choosing the style from either box listing will produce a dialog box that informs the user that the style encompasses both fill and line changes. Simply click Yes to enact both style changes. Click No to enact only one of the changes. The dialog boxes will always appear if the style affects more than one type of characteristic.

Tip   You can hide the new style from users by checking the Hidden Style feature. This action prevents the created style from appearing in the New Fill, New Line, New Text, and All Style boxes.

Note   Style changes only appear within saved stencil, template, and drawing files. You cannot access the new style simply by retrieving the Visio Drawing window.

Renaming a style

Once you've created a new style, you can rename it. For instance, you may come to your senses and realize that "Round-Red" is a terrible style moniker. Instead, you decide to rename the style "Just My Style." Here's how to rename it:

1. Select a shape that exhibits the style which you want to rename.

2. Choose Format ➪ Define Styles from the menu bar.

3. To rename the style, click the Rename button. Type the new name in the Rename Style dialog box and then click OK.

4. Click the OK button on the Define Styles dialog box.

Note   Basic style settings in Visio 2000, such as Normal, Guide, and Text Only, cannot be renamed or deleted.

Editing a style

Select the shape with the style that you wish to modify and then choose Format ⇨ Define Styles in order to retrieve the Define Styles dialog box (as shown in Figure 18-5). First, check the Preserve Local Formatting box in order to protect changes that you've made to a particular shape. This is necessary in order to preserve manual changes that you've made before the modification. For example, if you've colored a box yellow, you can keep that color by selecting this feature. Therefore, the shape will not return to a white color after you have applied the Normal fill feature. You can also keep text modifications involving font, style, and point size when using this feature. If you do not wish to keep these changes, then do not preserve the local formatting features.

In the Change section, select the applicable buttons. For instance, if you want the style to feature a different fill color, click the Fill button. If you would like to change the line weight, click the Line button. The Text, Line, and Fill buttons each take you to that category's respective dialog box. Choose the appropriate changes there, and then select OK. After finishing all procedures, click OK on the Define Styles dialog box.

Click here to rename a style

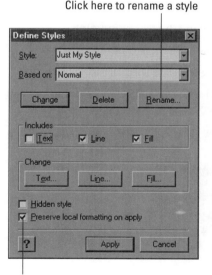

Check this box to protect your changes

Figure 18-5: The Define Styles dialog box

Tip   You can simultaneously edit the style of several shapes. Select all of the shapes. Next, make the necessary changes in the Define Styles dialog box. Finally, click the Apply button.

Note   Delete a style by selecting the Delete button and then clicking OK.

Using Shape Protection Features

Once you've formatted a shape, Visio 2000 helps you keep it intact. The Protection dialog box features prevent inadvertent hands from editing or deleting important shapes that are on your files. To access these features, click a shape and then select Format ➪ Protection. You can also right-click the shape and then select Format ➪ Protection from the pop-up menus. The Protection dialog box (as shown in Figure 18-6) contains the following ten features, which all enable you to restrict user access:

✦ **Width.** Prevents users from adjusting a shape's width

✦ **Height.** Prevents users from adjusting a shape's height

✦ **Aspect ratio.** Enables users to adjust a shape's height and width. However, the feature maintains the proportion between the two measurements.

✦ **X position.** Prevents any horizontal repositioning of a shape

✦ **Y position.** Prevents any vertical repositioning of a shape

✦ **Begin point.** Prevents users from moving a line's begin point

✦ **End point.** Prevents users from moving a line's end point

✦ **Rotation.** Prevents users from rotating a shape with the Rotation Tool

✦ **From selection.** Prevents users from selecting a shape when it is used in conjunction with the Protect Document dialog box's Shape box feature.

✦ **From deletion.** Prevents users from deleting a shape

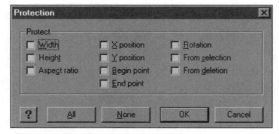

Figure 18-6: The Protection dialog box

These features enable you to protect lines, guides, and shapes. However, some of these features are designed specifically for one-dimensional objects. For example,

Begin and End Point protection features prevent other people from moving a line's protected point. Thus, others can only extend the line from the unprotected point or rotate the line from the protected point. Notice, too, that protected begin and end points appear gray instead of the usual green. That's how Visio 2000 designates which line points are protected.

Tip   To prevent others from resizing a line, select both the Begin and End Point boxes.

Cross-Reference   Don't forget to use both the Protect Document and Protect dialog boxes in order to protect a one- or two-dimensional object from being selected. The Protect Document dialog box can be accessed from the Drawing Explorer. To learn more about the Protect Document dialogue box, see Chapter 11. Also, see Chapter 34 for shape protection features involving Visio 2000 ShapeSheets.

Inserting Information into the Special Dialog Box

In Chapter 11, you learned how to apply data to a file's properties primarily for identification measures. Well, the same features hold true for shapes. This time, though, use the Special dialog box to insert ID data for each object within a drawing, including lines and guides. You can access the Special dialog box (shown in Figure 18-7) in one of two ways:

✦ Click a shape and then choose Format ➪ Special from the menu bar.

✦ Right-click a shape and then select Format ➪ Special from the pop-up menus.

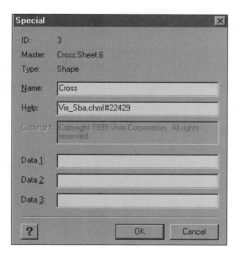

Figure 18-7: The Special dialog box

The Special dialog box contains nine categories:

✦ **ID.** Visio 2000 assigns numbers to each shape based upon the order that the shapes were placed in a drawing page. For example, the first shape drawn is labeled 1, the second 2, and so on.

✦ **Master.** Lists the name of the master

✦ **Type.** Indicates the object's type, for example, shape, or guide

✦ **Name.** By default, Visio 2000 uses the master's name here.

✦ **Help.** Help-related documentation

✦ **Copyright.** Insert creation date and ownership for shapes that you've designed; existing Visio 2000 masters already contain noneditable copyright information.

✦ **Data 1.** Type in descriptive information relating to that shape.

✦ **Data 2.** Type in descriptive information relating to that shape.

✦ **Data 3.** Type in descriptive information relating to that shape.

You can only edit the Name, Help, Data 1, Data 2, and Data 3 sections. The Copyright section only can be edited if you are creating a new shape. Once you finish inserting information, simply click the OK button. Anytime you select the Special dialog box for a specific shape, the inserted data for that shape appears.

Summary

This chapter discussed how to modify shapes in a simple and quick manner, formatting techniques for protecting certain drawing elements, and how to insert shape data. The following specific points were covered:

✦ Selecting multiple shapes by clicking a shape, and then simultaneously clicking and pressing the Shift key in order to highlight other shapes.

✦ Selecting Edit ➪ Select All in order to choose all objects on a drawing page.

✦ Editing the 24 colors available on the Color Palette.

✦ Using the Format Painter in order to copy a shape's fill, text, line or styles attributes to other shapes.

✦ Adjusting the settings on the Style dialog box to reset a shape's default features.

✦ Choosing Format ➪ Define Styles to create, modify, or delete a shape's styles.

✦ Using features in both the Protect Document and Protection dialog boxes in order to prevent another person from selecting a specific shape.

✦ Using the Special dialog box to insert information about a shape, such as its name and any helpful tidbits about how to use it.

Chapter 19 discusses methods for distributing and aligning shapes.

✦ ✦ ✦

Aligning and Distributing Shapes

Presentation is an essential element in all areas of communication. In fact, the way an idea is expressed is often as decisive to an audience's response as the idea itself. Therefore, most visual presentations, even in the business world, must display information in an aesthetically pleasing format. That's the purpose of Visio 2000 — to make business drawings both simple and professional looking. Aligning and distributing shapes is a major part of this process.

Alignment in Visio 2000 involves lining up two or more shapes vertically or horizontally, either by their edges or their centers. Shape distribution, on the other hand, enables users to insert an equal amount of space between a number of specified shape features, such as instances' edges, centers, or certain sides. Both of these processes add more balance to charts and diagrams. Other functions within Visio 2000 also contribute to the uniform placement of shapes, such as centering drawings and reversing ends. The functions discussed in this chapter are undoubtedly useful for a large number of business drawings. The aesthetic placement of shapes is an important element in making the art of presentation work for you.

Aligning Shapes

Almost all diagrams and drawings require aligning certain shapes with each another. You can rely on Visio 2000's rulers, grids, and guides to help you place objects, or you can use these features along with Visio 2000's automatic alignment functions. The choice is yours.

Using rulers and grids to align shapes

The most basic method of aligning shapes involves using rulers and grids as markers. For example, you can align two or more shapes by placing their top edges on the same horizontal grid or by lining them up with the same vertical ruler marking (see Figure 19-1). This is probably a method you've used since installing Visio 2000 onto your computer. It's relatively common and simple.

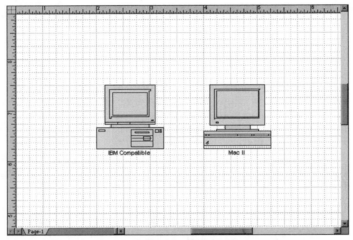

Figure 19-1: Use ruler markings and a grid line to align two computer images.

> **Tip**   You can choose to view—or not view—grids, rulers, and guides by clicking the appropriate name in the View drop-down menu.

Rulers and grids also enable you to align shapes by arranging them according to their centers. This can be difficult when dealing with shapes of different sizes. The key is to measure the shapes and then choose a spot to place them by symmetrically dividing each shape with grid lines and rulers (as shown in Figure 19-2). After you have placed the shapes, draw an imaginary line through them. Placing a line with the Line Tool and then clicking the Undo button will also work.

> **Tip**   Notice that dotted marks appear on both rulers. The dotted marks indicate where the center and outside boundaries of a selected shape are located. These markings move as you relocate the shape.

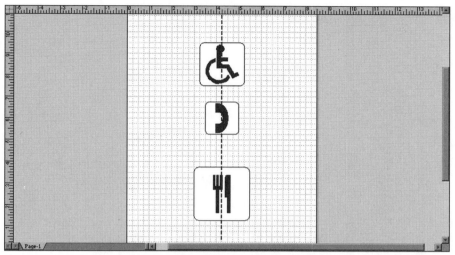

Figure 19-2: Align shapes by symmetrically dividing each instance with rulers and grids.

Using guides and guide points to align shapes

Guides make alignment somewhat easier. To create a guide, place your cursor on one of the rulers and then drag. A vertical guide appears from the vertical ruler. Dragging from the horizontal ruler produces a horizontal guide. The following exercise demonstrates how you can align several shapes with a guide:

1. Drop three shapes from a stencil onto your drawing page. Next, drag a guide from one of the rulers onto the page.

2. Place each shape onto the guide. If you want to line them up by their centers, drag each shape onto the guide until a small red box appears on its center connection point. The red box indicates that the shape has been glued to the guide. If you want to line up the shapes' edges, drag each shape onto the guide until a small red box appears on that edge's connection point.

3. Drag the guide to any place on the drawing page; the shapes will follow (see Figure 19-3). Align the guide with either grid lines or your ruler markings.

Guides make aligning shapes much easier than simply using rulers and grids. However, as you will learn a little later in this chapter, there is an even easier way. You probably figured that, though. Visio 2000 offers a multitude of methods for accomplishing tasks, all of them fairly simple, some more so than others.

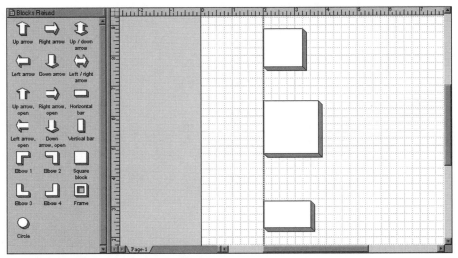

Figure 19-3: Guide shapes into alignment.

Note With guide points, users can align shapes near or on top of one another by simply gluing the guide point onto a shape's center connection point and then dragging the connection point over the center point of other shapes.

Cross-Reference See Chapter 10 for an in-depth discussion on how to use rulers, grids, and guides. Also, check out how dynamic grids and certain snap extensions can simplify alignment.

Arranging geographic map shapes

Aligning and juxtapositioning countries can be difficult. So many zigzagging borders are enough to intimidate anybody. Even those of us who are fairly knowledgeable concerning world geography usually still can't draw maps that look like honest-to-goodness maps; everything is out of proportion. Well, don't panic. You don't have to rush to the store and buy a world atlas; Visio 2000 does the thinking for you. In fact, Visio 2000 doesn't require you to be an artist or a geography teacher in order to use its Geographic Map template.

Aligning map shapes

Placing and sizing countries is so easy. Visio 2000 contains map shapes, all of which are in correct proportion to each other. Furthermore, Visio 2000 features will automatically arrange these shapes so that the shapes will appear just as they would on a map. Follow these steps to see Visio 2000 in action:

1. Select the New Drawing button and choose Map ➪ Geographic Maps in order to access the Geographic Maps template.

2. Click the Europe stencil title bar in order to view its contents. Next, drop the France, Germany, Ireland, Spain, Sweden, and Turkey map shapes onto the drawing page. Where you place them is not important. Notice, however, that all of the shapes are already realistically proportioned.

3. Select five of the shapes. Do this by clicking the first shape and then holding Shift while clicking the other four.

4. Right-click one of the shapes you've selected, or hold Shift if you are right-clicking the drawing page. Choose Arrange to Shape from the pop-up menu.

5. A small dialog box appears, prompting you with the message: "Select the shape that you want the other shapes aligned to, then click OK." Double-click the sixth shape, the one that you want to arrange with the selected shapes. Next, click the OK button in the dialog box.

Like magic, the shapes are proportioned accordingly (as shown in Figure 19-4). Spain and Germany are placed, as they are in real life, adjacent to France. Notice that Ireland, Sweden, and Turkey are not connected to any other shapes. However, they are placed as they would be on a map of Europe. In fact, the program arranges these shapes as if their surrounding shapes were on the drawing page. For example, if you compare your map to a map of Europe in a world atlas, you will see that the space between Turkey, Sweden, and Germany corresponds proportionately to the absent countries — as if they were actually there.

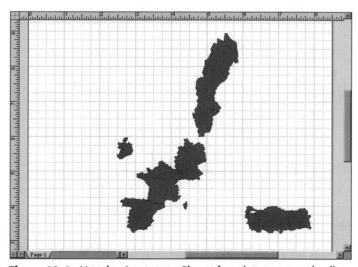

Figure 19-4: Use the Arrange to Shape function to properly align map shapes.

Tip

Use the Arrange to Shape feature to place rivers and other bodies of water in their actual locations.

Sizing map shapes to fit the drawing page

The countries are placed correctly, but you're still not satisfied. You want to enlarge and arrange the shapes so that they fill the page and remain in correct proportion to each other. No problem, just follow these simple steps:

1. Select all of the map shapes on the drawing page.

2. Right-click one of the shapes that you've selected, or hold down the Shift button if you are right-clicking the drawing page. Choose Arrange to Page from the pop-up menu.

3. The Arrange to Page dialog box emerges. Check the box next to "Size shapes to fill the drawing page." Next, click the OK button.

The shapes are now fitted to the drawing page (see Figure 19-5). There was no need to go through a tedious task of dragging and resizing shapes; Visio 2000 knows its geography.

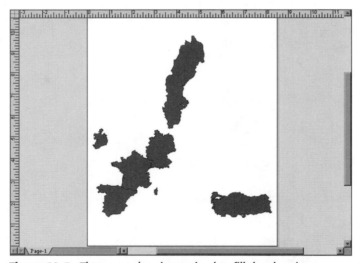

Figure 19-5: The same drawing resized to fill the drawing page

Tip To lay out all of the map shapes on a stencil, right-click one of the shapes and then choose Select All. Place that shape on the drawing page and the other shapes will automatically follow. Use the Arrange to Shape function to organize the shapes correctly. Apply the Arrange to Page function to fit the map shapes on your drawing page.

Applying the Align Shapes functions

Visio 2000's automatic shape alignment features allow you to arrange shapes with less dragging. You can find the Align Shapes functions on the Action Toolbar and the Tools drop-down menu. The Align Shapes feature is the first button to the left of the Action Toolbar. Select two or more shapes and then either click the button or the arrow button next to the shapes for further options. The options are arranged in the arrow button's drop-down menu in two sets of three. The top three icons represent horizontal alignments, while the bottom three icons represent vertical alignments (see Figure 19-6). Selecting Tools ➪ Align Shapes produces the same dialog box as clicking the Align Shapes button (see Figure 19-7). The options are visually larger than the options in the drop-down menu that was retrieved by the Align Shapes arrow button.

Figure 19-6: Click the Align Shapes arrow button in order to view its drop-down menu.

Aligning shapes vertically

You can align shapes vertically in three different fashions:

✦ Align shapes by their left sides

✦ Align shapes by their right sides

✦ Align shapes by their centers

Figure 19-7: Selecting the Align Shapes button pulls up this dialog box.

You can accomplish different looks with these three methods. The following exercise demonstrates how this works:

1. Drop two or more shapes onto the drawing page, preferably different-size squares and rectangles.

2. Drag one of the shapes to the top of the page.

3. Select the shape at the top of the page by clicking it. This is the shape with which all others will be aligned. Hold down the Shift key and click the additional instances.

4. Choose Tools ⇨ Align Shapes in order to retrieve the Align Shapes dialog box. You can also do this by clicking the Align Shapes button.

5. Select the first button in the Left/Right Alignment section of the Align Shapes dialog box, and then click the OK button. The highlighted shapes' left sides should line up vertically (as shown in Figure 19-8). Access the Align Shapes dialog box, choosing the other two selections in the Left/ Right Alignment section. Notice how each command displays the shapes.

Notice that various amounts of space exist between each of the aligned instances. This is because shapes are moved horizontally from the place where they're selected (as shown in Figure 19-8). Therefore, if two shapes are horizontally near one another, one of the instances may be placed behind another shape. To avoid playing unnecessary rounds of hide-and-seek, make sure that your shapes are never to the left or right of another instance when you use vertical alignment.

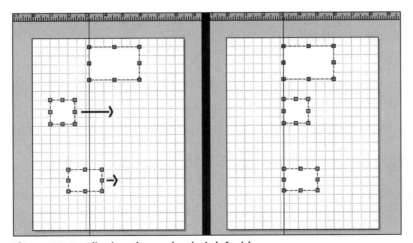

Figure 19-8: Aligning shapes by their left sides

Note   The first-selected shape becomes the target to which other shapes will align.

Tip Alignment features only line up shapes; they do not distribute an equal amount of space between aligned shapes. This is a function of the Distribute Shapes features.

Aligning shapes horizontally

Visio 2000 enables users to horizontally align shapes in three different fashions:

✦ Align shapes by their tops

✦ Align shapes by their bottoms

✦ Align shapes by their centers

Let's get started. Try aligning shapes horizontally by following these steps:

1. Drop two or more shapes onto the drawing page, preferably different-size squares and rectangles. If you still have the drawing used in the vertical alignment process, just use it.

2. Drag one of the shapes to the left of the page. Haphazardly place the others in a horizontal line.

3. Select the shape at the top of the page by clicking it. This is the shape to which all others will align. Hold down the Shift key and click the additional instances.

4. Choose Tools ➪ Align Shapes in order to retrieve the Align Shapes dialog box. You can also do this by clicking the Align Shapes button.

5. Select the first button in the Up/Down Alignment section of the Align Shapes dialog box, and then click the OK button. The highlighted shapes' tops should align horizontally (as shown in Figure 19-9). Access the Align Shapes dialog box again, choosing the other two selections in the Top/Bottom Alignment section. Notice how each command displays the shapes.

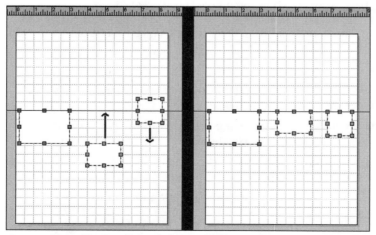

Figure 19-9: Aligning several shapes horizontally

Click the appropriate X button in the Align Shapes dialog box in order to cancel vertical or horizontal alignments.

Shapes, in these circumstances, are moved vertically from the point where they were selected (see Figure 19-9). Thus, if two shapes are vertically near one another, one of the instances may seek to play hide-and-seek. If you end up a couple shapes short after using the alignment function, this is what has happened. Avoid this problem by making sure that selected shapes are never to the top or bottom of another instance when you use horizontal alignment.

When you are in the Align Shapes dialog box, Visio 2000 will automatically attach a guide to the aligned shapes if you check the box next to "Create guide and glue shapes to it."

Once the instances are aligned, you can relocate the "train of shapes" without a guide — if they are selected. Just drag one of the shapes; the rest will follow.

Distributing Shapes

Alignment functions only align shapes by their edges or centers. Use the distribution features in order to place increments of equal space between instances, their sides, or their centers. Otherwise, the distances for the specified areas between aligned shapes will be uneven.

Using rulers, grids, and guides to distribute shapes

The most rudimentary way of distributing shapes involves using rulers, grids, and guides. You can measure the distance between instances with rulers and grids, and then drag the shapes equal distances apart. You can also glue certain shapes to guides and then relocate the shapes by dragging the guides. The following brief exercise shows you how this works:

1. Open any stencil and then drop three shapes from it onto a drawing page.
2. Drag a vertical guide onto the page, and glue it to one of the shapes on the far right of the drawing screen.
3. Distribute the shapes horizontally and place an equal amount of space between the shapes. For example, let's try three inches.
4. Drag the first and second shapes either left or right so that they are an inch apart. Use the rulers for assistance.
5. Attach the third shape to a guide. Drag the guide so that an inch separates it from the second shape. The result should resemble Figure 19-10.

The process is fairly simple, but it is still quite time-consuming. Such tasks have their time and place, particularly when you're distributing two shapes. But if you are distributing more than two shapes, this method can become tedious. In such instances — pun not intended — use the Distribute Shapes functions.

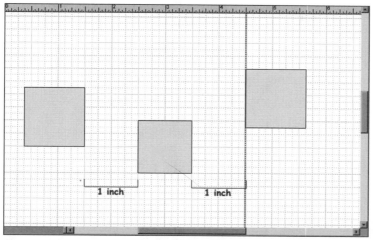

Figure 19-10: Manually distributing shapes

Applying the Distribute Shapes functions

The Distribute Shapes functions, like those for aligning instances, can be found on the Action Toolbar and the Tool drop-down menu. You must select three or more instances to use these features. The Distribute Shapes button is the second button on the left of the Action Toolbar. Selecting it pulls up the Distribute Shapes dialog box, which can also be accessed by choosing Tools ➪ Distribute Shapes. The arrow button next to the Distribute Shapes button retrieves a drop-down menu with four distribution options (see Figure 19-11). The top two options are vertical distribution formats and the bottom two options are horizontal distribution formats. The Distribute Shapes dialog box offers twice as many options (see figure 19-12).

Figure 19-11: The Distribute Shapes arrow button retrieves a drop-down menu that offers four distribution options.

Note Only four options in the Distribute Shapes arrow button's drop-down menu are available. Distribution by shapes' left sides, right sides, tops, or bottoms is not accessible.

Vertically distributing shapes

You can distribute shapes vertically in four formats:

✦ Arrange equal amounts of space between all selected shapes

✦ Arrange equal amounts of space between shape tops

✦ Arrange equal amounts of space between shape centers

✦ Arrange equal amounts of space between shape bottoms

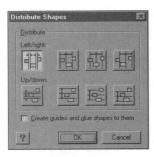

Figure 19-12: The buttons in the first row of the Distribute Shapes dialog box distribute shapes vertically.

Using distribute features is fairly simple. They work by taking the distance between the two farthest shapes and dividing the space equally between the selected instances. In the case of vertical distribution options, the two farthest shapes would be the shape at the highest end of the page and the shape at the lowest end of the page (see Figure 19-13). These two shapes will not move when Distribute Shapes features are used. However, the shapes in between these two will be arranged so that an equal amount of vertical space is distributed between each instance. For example, arranging the shapes in Figure 19-13 by their centers would result in the two middle shapes shifting so that there is equal space between their centers and the centers of the two outer shapes.

Note   If the instances are composed of different shapes and different sizes, only the first button in the Distribute Shapes dialog box will *always* distribute an equal amount of space between the instances.

Distributing shapes horizontally

Visio 2000 enables you to distribute shapes horizontally in four formats:

✦ Arrange equal amounts of space between all selected shapes

✦ Arrange equal amounts of space between the left sides of shapes

✦ Arrange equal amounts of space between shape centers

✦ Arrange equal amounts of space between shape bottoms

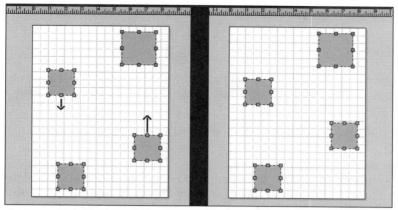

Figure 19-13: The farthest shapes do not move; only the middle shapes shift.

Horizontally distributing shapes works in the same manner as vertically distributing shapes. Therefore, the two farthest shapes — the one on the far right and the one on the far left — do not move. The shapes between these two shapes shift horizontally so that the specified space is distributed equally among all of the shapes. Both the Distribute Shapes dialog box or the drop-down menu retrieved by the Distribute Shapes arrow button can perform these functions.

The Distribute Shapes dialog box enables you to attach guides to each of the selected shapes — for both horizontal and vertical distribution. To do this, within the dialog box check the box to the right of "Create guides and glue shapes to them." This action places guides on each of the selected shapes. Furthermore, you can use the guides to move the shapes without having to distribute them again. To do this, just drag one of the guides that is attached to the outermost instance. The rest of the shapes adjust automatically (as shown in Figure 19-14).

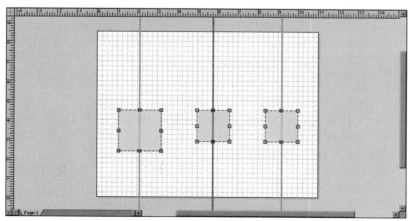

Figure 19-14: Automatic distribution with guides

The following exercise demonstrates how this works:

1. Open a stencil and drag three shapes onto the drawing page.

2. Select the three shapes and then choose Tools ➪ Distribute Shapes.

3. Click the first button on the left in the Left/Right section of the Distribute Shapes dialog box. This option distributes an equal amount of horizontal space between selected shapes.

4. Check the box labeled "Create guides and glue shapes to them." Click the OK button.

5. Each of the shapes now has a guide attached to it. Move the guide glued to either the shape located farthest to the left or the shape located farthest to the right. Notice that the space between the shapes adjusts automatically.

Note   You will be unable to access the guides-distribution feature if you have chosen not to view the guides. Undo the selection by choosing View ➪ Guides. Turning off glue in the Snap & Glue dialog box, however, does not prevent you from using guides in this circumstance.

Distribution features do not align shapes; they only coordinate an equal amount of space between specified areas. To align and distribute shapes, use both the Align Shapes and Distribute Shapes functions.

Arraying Shapes

Visio 2000 Technical includes the Array Shapes feature, a function not found in Visio 2000 Standard. Arraying shapes is a quick way to duplicate a shape into several rows and columns. For instance, you can design a floor of cubicles with this feature in just a few minutes (see Figure 19-15). Creating and aligning these seats can be a laborious affair, even with the Duplicate command. It's a piece of cake, though, with the Array Shapes feature.

The Array Shapes feature can array a variety of shapes, from trees for landscaping to seats for a company convention. In the following example, though, I'm going to use chairs, a useful shape for designing auditoriums. The following instructions will take you step-by-step through the arraying process:

1. Open the Office Layout template from Visio 2000 Technical.

2. Place the Chair shape in the drawing page. Use the Rotation Tool in order to rotate the shape so that a person sitting in it would be facing the top of the screen.

3. Select the shape and then choose Tools ➪ Array Shapes in order to pull up the Array Shapes dialog box (as shown in Figure 19-16).

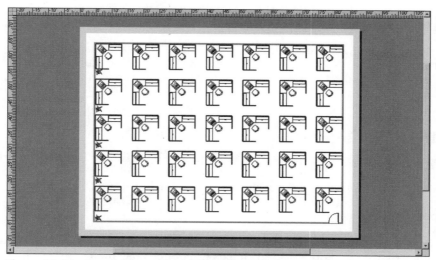

Figure 19-15: Use the Array Shapes function to lay out office cubicles.

4. In the Layout section, choose the number of columns and rows that you would like. You may also choose the amount of horizontal space that you would like either between shape centers or shape edges. Click the OK button when you're finished with the settings. This is how you begin laying out an auditorium, a useful feature for business conventions.

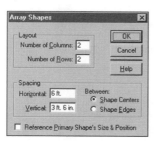

Figure 19-16: The Array Shapes dialog box

Check the box labeled "Reference Primary Shape's Size & Position" in order to use guides with the Array Shapes features. After selecting the OK button on the Array Shapes dialog box, a guide will run through the two outermost columns and rows. By moving a guide, you now can move, as well as distribute, an equal amount of space between the arrayed shapes. This is the process that was used to create the office cubicles in Figure 19-15.

Working with Other Shape-Coordination Tools

Besides alignment, distribution, and arrays, the Visio 2000 series offers other miscellaneous shape-coordination features. Many of these features can be found on Visio 2000 Standard. For example, users can update the alignment box and center drawings with little or no dragging of shapes.

Centering shapes

If you're looking for perfect page symmetry, then use the Center Drawing feature. As the name suggests, this command will center a selected shape, or shapes, in the drawing page. There's no dragging and no dialog boxes; just click the shape that you want to center and then choose Tools ⇨ Center Drawing. Presto! The shape is centered in the page.

You can, of course, center a group of shapes on a drawing page, even if they are not grouped. One or more selected shapes will not be placed on top of each other. Instead, Visio 2000 calculates the minimum sum width and minimum sum height of all the selected shapes, as well as the space between the shapes, and considers this the selected area. Therefore, the "selected" area — not the shapes — is centered on the drawing page (see Figure 19-17).

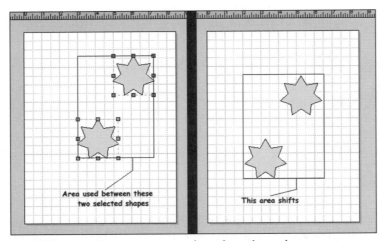

Figure 19-17: Visio 2000 centers the selected area between two selected shapes.

Updating the alignment box

The alignment box is composed of green dashes, which surround selected objects. If you do not see an alignment box highlighting your selections, then you have disabled the box. To activate it, go to the Behavior tab in the Behavior dialog box and check the box labeled "Show alignment box." Then click the OK button.

Sometimes alignment boxes become misaligned. This problem often occurs after resizing an instance or group of instances, or after adding or deleting shapes from a group.

In these cases, you can select an instance or group of shapes, and then choose Shape ⇨ Operations ⇨ Update Alignment Box in Visio 2000 Standard. You can access the feature in Visio 2000 Technical by selecting a shape and then choosing Tools ⇨ Update Alignment Box.

Cross-Reference　　See Chapter 24 for information on creating shape groups.

Summary

The applications covered in Chapter 19 will help you efficiently place shapes in balance with each other. Whether aligning or distributing instances, the features will come in handy throughout much of your business drawing career. Chapter 19 discussed the following points in detail:

✦ How to align shapes by using grids, rulers, and guides as markers.

✦ The Arrange to Shape function enables users to coordinate numerous geographic map shapes quickly and properly.

✦ The Arrange to Page function sizes geographic map shapes so that they will fit on the active drawing page.

✦ Visio 2000 offers six formats for automatically aligning shapes.

✦ Distributing space between shapes, their centers, or their edges by using rulers, grids, and guides.

✦ Visio 2000 offers eight formats for automatically distributing shapes.

✦ Upgrading Visio 2000 Standard to Visio 2000 Technical allows users to access the Array Shapes feature.

✦ How the Center Drawing function centers several instances on a drawing page.

✦ Using the Update Alignment Box function when adding or deleting shapes from a group.

You're on way to creating quality presentations. Chapter 20 instructs you on how to apply and use layers.

✦　　✦　　✦

Working with Layers

Everyone knows what layers are — or do they? Your junior high science class probably introduced you to the most popular notion. The teacher's lessons likely touched upon such things as sedimentary strata, various belts of ice and rock orbiting planets, and perhaps even a microscopic view of the enveloping rings that comprise an onion. Because of such common approaches, most people often think of layers strictly as overlapping objects. Visio layers, however, work differently. Unlike these examples, Visio 2000's layers have nothing to do with the overlapping positions of objects. Instead, Visio 2000's layers are tools used to categorize shapes by name and/or function. In short, Visio 2000's layers are employed solely as a means for organizing objects — not stacking shapes. If you're interested in overlapping objects, you'll need to take a look at Chapter 16.

Layers are an ordering principle within Visio 2000. The program allows users to create layers and then assign shapes to them. This feature comes in handy for several reasons. Primarily, people use layers when drawing maps and office layouts, diagrams whose dimensions will remain constant, although the locations of certain objects within those dimensions may change. For example, office workers may have the same size cubicle, but with Visio 2000 each employee can create different arrangements for his or her desk, file cabinet, plants, and so on. You can also use layers for data that may change within a flowchart or a CAD drawing. Layers especially make editing complex drawings easier because you can lock and highlight specific layers. You can even choose which layers to print, omitting those that you don't need. This chapter details how layers work within the basic editing process.

Note You can assign shapes, as well as objects such as guides and guide points, to layers.

Cross-Reference See Chapter 38 for information regarding CAD drawing layers.

Creating Layers

Well, it's time to get busy. You now know what layers are, so prepare to create a few. As with most of Visio 2000, the process is fairly simple and easy. The following steps are a straightforward approach to getting started:

1. Select View ➪ Layer Properties from the menu bar to access the Layer Properties dialog box.

2. Click the New button.

3. Type in a name for your layer within the New Layer dialog box (as shown in Figure 20-1). Once finished, click OK.

4. Click OK on the Layer Properties dialog box to finalize your selection.

Figure 20-1: The New Layer dialog box

Note Select the New button on the Layer dialog box to create a new layer, the All button to assign all of the available layers to selected shapes, and None to cancel all layer assignments for a selected shape.

The new layer can be ascribed to any shape on that drawing page. Unfortunately, you can only assign layers to the foreground or background pages that you have open. Layers can not be ascribed to more than one page at a time, even when working from the Drawing Explorer window.

Assigning shapes to layers

Two ways exist for assigning instances to layers. The primary difference lies in the order in which you establish the link. For example, you can first create the layer, add the shape, and then assign the instance to the layer. A quicker alternative enables you to first create the shape and then simultaneously add the layers and make the assignment. This chapter covers both methods.

If you've already created a layer with the method discussed in the "Creating Layers" section, your next step is to place a shape in the drawing page. Once you do that, you have four options for making the layer assignment:

✦ Select the shape and then the layer of your choice from the Layer box, which is located on the Format Shape toolbar. Simply click the arrow next to the box and then choose the layer.

✦ Select the shape and then choose Format ➪ Layer. Choose the appropriate layer from the Layer dialog box's left panel (as shown in Figure 20-2), or click the All button in order to assign all available layers to the shape. Click OK when finished.

✦ Right-click the shape and then choose Format ➪ Layer from the pop-up menu. This step retrieves the same Layer dialog box that you used in the previous option.

✦ Right-click your selected shape icon within the Drawing Explorer window to also access the Layer dialog box.

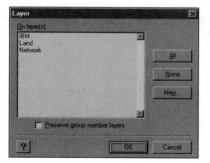

Figure 20-2: The left panel in the Layer dialog box reveals the layers currently available for that drawing page.

Of course, you can create a layer after you've created a shape. Simply select the shape and then choose Format ➪ Layer. You can also right-click the shape and then select Format ➪ Layer from the pop-up menu. Click the New button on the Layer dialog box. Type in the layer name in the New Layer dialog box. Click OK on the New Layer and Layer dialog boxes. Now the shape's new layer name is revealed in the Layer box, which is located on the Format Shape toolbar.

Note   Shapes drawn with stencils have predefined layers, while shapes drawn with the Standard drawing tools, such as the Rectangle Tool or Line Tool, are not assigned layers.

Chapter 15 contains more information on the Drawing Explorer window.

The Layer dialog box also contains the Preserve group member box. Checking this box allows shapes to maintain their individual layers when they are classified into a group layer. For example, you may create a company logo, placing it in a layer called "Clip Art." Next, you group the logo instance with other shapes, which happen to be on other layers. To avoid confusion, you label the group of shapes into a single layer. If the Preserve group member box is checked, all shapes within that group (including the company logo instance) will now be attached to two layers — the group layer and their previous layer. Without activating the Preserve group member box, all group shapes will belong to only one layer — the group layer.

Read Chapter 24 to learn more about creating shape groups.

Assigning masters to layers

To save time in assigning layers to instances, you may consider just assigning the master to a particular layer. This way all newly placed instances (those based on that particular master) will be assigned to the same layer as the shape's master.

Unless you've just created a new stencil, you will need to right-click the stencil title bar in order to alter the master's layer. Next, select Edit from the pop-up menu. Now you can reassign another layer to the master by following these steps:

1. Right-click the master icon whose layer you wish to edit and then select Edit Master from the pop-up menu.

2. Right-click the master within the Edit Master drawing window, selecting Format ⇨ Layer from the pop-up menu (see Figure 20-3).

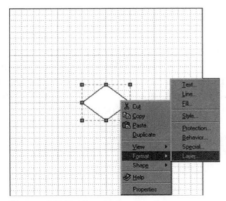

Figure 20-3: Preparing to change a master's layers

3. Click an appropriate button in the Layer dialog box (New, All, *or* None). or select the available layers in the left panel, depending on what you need.

4. Click the OK button on the Layer dialog box and then select Yes on the next dialog box in order to update the master. Now all future instances derived from that particular master will reflect the same layer changes.

Cross-Reference

See Chapter 15 for more information on editing stencil masters.

Selecting Multiple Layers

You can select multiple shapes by using the various techniques described in Chapter 18. Using the Select Special dialog box is the easiest way, though, to select shapes affiliated with one or more layers. Choose Edit ➪ Select Special to access the Select Special dialog box. Click the Layer radio button in the Selection By section. Next, highlight the layers that you want in the panel window, which is located to the right of the Layer radio button. Click OK. All objects belonging to the highlighted layers now are selected.

Adjusting Layer Properties

The Layer Properties dialog box (as shown in Figure 20-4) enables Visio 2000 users to manipulate various layer properties, including removing and renaming layers. Access the dialog box by selecting View ➪ Layer Properties. Notice that the dialog box contains nine buttons at the top of the viewing panel. These features and their corresponding properties are

✦ **Name**. Reveals the layer's name

✦ **#**. Lists number of shapes assigned to that particular layer

✦ **Visible**. Check to view all shapes assigned to that layer

✦ **Print**. Check to enable all shapes assigned to that layer to be printed

✦ **Active**. Check to incorporate additional nonlayered shapes to the chosen layer

✦ **Lock**. Check to prevent users from editing shapes assigned to certain layers

✦ **Snap**. Check to enable shapes on a layer to snap onto shapes of other layers

✦ **Glue**. Check to enable shapes of a layer to glue onto shapes of other layers

✦ **Color**. Check to highlight all shapes of a specific layer in one particular color

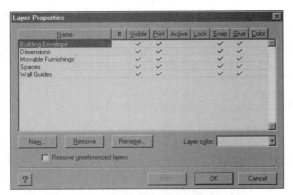

Figure 20-4: The Layer Properties dialog box

Note   By default, the Visible, Print, Snap, and Glue features are activated for all layers.

Clicking each of the buttons activates certain features. For instance, selecting the Name button enables you to rename the highlighted layer in the viewing panel. Clicking the # button reveals the number of shapes assigned to each listed layer. Selecting the other seven buttons activates the qualities described in the preceding list. You can also click the corresponding space below each button in order to place a check mark. Clicking the checkmark a second time deactivates the feature for the highlighted layer; however, clicking the buttons activates and deactivates that feature for all the listed layers. Next, click the Apply button to add the selected properties to the objects. You must click the OK button if no objects are selected.

Note   You can activate the Visible and Active features from within the Drawing Explorer window.

Two of the features, the Color and Active buttons, may require some clarification. The Color button, when activated, displays all object boundaries in the chosen color. The Layer Color box in the lower right-hand corner enables users to manipulate the color. You can choose additional colors from the box by selecting Custom. This gives users access to the Edit Color dialog box. Use the Color feature for redlining technical drawings or for taking a quick look at all objects categorized as a particular layer. For example, use color-coded shapes to analyze the latest changes to a flowchart.

The Active button functions somewhat differently. Activating a particular layer enables the program to automatically assign instances with no layers to the Active layer. For example, all shapes without designated layers that were drawn with Standard toolbar features, such as Ellipse Tool or Pencil Tool, will be assigned to the Active layer. Many shapes, such as those in the original Visio stencils, will not change because they already have preassigned layers.

Note Only so-called "No Layer" shapes that are drawn *after* placing a particular layer in Active mode are labeled with the activated layer.

Note You can view the following Layer properties from the ShapeSheet window: Visible, Print, Active, Lock, Snap, Glue, and Color.

Cross-Reference Chapter 34 includes detailed information on using ShapeSheets

Renaming layers

The Layer Properties dialog box offers two ways to rename a layer:

✦ Highlight the layer name that you want to change and then click the Name button.

✦ Highlight the layer name that you want to change and then click the Rename button.

Both actions result in calling forth the Rename Layer dialog box. Simply type in the new name and click the OK button in order to change the layer's name. Select OK on the Layer Properties dialog box to finalize the change.

Removing and deleting layers

Visio 2000 uses the terms "Delete" and "Remove" interchangeably. Both result in the same action — the removal of the selected layer and all related objects. The Remove button is located in the Layer Properties dialog box. Simply click the layer's name that you wish to delete and then click the Remove button. A small dialog box appears asking you if you're sure of your selection. Select Yes and then click the OK button in the Layer Properties dialog box.

Tip Check the Remove unreferenced layers box in order to delete layers within a drawing that do not have corresponding objects, such as shapes or guides.

You can also remove layers from the Drawing Explorer window. Right-click any of the components in the Layers folder, which is located in the Foreground and Background Pages folders. Select Delete Layer from the pop-up menu (as shown in Figure 20-5). The layer and all associated objects are instantly removed. That's all there is to it.

Figure 20-5: Removing layers with the Drawing Explorer

Summary

Layers, tools instrumental for organizing shapes, make editing complex flowcharts and office layouts more manageable. This chapter covered all basic aspects and techniques of Visio layers, including the following points:

✦ Layers are used to categorize objects; they have nothing do with stacking or positioning shapes.

✦ You can assign shapes to layers, as well as objects, such as guides and guide points.

✦ A layer can only be ascribed to one page at a time.

✦ The Drawing Explorer allows users to edit and delete layers from its window.

✦ You must use the Edit Master drawing window in order to assign masters to a layer.

✦ Some Layer Properties dialog box features prevent selected layers from being shown in the drawing window or from being printed.

✦ You can rename layers using either the Rename or Name buttons on the Layer Properties dialog box.

Chapter 21 discusses layout and routing functions. If you would like to read about some detailed examples of layers at work, check out Chapter 37.

✦   ✦   ✦

Using Layout and Routing Functions

Chapter 17 introduced the fundamentals of connectors, from a look at how dynamic glue works to a discussion of the three types of connection points. It also touched upon aspects of layout, such as line jumps and routing spacing. If you remember, I mentioned in Chapter 17 that these topics would merit a chapter of their own. Well, guess what? Here it is.

This chapter picks up where Chapter 17 left off, guiding you through numerous layout and routing techniques, especially those for automatic formatting. The information in this chapter will help you become an expert in connection efficiency and aesthetics. In fact, with the knowledge that you acquire in this chapter, you'll soon be creating organization diagrams with ever-so-tight organization and flowcharts that actually flow. So, what are you waiting for? Let's get connected.

Getting Connected

Visio connectors are key features for illustrating relationships. Without these one-dimensional shapes, many charts would lack the necessary linear logic for effective communication. Imagine trying to explain your company's manufacturing process with a bunch of jumbled pictures! Connectors bring order to the chaos. However, as you may have realized in Chapter 17, the connection process is rather diverse and can be at times, depending upon your approach, confusing.

Layout and routing is not rocket science, though. You have been working with connector placement and styles long before reading this paragraph. The "Using dynamic connectors," "Point-to-point connections," and "Shape-to-shape connections" sections will aptly prove this. Sure, you'll find a few new concepts, but for the most part, the material in these first few sections is old hat. That's why I believe these sections are a good starting point for getting "connected" to the layout and routing process.

Manually adjusting dynamic connectors and shapes

Before discussing the more complex aspects of layout and routing, I'm going to start with the fundamentals. In Visio 2000, only dynamic connectors can automatically reroute themselves and other shapes. These connectors, like other connectors, are used to create two types of shape connections: point-to-point, and shape-to-shape.

Thus far, the Visio 2000 Bible has discussed how to manually work with layout and routing techniques. For example, when you rotate a shape or drag it to a new position, you're changing its layout. The same can be said for rerouting a dynamic connector or connecting it to instances. These first sections, as I mentioned earlier, are a bit of a refresher course. I want to discuss simple shape adjustments and some basics of dynamic connectors. This information will lay the groundwork for the rest of the chapter.

Making simple shape adjustments

Visio 2000 offers many methods for manipulating shapes. In fact, much of this book pertains to that very subject. However, simple shape adjustments are the only thing necessary for much of your manual layout and routing needs. Just remember these three methods — if they're not already ingrained on your brain:

✦ Reposition a shape by dragging a shape from its center, generally where no handles are located.

✦ Extend a shape's height or width by dragging the appropriate midpoint handle.

✦ Resize a shape by dragging one of the instance's corner handles.

Using dynamic connectors

Dynamic connectors are an important part of the layout and routing process. How do you know if you're working with a dynamic connector? All connectors drawn with the Connector Tool and the Connect Shapes command are considered dynamic connectors. The Dynamic Connector shape, found on various stencils, is also one. Dynamic connectors are used for rerouting purposes and for creating placeable shapes, instances that automatically reposition themselves when they come into contact with other shapes and connectors. (To learn more about how dynamic connectors and placeable shapes interact, see the "Selecting a placement behavior format" section.)

Note

Visio 2000 automatically repositions placeable shapes when they cross paths with connectors and other shapes. A placeable shape must be linked to a dynamic connector.

Most people reroute dynamic connectors by selecting one of the connector's handles and then dragging the connector to where they want it. However, Visio 2000 offers several other methods. Table 21-1 briefly explains various ways to format dynamic connectors and their components. However, you won't have to worry about these methods when using automatic layout and rerouting.

Table 21-1
Formats for Positioning Dynamic Connectors and Their Components

Format	Method
Repositioning a connector from two instances to two other shapes	Drag the connector at any point other than its endpoints, vertices, and midpoints.
Repositioning a connector while maintaining the exact angles of the connector line segments and the two instances between the line segments.	Drag the connector's midpoint.
Extending a connector's length	Drag the connector's endpoint.
Adding a bridge to a connector	Hold down the <Shift> key while dragging the connector's midpoint.
Adding a vertex to a connector	Hold down the <Control> key while dragging the connector's midpoint.
Adjusting a vertex's position	Hold down the <Control> key while dragging the connector's vertex.
Adjusting a vertex's position without affecting the exact angles of the connector line segments	Drag the connector's vertex.

Point-to-point connections

You're probably already familiar with point-to-point connections, even if you are oblivious to the term. Point-to-point connections use static glue. Why do we call it "static"? Because the place where each connector's beginning and ending points "glue" to a shapes' connection points remains fixed. Therefore, no matter where you move the two connected shapes, the connector stays attached to the same points. However, static glue does not enable shapes and connectors to switch their original connection points.

Note

Remember that a dynamic connector can be used with both static and dynamic glue.

The following example demonstrates how static glue and point-to-point connections work:

1. Open the Basic Shapes stencil. One way to do this is by selecting File ➪ Stencil ➪ Block Diagram ➪ Basic Shapes.

2. Drag two Ellipses onto the drawing page, placing them horizontally adjacent to each other.

3. Select the Connector Tool and then draw a connector between the two shapes.

4. Click the Pointer Tool to stretch the connector to a connection point on each ellipse, as shown in the left drawing of Figure 21-1. Notice the red blocks that appear on the ends of the connector; these indicate that a point-to-point connection has been created.

5. Drag one of the ellipses anywhere on the drawing page. Notice that the connector may zigzag some, but it stays glued to the two shapes' same connection points, as the right drawing in Figure 21-1 shows.

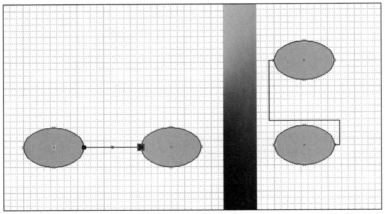

Figure 21-1: Static glue forces the connected points to remain the same, no matter where you move the two connected shapes.

The same "point-to-point" contact remains "static" in these instances. Not even super glue has this kind of binding power! The method, however, is rarely used because of the extensive connector lengths and zigzags that can form when moving connected shapes. You'll know when the method is right. If your page is cluttered with long, squirrelly connectors, then the point-to-point technique is not the option to implement.

Tip

Break any connection by dragging the connector's endpoint away from the shape's connection point.

Shape-to-shape connections

Whereas point-to-point connections use static glue, shape-to-shape connections require dynamic glue. This feature makes quite a difference in the layout and routing of shapes. In a word, shape-to-shape connections are more . . . dynamic. Two shapes utilizing this feature do not keep the same point of connection when moved. In fact, the connector tries to find the shortest distance between the two connected shapes' connection points! This is a far cry from the long, zigzagging connectors that can develop when using the point-to-point method.

See how these "smart" connectors complement Visio's patented SmartShapes, the customized masters found in Visio's stencils. The following exercise illustrates how shape-to-shape connections work:

1. If you've already closed the Basic Shapes stencil, reopen it.

2. Drag two Ellipses from the stencil onto the drawing page.

3. Select the Connector Tool button and then draw a connector between the two shapes. Drag the connector slightly toward each shape's center connection point — but do not connect it there (see the left drawing in Figure 21-2). Notice the two red squares that momentarily pop up around each shape; this indicates that a shape-to-shape connection has just been made.

4. Drag one of the shapes anywhere on the drawing page. Although the connector always remains connected to the two shapes, it attaches to them at different connection points (see the right-hand drawing in Figure 21-2).

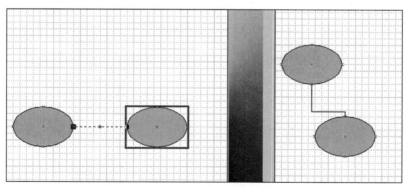

Figure 21-2: The shape-to-shape method enables a connector to choose the shortest path between two shapes.

Tip

You can also connect shapes by selecting both shapes and then choosing Tools ➪ Connect Shapes.

Cross-Reference

To learn more about dynamic glue and connectors, see Chapter 17.

Shape-to-shape connections are popular because they rarely crowd the drawing page, as their point-to-point counterparts can. The key to creating a shape-to-shape connection is to drag the connector to the middle of the shape, either on the center connection point or near it. If you move the connector onto the center connection point, the connector will connect at this point. However — as the example above indicates — if you just slightly move the connector toward the center of the shape, a shape-to-shape connection will develop on one of the shape's outer connection points instead of on the center connection point.

Layout and Routing Basics

In essence, the layout and routing process is the arrangement of shapes in conjunction with dynamic connectors. Both point-to-point and shape-to-shape connection techniques demonstrate the most basic aspects of this process. Ultimately, though, you'll want to find the most aesthetic and efficient manner for using these two connection methods and for using the various shape placements. This is when Visio 2000's automatic layout and routing methods come in handy. By simply clicking a button or filling in data within a dialog box, numerous shapes and connectors will automatically respond to your commands — without using a mouse to individually manipulate each figure.

The Layout & Routing Toolbar

When working with connectors, access the Layout & Routing Toolbar for additional support. Simply right-click anywhere on the right side of the Visio Drawing window's menu bar, and then select Layout & Routing from the pop-up menu. You can also access the Layout & Routing Toolbar by choosing View ➪ Toolbars ➪ Layout & Routing. The Layout & Routing Toolbar contains nine features, as shown in Figure 21-3. Many other dialog boxes have these features, as well.

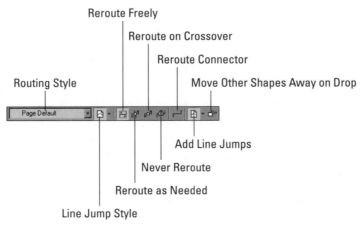

Figure 21-3: The Layout & Routing Toolbar

Following is a list of the nine features and their functions:

✦ **Routing Style box**. Lists available routing styles that you can choose

✦ **Line Jump Style**. Lists available line jump styles that you can choose

✦ **Reroute Freely**. Enables you to reroute connectors anytime and anywhere

✦ **Reroute as Needed**. Enables you to reroute connectors when they are crossing other connectors or shapes

✦ **Reroute on Crossover**. Enables you to reroute only two crossing connectors

✦ **Never Reroute**. Never allows you to reroute connectors

✦ **Reroute Connector**. Allows you to reroute connectors

✦ **Add Line Jumps To**. Enables you to add line jumps to specific types of lines

✦ **Move Other Shapes Away on Drop**. Automatically forces placeable shapes to move when another placeable shape is inserted into a drawing

Applicable sections concerning each feature are covered throughout this chapter. For example, if you are interested in more details about rerouting options, see the section "Rerouting connectors automatically." In general, remember that Layout & Routing Toolbar buttons are shortcuts for the same functions in various Visio 2000 dialog boxes.

Layout and Routing dialog boxes

Of course, Visio 2000 users have more connector-related options at their disposal than those provided on the Layout & Routing Toolbar. Four dialog boxes, presented in Table 21-2, contain applications and settings for connectors and their interactions with shapes. Notice that you can access the fourth dialog box via two methods, as well as from two locations: the Layout and Routing tab on the Page Setup dialog box, and the Layout Shapes dialog box. Just press the Spacing button on either of the dialog boxes in order to reach the Layout and Routing Spacing dialog box. Accessing the other three dialog boxes is fairly self-explanatory.

Table 21-2
Layout- and Routing-Related Dialog Boxes

Dialog Box	*Access Path*
Page Setup (Layout and Routing tab)	File ➪ Page Setup
Behavior (Connector tab, Placement tab)	Format ➪ Behavior
Layout Shapes	Tools ➪ Layout Shapes
Layout And Routing Spacing	Tools ➪ Layout Shapes
	File ➪ Page Setup

I discuss various aspects of each dialog box throughout the rest of the chapter. However, because of the overlapping nature of their features, the functions discussed in each section often are not exclusive to the dialog box that is under explanation.

Placing Connectors for Layout and Routing

Shapes and connectors are critical for all layout and routing procedures. They are the yin and yang of Visio 2000, if you will. In fact, without them drawing would be impossible. This section will first detail several ways to manipulate connectors, from routing styles and directions to overlapping and line jumps. Next, this section will discuss shape layout. But first, it's time to learn how to speak the language of linear logic.

Modifying routing styles

Visio 2000 offers numerous styles for your connectors. For example, you can use connectors that branch in right angles, slant, or simply appear straight. The connector styles can be manipulated from several dialog boxes, including the Route Style box on the Layout & Routing Toolbar. Just select the connector whose style you wish to modify. Next, click the down-pointing arrow next to the box. A drop-down menu appears, which contains the following styles:

Page Default	Tree
Right Angle	Organization Chart
Straight	Simple
Center-to-Center	Simple Horizontal-Vertical
Flowchart	Simple Vertical-Horizontal

Notice that some of the styles that appear from the Route Style box have blue arrows next to them. (I'll explain the significance these arrows in the "Applying routing directions" section.) Notice, also, that the Layout Shapes dialog box, the Connector tab on the Behavior dialog box, and the Layout and Routing tab on the Page Setup dialog box all contain preview screens in which you can view each style's appearance before implementing that style on the drawing page. Use the Style box in any of these dialog boxes. The style boxes, though, are located within different sections of each dialog box. See Table 21-3 for the exact locations.

Choose the style you like in the same manner as you would from the Route Style box, which is accessed from the Layout & Routing Toolbar. Just click the down-pointing arrow at the end of each box in order to scroll through your choices. The

Style you choose in the Page Setup dialog box will become your default style. The Layout Shapes dialog box, however, gives you the option to apply the new setting to only your selection or to the whole page.

Table 21-3 Routing Style Box Locations	
Dialog Box	**Location of Routing Style Box**
Page Setup (Layout and Routing tab)	Routing section
Behavior (Connector tab)	Line Routing section
Layout Shapes	Connectors section

Tip

To change the connector style to all of the connectors on a drawing page, select the new style from the Layout Shapes dialog box. Next, apply the new setting to the whole page by checking the Whole Page box, which is located in the upper right-hand corner of the dialog box. Finalize your decision by clicking the Apply button.

Applying routing directions

Remember the blue arrows you saw with some of the styles in the Route Style box of the Layout & Routing Toolbar? These indicate the connector direction for those particular styles. Not all styles have routing direction options, though. In fact, the following directions are available only for Flowchart, Tree, Organization Chart, and Simple styles:

Top to Bottom	Left to Right
Bottom to Top	Right to Left

You can also manipulate connector directions from the same dialog boxes that you used for modifying routing styles. The Direction boxes are even located in the same sections as are the routing boxes; Table 21-4 lists the locations. Notice that you cannot adjust the Direction box until an applicable style is called up in the Style box. After an applicable style is retrieved, you can scroll through four options. For example, try selecting the Bottom to Top direction for the Tree style. Using this format should result in a drawing similar to Figure 21-4.

Other factors, such as the style of shape placement, can affect routing directions as well. This will be covered in the "Placing Shapes for Layout and Routing" section.

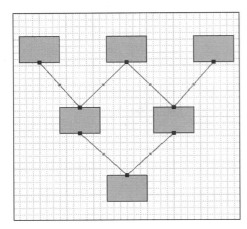

Figure 21-4: Combining a Bottom to Top direction with the Tree style

Table 21-4
Routing Direction Box Locations

Dialog Box	Location of Routing Direction Box
Page Setup (Layout and Routing tab)	Routing section
Behavior (Connector tab)	Line Routing section
Layout Shapes	Connectors section

Separating and overlapping routes

When working with a multitude of shapes and connectors, your drawing page can become cluttered and, sometimes, even confusing. Separating or overlapping certain connectors can help you avoid these problems.

You can automatically separate and overlap connector routes only from the Page Setup dialog box's Layout and Routing tab (as shown in Figure 21-5). Access the Page Setup dialog box by selecting File ➪ Page Setup and then clicking the Layout and Routing tab. The Separate and Overlap boxes are located in the upper right-hand corner of the dialog box, under the Routing section. If you click the arrows in the box, you'll notice each feature has four options, and each option indicates how connectors can be separated or overlapped.

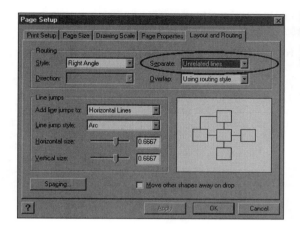

Figure 21-5: Select an option from the Separate box. You can only access this feature from the Page Setup dialog box.

The Specifications drop-down box offers the following four separating choices:

✦ **Unrelated Lines.** Separates lines that correspond to different shapes

✦ **All Lines.** Separates all lines, even those that correspond to the same shapes

✦ **No Lines.** Separates no lines whatsoever

✦ **Using Routing Style.** Separates routes as defined by the current or predefined connector style.

The Overlapping Specification list offers the following four options:

✦ **Related Lines.** Overlaps lines that correspond to the same shapes

✦ **All Lines**. Overlaps all lines, even those that do not correspond to the same shapes

✦ **No Lines**. Overlaps no lines whatsoever

✦ **Using Routing Style**. Overlaps routes as defined by the current or predefined connector style

Working with related lines

A few exercises will demonstrate differences between separating and overlapping connectors. For instance, the following steps contrast presentations between separating and overlapping all lines:

1. Open the Basic Shapes stencil, placing three Circles onto the drawing page (see Figure 21-6).

2. Select File ➪ Page Setup and click the Layout and Routing tab of the Page Setup dialog box.

3. Choose Related Lines from the Overlap box and No Lines from the Separate box. Click the Apply button and then the OK button.

4. Using the Connector button, place connectors from the left and middle circles' top connection point to the right circle's bottom connection point. Again, see Figure 21-6. The connectors should overlap.

Note For all of these routing, use the default Style designation (Right Angle) to end up with the same results as shown in the Figures.

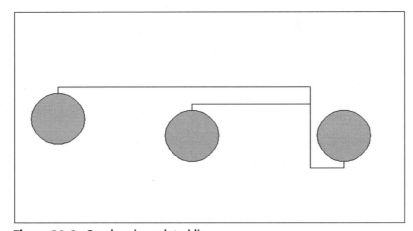

Figure 21-6: Overlapping related lines

5. Press the Undo button twice to remove the connectors.

6. Go to the Layout and Routing tab on the Page Setup dialog box once again. This time choose All Lines from the Separate box and No Lines from the Overlap box.

7. Using the Connector button, place connectors in the same manner as you did in Step 4. This time the connectors should be separated, except at the right circle's connection point. Compare Figure 21-7 with Figure 21-6.

Figures 21-6 and 21-7 demonstrate the same linear logic; in both cases, the left and middle circles are linked to the right circle using a point-to-point connection. The difference lies in presentation.

Working with unrelated lines

Whereas the preceding exercise applied to related lines, the next exercise demonstrates how to modify drawings with unrelated lines, in this case, two connectors that link two different shapes:

1. Open a new drawing page. Using the Basic Shapes stencil, place four circles on the drawing page, as shown in Figure 21-8.

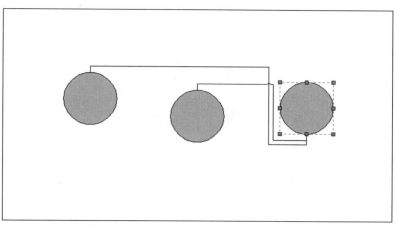

Figure 21-7: Separating all lines

2. Select File ⇨ Page Setup. Click the Layout and Routing tab of the Page Setup dialog box.

3. Choose Unrelated Lines from the Separate box and All Lines from the Overlap box. Click the Apply button and then the OK button.

4. Connect the top-left circle's right connection point with the bottom-left circle's right connection point. Connect the top-right circle's left connection point with the bottom-right circle's left connection point. As shown in Figure 21-8, the two connectors do not overlap.

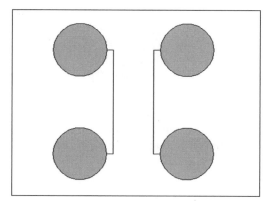

Figure 21-8: Separating unrelated lines

5. Press the Undo button twice to remove the connectors.

6. Go back to the Layout and Routing tab on the Page Setup dialog box.

7. Choose All Lines from the Overlap box and No Lines from the Separate box. Click the Apply button and then the OK button.

8. Use the Connector to draw the same connectors as you did in Step 4. The two unrelated connectors should now be overlapping, as shown in Figure 21-9.

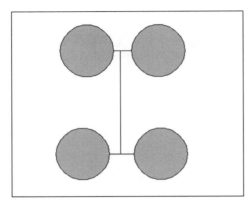

Figure 21-9: Overlapping unrelated lines

Overlapping or separating related lines does not affect a presentation's linear logic; however, overlapping unrelated lines drastically changes the linear logic of a presentation. Whereas Figure 21-8 shows two unrelated sets of shapes, Figure 21-9 has four interrelated shapes. The unrelated lines, when overlapped, become related.

Using line jumps

Sometimes, despite using the Separate feature, you have to deal with crisscrossing connectors. To avoid getting your lines crossed — literally — use line jumps. A line jump bows one of the crossing lines (as shown below in Figure 21-10), indicating that the two connectors are unconnected.

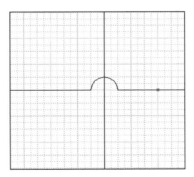

Figure 21-10: Line Jumps prevent unrelated connectors from appearing linked.

Adding line jumps

Visio 2000, by default, adds line jumps to horizontal crisscrossing connectors. However, you can choose not to add line jumps to connectors. Two dialog boxes enable you to control line jumps. The Connector tab on the Behavior dialog box allows users to decide if and when to add line jumps. The Layout and Routing tab on the Page Setup dialog box allows users to decide both when and to which connectors to add line jumps.

You can also choose how you would like to add line jumps from the Layout & Routing Toolbar. Click the small arrow next to the Add Line Jumps To button. Notice that a drop-down menu appears offering six options (see Figure 21-11). These same options can be found in the Page Setup dialog box's Layout and Routing tab on the Add Line Jumps To box. Following are the six options and their functions:

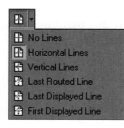

Figure 21-11: Select an option from the Add Line Jumps To button.

✦ **None.** No line jumps are added

✦ **Horizontal Lines.** Adds line jumps only to horizontal connectors that cross another connector's path

✦ **Vertical Lines.** Adds line jumps only to vertical connectors that cross another connector's path

✦ **Last Routed Line.** Adds line jumps to the most recently placed or edited connector within a crossing pattern

✦ **Last Displayed Line.** Adds line jumps to the most recently placed connector within a crossing pattern

✦ **First Displayed Line.** Adds line jumps to the first connector placed within a crossing pattern or on the connector

Note

Some lines are not 100 percent vertical or horizontal. A good example of this is a top-down diagram using tree-style connectors. In these cases, depending upon your selection, a line jump is added to the most vertical- or horizontal-oriented connector.

The Connector tab on the Behavior dialog box also enables users to control how line jumps are added. It offers five options that are somewhat different from the six options available from the Add Line Jumps To button. The following steps will access the five options:

1. Select the connector or connectors that you want to format.
2. Choose Format ➪ Behavior. Click the Behavior dialog box's Connector tab.
3. In the Line Jumps section, select an option from the Add box.
4. Click the OK button.

Following is a list of the five options and their functions:

✦ **As Page Specifies**. Adds line jumps according to the template's or program's default settings
✦ **Never**. Never adds line jumps to connectors
✦ **Always**. Always adds line jumps to connectors
✦ **Always to Other.** Always adds line jumps to the connector that intersects the selected connector
✦ **To Neither**. Does not add line jumps to the selected connector or to the connector that intersects the selected connector

Applying line jump styles

You can apply line jump styles from one of three different locations:

✦ The Line Jump button in the Layout & Routing Toolbar
✦ The Connector tab in the Behavior dialog box
✦ The Layout and Routing tab in the Page Setup dialog box

Simply select the connector to which you want to apply a line jump and then go to one of these locations. For example, click the down-pointing arrow next to the Line Jump button. Notice that ten line jump styles are available (see Figure 21-12). Just click the one that you wish to apply. You can also select these options from the dialog-box areas displayed in Table 21-5.

Figure 21-12: The available line jump styles

Tip

Default-size line jumps are difficult to see. I recommend viewing a drawing page from at least 100 percent magnification in order to see the changes you've made.

Table 21-5
Dialog Box Locations for Adjusting Line Jump Style

Dialog Box	Section	Edit Box
Page Setup (Layout and Routing tab)	Line Jumps section	Line Jump Style
Behavior (Connector tab)	Line Jumps section	Style

Modifying line jump sizes

To modify line jump sizes, go to the Line Jumps section in the Page Setup dialog box. Select File ➪ Page Setup in order to access the dialog box. Next, click the Layout and Routing tab. You can adjust horizontal and vertical line jumps from their respective controls (Horizontal Size and Vertical Size). Drag the arrow buttons on each control to the size you desire; sizes are listed in the edit box to the right of the buttons. You can also simply type in the size you want in the edit box. To apply the newly adjusted size, click the OK or Apply buttons.

Note

You can only size a line jump from 0 to 1 with the arrow buttons. However, the dialog buttons allow you to enter sizes up to 10.

Default horizontal and vertical line jump settings are 0.6667. Notice that the chosen line jump size corresponds to the fine grid spacing when it is viewed at 100 percent. This may be somewhat difficult to see with the default settings, so for now insert a horizontal line jump setting of **10**. At these settings, the horizontal line jump size spans ten grid-blocks (see Figure 21-13). Five of the blocks are to the left of the vertical connector and the other five are to its right. Notice that the height of a line jump is half of the line jump size. Thus, a horizontal line jump of ten, spans ten grid-blocks with a height apex of five.

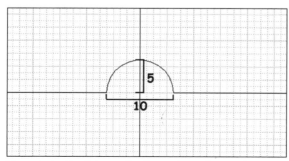

Figure 21-13: A large, horizontal line jump size

Note Line jump size changes are applied to all connectors on that page, regardless of whether the connectors are selected or not.

Rerouting connectors automatically

Rerouting involves "editing" a connector in such a manner as to have it form a path around other shapes. Rerouting helps prevent crossing instances and lines. Access the rerouting feature by selecting Format ⇨ Behavior. Next, select the Connector tab on the Behavior dialog box. In the Line Routing section, choose the rerouting format inside the Reroute edit box. Visio 2000 offers users the following four formats for rerouting connectors:

✦ **Freely.** Allows you to reroute connectors anywhere and anytime

✦ **As Needed.** Allows you to reroute connectors when they are crossing other connectors or shapes

✦ **On Cross-Over.** Allows you to reroute two crossing connectors

✦ **Never.** Never allows you to reroute a connector

Always remember that rerouting connectors and placing connectors are not the same processes. For instance, the rerouting feature enables users to place connectors anywhere, regardless of rerouting style. Rerouting concerns how you "bend" a connector, not where you manually place it. For example, draw a right-angle style dynamic connector that can be rerouted with the Freely format. Notice that you can drag part of the line (by one of its endpoints) so that it forms a right angle in the opposite direction from which the previous one appears (as shown in Figure 21-14). However, drawing a right-angle styled connector with the Never format is not possible. Although you can move the line as a whole, you cannot reroute part of the line so that it forms a right angle in the opposite direction from which it first appeared. Trying to do so changes the right-angle line into a straight line. These formats strictly affect rerouting connectors, not their placement.

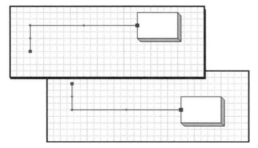

Figure 21-14: Rerouting a connector

Placing Shapes for Layout and Routing Purposes

Visio 2000 offers several layout and routing functions that provide ways to set placement behavior formats and placement styles, as well as to set several shapes' directions and patterns. This section will detail how to get the look you want in a lot less time by using these layout and routing functions.

Modifying placement behaviors

Placement behaviors refer to what Visio 2000 calls placeable shapes. Placeable shapes "force" dynamic connectors to route around them. Therefore, dynamic connectors do not cross placeable shapes. The Placement tab on the Behavior dialog box enables users to manipulate placeable features. Simply choose Format ⇨ Behavior in order to access the Behavior dialog box.

Selecting a placement-behavior format

To try selecting a placement-behavior format, draw two shapes and attach a separate dynamic connector to each. After selecting the shapes, you can choose which placement behavior format you'd like to apply. Pull up the Behavior dialog box and then select the Placement tab. A box labeled Placement Behavior is located at the top of this area. Click the adjacent arrow button to view the following three formats:

✦ **Lay Out and Route Around.** Dynamic connectors route around shapes

✦ **Do Not Lay Out and Route Around**. Dynamic connectors route through shapes

✦ **Let Visio Decide.** Dynamic connectors that are attached to other shapes will not route through shapes attached to dynamic connector

Note The Lay Out and Route Around function transforms instances into placeable shapes.

To see how each function works, complete the following exercise:

1. Choose Lay Out and Route Around, and then click the OK button.

2. Drag one of the open connector endpoints toward the other shape, as shown in Figure 21-15. Notice that the connector routes around the shape.

3. Now highlight both of the shapes again. Go back to the Placement tab on the Behavior dialog box. Choose Do Not Lay Out and Route Around, and then click the OK button.

4. Drag one of the open connector endpoints toward one of the shapes, as shown in Figure 21-16. Notice that the connector crosses over the shapes instead of routing around them.

5. Highlight both of the shapes once more. Go back to the Behavior dialog box. Select Let Visio Decide, and then click OK.

6. Drag one of the open connector endpoints toward a shape. Since both shapes are attached to a dynamic connector, the connector you're dragging should route around the shape. If you delete one of the shapes and then drag the connector toward the remaining shape, the connector will intersect the shape.

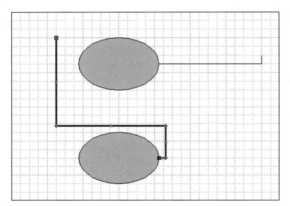

Figure 21-15: Using the Lay Out and Route Around format

Note   The Lay Out and Route Around format is the only one of the three placement-behavior formats that provides access to the rest of the Placement tab's features.

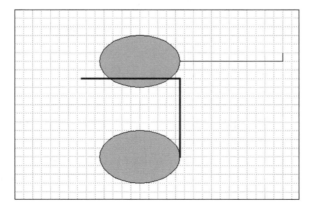

Figure 21-16: Using the Do Not Lay Out and Route Around format

Working with more lay out and route-around features

Selecting the Lay Out and Route format enables users to manipulate more features. For instance, you can manipulate features within three of the Placement tab's sections: Placement, Move Shapes on Drop, and Interaction with Connectors. Table 21-6 explains how each section works.

Table 21-6
Lay Out and Route Around Features

Placement Features	Function
Do Not Move During Placement	Using the Lay Out Shapes dialog box will not move the selected shape.
Allow Other Shapes to be Placed on Top	Enables Visio 2000 to place other shapes on top of selected shapes when the Lay Out Shapes dialog box is in use.
Move Shapes on Drop Features	**Function**
Move Other Shapes Away on Drop	Forces selected shapes to move when a placeable shape is inserted into a drawing.
Do Not Allow Other Shapes to Move This Shape Away on Drop	Does not force selected shapes to move when a placeable shape is inserted into a drawing.
Interaction with Connector Features	**Function**
Route Through Horizontally	Allows horizontal connectors to intersect with selected shapes.
Route Through Vertically	Allows vertical connectors to intersect with selected shapes.

New Feature Many of Visio 2000's placement features are new and cannot be found in Visio 5.0. In fact, Visio 2000's Behavior dialog box contains numerous additional options.

Many of these functions are self-explanatory. The Move Other Shapes Away on Drop feature is slightly more sophisticated than the other functions. It contains the following three options:

Plow as Page Specifies

Plow No Shapes

Plow Every Shape

The Plow as Page Specifies option forces selected shapes to move when a placeable shape is dropped in their way. The Plow No Shapes option also forces connectors attached to selected shapes to move when a placeable shape is placed in their paths. The Plow Every Shape option forces the selected shapes and their connectors to move when a placeable shape is dropped within their paths.

All of the features listed in Table 21-6 are used in conjunction with the Lay Out and Around format. Placement features allow you to "anchor" selected shapes onto the drawing page or to stack other shapes upon them. Move Shapes on Drop features enable you to quickly place shapes onto the page without wasting time moving or reformatting shapes. Interaction with Connector features allow users to route connectors through certain shapes. These options make the Lay Out and Around format more diverse and sophisticated.

Using automatic shape-connector placements

You can manipulate shape-connector placements from the Placement section in the Lay Out Shapes dialog box (shown in Figure 21-17). To access the feature, select Tools ⇨ Lay Out Shapes. The Placement section of the Lay Out Shapes dialog box contains three boxes: Style, Direction, and Depth. These features are discussed in the following sections.

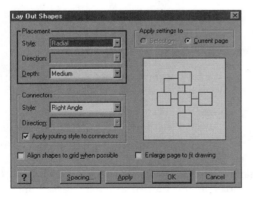

Figure 21-17: Adjust shape-connector placements from the Lay Out Shapes dialog box.

Applying various placement styles

Visio 2000 offers three different placement styles: Radial, Flowchart/Tree, and Circular (see Figure 21-18). These formats affect the overall arrangement of shapes on a drawing page. To implement a style, just select one from the Style box and then click the OK button. All shapes on the drawing page will be arranged in the selected style's format.

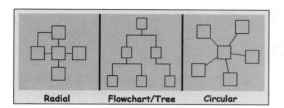

Figure 21-18: The Radial, Flowchart/Tree, and Circular placement styles

Note

Before implementing a placement style, you can view how each style will affect your drawing from the Lay Out Shapes dialog box's preview window.

Adjusting an arrangement's direction

The Flowchart/Tree placement style is the only one of the three styles that enables users to manipulate the overall direction of a group of shapes. Groups can be arranged as Top to Bottom, Bottom to Top, Left to Right, or Right to Left (see Figure 21-19). Use the preview window in order to view each arrangement. Once you're satisfied with your selection, click the OK button.

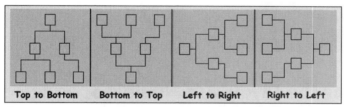

Figure 21-19: Four arrangements for the Flowchart/Tree style

Adjusting an arrangement's depth

The Depth option adjusts the amount of space between an arrangement of shapes. This feature comes in handy when working with a large arrangement of shapes, particularly when several shapes extend beyond the boundaries of a drawing page. Shallow is the least effective of the options, although it maintains the closest representation of the placement style format. Deep, by far, eliminates more extra space between the shapes — at the cost of a more aesthetically pleasing arrangement. However, it is usually required when having to squeeze several shapes onto a drawing page. The Medium setting, as you can guess, eliminates extra space better than the Shallow setting but not as well as the Deep setting. After choosing a depth, simply click the OK button in order to implement a depth format.

Note

Don't forget that you can also improve layout placement by checking two of the boxes in the Lay Out Shapes dialog box: Align Shapes to Grid When Possible and Enlarge Page to Fit Drawing.

Setting Layout and Routing Spacing Specifications

The Layout and Routing Spacing dialog box (shown in Figure 21-20) is the only place within Visio 2000 where users can adjust layout and routing spacing. The dialog box enables you to change such things as connector-to-connector spacing and connector-to-shape spacing. You can reach the Layout and Routing Spacing dialog box from only two other dialog boxes: the Layout Shapes dialog box, and the Layout and Routing tab on the Page Setup dialog box. In both cases, you must click the Spacing button at the bottom left-hand corner of either dialog box. This action pulls up the Layout and Routing Spacing dialog box.

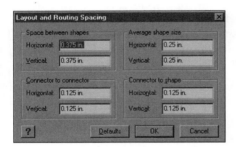

Figure 21-20: The Layout and Routing Spacing dialog box with its default settings

Understanding the Layout and Routing Spacing dialog box

The Layout and Routing Spacing dialog box contains the following four sections, each of which controls how shapes and connectors are placed upon a drawing page:

✦ **Average shape size.** Located in the top right-hand corner of the Layout and Routing Spacing dialog box. It quickly defines the average size of placeable shapes.

✦ **Space between shapes.** Located in the top left-hand corner of the dialog box. It enables users to adjust settings for the amount of horizontal and vertical space between two placeable shapes.

✦ **Connector to shape.** Located in the bottom right-hand corner of the Layout and Routing Spacing dialog box. It can adjust both horizontal and vertical distances between a connector and shape. Use connector-to-shape spacing to set the minimum distance desired between connectors and shapes.

✦ **Connector to connector.** Located in the bottom left-hand corner of the Layout and Routing Spacing dialog box. It sets, depending on other settings, the smallest possible amount of space allowed between connector points. You can adjust the distance a connector spans horizontally and vertically.

Coordinating spacing sizes

Try to coordinate *all* figures in the Layout and Routing Spacing dialog box for maximum effect. Use Table 21-7 for assistance. Generally speaking, every change in a particular spacing format's orientation size should be reflected in other spacing formats for that same orientation. For instance, if you're defining a horizontal "Average shape size" of 0.5 inches, then this change should correspond accordingly in the other horizontal spacing formats. The "Space between shapes" should, therefore, be 1.5×0.5 inches. The "Connector to connector" and "Connector to shape" formats should be 0.5×0.5 inches. Table 21-7 depicts the "Average shape size" variable as *a* or *b*, depending on the orientation.

Table 21-7 Coordinating Layout and Routing Spacing Sizes		
Spacing Format	*Horizontal Orientation*	*Vertical Orientation*
Average shape size	a	b
Space between shapes	$1.5 \times a$	$1.5 \times b$
Connector to connector	$0.5 \times a$	$0.5 \times b$
Connector to shape	$0.5 \times a$	$0.5 \times b$

Although coordination is usually necessary, remember that you need not change one orientation's sizes just because you modified the size of the other orientation. For clarification, the exercise below illustrates how you can effectively coordinate your spacing sizes:

1. Drop two Squares from the Basic Shapes stencil onto the drawing page. Link dynamic connectors between the instances. For maximum effect, place the instances wide apart.

2. Select Tools ⇨ Lay Out Shapes. Click the Spacing button on the Lay Out Shapes dialog box.

3. Look for the "Average shape size" section in the Layout and Routing Spacing dialog box. Type **0.5** in the Horizontal box. Type **0.75** in the Horizontal box of the "Space between shape" section. Type **0.25** in the "Connector to connector" and "Connector to shapes" Horizontal boxes. Leave the default settings in all of the Vertical boxes.

4. Click OK on the Layout and Routing Spacing dialog box. Next, click the Apply and OK buttons in the Lay Out Shapes dialog box. Notice that the connectors have been shortened so that the Squares fit horizontally on the drawing page (as shown in Figure 21-21). All spacing should correspond roughly to your settings.

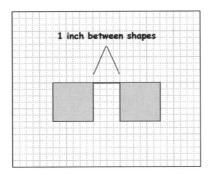

Figure 21-21: Using the horizontal Layout and Routing Spacing features

Summary

Chapter 21 covered a great deal of information about the layout and routing process. We'll put some of this knowledge to further use in Chapter 39. By then, you will be a Visio 2000 guru. But until that time, you might want to review the following points from Chapter 21:

✦ Placeable shapes are instances that automatically reposition themselves when they come into contact with other shapes and connectors.

✦ Point-to-point connections use static glue to attach two shapes to a connector.

✦ Shape-to-shape connections use dynamic glue to attach two shapes to a connector.

✦ The Layout & Routing Toolbar has nine useful functions.

✦ Four dialog boxes enable you to make layout and routing changes.

✦ Routing direction options are only available for Flowchart, Tree, Organization Chart, and Simple routing styles.

✦ Overlapping two unrelated lines creates a related connection.

✦ Use line jumps to avoid confusion with crisscrossing connectors.

✦ You can modify various line jump formats, including size and style.

✦ Rerouting connectors and placing connectors are different processes.

✦ The Lay Out and Route Around function transforms instances that are attached to dynamic connectors into placeable shapes.

✦ The Placement tab on the Behavior dialog box enables you to manipulate additional features when using the Lay Out and Route Around function.

✦ Visio 2000 offers three shape placement styles: Radial, Flowchart/Tree, and Circular.

✦ The placement depth feature comes in handy when working with a large arrangement of shapes, particularly when you're trying to fit a large number of shapes onto a drawing page.

✦ For best results, coordinate all of the spacing sizes on the Layout and Routing Spacing dialog box.

The next chapter covers methods for modifying shape behavior.

✦   ✦   ✦

Formatting Shape Behavior

I n the most ordinary sense, shape behavior runs the full gamut of Visio business drawing applications. For instance, positioning and enlarging instances are forms of shape behavior modification, as are aligning and distributing shapes. The same can be said of coloring shape lines, shadows, and fill, or manipulating ShapeSheet data. Needless to say, this chapter doesn't cover all of these aspects. Such features, instead, are discussed in other areas of this book. Since shape behavior, generally speaking, is what Visio is all about, I've divided the chapters and labeled them according to specific functions. This chapter, however, just contains miscellaneous aspects of shape-behavior formatting, involving features found on Visio 2000's Behavior dialog box.

New Feature   Visio 2000's Behavior dialog box contains more features than those offered by its predecessor, Visio 5.0.

Modifying Fundamental Shape Behavior Features

There are many ways in which the Shape Behaviors can be modified. Whether you want to reveal or hide shape features, run macros, or modify line jump styles, the Behavior dialog box is the place to go.

Adjusting basic shape behaviors

The most basic shape behaviors can be modified from the Behavior tab on the Behavior dialog box. You can change the interaction style of lines and boxes, reveal or hide shape features such as control handles and alignment boxes, and format resizing and group behavior.

Resetting Double-Click Operations

The Behavior dialog box's Double-Click tab enables Visio 2000 users to reset selection operations. For example, every time you double-click a shape, you can manipulate the program to open ShapeSheets, run macros, or view help topics for Visio instances. These are just a few of the double-click options.

Working with Connector and Placement features

Use the Connector and Placement tabs on the Behavior dialog box to format connectors and their relationships with shapes. Features on the Connector tab enable you to modify line-jump styles, line-routing styles and directions, as well as rerouting conditions. The Placement tab enables users to set various placement restrictions and control shapes' interactions with dynamic connectors. Many of these features were explained in Chapter 21, so I just briefly touch upon them here due to their location on the Behavior dialog box.

Note   To view the Behavior dialog box's Connector tab, you must first select a connector on the drawing page; otherwise, only the Behavior, Double-Click, and Placement tabs appear.

Cross-Reference   See Chapter 21 for details on manipulating features within the Behavior dialog box's Placement and Connector tabs.

Altering Basic Shape Behaviors

As mentioned above, the Behavior tab on the Behavior dialog box enables users to control some of the shapes' most basic elements. Access the feature by first selecting a shape, then choosing Format ➪ Behavior. The Behavior tab is the first of four tabs on the Behavior dialog box (as shown in Figure 22-1). It features the following options labeled in five different sections: Interaction Style, Selection Highlighting, Resize Behavior, Miscellaneous, and Group Behavior.

The following is a description of the contents of each section:

- ✦ **Interaction Style.** Use to give any instance a 1-D or 2-D shape style

- ✦ **Selection Highlighting.** Use to hide or reveal specific shape features

- ✦ **Resize Behavior.** Use to control how a group shape responds when the entire group is resized

- ✦ **Miscellaneous.** Use to prevent a shape from printing, and to add a shape to a group by simply placing the instance within that group

- ✦ **Group Behavior.** Use to format an assortment of shape group behaviors

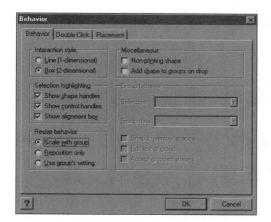

Figure 22-1: The Behavior tab is located on the Behavior dialog box.

Changing Interaction Styles

The two radio buttons in the Interaction Style section enable users to manipulate the dimension style of objects. For example, you can switch a 2-D box into a 1-D shape and vice versa for a line or connector. Although all Visio shapes are automatically coordinated accordingly (for example, closed-in shapes like boxes are labeled 2-D objects while connectors and lines are labeled as 1-D shapes unless you manually change the dimensions in this section), these features allow you to customize shapes for your purposes.

Note Three-dimensional shapes, such as those with perspective, are considered 2-D shapes in Visio 2000.

This brings us to the question that's most likely in the back of your mind: "Why would anyone want to change a Visio shape to its opposite dimensional style?" The particular reason depends on your drawing purposes, but, generally, such changes are made to save time and increase design efficiency. For example, changing a closed shape like a chair into a 1-D object allows you to do two things that you cannot do with most 2-D shapes. First, you can rotate the chair without using the Rotation Tool. Second, you can extend a shape's size, affecting its proportion. This new customization is handy because a 2-D shape must maintain its proportion during resizing. Such features, overall, make adjusting shapes more convenient, especially in cases in which rotation and such resizing techniques are required.

The following exercise shows you some ways to use 1-D style features for a 2-D shape:

1. Open the Basic Shapes stencil. Drop two Squares onto the drawing page.

2. Select one of the shapes and then choose Format ➪ Behavior.

3. Change the shape's interaction style from "Box (two-dimensional)" to "Line (one-dimensional)." Click the OK button.

4. Notice that the style has produced changes in that Square's handles. Instead of having eight handles, the Square now has two handles and a begin and an end point (see Figure 22-2).

5. Drag either of the handles, or the begin or end point; you can change the shape into a rectangle. If you try this with the other Square, you cannot reproduce the same results. Although you can adjust the Square's size, it nonetheless remains a Square.

6. Drag the newly formed rectangle's end point towards the top or the bottom of the screen. The shape can be rotated without using the Rotation Tool.

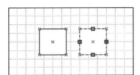

Figure 22-2: Turning a 2-D shape, like this Square, into a 1-D object results in a begin point (marked with an X) and an end point (marked with a +) being placed on it.

Note   Applying a 1-D style to a 2-D object does not change it so that it appears as a line or connector –– the shape only "behaves" like one. For example, you can glue the new shape to other shapes with its begin and end points. You can also drag the shape 360 degrees by those points. Yet the closed shape still looks like a closed shape, not a connector or line.

Tip   You can create 2-D master shapes with 1-D interaction styles. This means that every time you drop that shape, you will not have to make changes in the Behavior dialog box; the changes appear just as you saved the master.

Changing a line or connector into a 2-D shape is not done as often, probably due to the certain restrictions that develop from the modification. For instance, a 2-D line or connector cannot be rotated or glued to other objects. These aspects dramatically deter from a 1-D object's general purpose, since most of these objects are "connectors."

However, applying a 2-D interaction style to 1-D objects has some advantages. For instance, you can prevent people from moving connectors. The exercise below shows you how this works:

1. Open the Blank Drawing template. Next, draw a connector on the drawing page using the Connector Tool button.

2. Select the connector, then choose Format ➪ Behavior.

3. Change the connector's interaction style from "Line (1-dimensional)" to "Box (2-dimensional)." Click the OK button. The connector has developed new control handles.

4. Click on the Pointer Tool button. Try to drag the connector; it shouldn't budge. You will receive a message like the one shown in Figure 22-3 when tugging at the shape.

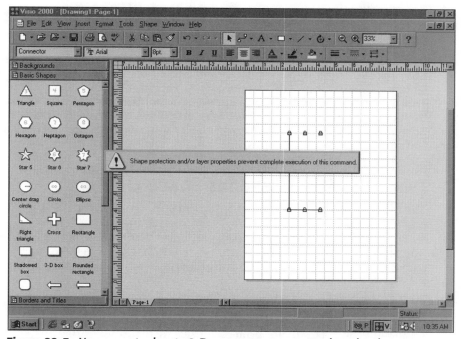

Figure 22-3: You cannot relocate 2-D connectors no matter how hard you try.

Deactivating Selection Highlighting

The Selection Highlighting section has features to use when selecting a shape. For example, clicking a shape enables you, in most cases, to view shape handles, control handles, and the shape's alignment box. These features are optional and, thus, can be turned off by unchecking the appropriate box in the Behavior dialog box's Behavior tab. Visio 2000, by default, activates certain features for certain shapes. Table 22-1 displays the default settings for most closed shapes, lines, and connectors.

Table 22-1
Default Selection Highlighting

Feature	Shape Handles	Control Handles	Alignment Box
Closed Shapes	Shown	Shown	Shown
Lines	Shown	Shown	Shown
Connectors	Shown	Shown	Not Shown

Using these features is easy. Select a shape, then choose Format ➪ Behavior. Uncheck the boxes in the Selection Highlighting section to deactivate particular features. Unchecking all three options prevents users from selecting that object. This is another method, other than format-protection measures, to keep coworkers from tampering with shapes. For example, turning off an object's shape handles prevents others from resizing that instance. You can check and uncheck all three features for specific 2-D shapes, lines, and connectors within a drawing.

Using the Miscellaneous Shape Options

The Miscellaneous section is located in the upper right-hand corner of the Behavior dialog box's Behavior tab. Two boxes are located there. The Non-Printing Shape feature prevents you from printing a particular shape when its box is checked. The Add Shape to Groups on Drop feature — when checked — enables you to drag a particular instance onto a shape group, automatically placing that instance within the group.

Creating Non-Printing Shapes

Although Visio 2000 will not print shapes using the Non-Printing Shape feature, you can still adjust a non-printable instance's placement and size. The exercise below demonstrates how all of this works:

1. Open a stencil, then drop a shape from it onto the drawing page.

2. Select the shape. Choose Format ➪ Behavior.

3. Check the Non-Printing Shape box, then click the OK button.

4. Drag the shape, adjusting its size and position.

5. Select File ➪ Print Preview. Notice that the page is blank; the non-printable shape does not show.

Adding a Shape to a Group

The next box, the Add Shape to Groups on Drop option, involves shape groups, a topic discussed in detail later in the book. For now, take a look at the exercise below to see how to use the feature:

1. Open a drawing page and the Basic Shapes stencil. Drop two shapes from the stencil onto the drawing page. Try to place them near each other.

2. Select both shapes; then choose Shape ➪ Grouping ➪ Group. Both shapes can now operate as one unit. (Notice that the alignment box surrounds both instances.)

3. Drag another shape onto the drawing page, placing it a few inches from the group.

4. Select the lone instance; then choose Format ➪ Behavior. Check the Add Shape to Groups box; then click OK.

5. The group will not accept the shape unless programmed to do so. Select the shape then choose Format ➪ Behavior again. Check the Accept Dropped Shapes box located in the Group Behavior section. Click OK to finalize your choice.

6. Drag the lone shape into the black box the surrounds the group (as shown in Figure 22-4). The shape is now part of the group. When you move the other shapes, the newest group member tags along.

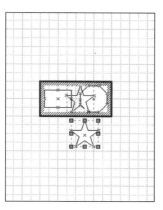

Figure 22-4: Initiating a new group member

Note   You must select all of the shapes so that you have access to the Accept Dropped Shapes area.

Working with the Group Behavior applications

The Group Behavior section enables users to dictate how a shape group responds to certain actions on the drawing page. You can manipulate various features, from selection options to snapping member shapes together. Use these options to customize shape group features.

Cross-
Reference

Refer to Chapter 24 for further details on creating and using shape groups.

Using the Selection feature

The Selection feature enables users to control how a group and its individual members are highlighted. Details for the function of each selection option are listed below. To choose one of the options, first create a group. After pulling up the Behavior dialog box, click the arrow button at the end of the Selection box, then choose an option. Click the OK button to implement the change.

+ **Group Only.** Only the group — not its individual members — can be selected

+ **Group First.** Clicking a group highlights the group; clicking again highlights the group member you've clicked on.

+ **Members First.** The group member you've clicked is highlighted; clicking again highlights the entire group

Note

The Group First setting is the default setting for newly created shape groups.

Setting group data options

Group data options affect how text is presented in shape groups. For example, the Hide setting does not allow you to view inserted test. The Behind Member Shapes setting places text behind shapes. The In Front of Member Shapes places inserted text on top of group members. The following exercise demonstrates how each works:

1. Open the Basic Shapes stencil. Drop three shapes onto the drawing page.

2. Convert the shapes into a group by selecting the shapes then choosing Shape ➪ Grouping ➪ Group.

3. While the group is still selected, click the Text Tool button. Type in the alphabet or a long sentence. The goal is to create letters on top of, and in between, the group members. Click the Pointer Tool after you're finished typing. What you've typed should appear in full because the default setting is In Front of Member Shapes.

4. Select the group, then access the Behavior dialog box's Behavior tab. Choose the Hide setting and then click OK. The text should disappear.

5. Go to the Behavior dialog box again, and this time select the Behind Member Shapes setting. Click the OK button. Text should appear behind the shapes, as shown in Figure 22-5.

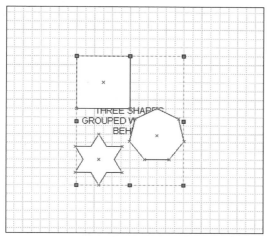

Figure 22-5: Placing text behind group members

 Chapters 29, 30, and 31 discuss in full detail creating and editing text.

Applying other Group Behavior options

Three other options are listed in the Group Behavior section. These features and their functions, listed below, pertain to group member and group text characteristics. Keep in mind that the Snap to Member Shapes and Edit Text of Group options are, by default, selected for groups. You can, however, make changes to those settings by unchecking the boxes.

✦ **Snap to Member Shapes.** Enables you to snap other shapes to a shape group's alignment box.

✦ **Edit Text of Group.** Enables you to edit text inserted into a shape group.

✦ **Accept Dropped Shapes.** Enables a shape group to incorporate another shape dropped with the group's boundaries — if the dropped shape is programmed to Add to Groups on Drop.

 When using the Snap to Member Shapes setting, make sure the Alignment Box's checkbox in the Snap To section of the Snap & Glue dialog box is activated.

Manipulating a group member's Resize Behavior

The Resize Behavior section is located in the bottom left-hand corner of the Behavior dialog box's Behavior tab, as shown in Figure 22-6. The features in this section are used to manipulate a group member's resizing characteristics. Therefore, depending on your selection, a particular group member may size differently when the group as a whole is being resized. For example, you can prevent one group member from being resized with the rest of the group.

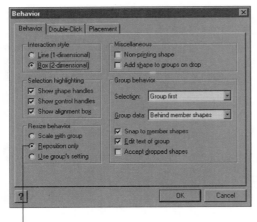

Figure 22-6: Using the Reposition Only setting on a group member

Click here to prevent a group member from resizing with the rest of the group.

Three radio buttons are located in this section: Scale with Group, Reposition Only, and Use Group's Setting. The last of these three options is the default setting for groups. The list below contains information on how all of these options work. Click one of the group members. Next, choose the setting you want from the Behavior dialog box and then click the OK button. Make sure that the Group First or Members First setting is chosen in the Selection section; otherwise, you will not be able to select individual group members.

✦ **Scale with Group.** Group member is resized and scaled proportionately with other group members

✦ **Reposition Only.** Group member is not resized with other group members, only repositioned

✦ **Use Group's Setting.** All group members are resized in a fashion that maintains their proportion to each other (default setting)

Cross-Reference Refer to Chapter 24 for an in-depth approach to manipulating shape groups.

Setting Double-Click Options

The second tab on the Behavior dialog box controls which actions are automatically performed when you double-click a shape. If you go ahead and double-click a shape, you will notice that a text block appears within the object. This is the default double-click setting. You can modify this setting by selecting a different option from the Behavior dialog box's Double-Click tab. Simply click the OK button to implement the new action. Now, every time you double-click a shape the action you've chosen will be performed.

Eleven different double-click settings are available, as shown in the list below. Only one of the features, The Open in New Window option, can be set simultaneously with the others. Therefore, you could, for example, right-click a shape to pull up a new window as well as a text block in the selected shape. However, you cannot couple any of the first ten options (those marked with radio buttons).

Note
You can program each shape within a drawing to perform a different right-click action.

✦ **Perform Default Action.** A text block opens within lines, connectors, and closed shapes.

✦ **Perform No Action.** No changes appear.

✦ **Edit Shape's Text.** A text block opens within lines, connectors, and closed shapes.

✦ **Open Group in New Window.** A new window opens containing the selected group.

✦ **Open Shape's ShapeSheet.** That shape's ShapeSheet window is opened.

✦ **Custom.** Changes made in the EventDblClick cell of the shape's ShapeSheet are applied.

✦ **Display Help.** Help topics for that shape are presented; used in conjunction with the Help feature on the Special dialog box.

✦ **OLE Verb.** The program enables you to use OLE options.

✦ **Run Macro.** The macro chosen in the Behavior dialog box runs.

✦ **Go To Page.** You are returned to the page chosen in the Behavior dialog box.

✦ **Open in New Window.** A new window of your drawing is opened. This option can be run simultaneously with any of the other right-click options.

Some of the options are not available to all shapes. For example, the OLE Verb feature can only be used when working with object linking and embedding shapes. The Open Group in New Window feature is only applicable to shape groups; therefore, you must double-click a shape group — not a shape — to open the group window.

Macros operate best with certain shapes. Read more about how macros work in Chapters 26, 27, and 28. The Run Macro option on Visio 2000 Standard offers an extensive number of Visio wizards and macros. They are as follows:

Organization Chart Wizard	Database Wizard
Timeline	Gantt Chart
Build Region	Import Flowchart Data Wizard
Chart Shape Wizard	Import Project Data
Color Schemes	Number Shapes
Custom Properties Editor	Organization Chart Converter
Database Export	Organization Chart Wizard
Database Refresh	Page Layout Wizard
Database Settings	Property Reporting Wizard
Database Update	Shape Explorer

Using Connector and Placement Features

The third and forth tabs on the Behavior dialog box contain features that enable you to manipulate the behavior of connectors and their interaction with other shapes. Select Format ➪ Behavior... to access the Behavior dialog box, then click either the Connector or Placement tab to view their contents.

Note To view the Behavior dialog box's Connector tab, you must first select a connector on the drawing page; otherwise, only the Behavior, Double-Click, and Placement tabs appear.

Cross-Reference See Chapter 21 for in-depth information on manipulating features within the Behavior dialog box's Placement and Connector tabs.

The Connector tab

The Connector tab is divided into two sections: Line Routing and Line Jumps. The first section enables users to dictate the style, direction, and rerouting capabilities of connectors. The options direct the way connectors attach to shapes, what Visio 2000 calls a connector's style. Ten style options are available, as listed below:

✦ Page Default

✦ Right Angle

✦ Straight

✦ Center to Center

✦ Flowchart

✦ Tree

✦ Organization Chart

✦ Simple

✦ Simple Horizontal-Vertical

✦ Simple Vertical-Horizontal

You can view each of these settings in the preview window (shown in Figure 22-7). Notice that only four of the styles permit you to edit their direction: Flowchart, Tree, Organization Chart, and Simple. You can arrange these styles from top to bottom, bottom to top, left to right, or right to left. Again, use the preview window to view how these settings affect the style's appearance.

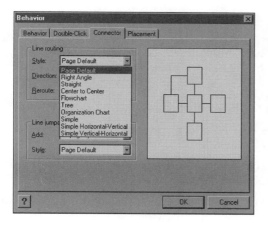

Figure 22-7: Use the preview window before implementing a line routing change.

The Line jumps section enables users to choose how and when line jumps are added. A line jump is a bridge-like arc that appears on one of two crossing connectors. Line jumps are used to prevent people from confusing two separate connectors as part of a related network. Select when and how you want to add line jumps from the Add options. Choose a line-jump style from the Style options. You can also access these options by selecting various buttons on the Layout & Routing toolbar.

The Placement tab

You must click a 2-D shape to access any of the features on the Placement tab. The page is divided into four sections: Placement Behavior, Placement, Move Shapes on Drop, and Interaction with Connectors. The Placement Behavior box controls the routing capabilities of dynamic connectors. The list below explains how each setting works. Only if you use the Lay Out and Route Around format will you have access to the rest of the Placement tab's features.

✦ **Lay Out and Route Around.** Dynamic connectors route around shapes.

✦ **Do Not Lay Out and Route Around.** Dynamic connectors route through shapes.

✦ **Let Visio Decide.** Dynamic connectors that are attached to other shapes will not route through shapes attached to dynamic connectors.

The other three sections are extensions of the Lay Out and Route Around format. The Placement and Move Shapes on Drop sections enable users to dictate how placeable shapes react to each other. The Interaction with Connectors section enables connectors to intersect with selected shapes.

Summary

In conclusion, you've learned how to manipulate various forms of shape, group, and connector behaviors. In this chapter, the following aspects of behavior formatting were discussed:

✦ Interaction styles enable you to assign any instance a 1-D or 2-D style.

✦ Selection highlighting options entail hiding or revealing a shape's control handles, shape handles, and alignment box.

✦ Non-printing shapes show up only on the Drawing window — not on the Print Preview window and printouts.

✦ You must use the Add Shapes to Groups on Drop and Accept Dropped Shapes features together.

✦ The Selection feature enables you to control how a group and its individual members are highlighted.

✦ Group data options let you hide text, or place it on top of, or behind, shape groups.

✦ Use the Snap to Member Shapes option to snap shapes to a shape group's alignment box.

✦ Activating the Edit Text of Group feature enables you to edit text inserted into a shape group.

✦ The Resize Behavior radio buttons are used to manipulate a group member's resizing characteristics.

✦ Eleven double-clicking options are offered on the Behavior dialog box's Double-Click tab.

✦ You also reviewed basic connector and placement behavior features.

The next chapter helps you understand ways to edit and customize shape properties and fields within Visio 2000. The chapter after that turns your attention again towards shape groups.

✦   ✦   ✦

Customizing Shape Properties

Visio 2000's shapes have the ability to hold information or data. In the last chapter you learned how to specify data for a shape. In this chapter you learn how to create, delete, or modify the custom properties of a shape that holds data.

All shapes can hold data in a custom property field. Most shapes in Visio 2000 already have one or more default custom properties already defined. This chapter first shows you how you can view these properties, then we discuss details on how to edit them. Later on in the chapter, I show you how to create new properties for a shape or delete a custom property from a shape. After that, I will show you how to do the same for a master on a stencil.

Creating, editing, and deleting custom properties is fairly easy to do in Visio 2000. But because of the large amount of information about custom properties, describing how to do so isn't as simple. In this chapter you will learn much better by working through the examples rather than just reading the descriptions. (Of course, you still want to read the descriptions first so you have a better idea of what you're doing in the exercise.)

About Custom Properties

Custom properties of a shape hold data. That data can be in text form or numeric form, stored in a number of different types and formats. Data types include string, number, fixed list, variable list, Boolean, currency, date, and duration. The format depends on the type. For example, string data can be stored in uppercase format, lowercase format, or normal format (uppercase and lowercase). Duration data can be in the format of weeks, days, hours, minutes, seconds, or a combination of hours and minutes, or minutes and seconds.

With these data types and formats you can store the following in a shape: costs, purchase dates, moving dates, names and addresses, process times, confirmations, virtually any form of data commonly used in business, electronics, travel, and so forth. Custom properties can even be connected to databases, which you will learn about in Chapter 28. When you put data into a custom property, Visio 2000 checks to make sure it's the correct format. If data is entered incorrectly, the program gives you an error message and requests the correct format. For example, if you accidentally try to enter a name in a property that's for holding currency amounts, the program blocks the incorrect data form.

Opening the Custom Properties Window

The Custom Properties Window is very similar in appearance and features to the Pan and Zoom Window you learned about in Chapter 9. It can be set to autohide, it can be made to float, or moved to any area of the workspace. When open, it displays the custom properties of the shape (or shapes) selected. If no shape is selected, it shows custom properties of the open page. If there are no custom properties defined for the selected shape(s), a warning message appears in the Custom Properties Window.

To open the Custom Properties Window, select View ➪ Windows ➪ Custom Properties from the Menu toolbar. The window opens in an open area of the workspace (as shown in Figure 23-1).

Note   The Custom Properties Window's data fields are shape-dependent. If the selected shape is a flowchart symbol, the window will display Cost, Duration, and Resources. On the other hand, if the selected shape is a couch or printer, the window will display Inventory Number and Owner.

To access the window controls, right-click the Custom Properties Window. The submenu has the same options as the Pan and Zoom window (Close, Float Window, and Autohide), plus two more: Autofit and Define Properties. The Autofit option allows the window to increase in size automatically if there is more content to show than it can fit in its normal size. In other words, if there are five custom properties and the window is sized to show three, then the window increases in size to show all five. In most cases you will want Autofit turned on. Clicking Define Properties is one way to access the Define Custom Properties dialog box, in which you can create, edit, or delete custom properties, discussed in detail later. For now, let's set up our first example.

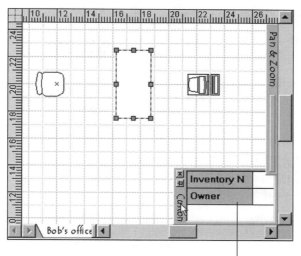

Custom Properties Window

Figure 23-1: When first opened, the Custom Properties Window may appear anywhere in the workspace.

Example: Open, move, and autohide Custom Property Window

Open a new project. Select Office Layout as the drawing type. Drag a desk, a chair, and a PC onto the page. From the Menu Toolbar select View ➪ Windows ➪ Custom Properties. This pops up the Custom Properties Window. Right-click this and select Float Window from the submenu. Move the Custom Properties Window to a convenient area in your workspace. Right-click it to bring up the submenu again. Select Anchor Window to set the window in its new place. To hide the window when it's not being used, select Autohide in the submenu. To bring out the window, move your cursor over the window's titlebar.

Select any of the three shapes on the page. Note that there are two custom properties already defined in the Custom Properties Window, which you can see if you look back to Figure 23-1. These are Inventory Number and Owner. These custom properties are predefined for all shapes on the Office Layout stencil. In a moment, you'll see how these can edit existing custom properties. First though, let's take a look at entering data in the custom property fields.

Entering data in the Custom Properties Window

You can enter data through the Custom Properties Window. Select the shape; in the Custom Properties Window select the custom property field and type in the data.

You can do this to several shapes (fingers permitting). Select the first shape, hold down the Shift key and select the remaining shapes. Go to the Custom Properties Window and select the custom property field to which you want to add data. Type in the data.

Pretty simple, isn't it? Let's try it in the next example.

Example: Entering data

Let's enter data for all three shapes simultaneously. Select one of the three shapes on the page. Hold down the Shift key and select the other two shapes. Go to the Custom Properties Window. Move your cursor over the Owner field. A tip pops up to tell you what type of information to enter. Click the Owner field. Type in the name **Bob** (as shown in Figure 23-2). Press Enter. The program automatically goes to the next empty field. Because the Inventory Number for each item should be different, we will enter those individually. Click the page to deselect the three shapes.

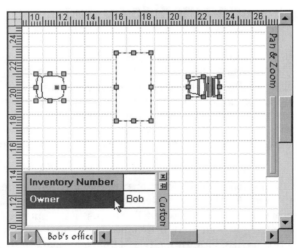

Figure 23-2: You can enter data directly into the Custom Properties Window.

Now click the desk. Go to the Custom Properties Window. The owner name is there. Click the Inventory Number field, and type in **DSK-943**. Press Enter. Now the desk has an assigned inventory number and is assigned to Bob. But Bob wanted a new desk, so let's assign this one to somebody else. Fortunately, editing information is easy. Save and keep this example ready.

Editing custom property data in the Custom Properties Window

To edit information entered in the Custom Properties Window, select the field with the data to be edited (with the correct shape or shapes selected) and enter in the new data. The new data overwrites the old.

Example

With the desk still selected, click the Owner field in the Custom Properties Window. Type in **Intern #9**. Enter it. The desk is now assigned to Intern #9. Save the example.

The Custom Properties Dialog Box

Another way you can enter data into a shape's custom properties is through the Custom Properties dialog box. This feature is useful primarily for inventory purposes. You can, for example, define ownership and assign inventory numbers to office furniture.

Opening the Custom Properties dialog box

There are two ways to open the Custom Properties dialog box. The first is to right-click a shape, which brings up a submenu. The bottom option on the submenu is Properties. Select Properties to bring up the Custom Properties dialog box for the shape selected. This method is advantageous because you always know that the dialog box is for the shape you right-clicked.

The second way to open the Custom Properties dialog box is to select the shape you want. From the Menu Toolbar, select Shape ➪ Custom Properties. This brings up the dialog box. If more than one shape is selected, this dialog box is for the first selected shape only.

The Custom Properties dialog box lists all of the defined custom property fields for a shape, along with entry fields for the input of data. Underneath the property fields is the prompt area, which displays the prompt for the selected field (as shown in Figure 23-3). This contains information that helps explain the type of data that needs to be entered in the selected field. At the bottom are three buttons: Cancel, which closes the box without making any changes; OK, which accepts all changes made and stores the displayed data in the custom properties; and Define, which opens the Define Custom Properties dialog box. The Define Custom Properties dialog box is discussed in the next section, after the following exercise.

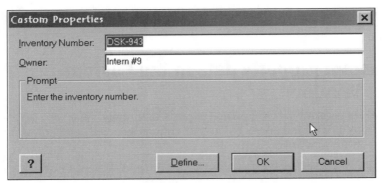

Figure 23-3: Data can be entered in the Custom Properties dialog box.

Exercise: Entering data in the Custom Properties dialog box

Right-click the PC shape in our exercise project. It doesn't matter what shape (if any) is selected before you right-click the PC. Select Properties from the submenu. The Custom Properties dialog box shows the Inventory Number field ready to accept data. Type **PC-143** in the data field. Click OK to accept the data. Notice that the Owner field still holds the name Bob. When we changed the Owner for the desk, it didn't affect the other shapes. Now, let's use the other method to open the dialog box for the chair shape.

Select the chair shape. From the Menu Toolbar, select Shape ➪ Custom Properties. The Custom Properties dialog box pops up. Once again the empty Inventory Number field is ready to receive the data. Type in **BB-123**. Select OK to accept the data. Now all three items have Inventory Numbers assigned to them. Save this example — it will be used to show how to change an existing custom property field.

Editing Custom Property Fields

With Visio 2000 you may edit, create, and delete custom shape property fields. You can change the type and/or format of the data to be entered, and change the name of the field. You can change the prompt for the data, and even change the data in the custom property field. You can create or delete a custom property. All of these changes can be done in the Define Custom Property dialog box.

This section covers editing an existing custom property for the purpose of familiarizing you with the use of the Define Custom Property dialog box. You'll also learn how to create a new custom property and define all of its aspects, and you'll see how to delete a custom property.

The two custom property fields discussed in the previous example both contained string data. String data can consist of letters, numbers, and most symbols. But what if you wanted to limit the Inventory Numbers field to numbers? With the data type set to string, anything can be entered as an inventory identification. We want to limit the Inventory Number field to whole numbers, a feat which can be accomplished in the Define Custom Property dialog box.

Opening the Define Custom Properties dialog box

Open the Custom Properties dialog box and select the Define button at the bottom of the dialog box. This opens the Define Custom Properties dialog box (as shown in Figure 23-4). The box includes several fields:

✦ **Label.** The name of the custom property selected. The ampersand denotes the shortcut key for the custom property's label.

✦ **Type.** The data type defined for the selected custom property. The selection arrow at the right of this field opens a drop-down menu listing all available data types.

✦ **Format.** The allowed format for the data type. Varies with the type of data selected. The arrow button at the right of this field opens a submenu that lists the available data formats for the data type selected.

✦ **Value.** Current data value stored in the custom property. If none has been entered, then the field may be empty or it may contain a predefined default value.

✦ **Prompt.** The pop-up tip that explains the custom property value field.

✦ **Properties.** This lists the defined custom properties for this shape and displays the Label, Type, Format, Value, and Prompt for each custom property. The highlighted custom property in this field shows in the upper fields where you can edit it.

The five Define Custom Properties buttons are:

✦ **? (Help).** The Help button. Brings up the Visio Help box.

✦ **New.** Creates a new custom property for the shape.

✦ **Delete.** Deletes the selected custom property.

✦ **OK.** Accepts all changes and exits the Define Custom Properties dialog box.

✦ **Cancel.** Exits the Define Custom Properties dialog box without making any changes.

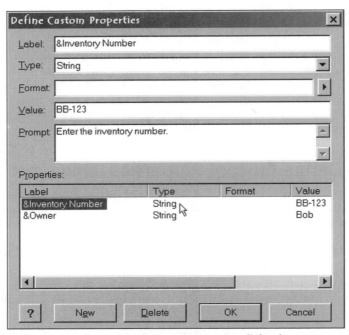

Figure 23-4: The Define Custom Properties dialog box

Editing an existing custom property

To edit an existing custom property, select the property in the Properties field. The property parameters appear in the upper fields. Select the field to edit and make the changes. For changes to Label, Value, and Prompt, simply type in the new information. For Type and Format changes, use the right-hand selection arrows to access the available choices. If you are changing both Type and Format, you need to alter Type before the Format. When you're finished, click the OK button to accept the new parameters.

Example: Editing an existing custom property

Select the PC on the drawing page. From the Menu Toolbar select Shape ⇨ Custom Properties. Click the Define button in the Custom Properties dialog box. This displays the Define Custom Properties dialog box. Imagine that your boss told you that all PCs are to have numeric inventory numbers only. Accordingly, you would need to change the data Type. Specify its Format, then update the Value.

In the Properties section, highlight Inventory Number. Click the down arrow at the right of the Type field (as shown in Figure 23-5). Select Number from the list. Click the arrow at the right of the Format field. Select Whole Number (3) from the submenu. Click the Value field. Delete the current entry, then type in **98765**. Select OK to accept the new values.

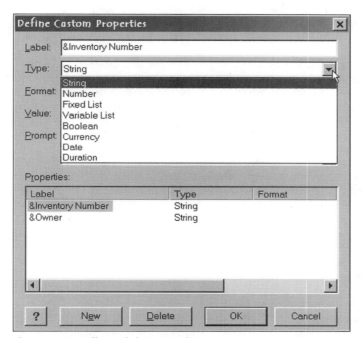

Figure 23-5: Allowed data Type list

Notice that the new value for the Inventory Number is displayed in the Custom Properties dialog box. Now try to enter an unacceptable value. Highlight the Inventory Number data field. Delete the current value and type in **XYZ-6**. Click the OK button. An Error box appears explaining that the entry must be a number.

Click OK on the Error box. Reenter **98765** in the Inventory Number field and click OK. Save the example.

Creating a new custom property

The New button at the bottom of the Define Custom Properties dialog box creates a new custom property with a default name in the Label field. Once created, you can change the name and specify the parameters for the new custom property. Following is an example.

Example: Creating a new custom property

Select the PC on the page from our previous example and open the Define Custom Properties dialog box. Click the New button. The new property is created with the default name of Property3. The Label field is highlighted, so let's go ahead and name the custom property. In this custom property we want to define what operating system this PC uses. Type the following in the Label field: **Operating&System**.

The ampersand defines the S to be the shortcut key for this custom property. The Format field is empty. If we don't enter a Format the system defaults to the most general format. Leave it as is because the user might be using both upper- and lowercase letters for the value of this property. Click the Prompt field and type in the following: **Enter this computer's Operating system**. Now this custom property is set. Once accepted and selected, the user can enter information on the operating system. For variety's sake, let's add one more new property.

Let's add a date-of-purchase custom property for the PC. Click the New button. Property4 is created. Change the Label to read: &Date of Purchase. For Type, select Date. For data Format, select 10/03/93. Notice that the information actually entered into the field is MM/dd/yy and not the numerical example Visio provides. Visio uses examples to ensure you understand the chosen format. Click the Prompt field and enter the following information in between the brackets: {**Enter the date of purchase. Example: 10/03/93**}. Don't enter the brackets into the field. Click the OK button to accept the changes.

Now enter values for the new properties in the workspace Custom Properties Window. Go to your example page. Select the PC shape. Open the Custom Properties Window, which should still be on your workspace. We left it on Autohide, so move your cursor over its titlebar to open it. Move your cursor over the Operating System label. The tip you typed will appear. Click Operating System to select the data field, and type in your current operating system name. Press the Enter key.

The program enters the information and automatically moves on to Date of Purchase. A button appears at the right of the Date of Purchase entry field. Click that button. A calendar appears! By using the calendar, users can pick a date without worrying about the correct way to enter it; Visio will do that for them! Pick a date from the calendar and press the Enter key. The program automatically cycles over to the Inventory number. Click the page to deselect the PC and leave all of the new data in its custom properties. Save the example. Now we have one more thing to learn in this section before moving on to the next: deleting a custom property.

Deleting a custom property

Deleting a custom property is easy. Select your shape. Open the Define Custom Property dialog box, select the custom property you want to delete, and press the Delete button.

Note   You cannot delete a custom property using the Delete key on the keyboard. You must use the Delete button in the Define Custom Properties dialog box.

Example: Deleting a custom property

Word has come down from upper management. Since chairs are often traded, moved, and replaced, they will no longer be assigned an owner. As a result, you must delete that custom property from the chair shape on the current page.

Select the chair shape in the example. Open the Define Custom Properties dialog box. Highlight the Owner custom property in the Properties field. Hit the Delete button at the bottom of the dialog box. Click the OK button, and save the example.

Now, you're going to learn about another way to modify custom properties before you put them on the page.

Using the Custom Properties Editor

We've created, edited, and deleted custom properties for previously placed shapes. But if you have several instances of a shape, wouldn't it be better to make the changes on the master shape before placing the shapes on the page? Visio 2000 enables you to modify the custom properties of a master, or the shapes on an active page, or shapes on another page using the Custom Properties Editor.

The Custom Properties Editor is the Godzilla version of the Define Custom Properties dialog box. It can modify shape masters on a stencil. It has additional options such as Ask on Drop, which asks the user to enter data when a shape is first placed on a page. You can use it to modify shapes on the active page or in an unopened page.

The Custom Properties Editor is one of Visio 2000's Wizards. There is only one way to open it.

Opening the Custom Properties Editor

From the Menu Toolbar, select Tools ⇨ Macros ⇨ Custom Properties Editor. This opens the wizard. The first screen of the wizard asks where you want to edit custom properties (as shown in Figure 23-6). There are three choices:

> Shapes in a stencil
>
> Shapes in the active drawing
>
> Shapes in another Visio drawing

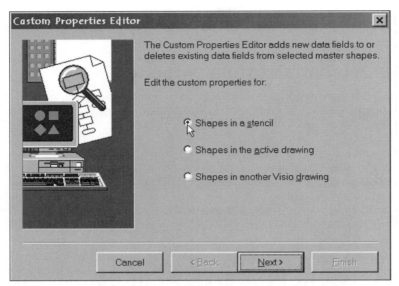

Figure 23-6: First screen of the Custom Properties Editor Wizard

Since we already practiced editing an active drawing, let's first work with editing a stencil before learning how the Custom Properties Editor works on an active drawing. Finally we'll look at how the Custom Properties Editor Wizard works on a closed Visio drawing.

Editing masters on a stencil

On the first screen of the Custom Properties Editor wizard, choose the Shapes in a stencil option. Then click Next. The following screen asks you to select a stencil to edit. Enter in the path and name, or (more likely) click the Browse button to go through the folders to find the stencil you want to edit. Once you find the stencil, click the Next button to go to the next screen.

This screen asks you whether you want to make a copy of the stencil to edit or to edit the original stencil. To be safe, always choose to Make a Copy, and edit that. This ensures that if anything goes wrong, your original is still intact and can be used to create another copy. After choosing Make a Copy to edit, hit the Next button.

Visio 2000 creates a copy of the stencil with a generic name (like Stencil1) and opens the next screen of the wizard (as shown in Figure 23-7). This screen enables you to choose any, some, or all of the shapes in the stencil to be edited. It has a list field with the names of the shapes on the stencil in it. There is a button for choosing All of the shapes and a button for choosing None of the shapes. Because the screen opens with all of the shapes selected, the None button is a quick way to deselect them before selecting any specific shapes for editing. If you want to make a change that will appear in all of the shapes, just click Next to continue. If you want to select one or some, but not all of the shapes, click the None button. Then, for one shape, click its name and select Next to continue. To select two or more shapes, select the first one. If all of the shapes you want are in a row, then hold down the Shift key and click the last of the shapes you want to modify. All the shapes in between will be selected as well. If the shapes aren't in a row, hold down the Ctrl key and select each shape to be modified. Once you have selected the shapes, click the Next button to continue.

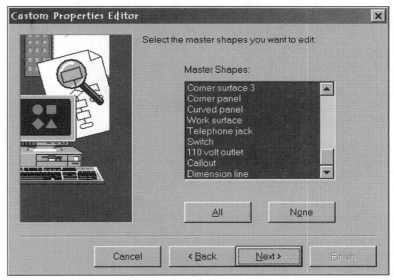

Figure 23-7: The Shapes selection screen of the Custom Properties Editor wizard

On the left of the next screen of the wizard, all of the master shapes chosen in the last step are shown (see Figure 23-8). On the right side is a field that displays the custom properties of the selected shapes from the left. If more than one shape is selected, the Custom Properties field shows the combination of the custom properties of the selected master shapes.

Below the Custom Properties field are the Add and Remove buttons.

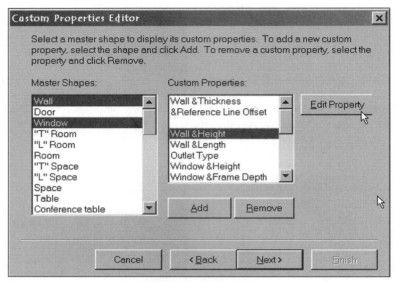

Figure 23-8: The Custom Properties selection.

The Add button

The Add button enables you to create a new custom property for the master shapes selected. It's similar to the New button in the Define Custom Properties dialog box. Clicking this button brings up the Add Property dialog box (as shown in Figure 23-9). There are three tabs in the Add Property dialog box.

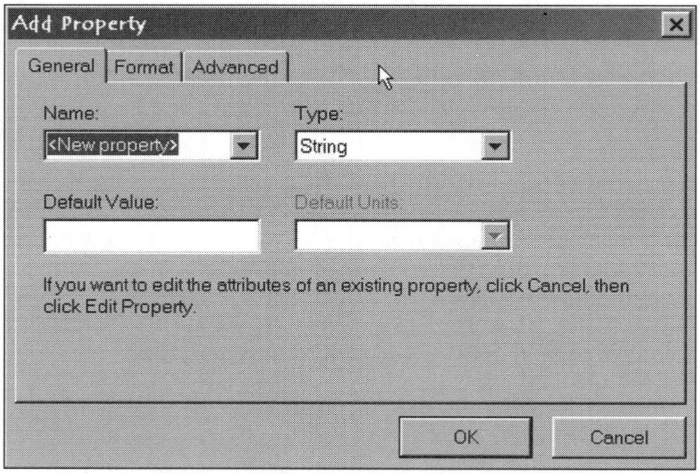

Figure 23-9: The Add Property dialog box has three tabs: General, Format, and Advanced.

The General tab has four input fields:

✦ **Name.** The Name field enables you to type in a name for the custom property. Notice a list arrow on the right side of this field. Clicking it displays a list of the existing properties for all the shapes on the stencil. Selecting one of these enables you to edit the existing custom property whose name you selected. Changes made by selecting a custom property name affect all master shapes with this property. To prevent confusion, I recommend using the Edit Properties dialog box to edit properties rather than the Add Properties dialog box.

✦ **Type.** The Type field enables you to select the data type for the custom property. Use the list arrow at the right of the field to open the list of available data types.

✦ **Default Value.** The Default Value field enables you to set a default value that will be assigned to any instances of the shape placed on a page. Depending on the type chosen and the format options chosen on the Format tab, this field may be grayed out (inaccessible).

✦ **Default Units.** The Default Units field enables you to set the units for the data type and format chosen. The list arrow at the right side of the field displays a list of appropriate units available for the chosen data type and format from which you may choose. Depending on the type chosen and the format options chosen on the Format tab, this field may be grayed out (inaccessible).

The Format tab has two input fields and one display field:

✦ **Type.** The Type field is a duplicate of the Type field from the General tab. Changes made here change on the General tab as well. It is placed here for ease of selection when making format decisions.

✦ **Format.** The Format (Display As) field lets you choose the inputted data's format. The available formats vary with data Type. Scroll down the available list to select a format.

✦ **Sample display.** The Sample display field displays an example of the data and format type chosen. Note that examples are not always available.

The Advanced tab has three input fields and two selection buttons:

✦ **Row Name.** The Row Name field enables you to specify where in the stencil the shape will appear. Placement is Automatic by default. This option should only be changed by advanced users and programmers. After all, who cares where the shape appears as long as it does?

✦ **Sort Key.** The Sort Key field enables you to specify the order in which the properties appear in the Custom Properties dialog box. Entering a 1 here will display the property first in the list.

✦ **Prompt.** The Prompt field enables you to enter a user prompt. This is where you specify to the user what data is expected and how to enter it.

✦ **Ask on Drop.** When checked, the Ask on Drop selection button asks the user to enter a value for this custom property when they drag the shape onto a page. This is a smart way to ensure that critical data is entered into a custom property when it is plopped on the page.

✦ **Hidden selection.** The Hidden selection button, when checked, hides the custom property from the user. This button is for applications in which the user may not need to, or should not, know about a particular property of a shape. It is most often used in security applications.

The Remove button

The Remove button deletes the custom properties selected in the Custom Properties field. It is basically the same as the Delete button in the Define Custom Properties dialog box.

The Edit Properties button

To the right of the Custom Properties field is the Edit Property button. This button enables the editing of the selected existing custom property. Clicking this button displays the Edit Properties dialog box. The Edit Properties dialog box is similar to the Add Properties dialog box. Upon opening, however, the Edit Properties dialogue box displays the custom property's current parameters. Read the Add Properties button section for information on this dialog box. You can only edit one property at a time. If more than one property is selected, the last custom property selected will be the one shown in the box.

Once you have finished adding, removing, and editing custom properties for the master shapes on the stencil, click the Next button to continue.

The penultimate screen of the wizard asks whether you want to preview the changes. Selecting Don't Show Preview and clicking Next takes you to the final screen of the wizard where you select Finish to close the wizard. Selecting Preview/Add lists and clicking Next takes you to the next screen of the wizard. Selecting Finish on this screen closes the wizard with no preview and saves the changes.

The Preview screen (if you selected to view it) has two list fields — the Master Shapes field and the Custom Properties field — and a set of option buttons. The left, or Master Shapes field lists all of the master shapes in the stencil. The Custom Properties field lists the custom properties for the selected master shape(s). You can choose to see all of the custom properties as they will exist for the shape(s) when finished, just the custom properties that will be added, or the custom properties that will be removed. Clicking the appropriate option button in the Show Properties section changes which custom properties will be shown, enabling you to review what you have added, what you have removed, and what the final list of custom properties will be for a shape or group of shapes. Clicking the Next button takes you to the finish screen. Clicking Finish closes the wizard and saves the changes.

The Finish Screen is your last chance to Cancel and leave the wizard without making the changes. Clicking Finish saves the changes and closes the wizard.

Editing shapes in the active drawing with the Custom Properties Editor

From the Menu Toolbar select Tools ➪ Macros ➪ Custom Properties Editor. Select the Shapes in the Active Drawing option and click Next to pop to the next screen of the wizard.

This screen shows a list with the master shapes of the shapes currently on your active page (as shown in Figure 23-10). You can select one or more of these to edit. You may select All or even None. After this, select Next to take you though a process nearly identical to the above process for editing a stencil. However, there are two differences: 1) you don't have to select a stencil, and 2) the shapes and custom properties available are limited to those currently on the active page. You will be asked if you want to make a copy or work from the original stencil. Choose copy, *always*. Since the process is already described in the Editing Masters on a stencil section, I won't repeat the same information here.

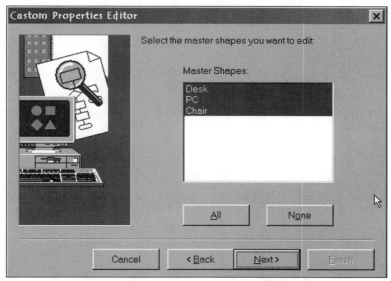

Figure 23-10: In an active drawing, you are limited to the shapes currently on the active page.

Editing shapes in another Visio drawing with the Custom Properties Editor

When you select this option, the next screen asks for the location of the page you wish to edit. You may enter the file path directly or browse to the page. Click Next to continue.

As with "Editing Shapes on the Active Page," your choices of shapes and custom properties are limited to what is on the page selected. Other than that, the process is the same as described in the previous section, "Editing Masters from a Stencil." Read that section for information on the editing process.

When you're finished editing, the page you selected will appear in your active workspace so you can verify changes to the custom properties with the Custom Properties Window.

Example: Using the Custom Properties Editor

Open the wizard and select a stencil to edit.

From the Menu toolbar, select Tools ➪ Macros ➪ Custom Properties Editor. On the first screen of the wizard, select Shapes in a Stencil and click Next. On the next screen, click the Browse button. Find the Solutions folder in the Visio program folder. Open it, then find and open the Network Diagram folder. Select the Basic Network Shapes stencil and click Open. Click Next at the bottom of the wizard screen.

On the next screen, double-check to make sure the Make a copy to edit option is selected (as shown in Figure 23-11). Do this to prevent the possibility of affecting the original. Click Next.

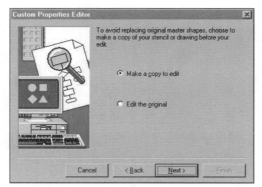

Figure 23-11: Select the Make a copy to edit option for precautionary reasons.

Since all the shapes are already highlighted on this screen, just click Next to continue.

It may take a moment for the next screen to appear. When it does, click Desktop PC in the Master Shapes field. Click Manufacturer in the Custom Properties field. Click the Edit Property button, then click OK in the Warning box that pops up. Remember that you're working on a copy, not the original.

Look through all three tabs on the Edit Properties dialog box, then return to the General tab. We will add a default manufacturer. Click in the Default Value field. Type in the following: **PhlieBienyte Inc**. Then, open the Advanced tab. Click in the Ask on Drop option box. If this shape is dropped on a page, it automatically asks for a manufacturer to be entered. If bypassed, PhlieBienyte Inc. will be the default value stored in it. Click OK to accept the changes.

Scroll down the Master Shapes list and select Dynamic Connector. It does not have any default properties in the Custom Properties list, so let's give it one. Click the Add button.

The Add Property dialog box opens with the General tab up and the Name field selected. In the Name field type: **Duo Dynamic Length**. Open the Format tab. From the Type list choose Number. Then, in the Format (Display As) field select One Decimal place w/ units. Return to the General tab and click the list arrow on the right side of the Default Units field. From the list select Inches (decimal). Now open the Advanced Tab. Click in the Prompt field and type the following: **Enter the length of the Duo Dynamic of the Dynamic Connector in inches using accuracy of one decimal place**. Then click the OK button at the bottom of the dialog box.

You have now edited a property and added a property. Now you just have to delete one.

In the Master Shapes list choose the Mouse. Then, in the Custom Properties field, select the Location property. Press the Remove button. Now you don't have to worry about the location of the mouse.

You've made your changes, so click the Next button. The Preview/Add list option should be pre-selected. If it isn't, select it. Click Next.

In the Show Properties section on the right, click To Be Added. Then, in the Master Shapes list, click the Dynamic Connector. The property you added shows up. Click any other master shape and the Custom Property list is blank. We did not add any other properties to any other shapes. Click the Mouse in the Master Shapes list. Nothing shows under the Custom Property list. Now go to the Show Properties section and click To Be Removed. The Location property you removed shows up. Now, in the Show Properties section click Final List. All the custom properties you left in the mouse shape show up, without the Location property.

Click Next. You are now at the Finish screen. Because this was only for practice, click Cancel to close the wizard without saving the changes. You have now edited, added, and deleted properties, and reviewed the changes.

On your own, edit the shapes in the exercise we were working on throughout this chapter. Remember to edit a *copy*, not the original. On the last screen, Cancel to exit without saving changes unless you are confident you will not confuse the new copy with the original. Then do the same for one of the examples we used earlier in the book that's not currently open in the workspace. This will give you practice in all of the areas the Custom Properties Editor can edit, and the subtle differences between them.

Now we have covered all the ways you can edit and view custom properties of a shape. Let's review what we learned.

Summary

You learned that custom properties of a shape can hold data in different formats and types. You saw how to open and use the following:

✦ Custom Properties Window, which resides in the workspace. You can use it to see the custom properties of a shape, or enter values for custom properties. You also learned how to use it to open the Define Custom Properties dialog box

✦ Custom Properties dialog box, which enables you to view custom properties for a shape, enter unique values, and open the Define Custom Properties dialog box

✦ Define Custom Properties dialog box, which enables you to edit, add, or remove custom properties for a shape. It also enables you to set parameters for a custom property such as Label, Type, Format, Value, and/or Prompt. You also learned to input values for a custom property in this dialog box.

✦ Custom Properties Editor, which enables you edit master shapes on a stencil, on an active drawing page, or in any Visio drawing page. This wizard enables you to edit, add, or remove custom properties for master shapes. You can define all of the custom property parameters that are in the Define Custom Properties dialog box, plus additional parameters such as Default Values, Default Units, Row Name, and Sort Key. Also, option settings Add on Drop and Hidden that enable you to make the shape ask the user for data or hide the custom property from the user.

With the ability to manipulate the custom properties of shapes you have an entirely new dimension of Visio 2000 and business under your control. In the next chapter, you will learn even more about shapes as you learn to create shape groups.

✦   ✦   ✦

Working with Shape Groups

Groups are a collection of shapes that function as one unit. For example, you can place a desk, computer, and chair into a group since each shape's placement is related and dependent upon one another. Therefore, rather than moving each shape individually, you can reposition the group in one step. Any time you are using several shapes that must behave as one unit, place the shapes in a group. This is true especially for office furniture and logos, such as the Techno Savvy Systems item created a couple of chapters ago.

You can construct groups from any type of shape, whether they consist of closed two-dimensional objects, lines, connectors, or all three. Grouping functions place shapes into one large two-dimensional unit. The objects' control handles and alignment boxes disappear; instead, one alignment box—with its own shape handles—surrounds the entire group. Users can then simply manipulate the shape group as a whole.

Grouping and Ungrouping Shapes

Grouping and ungrouping shapes is simple. In fact, you grouped a few shapes in Chapter 22 during the discussion on group behavior modifications. The task consists of creating a few shapes, selecting them, and then applying the Group function. To ungroup a shape group, select the group and click Ungroup. You can access these features from the Shape drop-down menu or the Action toolbar.

Placing shapes in a group

For starters, place a group of simple shapes and a connector onto the drawing page. Attach the connector to the shapes. Then arrange all three objects into a group. The following exercise is a step-by-step demonstration:

1. Open the Block Diagram template.

2. Drop the box and diamond shapes from the Blocks stencil onto the drawing page.

3. Drag the Line-Curve Connector between the two shapes. Connect the begin point to the box and the end point to the diamond. A small red box will appear over each shape's connection point when the attachment is complete.

4. Select all three shapes. A simple way to do this is to choose Edit ⇨ Select All.

5. Choose Shape ⇨ Grouping ⇨ Group. The shapes are now one happy group; no divisions or conflicts are noticeable. But sooner or later one will become jealous of another's success or wife. Anyway... an alignment box surrounds all three objects (as shown in Figure 24-1), indicating that they will act in unison.

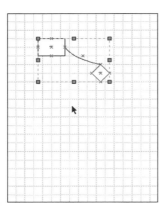

Figure 24-1: Each object's distinctive alignment box and/or shape handles have been replaced with the group's single alignment box and control handles.

Tip

Metafiles often contain complex and integrated graphic features, including bitmaps and text. Such characteristics sometimes make it difficult to edit or reposition these imported objects without first converting the metafile into a group. Do this by selecting the metafile image(s) then choosing Shape ⇨ Grouping ⇨ Convert to Group.

Ungrouping shapes

Grouping shapes is easy, but perhaps ungrouping them is even easier, for you do not have to create any objects and put them together — you just take them apart. Here's how:

1. Use the shape group created previously. Select the group by clicking any of the group shapes. You may have to do this twice depending on which Selection feature you have activated in the Behavior dialog box's Behavior tab.

2. Select Shape ➪ Grouping ➪ Ungroup (see Figure 24-2). The shapes have regained their individual characteristics. They can now be moved and deleted one by one.

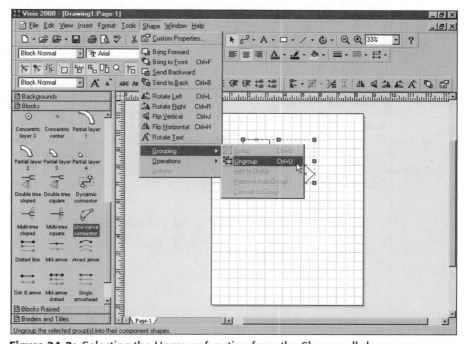

Figure 24-2: Selecting the Ungroup function from the Shape pull-down menu

If you do not see alignment boxes and handles on individual shapes, you probably need to adjust the selection highlighting features on the Behavior dialog box. See Chapter 22 for more details.

Editing Shape Groups and Their Members

Knowing how to group and ungroup shapes is only a small part of grouping applications. Situations and projects often demand editing groups and even group members. Visio 2000 enables program users to do both. The rest of this chapter is designed to show you how.

Selecting groups and group members

The Selection feature enables users to control how a group and its members are highlighted. By highlighted, I'm referring to a shape's handles and alignment box — properties that arise after clicking a shape and/or group. To choose one of the Selection options, you must first create a group. Next, choose Format ➪ Behavior to pull up the Behavior dialog box. Look on the Behavior tab for the Selection feature under the Group Behavior section. Click the arrow button at the end of the Selection box to view the options. Select one, then click OK to implement the change.

Group First is the default setting. With this option, when you first click a group shape, it highlights the entire group. Clicking again highlights the selected group member (see Figure 24-3). Notice that selected group members contain handles marked with X's. You can position or resize the selected shape, having minimal — if any — effects on the other shapes. The Members First setting events work in the opposite order of those for the Group First setting. Your first click on a group shape highlights that particular shape; clicking that shape again highlights the entire group. The Group Only setting only highlights the group, not its members.

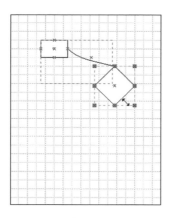

Figure 24-3: You can select individual group members.

Visio 2000 enables users to select more than just one group member. For example, after highlighting a group member, hold down the Shift key, then click another group member. The second shape's handles will become highlighted too — except they will be in light blue. Only the first selected shape, the primary selection, is highlighted in green. To highlight additional group members or even non-members, just press the Shift key and click another shape.

Making changes to a group member

You can make alterations to separate entities within a group without enacting changes to all group members. Visio 2000 allows you to format a group member's size, position, and resize behavior.

Manipulating a shape's size or position

Depending on the Selection setting, click the group member you wish to modify. The selected member contains handles marked with X's. You can resize or reposition the shape and it will still remain a part of the group. Drag the corner handles to resize the group member. To reposition an instance, click anywhere inside the shape other than on any handles, then drag the shape. Click outside of the group when finished.

Dragging a group member's handles does not affect other 2-D shapes (for example, closed shapes) within the group. Glued 1-D shapes (other than guides), however, are affected by such changes. Objects like 1-D lines and connectors must maintain an elastic attachment to the edited group member and its counterpart(s).

You can simultaneously apply shadows and fill to all group members by selecting the group and then using the appropriate feature. To make shadow, line, and/or fill color changes to an individual group member, click that particular shape and then implement the feature.

Resizing group members individually is not difficult. For example, click a particular member and then drag its shape handles. You cannot distort the shape's form, as with non-group members. A group member always maintains its proportion. Thus, dragging the middle shape handle of a square — when it's a group member — will not create a rectangle, only a larger or smaller square. You must remove a shape from its group to distort its length or width.

Notice that enlarging a group member shape sometimes causes it to exceed the group's designated alignment box (as shown in Figure 24-4). The problem is that the group's alignment box is not responding to the new changes. You can remedy this by selecting the group then choosing Shape ➪ Operations ➪ Update Alignment Box. The shape group's alignment box will then be placed around all group members.

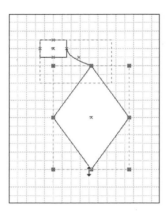

Figure 24-4: Resizing a group member may cause it to exceed the group's alignment box size; use the Update Alignment Box function to fix this problem.

Manipulating a group member's resize behavior

You just learned that you can resize individual group members as well as position them. You can also affect how a group member resizes with its group by adjusting its resize behavior. If you go to the Behavior dialog box's Behavior tab, and look in the Resize Behavior section, you will notice that the default setting for groups is Use Group's Setting. Selecting individual group members reveals that the same setting is applied to all group members. This setting enables grouped shapes (and the area between them) to size as one unit.

Table 24-1 describes how all three Resize Behavior functions work. Both the Scale with Group and Use Group's Setting functions behave similarly. However, applying the Reposition Only setting to a group member will only cause that shape to reposition. Thus, while resizing the group, the shape with the Reposition Only setting is only repositioned, not resized (as shown in Figure 24-5).

Table 24-1
Resize Behavior Options

Option	Function
Scale with Group	Group member is resized and scaled proportionately with other group members.
Reposition Only	Group member is not resized with other group members, only repositioned.
Use Group's Setting	All group members are resized in a fashion that maintains their proportion to each other (default setting).

The following exercise demonstrates how the Reposition Only feature works:

1. Open the Basic Diagram template.

2. Drop two squares and a circle onto the drawing page.

3. Place all three shapes into a group by first selecting them, then choosing Shape ➪ Grouping ➪ Group.

4. Select the circle shape. Next, choose Format ➪ Behavior. Look for the Resize Behavior section on the Behavior dialog box's Behavior tab. Click the radio button marked Reposition Only. Click the OK button.

5. Select the entire group. Drag a group handle to enlarge the group's size. Notice that all of the group members other than the one programmed to Reposition Only are becoming larger (see Figure 24-5).

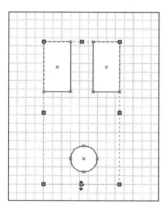

Figure 24-5: Using the Reposition Only setting

Deleting groups and group members

Several ways exist to delete groups and shape members from the drawing page. First, you can use the Drawing Explorer features. A more routine method involves selecting the shape or shape member from the drawing window and then either pressing the Delete key or choosing Edit ➪ Delete ➪ Selection. If you accidentally erase a shape or group, click the Undo button (located on Standard toolbar).

Cross-Reference

See Chapter 15 for more information on the Drawing Explorer.

Removing shapes from a group

Removing shapes from a group and deleting a group member are two different things. Whereas the first action merely discontinues a shape's inclusion with a group, deleting a group member erases the selected shape from the drawing page. You use the Remove from Group command to revoke a shape's group membership when it is no longer getting along with the other shapes or when bad press makes the shape's inclusion embarrassing to the group organization. Of course, most shapes don't instigate disputes, they are just no longer a useful component of the group. The shape should look on the bright side, though—at least it wasn't deleted!

An example may make understanding the removal process simpler. Say you have a file cabinet that you'd like to remove from your office suite. Select the file shape. The selected group member should be the only object highlighted. Next, Choose Shape ⇨ Grouping ⇨ Remove from Group. The file is no longer a part of your office furniture (see Figure 24-6). The rest of the objects (for example, desk, computer, and desk chair), however, remain in the shape group.

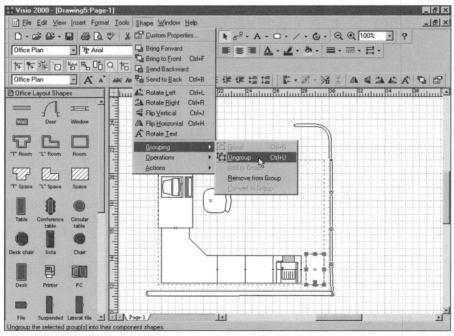

Figure 24-6: The file is no longer part of the group.

Adding shapes to a group

Your supervisor just notified you that she's ordered a larger file cabinet to replace the one removed from your office. All you need to do is update your Visio document accordingly. This time, drop the Lateral File shape from the Office Layout Shapes stencil near the rest of your office furnishings. Select the group in which you wish to add the shape and the Lateral File. Choose Shape ⇨ Grouping ⇨ Add to Group. Presto! The new file cabinet is part of the group.

Tip　Be sure that you know what size file cabinet the supervisor is sending; after all, Visio 2000 enables you to size office furniture. Using the Dimension Line instance for assistance, drag the Lateral File shape by its handles until it reaches the proper measurement.

Note　You cannot glue guides to a shape group and manipulate the group as you would a shape.

You can also add new shapes to a group by simply dropping them on the shape group. This action, however, requires adjusting features within the Visio 2000 program. For example, as acting city mayor, you need a visual document to reveal your plans to place a stoplight at the newest intersection. In Visio 2000, you can do this by applying the Add to Group command or using the Add Shape to Groups and Accept Dropped Shapes features. Let's use the latter method here:

Open the Directional Map template. Drop the Road Square and 3-Way shapes from the Road Shapes stencil onto the drawing page. Fit them together.

1. Select both shapes then choose Shape ⇨ Grouping ⇨ Group. Both shapes can now operate as one unit (notice that an alignment box surrounds both instances).

2. Drag the Stoplight shape (from the Transportation Shapes stencil) onto the drawing page, placing it a few inches from the group.

3. Select the Stoplight shape then choose Format ⇨ Behavior. Look for the Miscellaneous section on the Behavior tab of the Behavior dialog box. Check the Add Shape to Groups on Drop Box then click OK. See Figure 24-7.

4. Dragging the Stoplight to the intersection will not work yet; the group will not accept the shape unless programmed to do so. Select the group, then choose Format ⇨ Behavior again. Look for the Group Behavior section on the Behavior dialog box's Behavior tab. Check the Accept Dropped Shapes box. Click OK to finalize your choice.

5. Drag the Stoplight onto the 3-Way intersection. The shape is welcomed into the group — and you'll now most likely win a new term as mayor.

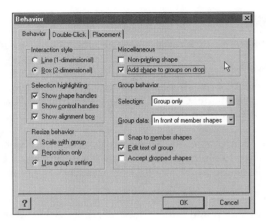

Figure 24-7: The Add Shape to Groups and Accept Dropped Shapes features are located on the Behavior dialog box's Behavior tab.

Positioning shape groups

As a whole, groups behave the same way as any typical 2-D shape does. In fact, you position groups (even those containing bitmaps and other imported objects) with the same methods you use with other shapes. The following placement features work the same with groups as they do for shapes:

The Rotation Tool button

Rotate Left button and command

Rotate Right button and command

Flip Vertical button and command

Flip Horizontal button and command

Reverse Ends command

Align Shapes buttons

Distribute Shapes buttons

You can also use the Bring Forward button, Send Backward button, Bring to Front button and command, and the Send to Back button and command to position groups behind, in front of, or in between other shapes and groups.

Cross-Reference   You can give a group a 1-D interaction setting. For more information on interaction styles as well as an explanation on how 1-D and 2-D shapes differ, see Chapter 22.

Summary

Overall, groups operate similarly to shapes. However, integrating related shapes prevents you from wasting needless time repositioning and modifying a horde of instances. Use the grouping techniques and functions presented in this chapter regularly to increase your drawing proficiency.

In conclusion, this chapter covered the following points:

✦ Groups are a collection of shapes that operate in a drawing as one unit.

✦ People place shapes into groups to avoid repositioning each group component; thus saving a lot of time.

✦ Groups, by default, are categorized as 2-D objects.

✦ The Group and Ungroup functions are commands on the Shape ⇨ Grouping drop-down menu, with corresponding buttons on the Action Toolbar.

✦ In many cases, you must convert a metafile into a group before repositioning or editing it.

✦ The Selection feature (found on the Behavior dialog box) controls the order in which you must click to select a group and its components.

✦ Resize Behavior options dictate how an individual shape resizes itself when you resize the entire group.

✦ Removing shapes merely takes an instance out of a group, whereas deleting a group member erases the selected shape from the drawing page.

✦ You can add shapes to a group by either applying the Add to Group command or dropping a shape into a group.

✦ Use the same tools and functions to reposition shape groups as you would to reposition shapes.

Group applications add a level of sophistication to the drawing process. Have fun practicing some more with them. In the next chapter, the last chapter of Part IV, I discuss shape operation functions that enable you to modify shapes, including combining, intersecting, and trimming instances.

✦   ✦   ✦

Using Shape Operations

Operations are additional Visio 2000 functions used to modify shapes and shape groups. None of these features can be found on the toolbars, only on the Shape drop-down menu (see Figure 25-1). Twelve operations are offered; you can view them by selecting Shape ➪ Operations. In general, these features affect how selected shapes interact with other shapes — sometimes in radical ways. Many operations enable you to dismember shapes, delete shape areas, or merge several shapes into one shape (in various ways). Depending on the shapes and the number of operations you use, the results can be endless. Overall, you will find these features important for creating a diverse amount of images and diagrams.

Applying Operations

Operations function in various ways. Classifying them into categories is difficult because of their range and sophistication. For instance, the Reverse Ends feature merely reverses the placement of a selected shape or shape group. Compare this function to the Fit Curve command, which transforms polygonal lines into splines, or the Union feature that merges two or more shapes into one indistinguishable shape. Obviously, not all operations merge or divide shapes.

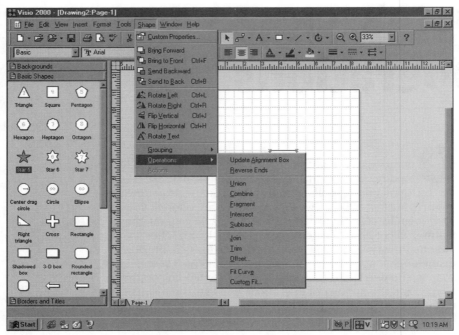

Figure 25-1: Shape Operation functions can only be found by selecting Shape ⇨ Operations.

Due to the variety and complexity involved with the subject matter, I discuss and include separate exercises for many of the 12 Visio 2000 operations. I also provide some tips on how you can integrate several operations on shapes for certain effects. You learn how to use these features with closed shapes, line segments, and groups. Though brief, the material is still quite extensive in scope. Therefore, I can promise you that after this chapter, working with shapes will never be the same. You'll finally realize how much fun creating your own shapes can be by using any of the following 12 operations:

Update Alignment Box	Readjusts a shape's or shape group's alignment box to reflect recent changes
Reverse Ends	Flips a shape or shape group both horizontally and vertically
Union	Merges overlapping shapes into one shape
Combine	Merges overlapping shapes into one shape, but deletes the area where the shapes intersect

Fragment	Divides overlapping shape areas into separate shapes
Intersect	Overlapping shape areas remain while the rest of the shapes are discarded
Subtract	All secondary selections are deleted; parts of the primary selection are deleted if they contain overlapping secondary selections
Join	Groups lines and shapes into one unit; joined shapes lose their fill, which can be reapplied but not to overlapping areas
Trim	Cuts shapes and lines at points where they intersect
Offset	Places two derivative shapes an equal distance from the selected object
Fit Curve	Transforms straight and polygonal lines into splines
Custom Fit	Maintains an imported object's line quality

Updating the Alignment Box

The Update Alignment Box function does not create or distribute shapes; it simply updates a shape's or shape group's alignment box. Sometimes when resizing or positioning a two-dimensional object, its alignment box fails to accommodate those changes. Snapping other shapes to the object's alignment box can then become a problem because they are not snapping where you want them. The Update Alignment Box operation solves this problem.

Problems with the alignment box are especially common with shape groups. Often, after resizing a group member, the group alignment box does not extend to the member's new boundaries (see Figure 25-2). In these cases, you must select the group and then choose Shape ➪ Operations ➪ Update Alignment Box. This action "reminds" the alignment box to reflect the recent change. The following exercise demonstrates how the process works:

1. Open the Basic Diagram template.

2. Drop a Square, Triangle, and Pentagon from the Basic Shapes stencil onto the drawing page.

3. Select the three shapes and then choose Shape ➪ Grouping ➪ Group.

4. Select the Triangle, drag it several inches from the group and then resize it.

4. Select the group. Notice that the alignment box needs updating. Choose Shape ➪ Operations ➪ Update Alignment Box. The alignment box then expands appropriately, as shown in Figure 25-3.

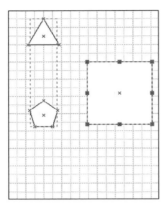

Figure 25-2: This group's alignment box needs updating

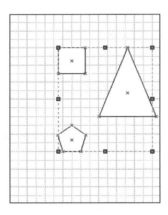

Figure 25-3: An updated alignment box

Reversing Ends

Like the Update Alignment Box command, the Reverse Ends operation is one of the simplest features discussed in this chapter. It works similarly to the Flipping methods present on the Action toolbar and Shape drop-down menu. In fact, applying the Reverse Ends operation creates the same result as implementing both the Flip Vertical and Flip Horizontal functions upon a shape or shape group. Here's an example:

1. Open the Blank Drawing template and then open the Clip Art stencil.

2. Locate the shape icon called Presentation. Drop it onto the drawing page. Notice that a man is on the left and the chart to which he's pointing is on the right (see Figure 25-4).

3. Select the Presentation instance if it's not already highlighted. Choose Shape ⇨ Flip Horizontal. The man is now on the right while the chart is on the left.

4. Choose Shape ⇨ Flip Vertical. The man is still on the right, but he and the chart are now upside down.

5. Click the Undo button twice to undo the Flip Vertical and Flip Horizontal features. The shape should now look exactly as it did in Step 2.

6. Select the Presentation shape if it's not already selected. Choose Shape ⇨ Operations ⇨ Reverse Ends. The man and the chart, besides being upside down, have switched sides (see Figure 25-5). This is the same result as having applied both the Flip Vertical and Flip Horizontal features in Steps 3 and 4.

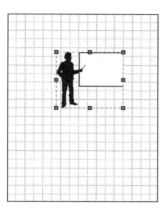

Figure 25-4: The original placement of the Presentation shape

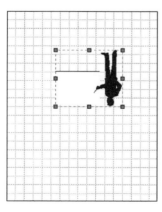

Figure 25-5: The Reverse Ends operation reverses a shape's or a group's horizontal and vertical presentation.

When you need to apply both the Flip Vertical and Flip Horizontal functions, save a step by using the Reverse Ends operation.

Uniting Shapes

The Union operation merges overlapping shapes into one shape. To understand this concept, imagine the boundaries of each shape "dissolving" where the instances overlap. The exercise below reveals how you can unite two triangles in order to create a star, a shape similar to the Star 6 shape in the Basic Shapes stencil:

1. Open the Blank Drawing template and then open the Basic Shapes stencil.

2. Drop two Triangles on the drawing page.

3. Apply the Flip Vertical command to one of the Triangles. Next, drag that shape onto the other Triangle until their two middle connection points overlap (as shown in Figure 25-6). If you wish, add fill to the shapes.

4. Select both Triangles and then choose Shape ➪ Operations ➪ Union. Both of the shapes will then merge to form a shape similar to the Star 6 shape in the Basic Shapes stencil (see Figure 25-7). Notice that all overlapping boundaries have meshed to form one shape.

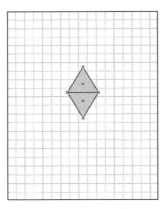

Figure 25-6: Overlapping two Triangles to create a star

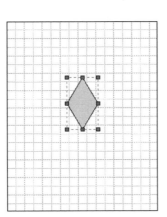

Figure 25-7: The newly created star

The Union feature enables you to create a variety of shapes — even those (of course), that you cannot find on Visio 2000 stencils. You can even apply the operation to shape groups, the subject of the next exercise:

1. Open the Blank Drawing template and then the Basic Shapes stencil.

2. Drop two Circles onto the drawing page. Situate them so that one Circle's left connection point coincides with the other's right connection point.

3. Select both shapes and then choose Shape ⇨ Grouping ⇨ Group to place the Circles in a group.

4. Drop a Square from the Basic Shapes stencil onto the drawing page. Do not place the Square in a group.

5. Drag the Square so that its center connection point coincides where the two Circles' connection points meet (as shown in Figure 25-8).

6. Select both the Square and the group of Circles. Choose Shape ⇨ Operations ⇨ Union. You should end up with a shape like the one shown in Figure 25-9.

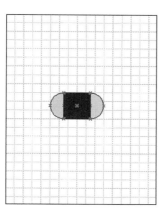

Figure 25-8: Dragging the Square onto the two Circles

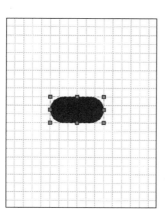

Figure 25-9: Uniting the Circle group and the Square

Many of the operations work just as well for groups as they do for shapes. You can, as demonstrated in the example above, even use them to form interactions between shapes and shape groups.

Note The Union operation can also be applied to overlapping members of a group. Simply select the group or the group members that you wish to merge and then apply the Union feature.

Combining Shapes

The Combine operation also merges shapes but in a way quite different from the Union function. Whereas Union meshes the bodies of overlapping shapes, Combine deletes the areas where shape bodies overlap. The exercise below demonstrates how this process works:

1. Open the Blank Drawing template and the Basic Shapes stencil.

2. Draw a rectangle (2 inches × 3 inches) with the Rectangle Tool.

3. Drop two Stars onto the rectangle. Place one of the Stars half inside and half outside of the rectangle. Place the other Star completely inside of the rectangle. You should have something similar to Figure 25-10.

4. Select all three shapes and then choose Shape ➪ Operations ➪ Combine. Notice that where the shapes overlapped one another, only the drawing page grid exists (see Figure 25-11).

Although some shape parts are deleted, the Combine feature merges all of the remaining shape parts into one shape. Like the Union operation, you can use the Combine feature on shape groups, as well.

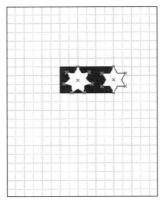

Figure 25-10: Placing two Stars onto the rectangle

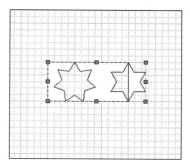

Figure 25-11: The Combine operation applies a "cookie-cutter" effect to areas of overlapping shapes.

Fragmenting Shapes

Whereas the Union and Combine operations transform several overlapping shapes into one shape, the Fragment operation breaks several overlapping shapes into even smaller shapes. Specifically, the Fragment command "fragments" or divides overlapping shape areas. This step-by-step example explains how the operation works:

1. Open the Blank Drawing template and then open the Basic Shapes stencil.
2. Drop a Circle onto the drawing page.
3. Drop a Triangle onto the Circle so that their center connection points coincide.
4. Select both shapes and then choose Shape ➪ Operations ➪ Fragment. The overlapping shape sections are transformed into shapes (see Figure 25-12). Each can be selected and dragged (as shown in Figure 25-13).

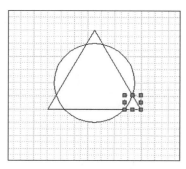

Figure 25-12: Creating fragments of an overlapping Triangle and Circle

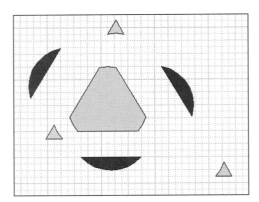

Figure 25-13: Space the fragments by dragging them.

You can do a number of things with the fragments. First, you can sort them in a particular pattern and then apply the Group command to keep them in place. You may even wish to overlap fragmented shapes in order to later form other shapes by implementing the Union function. For example, you can use fragments of the Star 7 sides, a Triangle, and a narrow rectangle to form a maple leaf. You can create all kinds of neat stuff.

Note Some people find that "fragmenting" three overlapping circles is useful in designing Venn diagrams.

Tip Transpose groups over one another and then use the Fragment operation. A number of interesting shapes and patterns will develop. Save all of your fragments in a separate drawing file. The components may become part of a project sometime down the road.

Intersecting Shapes

The Intersect feature works in the opposite way as the Combine function. Whereas overlapping sections of shapes were deleted when using Combine, only the overlapping areas remain in Intersect operations. The following exercise takes you through a step-by-step approach involving this feature:

1. Open the Blank Drawing template and then open the Basic Shapes stencil.

2. Drop two Circles onto the drawing page. Drag one circle so that its left connection point coincides with the other Circle's center connection point (as shown in Figure 25-14).

3. Select both Circles and then choose Shape ➪ Operations ➪ Intersect. A football-like shape will emerge where the two circles intersected (see Figure 25-15).

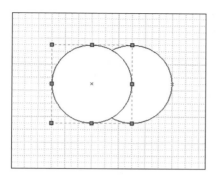

Figure 25-14: Placing two Circles onto the drawing page

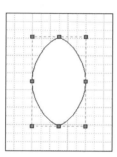

Figure 25-15: With the Intersect feature, the overlapping areas of the shapes remain, while the rest is discarded.

Note

Applying the Intersect operation to shapes that do not overlap results in the deletion of those shapes.

Subtracting Shapes

The Subtract operation enables you to subtract selected shapes from your primary selection (the first shape you select). The Combine feature, which acts similarly, still differs from the Subtract command in several ways. First, the Combine operation does not distinguish between primary and secondary selections (all the selected shapes other than the primary selection). Secondly, only overlapping areas are deleted with Combine features. The Subtract command, however, deletes all secondary selections. Parts of the primary selection are "subtracted" only if they overlap with those secondary selections.

Note

In regard to Group Operations, the first shape that you select is called a primary selection. Shapes selected after the first shape are referred to as secondary selections.

Use the Subtract feature to delete parts of a shape. The exercise below serves as an example:

1. Open the Blank Drawing template and then open the Basic Shapes stencil.

2. Drop a Rectangle and a 3-D Box on the drawing page. Place the box shape onto the Rectangle, so that half of it remains on the drawing page (as shown in Figure 25-16).

3. Select the Rectangle first. The green shape handles and alignment box indicate that it is your primary selection. Click the box while holding the Shift key. The light blue shape handles and alignment box indicate that it is a secondary selection.

4. Choose Shape ➪ Operations ➪ Subtract. The 3-D Box is now gone; the area where it overlapped with the Rectangle has been "subtracted" (see Figure 25-17).

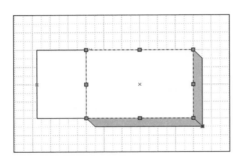

Figure 25-16: Placing a 3-D Box halfway on a Rectangle

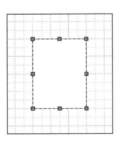

Figure 25-17: The Subtract command deletes all secondary selections, as well as the areas where they intersect with the primary selection.

The Subtract function is the only operation that distinguishes between primary and secondary selections.

Joining Line Segments

Although the Join operation can be used on closed shapes (for example, rectangles, circles, and triangles), it is primarily applied to line segments. The Join command can line up several line segments and then group them. Once enacted, the lines will operate as one unit. Use the operation in the example below:

1. Open the Blank Drawing template.

2. Draw two lines with the Line Tool, placing them about an inch apart.

3. Drag one of the lines so that it touches the other to form a 90-degree angle. Notice that you can click each line and that they operate as two different units.

4. Select both lines and then choose Shape ⇨ Operations ⇨ Join. The two lines now operate as one unit. An alignment box surrounds the joined segments (see Figure 25-18).

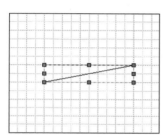

Figure 25-18: Joined lines have an alignment box around them.

The Join command transforms a group of one-dimensional lines into a two-dimensional object.

You can also join two-dimensional closed objects. The Join operation will maintain the geometry of the merged objects; however, the shapes will lose their fill. You can apply fill to the objects as a whole, but not to their overlapping areas (see Figure 25-19).

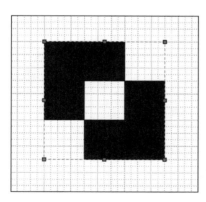

Figure 25-19: The Join operation affects the fill of two-dimensional closed objects.

Trimming Shapes

The Trim operation cuts or "trims" shapes where their lines intersect. For example, two line segments that intersect halfway through each other would be divided into four different line segments. Lines from two or more shapes are also cut at intersection points, as the following example demonstrates:

1. Open the Blank Drawing template and then open the Basic Shapes stencil.

2. Drop a Square and Triangle onto the drawing page. Place the Square so that its bottom-right connection point coincides with the Triangle's center connection point (as shown in Figure 25-20).

3. Select both shapes, and then choose Shape ➪ Operations ➪ Trim.

4. The shapes have lost their fill. You can drag each broken segment apart from their respective shapes (see Figure 25-21).

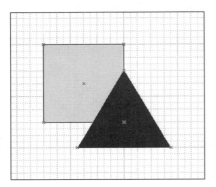

Figure 25-20: Placing a Square on top of a Triangle

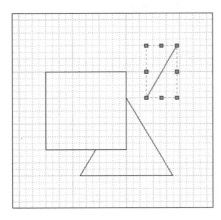

Figure 25-21: The "trimmed" Square and Triangle

Note   Although the Trim feature can break closed shapes into broken segments, all lines are assigned two-dimensional settings. Even one-dimensional line segments are transformed into two-dimensional objects after the Trim operation is implemented upon them.

Offsetting Shapes

The Offset command enables you to place two derivative shapes an equal distance from the selected object. For example, the Offset command can place a line one inch above and one inch below a horizontal line segment. If the selected segment is a vertical line, the Offset feature places equidistant lines to the left and right of the shape. You can also place shapes one inch to the inside and outside of a selected polygon. However, only a single line segment with no angles or intersections can be duplicated in size and length. Use the following example to further understand how the offsetting process operates:

1. Open the Blank Drawing template and then open the Basic Shapes stencil.

2. Drop a Pentagon from the Basic Shapes stencil onto the drawing page.

3. Click the Pointer Tool button. Size the Pentagon so that its alignment box covers 3 inches × 3 inches of the drawing page.

4. Select Shape ➪ Operations ➪ Offset. The Offset dialog box appears (as shown in Figure 25-22). Type **1** in the Offset Distance area. Click the OK button. Two new Pentagons should appear on the page, both one inch from the selected shape. The outside Pentagon is larger than the selected shape, while the inside Pentagon is smaller (see Figure 25-23).

Figure 25-22: The Offset dialog box

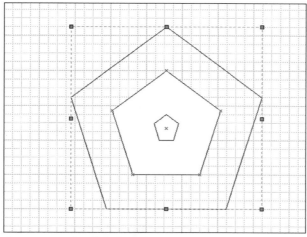

Figure 25-23: Offsetting Pentagons

Note   You can set the measurements in the Offset dialog box according to those defined on the Page Setup dialog box's Page Size tab. For example, if you're working with metric units, you can offset shapes by millimeters instead of inches.

Tip   If you set the offsetting distance too high for a closed shape, the inside shape cannot form. Instead, only several broken lines will develop in the given space. Avoid this by keeping in mind the measurements of your selected shape.

Applying the Fit Curve Function

The Fit Curve feature transforms straight lines into curves. The new line's path retains the same vertices of the original segment. Complete the exercise below to get an understanding of what the Fit Curve operation does:

1. Open the Blank Drawing template again, if you don't already have it open.

2. Click the Line Tool button. Draw an M-like shape. Connect each line so that vertices form between each segment (as shown in Figure 25-24).

3. Select Shape ➪ Operations ➪ Fit Curve. Notice that the straight lines now appear as splines (see Figure 25-25).

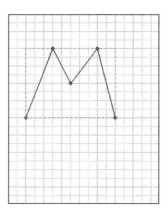

Figure 25-24: Vertices should appear between each line segment.

Note   The Fit Curve function cannot curve straight or angled connectors.

You can also apply the Fit Curve feature to closed two-dimensional shapes. Straight lines within a square or triangle are then curved so that the spline passes through the original shape's vertices. For example, using the Fit Curve operation on a Rectangle transforms it into an oval.

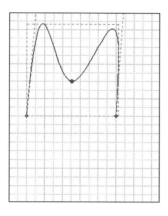

Figure 25-25: The Fit Curve operation turns straight lines into splines.

Custom Fitting Imported Shapes

The Custom Fit operation is used primarily on imported images. The operation's dialog box (shown in Figure 25-26) contains four elements that enable you to fit a shape onto the drawing page without affecting the image's overall quality.

✦ **Periodic Splines.** Creates splines to maintain some of the lines' smoothness

✦ **Circular Arcs.** Converts polygonal line vertices into circular arcs

✦ **Cusps and Bumps.** Maintains the crispness of image

✦ **Error Tolerance.** Sets the amount of error required for rendering the object's lines

Simply select the imported object and then choose Shape ➪ Operations ➪ Custom Fit to access the Custom Fit dialog box. Check the Periodic Splines, Circular Arcs, and Cusps and Bumps boxes in order to check or uncheck those features. Type in the error tolerance amount that you find acceptable.

Figure 25-26: The Custom Fit dialog box

Note   The greater the Error Tolerance setting, the more chance you have of increasing the imported image's size.

Tip   Some clip art images and bitmaps will require that you use the Ungroup feature before applying the Custom Fit operation.

Summary

Visio 2000 operations provide users with an extensive and advanced repertoire for modifying and creating shapes. In conclusion, this chapter covered the following points:

✦ Regularly update the alignment boxes that have edited shape groups within them.

✦ Applying the Reverse Ends operation creates the same result as implementing both the Flip Vertical and Flip Horizontal functions on a shape or shape group.

✦ The Union operation merges overlapping shapes into one shape.

✦ The Combine operation combines intersecting shapes into one shape, but deletes the areas where the shapes overlap.

✦ The Fragment operation divides or "fragments" overlapping shape areas into separate shapes.

✦ The Intersect operation deletes all shapes except in the areas where they overlap.

✦ The Subtract operation deletes all secondary selections, including parts of the primary selection that overlaps with the secondary selections.

✦ The Join operation groups lines and shapes into one unit.

✦ The Trim operation cuts or "trims" shapes and lines where they intersect.

✦ The Offset operations places two derivative shapes an equal distance from the selected object.

✦ The Fit Curve operation transforms straight and polygonal lines into splines.

✦ Use the Custom Fit operation to maintain an imported object's line quality.

This concludes Part IV. The next chapter discusses some of Visio 2000 Standard's numerous macros.

✦   ✦   ✦

Mastering
Visio 2000
Tool Option and
Macro Features

T his section offers chapters on Tool Options, key Visio
macros, and database wizards. Although the information
in these chapters is geared primarily for sophisticated
business drawing software users, the features discussed can
help professionals in all walks of life with overall convenience
and project efficiency.

Utilizing General and Advanced Tool Options

In this chapter, I show you how to manipulate user settings. These settings have to do with the appearance of Visio features and how Visio behaves . . . which is well, I hope.

The General Tab Options

To access the tool options, select Tools ⇨ Options from the menu bar. Here you have the opportunity to explore options on three of the tabs: General, Drawing, and Advanced.

The General tab, shown in Figure 26-1, features three groups of options: User options, Enable ScreenTips, and Color settings.

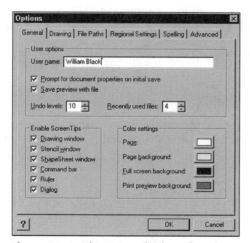

Figure 26-1: The General tab tool options

User options

The User options group on the General tab provides you with the following options:

✦ **User name.** Indicates the author of the file. In the text field, enter the author name. This is usually the name of the person working on the computer. This name appears in the Author section of File ⇨ Properties. The Properties dialog box appears the first time you save the file. The default name is the one registered when MS Windows was installed.

✦ **Prompt for document properties on initial save.** Specifies whether the properties for any particular file are displayed when you initially save the file.

✦ **Save preview with file.** Specifies that a preview is saved automatically whenever a file is saved.

✦ **Undo levels.** Sets the number of consecutive undoable actions or action levels. More memory is required to store a higher number of actions. You can set the number of undo levels up to 99, but no one makes that many mistakes in a row — do they?

✦ **Recently used files.** Enables you to specify the number of recently opened files listed on the File menu and in the Welcome To Visio dialog box that appears when you activate the Visio program. This list provides easy access to those recently used files, so it's a good idea to set this number to the maximum, which is nine in this case.

Enable ScreenTips

In the Enable ScreenTips group of options on the General tab, click the checkbox of any of the screen tip options you want activated. When you pause with the cursor over an item for which you've enabled this option, a screen tip comment identifying the tool or shape appears. You can activate screen tips for any of the following:

Drawing window	Command bar
Stencil window	Ruler
ShapeSheet window	Dialog

Note   When the user pauses the cursor over a shape that contains a hyperlink, the hyperlink appears in the screen tip instead of the shape comment.

Color settings

In the Color settings group of options on the General tab, select the colors for the page, page background, full screen background, and print preview background. The colors set for each appear on buttons next to each option. To change any of these color options, click the color button beside it. The Edit Color dialog box appears (see Figure 26-2), through which you can edit the basic color palette and create up to 16 custom colors.

Note These color settings affect Visio's appearance on your computer screen, not the actual colors of the shapes in a drawing.

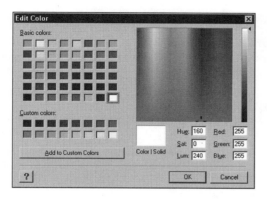

Figure 26-2: The Edit Color dialog box

The dialog box displays the basic MS Windows color palette. You can set the default color to any of the colors in the Basic colors section with just a click. If you prefer to build your own custom color, choose a color from the color picker or enter values for hue, saturation, luminosity, red, green, and blue. The selected color appears in the Color | Solid box. To add the color to the Custom Colors palette, click the Add to Custom Colors button.

Options on the Drawing Tab

The Drawing tab contains three groups of options: Text options, Drawing options, and Freeform drawing (see Figure 26-3). Let's take a look at each.

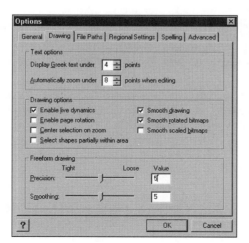

Figure 26-3: The Drawing tab tool options

Text options

The Text options group on the Drawing tab contains the following options related to the point size of your text:

✦ **Display Greek text under __ points.** When the text on screen is smaller than the point size you specify here, the text appears as a wavy line. This is known as *greeking the text* and has nothing to do with college fraternities. You can set this point size to any number up to 20 points.

✦ **Automatically zoom under __ points when editing.** When editing text, this option specifies to what size Visio magnifies the text. You can set the zoom to any number up to 20 points. Any larger than that, and you may need new glasses.

Drawing options

The following options are available in the Drawing options group on the Drawing tab:

✦ **Enable live dynamics.** When you resize or rotate a shape, you can see action as it occurs vice watching the box that bounds what you rotate until the action is complete.

✦ **Enable page rotation.** Enables you to use the rotation tool on the Standard toolbar to grab the corner of the currently displayed page to rotate the page. (This action is known as *dynamic page rotation*.)

✦ **Center selection on zoom.** Specifies that whatever shape was selected appears in the center of the window when you zoom in.

✦ **Select shapes partially within area.** If you prefer to select shapes using a selection net (that is, dragging to create a box around shapes you want to select on the drawing page), you can change the selection settings to also include shapes that are partially within the selection net.

✦ **Smooth drawing.** If unchecked, when you stretch a bitmap or other non-Visio object, you see a flicker.

✦ **Smooth rotated bitmaps.** If checked, when you rotate a bitmap, your Visio product cleans up the image through anti-aliasing and by adding colors as needed.

✦ **Smooth scaled bitmaps.** If checked, when you resize a bitmap, your Visio product cleans up the image through anti-aliasing and by adding colors as needed. To speed up performance, disable this option.

Freeform drawing

In the Freeform drawing group of options on the Drawing tab, you can set precision and smoothing controls for the line, arc, freeform, and pencil tools (see Figure 26-4). These tools are accessed from the Standard toolbar.

 Figure 26-4: From top to bottom: the line, arc, freeform, and pencil tools

The Precision slider bar controls the margin of error allowed while the freeform tool is drawing a straight line before it switches to drawing a spline. The indicator can be moved along the bar between Tight and Loose. The tighter you set the indicator, the more precise the margin of error; the looser you set it, the less precise the margin of error. The default is in the middle.

The Smoothing slider bar controls how precisely the mouse movements are smoothed while drawing a spline. The indicator can be moved along the bar between Tight and Loose. The tighter you set the indicator, the smoother the mouse movements; the looser you set it, the less smooth the mouse movements. The default is in the middle.

Options on the Advanced Tab

Three groups of options appear on the Advanced tab: User settings, Developer settings, and Stencil spacing (see Figure 26-5).

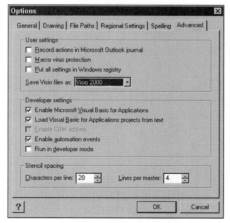

Figure 26-5: The Advanced tab tool options

User settings

In the User settings group on the Advanced tab, enable any of the following options by placing a check in the appropriate checkbox:

✦ **Record actions in Microsoft Outlook journal.** Specifies that your actions, such as editing a file, are recorded in the MS Outlook Journal.

✦ **Macro virus protection.** Checks macros for viruses. When this option is enabled, documents are run in design mode.

✦ **Put all settings in Windows registry.** Adds all possible application settings to the Windows registry. The default only adds certain settings to simplify the registry. These are usually nondefault settings and a few others, such as file paths, import and export filters, and last files.

✦ **Save Visio files as.** Specifies the default format files are saved in when you choose File ⇨ Save As. You can select either Visio 2000 or Visio 5.0 for the file format.

Developer settings

The Developer settings group on the Advanced tab provides options useful to program developers interested in writing programs to control the Visio application. Such programs can be written in MS Visual Basic for Applications (VBA) or any programming language that supports automation. A program can use automation to incorporate Visio drawing capabilities or to automate certain Visio functions. The options are as follows:

✦ **Enable Microsoft Visual Basic for Applications.** Enables VBA.

✦ **Load Visual Basic for Applications projects from text.** Select this option if you want your VBA project to work in drawings that were made in Visio 5.0 or later. Your VBA project is compiled when the file is loaded, but the compiled project is never saved.

✦ **Enable COM add-ins.** Enables you to load COM Add-Ins.

✦ **Enable automation events.** Select this option if you want to be able to send Visio events to Visio add-ons and VBA macros.

✦ **Run in developer mode.** Enables certain user interface functions for the development environment. The Show ShapeSheet command is added to a shape's right-click shortcut menu. This also provides a means for identifying which connection points are inward, outward, or both.

Stencil spacing

In the Stencil spacing group of options on the Advanced tab, you can specify the number of characters per line on a stencil shape and how many lines of text can appear below the shape.

The Characters per line setting dictates how many characters can appear on each line before the text wraps; the maximum number for this setting is 20. The higher the number set, the more spacing that appears between shapes, and therefore the fewer shapes you can see without scrolling in the stencil window.

The Lines per master setting dictates how many lines of text can appear below the shape before the text is truncated and appended with " . . . " marks, the maximum number being 4. As with the Characters per line setting, the higher the number you set, the more spacing that appears between the shapes, and therefore the fewer shapes you can see without scrolling in the stencil window.

Color Palette Dialog Box Options

A color palette is available for selecting colors for the lines, shape fills (the color and pattern inside a shape), and text on the active drawing. You can customize the colors that appear on this palette. To display the current color palette, select Tools ➪ Color Palette from the menu bar (see Figure 26-6).

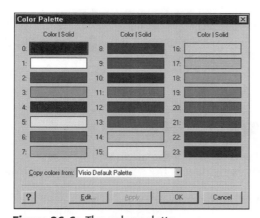

Figure 26-6: The color palette

Besides being able to select colors for your palette, you can choose a different color palette to use for the active file.

For lines, solid colors are used. For fills that don't have a pattern (item 0 or 1 in the Pattern lists in the Fill dialog box), the dithered version of the foreground color is used. For patterned and gradient fills (patterns 2 through 40), the solid color for the foreground and background colors is used.

Note   The default fill for Visio shapes is solid white.

With the edit button, you access an Edit Color dialog box. You can use the resulting dialog box to choose different colors. This dialog box behaves in exactly the same way as the one discussed in the "Color settings" section earlier in this chapter, except the settings in this dialog box affect the colors of the active drawing itself rather than those of the page or background.

If shapes in the file are formatted with a particular color, any edits you make to that color are then reflected in the formatting of those shapes. The colors you select or edit appear in the Color lists for the Fill, Text, and Line formatting dialog boxes.

Color | Solid

The heading Color | Solid refers to the solid colors displayed, 23 colors in all. In the Color lists, a 24th option is also included — no color.

If your display driver supports 16 colors, the left side of each color bar shows the color when dithered and the right side shows the closest solid color. If your display driver supports 256 colors or higher, you won't see dithered colors.

Copy colors from

The Copy colors from drop-down list toward the bottom of the dialog box displays a list of open drawing files and predefined color palettes. Choose from this list to copy a new color palette to the active drawing file.

Centering a Drawing on a Page

Another option available from the Tools option of the menu bar makes it easy for you to center a drawing on the drawing page. Choose Tools ➪ Center Drawing.

The drawing is automatically centered on the drawing page. If the drawing page and the printer page are the same size, the drawing is centered on the printed page also.

Tip You can adjust the margins if the drawing doesn't come out centered on the printed page.

Summary

In this chapter, you learned how to manipulate various user settings available through the Tools menu bar option. These settings affect the way Visio appears on your computer screen and how some of its functions behave. This chapter covered the following:

✦ User options related to document properties, undo levels, screen tips, and lists of recent files.

✦ Settings for changing the colors of Visio's screen appearance.

✦ Options for how small text can appear on the screen and how a number of drawing functions behave, including how precise the freeform drawing tool is and how smooth the mouse drawing functions are.

✦ Advanced settings for the save-as function, Visio action recording in the MS Outlook journal, and macro virus protection, as well as a variety of developer settings.

✦ Options for controlling the spacing of shapes on a stencil.

✦ Color palette customization and selection of colors for the lines, shape fills, and text on the active drawing file.

✦ Centering the drawing on both the screen page and the printed page.

The next chapter contains information on using key features of the tool macros.

✦　　✦　　✦

Utilizing Key Macro Features

In Chapter 23, I touched on custom properties. The key macro features include editing tools such as the Custom Properties Editor, the Shape Explorer, and timelines. In this chapter, you discover how to employ these powerful tools for editing the custom properties to create custom solutions tailored to your needs.

Using the Custom Properties Editor

You can edit existing custom properties, add new ones, or delete fields you don't need. You can also add custom properties to new shapes you create. Making your own custom solution is an advanced function and is associated with developing.

As a prerequisite for editing custom properties, you need to activate the developer mode by selecting Tools ➪ Options. Click the Advanced tab and select the Run in developer mode option. Click OK.

 Cross-Reference For more about developer options, see Chapter 26.

The Custom Properties Editor helps you select master shapes and add new data fields to them or delete existing data fields from them.

To access the Custom Properties Editor (shown in Figure 27-1), select Tools ➪ Macros ➪ Custom Properties Editor from the menu bar.

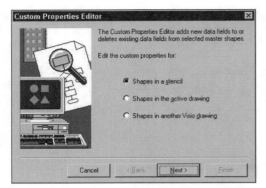

Figure 27-1: The Custom Properties Editor's opening screen

The first screen has three options:

✦ **Shapes in a stencil.** Choose this option and then choose a stencil in which to edit shapes.

✦ **Shapes in the active drawing.** Choose this option to edit shapes in an open drawing.

✦ **Shapes in another Visio drawing.** Choose this option and then choose a drawing in which to edit shapes.

Note If no drawing is open, the option Shapes in the active drawing is disabled.

Click Next to continue (as shown in Figure 27-2).

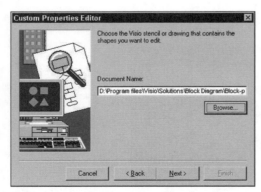

Figure 27-2: Choose a stencil or drawing.

Unless you had an active drawing open and chose to use it, the next screen prompts you to choose the stencil or drawing in which to edit shapes (see Figure 27-2). Use the Browse button to help you find the file.

After the name of the document you want to open appears in the text field, click Next. Visio loads the chosen file.

In the next screen, you are asked to indicate if you want to make a copy of the file or edit the original (as shown in Figure 27-3). Click Next, and Visio loads the property definitions for the shapes in the file.

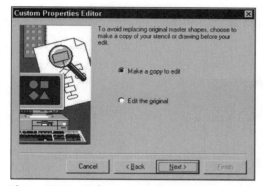

Figure 27-3: Make a copy of the file you wish to work on.

> **Tip**
>
> Unless you are sure you want to cross the editing Rubicon, do not change the original.

In the next screen, the master shapes that are in the stencil or drawing you selected are listed, as shown in the example in Figure 27-4. You can use the All button to select all the master shapes or hold down the control key and click the names of the master shapes that you want to edit. If you don't want to edit any existing shapes, use the None button. Click Next to continue.

The next screen displays two lists (as shown in Figure 27-5): the list of master shapes according to your previous choices and the list of custom properties. Notice that when you click each master shape, the Custom Properties list displays the custom properties of the particular master shape. The Custom Properties list is blank for those master shapes that have no custom property. Makes sense, doesn't it?

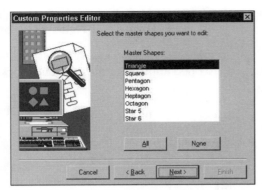

Figure 27-4: The list of master shapes from the chosen stencil or drawing

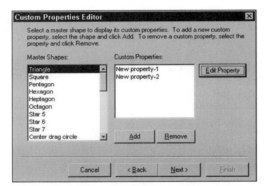

Figure 27-5: The list of chosen master shapes and the list of custom properties

Use the Add or Remove button to add or remove custom properties. Use the Edit Properties button to modify a custom property. The Edit Properties button is disabled when no custom property is listed.

When you press the Edit Properties button, a warning message appears. Please take note that what you change in the next dialog box can have far-reaching effects.

When you press OK, you get the same dialog box as when you press the Add button, as shown in Figure 27-6.

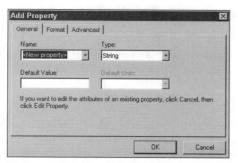

Figure 27-6: General tab in the Add Property dialog box

The Add Property General tab has the following four fields:

✦ **Name.** Enter a name for the new property.

✦ **Type.** Set a data type for the custom property value.

✦ **Default Value.** Give the property's initial value.

✦ **Default Units.** Set the unit type of the default value. The options in this drop-down list vary according to the default value entered.

Note

The Name field appears only in developer mode. In the Default Value field, you can enter a formula, but its value may be overwritten by the value you enter in the Custom Properties dialog box—even if you use the GUARD function to protect the formula.

The Add Property Format tab, shown in Figure 27-7, has three fields.

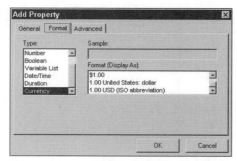

Figure 27-7: Format tab in the Add Property dialog box

✦ **Type.** Specifies a data type for the custom property value.

✦ **Sample.** As applicable, shows an example of the type.

✦ **Format (Display As).** As applicable, offers display options for the particular data type selected.

The Add Property Advanced tab has the following three fields:

✦ **Row Name.** Specify the name of the custom property's row in the ShapeSheet spreadsheet. For instance if you use the name Date or Size, the ShapeSheet spreadsheet shows the row name Prop.Date or Prop.Size, respectively. This option provides control over row naming for writing formulas, code, and so on and is a helpful tool for developers.

✦ **Sort Key.** Enter a number for each property. This establishes the order in which properties appear in the Custom Properties dialog box. The property with the number 1 will be the first in the Custom Properties dialog box that the user sees.

Note

In this dialog box, the properties appear in the order in which they were created.

✦ **Prompt.** Specify the explanatory text that appears when the particular property is selected.

✦ **Ask On Drop.** Enabling this checkbox option prompts users to enter custom property information for a shape when they create individual shapes or when they make copies of a shape.

✦ **Hidden.** Making a checkmark here indicates the property will be hidden from the user. The property will be visible only when you are running in developer mode. This option is useful for developers who need to store properties for specific purposes and want users to be unaware of them.

Note

Sort Key, Ask On Drop, and Hidden are available only in developer mode.

The Add Property Advanced tab can be seen in Figure 27-8.

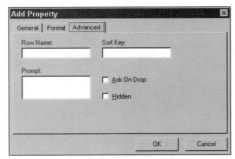

Figure 27-8: The Advanced tab in the Add Property dialog box

About Type options:

✦ **String.** Sets text as the custom property value. You can choose from Normal, Lowercase, and Uppercase text format.

✦ **Number.** Sets a number as the custom property value. The number may represent an amount in any of a variety of formats, including general numbers, whole numbers, numbers with up to four decimal places, and different types of fractions.

✦ **Fixed List.** Displays a drop-down list of items in the Custom Properties dialog box. To specify how the data is displayed, select this option from the Format tab. The Format (Display As) field becomes a list box with accompanying Add and Remove buttons to help you create a list.

✦ **Variable List.** Displays a drop-down list of items in the Custom Properties dialog box. To specify how the data is displayed, select this option from the Format tab. The Format (Display As) field becomes a list box with accompanying Add and Remove buttons to help you create a list.

✦ **Boolean.** Displays FALSE and TRUE as options that can be selected in the Custom Properties dialog box.

✦ **Currency.** Displays the system's regional currency settings. To specify how the data is displayed, choose from the options for how currency may be formatted in the Format (Display As) list.

✦ **Date.** Choose from a variety of date formats: short or long dates from the system settings or date and time from the system settings. Or, set a format for data and time independent of the system settings. The date and time can be displayed according to what options you choose in the Format (Display As) list. The choices include just about every possible way of expressing date and time.

✦ **Duration.** Displays elapsed time. You can choose from the options Weeks, Days, Hours, Minutes, Seconds, Hours and Minutes together, or Minutes and Seconds together.

From the Add Property dialog box, you return to the screen with the lists of master shapes and custom properties. What you have added is now included in the Custom Properties list. You can navigate among the master shapes and add or remove custom properties as you like. Once you have created the custom properties you want and set all the options for them, click Next.

In the next screen, you have the option to preview the list in which you've made changes (see Figure 27-9). If you elect, you can preview a list of the custom properties that you've added or removed, as shown in Figure 27-10. Here you can make final changes. Or, you may elect not to review the list, in which case you can click Finish.

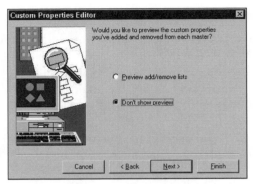

Figure 27-9: Choose to preview the list of custom properties.

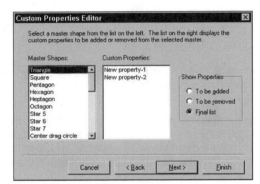

Figure 27-10: Review the list of custom properties added or removed.

The review screen is similar to the lists screen. However, it contains only those custom properties to be added or removed. You can elect to see only those properties to be added or those to be removed, as well as the entire final list.

When you are satisfied with the list, click Finish. If you want to make changes, move back to the list screen using the Back button and continue to add or remove custom properties.

Shape Explorer

Visio's Shape Explorer is a search tool through which you can locate shapes, stencils, template files, and wizards. It is a handy tool when you want to find one of these items but are unsure where to find it. You can use the search results list that is displayed in the Shape Explorer to add a shape to a drawing, open a stencil or template, or run a wizard.

Searching with Shape Explorer

To begin a search with Shape Explorer, select Tools ➪ Macros ➪ Shape Explorer from the menu bar. The main search dialog box appears, as shown in Figure 27-11.

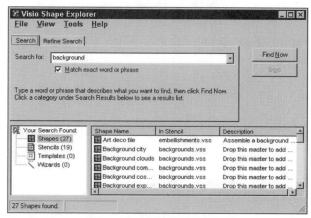

Figure 27-11: Visio Shape Explorer's main search dialog box

In the Search for field on the Search tab, enter a keyword, name, or phrase that targets your search.

If you want Shape Explorer to exactly match the word or phrase you entered (for example, to search for items associated with the word *station* but not those associated with *substation*), select the option Match exact word or phrase. To initiate the search, click the Find Now button. The Shape Explorer finds all references to your entry.

If you leave the Match exact word or phrase option unchecked, Shape Explorer looks for the word and all its variations.

You can refine your search through the Refine Search tab (shown in Figure 27-12) and limit the search to certain categories. For instance, to search for shapes and stencils only, you would check or uncheck the appropriate categories.

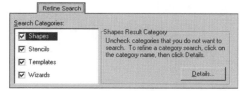

Figure 27-12: Visio Shape Explorer's Refine Search tab

You can also limit a Shape Explorer search to a particular database field by choosing a category and clicking the Details button on the Refine Search tab.

In the Details - Shapes dialog box (shown in Figure 27-13), you can limit the search to keywords in any of the database fields: Shape name, Status bar text, or Keywords. Leave unchecked any field that you do not want to search, and then click OK.

Figure 27-13: Details - Shapes dialog box

Choose another category in the Refine Search tab and click the Details button again to refine the search for that category. Repeat these steps for each category you want to search, and then click Find Now.

A list of search results at the bottom of the Shape Explorer dialog box is displayed. On the bottom left, the number of finds are listed per category.

Personalizing databases in Shape Explorer

When you enter a word or phrase, the Shape Explorer searches a database holding information related to each Visio shape, stencil, template, and wizard: name, description (status bar text), and some keywords. Make your search more efficient and run quicker by creating your own customized database that is a subset of the whole Visio database. You can compile this from stencils and templates you have created yourself. You can add customized keywords to Visio stencils or newly created stencils.

To create a personalized database in Shape Explorer, choose File ➪ Create User Database from the menu bar. The Create User Database dialog box appears (as shown in 27-14).

In the Database Name field, enter a name for your new database. In the Save database in section of the dialog box, select the location where you want the database file to be saved, and then click OK twice. The new filename appears in the File name list.

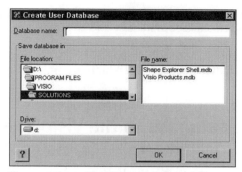

Figure 27-14: The Create User Database dialog box

Click OK and a message box appears, asking you if you want to add files to the database. Click the Yes button and the Add Files dialog box appears (shown in all its splendor in Figure 27-15).

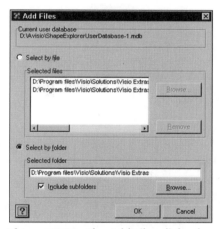

Figure 27-15: The Add Files dialog box

The two main options are whether to select by file or by folder. Choose the Select by file option to add individual files to the database, such as stencils, templates, or wizards. Click Browse to help you locate the file. Repeat this step to add additional files.

Choose the Select by folder option to add entire solutions to the database. Click Browse to help navigate to the folder that holds the solution you want, and then click OK. Repeat this step to add additional solutions. Place a checkmark in the Include Subdirectories checkbox to ensure that information from all the files inside the directory is included in the database.

Caution   It could take up to half an hour to perform this operation depending on the number of files you add to your personalized database and the speed of your computer.

The database that is created is formatted as an .mdb file, which is compatible with MS Access.

Adding your customized database to the Visio Shape Explorer search

You can add your customized database to the Shape Explorer search by accessing the Database Options dialog box from the Shape Explorer menu bar (Tools ⇨ Database Options).

At the bottom of the Database Options dialog box, under User Database, make sure the database to which you want to add files is indeed listed in the Location box (see Figure 27-16). If the database is not listed, click Browse to locate it.

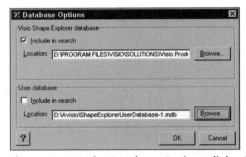

Figure 27-16: The Database Options dialog box

Note   You cannot add files to the original Visio database, only to a secondary database.

At the top of the Database Options dialog box, a check next to Include in search ensures that the original Visio database is included in the search. It should be listed in the Location field. You can actually choose another database to be the baseline database used for searches.

Note   You may add Visio files or solutions only to a database that was created in Shape Explorer.

Cross-Functional Flowcharts

You can use cross-functional flowcharts to show the relationship of a function among different parts of a business process or organizational units, such as departments, divisions, sections, or groups that are responsible for a particular part of a process. Figure 27-17 shows an example of such a flowchart. Shapes may be used to represent steps in the process. They may be placed in bands that correspond to functional units responsible for those particular steps or that represent levels of a process.

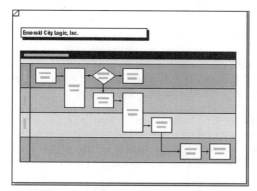

Figure 27-17: An example of a cross-functional flowchart

To open the Cross-functional Flowchart solution, choose File ➪ New ➪ Flowchart ➪ Cross-functional Flowchart from the main menu bar. The Cross-functional Flowchart Band Orientation dialog box opens, as shown in Figure 27-18, together with the Cross-functional Flowchart stencil.

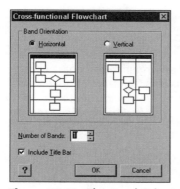

Figure 27-18: The Band Orientation screen

Choose the desired orientation for the bands in your flowchart. Set the number of bands, up to five. Indicate if you want to add a title bar to the top of the bands, and then click OK. The Band framework is generated. You can drag a functional band shape into the drawing to add additional bands as needed.

Tip   After you click the OK button in the Cross-functional Flowchart dialog box, you can add or delete bands, but you cannot change the orientation of the bands, nor can you add a title bar or bands with another orientation.

With an individual band selected, enter its label text. Position process shapes representing steps inside of or across bands to show their relative positions. Moving or inserting other bands should maintain this relationship. You can also position shapes to span two or more bands.

Tip   If you move or resize a band, a shape that spans multiple bands adjusts so that it continues its relative position in the band. If you insert a band between bands spanned by a shape, the shape resizes itself to span all three bands.

You can use the separator shape from the Cross-functional Flowchart stencil to establish relationships with the process steps to the right of or below them, depending on the flowchart orientation you specified. When you move a separator, you also move its associated shapes. From the Cross-Functional Flowchart Shapes stencil, drag a Separator shape to the place in the flowchart where you want to indicate a separation in the process. The shape spans across all the bands automatically.

Tip   If you want to shrink the distance between two separators, move the separator that is to the right or below (according to the flowchart orientation you selected) the other separator.

Tip   You can use PERT chart shapes in a cross-functional flowchart by choosing File ⇨ Stencils ⇨ Project Schedule ⇨ PERT Chart Shapes.

Organization Chart Converter

Use the Organization Chart Converter to convert an organization chart created in a previous version of a Visio product. To access this function, choose Tools ⇨ Macros ⇨ Organization Chart ⇨ Organization Chart Converter from the main menu bar. The first screen of the Organization Chart Converter appears, as shown in Figure 27-19.

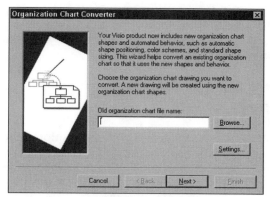

Figure 27-19: The first Organization Chart Converter screen

Locate the drawing created in a previous version of the progam by using the Browse button. When the Organization Chart Converter converts a file, it activates all the new behavioral functions available in the Visio 2000 organization chart. However, you can specify which behavior is to be activated by clicking the Settings button. A dialog box appears in which you can deselect the behavior you do not want to be activated and then click OK (see Figure 27-20).

Figure 27-20: The Organization Chart Converter settings screen

You can set what types of new behavior enabled by Visio 2000 will be activated in the converted drawing. Your choices are to activate new behavior for Shape position, Shape color, and Shape size. Click OK to return to the previous screen.

In the Organization Chart Converter, click Next. In the next screen, the Converter prompts you to indicate how it should deal with shapes that it cannot convert, such as shapes you created yourself or clip art. Select the options you want, and then click Finish. The chart is converted to the Visio 2000 mode.

Creating a Gantt Chart

Gantt charts are bar charts that show activities in terms of their duration, which is useful for managing, scheduling, and planning projects. With the Visio Gantt Chart solution, you can quickly and easily create, format, and modify complex Gantt charts.

To access the Gantt Chart solution, from the menu bar, select File ➪ New ➪ Choose Drawing Type, or select File ➪ New ➪ Project Schedule ➪ Gantt Chart. You can also access this solution through Tools ➪ Macros ➪ Project Schedule ➪ Gantt Chart.

The Gantt Chart Options dialog box appears. It contains options for you to set that determine how the chart represents information about a project.

The Gantt Chart stencil and toolbar open in the background as well.

Date

In the Date tab of the Gantt Chart Options dialog box (shown in Figure 27-21), choose the dates and units you want to use on the Gantt chart timescale. For a new Gantt chart, you can also choose the number of tasks on this tab.

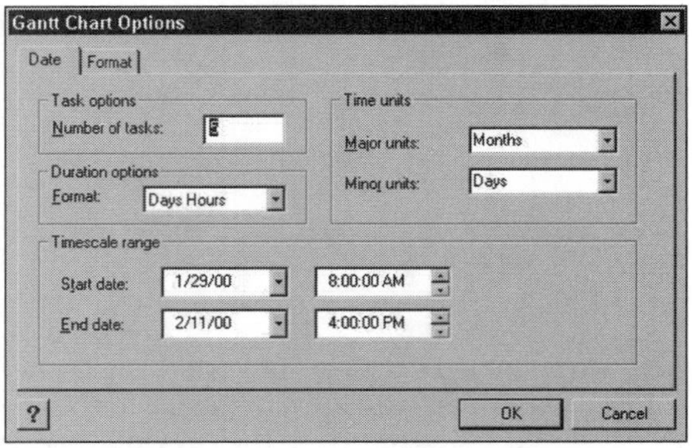

Figure 27-21: The Date tab on the Gantt Chart Options dialog box

Set the following options:

✦ **Number of tasks.** Set the number of tasks you want to start off with.

Note You can add more tasks later.

✦ **Major units.** Choose the largest time unit to be represented in the Gantt chart timescale from among these options:

Years   Weeks

Quarters   Days

Months   Hours

The major units appear above the minor units on the Gantt chart timescale at the top of the chart.

✦ **Minor units.** Choose the smallest time unit to be represented in the Gantt chart timescale. Your options are the same as for major units.

The minor units appear below the major units on the top of the chart.

✦ **Format.** Choose the time units in which you want the duration to be displayed in the duration column of the chart.

✦ **Start date.** Choose the date and time when the project is to begin. The date you set here is the starting date for the timescale of the chart.

✦ **End date.** Choose the last date and time you want to be displayed on the chart's timescale.

Note You can always extend the timescale to a later date if the project's schedule is changed.

For the Start date and End date fields, when you click the date's drop-down arrow, a calendar date picker appears; this puppy is aptly sketched in Figure 27-22.

Figure 27-22: The calendar date picker

Use the arrow buttons on the upper corners of the calendar to navigate among previous and subsequent months. Click the date you want, and it appears in the date field of the previous screen.

Format

Choose the formatting options you want for the taskbars, milestones, and summary bars of a Gantt chart in the Format tab of the Gantt Chart Options dialog box (see Figure 27-23).

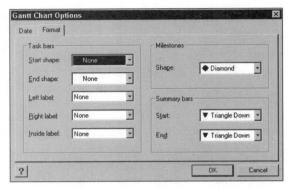

Figure 27-23: The Format tab on the Gantt Chart Options dialog box

Set the following options:

✦ **Start Shape.** Select the type of shape to appear at the start of all taskbars.

✦ **End Shape.** Select the type of shape to appear at the end of all taskbars.

✦ **Left Label.** Select the column heading text to appear as a label at the start of all taskbars.

✦ **Right Label.** Select the column heading text to appear as a label at the end of all taskbars.

✦ **Inside Label.** Select the column heading text to appear as a label in all the taskbars.

✦ **Shape.** Select the type of shape you want to use to represent all milestones.

✦ **Start.** Select the type of shape you want to appear at the start of all summary taskbars.

✦ **End.** Select the type of shape you want to appear at the end of all summary taskbars.

For choosing a type of shape, the default options are shown in Figure 27-23. Following is a list of all the shape types available:

None	Arrow Down
Diamond	Arrow Up
Triangle Down	Star
Up Triangle	Circle

For setting label text, you have the following options available (default options are shown in Figure 27-23):

Actual Duration	Task Name
Actual End	Task Notes
Actual Start	User Defined Decimal
Duration	User Defined Duration
End	User Defined Number
ID	User Defined Text 1
None	User Defined Text 2
Outline level	User Defined Text 3
Percent Complete	User Defined Text 4
Resource Name	User Defined Text 5
Start	User Defined Time

When you have set the options as you like, click OK and the Gantt chart is generated. I've provided an example for your perusal in Figure 27-24.

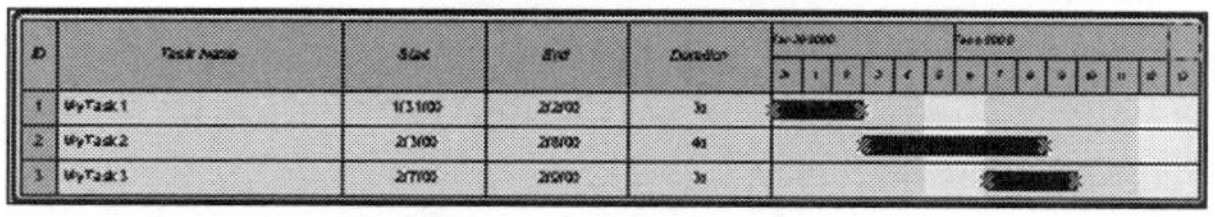

Figure 27-24: A Gantt chart

The Gantt Chart stencil has the same shapes as were used in creating the Gantt chart discussed in this section. You can use the shapes to add items to a Gantt chart.

The Gantt Chart toolbar

The Gantt Chart toolbar (shown in Figure 27-25) has clickable icons for the following options (left to right):

✦ **Navigation arrows.** Moves the timescale display. These consist of the Go to Start, Go to Previous, Go to Next, and Go to End icons

✦ **Find Task icon.** Locates a task on a large chart.

✦ **Insert Task icon.** Adds a task above an existing task you've selected.

✦ **Delete Task icon.** Deletes a task you've selected.

✦ **Promote Task icon.** Moves a selected task higher on the list.

✦ **Demote Task icon.** Moves a selected task lower on the list.

✦ **Link Tasks icon.** Sets dependencies via links between tasks.

✦ **Unlink Tasks icon.** Breaks the dependency links between tasks.

Figure 27-25: A Gantt Chart toolbar

These functions can also be accessed via the Gantt Chart menu bar option or via a right-click anywhere on the chart.

Changing timescale dates or units

You can extend the timescale and display more dates in the Gantt chart by selecting a Gantt Chart frame shape and clicking the solid line that surrounds the Gantt chart.

Drag the green selection handle at the right-center of the frame, and the frame extends to show more timescale units.

Replacing default task names and other default data

Replace the default task names with whatever names you want for your project's tasks. Also, replace the start date, end date, and duration for each task. You do this the same way as you would enter text in any Visio shape.

Note The end date is compared to the start date. Accordingly, you can never enter an end date earlier than the start date. Don't we wish our checkbooks included that function each new year?

Adding a new milestone

You can drag a milestone shape from the Gantt Chart stencil and drop it onto the drawing page between the tasks you want the milestone to precede and follow.

Tip You add a task row with a duration of 0 (zero) automatically when you add a milestone shape to the chart.

Configuring working time

From the menu bar, choose Gantt Chart ⇨ Configure Working Time, or from the right-click shortcut menu, access the Configure Working Time dialog box (see Figure 27-26).

Figure 27-26: The Configure Working Time dialog box

You can set which days are to be considered working days and what hour is the start and end of the work day. The Gantt chart makes sure that non–work days are not included in durations and the start and end times figure into the hourly timespans.

Creating dependencies between tasks

You can create dependencies between Gantt chart tasks by selecting the taskbars and milestones between which you want dependencies.

You can select multiple taskbars and milestones by right-clicking one of the selected shapes. Then, from the right-click shortcut menu, select Link Tasks from the shortcut menu.

The following are additional ways to set dependencies between tasks:

✦ Select two taskbars, and select Gantt Chart ⇨ Link Tasks.

✦ Select two taskbars, and, on the Gantt Chart toolbar, click the Link Tasks button.

✦ Drag the control handle on the right end of one taskbar and glue it to a connection point on the left end of the nearby taskbar.

✦ Drop a link lines shape onto the drawing page and glue its endpoints to the taskbar's connection points.

Add a title and legend

You can add a title and legend to your chart by dragging a title shape from the Gantt Chart stencil onto the drawing page and positioning it on top of the chart. Select the title shape and enter text for the title.

You can add a legend to the chart by dragging a legend shape from the Gantt Chart stencil onto the drawing page. Select the legend shape and click the area of the shape where you want to add text. Then enter the text you want.

You can add a date field to the legend shape by selecting the legend shape and clicking the area of the shape where you want the date field to appear. From the menu bar, select Insert ⇨ Field. For category, select Date/Time; for Field, select the type of date you want; and for Format, select the format in which you want the date to appear. Click OK when you are done.

Printing the Gantt chart

Even the simplest Gantt chart is usually larger than one regular-sized printer page, so your chart should be printed, or tiled, across several pages. Before you print, adjust the Gantt chart so that it fits on the drawing page.

You can also resize the drawing page so that the chart fits. Select File ⇨ Page Setup. Click the Page Setup tab. For Page Size, select Size To Fit Drawing Contents. Click OK.

The page size adjusts to fit the drawing without any margin. It may look as though you zoomed in on the drawing on the screen.

Another option for adjusting the drawing so that the Gantt chart fits is to modify the margins or center the drawing on the printed page.

Via Page Setup, click the Print Setup tab. For Print Zoom (All Pages), select one of the following:

✦ Reduce the size of the drawing by selecting Adjust To and entering a number less than 100.

✦ Enlarge the size of the drawing by selecting Adjust To and entering a number greater than 100.

✦ Set the drawing to print across multiple sheets of paper by selecting Fit To. Enter the number of pages across and down on which you want the drawing to be printed.

Be sure to preview the drawing to see if your drawing page and printer paper are as expected. Also, in Page Setup, make sure the printer page and drawing page orientations are the same. You can also set the margins to control the overlap between printed pages.

Exporting Gantt chart data

You can export the data from your Gantt chart in a format compatible with Microsoft Project. The exported file will have the extension .mpx. The Export function exports the data from all the data columns, including the customized data columns that contain categories of data you set yourself.

To export Gantt chart data, be sure to have the file from which you want to export data open.

From the menu bar, select Gantt Chart ⇨ Export. A Save As dialog box appears. Enter a name for the file, including an .mpx suffix. Select the location where to save the file, and click Save. The data is exported to this file in Microsoft Project (.mpx) format.

Importing project data

You can import data about a project into a Gantt chart from files with any of the following formats: .mpx, .txt, .xls, or .csv

In the Import Project Data function, you can also create data in either a text file or MS Excel Workbook.

From the menu bar, select Gantt Chart ⇨ Import. The Import Project Data dialog box appears (see Figure 27-27).

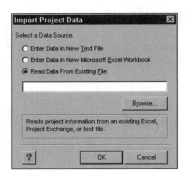

Figure 27-27: The Import Project Data dialog box

You can choose to enter data in a new text file, enter data in a new MS Excel Workbook, or read data from an existing file.

Entering data in a new text file

If you choose to enter data in a new text file, when you click OK, the Notepad application opens in a text (.txt) file template. Follow the format provided for entering data in this template. The format looks like this:

Task #,Task Name,Duration,Start Date,End Date,Dependency,Resource

Note   For more information about creating data files in the text file format, see Chapter 28.

When you are finished, save the file and close it. In Visio, run the Import Project Data function again, but this time choose to have data read from an existing file. Click OK, and the Gantt chart is generated.

Entering data in a new Microsoft Excel Workbook

If you choose to enter data in a new MS Excel Workbook, when you click OK, the MS Excel application opens in an .xls template. Follow the Excel format provided for entering data in this template. The column headings are the same as the text format fields.

Note   For more information about creating data files in the MS Excel format, see Chapter 28.

When you are done entering data, save your work, and then click the Gantt Chart icon in the MS Excel toolbar or choose the option from the Tools menu.

Reading data from an existing file

If you already have a data file from which you want to generate a Gantt chart, click Browse to locate the file. You can create a Gantt chart in Visio from data from another program, such as Microsoft Project.

Tip

For Milestones, specify only a start date and include blank placeholder fields (or columns in Excel) for those fields (or columns in Excel) with no data in them. For Dependency, use the task number that the current task depends on. For Durations, specify "D" for days, "W" for weeks, or "M" for months. For Resource, use anything, including names or numbers of people. Data for Resource appears in your Gantt chart when you add a Resource column to the chart.

Creating a timeline

You can create a timeline like the one shown in Figure 27-28 with shapes from the Timeline stencil. You can quickly make linear timelines that show milestones and events over the duration of a project or process. Timelines help to show a sequence of events or a history of events. You can also use a timeline to show a summary of a more complicated chart.

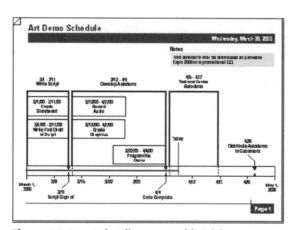

Figure 27-28: A timeline created in Visio

To create a timeline, select File ➪ New ➪ Project Schedule ➪ Timeline from the menu bar. The Timeline stencil appears alongside an empty drawing page. From the Timeline stencil, drag a timeline shape onto the drawing page. Access the Configure Timeline dialog box (shown in Figure 27-29) via the right-click shortcut menu.

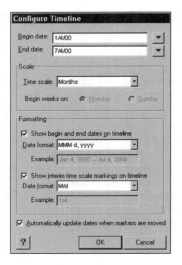

Figure 27-29: The Configure
Timeline dialog box

Specify settings for the beginning and ending date for the timeline, the time scale, and date and time scale formatting. Set how the milestones and interval marker shapes are to behave when you move them.

You can automatically update the dates on your marker, milestone, and interval shapes when you move them by enabling the Automatically update dates when markers are moved option. Click OK.

You can add milestones, intervals of time, and more using the shapes of the Timeline stencil. Timeline intervals have a similar dialog box for making settings. Use the right-click shortcut menu on the interval shape to access the options.

You can use a Today Marker or elapsed time shapes from the stencil to show the current date and elapsed time.

Note   If you drag a milestone, interval or Today Marker, and so on outside a timeline shape's boundary, it will not be linked to the timeline. The only way to enter data for the shape label is to edit the text.

Numbering Shapes in a Drawing

You can start shape numbering on a drawing page and set the starting number and numbering method with the Number Shapes option. Access it from the menu bar by selecting Tools ➪ Macros ➪ Visio Extra ➪ Number Shapes. The Number Shapes dialog box appears (see Figure 27-30).

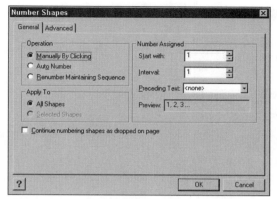

Figure 27-30: The General tab on the Number Shapes dialog box

In Operations, specify whether you want to number the shapes manually or automatically, or maintain the numbering sequence.

Choosing the Manually By Clicking option and clicking OK opens the Manual Numbering dialog box, which stays open while you number shapes by clicking them and drop new shapes from a stencil onto the drawing page.

Choosing the Auto Number option numbers shapes by default, from left to right and then top to bottom on the drawing page. You can change the automatic numbering sequence through the Advanced tab in this dialog box.

Choosing the Renumber Maintaining Sequence option renumbers the shapes on a page and maintains the existing numbering sequence. By default, renumbering allows duplicates in the sequence. You can change the default through the Advanced tab in this dialog box.

Decide to apply the numbering to all shapes or selected shapes. Select the starting number, interval, preceding text, and preview options.

In the Advanced tab (shown in Figure 27-31), set the following options for numbering and renumbering shapes.

Choose either Before shape text or After shape text to specify if the number is to be displayed on the shape before or after any text you add.

The All Layers option applies shape numbering to all shapes on the drawing page regardless of which layer the shapes are on.

Selected Layers applies shape numbering only to shapes on the layers you select from the list underneath.

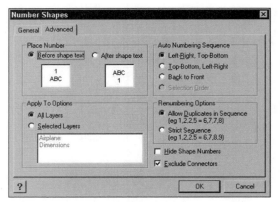

Figure 27-31: The Advanced tab on the Number Shapes dialog box

The Auto Numbering Sequence options are Left-Right, Top-Bottom; Top-Bottom, Left-Right; and Back to Front. This enables Visio to number shapes according to the order in which they were put on the page. You can change the order for a particular shape by selecting the shape and choosing Shape ➪ Bring Forward, Shape ➪ Bring To Front, Shape ➪ Send Backward, or Shape ➪ Send To Back.

The Allow Duplicates In Sequence option indicates that when shapes are renumbered, the original sequence is to be kept, even if the sequence includes duplicate numbers.

The Strict Sequence option indicates that when shapes are renumbered, duplicates are eliminated.

The Hide Shape Numbers option hides the numbers on shapes so that they don't appear on the drawing page or in print.

The Exclude Connectors option excludes the connector shapes in a connected drawing, such as a flowchart or network diagram, from receiving numbers. Deselect this option if you want connector shapes to be included in the numbering.

Summary

In this chapter, you have learned about many of Visio's key macro features. Specifically you have examined the following:

✦ How to edit shape properties with the Custom Properties Editor

✦ How to use the Shape Explorer to find shapes and modify/create shape databases

✦ How to create cross-functional flowcharts

✦ How to use the Organization Chart Converter to convert organizational charts from previous versions of Visio

✦ How to create a Gantt chart

✦ How to import project data from various outside sources

✦ How to create a timeline and number shapes in your drawing

The next chapter covers creating projects based on information from a database.

✦   ✦   ✦

Creating Projects Based on Information from a Database

Visio charts and diagrams can be connected to information from databases with the help of Visio's database-related wizards. Wizards provide faster and more efficient ways to get your work done. Think of them as miniprograms that walk you through a set of choices and make sure all the steps connected to a process are covered. Visio 2000 offers a variety of innovative database-related wizards:

✦ Database Wizard

✦ Database Export Wizard

✦ Import Flowchart Wizard

✦ Organization Chart Wizard

✦ Property Reporting Wizard

Without the help of these wizards, connecting Visio charts and diagrams to information from databases would be a labor-intensive chore. Wizards make all the connections between data by prompting you for the information they require instead of you having to write it all in programming code.

Introducing Database-Related Visio Wizards

When you activate a wizard, you get an introductory screen telling you the basics about that wizard. On the bottom of the screen are navigation buttons. You click the Next button to move to the next screen. Each of the following screens offers you choices to make, fields to fill in, browsing links to find files, and more. When the choices of a screen are more complex, a More Info button often appears alongside the navigation buttons. Clicking the More Info button opens a help screen related to the wizard screen.

With the Database Wizard, linking information from Visio shapes to databases makes it possible to do more with Visio than generate charts and drawings. It means you can create charts and drawings based on information collected in a database, or you can link shapes in a drawing to records in a database (see Figure 28-1). Also, you can adjust the chart to changes made in the database by adding actions and events to Visio shapes and pages. The Database Export Wizard helps you export custom property field data for every shape, or for selected shapes, in a drawing to a table in an ODBC-compliant database.

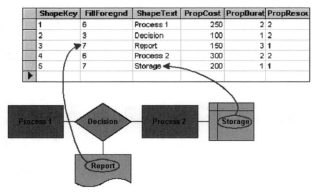

Figure 28-1: Shapes in a Visio drawing can be linked to database information.

The Import Flowchart Wizard helps you automatically generate a flowchart from information in a text file or in MS Excel format. It enables you to create a database or use an existing one to create a flowchart. The Organization Chart Wizard helps you generate an organization chart from an information file such as a text file, MS Excel file, Microsoft Exchange Server directory, SAP/R3, or other ODBC-compliant data sources.

After you enter data for the properties associated with your network shapes, the Property Reporting Wizard helps you to generate reports based on the data.

Because linking Visio shapes with database information is sophisticated, often resulting in mistakes that are sometimes pretty hard to identify, the database-related wizards in Visio really make these tasks a lot easier. Although some of the wizards may become more useful to you than others depending on your needs, they all show you how versatile Visio 2000 is. In short, database-related wizards are useful for getting through a sequence of steps to perform a multiple-stage or complex database-linking task.

In other parts of this book, I give examples of what can be represented in Visio drawings and charts. A lot of the same information depicted in a Visio drawing may be kept in a database for statistical purposes. It is useful to have the information in both formats. However, situations are constantly changing, and information has to be updated to reflect such changes. Once you have gone to the trouble of building a body of data or creating a complex chart, what do you have to go through to update changes? By linking a Visio drawing to a database, updates can be communicated between them. Or, by basing a drawing on a database, you can organize information in a Visio format with ease. Wizards make both processes less complicated. Similarly, exporting data or creating a database based on information held in Visio format by way of a wizard means that you can save a lot of time and effort.

Starting with a Database-Related Wizard

Before you can use any of Visio's database-related wizards, you have to know something about the types of databases with which Visio 2000 can work. Let's take a look.

Some of the Visio wizards are about helping you create charts from data files. Three primary types of data files are used: text files, MS Excel workbooks, and ODBC-compliant data sources. The first two are basic database file types that you can use directly to make data files in the framework of some Visio wizards. ODBC-compliant data sources are an international standard database format that makes importing and exporting data compatible.

In order for you to really understand how to make these types of data files properly, let's examine the essentials of the different types of data files that Visio uses.

Visio's sample data files

Visio's sample files include a variety of samples of Visio drawing files and templates. See Appendix C for a comprehensive list of the sample files. Visio sample files also includes sample data files so you can model your own on them. These sample files are located in the Samples directory where Visio is installed, as indicated here:

- ✦ Samples ➪ Flowcharts:
    - Sample Flowchart Data.txt
    - Sample Flowchart Data.xls

- ✦ Samples ➪ Organization charts:
    - Sample Org Chart Data.txt
    - Sample Org Chart Data.xls

✦ Samples ➪ Project schedule:

- Sample Gantt Chart Data.txt
- Sample Gantt Chart Data.xls

✦ Samples ➪ Visio Extras:

- DBSample.mdb (an Access 95 file containing tables of data and queries that create views and summaries of the data in the tables)

Tip   Make a copy of the sample files you want to experiment on with a wizard. Keep the originals for future experimentation or as models from which to copy the format.

Text files

In text files, you write information in lines similar to regular text, and certain punctuation marks or keystrokes — such as a tab — serve to designate where one piece of information ends and another begins. Each piece of information is held in a *field* between the punctuation marks. The punctuation marks are called *field separators*.

You can use a comma (,) or a semicolon (;) as a field separator, or you can use the Tab key or the Return key between fields to insert field separators. In the Visio wizards, you find screens that prompt you to indicate what mark the file you want to use as its field separator. If you are creating a data file through the Visio wizard, Visio advises you use commas (,) as field separators. When the Visio wizard prompts you to indicate which marks you want to use as field separators, choose the comma.

You may be asked to identify types of information and indicate values for each. Quote marks (") are used for indicating what a value is supposed to be. For example, if in the text file you have to tell Visio what template you want to use, you would be prompted like this:

Template, "Template Name"

Anything written between the quote marks indicates the actual value for or definition of what precedes the quotes — in this case, template. Here, you would specify a value for the template like this:

Template, "Basic Flowchart.VST"

In this case, Visio knows it should use the Basic Flowchart.VST template to create the flowchart.

It is important to use punctuation correctly when you are writing the data and marking values or separations between fields. If the marks aren't exactly right, the program reads the information incorrectly. For example, if you add an extra comma by mistake, the program treats it as defining a separate field.

MS Excel workbooks

The Visio 2000 wizards are great tools for creating charts and diagrams based on your MS Excel data files. But, in order to use Visio with MS Excel files, you have to have MS Excel installed on your computer. In Visio charts based on MS Excel files, each cell or field cannot contain more than 64 characters. Visio does not recognize information beyond the 64th character. However, 64 characters should be ample for your data file needs.

In creating an MS Excel database file from which to base a chart, Visio supplies MS Excel data templates. In each of them, the columns and their headings are already set up. Enter the information in the cells underneath each heading, save and close the file, and Visio creates a chart accordingly. When the MS Excel data template is opened, you can alter the column headings to read as you like or add more.

For Excel files, the Database Wizard creates tables through the Define table option. In Excel 5 or later, newly created tables are stored on separate sheets (or pages) in the Excel file. These tables are accessed by tabs on the bottom of the MS Excel screen. The records are marked as a named range. To access an existing table in an Excel file via ODBC, you must create a named range in the Excel file. This named range must include all the rows and columns utilized in the table. The first row of the named range is used as the table's column headings.

About ODBC-compliant data sources

Open Database Connectivity (ODBC) is Microsoft's standardized database interface. It uses a database language called Structured Query Language (SQL), an international standard interface for relational databases through which programs can access, view, and modify data from databases in order to read, insert, update, and delete data. ODBC-compliant data sources include the following:

DBASE	MS SQL Server
FoxPro	Oracle SQL Server
MQIS	Paradox
MS Access 7.0	Text files
MS Access 97	Visual FoxPro Database
MS Excel	Visual FoxPro Tables

A database that is an ODBC data source works with Data Source Name (DSN) files. These are file-based data sources that can be shared among users who have the same drivers installed so they have access to the database. These data sources need not be dedicated to a particular user or local to a particular computer.

Creating a DSN sounds complicated and foreign to the average user. So, to make it possible for anyone to connect between Visio shapes and various types of databases, including the ability to update information between the two, Visio provides the database-related wizards for creating the connections and building the script for the user.

In the Database Export Wizard, Visio provides a way to export data into forms that are compatible with other database programs. To be able to export data in ODBC format makes the databases importable by all the database programs following this international standard.

If you want to use data files from a program other than those mentioned here, you have to check that the database is an ODBC-compliant data source before you begin with a Visio wizard. Check if your database program is ODBC compliant by consulting the program's documentation.

Note   Although Visio provides all you need to interact with database files, it does not provide any of the database programs listed earlier. If you want to use a database file for linking with Visio shapes in a drawing, you must have the appropriate database drivers installed on your computer. For ODBC-compliant databases, you must have the ODBC components.

What is not supported by the database-related wizards

The database-related wizards do not support the following:

✦ Visio cells and fields cannot store ODBC strings longer than 64 characters.

✦ Visio cells and fields cannot store ODBC binary fields longer than 32 characters.

✦ Because Visio stores numeric values as double floating-point numbers internally, numbers with a large degree of precision are stored as approximate values.

✦ For the Excel ODBC driver, Visio does not support the deletion of rows. The Database Wizard works around this by setting text fields to #ROW DELETED# and numeric fields to 0 to mark rows as deleted. Text field values of 0 and #ROW DELETED# are treated as invalid keys for wizard operations such as Select, Refresh, and Update.

✦ For MS Access, Visio cannot reflect updates in the replication IDs.

✦ Visio cannot support database key fields of the SQL_TIMESTAMP type.

✦ For Informix, Visio cannot reflect updates in the Timestamp fields.

Database Wizard: The Details

With the Database Wizard, you can create charts and drawings based on information collected in a database, or you can link shapes in a drawing to records in a database. You can also create events and actions for the Visio shapes and pages to communicate updates between a Visio drawing and the database to which it is linked.

Before you use this wizard, you must have the appropriate components and database drivers installed on your computer, as well as a Visio master that has a corresponding ShapeSheet cell for every field in the database.

Assuming you have these, let's examine how the Database Wizard guides you through these options. First of all, to access the Database Wizard, from the menu bar select Tools ⇨ Macros ⇨ Visio Extras ⇨ Database Wizard. The initial screen appears, offering three basic options:

✦ **Link shapes to database records.** Links Visio shapes, ShapeSheet cells for a master, or individual shapes to fields in a database table.

✦ **Create a linked drawing or modify an existing one.** Creates a new linked drawing, opens an existing one, or adds actions to a linked drawing page for keeping values in the database and ShapeSheet synchronized.

✦ **Generate new masters from a database.** Creates masters based on an existing master and a table of information and stores the new masters on an existing or new stencil.

Linking shapes to a database record

Choose the Linking shapes to a database record option and click Next to continue. On the next screen, you have another three options to choose from about the type of shape for which you want to define links:

✦ **Shape(s) in a drawing.** If you want to link a particular shape on a page to a particular record in a database, choose this option.

✦ **Master(s) On a document stencil.** If the drawing file already exists, choose this to be able to modify the existing drawing file.

Note The changes won't be available outside of the drawing file.

✦ **Master(s) on a Visio Stencil.** If you haven't created a drawing file yet or you want to be able to use the masters in multiple drawings, choose this option.

Note Notice the option for making a copy of the stencil, rather than using the original. It is a good idea to keep this option enabled and use a copy. (This option is enabled by default.)

Shape(s) In A Drawing

If on the previous screen you selected Shape(s) In A Drawing, click Browse in the resulting dialog box (shown in Figure 28-2), and locate the drawing file you want to use. For Page, select the page that contains the shapes you want to link. For Shape Name(s) And ID(s), select from the list the specific shape you want to use. To select more than one shape on the Visio drawing, click the Select Shapes button. You get a message box requesting you select the shapes that you want. When you are done, click the OK button. You are returned to the wizard screen. Click Next to continue.

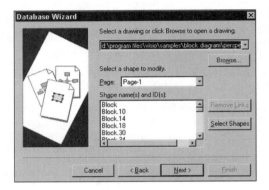

Figure 28-2: Choose a drawing and select a specific individual shape.

Master(s) On A Document

If on the previous screen you selected Master(s) On A Document, click Browse in the dialog box (shown in Figure 28-3), and locate the drawing file you want to use. For Choose Master(s) To Modify, select the master you want to use. Click Next to continue.

Figure 28-3: Choose a drawing and select a master to use.

Master(s) On A Visio Stencil

If on the previous screen you chose Master(s) On A Visio Stencil, click Browse in the next Window (see Figure 28-4), and locate the stencil you want to use. Click a checkmark in the Open Copy checkbox (unless you know what you are doing and want to change the original stencil). For Choose A Master To Modify, select the master you want to use. Click Next to continue.

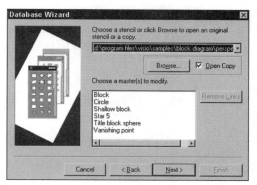

Figure 28-4: Choose a drawing, locate a stencil, and select a master.

Note You can use the Remove Links button to remove from the selected shapes any existing links to other database information.

ODBC data source

The next screen prompts you to choose an ODBC data source (as shown in Figure 28-5). If the database you want to choose is not listed on this screen, the database may not defined as an ODBC data source.

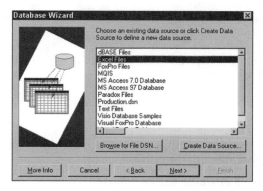

Figure 28-5: Choose an ODBC data source.

From the list, select the data source that represents the database you are using. As needed, you can select a DSN file by using the Browse for File DSN button.

Or, you can define an existing database as an ODBC data source by clicking the Create Data Source button, and then follow the instructions on subsequent screens.

Tip If you make a mistake and choose the wrong file or are for any reason unhappy with the file you choose, to choose a different ODBC data source, you have to quit not only the wizard but also Visio. Only by opening Visio again can you reset the connection with the ODBC data source.

Creating a new data source

When you click the Create New Data Source button, a sequence of screens to help you create a new data source begins. The first screen prompts you to select a type of data source (see Figure 28-6).

Figure 28-6: Select a type of data source.

In the next screen, if you have Microsoft Office 97 or 2000, a list of drivers for database programs appears in the Create New Data Source dialog box. Select the driver for the program in which you created your database, and then click Finish.

If you have Microsoft Office 95, a list of drivers for database programs appears in the Add Data Source dialog box. Select the driver for the program in which you created your database, and then click Finish.

In the Create New Data Source dialog box, select a type of data source from the following options:

- ✦ **File Data Source (Machine independent).** Appropriate for network users if you want the database to be available to other people on other computers.

- ✦ **User Data Source (Applies to this machine only).** Choose this if you are to be the only one using the database.

- ✦ **System Data Source (Applies to this machine only).** Appropriate if you use a log-in/password system and want the database to be available to everyone who uses the current computer.

Choose the appropriate option and click Next to continue.

In the next screen, you select the driver of the database program to be the new data source. Click Next, and then click Finish.

If you choose the File Data Source or System Data Source option, an extra screen appears asking you to name the new data source file. You can also use the Browse button to access the data source directory. (The default location for DSN files is c:\Program Files\Common Files\ODBC\Data Sources.) Type a name or choose an existing file. Click Save. The information is displayed for you to check on the next screen. To modify it, click Cancel. If it is OK, click Finish.

The next screen is the ODBC Setup dialog box. It is customized for whatever database type you choose. Enter a source name and description, and then click OK. The database is now defined as a data source and stored in DSN format (as indicated by the extension .dsn).

The wizard screen also has a Browse for File DSN button. Use it to access an existing DSN file.

You are returned to the wizard, where your new data source now appears in the list. Select your newly created data source from the list, and then click Next.

In the next screen, you are prompted to choose a database object to connect to and set the following options:

✦ **Database.** Choose the database containing the object to which you want to link. This option is available only for ODBC-compliant database programs (listed earlier in this chapter) in which connecting to a DSN data source gives you access to multiple databases.

✦ **Owner.** If you are working on a network, this option enables you to choose from the drop-down list. Choose All Users or the name of an object creator. Choosing a specific creator filters the number of objects that are displayed in the list. This option is available only for ODBC database programs in which you can specify an object creator.

✦ **Object Types.** Click the checkbox of the type of object to which you want to link a Visio shape or drawing on a page. This can be a database table, a database view (query), a system table, or an alias name for a table. If you haven't created the table yet, click Define Table button.

✦ **Define Table.** Click the Define table button if you have no database object defined or if you want to create a new table. You can define a table within the process of the Database Wizard. (See the section that follows, "Define Table options.")

✦ **Database Objects.** Lists the tables, views, system tables, or aliases available in the selected database file, according to the items you have checked under Object Types. From the list, choose what you want to link to generate the new masters. For more details about database objects, see your database program documentation.

Set the options, and click Next to continue.

Define Table options

Set the follow options when defining a table:

✦ **Data Source.** This name reflects the data source you selected on one of the previous wizard screens.

✦ **Table Name.** Enter the name of the new table you want to define.

✦ **Name.** Enter the name of a field you want to add to the new table.

✦ **Type.** Select a data type for the field specified under Name. The data types you can choose depend on the database driver associated with the database to which you are linking.

✦ **Length.** Enter the size in bytes of a variable length field.

✦ **Decimal.** Enter the number of decimal places supported by the field. This applies only to numeric fields that are not integers.

✦ **Fields.** Lists the fields in the new table you are defining.

✦ **Primary Key.** Select this option if the field specified under Name is part of the primary key (a field or fields that uniquely identify each record) for the database table.

✦ **Unique.** Select this option if the field specified under Name cannot have duplicate values.

✦ **Required.** Select this option if the field specified under Name cannot have a null value.

✦ **Add.** Select this option to add the field specified under Name to the table you are defining.

✦ **Remove.** Removes a selected field from the table you are defining.

To define a table, type the name you want to give the new table in the Table Name field. To create fields for the new table, give each field you want to be in the new table a name in the Name field. From the Type drop-down list, specify the type of field you want it to be. Enter values for the other parameters as needed. To add the new field to the list, click the Add button. To remove a field from the list, click the Remove button.

Note For more details about defining database tables, see your database program documentation.

When you are finished with defining the table, click Next. You are returned to the screen in which you choose a Database Object. When you are finished with selecting all the options, click Next to continue.

The next screen asks you to choose the number of fields for the primary key of the selected table.

What is a primary key?

A *primary key* is a unique identifier that ensures the database record is one of a kind. Sometimes different items have the same name and features. The primary key functions to differentiate the data. For example, you could have two employees with the same name or more than one piece of equipment of the same type. For the employees, you can specify both an employee number and name as the primary keys. For the pieces of equipment, you can specify an equipment number and name as the primary keys.

PIC match primary key field

You can designate up to five fields to make up the primary key (see Figure 28-7). From the drop-down list, select a number and click Next to continue. In the next screen, shown in Figure 28-8, you choose the primary key field from the database table (such as employee number and name). Click Next to continue.

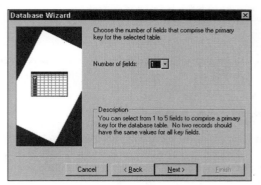

Figure 28-7: Choose the number of fields that compose the primary key for the selected table.

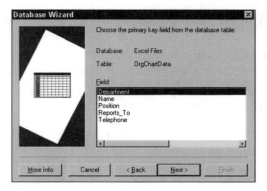

Figure 28-8: Choose the primary key field for the selected table.

In the next screen, you choose a default value for each primary key you selected in a previous screen or click the None button (as shown in Figure 28-9). By assigning values for each primary key, you associate the shapes with particular records in the database. By choosing None, you associate the shapes with fields in the database, not particular records or specific data. Click Next to continue. In the next screen, you choose event and action options for the Visio shapes to communicate updates between a Visio drawing and the database to which it is linked.

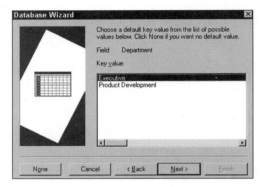

Figure 28-9: Choose a default value for each primary key you selected in a previous screen.

Note The name of the database and the table that you selected in a previous screen appear on this screen.

Adding actions and events to a shape

If you add shape events, you define how a linked shape responds when it is copied or dropped into a page (see Figure 28-10). Under the Shape Events heading, enable the option Include an on drop event with the shape. To define how a linked shape responds, choose between the following:

✦ **Refresh shape on drop.** If you are linking particular shapes, this causes updating for the linked ShapeSheet cells for each copy you create when you duplicate the particular shape.

If you are linking a master, this causes automatic updating for the linked Shape Sheet cells for each instance you create when you drop a linked master.

✦ **Select record on drop.** If you want to select a new database record every time you copy a particular shape or drop a linked master, select this option.

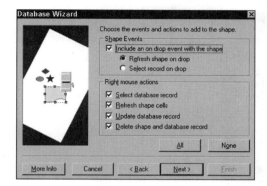

Figure 28-10: Choose the events and actions to add to the shapes.

Under the Right mouse actions heading, select those options you want to be added to the linked shape's shortcut menu (accessed when you click the right mouse button on particular shapes). The options are as follows:

✦ **Select database record.** Specifies a new database record to be linked to the shape.

✦ **Refresh shape cells.** Refreshes the values in the shape's ShapeSheet cells to reflect changes in the database.

✦ **Update database record.** Updates the fields in the database to reflect changes in the shape's ShapeSheet cells.

✦ **Delete shape and database record.** Adds a command to delete the shape and its linked database record.

When you are finished choosing the events and actions to be added to shapes, click Next to continue.

The next screen prompts you to choose the shape cell to be used for storing the primary key field value. The primary key fields that you set in a previous screen now appear in the upper part of this screen. For each primary key field, select the ShapeSheet cell where the values for these fields are going to be stored. Click Next to continue.

The next screen asks you to match up the remaining ShapeSheet cells with the database fields (see Figure 28-11). You select a cell from the Cells list, select a database field from the Database Fields list, and then click Add. The link created between the ShapeSheet cell and the database field appears in the Links list. Use the Remove button to remove any link from the Links list.

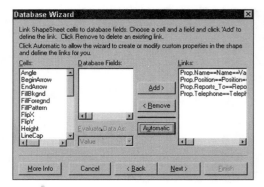

Figure 28-11: Match up the remaining ShapeSheet cells with the database fields.

You can also use the Automatic button to automatically link all fields with matching ShapeSheet cell names. If no names match, a Custom Property ShapeSheet cell is automatically created to correspond with the database field names. Click Next to continue.

The final screen appears announcing that the Database Wizard will now link Visio shapes to database records based on the selections you made throughout the wizard. The selections are summarized in the screen for you to look over. If you are satisfied with the information, click Finish, and the links are created. If you are not satisfied with the information, you can go back through previous screens to make changes in your selections. Click the Back buttons until you reach the screen in which you want to begin making modifications.

Creating a linked drawing or modifying an existing one

When you want to create a drawing that is a graphical representation of a database table, use the second option in the beginning of the Database Wizard: Create a linked drawing or modify an existing one. You can create a new linked drawing, open an existing one, or add actions to a linked drawing page for keeping values in the database and ShapeSheet synchronized.

Starting from the beginning of the Database Wizard, choose the second option and click Next to continue. On the next screen, you have another three options from which to choose:

✦ **Create a drawing which represents a database table.** Select this option to create a drawing that is a graphical representation of a database table.

✦ **Open an existing database drawing.** Use this option to open a drawing that you previously linked to a database table. The sequence of screens is similar to others mentioned in this chapter.

✦ **Add database actions and events to a drawing page.** Select this option if you want to add right mouse actions and NOW function events to a page that enable you to manually communicate changes in a drawing to a database and vise versa.

Let's examine the first of these options. Choose the option Create a drawing which represents a database table, and then click Next to continue.

In the next screen, choose between creating a new drawing file or modifying an existing one. If you choose to create a new drawing, the following screen asks you to choose a template and provides a Browse button to help you select one. Click Next to continue.

If you choose to modify an existing one, in the next screen, click the Browse button to select a drawing file. If the existing drawing you choose already contains links to a database, you can remove those links by clicking the Remove Links button. Click Next to continue. The next screen informs you that when you click Finish, all the links will be removed and you will have to run the Database Wizard again to add new database links to the drawing. When you run the wizard again, follow the same choices in the screens that appear. This time, because you already removed the previous links, just click Next to continue.

The next screen asks you to choose to either create a new page or modify an existing page inside the drawing file. You can choose from the existing pages listed in the drop-down menu. Click Next to continue.

The next screen prompts you to specify the options to use for how to monitor this drawing. (See the section "Database Drawing Monitor" toward the end of this chapter.) Choose from the following options for monitoring communication between the linked drawing and database:

✦ **Automatically distribute shapes on the page.** Arranges the shapes in rows and columns on the page. One shape represents each database record.

Note

Leave this option unchecked when the database table includes fields that specify shape location (that is, if the database records are going to be linked to the PinX and PinY cells in the Shape Transform section of the ShapeSheet spreadsheet). Instead, shapes appear on the page at the designated PinX and PinY locations. If PinX and PinY are not linked and you don't enable this option, all shapes are positioned at 0,0. You move them into the position you want later.

✦ **Automatically scale the drawing page.** Sets the page size to exactly accommodate the shapes the page is going to distribute. (This option is enabled only if the option Automatically distribute shapes on the page is selected.)

Note

When you don't select this option, shapes may be drawn outside page boundaries. If you are creating linked shapes that include text, such as business cards, don't enable this option because the text may not be scaled correctly when you scale the page.

✦ **Launch the drawing monitor on document open.** Activates the wizard's Drawing Monitor each time you open this linked drawing. The Monitor manages communication between the drawing on a page and the database table. When the Monitor is activated, the changes that you make to shapes in the drawing are automatically reflected in database records.

Note

If you want to make changes in the drawing on a page without automatically affecting database records, don't check this option. You can still manually communicate changes between the drawing and the database table by choosing Tools ➪ Macros ➪ Visio Extras ➪ Database Refresh or Database Update.

✦ **Add 'launch monitor' right mouse action to the page.** Adds a Launch Monitor command to the right-click shortcut menu of the page. You can activate the Drawing Monitor by right-clicking the page and choosing the Launch Monitor command.

✦ **Access the database table in read-write mode.** Makes sure any changes made in the drawing's page are updated in the database and vice versa. If you don't want drawing changes to affect the database, don't check this option. The file is then treated as read-only.

✦ **Automatically refresh page based on global setting.** By choosing Tools ➪ Macros ➪ Visio Extras ➪ Database Settings, you can set a global refresh interval that applies to all your drawings that are linked to databases. (The refresh interval is the amount of time that elapses before changes made to a database are automatically updated in its linked drawing.)

Note

If you want the global refresh setting to apply to the drawing on the selected page, select this option. If you want to refresh the drawing by clicking Refresh on the Drawing Monitor, don't enable this option. See the section "Database settings" toward the end of this chapter.

Select any of the options you want to have in this drawing. Click Next to continue. The next few screens are the same as described previously. You are prompted to choose an ODBC data source to which to export the generated data. See the section "About ODBC-compliant data sources" earlier in this chapter.

When you finish with the database source–related screens, the next screen asks you to select a Visio master shape to represent records from the data source. For Stencil, choose the stencil that contains the master you want to use for the automatically generated shapes. Use the Browse button to choose the file you want.

For Masters, choose the master that is to be used for the automatically generated shapes, and then click Next.

Every field in the database is represented by a corresponding ShapeSheet cell in the master you select. Click Finish.

Cross-Reference See Chapter 34 for details on understanding and using ShapeSheets.

Adding database actions and events to a page

You can also create events and actions for the pages in a Visio file to communicate updates between a Visio drawing and the database to which it is linked. For example, you may have a page with a lot of shapes that are linked to fields in a database. It can be useful to be able to refresh the shapes in a page all at once to reflect the changes in the database to which they are linked. You can accomplish this through the Database Wizard by adding database actions and events to the page's right-click shortcut menu.

On the first screen, click Next. On the second screen, choose the Create a linked drawing or modify an existing one option (as shown in Figure 28-12). Click Next to continue. In the next screen, choose the Add database actions and events to a drawing page option (see Figure 28-13). Click Next.

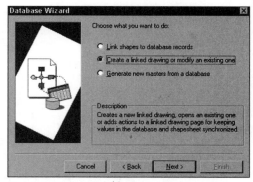

Figure 28-12: Choose the option Create a linked drawing or modify an existing one.

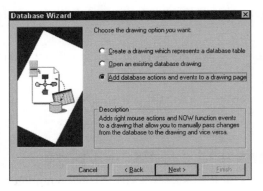

Figure 28-13: Choose the option Add database actions and events to a drawing page.

In the next screen, use the Browse button to locate the Visio drawing file for those pages to which you want to add database actions and events. After the wizard shows the name of the selected file in the text field, the file's pages are listed in the Choose the drawing page to modify field (see Figure 28-14). Select the page you want to change. The file is opened in Visio behind the wizard screen. Click Next to continue.

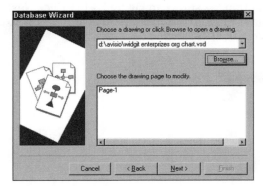

Figure 28-14: Choose a drawing and then which page to modify.

In the next screen, you choose how you want the shapes in the page and the database to be updated (see Figure 28-15).

Two page action options exist. When you enable these options to add the actions to a page, you can access the actions through the page's right-click shortcut menu.

Note   No shapes should be selected. Click an empty part of the display.

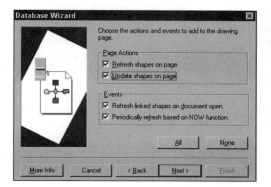

Figure 28-15: Choose the actions and events to add to the drawing page.

✦ **Refresh shapes on page.** Adds the Refresh command to the page's shortcut menu. When you right-click the page and choose Refresh linked shapes, all the values in the shape's ShapeSheet cells are refreshed at once to correspond to changes in the values in the database records to which they are linked.

✦ **Update shapes on page.** Adds the Update command to the page shortcut menu. When you right-click the page and choose Update linked records, all the values in the database records are updated at once to correspond with the changes made to the values in the ShapeSheet cells to which the records are linked.

Two Events options are also available on the same screen. When you add an event to a page, you define how shapes in the drawing on that page respond to specific user actions as explained here:

✦ **Refresh linked shapes on document open.** Every time you open the drawing file, the ShapeSheet cell values for all the shapes in your drawing file are refreshed to reflect any changes in the values in their linked database records.

✦ **Periodically refresh based on NOW function.** Refreshes the ShapeSheet cell values for all the shapes in a linked drawing file at NOW function-defined intervals. The values in each shape's ShapeSheet cells are updated to reflect any changes in the values in the linked database records. If you choose this option, double–right-clicks of the page start or stop the continuous refresh.

Note No shapes should be selected. Double–right-clicks to an empty part of the display activate the start or stop.

To select the options, click the checkbox next to the option you want to select. You can select all the options by clicking the All button or indicate you don't want any of the options by clicking the None button. Click Next to continue.

The final screen gives you a summary of information about the file and options you selected for you to review (as shown in Figure 28-16). If you are satisfied with them, click Finish. If you want to modify something, use the Back buttons to move back through the screens until you find the screen in which you want to make changes. To make the options available, right-click anywhere on the page (see Figure 28-17).

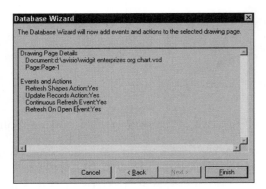

Figure 28-16: The summary on the final screen

Figure 28-17: Right-click anywhere empty on the page, and the menu pops up with the options you set.

Generating new masters (shapes) from an existing database

Select Next on the first screen of the Database Wizard. On the second screen, choose Generate new masters from a database. Click Next to continue.

Click Browse, and then locate the stencil that contains a shape you want to use as the basis for all the new masters. Under Masters, select the name of the shape. Click Next.

From the list, select the data source that represents the database you're using. If necessary, create a data source. The sequence of screens follows the same pattern as the previous wizards discussed in this chapter. (See the "About ODBC-compliant data sources" and "ODBC data source" sections in this chapter.)

In the screen that prompts you to choose the database link and naming options for the new master (see Figure 28-18), select from the following options:

✦ **Keep database links in new masters.** If enabled, keeps the capability to change a record in the database by right-clicking a shape that corresponds to it.

✦ **Generate names from primary key fields.** Select this option to be able to use the primary key fields to generate the shape names.

✦ **Base names on the original Visio master**. If you prefer to be able to have the shape names automatically created based on the master you select, choose this option.

Choose an option and click Next to continue. The options in the next few screens are the same as in the previous section.

The next screen asks you to match up the remaining ShapeSheet cells with the database fields (see Figure 28-19). You select a cell from the Cells list, select a database field from the Database Fields list, and then click Add. The link created between the ShapeSheet Cell and the database field appears in the Links list. Use the Remove button to remove any link from the Links list.

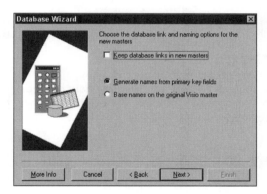

Figure 28-18: Choose the database link and naming options for the new master.

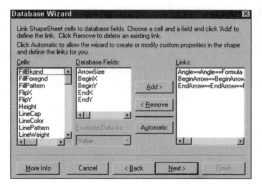

Figure 28-19: Match up the remaining ShapeSheet cells with the database fields.

You can also use the Automatic button to automatically link all fields with matching ShapeSheet cell names. If no names match, a Custom Property ShapeSheet cell is automatically created to correspond with the database field names. Click Next to continue.

The next screen asks you to choose if you want to create a new stencil or append the new shapes to an existing stencil. If you choose the Append to an existing stencil option, the Browse button is activated for you to choose the file you want. Click Next to continue.

The final screen appears announcing that the Database Wizard will now create a new set of Visio masters based on the selections you made throughout the wizard. The selections are summarized in the screen. If you are satisfied with the information, click Finish, and the links are created. If you chose to create a new stencil, the new stencil appears in the Visio display. When you close it, it prompts you to give the new stencil a name. If you chose to append the new shapes to an existing stencil, the new additions appear on the stencil selected.

If you are not satisfied with the information in the final screen's summary, you can go back through previous screens to make changes in you selections. Click the Back buttons until you reach the screen in which you want to begin making modifications.

Database Export Wizard

The Database Export Wizard helps you export custom property field data for every shape or for selected shapes, as well as for other ShapeSheet cells in a drawing, to a table in an ODBC-compliant database.

How Visio shapes relate to records, tables, and fields in a database

If the shapes in your drawing have custom property fields in which you have entered data, you can generate a database table to represent that data with the Database Export Wizard.

A record or row in the database table represents each shape in the drawing, and a field or column row in the database table represents each custom property or ShapeSheet cell. The data that you enter in the custom properties or in ShapeSheet cells appear as values in the database table cells.

For more information on Custom properties, see Chapter 23.

A good reason to use the Database Export Wizard is to create an inventory report based on the data stored in the shapes custom property fields in an office layout. You can generate different inventory reports for different groups of items that are represented by different types of shapes as well as for the data that you assign to each shape in custom properties. For instance, if you wanted to create a report on furniture inventory or computer equipment, you could select the shapes for the items you need for a particular report.

With this wizard, you can generate a new database, overwrite data in an existing database table, or insert a new table into an existing ODBC-compliant database. This wizard works with any ODBC-compliant database application. You can define an existing database as an ODBC data source within the Database Export Wizard. Also, when you use the wizard to create a new database, you can also define that database as a data source.

Using the Database Export Wizard

You can export data for every shape in the drawing or for selected shapes. You can take advantage of different ways to organize your drawing by using separate pages and layers to group items.

You can select the shapes with data you want to export by placing those shapes on one or more layers.

For drawings with more than one page, the wizard only performs its functions on one page at a time. For an additional page, you have to start with the Database Export Wizard again and choose the second page.

You can run the Database Export Wizard by selecting Tools ➪ Macros ➪ Visio Extras ➪ Database Export. The opening screen introduces you to the Database Export Wizard. Click Next to continue.

In the next screen, choose a drawing from the drop-down list of open drawings or use the Browse button to choose a different drawing file. If the file has more than one page, they are listed in the box beneath the drop-down list. Choose the page from which you want to generate and export a database (see Figure 28-20). Click Next to continue.

The third screen asks you to choose between All shapes on the page, Selected shapes on the page, or All shapes on one or more layers (see Figure 28-21).

Figure 28-20: Choose a drawing file and page from which to generate and export data.

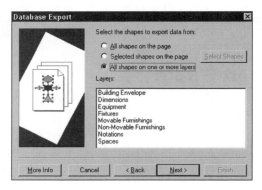

Figure 28-21: Choose between All shapes on the page, Selected shapes on the page, or All shapes on one or more layers.

If you choose the Selected shapes on the page option, the Select Shapes button is activated. Click it and a dialog box appears telling you to select shapes from the page. When you are done, click the OK button. You are returned to the wizard screen. Click Next to continue.

Tip   To select multiple shapes, hold down the Shift key while you click the shapes.

If you choose the All shapes on one or more layers option, the layer list appears below the options. In it are listed all the existing layers in the selected drawing. Choose the layers containing the shapes you want. Click Next to continue.

Tip   To select more than one layer, hold down the Shift key and you can select consecutive layers, or hold down the Control key and select any of the layers.

Cross-Reference   See Chapter 20 for a quick refresher on assigning shapes to layers.

The fourth screen prompts you to select the data you want to export into a database (as shown in Figure 28-22). You can choose to display all the cells in the ShapeSheet spreadsheets of the shapes for which you're exporting data in the list box by selecting the Show all Cells checkbox. If the checkbox is not checked, only the shapes' custom property fields are listed.

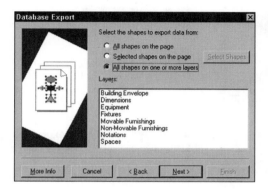

Figure 28-22: Select the data you want to export.

Use the Add button to add individual list items to the Cells and Fields to Export list. Use the Add All button to add the entire list. Use the Remove and Remove All buttons to remove items from the Cells and Fields to Export list.

When you export, the wizard determines the most appropriate data type for each cell or field for the information you are exporting. You can change the data type settings, and you can specify how you want to interpret the data (for example, as a formula, value, number, or number with a particular set of units). Click Next to continue.

The fifth screen asks you to choose an ODBC data source to which you want the generated data exported. If the database to which you want to export is not listed on this screen, the database may not be defined as an ODBC data source. You can define an existing database as an ODBC data source by clicking the Create New Data Source button, and then follow the screens. For more information about ODBC data sources, see the section "About ODBC-compliant data sources" earlier in the chapter.

Depending on the type of data source you have chosen, the next screen asks you to select a specific file to which you want the data to be exported (see Figure 28-23). Select a file and click OK.

Now you must specify the export table details (as shown in Figure 28-24). You indicate the name of the database table to which you want the shape data exported. (In some database programs like Excel, different tables appear on worksheets or separate pages.) Also, choose the type of data you want in the key field for the database table. (The key field is the field that uniquely identifies each shape.)

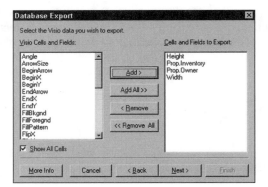

Figure 28-23: Select a specific file to which you want the data exported.

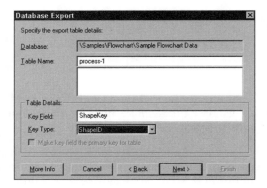

Figure 28-24: Specify the export table details.

Let's look at the fields appearing on this screen:

✦ **Database.** The name of the ODBC data source you selected on the previous screen.

✦ **Table Name.** If the database has tables, they are listed in the text box. If you want to export shape data to an existing table, select a table from those listed in the text box. The name appears in the text field just above it. The exported data replaces the previous data. If you want to create a new table to receive the exported shape data, enter a name for the new table in the text field just above it.

✦ **Key Field.** The wizard creates a key field in the database table called Shape Key. You can enter a different name for the field. The key field is the field that uniquely identifies each shape.

✦ **Key Type.** You can choose either ShapeID or GUID.

ShapeID is a number assigned to a shape by Visio according to the order in which the shape was created on the page. Because ShapeID is assigned by the order the shapes were created, if you delete a shape, and then add another shape, the second shape assumes the same ShapeID as the deleted one.

A GUID is a unique null-terminated 39-character string that is assigned to each shape when you export its data.

✦ **Make key field the primary key for table**. Making the key field a primary key field can increase the speed with which your database program can access the field. Because not all database programs can make fields primary key fields, for some database types, this option is disabled.

After you have set all the options in the screen, click Next.

The next screen asks you to specify the export mapping details (as shown in Figure 28-25). You set how you want the data to be interpreted in the database table.

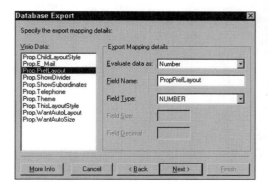

Figure 28-25: Specify the export mapping details.

For each ShapeSheet cell or custom property field from which you are exporting data, the wizard assigns a data type and a name, type, and size for the field the data is to reside in inside the database. The screen opens with default values assigned in each field. Change the defaults as you wish. Let's examine the fields on the screen and their choices:

✦ **Visio Data.** Select from the items listed here. Check if you want to remain with the default values in the other fields or make changes.

✦ **Evaluate Data As.** Choose how you want the data from the selected cell or field evaluated in the database: as a value, a formula, or by various types of measurements such as degrees, inches, or meters.

✦ **Field Name.** By default, the field name or column heading for the database field is the cell or field name as derived from the shape. You can change the name if you want.

✦ **Field Type.** Choose a type for the database field. The choices are CURRENCY, DATETIME, LOGICAL, NUMBER, or VARCHAR.

✦ **Field Size.** Enter a number that indicates how many characters a person can enter in the database field.

✦ **Field Decimal.** Enter a number that indicates how many digits to the right of the decimal point a person can enter in the database field.

Note This option is only available when the database table includes a SQL_NUMERIC or SQL_DECIMAL field.

When you are finished setting the values for the fields, click Next to continue. The next screen prompts you to select the Add export right mouse action to the drawing page option if you want to be able to re-export data to the database table by using a right mouse action (see Figure 28-26). Click Next to continue.

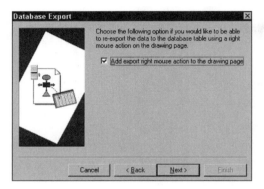

Figure 28-26: Specify the export mapping details.

The next screen enables you to examine the list of what is to be exported based on the selections you have made. To modify any of your selections, use the Back button to retrace your steps through the screens. If you are satisfied with the list, click Finish (see Figure 28-27). The data is exported to the selected file. To check the results, you have to open the database file in the appropriate application.

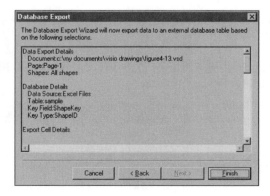

Figure 28-27: When you're ready to export, click Finish.

Import Flowchart Data Wizard

You can use the Import Flowchart Data Wizard to generate a Visio flowchart from data in an existing text (.txt) or MS Excel (.xls) file. Or, you can create a new data file (either a text or MS Excel file) and then use it to generate a flowchart.

You can run the Import Flowchart Data Wizard by accessing it from the menu bar (Tools ➪ Macros ➪ Flowchart ➪ Import Flowchart Data Wizard). The opening screen introducing you to the wizard appears. Click Next. The next screen offers you three options:

✦ **Enter Data in New Text File.** Opens a new text file where you can prepare data on which to base your Visio flow chart.

✦ **Enter Data in New Microsoft Excel Workbook.** Opens a template file in MS Excel that helps you prepare a data file on which you can base the Visio flowchart.

✦ **Read Data from an Existing File.** Enables you to choose either a text or MS Excel file that you have already prepared and then bases the new Visio flowchart on it.

Depending on your choice, the wizard takes you through preparing a data file or choosing an existing file and then displays a screen that asks you to choose a template for your flowchart. You have two options: Use a Vision Basic Flowchart Template or Use a Custom Template. The second option enables you to choose an existing custom template. Visio prepares the flowchart according to the template. Before going on, let's go over what you need to know about preparing a data file in either a text or MS Excel format.

Preparing a data file in a text format

If you want to prepare data in a text file, select the Enter Data in New Text File option and click Next. In the next screen, choose a template and click Next. The New Text File screen appears, giving you directions about what comes next and asking you to name the new data text file. When you click Next, a text file opens. This text file has directions on how the data file needs to be prepared. On the bottom of this text file, you are told to start the actual data file below the indicated line. Don't bother to edit information above the line. Visio knows to ignore it.

The text file must contain information about what template and which master shapes you want to use, how many instances of each master shape you want to include in the drawing, and to which shapes you want to connect. If you want to add custom properties to the master shapes, the text file has to include custom property information also.

What is between each quote mark (") represents the value of an item. Remember that the punctuation has to be exact for the data in the file to be read correctly. (For more information, see the section "Text files" earlier in this chapter.)

The first line should indicate which template you want to use:

> Template,"Template Name"
>
> (For example, Template,"Basic Flowchart.VST")

For choosing what Master Shapes you what to use, next add a line for each master shape you want to use:

> Master,"Master Name","Stencil Name"
>
> (For example, Master,"Process","Basic Flowchart Shapes.VSS")

If you want to add custom properties to master shapes, for each custom property you want to add to each master, include a line like this:

> Property,"Master Name","Property Name","Label","Prompt","Type","Format", "Value","Hidden","Ask"
>
> (For example, Property,"Process","Cost","Cost of Process","Enter cost in US dollars",,,,,)

For placing shapes on the drawing page, add a line like the following for each shape you want to place on the drawing page:

> Shape,"Shape Name","Master Name","Shape Text","ShapeX","ShapeY", "Width","Height","Cost","Duration","Resources"
>
> (For example, Shape,"MyShape1","Process","This is my shape's text",,,,,"1.05","4 hours","Some resources")

Note   If left blank, Visio determines the appropriate ShapeX, ShapeY, Width, and Height (the position and size of the shape).

For connecting shapes, add a line for every two shapes you want to connect like this:

> Link,"Link Name","Master Name","Link Text","From Shape (or Connector) Name","ToShape(or Connector) Name"
>
> (For example, Link,"MyLink1","Connector","some text","MyShape1", "MyShape2")

When you are done with the data file, save it and close it. Go back to the Visio Tools ➪ Macro ➪ Flowchart ➪ Import Flowchart Data Wizard and open it. This displays the introductory screen. Click Next and you get back to the New Text File screen. The name of the text file you have just prepared is in the name field. Click

Finish, and the wizard creates the flowchart based on the data file. But, before it does, the Visio File Converter window appears (as shown in Figure 28-28). Here you have to designate what the field separator, text delimiter, and comment character are.

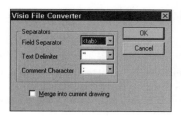

Figure 28-28: The Visio File Converter window

Each has a drop-down menu for you to tell Visio what you used in the data file. If you used the Flowchart database text file template, choose comma (,) for the field selector. Enable the checkbox option at the bottom of the screen if you want to merge with a currently opened drawing. If you do not check this option, Visio makes a new chart.

Preparing a data file in an MS Excel format

To prepare data in an MS Excel file, select the Enter Data in New Microsoft Excel Workbook option and click Next. In the next screen, choose a template and click Next. The next screen explains about what is going to happen. When you click Next, MS Excel is then activated, and the template you specified opens in it. Fill in the fields as you wish. When you are done, save the file and select the Tools option from the toolbar. From the menu that appears, choose Visio Import Flowchart Data Wizard. You are returned to the wizard. Click Finish, and the Visio File Converter window appears. Here you have to designate what the field separator, text delimiter, and comment character are. According to the options you set, the wizard creates the flowchart based on the data file.

Organization Chart Wizard

Say you want to make a chart that shows the employee structure of your company or organization, or the chain of command in your Boy Scout troop. You can make a data file with information about personnel, and from it the Organization Chart Wizard helps you generate a chart that shows the organization's hierarchy.

Choose the option to base the chart on an existing data file. Click Next to continue. The Organization Chart Wizard uses the fields from your data file to create custom property fields associated with the shapes in the organization chart it generates.

Each row in the data file represents information about one employee or member. Therefore, that row corresponds to one shape in the organization chart.

In many databases, such as MS Excel, MS Access, and Lotus 123, the fields are arranged in columns. You designate which of the columns or fields are to be incorporated in Visio shapes' custom property fields and associated with each shape in the chart as well as what is displayed in the shape. For each employee or member listed, a value is assigned for each of the data fields. These values are what the wizard puts into the custom property fields associated with a specific organization chart shape.

For example, say your data file contains a row for an employee named Joe Black. His name appears on the shape that represents him in the chart. In the wizard, his telephone number, x5678, which is contained in a data field, can be designated as a custom property field. The shape representing Joe Black in the chart would include a Telephone Number custom property field with the value x5678.

Using the Organization Chart Wizard

You can run the Organization Chart Wizard by accessing it from the menu bar (Tools ⇨ Macros ⇨ Organization Chart ⇨ Organization Chart Wizard). The first screen introduces you to the Organization Chart Wizard. The second screen prompts you to choose one of two options, you can base the chart on an existing data file or you can create the data file as you go through the wizard.

Let's create an organization chart based on an existing data file. In the second screen, choose the first option, Information that's already stored in a file or database. Click Next. In the next screen, you can choose between three data file options:

✦ A text Org Plus (.txt) or MS Excel file

✦ An MS Exchange Server directory

✦ An ODBC-compliant data source

According to the type of existing file that you want to base the drawing on, choose an option. Click Next to continue. In the next screen, enter the location and name of the information file. Or, use the Browse button to help locate the file. Click Next.

Tip   If you have used this wizard before, the filename of the last file you used is listed in the text field. If you have changed any data in the file, you should use the Browse button and select it again. This way the wizard updates itself.

The next few screens are the part of the wizard that asks about the information it needs to know in order to make the connection between the information in the database file and the shapes the wizard generates. Figure 28-29 shows an example of one of these screens.

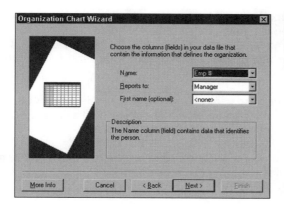

Figure 28-29: Designating the fields for the unique identifier and the person to which each reports

What type of data does the Organization Chart Wizard require?

The Organization Chart Wizard creates a hierarchical chart based on the required data field that indicates a unique identifier. That is, for each employee or member listed in the database, this field's entry identifies the person uniquely. It could be a person's name, but often more than one person has the same name. To make sure that each line item is one of a kind, many database systems use an identification number as a unique identifier.

The other crucial piece of data the wizard needs to know is to whom the employee or member reports. This field establishes the hierarchy of the organization. The field must contain each manager's or higher up's unique identifier (name or an identification number). The person at the top of the organization has no one to report to and therefore appears at the top of the chart. The database field for his manager or higher up should be left blank.

This screen has three fields with drop-down lists from which to make choices:

✦ **Name.** Choose the database field that is the unique identifier for the employee or member.

✦ **Reports to.** Choose the database field that indicates the manager's or higher up's unique identifier, whether that identifier is a name or an identification number.

✦ **First name (optional).** The First Name field is optional. It is there to help you create a unique identifier if you have personnel with the same last name but different first names, and you are using the name field as the unique identifier.

Because titles and tasks are generally organized differently in various companies, volunteer groups, and so on, you can name these required fields as you desire. This way the fields need not be named Name and Reports_to. The wizard gives you an opportunity to identify which of your field names provide information for the identifier, name, and who he or she reports to.

Note For an MS Excel file, make sure the database field names are in the first row. If you use the first rows for a headline before a row with the actual field names, the wizard does not register the field names in the appropriate places.

In the example in Figure 28-29, I have picked the database field, Emp# (indicating the unique identifier as the employee number), for the Name field and the database field, Manager, for the Reports to field.

For your work, select the database field appropriate for each wizard field and click Next to continue. The next screen asks you to choose the data fields whose values you want displayed in the chart (see Figure 28-30).

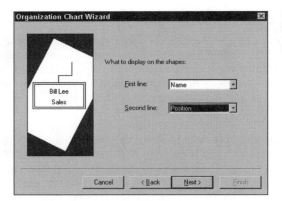

Figure 28-30: Designating the fields whose values you want to appear in the chart

Here, too, all the database fields are listed. The wizard can put up to two lines into the shapes it generates. It takes the values from the two fields you indicate here and puts them into the shapes. Although you can choose from any of the fields listed, you probably want to choose the database fields that indicate the name of the employee or member and his position. Choose the appropriate database fields and click Next.

Note You can always add more information in the shapes after the chart is generated, if you wish.

In the next screen, you choose the database fields that you want to add to the organization chart shapes as custom property fields.

Your database may include other information such as title, department, telephone numbers, and so on. The wizard includes the option of storing it with the shape as needed in the shape's custom property fields.

Let's take a detour and go back to what happens when you want to create the database while using the wizard, and then return to what happens just before the wizard creates the organization chart.

Creating an organization chart from data entered with the Wizard

If you want to create an organization chart from data entered through the Organization Chart Wizard, in the second screen select the option *Information that I enter using the wizard*. The next screen asks you to choose a type of file for entering data. Choose from MS Excel or delimited text, and then give the file a name.

Creating a database text file

Say you want to make a text file. Choose the Delimited text option and click Next. A text file template opens. But before it does, you get a message telling you that you should type over the sample text to create your data file.

The sample text looks like this:

> Name,Reports_To,Position,Department,Telephone
>
> Joe Sampleboss,,CEO,Executive,x5555
>
> Jane Samplemgr,Joe Sampleboss,Development Manager,Product Development, x6666
>
> John Samplepos,Jane Samplemgr,Software Developer,Product Development, x6667

The first line defines the field types or headings. Each line following is a single record that you write over with real data. The sequence of the data corresponds to the sequence of the headings in the first line. Notice that the CEO actually reports to no one, so the Reports_to field is blank. Don't forget to save the file before closing it and returning to the wizard.

Creating a database MS Excel file

Say you want to make an MS Excel file. Choose the MS Excel option and click Next. An MS Excel file template opens. But before it does, you get a message telling you that you should type over the sample text to create your data file.

Note For an MS Excel file, the database field names must be in the first row. Do not add a headline into rows above the row with the actual field names; if you do, the wizard will not register the field names in the appropriate places.

When you are done with entering the data, click the Save button. Close MS Excel. You are returned to the wizard.

Tip   You can make a copy of the file before you go to the next step, regardless of whether it's a text file or MS Excel file. Save the file in another name and then open the original file. This way, if you make an error and accidentally overwrite the file, you have a copy. If you click Next and an error occurs in the data file, Visio informs you with a message box. When you click OK, and then click the Back button, you do not go back to the data file. You have to exit Visio and then go back to the file to fix errors or open a new file. Here's a trick for getting around this: Open a new file from the wizard, and then open your saved file from the file editor. Fix the errors. Rename the saved file in the name of the new file. Close and continue with the Visio Organization Chart Wizard.

Before the wizard creates the organization chart

When working with an existing database or creating a database through the wizard, Visio offers help if your organization has more employees than can be displayed in a single page. Visio asks you to choose between letting it automatically break up the chart across pages or manually breaking up the chart yourself. If you let Visio do it, it then generates a chart.

If you choose to do it yourself, the next screen displays a list of pages in a table. It tells you the page number, the name of the employee at the top of the page, and the additional levels. Just click Finish.

Modifying the chart through the wizard

If you are not happy with the way the generated chart appears, you can modify the chart with the wizard. Open the Organization Chart Wizard again. Choose the database file again and go through the preceding screens. Choose to separate the pages yourself. You can add a page or modify a selected page. A screen appears in which you can specify the organization levels to appear on the selected page. You can experiment with it to see how the results come out. Go back through the wizard again until you are happy with the results.

Tip   Once the chart is generated, the Organization Chart toolbar appears. You can also modify the appearance of the chart through the options on this toolbar.

Adapting SAP/R3 databases for use with Visio Organization Chart Wizard

Visio can be used to generate charts from personnel data files created in SAP/R3, the integrated suite of software application modules that manage comprehensive financial, manufacturing, sales and distribution, and human resources functions essential to corporate operations. To adapt SAP/R3 data files for use with Visio, follow these steps:

1. Familiarize yourself with how to set up an organization chart data file and how the data needs to be structured so that the wizard can read it.

2. Choose between past, present, and future time periods that the organization chart is to represent. Make sure you choose the right settings that will generate a report based on the time period you want.

3. From the Human Resources Master Data in SAP/R3, create a report.

You need the following *infotypes* — Visio's term for a field information type — and fields from the Human Resources Master Data for the report:

Key Field infotype	Position # field
Personnel # field	Personal Data infotype
Org Assignment infotype	Last Name field
Description of Position field	First Name field

Now, from the Organization Management Data in SAP/R3, create another report. You need the following infotypes and fields from the Organization Management Data for the report:

✦ Object Name infotype

✦ Object ID field

✦ Object Name field

✦ Relationships infotype

✦ Relationships Between Objects field (specify the Reports To relationship)

✦ Relationship Specification field (if you want to specify Active or some other type of relationship)

✦ Type of related object field

✦ ID of related object field

From these two reports, you can now generate flat data. Here's how:

1. Import the flat data files into an ODBC-compliant database application. (You can use MS Excel.)

2. If you want both names to appear on organization chart shapes, combine the Last Name and First Name fields into one Name field in the first report file. Delete the Last Name and First Name fields.

3. Generate a new field in the first report called Manager Position # by running a query that compares Position # fields in the first and second reports.

4. Generate a new field called Manager Name by running a query that compares the Manager Position # field with the Position # field in the first report.

5. Check the data in the first report for errors that can cause problems for the Organization Chart Wizard. Make sure that no duplicate personnel ID numbers or manager position numbers exist. Make sure that the Manager Position # field for the person at the top of the organization chart is empty.

6. Save the first report so that the Organization Chart Wizard can read the data it contains to generate an organization chart.

7. Next, the wizard prompts you to choose fields from your data file that correspond to Name, Reports_To, and Unique ID. For the Name field, choose the SAP/R3 field Names; for Reports_To, choose the SAP/R3 field Manager Position #; and for Unique ID, choose the SAP/R3 field Personnel ID#s.

Property Reporting Wizard

The Property Reporting Wizard generates reports from custom property data stored in the shape of a chart or diagram. You can use the custom properties of the shapes to store all sorts of useful data about which you have designed a diagram or chart. You can use the Property Reporting Wizard to gather the stored custom property data and produce a report from it. The types of information or reports that can be made with these tools are inventory reports, such as bills for materials and supply inventories; or Numeric reports, such as cost totals or averages.

Custom property data

A custom property data field is itself a database field in which you can enter information relevant to a shape. Many Visio masters come with custom property fields already assigned. You can run the Property Report Wizard by accessing it from the menu bar (Tools ⇨ Macros ⇨ Visio Extras ⇨ Property Report Wizard).

The first screen introduces you to the Property Report Wizard. Click Next to continue. In the second screen, the Wizard prompts you to select shapes for reporting (as shown in Figure 28-31). You can report on all shapes on all pages of a drawing, or you can report on selected shapes.

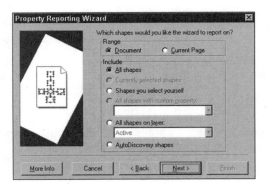

Figure 28-31: Select the shapes on which you want a report.

To select the range, choose one of these options:

✦ **Document.** Reports on all shapes from all pages of your drawing. (If you only have one page in the Visio drawing, this option is disabled.)

✦ **Current Page.** Reports only on shapes that are on the page you currently have displayed.

Select which shapes you want to include by choosing one of these options:

✦ **All shapes.** Reports on all shapes on all pages of your drawing.

✦ **Currently selected shapes.** Reports on shapes you selected before you started the wizard.

✦ **Shapes you select yourself.** While the wizard waits in the background, you click the shapes in your drawing on which you want a report. The shapes you select can be on different drawing pages.

✦ **All shapes with custom property.** Reports only on shapes with a specific custom property field (for example, cost). Choose the property you want from the list.

✦ **All shapes on layer.** Reports only on shapes assigned to a specific layer. (A layer is a named category of shapes.)

✦ **AutoDiscovery shapes.** Reports on the IP addresses and other network-related data associated with shapes in a network diagram generated dynamically from a network using AutoDiscovery technology.

Make your choices and click Next to continue.

Using Layers for refining inventory or numeric reports

When you want to create more than one report for a drawing, you can use layers to separate the shapes into categories, and then generate reports based on the categories.

For example, in a process flowchart, you can assign the shapes associated with each subprocess to a separate layer. This way you can easily generate an inventory report for the entire process that lists the cost, time, and resources associated with each phase. You can also generate separate numeric reports for each subprocess that calculate the total or average costs for each step in the subprocess.

The additional layers are hidden, so they do not affect the appearance of your drawing. The shapes are put in a category that you can select, hide, lock, print, or color separately. To put the shapes connected with a report on one layer also makes it easier to update the report.

Cross-Reference   For more information about layers, see Chapter 20.

Setting the report's appearance

In the next screen, you choose the property or properties to include as data columns in your inventory or numerical report (see Figure 28-32). The Properties included in your report become the column headings, or fields, in a spreadsheet.

Use the buttons to insert items from the Properties list into the Include list or remove items from the Include list. When you are finished, click Next. On the next screen, choose the type of report you want to create (see Figure 28-33). The choices are Numerical or Inventory.

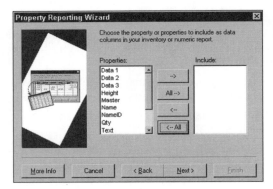

Figure 28-32: Select the properties you want to appear as data columns in your report.

Figure 28-33: Choose the type of report you want to create.

For numeric reports, you can specify one of the standard calculations (Total, Average, Median, Minimum, and Maximum), and the results of the calculation are displayed in the spreadsheet. If you choose Custom, you can enter formulas for advanced calculations to be in appropriate spreadsheet fields in your report.

For Numeric reports, the wizard automatically includes these column headings in the spreadsheet:

Page Name

Shape Name

Shape Text

The information under these column headings is required to identify the shapes. The wizard takes some of the data (the column headings and the calculation results) from the spreadsheet and displays it in a report shape in your drawing. If you add formulas to the spreadsheet, select the fields you want the report shape to include before you click Next to exit the spreadsheet.

For inventory reports, if you specify Basic Inventory, the results of the inventory are presented in the spreadsheet. If you want to group duplicates of individual shapes (shapes that share the same master), select the Total Identical Items option. Leave this option disabled to list each shape separately.

When you click Next, the wizard collects the appropriate inventory data and displays it in a report shape in your drawing. Save your spreadsheet as a text file or MS Excel file by clicking the Save icon in the upper-left corner of the display (see Figure 28-34).

Property Reporting Wizard

Below is the raw data for your property report. To save this information in either Microsoft Excel (XLS) or text (.TXT) format, click the Save button below.

	Department	Name	Name	NameID	Position	ow
1	Executive	Executive	Executive	Sheet.1	CEO	
2	Accounting	Manager	Manager	Sheet.2	Accountant	
3	Accounting	Position	Position	Sheet.3	Bookkeeper	
4	Office Administrat	Position.4	Position.4	Sheet.4	Secretary	
5	Product Develop	Manager.5	Manager.5	Sheet.5	Development Ma	
6	Product Develop	Position.6	Position.6	Sheet.6	Software Develo	
7	Product Develop	Manager.7	Manager.7	Sheet.7	Senior Technical	
8	Product Develop	Position.8	Position.8	Sheet.8	Technical Writer	
9	Product Develop	Position.9	Position.9	Sheet.9	Software Develo	
10	Product Develop	Position.10	Position.10	Sheet.10	Software Develo	
11	Product Develop	Position.11	Position.11	Sheet.11	Administrative As	
12	Product Develop	Position.12	Position.12	Sheet.12	Software Develo	
13	Product Develop	Position.13	Position.13	Sheet.13	Software Develo	
14	Product Develop	Position.14	Position.14	Sheet.14	Software Develo	

Cancel | < Back | Next > | Finish

Figure 28-34: A data spreadsheet

Note

You can only navigate the spreadsheet after you have clicked one of the fields.

To display data in your report selectively, hold down the Control key and click the columns that contain the data you want displayed. If you select no columns, they all appear on the report. Click Next to continue.

In the next screen, enter a title for your report, and from the drop-down list of pages in your drawing, choose the page you want the report shape to appear on (see Figure 28-35). Where applicable, select the options for including subtotal reports for the shapes on each page and for displaying column headings. Click Next to continue.

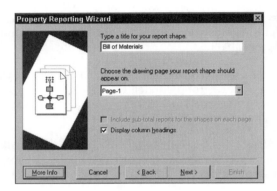

Figure 28-35: Give your report a title and choose on what page you want the title to appear.

The next screen asks you to choose the additional information you want displayed in your report shape (see Figure 28-36).

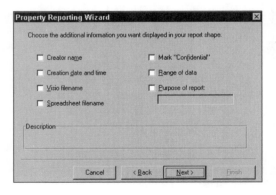

Figure 28-36: Choose additional information to be displayed in your report shape.

Let's examine the options:

✦ **Creator name.** Lists the Author information in the File ➪ Properties menu.

✦ **Creation date and time.** Lists the date and time the file was created according to the date and time settings in your computer.

✦ **Visio filename.** Lists the name of the Visio file on which the report is based.

✦ **Spreadsheet filename.** Lists the name of the spreadsheet file on which the report is based.

✦ **Mark "Confidential".** Labels the report Confidential.

✦ **Range of data.** Displays the layer name or custom property on which the report is based, or indicates that all shapes are included.

✦ **Purpose of report.** In the field provided, enter the purpose of the report.

Click the checkboxes of the items you want to select them, and then click Next to continue. The final screen tells you that you have answered all the questions necessary to create your property report. To generate the report shape, click Finish. The report shape appears in a layer on the page, as shown in Figure 28-37.

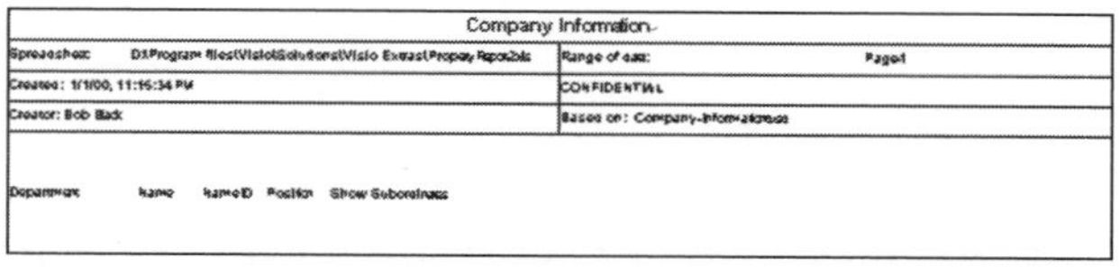

Figure 28-37: A generated report shape

Examining Other Database-Related Visio Extras

You should know about these four important functions:

Database Settings

Database Refresh

Database Update

Database Drawing Monitor

Database Settings

You can set certain aspects of ODBC behavior through the Database Settings menu. Access this menu from the menu bar (Tools ➪ Macros ➪ Visio Extras ➪ Database Settings).

When you have linked Visio shapes or drawings to databases created in ODBC-compliant applications, the settings control how the drawing monitor communicates changes to the database. The settings are global, applying to all the drawing-database links you have established. You can override the global settings in the process of establishing a link between a database and a drawing. Or, you can disable it in the drawing monitor (see Figure 28-38).

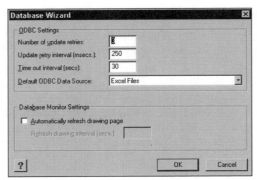

Figure 28-38: The Database Settings screen

Let's examine the options:

✦ **Number of update retries.** Enter the number of times you want to try updating a database based on changes to a drawing to which the database is linked if the first attempt fails.

✦ **Update retry interval (msecs).** Enter the number of milliseconds between update attempts.

✦ **Time out interval (secs).** Enter the number of seconds after which the update attempts time out.

✦ **Default ODBC Data Source.** Choose the ODBC data source you want the Database Wizard to link to by default. When you are using the wizard to link a shape to a database, you can choose a different data source.

✦ **Automatically refresh drawing page.** Select this option to refresh data based on changes from a database to a drawing according to the interval you specify in the next option.

✦ **Refresh drawing interval (secs).** Enter the number of seconds (for example, 20 seconds) that should elapse before changes to a database are communicated to a drawing. If it takes longer than the time you type to actually refresh a drawing, the Visio application adjusts the time accordingly.

You can modify these settings anytime.

Database Refresh and Database Update

You can manually communicate changes between the drawing and the database table by choosing Tools ➪ Macros ➪ Visio Extras ➪ Database Refresh or Database Update. Database Refresh refreshes the values in the shape's ShapeSheet cells to reflect changes in the database. Database Update updates the fields in the database to reflect changes in the shape's ShapeSheet cells.

Database Drawing Monitor

When you open a drawing that already has the option to refresh its data on opening the file, the screen in Figure 28-39 appears.

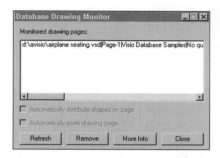

Figure 28-39: The Database Drawing Monitor screen

The option Launch the drawing monitor on document open, mentioned first in the section "Creating a linked drawing or modifying an existing one," activates the wizard's Drawing Monitor each time you open this linked drawing. The Drawing Monitor manages communication between the drawing on a page and the database table. When the Monitor is activated, the changes that you make to shapes in the drawing are automatically reflected in database records.

Note　If you want to make changes in the drawing on a page without automatically affecting database records, don't select this option. You can still manually communicate changes between the drawing and the database table by choosing Tools ➪ Macros ➪ Visio Extras ➪ Database Refresh or Database Update.

The Drawing Monitor manages the links between the shapes in the drawing and records in a database. For instance, if you delete a shape, the Drawing Monitor makes the change in the database table and deletes the corresponding record. If you add a shape, the Drawing Monitor adds an appropriate record to the database table. Changing a value in one of the shape's linked cells results in the Drawing Monitor making the change in the database table, altering appropriately the value in the corresponding record.

For the Drawing Monitor to function, you have to set the "Automatically refresh drawing page option" in the Database Wizard dialog box. You access this particular dialog box by selecting Tools ➪ Macros ➪ Visio Extras ➪ Database Settings.

How does it work?

When you change a shape, the Drawing Monitor compares Visio's cell values with the database record values. If the database record values have been changed, a screen appears in which the Drawing Monitor asks you to either discard the shape changes and revert to the values in the database or update the database record based on values from the shape.

The following items appear on the screen:

✦ **Monitored Drawing Pages.** The opened linked drawing pages are listed. The Drawing Monitor can monitor the database links for several pages at one time.

✦ **Automatically Distribute Shapes On The Page**. If you enable this option, it arranges the shapes in the drawing selected in the Monitored Drawing Pages list in rows and columns on the page.

If the database table includes fields you have linked to the PinX and PinY cells in the Shape Transform section of the ShapeSheet spreadsheet, do not activate this option. Otherwise, these shapes will be dropped at the PinX and PinY locations.

✦ **Automatically Scale Drawing Page**. Sets the page size to accommodate the shapes in the pages selected in the Monitored Drawing Pages list.

✦ **Refresh.** Copies the new values from database records into the corresponding ShapeSheet cells, and adds new shapes based on newly created database records, distributes shapes on the page, or scales a page for the drawing selected in the Monitored Drawing Pages list.

✦ **Remove.** Removes a selected drawing from the Monitored Drawing Pages list. The Drawing Monitor then stops monitoring the link for the drawing on the page you have removed.

✦ **Close.** Closes the Drawing Monitor and stops monitoring the links between any open drawings and their linked databases.

If you close the screen, you must do one of the following if you want to reopen the Monitor: Run the Database Wizard, and then choose the Create a linked drawing or modify an existing option. Or, right-click the page, and then choose Launch Drawing Monitor, if you added this option to the shortcut menu in the wizard.

Learn how to adjust the stencil windows and further manipulate stencil masters in Chapter 15.

Summary

This chapter covered all the database-related wizards in Visio 2000 Standard. I walked you through each wizard step by step to demonstrate what you can use them for and how to perform database-related tasks without having to write programming code.

I covered the following subjects in this chapter:

✦ Working with different types of databases in Visio

✦ Creating database-related actions and events for Visio shapes and pages

✦ Communicating updates between a Visio drawing and its related database

✦ Creating charts and drawings based on information collected in a database

✦ Linking Visio shapes in a drawing to records in a database

✦ Exporting custom property field data for every shape, or for selected shapes, in a drawing to a table in an ODBC-compliant database

✦ Generating reports with Property Reporting Wizard

You can find more information about the various Visio components that are affected when a Visio drawing is linked to a database throughout the book. The next chapter introduces you to formatting and aligning text and shows you how to set paragraphs and margins and use special features such as bullets, tabs, and background color.

✦   ✦   ✦

Creating and Manipulating Text

Part IV covers functions instrumental in creating and formatting text. In particular, I discuss methods for editing text position, color, font, size, and style. Readers are also introduced to Visio 2000's Spell Check feature, along with ways to add bullets and set margins.

Basic Text Functions

Now that you understand how to use the drawing tools and the numerous shapes within Visio 2000, you can begin to add text. No matter how detailed a drawing is, using text for descriptions, labels, data, addresses, names, dimensions, and notations will help clarify and enhance the drawing's level of detail. The result — a drawing that becomes a vital source of information.

This chapter discusses the essential tools and features used to create and to manipulate text. Not only will this chapter cover basic methods for entering text, but it will also detail how to manipulate predefined text styles, as well as how to create your own style.

Without text, your drawing solely consists of lines, shapes, and images. Mere one-dimensional strokes, striving to communicate information, but often not delivering the complete picture. Let's give those lines and shapes a helping hand. Let's add detail and data to those drawings. Let's bring in a few notes for clarification. Let's learn how to add text to our drawings!

Inserting Text

Visio 2000 enables you to insert text into your drawings in several ways. You can type text, use system information, or incorporate in-depth features, such as linking text in a shape to information located in databases. For our purposes, we will discuss the basic methods, hence, the title of this chapter, "Basic Text Functions." This chapter will cover how to

✦ use the Text Tool in order to enter text into a text-only field, which is a stand-alone shape with no visible lines. The Text Tool is useful for notes, dimensions, titles, addresses, and lists.

✦ use the Text Block Tool not only to create a shape, but also to edit the text block, perhaps adding descriptions, data, and important information to objects.

✦ add text to a Visio shape, including connectors.

Note   Not all Visio shapes allow text insertion. Some shapes located within templates automatically generate associated text from their custom properties. In addition, some shapes are locked against adding text. For these locked shapes, Visio lets you know by displaying a message that text cannot be added.

Using the Text Tool

Before I go any further and describe how to use the Text Tool and the Text Block Tool, let's make sure that you know where these items are located on the Standard toolbar (as shown in Figure 29-1). The Text Tool is showing, and clicking the down-arrow next to the Text tool will reveal the Text Block Tool.

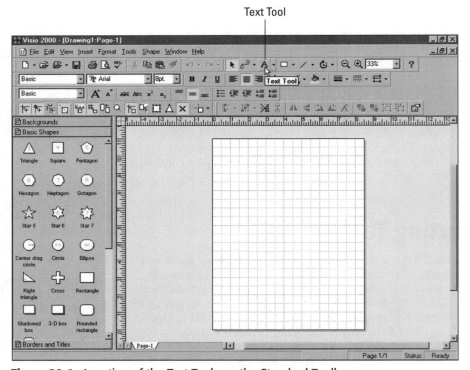

Figure 29-1: Location of the Text Tools on the Standard Toolbar

Your drawing is sitting there in front of you. All you want to do is to add a few notes to help clarify a process, or simply insert the name of a company and its address. Perhaps you just want to list some pricing information, or even add the title of the drawing. But you're just not sure how to insert this information. Well, let's find out.

To insert text in a text-only shape, click the Text Tool button on the Standard Toolbar. Move the cursor to where you want text to be placed and then click the mouse button. (Or, if you want, you can click and drag the cursor until the text block is the size that you need and then release the button.) A dotted-line box is displayed with the cursor flashing. At this point, you can enter your own text, or enter text available to you based on existing file properties and system information.

Once you are finished entering the desired text, you can either click outside the text area or press the Esc key. If you use the Esc key, the text will remain selected, which is indicated by green anchor blocks around the edge of the text-only shape.

If you decide you want to insert text that is available to you through file and system information, select Field from the Insert menu. You are presented with the Field dialog box (see Figure 29-2).

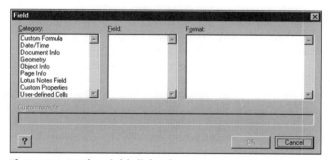

Figure 29-2: The Field dialog box

From the Field dialog box, you can insert information associated with the following nine categories:

✦ **Custom Formula.** Enter the formula in the Custom Formula text box at the bottom of the window. To create a formula, use the same functions you use in the ShapeSheet spreadsheet.

✦ **Date/Time.** Uses system information to track Creation Date, Creation Time, Current Date, Current Time, Last Edit Date, Last Edit Time, Print Date, and Print Time.

✦ **Document Info.** Uses information entered in the Properties dialog box to track Creator, Description, Folder, Filename, Keywords, Subject, and Title.

✦ **Geometry.** Uses a shape's width, height, and angle information. Use the Width field for dimension lines or the Angle field to show how far a shape is rotated from its original position. Use any Geometry field to automatically update technical specifications in a drawing.

✦ **Object Info.** Uses information entered in the Special dialog box to track Data 1, Data 2, Data 3, ID, Master, Name, and Type.

✦ **Page Info.** Uses information entered in the Page Properties tab of the Page Setup dialog box or information entered in the Properties dialog box in order to track Background Name, Number of Pages, and Page Number.

✦ **Lotus Notes Field.** Uses information entered in the Lotus Notes Field dialog box to manage information, such as shape details, shape measurements, and date of creation.

✦ **Custom Properties.** Uses custom properties stored in the Custom Property section of the selected shape's ShapeSheet spreadsheet. Define Custom Properties to associate the type of information you want identified with a shape. For example, you can associate a serial number with a piece of equipment.

✦ **User-defined Cells**. Uses information entered in the Value cell of the User-defined Cells section in the shape's ShapeSheet spreadsheet.

Some of the categories may have additional Fields and Formats that you need to select. For example, if you choose the Geometry category, the Field box displays Height, Width, and Angle as options. And if you choose Angle, you then have the options of General, Radians, and Degrees as a Format. Once you have made your selection, simply click OK. The appropriate information will be displayed in the text block.

Note Field information is automatically updated when you change a drawing.

Using the Text Block Tool

The Text Block Tool performs the same text inserting operations that were described in the "Using the Text Tool" section.

Click the down arrow next to the Text Tool button on the Standard Toolbar. From the drop-down menu, select the Text Block Tool. Now move the cursor to where you want to place text and then click the mouse button. Or, you can click and drag the cursor until the text block is the size that you need and then release the button. A dotted-line box is displayed with the cursor flashing. At this point, simply enter your text as described in the "Using the Text Tool" section. Once you are finished inserting text, click outside the text area.

Note The Text Block Tool not only can insert text, it also can rotate, position, and resize a selected text block. To learn more about these latter three functions, check out the "Rotating, Positioning, and Resizing a Text Block" section.

Adding text to a Visio shape

Aside from using the Text Tool and the Text Block Tool, you can also insert text into a diagram by simply adding the text to a Visio shape. First off, you need a Visio shape on your page. Next, simply double-click that shape. The text block will open and the cursor in the shape will flash. Now you are ready to insert text. Enter the text as described in the preceding two sections.

Finding and Replacing Text

So now there's text in your diagram, and you need to find a certain word, phrase, or even special characters, such as manual returns and tabs. You might even need to replace any or all occurrences of an item with a new word or phrase. No problem, you can do both.

Searching for text

To search for text items, select Find from the Edit menu. In the Find dialog box (see Figure 29-3) type the word or phrase that you're searching for in the "Find what" text field. Or, if you are looking for that special character, click Special and then choose the appropriate option, such as a manual return, tab, or caret. Select the Search and Match options that you want. After you are satisfied with your search criteria, click Find Next.

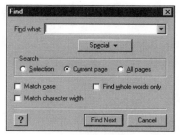

Figure 29-3: The Find dialog box

If Visio finds your item, it will highlight the item and then go to the place in the document where the item is located. Click Cancel in order to close the Find dialog box so that you can edit the word or phrase, or click Find Next in order to find the item's next occurrence. Once all the instances of your search are found, Visio will display a message that the search process is finished. If the item was not found, Visio will display this same message. Click OK and then click Cancel to close the Find dialog box.

Replacing text

Finding the text item was fine, but now you need to take it one step further. Not only do you need to find all of the occurrences of a word or phrase, but you also want to replace the occurrences with a new selection, without having to type it in each time. Well, that's when you use the Replace feature.

Select Replace from the Edit menu. In the Replace dialog box (see Figure 29-4) type the word or phrase that you want to replace in the "Find what" field. Or, click Special in order to specify a special character, such as a tab, or caret. In the "Replace with" field, type the word or phrase that you want to use instead of the text entered in the "Find what" box. Or, enter a special character by clicking Special and selecting an option, such as a tab, or caret. Select the Search and Match options that you want, and then click either Find Next or Replace All.

Find Next takes you to the next instance of the word, phrase, or special character. You then have the choice of replacing that occurrence with the new item (click Replace), replacing every occurrence with the new item (click Replace All), or not replacing the occurrence and moving to the next instance (click Find Next).

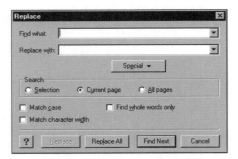

Figure 29-4: The Replace dialog box

When Visio has finished searching for and replacing the text item, it displays a message box that informs you that the search is complete. Simply click OK and then click Cancel in order to close the Replace dialog box.

Selecting Text

Once you have text in a diagram, you can manipulate it. However, before performing any text alterations, you must first select text. You can select any or all text within a text-only shape and within a Visio shape by using the following procedures:

✦ To select all of the text in a block, regardless if it is in a text-only shape or a Visio shape, double-click the shape. Or, select the shape and then press F2.

✦ To select part of the text in a text block, double-click the shape and then drag the insertion point.

✦ To select a word or paragraph, double-click the shape and then double-click a word or triple-click a paragraph.

Note You can also use Arrow keys while depressing the Shift key in order to select blocks of text.

If your drawing's View size is less than 100 percent, when you select text, the drawing enlarges to 100% so that you can clearly view the text. Once you click outside of that shape or text block, your drawing will return to its original magnification.

Rotating, Positioning, and Resizing a Text Block

What if you need to rotate a text block to a slanted angle, maybe even a 90-degree angle? Or, you might have to resize a text block so that it can accommodate more text. Maybe you will have to move a text block away from a shape. Well, all of this is easily done using the Text Block Tool.

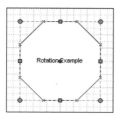

Figure 29-5: Rotating a text block

Note Notice the four round corner points of the selected text block (as shown in Figure 29-5). The appearance differs from the square points that result from using the Pointer Tool when selecting a block. Also notice the black *rotation pin* in the center of the block.

First, click the Text Block Tool button on the Standard Toolbar. Select the text block that you want to manipulate by clicking it. To rotate the shape's text block, place the mouse pointer over one of the block's four round anchor points (called *rotational handles*). The pointer changes to a circle with directional arrows. Click and drag a rotation handle clockwise or counterclockwise until it reaches the position that you want. Release the mouse button.

There is another way to rotate your text; however, it has its limits. If you want to rotate your text in increments of 90 degrees in a counterclockwise rotation, right-click over your selected text block and then select the Shape ➪ Rotate Text option.

To position a shape's text block, place the mouse pointer over the black center rotation pin. The pointer changes to two small rectangles, one lighter than the other. Click and drag the rotation pin until the text block is in the position that you want. Release the mouse button.

Note   Most Visio shapes have a rotation pin that allows you to easily move and reposition text.

To resize a shape's text block, place the mouse pointer over one of the square anchor points (called *selection handles*). The pointer changes to a small line with arrowheads at each end. Click and drag on the selection handle until the text block is the size that you want. Release the mouse button.

Performing Text Editing Functions

As in other Windows applications, you can perform the typical editing actions, such as Delete, Copy, and Paste. You can select any text in your diagram and perform a text action on it.

Note   As in any typical Windows application, you can perform each text editing operation with a keyboard, with onscreen menu options, or by accessing a pop-up menu by right-clicking your mouse. The remainder of this section will focus on keyboard methods because they are the quickest methods. However, if you are more comfortable using menu options, use the Copy, Cut, Paste, and Delete ➪ Selection options available under the Edit menu; or the Cut, Copy, Paste, and Duplicate options contained within the right-click pop-up menu.

In addition, you can repeat any text actions by pressing the F4 key.

Deleting text

Before this chapter, there was no text on your diagram. Well, there might have been, but it certainly wasn't inserted with the flair and expertise you've learned here — it's kind of like the difference between a wobbly pass heaved by Jim Plunket and a bullet rifled by Peyton Manning. I now return you to your regularly scheduled book.

As I was saying, there was no text on your diagram. Now all of the sudden you run into a situation where there is too much text or the information is no longer valid and you want to delete, cut, or remove it from the diagram. You can delete parts of or the entire text.

To cut selected text and place it on the Windows Clipboard, first select the text and then simultaneously press the Ctrl and "X" keys, or simply press the Delete key.

To delete an entire text-only shape, first select the shape with the Pointer tool on the Standard Toolbar, and then simultaneously press the Ctrl and "X" keys, or simply press the Delete key.

Copying and pasting text

Visio 2000 can copy existing text and then paste it into your diagram. You can copy and paste selected text or an entire text shape.

To copy text to the Windows Clipboard, first select the text and then simultaneously press the Ctrl and "C" keys.

To copy a text shape, first click the shape and then simultaneously press the Ctrl and "C" keys.

To paste the copied text or a text shape, first click where you want to place the insertion point and then simultaneously press the Ctrl and "V" keys.

 Note If you copy text from another program and then paste it to you diagram, any formatting information will be lost.

Selecting a Font

Getting tired of your default font? No problem. Visio 2000 has several methods for changing fonts. However, regardless of which of the following three methods you use, you must first select the text that you want to change. (If you've forgotten how to select text, refer to the "Selecting Text" section.)

✦ Go to the Font field located on the Format Toolbar (see Figure 29-6) and click the down arrow to the right of the box. From the drop-down menu, select the option that you want.

Font field

Figure 29-6: Using the Font field on the Format Toolbar

✦ Select Text from the Format menu. The Text dialog box appears (see Figure 29-7). From the Font tab, click the down arrow located to the right of the Font box. From the drop-down menu, select the option that you want and then click OK, or press the Enter key.

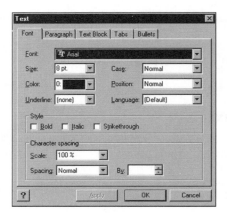

Figure 29-7: Accessing fonts from the Text dialog box

✦ With the mouse pointer positioned over your selection, right-click and select Format ➪ Text. Once again, the Text dialog box appears. Perform the same operation with the Text dialog box as in the previous paragraph.

Adjusting Text Size

Depending on the size of a shape or the number of objects in a diagram, you may need to adjust the size of text by changing font sizes.

As with most operations, there are several ways that you can accomplish the task. Following are four methods for changing font sizes. However, regardless of which method you use, you must first select the text that you want to change. (If you've forgotten how to select text, refer back to the "Selecting Text" section.)

✦ Go to the Font Size field located on the Format Toolbar (see Figure 29-6) and click the down arrow to the right of the box. From the drop-down menu, select the option that you want. Or, click inside the Font Size box, highlighting the displayed numeral. Enter a new font size and then press the Enter key.

✦ From the Format Text Toolbar (see Figure 29-8) click either the Increase Font Size or Decrease Font Size button until the text is the desired size.

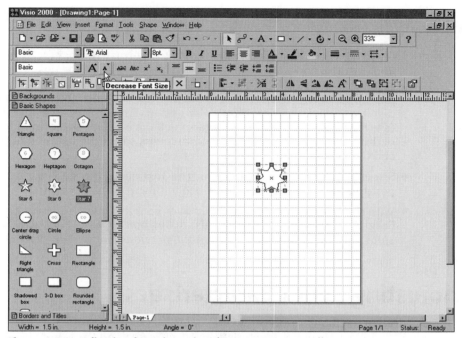

Figure 29-8: Adjusting font size using the Format Text Toolbar

✦ Select Text from the Format menu. The Text dialog box appears (see Figure 29-7). From the Font tab, click the down arrow located to the right of the Size box. From the drop-down menu, select the option that you want. Or, click inside the Size box, highlighting the numeral that is displayed. Enter a font size. Once you have entered a size, click OK, or press the Enter key.

✦ With the mouse pointer positioned over your selection, right-click and select Format ⇨ Text. Once again, the Text dialog box appears. Perform the same operation with the Test dialog box as in the previous paragraph.

Adjusting Text Color

Visio 2000's default color is black. However, at times colored text can add vital information to a diagram. Maybe a red font can signify a CAUTION or WARNING message. Or, you may want to identify changes with a particularly colored font. Whatever the reason, Visio 2000 offers several methods for changing font colors. Before using any of the three following methods, as with other font functions, you must first select the text that you want to change. (If you've forgotten how to select text, refer back to the "Selecting Text" section.)

✦ Go to the Font Color button located on the Format Toolbar (see Figure 29-6) and click the down arrow to the right of the button. (If the desired color is displayed on the button, then simply click the Font Color button.) From the pop-up swatches palette, click the new color. If the desired color is not displayed, click the More Text Color option. This displays the Text dialog box (see Figure 29-7). From the Font tab, click the down arrow located to the right of the Color box. From the drop-down menu, select the option that you want and then click OK, or press the Enter key.

✦ Select Text from the Format menu. The Text dialog box appears. At this point, perform the same steps as described in the previous paragraph.

✦ With the mouse pointer positioned over your selection, right-click and select Format ➪ Text. Once again, the Text dialog box appears. Follow the same steps with the Test dialog box that the previous two paragraphs outlined.

Adjusting Font Characteristics

In addition to changing fonts, text size, and text color, Visio 2000 enables users to alter the following font characteristics: Case (Normal, All Caps, Initial Caps or Small Caps), Position (Normal, Subscript, Superscript), Style (Bold, Italic, Strikethrough), Character Spacing, and Character scale. All of these font characteristics can be changed from the Text dialog box.

As with the previously discussed font functions, first select the text that you want to change. (If you've forgotten how to select text, refer back to the "Selecting Text" section.) Next, select Text from the Format menu. Or, with the mouse pointer positioned over your selection, right-click and select Format ➪ Text. Then click the Font tab and try the following methods for changing the five font characteristics:

✦ To change the case of text, click the down arrow to the right of the Case box. From the drop-down menu, select the option that you want and then click OK, or press the Enter key. If you want to change your text selection to small caps, you could also click the Small Caps button located on the Format Text Toolbar.

✦ To change text position, click the down arrow to the right of the Case box. From the drop-down menu, select the option that you want and then click OK, or press the Enter key. Or, click the Superscript or Subscript buttons on the Format Text Toolbar.

✦ To change the style of text, select the appropriate box within the Style area and then click OK, or press the Enter key. Or, click the Bold, Italic, or Underline buttons on the Format Toolbar, or the Strikethrough button on the Format Text Toolbar.

✦ To change character scale, click the down arrow to the right of the Scale box. From the drop-down menu, select the option that you want and then click OK, or press the Enter key.

✦ To change spacing between each character, click the down arrow to the right of the Spacing box. From the drop-down menu, select the option that you want. Next, click the down arrow to the right of the By box and select a desired spacing increment. When you're satisfied with the choices, click OK, or press the Enter key.

Changing a Text's Style

Visio 2000 comes with predefined text styles. However, you can create your own styles. Visio shapes have styles linked to them. Each style has its own particular text characteristics, and its own line or fill attributes.

To change the style of a text selection, first select the text. Then go to the Text Style box on the Format Text Toolbar and click the down arrow to the right of the box. Select the appropriate style that you want.

Manipulating Text Styles

Visio 2000 offers predefined text styles, so if you don't like a style's feature, you can change them. Or, you can create a new style.

Modifying a predefined style

To modify a predefined text style, select Define Styles from the Format menu. The Define Styles dialog box appears (see Figure 29-9).

Figure 29-9: The Define Styles dialog box

Click the down arrow to the right of the Style list and select a style that you want to edit. To rename a style, click Rename, type a new name for the style, and then click OK. To change a style's settings within the Change area, click the attributes that you want to edit. When the Change button becomes available, click it. Then click Apply.

Tip   If you change a style and don't want it to be visible from the Style list, select the Hidden Style box.

Creating a new text style

Sometimes it's easier to create a new style, rather than changing an existing style. To define a new style, select Define Styles from the Format menu. From the Style list, select the <New style> option , and then type a name for the new style.

To base the new style on an existing style, choose that style from the Based On list.

In the Includes section, select the attributes that you want your new style to include. A style can include formatting from any combination of the three attributes within the section.

In the Change section, click the Text, Line, or Fill buttons in order to alter the settings for that attribute. Select the settings that you want for each attribute that you selected in the Includes section.

Tip   If you create a style and don't want it to be visible from the Style list, select the Hidden Style box.

After selecting the settings that you want, follow one of the three following procedures:

- ✦ Click Apply to add the new style. Apply it to selected shapes, and then close the dialog box.
- ✦ Click OK if no shapes are selected to add to the new style, and then close the dialog box
- ✦ Click Add to add the new style and to continue working on styles in the dialog box.

Summary

This chapter covered all of the basic, but also essential, information and operations concerning text. The more you use Visio 2000, the easier it will become to use these operations. Before long, you won't think twice about how to change a font or its size. But just in case you've forgotten something, following is a quick review of the major points discussed in this chapter:

✦ How to insert text into diagrams by using either the Text Tool or the Text Block Tool, or simply double-clicking a Visio shape and then inserting the text.

✦ Using the Find option in the Edit menu in order to search for text. You can also use the Replace option in the same menu to not only find a particular word, phrase, or special character, but also to automatically replace the item with a new text item.

✦ Performing the typical text editing operations (cut, copy, and paste) by using the same features available in all Windows applications.

✦ Using the Text dialog box to change a text's font characteristics, such as a font's size, color, and style, or the font itself. You can also access these characteristics from the Format and Format Text Toolbars.

✦ How to use Visio 2000's predefined text styles, how to modify these styles, and how to create your own text styles.

The next chapter covers methods for formatting and aligning text.

✦   ✦   ✦

Formatting and Aligning Text

The last chapter introduced you to the Text Tool and its uses, including how to create text objects on a drawing page. This chapter covers formatting text blocks as a whole and as paragraphs. Proper formatting and aligning of page text goes a long way toward giving your presentation a professional appearance. This chapter details many ways to create more appealing text.

First, let's review how to retrieve the tools that you will need.

Toolbar Text Commands and the Text Dialog Box: Review

As you learned in previous chapters, the Format toolbar and the Format Text toolbar contain various text formatting commands. These toolbars can be accessed through the View command on the Menu toolbar. This chapter describes the following text formatting commands on the Format toolbar: Align Left, Align Right, Align Center, and Fill Color. On the Format Text toolbar, this chapter covers Align Top, Align Middle, Align Bottom, Bullets, Increase Indents, Decrease Indents, Decrease Paragraph Spacing, and Increase Paragraph Spacing.

The Text dialog box also offers these commands, as well as other commands. Because the Text dialog box offers more formatting options than the toolbars, it often is better to use it instead of the toolbars. Also, displaying toolbars reduces available workspace. I recommend that you pick one of the following ways to open the Text dialog box and then make it the standard method for formatting text in most of your projects.

Opening the Text Option box

The Text dialog box is a dialog box containing format, alignment, and other text tools. Remember that the Text dialog box will operate on the selected text or text-containing shape. So make sure you have made your selection *before* opening the Text dialog box.

The following two methods can open the Text dialog box:

✦ Select Format ➪ Text from the Menu toolbar.

✦ Right-click the selected text or text-containing shape. Then select Format ➪ Text from the pop-up menu.

Text dialog box tabs

The Text dialog box has five tabs: Font, Paragraph, Text Block, Tabs, and Bullets (see Figure 30-1). The rest of this chapter will discuss all these tabs, except the Font tab, which I covered in the previous chapter.

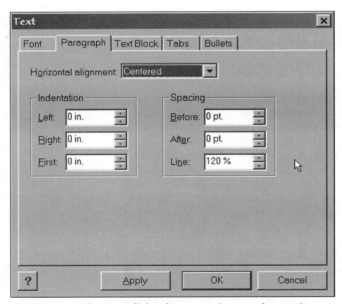

Figure 30-1: The Text dialog box contains text-formatting commands in five tabs.

Changing Paragraph Justification

Visio 2000 allows you to use either the Format toolbar or the Text dialog box to justify text blocks to right, left, or center.

Justification using the Format toolbar

From the Format toolbar, select the Align Left, Align Right, or Align Center button. Visio 2000 will justify to the left, right, or center, respectively.

Note　When using lower screen resolutions (such as 640 × 480), some Format toolbar buttons may not be visible. The Align Right and Align Left buttons are among the first to be cropped off. To gain access to these buttons, either delete other toolbar buttons, or set your screen to a higher resolution.

Justification using the Text dialog box

Open the Text dialog box as described earlier in the chapter, and select the Paragraph tab. At the top and center of the Paragraph tab is a selection field labeled Horizontal Alignment. To change justification, click the selection arrow on the right side of the field and choose Left to justify to the left, Right to justify to the right, or Centered to center-justify. Click Apply or OK in order to set the text block to its new justification.

Justified and Forced Justified options in the Text dialog box

The Text dialog box contains two horizontal alignment options that are not available on the Format toolbar: Justified, and Forced Justified.

If you select Justified, the text in the text block will space itself to align evenly with both sides of the text box. The last line will be justified to the left if it's not long enough to easily extend to both sides.

If you select Forced Justified, the text in the text block will space itself to align evenly on both sides to the width of the text box — including the last line. So, if the text block is much wider than the last line is when the last line has normal spacing between its words, then the Forced Justified option will end up spacing the words far apart in order to make the last line justify with both sides of the text box. You may need to reword the paragraph to prevent this.

Example: Paragraph justification

Start a new drawing. Select Basic Flowchart from the New Drawing submenu. From the Basic Flowchart Shapes stencil, select the Auto-height box shape and drag it onto the page. The box already has default text inside it. The text is center justified by default. If your Format toolbar is not already available, select it in the View ➪ Toolbar ➪ Format menu. Verify that the text shape is still selected. From the Format toolbar, select the Align Left button (as shown in Figure 30-2). You'll see the text line up evenly on the left side of the text box. Next, select the Align Right button. The text is now evenly aligned on the right side of the text box. Finish by selecting the Align Center button in order to return the text to its original position.

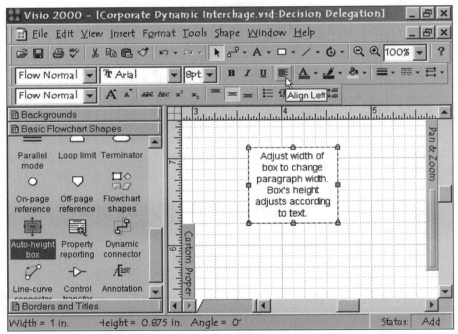

Figure 30-2: Selecting the Align Left button on the Format toolbar

Next, verify that the text shape is still selected. From the Menu toolbar, select Format ➪ Text. Click the Paragraph tab in the Text dialog box. Find the Horizontal Alignment field in the top-center of the Paragraph tab section. Click the menu arrow on the right side of the Horizontal Alignment field. From the menu, select Justified. Click OK. Notice that the letters in every line, except the last line, are spaced so that the lines are evenly aligned on both sides. The last line stayed short. Let's change that.

Right-click the text shape. From the pop-up menu, select Format ➪ Text. Select the Paragraph tab. Click the menu arrow in the Horizontal Alignment field. Choose the Forced Justified option. Click OK. Notice that the last line spreads to reach both sides of the text box, and it looks rather odd. This is why you should be careful with this option. Let's modify the box for a better fit.

Grab a size handle on either side of the text box. Slowly stretch the box until the last line runs back into the preceding line. Now, the new last line looks fine. Save this example for use in the next section.

Changing Paragraph Spacing

Spacing between paragraphs can be set in any of the three following ways:

✦ Place a space before the beginning of every paragraph, except the first paragraph.

✦ Place a space after the end of each paragraph, except the last paragraph.

✦ Place a space both before and after each paragraph, except before the first paragraph and after the last paragraph.

Note   To set spacing before the first or after the last paragraph, you must adjust margins.

Using the Format Text toolbar buttons

The last two buttons on the Format Text toolbar are the Decrease Paragraph Spacing button and the Increase Paragraph Spacing button (as shown in Figure 30-3). Clicking these will decrease (down to 0 points) or increase the space between paragraphs. These alterations change the amount of space before *and* after each paragraph in 2-point increments. (1 point equals 1/72 inch). That's 2 points before *and* 2 points after, equaling a 4-point (or 1/18 inch) increase or decrease of space between each paragraph. The 2-point increment is fixed. It cannot be changed from the Format Text toolbar. However, it can be changed from the Text dialog box.

Decreasing paragraph spacing
To decrease paragraph spacing in a selected text block by 4 points (1/18 inch.), click the Decrease Paragraph Spacing button on the Format Text toolbar.

Increasing paragraph spacing
To increase paragraph spacing in a selected text block by 4 points (1/18 inch), click the Increase Paragraph Spacing button on the Format Text toolbar.

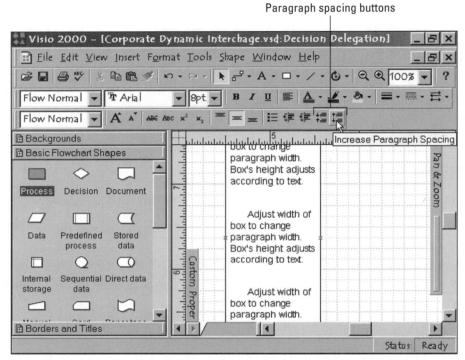

Figure 30-3: The Paragraph Spacing buttons are located on the far right of the Format Text toolbar.

Using the Text dialog box to change paragraph spacing

Open the Text dialog box. Select the Paragraph tab. The Spacing section, with three input fields, is located on the right side of the Paragraph tab's dialog box (as shown in Figure 30-1). Right now, we are concerned with the Before and After input fields.

By default, the Before and After input fields use points as their units of measure. You can replace points with inches, feet, centimeters, or meters by substituting the point's abbreviation (pt.) with the standard abbreviation for the new unit of measure (in. for inch, ft. for feet, cm. for centimeter, and m. for meter). Visio 2000 allows you to assign different units of measure to each field. However, I can't think of a good reason to do so. Generally speaking, if you change the measurement unit in one input field you should use that same measurement unit in the other input field so as to avoid confusion.

By default, the amount of Before and After spacing is set at 0 points. You can change both settings, either by clicking the up- and down-arrow buttons at the right of each field, or by entering a value directly into a field.

Using scrolling arrows

The scrolling arrows increase and decrease paragraph spacing amounts in 6-point increments (or 0.5-pica, 0.0833-inch, 0.0069-feet, 0.2217-centimeter, or 0.0021-meter increments, depending upon which unit of measure you use). Unfortunately, these values do not all correspond to the same exact size, although they are close. However, regardless of which unit of measure you choose, after you have reached the amount of spacing that you want, select the Apply button to accept the value, and then keep the Text dialog box open in case you would like to make further changes. Or, click the OK button in order to both accept a value and close the Text dialog box.

Note   The scrolling arrows allow a negative spacing value. However, a negative spacing value results in overlapping text lines.

Inputting values directly

You can type a specific value directly into the input field. Click inside the Before or After fields, and delete the current value. Then type in the new value. Remember to keep the measuring unit designation that you want. If you do not designate a measuring unit, it will be set to either the last unit of measurement used. After you have typed a spacing amount and a unit of measurement into the Before field or the After field, select the Apply button in order to accept the value, and then keep the Text dialog box open in case you would like to make further changes. Or, click the OK button in order to both accept the value and close the Text dialog box.

Example: Paragraph spacing

Let's pick up where we left off in the example for paragraph justification. Open the Format Text toolbar by selecting View ➪ Toolbars ➪ Format Text. Locate the Decrease Paragraph Spacing and the Increase Paragraph Spacing buttons on the right side of the toolbar. Because the text box that opens contains only one paragraph, you'll need to create more text.

Double-click inside the text box on the page. This should select the entire section of text. Copy the selection, and then click the end of the text in the text box in order to place a blinking cursor line there. Press the Enter key, and then paste the copied selection. Press the Enter key again. Paste again. You now should have three paragraphs in the text box shape.

Click the Increase Paragraph Spacing button on the Format Text toolbar. Notice the new spacing between the paragraphs. Click the Increase button twice more. Now you have a fair amount of space between the paragraphs. Next, click the Decrease Paragraph Spacing button several times. After the spacing has returned to its original amount, it will no longer decrease. Also, notice that each increase and decrease occurred in the set increment.

Next, position the text box shape to the far-right side of the open work area. Right-click the text box shape. Select Format ➪ Text to bring up the Text dialog box. Position the Text dialog box so that you can simultaneously view it and the text box shape. Select the Paragraph tab. Locate the Spacing section on the right side and the scrolling arrows to the right of the Before and After input fields. In the Before field, click the up-arrow button. Click Apply. Now, in the After field click the up-arrow button. Click Apply. In the Before field, click the down-arrow button. Click Apply. Repeat for the After field.

Click inside the Before input field. Remove the point-unit designator (pt.) and replace it with **in.**, for inches. Now experiment with the up- and down-arrow buttons. Remember to use the Apply button, not the OK button, in order to activate your changes. Notice that the unit designator in the After field still works in its original points setting. Click inside the After field, remove **pt.** and replace it with **cm.**, for centimeters. Experiment with the spacing settings, using the up- and down-arrow buttons.

Click inside the Before input field. Delete the contents of the entire field and enter **17 pt.** Click Apply. Click inside the After input field and delete the field's contents. Enter **0.0003 m.**, where **m.** stands for meters. Click Apply.

Click OK to close the Text dialog box and then save the example. We'll use it later in the chapter to learn how to enter a nonstandard unit into the Before and After fields.

Changing Line Spacing

You can change the spacing between lines in a paragraph only by using the Text dialog box. The Paragraph tab of the Text dialog box has a section called "Spacing." Within the Spacing section is an option labeled Line. Its field is set in percentages. By default, it's set at 120%, which means that the space from the bottom of a line of text to the bottom of the next line of text is 20% larger than the font size. So, if you set the line spacing to 100%, the bottom of one line of text would touch the top of the next. If the percentage were set to less than 100%, the text would overlap.

You can change the line-spacing percentage with the scroll arrows at the right of the Line input field. When you click a scroll arrow, the percentage increases or decreases in 10-percent increments. The scroll arrow settings have minimum values of 10% and maximum value of 1,000%.

Of course, if you want to use a spacing amount that is not divisible by ten, you can type the amount directly into the field. The minimum-allowed type-in value is 1% . I am aware of no maximum value. (I gave up after passing 111,111%.)

Let's return to the example that we used in the "Example: Paragraph spacing" section. Open the Text dialog box and position it so you can simultaneously view it and the text-box shape. Select the Paragraph tab. In the Spacing section, locate the Line input field. Click the up-scroll arrow at the right of the Line input field. Click Apply, and notice the change in line spacing.

Now click the down-scroll arrow three times in order to bring the percentage to 100%. Notice that the tops of the tallest letters will, in a few spots, just touch the bottom of some letters in the line above. Click inside the Line input field and set it to **33%.** Click Apply. What a mess! Click the up-scroll arrow in the field. Notice it jumped to 40%, not 43%. Return the line spacing to 120% and click OK. Save this example.

Changing Paragraph Indentation

You can change the size of paragraph indentation by using the Increase and Decrease Paragraph Indentation buttons on the Format Text toolbar, or by using the Text dialog box. Let's look at the toolbar buttons first.

Using Format Text toolbar buttons

The Increase and Decrease Paragraph Indentation buttons are located just to the left of the Increase and Decrease Paragraph Spacing buttons on the Format Text toolbar (as shown in Figure 30-4). The Increase Paragraph Indentation button increases the indentation to the left of every line of text in a selected text box by 1/4 inch. The Decrease Paragraph Indentation button decreases the indentation to the left of every line of text in a selected text box by 1/4 inch.

Note that this technique does not indent the first line only. To indent only the first line, or to indent from the right side, or to indent in increments other than a quarter inch, use the Text dialog box.

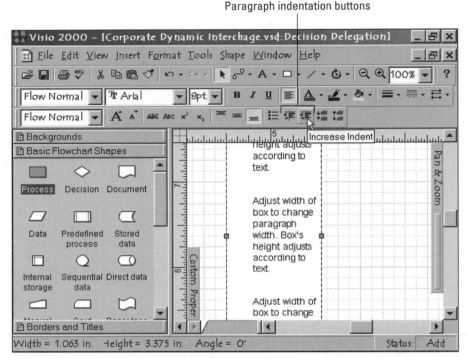

Paragraph indentation buttons

Figure 30-4: The Paragraph Indentation buttons, just to the left of the Paragraph Spacing buttons, work on every line of a selected area, not just the first line.

Example: Changing paragraph indentation using Format Text toolbar buttons

Return to the example in the "Changing Line Spacing" section. On the Format Text toolbar, locate the Increase Paragraph Indentation and the Decrease Paragraph Indentation buttons. Select the text-box shape. Click the Increase Paragraph Indentation button. Notice that it indents every line in the text. Click the Increase Paragraph Indentation button again. Then click the Decrease Paragraph Indentation button twice in order to return the paragraphs to their original nonindented format. Save this example.

Using the Text dialog box

At the left side of the Paragraph tab in the Text dialog box is the Indentation section, containing three input fields. The Left input field sets the paragraph indentation from the left side of the selected text box for every line of text in the text box. The Right input field sets the paragraph indentation from the right side of the selected text box for every line of text in the text box. The First indentation input field sets the paragraph indentation from the left side of the selected text box for first line of every paragraph in the text box. If both the Left indentation and First indentation are set, the total amount of indentation for the first line of every paragraph will be the First indentation amount plus the Left indentation amount.

The default indentation amount in all fields is 0 inches. The available measurement units are the same as for Paragraph Spacing: inches, feet, centimeters, meters, and points. The scroll arrows change by the same increments as with paragraph spacing. The default jump for inches is 0.1 inch; for feet, 0.0083 feet; for centimeters, 0.254 centimeter; for meters, 0.0025 meter; for points, 7.2 points; and for the mysterious *p*, 0.6 *p*.

You can also set negative indentations. However, be careful. Negative indentation may cause text to be incorrectly positioned within its shape. One practical use for a negative indent is to have the first line of a paragraph start to the left of the rest of the paragraph's alignment. To do this, set the First indentation as the negative of the Left indentation. With this setting, the First indentation cancels out the Left indentation, so the first line starts at the left side of the text box.

The scroll arrows can set indentations from –10 inches to 10 inches, or in corresponding amounts for the other units of measure that the Text dialog box accepts. For values typed directly into the Indentation input fields, however, I have found no limits. (Of course, there are no practical reasons for enormous indentations.)

Example: Changing paragraph indentation using the Text dialog box

Return to the example used in the "Example: Changing paragraph indentation using Format Text toolbar buttons" section. Select the text-box shape. Open the Text dialog box and then select the Paragraph tab. Position the Text dialog box so that you can simultaneously see it and the text-box shape. Locate the Indentation section on the left of the Paragraph tab. Click the up-arrow button on the Left input field. Click Apply. Notice that this indentation is smaller than the indentation created with the toolbar buttons. Next, click inside the Left input field and change the value to **0.25 in.** Click Apply. Now you have the same indentation that was produced using the toolbar buttons. Click the up-scroll arrow on the Right input field. Click Apply. All lines are now indented on both sides. Return the values for both Right and Left indents to **0 in.** Click Apply. Click inside the Indentation/First input field and delete the value and unit. Enter **0.5 cm**. Click Apply. Now you have indentation on the first line only. Save this example.

Vertically Aligning Text

When you have text inside a shape that is larger than the text block, you may want to place the text at the top, bottom, or in the middle of the shape. Visio 2000 enables you to do this with either the Text dialog box or the alignment button on the Format Text toolbar. Let's look at the toolbar first.

Using Format Text toolbar buttons

Located to the left of the Paragraph Indentation buttons on the Format Text toolbar are, reading from left to right, the following three Vertical Alignment buttons: Align Top, Align Middle, and Align Bottom (see Figure 30-5). To use these buttons, first select the shape containing the text that you want to align. Then click the appropriate button in order to align the text to the top, middle, or bottom of the shape.

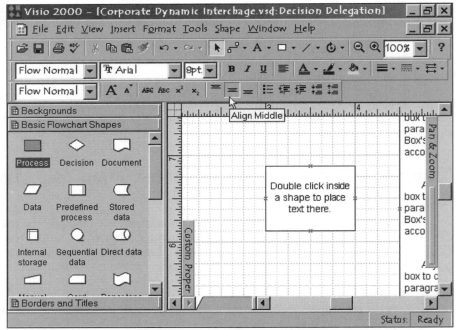

Figure 30-5: The Vertical Alignment buttons are located near the middle of the Format Text toolbar.

Remember that when you first enter text into a shape, it is aligned in the middle by default.

Example: Aligning text using the toolbar buttons

Return to the example used in the "Example: Changing paragraph indentation using the Text dialog box" section. The current shape has automatically sized itself around the text block within it. We need a shape that does not do this. From the Basic Flowchart Shapes stencil, grab the Process shape. Drag it onto the page and double-click inside the shape. A blinking cursor line should appear inside the shape. Make sure your font size is set at 8 points. Type in the following: **Double-click inside a shape to place text there.** Click outside the shape to set the type. This should result in three lines of text inside the shape. The shape's default size is about five 8-point lines.

Locate and click the Align Bottom button on the Format Text toolbar. The text moves to the bottom of the shape. Click the Align Top button. The text moves to the top of the page. Click the Align Middle button. The text returns to its default position. Save this example.

Using the Text dialog box

The Vertical Alignment option is located within the Text Block tab of the Text dialog box. It is the top section on that tab (as shown in Figure 30-6). To select an alignment, click the menu arrow to the right of the Vertical Alignment input field. Choose Top, Middle, or Bottom. Then either click the Apply button to accept the value and keep the option box open, or click the OK button to accept the value and close the option box.

Example: Using the Text dialog box

Return to the example from the "Example: Changing paragraph indentation using the Text dialog box" section. Make sure the Process shape is selected. Open the Text dialog box and select the Text Block tab. Click the menu arrow located on the right side of the Vertical Alignment input field, and choose Top. Click OK. The text in the shape is now aligned to the top. Save this example.

Adjusting Margins

Margins for text within a shape can only be adjusted with the Text dialog box. The margins section is located within the Text Block tab in the option box, directly underneath the Vertical Alignment section. Like the paragraph indentation and spacing input fields, the margin input fields can be set to centimeters, meters, inches, feet, or the mysterious *p*. By default, all margins are set at 2 points.

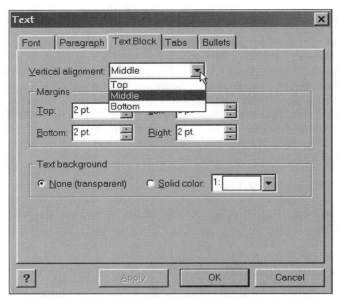

Figure 30-6: The Vertical Alignment section is located at the top of the Text Block tab.

When you use the scroll arrows, the value changes in jumps. I have found, however, that the jumps are not always uniform. So be careful and keep an eye on the values that the fields display, rather than simply counting clicks on the scroll arrows. Of course, you can always enter values directly, which avoids confusion.

As with the other input fields, to type in a specific value click the cursor inside the field and replace the old value with a new value, and if applicable, a new measurement unit. Then click either Apply or OK in order to accept the new setting.

Note   Be careful when setting margins. Overly wide margins can cause the text to appear outside of the shape. Conflicting margins (for example, margins with no space between them) can cause text to appear in odd places on the page or not at all.

Return to the same example you've been using. Select the Process shape. Scroll the workspace window until the Process shape is located on the far-right side of the workspace. Open the Text dialog box. Position the box so that you simultaneously can view it and the shape. Select the Text Block tab. In the Margins section, click inside the Top input field. Change the value to **0.5 cm**. In the Left input field, click the up-scroll arrow once. The left margin should now be **7.2 pt.** Click Apply. Now, even though in the last exercise you selected Top in the Vertical Alignment field, the new margin now pushes the text down slightly lower than center. The left margin has the text pushed slightly to the right. Change the Right margin to **0 pt.** and click Apply. The text now has enough room to rearrange itself, pushing up against the right side of the box. Return all of the margins to their default value of **2 pt.**. Click OK. Save this example.

Adjusting Background Color

You can add flair and style to your drawings by inserting background color behind text that is inside a shape, such as color coding different parts of a flow chart in order to improve readability and help readers organize information.

Background colors can be added either by clicking the Fill Color button on the Format toolbar, or by using the Text dialog box: When you click the Fill Color button, it fills the selected shape with the color that you've chosen. If text extends outside of the shape, that part of the text will not have color behind it.

In the Text dialog box, use the Text Background option for placing color behind a text block. The background color will not fill the entire shape. So, if the text block is not the same size or shape of its container shape, some areas around the text block will not be colored or will be a different color.

 Tip Use both of these options together to create multicolored shapes, giving you more options for color-coding processes and diagrams.

Using the Fill Color button

The Format toolbar contains three buttons that are labeled with a color bar. The button on the right is the Fill Color button. After you open Visio 2000, the color shown on the Fill Color button is yellow. When you use the button, its color will change to the last color chosen from the Colors submenu.

To fill a shape with the color shown on the Fill Color button, first select the shape that you want to color. Then click the Fill Color button.

To fill a shape with a color other than the color shown on the button, first select the shape. Then click the submenu arrow on the right side of the Fill Color button (as shown in Figure 30-7). The Colors submenu will appear. Select any of the 16 colors shown in the submenu, or choose No Fill Color for a transparent background. If you want a wider variety of colors, select More Fill Colors in order to open the Fill Colors option box. The color you choose will become the new color for the Fill Color button.

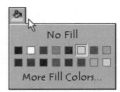

Figure 30-7: The More Fill Colors
submenu of the Fill Color button

**Cross-
Reference**

For more information on using the color palette to set colors for the Fill option
box, see Chapter 18.

Example: Using the Fill Color button

Return to the example from the "Adjusting Margins" section and select the Process
shape. Since the Fill Color button is set to yellow by default, let's use that color.
Click the Fill Color button. The process box is now yellow. Now select the Auto-
height box on the page. Click the submenu arrow on the right side of the Fill Color
button, and choose the light-blue color square. The Auto-height box, as well as the
Fill Color button's color bar, is now light blue. Save this example.

Using the Text dialog box

The Text Background option is located within the Text Block tab of the Text dialog
box. It offers two choices for text background: None (transparent) and Solid Color.

The Solid Color option has a submenu selection arrow located to the right side of
its input field. Clicking this arrow opens a submenu with 23 preset colors, space for
two custom colors, and the Custom color option. To choose one of the preset
colors, just click it, and select Apply or OK.

To create a custom color, click the Custom color option. This opens up the Edit
Color option box. From this option box, you can create a custom color by either
clicking the appropriate spots on the rainbow hue boxes, or by typing values into
the six color-control input boxes at the bottom-right of the option box.

Example: Using the Text dialog box

Select the Auto-height box in the example (it should still be light blue). Open the
Text dialog box and select the Text Block tab. In the Text Background section, click
the radio button beside the Solid color option. Click the submenu arrow at the right
of the Solid color field, and choose the second color: Red. Click OK. As you can see,
red appears only behind the area of the text. The text is not the same size as the

box because of margin and justification settings. Therefore, some areas of light blue appear around the red text area. This procedure can help you create multicolored shapes for the color-coding of processes. Save this example.

Setting Tabs

If a shape has much text, you may want to set tabs in order to group the text into sections. The Text dialog box and the Text Ruler enable you to set tabs. The Text Ruler can set tabs for specific selected paragraphs within a text block. The Text dialog box sets tabs for an entire text block.

Opening the Text Ruler

To open the Text Ruler, first select a text shape. Double-click inside the shape in order to edit the text. Then right-click the text, and from the pop-up menu select Text Ruler. The ruler will appear at the top of the shape (as shown in Figure 30-8). Select the paragraphs to which you want to add tabs. Look at the Tab button, located to the left of the Text Ruler. It displays one of the following four as the current tab style: Left, Right, Center, and Decimal. Click the Tab button in order to change the tab style. *L* indicates Left Tab, backward *L* indicates Right Tab, upside-down *T* stands for Center Tab, and upside-down *T* with a dot to its right indicates Decimal Tab.

Note   Decimal tabs are used to align columns of numerical data that usually contain decimals.

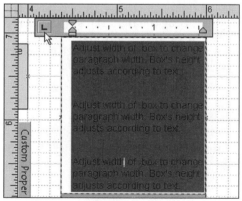

Figure 30-8: The Text Ruler appears at the top of the selected text shape.

Using the Text Ruler

The Text Ruler enables users to set tabs, change the position of tab stops, and remove tab stops.

To set tabs, click a button on the Text Ruler in order to select a Tab style. Then click the ruler at the position where you want the tab. Then click outside the shape in order to close the Text Ruler and set the tab.

To change the position of a tab stop, first open the Text Ruler. Select the paragraph or paragraphs that you want to edit. Drag the tab icon on the Text Ruler to a new position. Click outside of the shape in order to close the ruler and set the tab.

To remove a tab stop, first open the Text Ruler. Select a paragraph that you want to edit. Grab the tab icon that you want to remove and drag it off the ruler. Click outside the shape to close the ruler.

Example: Using the Text Ruler to set tabs

Return to the example from the "Example: Using the Text dialog box" section and select the Auto-height box. Grab a sizing handle on any side of the shape and drag it out until the paragraphs inside the shape are three lines long. This should give you a width of about 1 1/2 inches, enough for working with tab settings.

Double-click the text in the box and then right-click it. From the pop-up menu, select Text Ruler. The ruler will be at the top of the shape. The Tab button on the left of the ruler should show the *L* symbol, for a left tab. Click your cursor on the ruler about 1/2 inch from the ruler's left side. Next, click the Tab button on the ruler until it displays a backward *L,* representing a right tab stop. Click the ruler just to the right of the left tab stop that you placed there. Of course, the right tab stop is too close to the left tab stop to be of any use. Drag the right tab stop so that it is about 1/4 inch from the right border. Next, click the Tab button until you have a center tab, an upside-down *T*. Click about midway on the ruler. Click outside of the shape in order to close the ruler and set the tabs. Save this example.

Using the Text dialog box

The Text dialog box has a tab entitled Tabs (as shown in Figure 30-9). The "Tab stops" field is located on the left side of the Tabs tab. It lists the current tab stops for the selected text block.

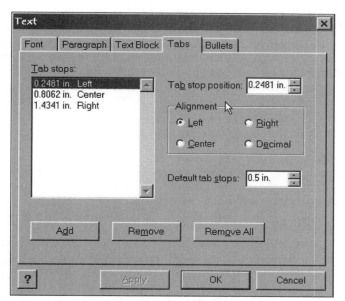

Figure 30-9: The Tabs tab in the Text option box

The "Tab stop position" input field is located in the top-right corner of the Tabs tab. It sets the position for the selected tab stop. Like other input fields discussed in this chapter, the "Tab stop position" input field accepts measurements in inches, feet, centimeters, meters, points, and the mysterious *p*. The scroll arrows located on the right side of the "Tab stop position" input field can increase or decrease the value displayed in the field. Or, simply type a new value into the field in order to change the current value.

The Alignment box is located below the "Tab stop position" input field. Use the four Alignment options to set or edit the style of a tab stop by simply clicking the button beside either Left, Right, Center, or Decimal.

Below the Alignment box is the "Default tab stops" input field. The input field sets the size of the tab stop that is activated when a user presses the keyboard's Tab key.

At the bottom of the Tabs tab are the Add, Remove, and Remove All buttons. Clicking Add creates a duplicate tab of any tab already selected in the "Tab stops" field. The values of the new tab can be changed by using the input fields discussed in this section. The Remove button deletes the tab stop that is selected in the "Tab stops" field. The Remove All button deletes all tabs.

Example: Setting tabs using the Text dialog box

Select the Auto-height box, which was used to set the tabs in the "Example: Using the Text Ruler to set tabs" section. Open the Text dialog box and select the Tabs tab. The left tab should already be selected in the "Tab stops" field. Change it by click the "Tab stop position" field's down-scroll arrow. Next, change the tab type in the Alignment section by clicking the radio button beside Decimal. The left tab is now a decimal tab. We don't need this right now, so while it is still selected, click the Remove button.

The Center tab in the "Tab stops" field should now be selected. Create a new tab by clicking the Add button, which will duplicate the Center tab. Click Left in the Alignment section in order to make it a left tab stop. Click inside the "Tab stop position" field and change its position to **0.6 cm**. Click Apply. Now there is a new left tab with metric spacing.

We will not need tabs for the rest of the examples in this chapter. Click the Remove All button. Click OK. Save this example.

Adding Bullets

Bullets can be added to a list by using the Text dialog box, or by clicking the Bullets button on the Format Text toolbar. Each of these techniques has its advantages and disadvantages. Sometimes you'll need to use both methods in order to accomplish what you want. I'll talk a little about the advantages and disadvantages of each method before describing their use. First let's look at the Bullets button.

The Bullets button

The Bullets button is located on the Format Text toolbar between the paragraph Indent buttons and the paragraph Align buttons (as shown in Figure 30-10). To use the Bullets button, first select the portion of text to which you want to add bullets. Next, click the Bullets button.

When you use the Bullets button on the Format Text toolbar, it adds bullets in front of the selected text inside a text block. This process allows you to place a bulleted list within a larger text block. The style of bullets, however, defaults to the style selected the last time the Text dialog box was used. (If no style was previously selected, the default is dot-style bullets.) So, if you want a particular style of bullet, you must first use the Text dialog box to set the style, and then use the Bullets button to insert the bullets. You may be wondering why you can't just use the Text dialog box all the time for setting bullets. Read on.

The bullets button

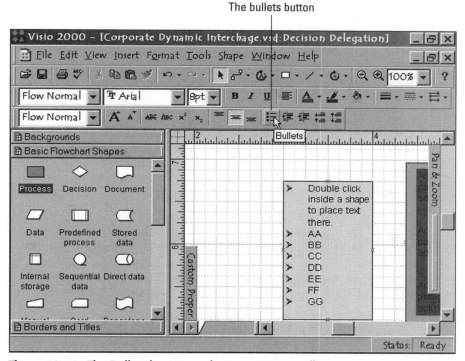

Figure 30-10: The Bullets button on the Format Text toolbar

The Bullets tab of the Text dialog box

The Bullets tab offers seven types of bullets, as well as a None option for removing bullets from a list (see Figure 30-11). A Custom bullets input field at the bottom of the tab allows users to enter specific characters to be used as bullets.

To add bullets to a selected text block, simply click the bullet style that you want, and select Apply or OK. To remove bullets from a selected text block, click None, and select Apply or OK. To add custom bullets, click inside the Custom input field. Type in the character or characters that you want to use as bullets. Then select Apply or OK.

The Bullets tab allows users to choose any type of bullet, regardless of what type was last used. However, this method adds bullets to the *entire* text block, even if only a portion of the text has been selected. So, if you want to add bullets to an entire text block, use the Bullets tab. Also, use the Bullets tab if you need to remove bullets from text blocks, or to set the style of bullets used by the Bullets button on a particular section of a text block.

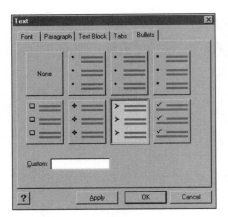

Figure 30-11: The Bullets tab offers seven standard bullet styles and a None option.

A helpful hint: Using a disposable list object

One way to verify the current bullet style, or to more easily change bullet styles, is to create a disposable shape with a short list in it. The list need be no longer than two items, and the items need only be one letter long. Drag a convenient shape onto an unused portion of the page and type a short list into it. Then, whenever you need to add bullets to a portion of a text block, first select your disposable object. Use the Bullets tab in the Text dialog box to set the style of bullets. Add those bullets to the disposable list. Next, go to the text block that you are working on and select the portion of the text block that you want to bullet. Click the Bullets button on the Format Text toolbar to add bullets only to that section of text. Using this method, you can even install several different types of bullets on multiple lists, all inside one text block.

Example: Using both methods to add bullets

Let's finish this section by doing a little fancy bullet work. Select the Process shape in the example. Double-click it in order to edit the text. Move your cursor line to the end of the text block. Press Enter and type **AA**. Press Enter again and type **BB**. Press Enter again and type **CC**. Follow this pattern until you have typed **GG**. You now have a text block with a paragraph followed by a seven-item list. The text probably extends beyond the bottom of the shape. Select the shape, grab the bottom sizing handle, and pull it down until the shape contains the entire list.

Now, let's add bullets to the first part of the list. Double-click inside the Process shape in order to enter text. Select AA through CC. Click the Bullets button on the Format Text toolbar. Dot-style buttons (the default) appear in front of AA, BB, and CC. For the rest of the list, however, we want to use a different button. So, use the auto-height box shape as our disposable list.

Select the auto-height box shape. Open the Text dialog box and select the Bullets tab. Click the Check bullets button, the last button, located on the bottom-right. Click OK. Each of the three paragraphs now has a checkmark-style bullet in front of it. If we had selected only two of the three paragraphs with this method, all three would still be bulleted.

Double-click the text in the Process shape. Select DD through GG. Click the Bullets button on the Format Text toolbar. Click outside the shape to deselect. Now you have two different bullets used within the list, and no bullets in front of the paragraph. You've just learned how to use both bullet methods to do fancy bulleting on lists. Have fun!

Summary

This chapter discussed text-formatting techniques that help Visio 2000 create professional-looking and eye-catching reports, lists, processes, flowcharts, and more. The following points were covered in detail:

✦ How to open the Text dialog box and the Text Ruler.

✦ Justifying paragraphs to the left, right, or center by using either toolbar buttons or the Text dialog box. Also, how to use the Text dialog box to justify text to both borders and how to force justify text.

✦ Increasing or decreasing spacing between paragraphs with toolbar buttons or the Text dialog box.

✦ Adjusting spacing between lines in a paragraph by using the Text dialog box.

✦ Increasing or decreasing indentation of entire paragraphs by using toolbar buttons or the Text dialog box. Using the Text dialog box to indent the first line of a paragraph.

✦ Aligning text to the top, bottom, or middle of its container shape with toolbar buttons or the Text dialog box.

✦ Adjusting margins on top, bottom, and both sides of a shape by using the Text dialog box.

✦ Placing color behind text in a shape by using the Fill button. How to only place color behind existing text by using the Text dialog box. How to use both of these methods in order to create multicolored text shapes, and how to select different background colors

✦ Setting the four tab types with the Text Ruler or the Text dialog box.

✦ How to add bullets to entire text blocks by using either the Bullets button or the Text option block. How to set bullet style with the Text option block. Setting bullets for a portion of a text block by using the Bullets button, and how to use a disposable text object to combine both methods and create fancy bulleting.

At this point in the Visio 2000 Bible, you've been exposed to almost all you need to know about formatting text with Visio 2000. But there's just a little more to know: How to use spell checkers, dictionaries, and other languages. The next chapter covers these points.

✦　✦　✦

Spell Checking Text

You have just created a masterpiece, an organizational flowchart of your company. However, before you send the work of art off to the laser printer and place it on display for the world, let us check the spelling.

When you invoke the Spelling check tool, you have the ability to

✦ Review the spelling of text in shapes, data fields, and summary information within the Visio active drawing.

✦ Examine the entire drawing, a specific page, or highlighted text.

✦ Customize a user dictionary that contains words specific to your company.

✦ Create an assortment of dictionaries, each with a different design in mind, and then call upon them in that moment of need.

Invoking the Spell Check Tool

There are a few ways that you can go about invoking the Spelling check tool. The easiest ways to spell-check an active drawing are as follows:

✦ Click the Spelling button from the Standard toolbar as shown in Figure 31-1, or

✦ Press the F7 key, or

✦ Select Tools ➪ Spelling

Click this button to check spelling

Figure 31-1: The Spelling icon

After selecting one of the previous options, and if Visio discovers an error or a word not found in its dictionary, the Spelling dialog box opens.

In the document, hiding behind the newly displayed Spelling dialog box, is the word in question, brilliantly highlighted.

If no misspelled words were found, a message window will inform you that the spell check process has been completed. Click OK.

Examining the Spell Check Features

Now let's take a look at the features and options contained in the Spelling dialog box as shown in Figure 31-2.

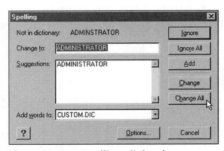

Figure 31-2: Spelling dialog box

The Spelling dialog box contains the following fields:

- ✦ **Not in dictionary** displays the word in question.

- ✦ **Change to** enables you to type in the new word(s) or select a word from the Suggestions list to replace the misspelled word.

- ✦ **Suggestions** lists replacement words from the open dictionaries.

- ✦ **Add words to** provides a list of available dictionaries to which you can add the word. For example, a product name might not be in the dictionary.

Additionally, the following buttons provide choices during the checking process:

✦ **Ignore** disregards the word and continues the checking process.

✦ **Ignore All** disregards all instances of the word and continues the checking process.

✦ **Add** copies the word in question to the dictionary displayed in the "Add words to" box.

✦ **Change** replaces the word in question to the one in displayed in the "Change to" box.

✦ **Change All** replaces all instances of the word in question to the one in the "Change to" box.

✦ **Options** displays the Options dialog box, where you can specify default settings for the Spelling command. This feature can also be found by selecting Options from the Tools menu and then clicking on the Spelling tab.

✦ **Cancel** closes the Spelling dialog box; however, this does not cancel or undo any changes that you have made.

Note   Although the Spelling check tool can save you from making an embarrassing error, it cannot save you from all mistakes when it comes to spelling. The Spelling check only checks for spelling errors, *not* grammatical errors.

For example, you might type the sentence *"The following is a list of there known prices."*

Because *there* is spelled correctly, the Spelling check tool will not catch the error, although, as we all know, the correct spelling is *their* — or was that *they're?* So be careful.

Understanding the User Dictionary

Here's a nifty feature that helps when you run Spelling check. Let's take a look at an example of a real-life scenario: Every time you use the spell check, the whatchamacallit widget keeps getting caught as a spelling error. You checked the marketing brochures and engineering drawings, and *whatchamacallit* is the exact name and spelling of the product. Well, remember our discussion on the Spelling check features? We described the "Add words to" field, where we have the option to select a dictionary to which we can add the word in question. Guess what. That's where we can take care of this, by creating our very own user dictionary and adding unique words to it.

You're probably wondering, "What dictionary is being used now?" And probably, "How can I create my own dictionary for the company?" Well, I'm glad you asked.

Visio uses its own dictionary, stored in the Visio\Systems\Spelling folder. And any dictionaries that you create will also be stored in this folder. Now, if you want to use an existing Microsoft Word dictionary, refer to your Word documentation to find the location of these dictionaries.

Creating a New User Dictionary

To answer your question on how to create your own dictionary, first select Options from the Tools menu. Click the Spelling tab. Within the User dictionaries area, click Add. In the File name box, type a name for the dictionary, and then click Open. Click OK.

Now that we've created our own user dictionary, the next time you run Spelling check and the whatchamacallit widget is displayed, instead of just nervously clicking the Ignore or Ignore All button, select the unique dictionary that you created within the "Add words to" field and then click Add. This stores the widget name in that user dictionary. The result—whatchamacallit will not get displayed as a spelling error, unless, of course, you misspell it.

Deactivating a user dictionary

We just learned how to create a user dictionary and now you want to make it inactive? What gives—can't make up your mind? Well maybe you have a few dictionaries for specific industries or products and you don't want to use them all at the same time. Well, whatever your reason, you can deactivate a dictionary by selecting Options from the Tools menu. Click the Spelling tab. Within the User dictionaries area, click the dictionary that you want to deactivate and then click Remove. Click OK.

Note   By hitting Remove, you do not delete the file. You just keep the dictionary from appearing in the "Add word to" list in the Spelling dialog box. You can always make the dictionary active at another time by adding it again.

Changing the Language for Spell Check

We're going international! However, before we send our drawings across the waters, let's check our spelling and make sure that we don't offend anybody.

First, select a language for your text. (Select Text from the Format menu or right-click and select Format ➪ Text from the pop-up menu.) In the Text dialog box, click the Font tab. Within the Language field, select the desired language and then click OK.

Once you select a language (such as German), when you invoke the Spelling check tool, the appropriate spelling file (such as the German dictionary) is used to check the spelling of text.

Summary

All in all, the Spell check tool is not very complicated. But don't be fooled by its simplicity, for it is a very useful tool and should be used whenever you plan to print or distribute your Visio pages for public consumption. It could save you or your company from an embarrassing or costly moment.

✦ Remember, before you distribute a page, reach for that Spelling button on the Standard toolbar, or press F7, or select Tools ➪ Spelling.

✦ Create your user dictionary to include unique words used within your company or profession.

The next chapter covers how to insert various objects in Visio files, including pictures, controls, and graphs.

✦　　✦　　✦

Inserting and Exporting Drawings

◆ ◆ ◆ ◆

◆ ◆ ◆ ◆

This section contains information on importing objects (e.g. pictures, graphs, and hyperlinks) into Visio files and exporting Visio documents into various file formats, including GIFs, JPEGs, and TIFFs. You also learn how to edit objects and work with linked objects.

Inserting Objects

Y ou can enhance your Visio drawings by adding objects of all types. These can range from images created in programs like Photoshop to spreadsheets, Microsoft Word files, or even comments you add to annotate your drawing. Visio can even use the Microsoft Windows feature of Object Linking and Embedding to insert objects you can edit in Visio, or update automatically when modified by the original application.

This chapter deals exclusively with inserting objects from other applications into Visio. However, you can also insert a Visio drawing into another application. Individual applications have their own procedures for inserting and importing files, but the Object Linking and Embedding (OLE) methods described later in this chapter work similarly in any OLE-compatible application. For more information on exporting Visio drawings, see Chapter 33.

Inserting Comments

Comments are unformatted text notes you attach to drawings or objects on drawings as a way of annotating your work. Comments appear when the cursor pauses over an object (except in Full Screen View), in much the way that a ScreenTip pops up when you move the cursor over a toolbar button. Comments do not print along with the drawing; they are notations viewable only within Visio itself. Nor do comments appear when the cursor is placed over an object that contains a hyperlink (See "Inserting Hyperlinks" later in this chapter). There are dozens of useful things you can do with comments. Try these on for size:

✦ **Notes to yourself.** Comments make great reminders, especially for works-in-progress. If you have to end a session before a complex object is finished, add a comment to it about the work that remains to be done. The next time you open the drawing, a quick tour over the objects it contains can refresh your memory about what you planned to do next.

✦ **Notes to others.** Perhaps others in your organization will be using your drawing as a template for their own work. Well-placed comments can offer tips on what each object is supposed to do, or perhaps provide instructions on how to carry out a task with that object (such as enlarging a logo to fill a certain space).

✦ **Improve collaboration efforts.** Any organization larger than one person will often need to circulate documents such as proposals, letters, or drawings for comments or approval. Visio's comment feature makes it easy for individuals to add their own annotations about a drawing. A set of initials within the comment can show who made it. Comments can be edited at any time, so as a drawing is circulated multiple times, the annotations can be updated.

✦ **Provide helpful labels.** You can apply labels to drawings, such as maps, as an aid for anyone viewing your drawing in Visio. For example, a map might already include basic text labels, such as Robinson Memorial Hospital or City Hall. You could include a pop-up comment with the address and/or phone number of each building. The result? Your basic map is uncluttered and can be printed out with only the basic information. However, fellow Visio users can benefit from the extra notes you provide.

Adding a comment

To add a comment to a shape, select the shape you want to annotate. If you select more than one shape, Visio assigns the same comment as a separate, individual comment to each shape (see the following Tip). Then choose Insert ➪ Comment. The dialog box shown in Figure 32-1 pops up. Enter the comment you want, of any length, and click OK when finished.

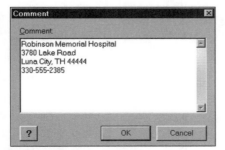

Figure 32-1: Comment dialog box

Only the first five or six lines of the comment are visible in ScreenTip mode. View longer comments (you can add pages and pages of text if you like) by editing the notation.

Tip   You can apply the same comment to several shapes as a shortcut, but still edit them separately later. For example, in a floor plan you could select all the objects representing furniture and type in a comment like "All furniture items can be moved around the floor plan at will." All of those objects would then have that comment attached. Even so, you could edit individual notations, adding information like "This represents a couch" or "This wooden desk has four drawers" to customize individual notes.

To add a comment to a page, make sure nothing on the page is selected. If an object does happen to be selected, click in an empty area of the page to deselect it. Choose Insert ➪ Comment and type your annotation. Page comments do not pop up when the cursor is over the page. The only way to view a page comment is to place the cursor on the page (without selecting an object) and choose Insert ➪ Edit Comment. If you think about it, that makes a lot of sense. You wouldn't want page comments popping up every time you let the cursor remain idle on an empty portion of the page, would you?

Note   If you press Enter while typing a comment, Visio assumes you are finished entering the text. If you really want to place text on different lines, press Ctrl+Enter at the end of a line.

Editing or deleting comments

To edit a comment, select the object or display the page with the comment you want to edit. Then choose Insert ➪ Edit Comment, make your changes, and click OK. Yes, I know that editing text from the Insert menu rather than Edit menu seems strange, but that's the way it works with Visio comments.

To delete a comment, select the object or display the page containing the comment you want to remove. Then choose Edit ➪ Delete ➪ Comment. (No, you don't have to use the Insert command. Using Insert to delete something makes as much sense as using the Windows Start menu to stop a computer.)

Inserting Bitmapped Pictures

You can insert bitmapped images such as photos or images created with programs like Adobe Photoshop. Of course, you can't edit the individual components of an image you've added; once a bitmapped picture has been inserted onto a Visio drawing, all you can really do with it is move it around, put it on a particular layer, or resize it.

Still, the ability to add a bitmap picture to your drawing can be useful. You might want to do this to add a picture of an actual product to a diagram of the product, or to insert a complex graphic such as a logo. If you do need to create a Visio object of a graphic that you already have as an image, you can import the picture and use it as a template to trace your Visio version. Figure 32-2 shows a drawing with a picture inserted into it.

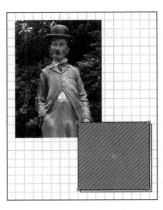

Figure 32-2: A picture inserted into a drawing

The kinds of bitmap formats Visio can import include the following:

✦ **gif.** Graphics Interchange Format

✦ **jpg.** Joint Photographic Experts Group

✦ **pct.** Macintosh Picture File Format

✦ **png.** Portable Network Graphics

✦ **tif.** Tag Image File Format

✦ **bmp, dib.** Windows Bitmap

✦ **pcx.** PC PaintBrush Bitmap

To insert a bitmapped picture, choose Insert ⇨ Picture. A standard File Open dialog box (in this case titled Picture, as you can see in Figure 32-3) appears. You can navigate around your hard disk using standard Windows exploration tools until you find the file you want to import. All the file formats that Visio can import are filled in for you in the "Files of type" box. By default, all those kinds of files are visible in the contents window. If you'd rather view only one type of file format, choose the format from the drop-down list next to the Files of type box. Click the Open button when the file you want appears in the File name box.

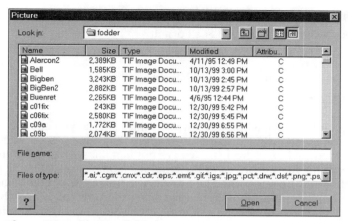

Figure 32-3: Picture dialog box

Inserting Other Graphics

Visio can insert a wide variety of other graphics formats in addition to bitmaps. You can grab many different vector, or line-oriented formats, including Adobe Illustrator files, AutoCAD drawings, CorelDRAW files, Encapsulated PostScript graphics, and other formats. This kind of picture is imported as a single object which you can move and resize just as you can a bitmapped picture. However, in many cases you can break down the graphic into its component shapes, which you can then manipulate individually in much the same way that you modify Visio's native shapes. Visio can import the following kinds of graphics files:

✦ **af3, af2.** ABC FlowCharter 2.0, 3.0, 4.0

✦ **ai.** Adobe Illustrator File Format

✦ **dwg.** AutoCAD Drawing File Format

✦ **dxf.** AutoCAD Drawing Interchange

✦ **cgm.** Computer Graphics Metafile

✦ **cmx.** Corel Clipart

✦ **cdr.** CorelDRAW Drawing File Format, version 3.0, 4.0, 5.0, 6.0 and 7.0

✦ **cfl.** CorelFLOW 2.0

✦ **eps.** Encapsulated PostScript

✦ **emf.** Enhanced Metafile

✦ **igs.** Initial Graphics Exchange Specification

✦ **drw.** Micrografx Designer Version 3.1 File Format

✦ **dsf.** Micrografx Designer Version 6.0 File Format

✦ **ps.** PostScript File

✦ **txt and .csv.** Text and Comma Separated Values

✦ **wmf.** Windows Metafile

Most of these formats are converted to Windows Metafiles, which you can ungroup to their original shapes by choosing Shape ➪ Grouping ➪ Ungroup, or by pressing Ctrl+U as you do with normal Visio groups. If you're not familiar with other kinds of drawing programs, you may be surprised at the results in some cases. Objects that look like a single entity may be ungrouped into dozens or hundreds of component pieces. For example, a gradient or fountain fill (as some programs call it) may be ungrouped into a large number of individual bands, each with a slightly different color. Or, text may appear as outlines.

Conversion Options

Depending on the format of the graphic file you're importing, Visio may show you a dialog box like the one in Figure 32-4. With bitmap files, you'll see only the Color Translation options. The Retain Gradients, Retain Background, and Emulate Line Styles options appear only if you're importing .cgm, .eps, or .pct files. Other file formats import directly with no need for this dialog box.

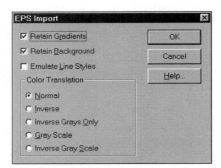

Figure 32-4: Import picture options

The following import options are only available for .cgm, .eps, and .pct files:

✦ **Retain Gradients.** When this box is checked, Visio recreates the gradients in the original image. If unchecked, Visio fills the object containing the gradient with the last color of the gradient.

✦ **Retain Background.** When this box is checked, Visio preserves the background color of the original image. Visio creates a background rectangle in that color, and overlays the image on top.

✦ **Emulate Line Styles.** When this box is checked, Visio draws thick or patterned lines as polygons rather than as simple lines to ensure that they match the line styles of the original file.

Color translation options for all file types include the following:

✦ **Normal.** When this box is checked, Visio tries to match the colors of the original image.

✦ **Inverse.** This option tells Visio to reverse the colors of the image. For example, black becomes white; dark blue becomes light yellow, and so forth.

✦ **Inverse Grays Only.** This option retains the colors of the original image, but reverses their black, white, and gray values. So, dark blue becomes light blue, light red becomes dark red, and so forth.

✦ **Gray Scale.** This choice converts all colors of an object to their gray values, which is useful if you want to preview how an image will appear on a monochrome printer.

✦ **Inverse Gray Scale.** This option is the equivalent of using the Gray Scale and Inverse choices simultaneously. Visio converts the object to gray and then reverses the tones, negative-style.

Inserting Clip Art

Clip-art images are simple graphics, often just line drawings or cartoons, that you can use in your Visio drawings. The term comes from printed clip books of public domain or licensed artwork that could be snipped out and pasted into layouts (back in the days when layout was done on boards rather than a computer display). Visio uses the Microsoft Clip Gallery as a source and repository for its clip art, so this feature will only work if you have installed Microsoft Office and elected to include some clip art. You can insert any of the clips furnished with Office or other applications that use the Clip Gallery, add clips from other applications, or stockpile clips from Microsoft's online resource.

To insert a clip, choose Insert ➪ Clip Art. The Microsoft Clip Gallery dialog box appears, as shown in Figure 32-5. You can then search for specific clips, browse categories of clips, insert clips from other applications, or download more clips from Microsoft's Web site.

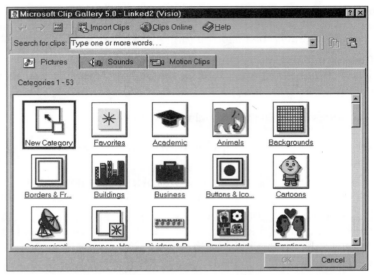

Figure 32-5: Microsoft Clip Gallery is available within Visio if you've installed Microsoft Office and its clip art.

To search for a clip, type one or more keywords into the "Search for clips" box and press Enter. The gallery displays a preview of the first clip it finds matching your keywords. If you want to continue to the next clip, click the Keep Looking button. When you find a clip you want to use, click the Copy button in the Clip Gallery dialog box, or press Ctrl+C. Then click OK to return to Visio to view the inserted clip.

To browse clips, scroll through the list of categories and click the one you want to browse. As you look through the clips, a ScreenTip with more information about the clip appears as the cursor passes over it. You may highlight a clip, press the Copy button in the Clip Gallery dialog box, or press Ctrl+C. Click OK to return to Visio.

Tip

If you left-click a clip, a shortcut menu appears with four choices: Insert Clip, Preview Clip, Add Clip to Favorites, or Find Similar Clips. If you right-click a clip, you'll see a different shortcut menu with the choices Insert, Copy, Delete, Recover (deleted clips), Select All (of the clips in the category), and Clip Properties (to view the clip's description, keywords, and the categories in which it appears).

Click the Import Clips button to add clips to the Gallery from other applications. A dialog box appears to let you browse for clips.

Click the Clips Online button to visit a Microsoft Web site with additional clip art you can download directly into your Clip Gallery.

Inserting Microsoft Graphs

When you choose Insert ⇨ Microsoft Graph, Visio does its magical editing-in-place trick and replaces its own menus and tool bars with those for the Microsoft Graph application. You can then use Graph's tools to replace the information in the sample datasheet that appears, as shown in Figure 32-6.

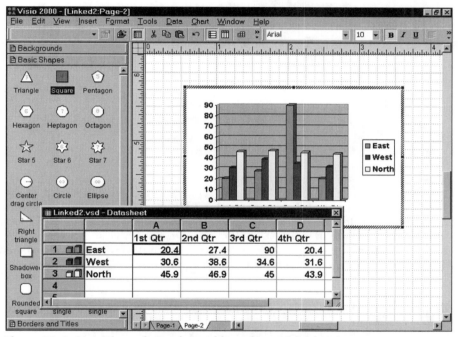

Figure 32-6: Use Microsoft Graph to add graphs to Visio drawings.

The datasheet is a kind of spreadsheet that contains the information you want to graph, including labels in the x and y directions, and the cells with the actual data. As you work, you can right-click each cell to produce a shortcut menu with editing options, such as Cut, Copy, Insert (rows or columns), format numbers, or adjust the font, font style, and font size.

If you already have a spreadsheet you'd like to use to create the graph, you can import it by selecting Edit ⇨ Import File. When you're finished building your datasheet, choose Chart ⇨ Chart Type to select the kind of chart you want to build from the dialog box shown in Figure 32-7.

Figure 32-7: Choose the kind of chart you want.

There are 14 varieties of charts, and each type has up to seven different variations to choose from. If none of these meet your needs, click the Custom Types tab and choose from a gallery of interesting alternatives with names like Pie Explosion and Tubes, as you can see in Figure 32-8. When you've chosen your chart type, click OK to return to Microsoft Graph. Click in the drawing window when you're finished with your datasheet to exit Microsoft Graph and return to Visio's default menus.

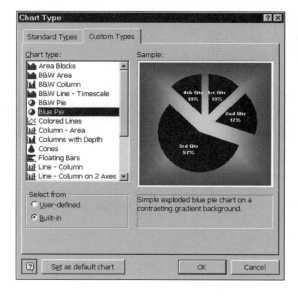

Figure 32-8: Select a custom chart type.

Inserting with Drag-and-Drop

After you've finished working on an object in its original application, you'll often want to insert it in your Visio drawing. If you have Visio and the other application open at the same time, you can do this easily. Just reduce each application to a window that's smaller than the full screen and arrange them so that both are visible. Then, highlight the object you want to insert to Visio, hold down the mouse button, and drag it to the Visio window. When the cursor enters the Visio workspace, it changes to a pointer with a plus sign, indicating that the dragged object will be copied. Release the mouse button when the selection is over the drawing, and it will be duplicated. Figure 32-9 shows a drag-and-drop copy in progress.

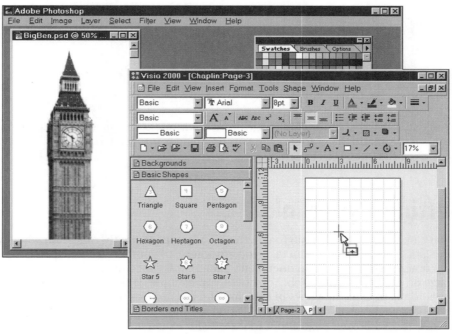

Figure 32-9: Drag-and-drop objects to copy them to Visio.

You can crop graphics that you've inserted into a Visio drawing using the Crop tool, which you'll find in the Visio Standard toolbar, doubled up with the Rotation tool. If the Rotation tool is visible instead of the Crop tool, click the down arrow next to the icon and choose the Crop icon instead.

Note   The Crop tool is generally used for imported graphics. You can't use the Crop tool on Visio shapes unless you copy them to the Clipboard (use Ctrl+C), and then paste them back in as a graphic using Edit ⇨ Paste Special. As a source for the object, choose Picture (Enhanced Metafile). That converts the Visio shape to a graphic object you can crop.

To crop a graphic, choose the Crop tool and click the object. Green control handles appear. You can drag these handles to resize the border around the graphic. The graphic remains the same size, so adjusting the borders has the effect of clipping off parts of the image, as you can see in Figure 32-10.

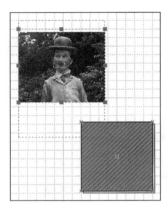

Figure 32-10: Cropping an image

You can move the underlying image around within the cropped borders by moving the cursor inside the graphic. The cursor changes into a hand, and you can click and drag the image to reposition it.

Inserting Hyperlinks

You can insert a link in Visio that activates a "jump" to another location whenever the link is clicked. A link can take you anywhere; to another Visio page in the same document, a different Visio document, a Microsoft Office document, or even to a page on the World Wide Web. You could, for example, create a large-scale map with hyperlinks to close-up views of each area on the map, or to pages that explain about company facilities in those areas. Clicking in Ohio on a U.S. map could transport you to a World Wide Web page about that state, for example.

Links to different pages in the same Visio document or to another Visio document are called *internal* links, because Visio is able to handle the jump entirely on its own without help from another application. You can use internal links to create interactive Visio documents that include explanatory text, more detailed graphics, or any other type of information you like. An *external* link is one to any non-Visio document, whether it's a Microsoft Word file, a graphic created by another application, or a Web page. Because working with hyperlinks in Visio documents and in World Wide Web pages is basically the same, I'll reserve the subject of creating and inserting links for the discussion of Web page design in Chapter 35.

Inserting Other Kinds of Objects

Visio uses a special Microsoft Windows feature called Object Linking and Embedding (OLE) to provide a particularly powerful way of inserting and working with objects. You'll find OLE a timesaver, because it lets you edit objects in place, or makes it possible for you to have objects updated automatically when they are modified in their original application.

Linking

Linking enables you to use consistently updated versions of text, spreadsheet cells, graphics, or other objects in many different Visio drawings. For example, you can insert a chart and link it to the original spreadsheet cells in Microsoft Excel used to create the chart. As the spreadsheet is revised, the chart is also updated. Each time the original document is revised, all linked versions are also updated. So, if you wanted to use a logo created in Photoshop in many different drawings you could do so, yet anytime the logo is changed in Photoshop, the new version will be used in every Visio document that links to the logo. The reverse is also true: to edit a linked object, you must return to the original file where the information originated, and edit it there.

Embedding

Embedding places a copy of the information or file in your Visio drawing. The copy becomes an independent version of the original information; editing the data in the original application has no effect on the copied version in the additional document.

However, you can make any edits to the copied data in the new document without opening the original application. For example, you can edit an image file placed in a Visio drawing without switching to Photoshop. This is known as *editing in place*. Visio's menus and toolbars change to those of the originating application.

Link or embed?

To decide whether to link or embed, look at how you plan to use the drawing. If you want to insert a range from a spreadsheet and have that information updated consistently, use linking. If, on the other hand, you have information such as a graphic that changes often within one Visio drawing, use embedding so you can edit the object directly. You can link or embed objects between many different OLE-compatible Windows applications.

Keep in mind that the road runs both ways. Not only can you link or embed an object created by another application in a Visio drawing, but a Visio document can in turn be linked or embedded in other OLE-compatible Windows applications.

Adding an embedded object

To insert an embedded object using OLE, choose Insert ⇨ Object to access the Insert Object dialog box, shown in Figure 32-11. Because an embedded object becomes part of your Visio drawing, you can choose to embed an existing file that you've already created with another application, or to create a new file from scratch using the other application.

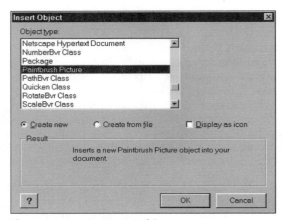

Figure 32-11: Insert an object.

If you want to create a brand new file, click the "Create new" button to reveal a scrolling Object type list with more than 50 different types of objects you can insert. These include many familiar ones, such as Adobe Photoshop Images, and quite a few objects (such as controls) that are mostly of interest to developers. Click OK and Visio creates an empty file of that type in your drawing, and then adds the menus and toolbars of the program that creates the file to Visio's own interface. That is, if you elect to create a new embedded CorelDraw object, the menus and toolbars of CorelDraw replace those of Visio. You can work with the object using those tools. Click outside the object to stop editing in place and return to Visio's interface. If the program is running full-screen, you must use File ⇨ Exit to return to Visio.

To embed an existing file into a Visio drawing, click the "Create from file" button instead. The dialog box changes to resemble the one shown in Figure 32-12

Browse to the file you want to embed, click the Open button, and click OK when you've returned to the Insert Object dialog box. The file you selected is now embedded in your Visio drawing, but you can still edit it in place using the original application by double-clicking the object.

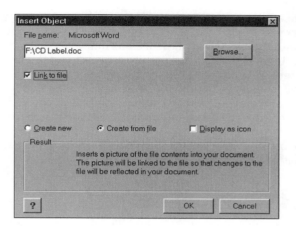

Figure 32-12: Embed an existing file into a Visio drawing.

To edit an embedded object in place, the original application must be installed on the computer. If you move a Visio drawing to another computer that doesn't have the required application, you won't be able to edit the object. To work around this problem, choose Object from the Edit menu (the choice may also appear as Artwork Object or another variation, depending on the kind of object) and select Convert to convert it to another format that can be edited on that system.

Adding a linked object

When you add a linked object to a Visio drawing, you're actually inserting only a reference to the original file. You already know that linking enables you to update an object in the original application any time you like, and Visio always includes the updated version the next time it opens a drawing that includes it. Another advantage of linking is that the pointer back to the original file doesn't significantly increase the file size of the Visio drawing. You can link dozens of objects in a single drawing and still maintain a reasonable file size; in contrast, the same drawing with all those objects embedded would be much larger.

There are two disadvantages to linking. First, you can't use editing in place with a linked object. You must go back to the original application to make changes. Second, because a reference to the linked file rather than the file itself is included in the drawing, if you move the file, you must update the link to reflect the new location. Similarly, any time you move a drawing containing linked objects, you need to take those objects along with the Visio file. Linking is best when a document won't be moved around a lot, or you don't mind updating the links. Embedding is best if you want the drawing to be self-contained and easily transportable.

To insert a linked file into a Visio drawing, choose Insert ➪ Object and click the "Create from file" button. Then, browse to the file you want to link. So far, the steps are exactly the same as for embedding an existing file. To create a link rather than embed the file, you must remember to click the "Link to file" box. Then click OK to return to your Visio drawing with the file linked. If the file has multiple pages, the first page appears in your drawing. Visio displays a picture representing the linked file, not the file itself. This picture will change to reflect changes made to the original only when it is updated, usually each time the drawing is loaded into Visio. Visio can update linked objects automatically when they are loaded, or you can do this manually. I'll show you how to manage links and updates later in this chapter.

Note   Check the "Display as icon" button if you want the icon for the originating program to appear in the drawing instead of a picture of the data itself.

Linking and embedding with cut-and-paste

You don't need to use Visio's Insert menu to link or embed files. If you have both Visio and the application that created the object you want to insert open at the same time, you can insert the object using simple cut-and-paste techniques. Often, that can be quicker than saving the external file and then navigating to it with a dialog box.

To link or embed an object, first go to the application that created the object. Highlight the information you'd like to link or embed in your Visio drawing. Then choose Copy from the application's File menu, or press Ctrl+C.

Then, switch to Visio and choose Edit ⇨ Paste Special. The Paste Special dialog box shown in Figure 32-13 appears. When you click the Paste button, Visio inserts the object as an embedded object, that is, one that becomes part of the Visio drawing but is still editable in its original application.

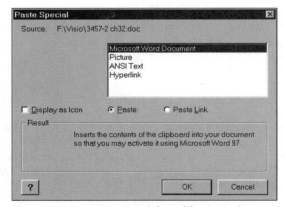

Figure 32-13: Paste Special enables inserting objects either as linked or embedded objects.

In that case, you must choose what kind of file you want the object inserted as, in order to determine which application's tools will be used to edit it. The Paste Special dialog box provides a list of compatible formats for the object you've selected. The list varies by type of object. For example, you may be able to paste an image as an Adobe Photoshop Image, picture, Windows Device Independent Bitmap, or another format. You may be able to paste text from a Word document as a Word document, text, picture, or another format. If you choose Paste Link instead, Visio inserts a picture of the object in your drawing and includes a link back to the original file. The linked object can be updated like any other linked object in a Visio drawing.

Whether you are linking or embedding, you can check the Display as Icon box to use an icon representing the object's original application rather than a picture of the object itself. Click OK when you're finished to link or embed the object in your drawing.

Editing an object

Editing a linked or embedded object is simplicity itself. If the object is linked, simply go back to the originating application, load it, and make any changes you like. The modifications will be reflected in your Visio drawing when you update it, either automatically or manually, as described in the following section.

To edit an embedded object, double-click the object in the Visio drawing. Visio's menus and toolbars will be replaced with those of the originating application (assuming that application is available on the computer you're using). As I mentioned earlier in this chapter, click outside the object when you're finished to return to the Visio drawing, or use File ➪ Exit if you're in full-screen mode.

Managing your links

Every time you open a Visio drawing containing a linked file, Visio can update its information to make sure it is using the latest version of the file. When you create a link, Visio sets it by default to update automatically. That is, each time the file is opened, Visio checks the original file, and if it has been modified, Visio uses the updated information.

If you like, you can prevent Visio from doing this. In that case the linked file will be updated only when you do it manually. You might want to switch to manual updating if the original files won't be available for some reason. Perhaps you decided to take a drawing with you on a trip for editing in your laptop, and don't want to take all the linked files along, too. Select one object on the page containing links you want to switch to manual update mode, and then choose Edit ➪ Links. The paths to all the links on that page appear in the Links dialog box, shown in Figure 32-14. Choose any of the links you want to switch to manual updating, and click the Manual button in the Update area of the dialog box.

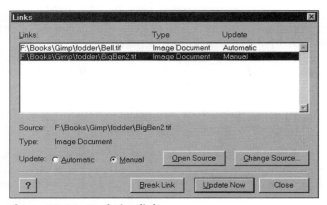

Figure 32-14: Updating links

As I mentioned, any time you move a drawing or the files linked to it, you must update the path to the links. Fortunately that isn't difficult. If you open a drawing that includes a linked object that Visio can't find, either because it moved or the Visio drawing was relocated, Visio asks you to update the links manually. To do that, choose Edit ➪ Links to work with the Links dialog box, as before. Click the Change Source button and navigate to the file's location.

Tip If you want to edit a file, click the Open Source button to open the file in the program that created it.

If you find a Visio drawing is being moved often and want to avoid the need to update links, you can convert a linked object to an embedded object. Just click the Break Link button in the Links dialog box. A dialog box appears, asking you to confirm the action. Click Yes, and Visio converts the object to an embedded object.

Summary

In this chapter you learned how to insert a variety of different kinds of objects into a Visio drawing. You learned how to add comments to drawings to serve as annotations or explanatory material. You discovered how easy it is to insert pictures, clip art, and graphs. Overall, this chapter explained the following points:

    ✦ How to insert and edit comments.

    ✦ Pictures in a variety of formats can be inserted.

    ✦ Trim graphics using the Crop tool.

    ✦ Use Microsoft Graph to add graphs to a drawing.

✦ Insert linked objects into drawings so the objects can be updated in their original application.

✦ Edit embedded objects right within Visio.

✦ Link or embed objects using either Insert or copying and pasting.

The next chapter covers exporting drawings.

✦   ✦   ✦

Exporting Drawings

While Visio can import many different file formats, you'll need to export your Visio drawings and shapes to use them in other applications. Exporting translates the components of the Visio document into a format that the other application can understand, using a software module called a filter. In some cases, many of the attributes of the drawing's shapes are retained and can be edited in the other application. In other cases, exporting to a particular format simply creates a "picture" of the drawing with no editable objects.

This chapter explains your exporting options and shows you how to transport Visio drawings to other applications with maximum flexibility.

Why Export?

If you can, use Object Linking and Embedding (OLE) instead of exporting a graphic. In most cases, you should only export a Visio object as your last resort. That's because when a file is exported, it undergoes a conversion that tries to translate all the features of the original file to the equivalent features of the new format. Not all formats support all graphics features, so anytime you export a Visio document or shape, you run the risk of having the appearance change or of losing some editable attribute.

For example, Visio's gradient fills are defined using algorithms created for Visio. Other applications use different definitions for gradient fills, so Visio objects containing them may look very different when exported and then imported into another program. The problem is compounded by the fact that when the destination application imports your file, it may make some changes of its own.

In addition, once you export a Visio object to another format, you can no longer edit it in Visio without re-importing it. If you make any changes in the destination application and then decide to use the graphic in Visio again, you'll face all the limitations of imported graphics discussed in Chapter 32.

However, sometimes you can't avoid exporting a Visio graphic. There are several reasons why you might turn to this option. First, you may want to use the Visio graphic in an application that doesn't support OLE2. Perhaps you're running an older, Windows 3.x application. Pre-Windows 95 applications used a 16-bit version of OLE that isn't compatible with the modern OLE2 release. So, you simply may not be able to link or embed the object in the target application.

Second, you may want to use the graphic on a computer that doesn't have Visio available for an OLE transfer. For example, you might want to share a document with a colleague who doesn't use Visio, either because the colleague doesn't own the product, or because he or she is using an operating system, such as MacOS or Linux, for which Visio is not available. Importing the Visio graphic as a file is the only option.

In contrast, when you use OLE, the translation is often less traumatic and more consistent, as OLE-compliant applications are specifically designed to exchange information smoothly.

What Formats Can You Use?

You can export Visio graphics into the following formats. If you compare them to their counterparts in Chapter 32, you'll see that Visio can export in fewer formats than it can import. That's because, from a Visio design standpoint, making Visio as flexible as possible in *using* different kinds of information is much more important, in most cases, than finding ways to let other applications use Visio graphics. The goal is to make the best Visio drawings possible, not enhance documents created by other applications.

Exportable Bitmap File Formats are as follows:

✦ **gif.** Graphics Interchange Format

✦ **jpg.** Joint Photographic Experts Group

✦ **pct.** Macintosh Picture File Format

✦ **png.** Portable Network Graphics

✦ **tif.** Tag Image File Format

✦ **bmp, dib.** Windows Bitmap

✦ **pcx.** PC PaintBrush Bitmap

Other Exportable Graphics Formats are:

✦ **ai.** Adobe Illustrator File Format

✦ **cgm.** Computer Graphics Metafile

✦ **eps.** Encapsulated PostScript

✦ **emf.** Enhanced Metafile

✦ **html.** Hypertext Markup Language

✦ **igs.** Initial Graphics Exchange Specification

✦ **ps.** PostScript File

✦ **wmf.** Windows Metafile

Exporting Specific File Types

This next section explains how to export Visio objects to various file formats. Some of the file formats listed previously are either not common, used for specialized applications, or don't produce particularly useful results when Visio graphics are exported to them. So, I'm going to confine the detailed explanations to the most widely used formats.

Exporting bitmapped files

There are five frequently-used bitmapped file formats: tif, pcx, jpg, gif, and bmp, plus a sixth, png, that could see increased use in the future. All can be exported using the same basic techniques. First, you'll need to choose which format is best for your target application.

To export a Visio drawing or object as a file in one of the bitmap formats, you first must select the page or objects you want to export. To export an entire page, display the page, clicking in an empty area to make sure nothing is selected. To export only specific shapes, select the shapes you want to export by clicking the first shape and shift-clicking each shape you want to add.

Then choose File ➪ Save As to access the dialog box shown in Figure 33-1.

Type in a name for the file and choose the file type from the "Save as type" drop-down list. Click Save, and an output filter dialog box appears. The options for each dialog box vary depending on the file format you are using.

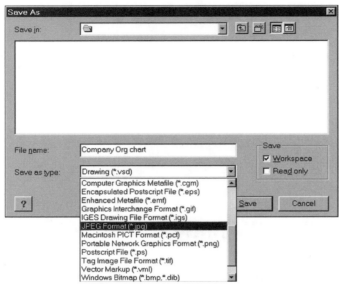

Figure 33-1: To export a file, you'll need to access the Save As dialog box.

TIFF Output Filter Setup

The format known as tif, or TIFF, is named for an abbreviation of Tagged Image Format File. TIFF files, which generally have the file extension .tif, are the most common of the standard file formats. If a software program is able to load a bitmapped format other than its own specialized file type, that other format is probably TIFF. Keep in mind that there are various types of TIFF files, including compressed TIFF, uncompressed TIFF, and TIFF Packbits. Not all software supports all the TIFF types. Visio includes options that let you save TIFF files with a maximum of compatibility.

The TIFF format specifications were first developed in 1986. The format is called TIFF because each file includes collections of information, called tags, which describe the file type. A tag can provide information on resolution, number of bits used per pixel, and many other descriptors. The basic data needed to handle a file is included in a standardized set of tags that can be interpreted by any application.

However, applications can create their own tags with information that the application wants to store with the file. A simple example of this would be a longer descriptive name or caption that is displayed when the file is loaded. These special tags are ignored by applications that don't understand how to read them, which means that you can exchange TIFF files between older versions of an application and newer, enhanced versions of the same software. Totally different programs can also read many TIFF files created by other applications.

Problems arise when new types of tags include important information that the application must understand in order to reconstruct the image. For that reason, you'll sometimes find TIFF files that can't be read by other software easily. For example, TIFF files can contain information about alpha channels, or masks created by programs like Photoshop, but other applications may not be able to read or use this information.

Four standardized TIFF formats used by many applications are classified as: B (black-and-white or binary information only), G (gray scale), P (palette, with a particular number of different colors), and R (red, green, blue (RGB) color). TIFF files can be compressed or uncompressed. If you plan to import files into another program, particularly a desktop publishing package, but you don't know what kind of application will be importing your Visio graphic, you should use uncompressed TIFF format. More disk space is required, but you'll avoid having to reload the file into the program that created or captured it, and then saving it again in the compatible format.

The standard options for the TIFF Output Filter Setup dialog box are shown in Figure 33-2. You must choose from Format, Resolution, Size, Data Compression, and Color Translation.

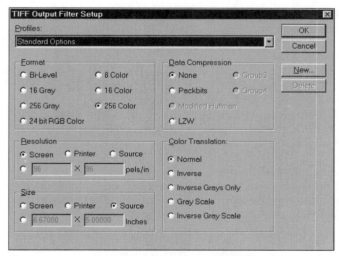

Figure 33-2: TIFF Output Filter Setup dialog box

Format actually refers to color depth, or the number of different colors in your image. You can select from Bi-Level (black and white only, with no grays or colors); 16 or 256 grayscale; 8, 16, or 256 color; or 24-bit (16.7 million) color. Visio selects the color palette for each of these options without input from you, so 24-bit color is often the best choice, if your destination application supports it and includes tools for reducing the number of colors to the desired number.

Resolution determines the resolution of the exported image in picture elements, abbreviated pels or pixels (also referred to as dots-per-inch or dpi). If you click the Screen button, Visio uses the current screen resolution for your display, for example 72 ppi/dpi for 14-inch screens or 96 ppi/dpi for larger displays.

If you click the Printer option, Visio bases the resolution on your system's current printer resolution setting. This option optimizes the image for printout. Choosing Source lets the destination application determine what resolution to use. There's a fourth, unnamed button that enables you to enter custom values for resolution. The value you enter must be between 32 and 400 pixels per inch.

Size enables you to specify the size to display the file. The Screen button sets the size at the largest that fits in the display screen without altering the shape of the object. The Printer button bases the size on the current paper size specified for your printer. Choosing Source lets the destination program determine the size, while the unnamed button enables you to enter a custom dimensions in inches.

Data Compression specifies whether the file will be compressed or not. Choose None if you think the destination program may not be able to accept compressed files. Use either Packbits or LZW (for Lempel-Zev-Welch, the originators of the compression algorithm) if you want to squeeze the file down to a smaller size.

Color Translation options are the same as described under importing files in Chapter 32. When the Normal box is checked, Visio tries to match the colors of the original image exactly. The Inverse button reverses the colors of the image. For example, black becomes white, dark blue becomes light yellow, and so forth. Click the Inverse Grays Only button and Visio retains the colors of the original image, but reverses their black, white, and gray values. So, dark blue becomes light blue, light red becomes dark red, and so forth.

The Gray Scale button converts all colors of an object to their gray values, which is useful if you want to preview how an image will appear on a monochrome printer. The Inverse Gray Scale option is the equivalent of using the Gray Scale and Inverse choices simultaneously. Visio converts the object to gray, and then reverses the tones, negative style.

When you've made your choices, click OK to finish exporting the file.

PCX Output Filter Setup

PCX is the second-most-common file format. ZSoft developed it for their now-defunct line of pre-Windows graphics products, which included PC Paintbrush. PCX was originally a binary file (black/white only) format. Gray scale and 24-bit color capabilities were added later. While not as flexible as TIFF, PCX is widely used and, today, extremely standardized, so it can make a workable exchange medium between Visio and another application.

Most current software supports PCX format version 5, which includes custom color palettes that can be tailored to a specific image. Earlier versions used a standard color palette and ignored the custom colors. Visio supports 256 color PCX.

The PCX Output Filter Setup dialog box, shown in Figure 33-3, is similar to the TIFF dialog box, with two exceptions.

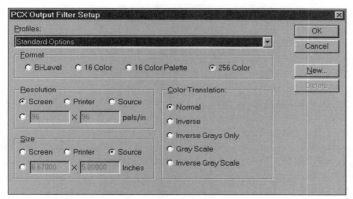

Figure 33-3: PCX Output Filter Setup dialog box

From the Format options, you may choose only Bi-Level (black and white), 16 color standard palette, 16 color custom palette created by Visio, or 256 colors. Visio does not support 24-bit color for PCX files.

PCX files are always compressed using a standard algorithm, so there are no data compression options to choose from.

JPG Output Filter Setup

The JPG Output Filter Setup dialog box, shown in Figure 33-4, is similar to the TIFF dialog box with the following exceptions.

From the Format options, you can choose only between grayscale (monochrome) or 24-bit color (YCC Color). JPEG does not support other color depths.

Instead of Data Compression, you can choose a Quality level, which is the same thing; the higher the JPEG quality, the lower the compression, and vice versa. You can leave the Default button checked, or click the other button and type in a percentage from 1% (incredibly small and incredibly rotten) to 100% (virtually as good as a TIFF or PCX file). The actual amount of space saved at each setting depends on the content of the object, so if you're looking for a specific file size, you'll need to experiment.

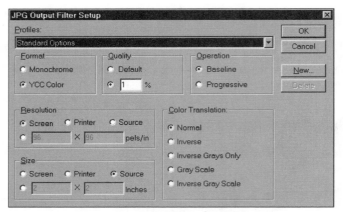

Figure 33-4: JPG Output Filter Setup dialog box

Operation specifies whether you want a conventional JPEG image or a progressive JPEG image, which is akin to the interlaced option of GIF files. When viewed with a compatible Web browser, a progressive JPEG image displays in low quality as the download begins, gradually becoming sharper as the download is completed.

GIF Output Filter Setup

GIF, also known as CompuServe Graphics Interchange Format, was developed as a way to provide reasonably-sized image files that could be downloaded at modem speeds as slow as 2400 bits per second, and viewed on pre-Windows PCs and Macintosh computers (as well as the other computers that existed in the 1980s). GIF uses color palettes of 256 or fewer colors, and a lossless data compression scheme called LZW, after its developers Lev, Zempel, and Welch.

GIF has an optional encoding method called interlacing, similar to JPEG's progressive format, in which an image is saved as four alternating (or interlaced) sets of lines. As the image is downloaded, first a coarse representation showing only 25 percent of the information is displayed (these days, most often in a Web browser), followed by 50 percent, 75 percent, and 100 percent versions. This gives visitors to a Web site an idea of what the image looks like before it downloads completely.

The GIF Output Filter Setup dialog box, shown in Figure 33-5, has many of the same options as the other bitmap format boxes, with a few variations.

Background Color and *Transparency* options enable you to choose one color (and only one) that will be displayed as the background of the image, or which will be seen as transparent in a Web browser, letting the background color or graphic "behind" the image show through. In either case, you can select the Default choice (which is white for background and no transparent color for transparency), or click the User Define button and type in separate red, green, and blue values.

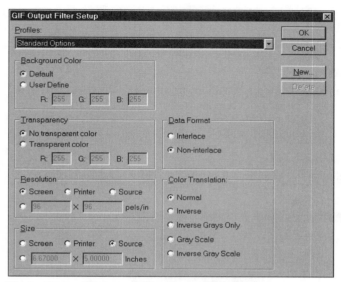

Figure 33-5: GIF Output Filter Setup dialog box

You can determine the RGB values of a color in Visio's Color Palette dialog box. Choose Tools ⇨ Color Palette and click the Edit button. In the Edit Color dialog box, shown in Figure 33-6, the RGB values of the selected color appear at the lower right.

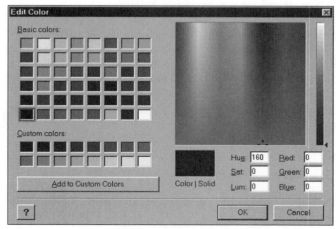

Figure 33-6: Use the Edit Color dialog box to discover RGB values.

Data Format enables you to choose from a conventional noninterlaced GIF, or one that is interlaced and displays at increasing sharpness as the download continues, much like a progressive JPEG image.

PNG Output Filter Setup

PNG was developed as an alternative to GIF, combining small file sizes with a greater number of colors, plus interlacing and a more versatile transparency capability. Because most browsers in use don't support PNG, this format has languished. You may have some application for exporting to PNG, however.

The PNG Output Filter Setup dialog box, shown in Figure 33-7, is more or less similar to the GIF dialog box, with the addition of an option for 24-bit color.

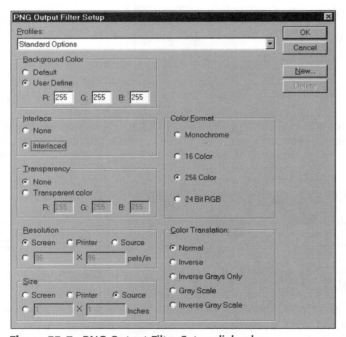

Figure 33-7: PNG Output Filter Setup dialog box

BMP Output Filter Setup

BMP is the standard Windows bitmap format, used for things such as wallpaper and as a format for Windows Paint. There are several versions of the BMP format, including the 24-bit Windows BMP and OS/2 formats, neither of which can be compressed to reduce file size; and BMP RLE, which can include only 256 or fewer colors, but can be compressed. A variation on the BMP file is the device-independent bitmap (DIB) format, used for computer multimedia systems.

The BMP Output Filter Setup dialog box, as seen in Figure 33-8, shares the Resolution, Size, and Color Translation options of the other bitmapped formats, but has some twists of its own.

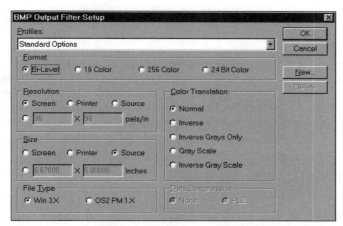

Figure 33-8: BMP Output Filter Setup dialog box

The *Format* and *Data Compression* areas of the dialog box work together. You can have 16 or 256 Color with data compression set to either None or RLE (run-length encoding, a compression scheme). If you choose Bi-Level (black and white) or 24 Bit Color (16.7 million colors), data compression becomes unavailable.

File Type offers the choice of Windows 3.X (the most common type) or OS2 PM (presentation manager) 1.X if you need special compatibility with OS/2.

Exporting other graphics formats

While bitmapped files are nothing more than a picture of your Visio object, other formats can export objects in a form that can be edited, to one extent or another, by the target program. You'll find this capability useful if you have a Visio drawing or shape that you want to work with in a program like Adobe Illustrator or CorelDraw.

Metafile formats

Metafile formats were created as intermediate file formats for transporting data between one application and another using the Windows Clipboard, OLE, or other methods. Often, metafiles are created and used only within memory, and copied to a hard disk only when they become too large for memory, or when you elect to save them. Because metafiles were designed expressly for data interchange of both bitmapped and outline graphics (like those produced by Visio), they have a remarkable degree of compatibility. For example, Visio doesn't have, or need, a setup dialog box for either Windows Metafile Format (WMF) or its successor, Enhanced Metafile Format (EMF).

Computer Graphics Metafile (CGM) format was an early version dating from the MS-DOS days of PC computing. Visio's CGM Output Filter Setup dialog box, shown in Figure 33-9, has the standard Color Translation options, as well as a Line Mode that determines how the ends of lines are represented. Stroked bases line-ends on those types of endings that the destination program already offers or can emulate. Device provides fewer, faster-drawing line-ends.

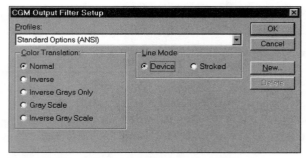

Figure 33-9: CGM Output Filter Setup dialog box

The original WMF format was developed to store both vector and bitmap data. Vector information, like Visio documents, is stored as commands used by the Windows Graphics Device Interface (GDI) to draw images. Bitmapped information is stored in a WMF as a device-dependent bitmap (with parameters associated with the device used to display it), or as a device-independent bitmap (DIB) which can be rendered by any device, regardless of resolution or size.

WMF is a 16-bit format that originally appeared with Windows 2.0 in the 1980s. The EMF version is a 32-bit upgrade with an enhanced color palette and support for Windows 95/98/NT/2000's 32-bit GDI commands.

As I mentioned previously, when you save a file in either WMF or EMF format from Visio, no dialog box appears. The file is exported automatically in the optimized metafile format. However, that doesn't mean that a program that can import WMF or EMF files will be able to handle the graphic with the same aplomb as Visio. There are several limitations to metafiles. The main potential problem is that rotated metafiles can produce unpredictable results when ungrouped or cropped.

Encapsulated PostScript/Adobe Illustrator

PostScript is a page description language (PDL) developed by Adobe Systems and licensed or emulated by other manufacturers. Because PostScript uses outlines for fonts and graphics, it provides great flexibility in sizing images, because a description of how to draw the image rather than a bitmap is used. And, like all vector formats, Visio's PostScript files can be scaled up or down without losing resolution.

Where PostScript describes how to draw a full page, a variation called Encapsulated PostScript (EPS) can be used to describe individual shapes and groups of shapes (as well as a complete page), just like Visio's native file format. For that reason, many drawing and illustration programs, such as Adobe Illustrator or CorelDraw, use EPS either as a main format or as an alternative.

EPS files can contain both vector outlines as well as a compressed bitmap such as TIFF or PICT images, and a lower-resolution preview image that can be used as a viewing and positional aid in a program that can't represent PostScript images directly.

Visio uses the same dialog box to create both generic EPS files and those intended for export to Adobe Illustrator (which end in an .ai file extension). The dialog box is shown in Figure 33-10.

You can select either generic EPS or Adobe Illustrator EPS from the Profiles drop-down list. With either you can choose Color Translation, Line Cap and Resolution options discussed earlier. The other options include Background Rectangle, Optimize for Color Printer, Include AI Format, Include TIFF Preview, Format, and Data Compression.

Background Rectangle determines whether Visio includes a rectangle that can be used to represent the image in the target application.

Optimize for Color Printer produces a file that looks best at the current printer resolution of your computer.

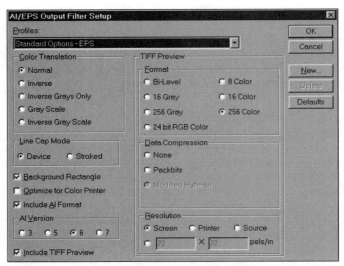

Figure 33-10: AI/EPS Output Filter Setup dialog box

Include AI Format tells Visio to create a file compatible with Adobe Illustrator. In the AI Version area below, you can select a release of Adobe Illustrator from 3.0 to 7.0. The higher the release number, the more features the file can include, but you must be using at least that release of Adobe Illustrator to later import the file into Illustrator.

Include TIFF preview tells Visio to include a TIFF preview image.

Format refers to the TIFF preview. You can choose either Bi-Level (black and white); 16- or 256-tone grayscale; 8, 16, or 256 Color; or 24 bit RGB (16.7 million) Color versions.

Data Compression enables you to choose from None or Packbits. With a Bi-Level format only, you can also choose from an additional compression scheme called Modified Huffman, which can produce particularly small files with black-and-white images.

PICT/IGS

PICT and IGS are formats used in some applications (PICT is the native Macintosh format) and can include both vector and bitmapped information. The PICT Output Filter Setup dialog box, shown in Figure 33-11, includes Color Translation, Line Cap Mode, and Background Rectangle options, which we've already discussed. The IGS dialog box, shown in Figure 33-12, is basically the same, but also offers a Fill Mode option that performs the same function as Line Cap Mode, but for object fills.

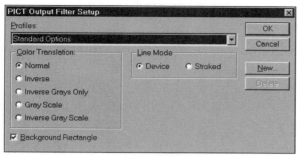

Figure 33-11: PICT Output Filter Setup dialog box

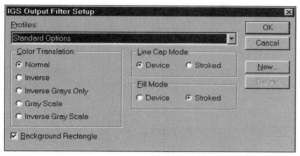

Figure 33-12: IGS Output Filter Setup dialog box

Summary

In this chapter you learned how to export Visio documents and shapes in formats that can be loaded by other applications. You learned the following important facts:

✦ Exporting isn't as compatible as OLE, but may be necessary when OLE isn't practical.

✦ Each format has its own setup dialog box that enables you to choose the options for the exported file.

✦ Bitmapped files can be saved using various color depths, resolutions, and compression schemes.

✦ Vector art formats can preserve many of Visio's features for editing in the target program.

In the next chapter, you learn how to use the Visio ShapeSheets feature.

✦　　　✦　　　✦

Applying Visio's Extensive Business Capabilities

◆ ◆ ◆ ◆

◆ ◆ ◆ ◆

Part VIII covers some of *Visio 2000's* key business drawing applications. You learn how to use ShapeSheets for directly editing shape numerical and function data. The use of HTML files, hyperlinks, and *AutoCAD* drawings are discussed in areas. Along with engineering and Web page design, I review other fields in which Visio software is typically found useful.

Understanding and Using ShapeSheets

In Part IV, you learned how to modify master shapes to organize them into groups or give them new outlines, sizes, orientations, and behaviors. However, sometimes the thousands of master shapes available with Visio and its templates won't be enough for a specific application. Perhaps you have a company logo you'd like to use as a SmartShape. Or, you might be a product developer creating templates for a specialized application. If that's the case, you can create a new master shape with the exact characteristics you want by modifying its ShapeSheet. Working with ShapeSheets is a complex process best left to developers, rather than the typical Visio user. However, in this chapter I can give you a good idea of what's involved. You learn what a ShapeSheet is, and what sort of skills you must have to modify its contents.

What Are ShapeSheets?

As you may know, Visio shapes are a kind of *vector* art, like that produced by other drawing programs such as Adobe Illustrator or CorelDraw, rather than *bitmapped* or *raster* art, like that produced by Adobe Photoshop, Corel Photo-Paint, and similar image editors. Although bitmapped images are nothing but a collection of pixels defined by their position, brightness/darkness, and hue, vector objects such as those used in Visio are represented by mathematical formulas.

The Visio shapes you see on the screen are actually graphical representations of those formulas, which define beginning and end points for the lines and curves that make up the object, the distance between those points, and other information that determines how the shape behaves when you do something with it, such as make it larger or smaller.

Every Visio shape, as well as other objects, such as object groups, objects you've linked or embedded from other applications, guide lines and guide points, and even Visio pages and documents, has its own ShapeSheet. A ShapeSheet is a collection of information about a shape, arranged in a spreadsheet or table format of rows and columns. The ShapeSheet controls both the way Visio creates the shape and the way the shape behaves on the drawing page. All default characteristics of a shape are incorporated, from its dimensions to the position of the angle of rotation. ShapeSheets can also include formulas that determine how the shape acts when resized or moved.

You can edit this basic information by changing the formulas in the ShapeSheet. This is usually a task for developers, because the process requires a good understanding of how objects are formed, and how to change them using mathematical formulas.

Parts of a ShapeSheet

You can display the ShapeSheet window for any object on a drawing by selecting the object and choosing Window ➪ Show ShapeSheet. The ShapeSheet window for a square is shown in Figure 34-1.

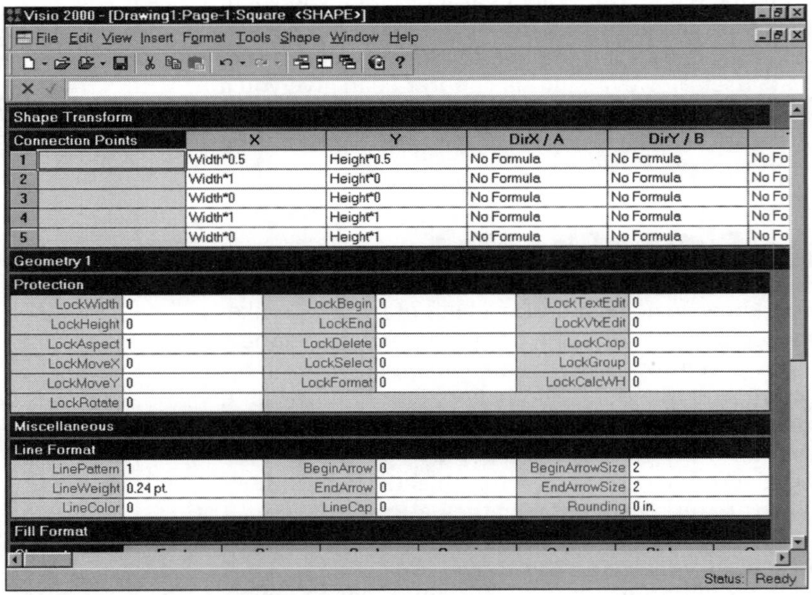

Figure 34-1: ShapeSheet for a square

If you plan to work with ShapeSheets extensively, you might want work in Visio's developer mode, which adds the command Show ShapeSheet to the shortcut menu that pops up when you right-click an object. To activate developer mode, choose Tools ➪ Options, and click the Advanced tab to produce the dialog box shown in Figure 34-2. Click the Run in developer mode checkbox, and then click OK to return to your drawing. You can also choose View ➪ Toolbars and click the Developer toolbar to make visible the Show ShapeSheet button (as well as other developer-oriented buttons).

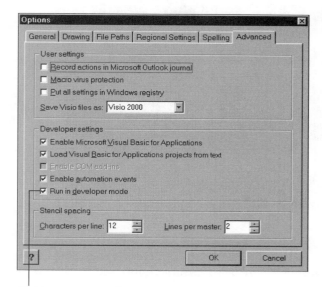

Figure 34-2: Turning on developer mode

Click here to turn on Developer Mode

The ShapeSheet consists of tables called *sections*, each of which contains information about a particular object property. Not all ShapeSheets contain all of the types of sections available, because some might not apply to a particular object. Because so many different tables, or sections, exist in a ShapeSheet — even for one as simple as a basic square — you usually have to scroll through the window to find the table you want to work with. You can also click the Maximize box in the upper-right corner of the window to fill your screen with the contents of the ShapeSheet window.

Showing and Hiding Sections

Visio includes a helpful window-shade mode that squeezes ShapeSheet information into a more usable area. If you click the title bar of any section, it collapses to nothing more than the title bar if the section is shown in full; if it is already collapsed, clicking the title bar expands it to full size again. Figure 34-3 shows a ShapeSheet that has been expanded to full screen size, with some of its sections collapsed.

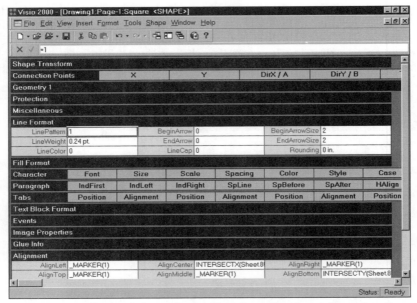

Figure 34-3: Full-screen ShapeSheet with collapsed and uncollapsed sections

You can also show or hide sections completely. Right-click the title bar of any section in a ShapeSheet, and choose View Sections from the shortcut menu. A dialog box like the one shown in Figure 34-4 appears. Sections not available in that ShapeSheet are grayed out.

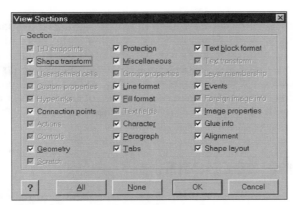

Figure 34-4: Selecting sections to view

1. Put a checkmark in the checkbox next to any section you want to make visible. Uncheck the checkbox to make the section invisible. This step does not remove the section; it only shows or hides it in the ShapeSheet window.

2. Click the All or None buttons to make all or none of the sections in a ShapeSheet visible.

3. Click OK when finished to return to the ShapeSheet window.

When a ShapeSheet is visible, you can make it active by clicking in it. When the sheet is active, the menus in the menu bar at the top of the screen change to provide commands appropriate for working with a ShapeSheet. For example, the Edit menu is modified to provide commands for adding rows, deleting table sections, and so forth.

In addition, a formula bar, which looks and acts like the formula bar in spreadsheet programs such as Microsoft Excel, appears below the main toolbars. When you click a cell in any of the tables, the content of that cell appears in the formula bar. You can modify the content by editing it in the cell itself or by entering the values you want in the formula bar.

There's a very good reason for giving you both options. You can change the ShapeSheet view so that each cell in a table shows either the current values for that cell or the formula itself. Select View ⇨ Values or View ⇨ Formulas to toggle between the two views. You may want the ShapeSheet to display all the formulas to give you an overview of every formula in a section. Then, when you're ready to make changes to specific cells, you may want to switch the ShapeSheet to Values view and make the actual modifications in the Formula bar. As you do so, the changed values are shown on the ShapeSheet. Figure 34-5 shows the ShapeSheet with both values and formulas displayed.

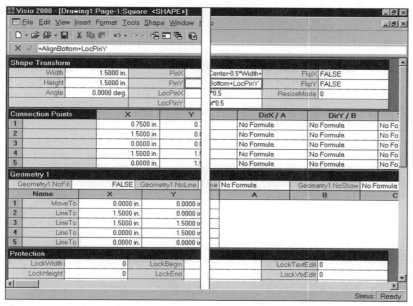

Figure 34-5: ShapeSheet with values (left) and formulas (right) displayed

Displaying ShapeSheets

Slightly different methods are available for displaying a ShapeSheet of an object already placed in a drawing or a master object positioned on a stencil, or the ShapeSheet associated with a document, page, or style.

Viewing an object's ShapeSheet

You can view the ShapeSheet for any object in a drawing, including shapes, lines, guide points, and guides.

1. Select the object in a drawing. If the object is combined into a group, click the group first, and then click the object with which you want to work.

2. Click the ShapeSheet button if you've activated it (as described in the previous section), or choose Window ⇨ Show ShapeSheet.

3. If you've activated developer mode, you can also view the ShapeSheet by right-clicking the object and choosing Show ShapeSheet from the shortcut menu that appears.

Viewing a group's ShapeSheet

Visio creates a ShapeSheet for an entire group; however, the ShapeSheet displays properties only for the entire group, not individual objects within the group.

1. Select the group with which you want to work. Make sure the entire group is selected, not just one object within the group.

2. Click the ShapeSheet button, if visible; otherwise, choose Window ⇨ Show ShapeSheet.

3. If you've activated developer mode, you can also view the ShapeSheet by right-clicking the group and choosing Show ShapeSheet from the shortcut menu.

Viewing a master object's ShapeSheet

You can work with ShapeSheets associated with master objects on stencils, either standalone stencils or those that are part of a Visio document. If you want to view the ShapeSheets of master objects in a drawing that is already open, you can also use the method described in the next section, "Viewing the ShapeSheet of a document, page, or style."

1. If the master object is contained in a standalone stencil, open the stencil using File ⇨ Stencils ⇨ Open Stencil. Navigate to the stencil you want, and open it.

2. If the master object is contained in a Visio document, open the document using File ⇨ Open. Navigate to the document you want, open it, and then make sure the stencil is visible by choosing Window ⇨ Show Stencil.

3. Right-click the master object in the stencil, and choose Edit Master from the shortcut menu that appears.

4. When the new drawing window opens with the master object displayed, click the Show ShapeSheet button if you've activated it, or choose Window ⇨ Show ShapeSheet. If you activated Developer Mode as described in the previous section, you can also right-click the window and choose Show ShapeSheet from the shortcut menu.

Viewing the ShapeSheet of a document, page, or style

You can view the ShapeSheets associated with a document, page, or style using the Drawing Explorer. You can also use this method as an alternative way of accessing a master object's ShapeSheet.

1. Open the document containing the ShapeSheet you want to view.

2. Choose View ⇨ Windows ⇨ Drawing Explorer. The Explorer appears (see Figure 34-6).

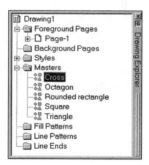

Figure 34-6: Drawing Explorer

3. Navigate through the Explorer to find the document, page, style, or master shape you want to view a ShapeSheet for.

   • If a plus sign appears next to a folder, click it to expand the folder and show the subfolders inside it.

   • If a minus sign appears next to a folder, click it to collapse the folder and hide its contents.

4. When you find the document, page, style, or master shape associated with the ShapeSheet you want to view, right-click the object and choose Show ShapeSheet from the shortcut menu.

Modifying ShapeSheets

If you want to modify a ShapeSheet, you should be an experienced developer, or, at the least, willing to study to get the knowledge you need to change ShapeSheets. Much of the information you need is contained in the Developer Reference document, included as a Portable Document Format (PDF) file on the Visio CD-ROM in the Docs folder. You can view the reference guide or print it using Adobe Acrobat Reader. If your computer doesn't have Acrobat Reader already installed, you can find it in the Acrobat folder on the Visio CD-ROM.

If you just want to play with ShapeSheets or enjoy the thrill of learning by trial and error, you can create an expendable document to work with. Display the shape you're working with in one window, and view its ShapeSheet side-by-side. You have more than 30 different sections to play with.

If you're math-oriented, you'll probably be able to figure out what the different formulas do. See what happens when you change a formula controlling one characteristic or another. For example, geometry sections describe the paths of the lines and arcs that make up an object. Individual rows in the section describe the position of the vertices that join these lines and curves. If you remove a particular row, the vertex vanishes, leaving a straight line between the vertices described by the rows above and below the one you removed. Similarly, if you add a row and enter a set of coordinates, a new vertex appears between the two described by the rows above and below.

Conversely, you can change the shape of the object in the drawing window and watch what happens to the formulas in the associated ShapeSheet section.

Some of the easiest sections to understand include the following:

✦ **Alignment.** How an object is aligned with its guide or guide point.

✦ **Character**. How the text added to an object should be formatted.

✦ **Controls**. The x and y coordinates of the object's control handles.

✦ **Fill format.** Patterns, foreground and background colors, and drop shadows associated with an object.

✦ **Geometry**. Coordinates of the vertices of the lines and curves that outline the object. Separate geometry sections are included for each path in an object.

✦ **Hyperlinks.** Links that jump to another object, page, or World Wide Web site when the object is clicked.

✦ **Image Properties.** Brightness, contrast, and other properties of bitmapped images inserted into a Visio drawing.

✦ **Layer Membership.** Names of the layers to which an object is assigned.

✦ **Layers.** Descriptions of the object's layers.

✦ **Line format.** Describes all the attributes of a line, including weight, color, and type of line ends.

✦ **Paragraph.** Indentations, line spacing, and other paragraph formatting.

✦ **Text Block Format.** Alignment and margins of text in a text block.

Visio's ShapeSheets operate much like spreadsheets. Although you can make many changes simply by modifying the values in an existing formula, to create new shapes and behaviors, you need to learn the functions available. These include familiar math functions (such as SUM, SIN, or COS) as well as functions created especially for Visio (such as GRAVITY). You'll find a full list of functions, their arguments, and how to use them in the Developer Reference.

As with spreadsheets, you can link a ShapeSheet's cells to a database of information, so the shape and behavior of an object can be varied based on updated information in the database. Conversely, if you change these attributes in the Visio drawing, the database can be updated to reflect that. Visio's Database Wizard, accessed by choosing Tools ➪ Macros ➪ Visio Extras ➪ Database Wizard, can lead you through linking a ShapeSheet's cells to the fields of a database. The Visio Database Wizard is shown in Figure 34-7.

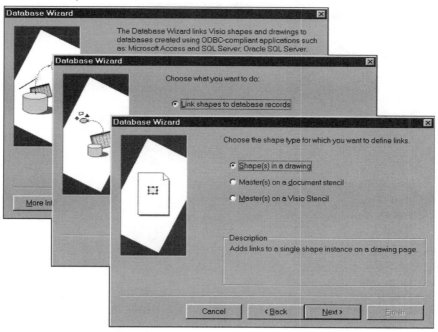

Figure 34-7: Visio Database Wizard

Printing a ShapeSheet spreadsheet

If you want to have a hard copy of a ShapeSheet to use as reference, you can easily print it.

1. Select the object you'd like to document.

2. Choose Tools ➪ Macros ➪ Visio Extras ➪ Print ShapeSheet. The Print ShapeSheet dialog box shown in Figure 34-8 appears.

3. Put a checkmark next to the sections you'd like to print, or click All to choose all of them.

4. From the Print To drop-down list, choose whether you want to copy the ShapeSheet to your printer, the Windows clipboard, or a print file.

5. Click OK.

6. Choose number of copies and other print properties in the Print dialog box.

7. Click OK to finish.

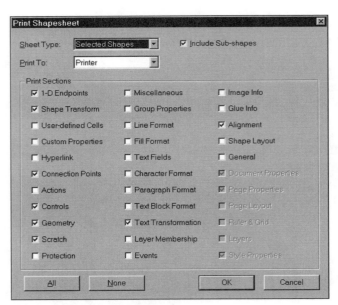

Figure 34-8: Print ShapeSheet

Summary

In this chapter, you looked at how Visio uses ShapeSheets and how you can modify them. You learned the parts of a ShapeSheet, as well as techniques for the following:

✦ Showing and hiding sections

✦ Displaying ShapeSheets

✦ Modifying ShapeSheets

✦ Printing ShapeSheets

If you are an experienced developer, you can use Visio's ShapeSheet capabilities to create your own powerful master shapes.

Go on to the next chapter to learn about Web Page Design with Visio.

✦　　✦　　✦

Web Page Design with Visio

What hath Tim Berners-Lee, creator of the World Wide Web, wrought? The Web and the hypertext markup language (HTML) pages that display its content have become much more than a way of distributing scientific papers. The Web page has become a fundamental conduit for transmitting information of all types, and not only on the Internet. Companies are using HTML on office networks to distribute business documents. Web pages can function offline as help files, because their hyperlinks make jumping from one topic to another easy. Through HTML, articles and books are being distributed in a format that can be read by anyone, using any computer platform that has a browser — and they all do! We're even seeing HTML serving as a word processing format for programs such as Microsoft Word.

So, Visio's HTML capabilities are important not only because they provide a gateway to using Visio drawings on the Web, but because drawings with hyperlinks can be enhanced documents that do more and better things than plain old "flat" drawings. This chapter explains both how you can use Visio to create Web pages for the Internet and how to apply its capabilities to other kinds of linked documents.

Visio and Web Pages

Visio's HTML page creation features are powerful. You can save drawings in formats that you can include on your Web pages, or have Visio create ready-to-run Web pages that duplicate your drawings — including any hyperlinks you may add to jump from page to page or Web site to Web site. Visio's HTML pages can include JavaScript instructions (written for you by Visio) that can perform an amazing number of functions.

There's not enough room here to explain the fundamentals of HTML or how to design Web pages. Hundreds of other books do just that. If you already have a good grasp of Web development, I can show you how to apply Visio's capabilities to your work.

The first step, of course, is to create the drawings that you want to use with your Web pages. You then need to figure out how to join the drawings with useful hyperlinks that can whisk visitors to your Web site from one page or object to another. Finally, you create those hyperlinks.

Note　Your final destination for a drawing with hyperlinks doesn't have to be the Web. You can create Visio drawings with links to other pages in the same drawing, other Visio drawings, non-Visio documents, or the Web. However, the techniques for inserting and using hyperlinks are the same in each case.

Inserting Hyperlinks

As I mentioned in Chapter 32, you can insert a link in Visio that "jumps" to another location whenever the link is clicked. The location can be virtually anywhere local or in hyperspace, including another page in the same Visio document, a page in a different Visio document, a page in a Microsoft Office document, or even to a page on the World Wide Web. You could, for example, create a large-scale map with hyperlinks to close-up views of each area on the map, or to pages that explain about company facilities in those areas. Clicking in Ohio on a United States map could transport you to a World Wide Web page about that state, for example.

Links to different pages in the same Visio document or to another Visio document are called *internal links*, because Visio is capable of handling the jump entirely on its own without help from another application. You can use internal links to create interactive Visio documents that include explanatory text, more detailed graphics, or any other type of information you like.

An *external link* is one to any non-Visio document, whether it's a Microsoft Word file, a graphic created by another application, or a Web page. In this case, Visio automatically opens the application that Windows runs by default for the kind of file in question, using the file's extension and Windows' built-in list of applications associated with each extension. That is, files ending in .pcx might be associated with Photoshop, Windows Paintbrush, Corel PhotoPaint, or a similar image editing application. Files ending in .doc might be associated with Microsoft Word, Word Pad, or another word processing program. To see a list of applications and the extensions they are associated with, open any Windows folder from the Windows Explorer or My Computer, and choose View ➪ Options, click the File Types tab, and highlight a file type.

Linking an object or page

To insert a hyperlinked object or to link to a page, first make sure you save the document you're working on. This is necessary because you must have a file on your hard disk to link to. Next, select the object you want to serve as the link. Or, if you want to link to a page rather than an object on a page, click an empty area of the page.

What can you link to? Visio's linking capabilities aren't really complicated, but they can be confusing. Table 35-1 provides a summary of what you can and can't link to. Instructions on how to create those links follow.

Table 35-1 Visio Hyperlinks	
Source	**Destination**
From a Visio drawing to a location in the same drawing	A file address is not needed; you must specify a subaddress consisting of a specific page or a specific object on a page in the same drawing. You can optionally select a standard zoom setting.
From a Visio drawing to a location in another Visio drawing	Specify only the file address, and Visio jumps to the first page of the drawing. You may also specify a subaddress pointing to a specific page or a specific object in the drawing, and optionally use a standard zoom setting of your choice.
From a Visio drawing to a Microsoft Office document	You must specify the file address. Visio jumps to the first page of the Office document. A subaddress to a specific page is not allowed.
From a Visio drawing to a World Wide Web page	You must specify the URL of the Web page, either as an absolute address or as an address relative to the location of the Visio file.

After you've selected the page or object to jump from, choose Insert ➪ Hyperlinks or press Ctrl+K to access the dialog box shown in Figure 35-1. If you have a lot of links to add, you may want to make sure the Web toolbar is visible by choosing View ➪ Toolbars ➪ Web. You can then add a link by clicking the Insert Hyperlinks button at the left edge of the toolbar (or the top edge if you dock the toolbar at the side of your Visio window.) Next, you enter some information to create your link.

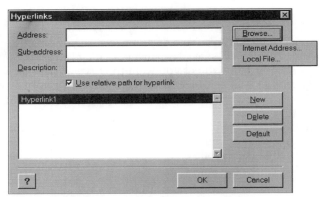

Figure 35-1: Enter information for hyperlinks here.

Note   You may not need to use Visio's Web toolbar, because its functions are limited. However, it's there if you need it. It includes an Insert Hyperlinks button (but pressing Ctrl+K is always faster), a pair of Forward and Back arrows to move between pages you've joined with hyperlinks, and a Visio on the Web button that opens your default browser and whisks you to the Visio Web site (if you're logged onto the Internet, of course).

Address

In this box you should type or browse to the destination address of the document to which you're linking. If you're linking to an object or page within the same document, you can skip this step and jump down to the instructions for including a subaddress, which appear in the following section. To Visio, an empty Address box means "this document."

If you're linking to a page or object in another document, you need to specify the document in the Address box. You can enter the path to the document if you know it, but more often you want to click the Browse button to navigate to the document being linked. Clicking the Browse button offers two choices, Internet Address and Local File, as shown in Figure 35-1.

If you click Internet Address, you must be connected to the Internet. In this case, Visio opens your browser, which you can use to navigate to the Web page to which you'd like to link. Visio updates the Address box with the URL of the page you're currently viewing.

If you click Local File, you can navigate your hard disk to the file you'd like to link to, as shown in Figure 35-2. Click Open to add the link. If the document is a file other than the current one, Visio inserts its name into the Address and Description boxes. You can choose the current document in this dialog box if you like, although it's not necessary. As I said, if you don't specify a filename, Visio assumes you mean the current document, in which case Visio leaves the Address box empty and fills in the current document's name in the Description box.

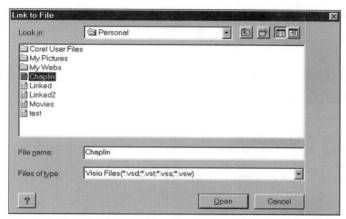

Figure 35-2: Add a file here.

Subaddress

If you're linking to the current Visio document, you must supply a subaddress that refers to a specific page or object in the document. If you're linking to another Visio document (but not a Microsoft Office document or Web page), you have the option to link to a specific shape or object in the target document, rather than let Visio default to the first page. Click the Browse button next to the Subaddress box to produce the Hyperlink dialog box shown in Figure 35-3.

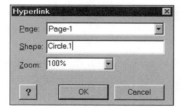

Figure 35-3: Add a subaddress.

If you want to link to a page in the document, the process is simple. The Page box includes a drop-down list with every page in the document to which you're linking. Just choose the page you want.

If you want to link to a specific object on a page, you must know the name of the object. It would be nice if all a selected page's objects were listed in the Shape box, but they are not, so you must find the name on your own. View the page with the object to be linked to, right-click the object, and choose Format ⇨ Special. The name of the object appears in the Name box of the Special dialog box, shown in Figure 35-4.

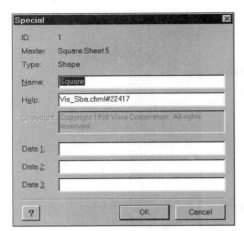

Figure 35-4: Finding out the name of an object on a page

The name will be something like Ellipse or Circle — the same name as shown on the drawing template. If more than one example of a shape appears, the shape will have a number in its name — for example, Ellipse.4 or Circle.3. It's also possible you or someone else has previously used Format ➪ Special to apply your own name to the shape. Just enter the current name in the Shape text box.

Any time you link to a subaddress, either in the same document or in a different Visio document, you can specify the zoom level Visio uses to display the shape or page you're linking to. This is a handy feature if you want to provide a closer look at an object through a link. Choose a standard (not custom) value from the drop-down Zoom list. Click OK when you're finished with the Hyperlink dialog box to return to the Hyperlinks dialog box (nobody said this step wasn't confusing), where the subaddress is filled in for you.

Description

The text in the Description box is displayed as a screen tip when the cursor hovers over the linked object. The default text is the name of the file being linked to, but you can enter any information you like here.

Use relative path for hyperlink

This innocent-looking checkbox is used to determine how Visio figures out where the hyperlink leads to. If the box is unchecked, Visio always uses the complete file path or Internet path you specify in the Address box, such as C:\Program Files\ Visio\Documents\Map1.vsd or http://www.dbusch.com/index.htm.

If you check the box, Visio bases the link on information you specify in the document's Properties sheet. To add this information, choose File ➪ Properties and click the Summary tab. Enter the address you want to use in the Hyperlink Base text box, shown in Figure 35-5.

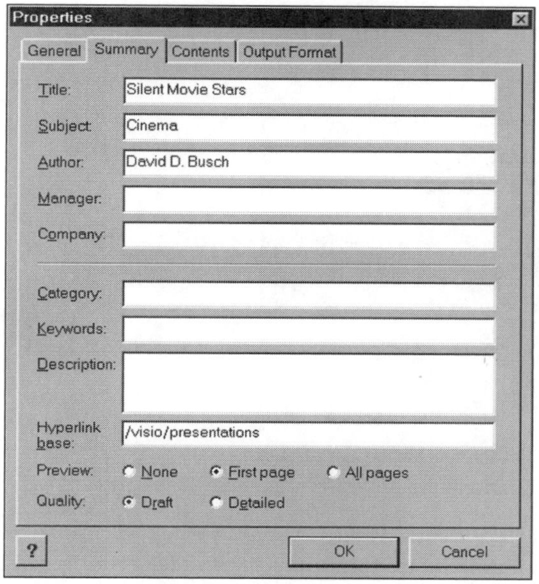

Figure 35-5: Enter a hyperlink base.

Next, when the Use Relative Path for Hyperlink option is enabled, Visio completes the path of the link using the path you enter in the Hyperlink Base text box.

A relative link points to the location of the linked file in relation to the Visio drawing or HTML page. For example, a link pointing to graphics\logos\logo1.jpg would indicate a file called logo1.jpg, located in the graphics/logos subdirectory inside the directory or folder when the current document is located. This means you don't really need to know the entire directory structure of the location for your document or Web page; you only need to know what files will reside in the same directory and in the directories underneath that directory.

An absolute link points to a file's complete location, such as c:\webpages\chaplin\ graphics\logos\logo1.jpg or http://dbusch.com/chaplin/graphics/logos/logo1.jpg. This kind of link is less flexible. When you move the files that the link points to you must always change the link. However, an absolute link is more or less unbreakable once you've taken the time to set it up.

Link List

The Link List window can contain a particular object or several links to other objects in the same document or to another document. The first link in the list is the default link, and is the link used if the host document is saved in HTML. If the Visio document is saved in Visio format, all the links are shown when right-clicking the object containing the link; you can jump to any of the links by selecting it from the short-cut menu, as shown in Figure 35-6.

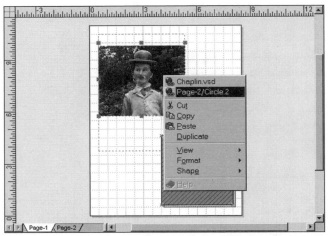

Figure 35-6: Right-click and jump to any link shown.

The buttons beside the Link List can be used to add a new link for an object that already has a link, delete an unwanted link, or set one of the links as the default link, moving it to the top of the list.

Choosing a shape for a link

You're free to link from any Visio shape, but a few professional-looking smart buttons are included for this purpose in the Borders and Tiles stencil in the Basic Drawing template. These include a hyperlink button and two types of hyperlink circles, each with some nifty functions built in. When you drag one of these shapes to your drawing, they spring into action, producing a Custom Properties dialog box like the one shown in Figure 35-7.

You need to choose the kind of icon you want from the drop-down Icon Type list. The icons you can choose from include Back, Forward, Down, Up, Directory, Home, Help, Info, Mail, Photo, Search, and None. When you click OK, the Hyperlinks dialog box described earlier appears automatically so you can create a hyperlink for the button.

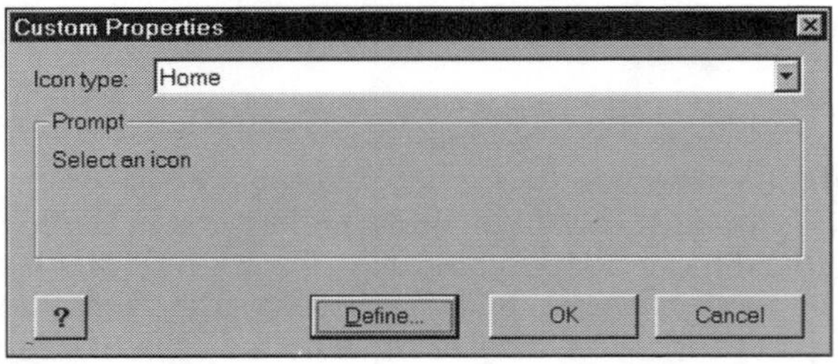

Figure 35-7: Choose custom properties for Visio's hyperlink button.

Saving for the Web

Visio actually gives you two options for saving drawings for use on Web pages. The easiest way is to save them as an image file that's compatible with browsers, using a format such as JPEG, GIF, or PNG. You can do this when all you want is an image of the drawing to use on an existing Web page, you don't care about hyperlinks or other special features, and you want to display the image in a size that will fit most browser windows. You also may want to export the drawing as an image file when you want to export only part of a drawing.

Or, you can save the drawing as one or more HTML pages, with all the hyperlinking, automatic resizing to fit a browser window, and other features Visio can provide. When you save a drawing that consists of one page, Visio creates a single Web page that contains the drawing and any hyperlinks within it. If your drawing has multiple pages, Visio creates a Web page for each drawing page and adds navigation buttons to enable you to move between them, as shown in Figure 35-8.

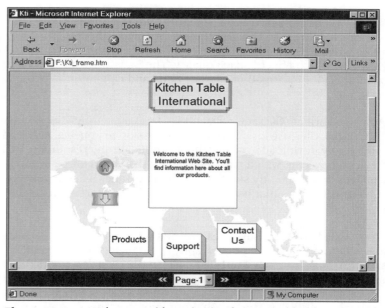

Figure 35-8: A Web page with navigation buttons added by Visio

Saving as an image

To save a file as an image, choose File ➪ Save As. Select .jpg, .gif, .png, or .vml in the Save as File Type list, and then click Save. The one of three Output Filter Setup dialog boxes appears (the .jpg version is shown in Figure 35-9). Choose the options you want, and then click OK.

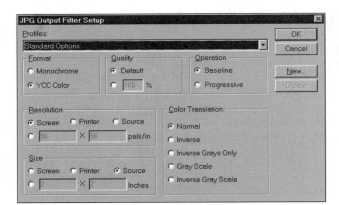

Figure 35-9: Specify image options with the Output Filter Setup dialog boxes.

Note

Information on using the Output Filter Setup dialog boxes to export images appears in Chapter 33.

If you've designed Web pages before, you probably understand the differences between the various file formats. The first three formats are all bitmapped formats, which means that when an image is enlarged or reduced, some pixels have to be created or discarded, which affects image quality. The fourth format, VML, is based on the same kind of vector information used in Visio, and can potentially provide higher quality.

Graphics Interchange Format (GIF) is the default file format used by Visio to save images for HTML pages. GIFs use lossless data compression to squeeze images down to a smaller, more easily downloaded size without sacrificing any resolution. GIFs are limited to 256 colors, however, which makes them less than ideal for continuous tone photographic images, but eminently suitable for Visio drawings, which typically contain 256 or fewer hues. GIFs that have fewer than 256 colors are even smaller and more compact.

The Joint Photographic Experts Group (JPEG) format was developed by a consortium of organizations with interests in the photography and imaging industries. JPEG was designed to allow for small file sizes while displaying more than 256 colors (up to 16.7 million colors, in fact), but at the cost of losing some image information.

The key to the success of JPEG is the fact that our eyes don't really notice all the details in images, rather they tend to blend pixels into recognizable form. As a result, images can be created that discard some information, making the file much smaller, but still allowing a decent quality graphic. You might want to use JPEG if your Visio drawing includes graphics from Photoshop or a similar image editor.

Portable Network Graphics (PNG) format was developed to combine the advantages of GIF and JPEG without using the copyrighted compression algorithms that GIF is built upon. Although PNG can produce sharp, full-color images, the format is still not supported by most browsers and is little used today.

Vector-Based Markup Language (VML) is a format developed by Microsoft, Visio, Autodesk (makers of AutoCAD), and Hewlett-Packard. It's a kind of extensible markup language (XML) that can reproduce an image without changing it from vectors to a bitmap. That means the image can be enlarged or reduced at will without sacrificing quality. In practice, VML provides a way to produce "zoomable" images that can be viewed in multiple sizes. However, at this time VML files can be viewed only by Microsoft Internet Explorer 5.0 or later, so if your HTML files are to be viewed by another browser, you should choose one of the other formats, or take advantage of VML's alternate format capabilities.

Note   When you choose VML as you save a Web page, the VML Settings dialog box appears. Select the Provide Alternate Bitmap checkbox, choose the format from the Graphics Format drop-down list, and click the Filter Settings button to make Filter Settings adjustments as described in Chapter 33. Click OK to finish.

Saving as HTML pages

To save a drawing as one or more HTML pages, choose File ➪ Save As. Select HTML Files from the Save As Type drop-down list and enter a filename for the pages, ending with the .htm or .html extensions. The Save As HTML dialog box, shown in Figure 35-10, appears. Choose from these options:

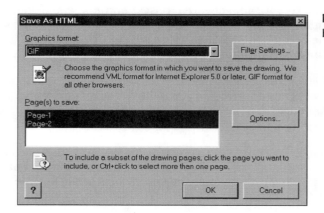

Figure 35-10: Save As HTML dialog box

✦ **Graphics Format.** Choose from the drop-down list the graphics format you want Visio to use to save the images in the drawing. GIF is the most compatible, as it can be viewed in all graphics-capable browsers. Click the Filter Settings button to set the output filter options discussed in Chapter 33.

✦ **Page(s) to Save.** Highlight the pages you want to save by clicking a page and then Ctrl+clicking additional pages to add them to the list of pages to be converted. If you want to use image maps, click the Options button. The options for image maps are discussed in more detail later in this chapter.

Click OK when you've selected your options. Visio creates one or more Web pages, including the HTML code for each and separate image files (in the format you selected) for each of the images on the page. Visio also creates graphic files for any navigation buttons it includes on your HTML pages. If you've specified image maps, it creates an image map file (as described in the following section). After Visio has saved your pages in HTML format, you are asked if you'd like to view the new pages. Click Yes if you want Visio to open your Web browser and show you the pages.

Image Maps

Most hyperlinks on a traditional Web page consist of a highlighted area of text, or else a graphic image. Both usually are associated with only one hyperlink. (As I mentioned earlier, a Visio drawing with hyperlinks can include several links for each object, but an HTML page converted from that drawing can have only one hyperlink active.)

Image maps are a way of doing an end-run around this limitation, enabling you to treat an entire graphic, such as a Visio drawing, as a map that includes embedded "hot spots" visitors click to activate a hyperlink. Each defined area in the graphic can jump to a different object or page.

So, an image map is nothing more than a graphic that has been divided into areas or regions a browser or Web server can recognize. It uses "borders" you define using a simple X-Y coordinate system. An image map could use an actual map as a graphic — say, an outline of the United States, with each state or region corresponding to a hyperlink to some information about that area.

However, clickable image maps are perhaps the most under-used, least understood, and most often badly applied graphic elements you're likely to find on a Web page. Even so, you can use Visio to help you put these graphics to work effectively if you follow a few guidelines.

Visio makes image maps much less complex to create, which is a blessing because the information about the hot spots is not embedded in the image file itself, but in a separate text file, called a *map file,* that stores the coordinates of the hot spots within the image.

A good image map should convey some information about the links nestled inside the image, and, most importantly, look enough like an image map to invite clicking. Visitors find nothing more frustrating than click-worthy images that contain no links, or hidden image maps that are stumbled upon by accident. An actual map, a dashboard full of buttons, a control panel, or similar graphics all make good image maps. Abstract shapes, unlabeled images, and large files that take a long time to download are poor choices for this technique. And don't forget to include text links for non–image-capable browsers: If all your links are embedded in image maps, even a Netscape Navigator user who has shut off image display will be lost on your page.

How image maps work

If you understand basic HTML, you'll see that image maps require no magic spells. The secret is in a simple ASCII file that contains little more than the coordinates of points defining any regions you want, and the URL or link to be activated when a visitor clicks inside that area. A typical map file might look like this one:

```
<MAP NAME="usa">
<AREA SHAPE="rect" COORDS="245,355 385,355"
HREF="colorado.htm">
<AREA SHAPE="polygon"
COORDS="201,331,281,339,291,283,359,334,294,357,198,358"
HREF="ohio.htm">
</MAP>
```

This file creates an image map named "usa" and defines two areas within it — a rectangular region suitable for a regularly shaped area such as the state of Colorado, and a six-sided polygon that hugs the borders of Ohio. Once the image map is deposited in the proper location (which can vary, depending on whether you're creating a client-side or server-side image map), an HTML reference in your Web page like the following displays the graphic on your page, and points toward the ASCII map file.

```
<IMG SRC="usa.gif" BORDER=0 ALT=" USA Image Map" USEMAP=#usa">
```

The ALT tag is a courtesy for those viewing your page without graphics, as mentioned earlier in this chapter.

Client-side vs. server-side image maps?

Originally, the only way to implement image maps was through use of maps that reside on the Web server. The server sees when you've clicked a hot spot in a downloaded graphic and handles requests for the hyperlinks specified.

Because all the work is done on the server, a server-side image map must use a common gateway interface (cgi) script on the server that tells the server how to handle the map. Server-based image maps can slow down when the Web server is overloaded, and frequent access to maps can contribute to the overload.

Today, client-side image maps are more common, because they have several advantages. Client-side image maps require nothing more than a map file on your site, appropriate HTML code to access the map, and, on the visitor's end, Netscape Navigator, Microsoft Internet Explorer, or another browser compatible with the client-side map. The browser itself handles keeping track of where the cursor is on the image map and jumping to the hyperlinks when you click.

Another advantage is that client-side image maps can be tested and debugged locally, rather than on your server. As a bonus, as visitors pass their cursor over hot spots in your map, actual labels describing the link (rather than just coordinates, which is the case with server-side maps) appear. All the work is handled by the browser, which determines which URL is requested, and passes the request on to the Web server.

Image maps in Visio

The details of creating map files manually are beyond the scope of this book, but here are the basics. The map files used with image maps are ASCII files filled with numbers. That's because they must contain a set of coordinates for each vertex of the shape that defines every area of the map. For a rectangle, that might be by simply defining the two opposite corners (such as 0,0 and 50,50). A circle is defined by specifying the coordinates of its center, plus its radius in pixels. Regular or irregular polygons are defined by specifying every vertex. For server-side maps, two common sets of syntax rules are available for defining these shapes. You must use the form compatible with your server.

To save a Visio drawing with image maps activated, click the Options button in the Save As HTML dialog box to view the dialog box shown in Figure 35-11. Click to place a checkmark in the Enable Image Maps checkbox, and select either the Client Side or Server Side button, as appropriate. If you choose the Server Side option, you can enter a URL that points to the map file, and select either NCSA or CERN syntax. Visio then creates the image map file for you automatically. You must move this map to your server to activate the image map feature.

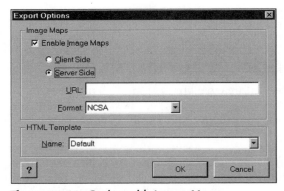

Figure 35-11: Saving with Image Maps

Summary

In this chapter, I showed you the basics of creating Web pages with Visio. The chapter covered the following topics:

✦ Visio can create Web pages as well as Visio documents with hyperlinks.

✦ Hyperlinks can jump from any object or page to another object or page in a Visio document, a non-Visio document, or a page on the World Wide Web.

✦ Hyperlinks can control the zoom level that an object jumped to is zoomed at.

✦ Visio can save as HTML pages and its graphics in JPEG, GIF, PNG, and VML formats.

✦ Clickable image maps can provide a more intuitive way to jump around a Web site.

✦　　✦　　✦

Working with AutoCAD Drawings

This chapter should be of particular interest to you engineering types out there. Come on, "techies" — you know who you are! Just because a particular comic strip character tends to shine a little humor on the profession doesn't mean that you have to go into hiding. We won't do that to you here. Anyway, to those of you who need to use Visio 2000 in conjunction with AutoCAD files, the information in this chapter will prove to be quite useful.

With Visio 2000, you can introduce an existing AutoCAD drawing (in one of several particular formats) to your Visio drawing to serve as a background or add detail. Once the AutoCAD image is in the new Visio drawing, you can add Visio shapes to it, crop it, or use layers to show or hide review comments.

At this point you might be thinking, "That's all fine and good, but what about editing the AutoCAD drawing once it's in Visio? Can I change any of the objects that I just brought in?" Well, since you asked, the answer is "Yes, you can!" In this chapter, you find out how to convert your AutoCAD drawing to Visio format, which you can then edit to your heart's content.

Finally, you may feel the need to bring the Visio drawing into your AutoCAD program. Well, you are able to do that, too. This chapter shows you how to convert your Visio 2000 drawing to AutoCAD format.

So, for all you AutoCAD users out there, just sit back in your cubicle and relax. The following chapter provides all the information you need to merge your AutoCAD files with Visio 2000 and vice versa.

Importing AutoCAD Drawings for Display

You may have many reasons for wanting to bring your AutoCAD files into Visio:

✦ **You need a way to review AutoCAD files.** Your organization may use AutoCAD for their technical diagrams. However, you've been asked to review a drawing and make redlines to it or comment on some feature. You could open that AutoCAD file in Visio 2000, create a layer, and make your comments on that layer.

✦ **You want to use the AutoCAD image as a background**. You've just been given the task of rearranging the layout of your group's work area. If you had the floor plan in an AutoCAD format, you could open the file as a background image and then start to drop and rearrange Visio shapes, from the included stencils, over the floor plan.

✦ **You want to show enlarged, "detailed" views.** You feel that a callout or closer look at the detail of a machine part is just what you need to convey the proper information. Insert the AutoCAD drawing into your Visio drawing and bring intricate details closer to a viewer.

 Note

The AutoCAD drawing that you import is a *copy* of the original file. Any changes you make to the image, once it is in Visio, do *not* affect the original file!

Importable AutoCAD formats

Before you start to wonder what AutoCAD formats you can import, let me simply list them:

✦ DWG and DXF file formats generated by Autodesk AutoCAD and other CAD programs

✦ Bentley MicroStation DGN file format

Reviewing AutoCAD files

If you frequently review engineering drawings and need to make comments or updates, you can bring the AutoCAD file into Visio 2000 and make your comments on a new layer. In Visio, select Open from the File menu, or click the Open button on the Standard Toolbar. The Open dialog box appears (see Figure 36-1).

Click the down arrow to the right of the Files of type field. From the drop-down menu, select AutoCAD Drawing (*.dwg, *.dxf) or MicroStation Drawing (*.dgn).

Toward the top of the Open dialog box, to the right of the Look in field, click the down arrow to locate the folder that holds the file that you want to import, select the file, and then click Open. The CAD Drawing Properties dialog box (as shown in Figure 36-2) opens.

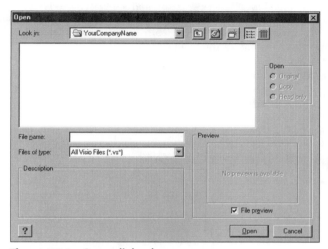

Figure 36-1: Open dialog box

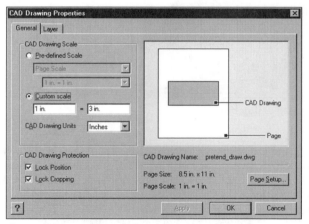

Figure 36-2: CAD Drawing Properties dialog box

Click OK to close the CAD Drawing Properties dialog box. You can now create new layers to mark up or add review comments to. Remember to save your file when you are finished with the review process.

Using the AutoCAD file as a background

This section guides you through the process of bringing an AutoCAD drawing into your Visio file to use it as a background image. Once the drawing is inserted, you can add Visio shapes, comments, and layers.

Note When importing a DWG drawing, any added Visio shapes snap to objects in the AutoCAD image. To prevent this from happening, lock the Visio layer containing the imported AutoCAD image. This stops you from inadvertently selecting and moving the AutoCAD image instead of the Visio shape.

Before you import the AutoCAD image, create a blank Visio drawing that has the page size and drawing scale that you want. In the blank drawing, select CAD Drawing from the Insert menu. The Insert CAD Drawing dialog box appears (see Figure 36-3).

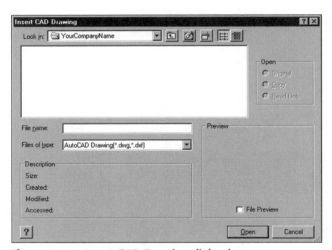

Figure 36-3: Insert CAD Drawing dialog box

To the right of the Files of type field, click the down arrow. From the drop-down menu, select AutoCAD Drawing (*.dwg, *.dxf) or MicroStation Drawing (*.dgn). Find the file that you want to use as your background image and click Open. The CAD Drawing Properties dialog box opens.

Tip If you are planning to add Visio shapes on top of the AutoCAD image and scale is important, remember to set the scale of the AutoCAD drawing to the same scale as that of the Visio drawing. For information on scaling options, check out the section "Editing the Imported AutoCad Drawing" later in this chapter.

On the General tab, select the Lock Cropping and Lock Position checkboxes to prevent accidental cropping or moving of the drawing as you work on it. Click OK.

Remember what I said earlier about locking the layer? Well, you are at the point where you can do this. If you want to lock the Visio layer containing the AutoCAD image, right-click the inserted drawing and, from the pop-up menu, select View ➪ Layer Properties. Click the Lock column for that specific AutoCAD drawing layer and then click OK.

Using the AutoCAD file for detail

You can import an AutoCAD file to get a closer look at the fine elements of a machine part or detail within a floor plan. Begin by opening the Visio file that needs the added detail. From this drawing, select CAD Drawing from the Insert menu. The Insert CAD Drawing dialog box opens.

To the right of the Files of type field, click the down arrow. From the drop-down menu, select AutoCAD Drawing (*.dwg, *.dxf) or MicroStation Drawing (*.dgn). Find the file that you want to use and click Open. The CAD Drawing Properties dialog box opens.

Review the size and position of the AutoCAD drawing on the Visio page. If you feel some modifications are needed, adjust the AutoCAD drawing scale on the General tab to increase or decrease the image.

On the General tab, you need to deselect the Lock Position and Lock Cropping boxes; otherwise, you won't be able to crop or move the imported AutoCAD image. When ready, click OK to start working with the image.

✦ If you need to reposition the AutoCAD image, simply select and drag the drawing to where you want it.

✦ If you need to crop or pan the AutoCAD image, check out the next section, "Editing the Imported AutoCAD Drawing."

Once you are satisfied with position and appearance of the AutoCAD drawing, remember to lock the drawing again so that you can't inadvertently move or crop it while you work on the Visio page.

Editing the Imported AutoCAD Drawing

Now that you've learned how to insert an AutoCAD drawing into your Visio drawing, you can edit this image by doing the following:

✦ Add Visio shapes

✦ Adjust the scale

✦ Show and hide layers

✦ Crop and pan the image

Adjusting an image's scale

When importing an AutoCAD drawing, Visio automatically picks a scale that enables the entire image to fit on the Visio page. You have the option of increasing or decreasing the scale, and you can also match the scale of the AutoCAD image to the Visio page.

Altering the scale of the AutoCAD image

To change the scale of an inserted AutoCAD drawing, right-click the inserted drawing. From the pop-up menu, select CAD Drawing Object ⇨ Properties. The CAD Drawing Properties dialog box opens. On the General tab, select a scale setting (see Table 38-1).

<table>
<tr><td colspan="3" align="center">Table 36-1
CAD Drawing Scale Options</td></tr>
<tr><td>*Option*</td><td>*Does What?*</td><td>*Use When?*</td></tr>
<tr><td>Pre-defined Scale: Page Scale</td><td>Matches the CAD drawing scale to the Visio drawing scale.</td><td>You want to add Visio shapes on top of an AutoCAD drawing.</td></tr>
<tr><td>Pre-defined Scale: Architectural Civil Engineering Metric Mechanical Engineering</td><td>Uses predefined industry-standard scales.</td><td>You want to add annotation shapes or text blocks to the imported drawing. Does *not* properly scale Visio objects that represent physical objects (such as office furniture).</td></tr>
<tr><td>Custom Scale</td><td>Uses the scale that you enter.</td><td>Anytime you want to set your own scale.</td></tr>
</table>

Cross-Reference   For more detailed information on scales, see Chapter 16.

Now is the time to check out the preview image on the right side of the dialog box (refer back to Figure 36-2 for an example). Take a look at the AutoCAD drawing compared to the Visio drawing page. If the AutoCAD drawing does not fit on the Visio page, you might want to try the following:

✦ Pick a smaller CAD drawing scale or Visio drawing scale.

✦ Select a larger page size — click Page Setup, and then click the Page Size tab. Pick another option within the Page size area. Click OK to apply the new settings and close the Page Setup dialog box.

When you are satisfied with your settings, click OK. If you set your AutoCAD drawing scale to a different scale than the Visio drawing scale, the CAD Drawing dialog box pops up (see Figure 36-4). Select the Continue without matching scale option and then click OK.

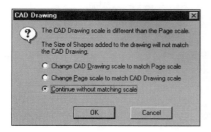

Figure 36-4: CAD Drawing scale verification dialog box

Showing layers

When you import an AutoCAD drawing into your Visio drawing, you may want to hide a comment layer or an outdated version of redlines. (Whatever the reason might be, I'm not here to judge!) To hide or show a layer or level, right-click the AutoCad image while in Visio. From the pop-up menu, select CAD Drawing Object ⇨ Properties. The CAD Drawing Properties dialog box opens. Click the Layer (or Level) tab. To hide the layer, deselect the Visible column. To show the layer, select the Visible column.

Cropping and panning the imported image

When you bring an AutoCAD drawing into your Visio drawing, you may not want to view the entire image. In such a case, you need to crop the AutoCAD drawing. To crop the drawing, select the Crop tool from the Standard toolbar (found under the Rotation tool). Click the AutoCAD drawing. Perform the usual cropping process (drag the square selection handles on the drawing's border until you can see only the part of the drawing that you want). If you need to pan (or reposition) the drawing within the CAD drawing border, click inside the border and drag the drawing.

Converting AutoCAD Objects to Visio Format

To make any changes to an object in Visio, that object must be a Visio shape. This means that when you are importing an AutoCAD drawing into a Visio file, you cannot, say, resize, remove, or edit any of the objects from the AutoCAD drawing without first changing those objects into Visio shapes. To do so, you must convert the AutoCAD drawing layer or level that contains the objects you want to manipulate.

Tip Convert only the layer that contains the objects you need to access. An unconverted AutoCAD drawing is quicker to deal with and usually results in higher image quality.

To convert an imported AutoCAD layer, right-click the drawing. From the pop-up menu, select CAD Drawing ➪ Convert. The Convert Wizard – Step 1 of 3 dialog box opens (see Figure 36-5).

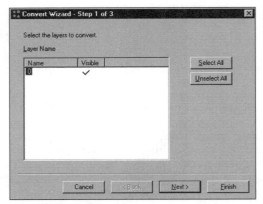

Figure 36-5: Convert Wizard – Step 1 of 3 dialog box

Select the layers or levels that you want to convert (if making multiple selections, use Ctrl+click). Click Next. The wizard advances to the next dialog box.

Select whether to hide or delete the original layers or levels, and then click Next. The wizard proceeds to the final dialog box.

Select how you want to convert the objects and click Finish. Presto-chango, like magic, the objects on the specified layer(s) or level(s) are converted.

Exporting Visio Files into AutoCAD Formats

Just as you were able to easily bring an AutoCAD drawing into Visio, you can also export a Visio drawing into the an AutoCAD program in the following formats:

✦ DWG and DXF file formats generated by Autodesk AutoCAD and other CAD programs

✦ Bentley MicroStation DGN file format

When converting a Visio file into an AutoCAD format, Visio 2000 takes the current Visio drawing page and converts it. So if you have multiple pages in your Visio drawing, you must then convert each page individually.

To convert a Visio drawing, go to the page that you want to convert. Select Save As from the File menu. The Save As dialog box opens. To the right of the Save as type field, click the down arrow. From the drop-down menu, select AutoCAD Drawing (*.dwg, *.dxf) or MicroStation Drawing (*.dgn).

In the File name box, enter the new name of the file. Toward the top of the dialog box, click the down arrow to the right of the Save in field to locate the folder that you want to put the file into. Select the appropriate folder and then click Save. The converted Visio file is converted and saved.

Summary

This chapter presents all the necessary information that you need to bring AutoCAD drawings into Visio 2000, as well as to save your Visio 2000 drawings for use in an AutoCAD program. The following points were discussed:

✦ You can import DWG and DXF formats generated by Autodesk AutoCAD and other CAD programs into your Visio 2000.

✦ When working with imported AutoCAD drawings, it is quicker to use unconverted layers.

✦ You can add Visio shapes to imported AutoCAD drawings, as well as crop and pan, hide or show layers or levels, or rescale the imported drawing.

✦ You can export your Visio 2000 drawing into DWG and DXF formats for use in AutoCAD programs.

In the next chapter, I cover other areas of business where Visio 2000 can be used to enhance and revolutionize visual presentations.

✦　　✦　　✦

Using Visio 2000 in Other Fields

Visio 2000 caters to a multitude of different business fields
and skill levels. Two diverse company departments, such
as public relations and accounting, can use the program for
everyday tasks. In addition, the software offers a number of
drawing tools for both simple and advanced computer users.
For example, a Visio 2000 novice can create a professional-
looking No Smoking sign in seconds. More advanced users may
use the Visual Basic Editor (shown in Figure 37-1) to create a
Microsoft Visual Basic for Applications program involving
event procedures and ActiveX controls.

The sophistication, scope, and design possibilities afforded in
Visio software are too numerous to discuss in detail with just
one book, much less a chapter. The purpose of this section is
to sum up some of Visio's most basic uses. Previous chapters
detail how Visio software is pertinent to engineering and Web-
based fields. I would like to further acquaint you with a couple
more ways Visio 2000 can help you with visual communications.
Some of these are simple; others are a little more complex.

Figure 37-1: Visio 2000's Visual Basic
Editor is one of the tools geared towards
advanced computer users.

Completing Simple Graphic Design Tasks

Numerous desktop publishing programs inundate office retail store shelves. The really good thing about Visio 2000 is that you don't have to be an artist or graphic designer to get the most out of it. The program differs from a lot of its counterparts in two ways: It is designed for nonartists, and the software is used primarily to create business presentations involving charts and diagrams. Although you can import CorelDRAW!, Adobe Illustrator, and Windows bitmap files into Visio drawings, many people use such features for things like personalizing a corporation's organization chart with photographs of each department head or sketching a company logo.

Visio 2000 also enables users to create signs, awards, business cards, and maps. For example, the Clip Art, Embellishments, and Symbols stencils (found in the Visio Extras solutions folder) come in handy for creating nifty signs to be placed in the office or at conferences (see Figure 37-2). One could even create a simple brochure for company luncheons. The Marketing Clip Art stencil (Charts and Graphs template and Marketing Charts and Diagrams template) contains a variety of SmartShapes, from credit card logos to a 1st Place ribbon image. You can even find a cash cow there!

Figure 37-2: The coffee machine is this way.

Note   You can design your own business cards and fax coversheets by using the Form Design template.

Tip Use additional features to spice up your drawings. The Insert drop-down menu enables you to import pictures and insert Word Art into drawings.

Visio does not stop with SmartShapes and clip art. The Word Art features are worth checking out if you feel the need to come up with some eye-catching text. Select Insert ➪ Word Art to access the special window (shown in Figure 37-3). Type your text in the Enter Your Text Here dialog box. Adjust the style, font, and font size from the three drop-down lists in the upper-left corner of the screen. The Word Art toolbar on the right contains buttons that enable you to control text placement, tracking, shading, shadow, and special effects. Once you've finished inserting Word Art, just click the drawing page to return to the drawing window.

Figure 37-3: Creating text on the Word Art window

Plenty of tools are available for just about any business drawing project imaginable. You can use Visio 2000's various toolbar buttons, several ornamental stencils, an editable color palette, the Color Schemes and Shape Explorer macros, Word Art, and importing capabilities to get the job done. The program caters to a variety of basic graphic design methods, ideal for creating maps and business cards or more simple fare such as signs and calendars.

Creating Marketing Diagrams and Charts

One of Visio 2000's many strengths lies in its extensive capabilities for designing and editing marketing diagrams and charts, as shown in the example in Figure 37-4. This is a well-known fact among the business world. Visio helps people create a wide range of marketing diagrams, some of which are listed here:

Bar graphs	Pie charts
Circle-spoke diagrams	Process charts
Feature comparison charts	Step charts
Line graphs	Venn diagrams
Matrices	3-D pyramid charts
Onion diagrams	

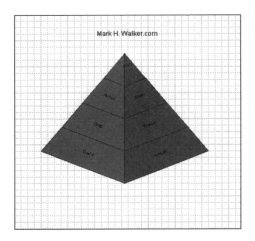

Figure 37-4: Designing a 3-D pyramid chart

Note Don't forget that Visio 2000 permits you to import Microsoft Excel graphs into a drawing.

Visio 2000 charts and diagrams make it possible to create presentations on product development costs, sales and pricing analyses, product feature comparisons, and a strategic look at advertising demographics. In fact, just about anything needed to explain the elements of supply and demand is at your fingertips. The Chart Shape Wizard enables you to create extendable and stackable shapes. The Charts and Graphs template and the Marketing Charts and Diagrams template (both found in the Forms and Charts solution folder) contain a variety of SmartShapes, many of which contain special editing options (see Figure 37-5). Just install Visio 2000 on your marketing associates' computers, and they will feel like kids in a candy store.

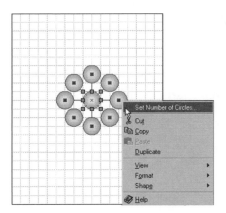

Figure 37-5: Right-clicking the Circle-Spoke Diagram shape enables you to set the number of circles that appear within it.

Designing Presentations for Genealogy Studies

As mentioned earlier, Visio helps you create company organization charts. You can arrange production teams, management, and various departments in a hierarchical scheme with either the Organization Chart template or the Organization Chart Wizard. The Organization Chart toolbar (shown in Figure 37-6) controls the routing direction, and the Behavior dialog box's Connector tab contains additional features that you can manipulate. To add a personal touch, some public relations departments even choose to place accompanying pictures of executives in corporate organization charts.

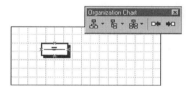

Figure 37-6: Use the Organization Chart toolbar to dictate a project's layout.

Organization charts, however, can be used for more than detailing a company's chain of command. Universities and museums would likely find Visio 2000 a valuable aid in conducting genealogy studies. College sociology professors, for example, could use the program to document the lineage of prominent Irish immigrants in the Boston area. Paleontologists could design museum presentations detailing certain dinosaurs' evolutionary trees during the Cretaceous Period. Visio software is capable of similar approaches in various scientific fields. Therefore, a museum's public relations department can assist the institution in charting its board of directors — as well as the direction of history.

Managing Projects

Project management tools, like those used to create marketing charts and diagrams, are an integral part of Visio software. After all, a company's financial stability is dependent on how well its project managers guide a product's course of development. As the old saying goes, time is money, and money is time. Visio 2000 provides several project management aids to help managers stay on course:

Calendar template	Import Project Data macro
Gantt Chart macro	PERT Chart template
Gantt Chart template	Timeline template

These tools range from the simple (for example, calendars) to the sophisticated (for example, Gantt charts). Overall, Project Schedule solutions help users set project milestones, coordinate integrated tasks for several teams, and document the start and end dates for all project-related activities. Gantt charts are the most complex forms of project scheduling. They have many advantages, however, one being that you can use data from Microsoft Excel to create a Gantt chart. They also are extremely easy to update.

Due to its sophistication, I'd like to take you through a brief tour using the Gantt Chart template. First, select File ➪ New ➪ Project Schedule ➪ Gantt Chart. Notice that a Gantt Chart Options dialog box immediately pops up on the screen (see Figure 37-7). Adjust the settings on the Date tab for the Task options, Time units, Duration options, and Timescale range sections. Click the Format tab to modify such items as taskbars, summary bars, and milestones. Once finished, click the dialog box's OK button.

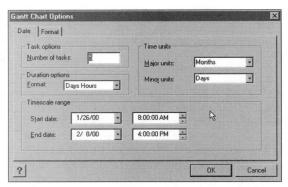

Figure 37-7: Changing settings on the Gantt Chart Options dialog box

The drawing window contains a Gantt Chart toolbar and a Gantt Chart heading on the menu bar. Although they feature some different functions, many of them overlap. For example, you can link, promote, and insert tasks from both locations. Edit the Gantt chart's tasks from either place, and manipulate the figures and duration bar on the chart itself (shown in Figure 37-8). Just click a cell and type the changes you want. Click outside the chart when you finish editing that particular cell. Due to the Gantt chart's interactive nature, changes made to one cell are automatically reflected in related cells. After creating your new chart, save it as you would any other Visio document.

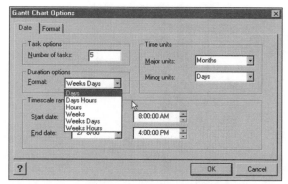

Figure 37-8: Changing the number of days in the duration cell automatically changes the start and end dates as well as the duration bar's length.

Note   You can import and export data into your charts from the Gantt Chart drop-down menu (Gantt Chart ⇨ Import and Gantt Chart ⇨ Export).

Gantt charts, PERT charts, timelines, and calendars provide some of the best means of keeping your projects on schedule. You can hand them out or e-mail them to respective team members, subordinates, and supervisors. With effective communication, all the snags that accompany projects can thus be handled swiftly and efficiently.

Working with Architectural Designs

Architects and construction consultants commonly use Visio products to create building plans. Although users can design office layouts with Visio 2000 Standard, additional features in Visio 2000 Technical (for example, array functions and more architectural templates) make it the program of choice for numerous people within the construction industry. As with Visio 2000 Standard, Visual 2000 Technical enables users to adjust window, door, and wall settings by right-clicking those items and selecting the appropriate functions from the pop-up menu. Details such as the placement of jacks, columns, and furniture can be made with just a few clicks (see Figure 37-9). Designing offices and homes is easy — and fun.

Note   The Architecture Page Properties dialog box in Visio 2000 Technical enables you to specify space measurements as well as those for doors, windows, and walls.

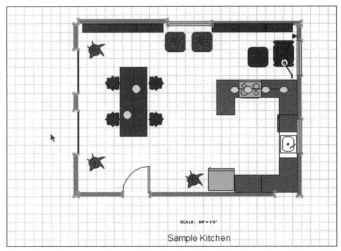

Figure 37-9: Making a few home improvements with Visio 2000 Technical Edition

Analyzing Information Systems

Another popular use for Visio products involves the analysis of information-based systems. Various Visio 2000 Standard templates in the Network Diagram and the Flowchart solution folders provide tools for simulating both hardware and software system processes. Check out Visio 2000 Professional and Visio 2000 Enterprise; they contain more applications geared for handling these tasks.

Tip　You can insert fields into objects by selecting a shape and then choosing Insert ⇨ Fields. Information such as Lotus Notes data, custom formulas, and the selected object's angle can be inserted into various shapes.

Summary

Visio 2000 is a multifaceted business-drawing software series. It can handle a diverse range of business presentations, from cartography to landscaping. Though hardly exhaustive, this chapter outlines some general applications of Visio products and discussed the following points:

✦ You can create signs, awards, business cards, and brochures with Visio 2000 templates.

✦ Visio 2000 Standard offers over ten different types of marketing chart and diagram applications

✦ Organization charts can be used for genealogy studies.

✦ Changes made to a Gantt chart cell are automatically updated in other parts of the table.

✦ Visio 2000 Technical is a popular tool for handling architectural layouts.

✦ Visio 2000 Professional is designed to handle sophisticated system analyses.

Refer to the appendixes for keyboard shortcuts, drawing examples, and the like.

✦   ✦   ✦

Installing Visio 2000

APPENDIX

◆ ◆ ◆ ◆

In This Appendix

Installing Visio 2000

Optimizing Visio 2000

Potential Problems

◆ ◆ ◆ ◆

Visio 2000 installation is not difficult, but there are a few points to consider. Following are some tips for installing Visio 2000.

Installing Visio 2000

Visio 2000's installation is straightforward. If your computer's Autorun function is enabled, the installation screen (as shown in Figure A-1) will appear after you insert the CD.

Figure A-1: The Installation Screen for Visio 2000 Technical Edition

Click Install Visio 2000 to install the program. You may also install the Visio 2000 interactive training sampler or tour the Visio 2000 working environment. Installing the Visio 2000 interactive training sampler installs a segment of Visio 2000's excellent interactive trainer (as shown in Figure A-2). This is a great tool for helping less experienced Visio users get up and running with the basics of Visio 2000.

Tip   Make sure you exit all programs before installing Visio 2000 (or anything else, for that matter). Don't forget to exit programs in your start tray, such as virus protection or automatic download agents.

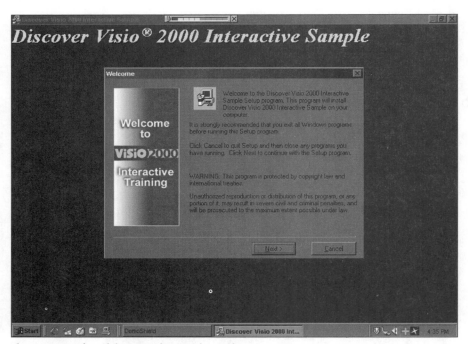

Figure A-2: The Visio 2000 interactive trainer

Touring the Visio 2000 Working Environment

Clicking "take a tour of the Visio 2000 working environment" retrieves the "Touring the Visio 2000 interface" window, as shown in Figure A-3. Although this window lacks the depth of the interactive trainer, it can familiarize you with some of Visio 2000's basic terms.

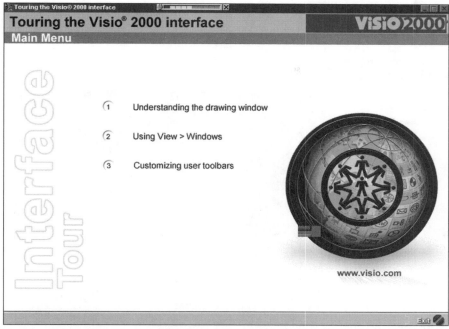

Figure A-3: The Touring the Visio 2000 interface window

The window presents three options:

✦ Understanding the drawing window

✦ Using View ⇨ Windows

✦ Customizing user toolbars

Understanding the drawing window

Selecting "Understanding the drawing window" displays the Visio 2000 drawing window, as shown in Figure A-4. The window lists Visio 2000 features, terms, and toolbars on the left of the screen. These items are "hot," indicated by your mouse morphing into a pointer finger when it passes over one of these items. Clicking an item will highlight the applicable portion of the drawing window. Clicking the icon in the bottom right of the screen returns you to the main menu.

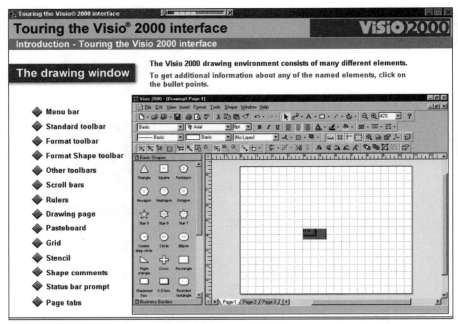

Figure A-4: The drawing window

The View ➪ Windows explanation

Clicking Using View ➪ Windows from the "Touring the Visio 2000 interface" Main Menu retrieves the drawing window shown in Figure A-5, with the following four windows displayed over it:

✦ Document Explorer window

✦ Size & Position window

✦ Pan & Zoom window

✦ Custom Properties window

Clicking any of these four windows not only highlights the window, but also displays an explanation of the window's function across the top of the page. Once again, clicking the Main Menu icon in the bottom right of the screen returns you to the Main Menu.

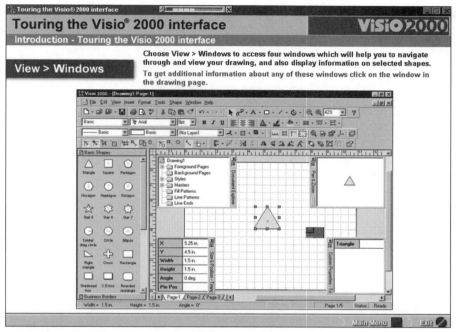

Figure A-5: The View ➪ Windows Section of the Visio 2000 tour

Customizing user toolbars

Visio includes numerous user-friendly toolbars. From the Standard toolbar to the semicomplex Developer toolbar, Visio has a toolbar for everyone. Well, almost everyone. People are unique, and accordingly want unique toolbars. And for these people, Visio 2000 provides a tutorial that explains how to customize its toolbars.

To open the tutorial, from the Main Menu click "Customizing user toolbars." The window shown in Figure A-6 appears. The window is similar to the windows described in the "Understanding the drawing window" and "The View ➪ Windows explanation" sections.

Note the Next and Back buttons at the bottom of the screen. Use these buttons to page through the tutorial or flip back to a point that you wish to review. After you have finished the tutorial, click Main Menu to return to — you guessed it — the Main Menu.

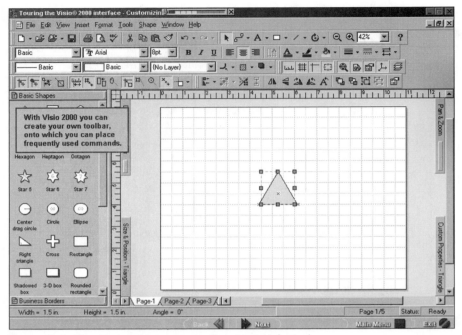

Figure A-6: The Customizing user toolbars' tutorial window

Installing Visio 2000: Updating FILES

Return to the main installation screen. If you choose to install Visio 2000, the screen immediately displays the Windows System Updater. Visio 2000 needs Windows files with specific updates in order to operate properly. The updater checks for these files. It also installs Internet Explorer 5.0. Installing Internet Explorer 5.0 does not change your default browser, but it is required in order to view Visio 2000's help files.

Note   To use Visio 2000 Standard Edition, you must be running one of the following 32-bit Microsoft Windows operating systems: Microsoft Windows 95, Microsoft Windows 98, or Microsoft Windows NT 4.0 (Service Pack 3 or later).

Accepting the updater's proposal splashes the user proposal. Click OK and Visio 2000 updates your system and installs Internet Explorer 5.0. You'll now need to restart your computer. Restart it, and Visio transfers you to the setup program.

Installing Visio 2000: Program Installation

Once the computer restarts, it will ask you to verify another user agreement and enter the product serial number. The Visio 2000 program setup screen, shown in Figure A-7, allows you to pick one of the following three installation options:

✦ **Typical Install** includes the files that most users will use.

✦ **Compact Install** conserves space but limits the program's capabilities.

✦ **Custom/Complete Install** allows the user to choose which options to install.

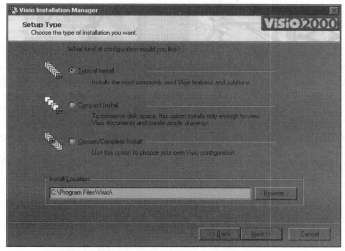

Figure A-7: The Installation Options window

Note   If you have bought a Visio upgrade and have an older version of Visio on your computer, the upgrade will install an updated version. If the Visio upgrade does not detect an older version, it asks for the serial number of the product that you want to upgrade. Enter the serial number to continue.

If you select Custom/Complete Install, the Visio installation manager displays the Custom Setup window. From this window you may choose which features you wish to install. After you select an option, Visio indicates what the option does and how much hard-drive space the option occupies.

Clicking Next displays the options that you have chosen. Clicking Next again installs Visio 2000 with your chosen options.

Placing a Visio Icon on the Word, PowerPoint, or Excel Toolbar

To install the Visio 2000 icon on a Microsoft Word, Excel, or PowerPoint toolbar, run the Insert Visio Buttons.exe file in the \Visio\System\Custom folder.

This procedure installs the Visio button on the toolbar of one of the following Microsoft Office applications:

✦ Microsoft Word 95, 97, and 2000

✦ Microsoft Excel 95, 97, and 2000

✦ Microsoft PowerPoint 2000

With one click of a Visio 2000 icon that is installed on an application's toolbar, a selected Visio drawing will be embedded into that application. An application's Insert ➪ Object command also accomplishes this.

Note   If the Visio\System\Custom folder is not present in your installation of Visio 2000, run the Add/Remove Programs utility in the Windows Control Panel, choose Visio 2000, and click the Add/Remove button. In the Visio Installation Manager, select the Add/Remove option, and then click the Microsoft Office Integration option from the list of features.

✦   ✦   ✦

Visio 2000 Keyboard Shortcut Combinations

Table B-1
Basic Function Keyboard Shortcuts

Function	Keyboard Shortcut
New Drawing	Ctrl+N
Nudge Selected Shape	Press one of the four arrow keys
Open dialog box	Ctrl+O
Page dialog box	F5
Page Setup (Print Setup tab)	Shift+F5
Print dialog box	Ctrl+P
Save dialog box	Ctrl+S
Save As dialog box	F12
Save Workspace dialog box	Alt+F12
Selecting menu bar functions	Alt (or F10)+the four arrow buttons; press Enter when you find the correct function on the drop-down menu
Visio Help Window	F1

Table B-2
Connection Function Keyboard Shortcuts

Function	Keyboard Shortcut
Connection Point Tool	Ctrl+Shift+1
Connector Tool	Ctrl+3

Table B-3
Edit Function Keyboard Shortcuts

Function	Keyboard Shortcut
Copy	Ctrl+C
Crop Tool	Ctrl+Shift+2
Cut	Ctrl+X
Duplicate	Ctrl+D
Paste	Ctrl+V
Pointer Tool	Ctrl+1
Redo	Ctrl+Y
Repeat	F4
Select All	Ctrl+A
Stamp Tool	Ctrl+Shift+3
Undo	Ctrl+Z

Table B-4
Field Function Keyboard Shortcuts

Function	Keyboard Shortcut
Insert Field	Ctrl+F9
Insert Height Field	Ctrl+Shift+H
Insert Rotation Angle Field	Ctrl+Shift+A
Insert Width Field	Ctrl+Shift+W

Table B-5
Hyperlink Function Keyboard Shortcuts

Function	Keyboard Shortcut
Hyperlinks dialog box	Ctrl+K
Navigate Back	Alt+ ←
Navigate Forward	Alt+ →
Navigate to Next Page	Ctrl+PgDn
Navigate to Previous Page	Ctrl+PgUp

Table B-6
Line Function Keyboard Shortcuts

Function	Keyboard Shortcut
Arc Tool	Ctrl+7
Freeform Tool	Ctrl+5
Line dialog box	Shift+F3
Line Tool	Ctrl+6
Pencil Tool	Ctrl+4

Table B-7
Macros Keyboard Shortcuts

Function	Keyboard Shortcut
Macros dialog box	Alt+F8
Visual Basic Editor	Alt+F11

Table B-8
Shape Formatting Keyboard Shortcuts

Function	Keyboard Shortcut
Align Shapes dialog box	F8
Bring to Front	Ctrl+F
Ellipse Tool	Ctrl+9
Fill dialog box	F3
Flip Horizontal	Ctrl+H
Flip Vertical	Ctrl+J
Group	Ctrl+G
Rectangle Tool	Ctrl+8
Rotate Left	Ctrl+L
Rotate Right	Ctrl+R
Rotation Tool	Ctrl+0
Send to Back	Ctrl+B
Ungroup	Ctrl+U

Table B-9
Snap & Glue Function Keyboard Shortcuts

Function	Keyboard Shortcut
Glue Tool	F9
Snap Tool	Shift+F9
Snap & Glue dialog box	Alt+F9

Table B-10
Text Formatting Keyboard Shortcuts

Function	Keyboard Shortcut
Beginning double quotation mark	Ctrl+Shift+[
Beginning single quotation mark	Ctrl+[
Bold type	Ctrl+Shift+B
Bullet	Ctrl+Shift+8
Copyright symbol	Ctrl+Shift+C
Discretionary hyphen	Ctrl+-
Em dash	Ctrl+Shift+=
En dash	Ctrl+=
Ending double quotation mark	Ctrl+Shift+]
Ending single quotation mark	Ctrl+]
Italic type	Ctrl+Shift+I
Nonbreaking backslash	Ctrl+Shift+\
Nonbreaking hyphen	Ctrl+Shift+-
Nonbreaking slash	Ctrl+Shift+/
Paragraph marker	Ctrl+Shift+7
Registered trademark symbol	Ctrl+Shift+R
Section marker	Ctrl+Shift+6
Small caps	Ctrl+Shift+Y
Spelling Check	F7
Subscript	Ctrl+Shift+X
Superscript	Ctrl+Shift+Z
Text dialog box (Font tab)	F11
Text dialog box (Paragraph tab)	Shift+F11
Text dialog box (Tabs tab)	Ctrl+F11
Text Tool	Ctrl+2
Text Block Tool	Ctrl+Shift+4
Underline type	Ctrl+Shift+U

Table B-11
Viewing Function Keyboard Shortcuts

Function	*Keyboard Shortcut*
Pan Drawing Page	Ctrl+Shift+Right Mouse Button while dragging page
View Page at Actual Size	Ctrl+I
View Whole Page	Ctrl+W
Zoom dialog box	F6
Zoom In on Drawing Page	Ctrl+Shift+Left Mouse Button
Zoom In on Selected Area	Ctrl+Shift+Left Mouse Button while dragging a rectangle around area
Zoom Out on Drawing Page	Ctrl+Shift+Right Mouse Button

Table B-12
Window Function Keyboard Shortcuts

Function	*Keyboard Shortcut*
Cascade Window	Alt+F7
Tile Window Horizontally	Shift+F7
Tile Window Vertically	Ctrl+Shift+F7

✦　　✦　　✦

Visio 2000 Drawing Examples

Unlike many of the examples in this book, the examples in this appendix help users apply numerous Visio 2000 applications in one project. For instance, the geographic-map exercise covers various ways to format lines, arrange map shapes, and add color to objects. The exercise on organization charts includes instructions on inserting hyperlinks, shadows, and backgrounds. Although some of the examples in this appendix are complex, *all* of them—from the simple to the sophisticated—serve as brief guides for exploring the rich diversity that Visio 2000 offers. Due to the extensive range of Visio 2000's capabilities, this appendix is hardly an exhaustive account of the program's uses. However, the figures and step-by-step instructions can help you gain ideas and insights for your own projects.

Designing a Business Card

You created a logo for a fictional company called Techno Savvy Systems Chapter 15. Well, as a fictional employee at a fictional company, your fictional supervisor has suggested that you create your own business cards with Visio 2000. The finished product should look something like the example in Figure C-1.

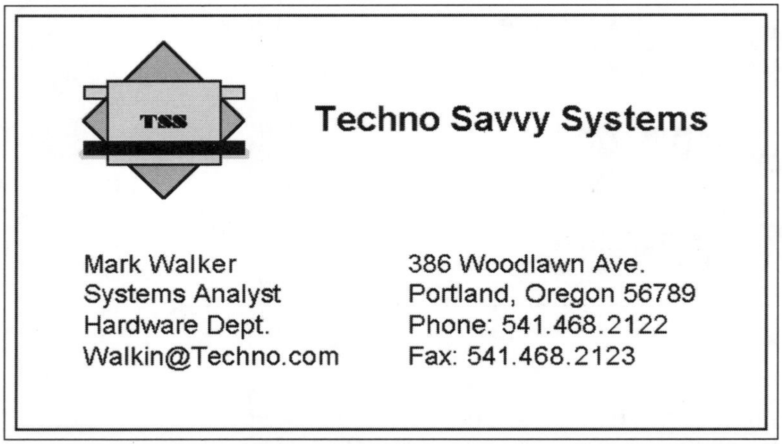

Techno Savvy Systems

Mark Walker
Systems Analyst
Hardware Dept.
Walkin@Techno.com

386 Woodlawn Ave.
Portland, Oregon 56789
Phone: 541.468.2122
Fax: 541.468.2123

Figure C-1: Techno Savvy business cards

Setting up the page

You'll need the business card shape to get started. It's in the Form Design template. Follow these instructions to access the shape:

1. Open Visio 2000 Standard.

2. Select File ⇨ New ⇨ Forms and Charts ⇨ Form Design.

3. Drag the Business Card shape from the Forms Shapes stencil onto the drawing page.

Inserting information

The business card shape is basically just a business card template. You have to add information in the designated areas. Follow these steps in order to add the information:

1. Double-click the business card shape to zoom in on it.

2. Click the area labeled Company Name. Type **Techno Savvy Systems** in its place.

3. Click the area in the bottom left of the card and type your name, position, department, and e-mail address.

4. Click the area in the bottom right of the card and type the company's address, phone number, and facsimile number. Remember that you can change the font size, type, and color, if you wish.

Placing the company logo on the card

It's time to put that nice logo to use. I just hope you haven't forgotten where you saved the Techno Savvy stencil. If you're ready, follow these steps to place the logo on your card:

1. To make room for the logo, shift the company name to the top right-hand corner of the page.

2. Access the Techno Savvy stencil you created in Chapter 15. Drop the Techno Savvy Systems logo near the top left-hand corner of the card. Resize the logo by dragging its corner control handles.

Duplicating cards

The card is complete, but your boss won't be happy if you waste printer paper. I'm sure one card on a full sheet of paper is not what she had in mind. Instead, fill the entire page with copies of your card. You will please your supervisor — not to mention the trees, whose lives you just saved. Follow these brief steps to receive your fictional raise:

1. Select the business card shape and then choose Edit ➪ Duplicate. You will have to repeat this several times.

2. Space the shapes on the drawing page. Now you can print several cards on one page. First, though, save the cards using the Save As function.

Creating a Pie Chart

You're a marketing executive for the pretend toy-manufacturer Larry's Toys. Your make-believe CEO, Larry, wants you to give a presentation on December's impressive holiday sales. One of the charts accompanying your report needs to visually break down the company's sales according to category (as shown in Figure C-2). I think Larry is hoping some dividends show up so that he can build the tree house of his dreams.

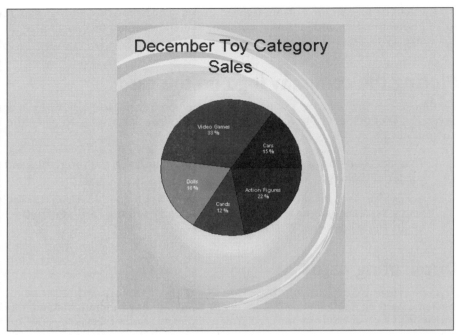

Figure C-2: Percentage of toy sales by category

Setting up the page

Use the Charts and Graphs template for your presentation. Locate and open the document by following these instructions:

1. Open Visio 2000 Standard.

2. Select File ⇨ New ⇨ Forms and Charts ⇨ Charts and Graphs.

Placing a pie graph on the page

Larry's company produces, distributes, and sells five categories of toys. Follow these steps to insert the appropriate number of pie slices and then center the chart upon the drawing page:

1. Drop the Pie Chart shape from the Charting Shapes stencil onto the drawing page.

2. A Custom Properties dialog box prompts you for the number of slices that you need. Click the button next to the edit box and select 5 from the available listings.

3. Drag the shape's corner control handles in order to enlarge it.

4. Select the shape and then choose Tools ➪ Center Drawing in order to center the pie graph upon the drawing page.

Resizing pie slices

Visio 2000, by default, assigns the same percentage to each pie slice, the total equaling 100 percent. Larry's toy sales, though, are not so nice and even. Follow these steps to resize the pie slices so that the percentages reflect actual sales:

1. Select the pie chart shape and then right-click.

2. Choose Set Slice Sizes from the pop-up menu.

3. Type a number for each of the five slices listed in the Custom Properties dialog box (for example, 15, 33, 18, 12, and 22). Once all new numbers tally to 100, click the OK button.

Naming pie slices

Each pie slice represents a toy category; however, Visio 2000 only lists percentages for each slice. You must insert category names into the chart. Follow these steps to name each pie slice:

1. Click the Text Tool button. Click the percentages in each pie slice. Type a name of a toy in front of each percentage. After inserting each name, hit <Enter> in order to place the percentages on a separate line.

2. If you're looking for inspiration, here are some categories worth considering: Cars, Video Games, Dolls, Action Figures, and Cards. You may have to adjust the font size, though, to keep things neat.

Adding finishing touches to your pie chart

The pie chart looks wonderful, but it still needs something. How about a title? And, while you're at it, a background would look good, too. Just follow these steps:

1. Click the Text Tool button again. Click near the top of the page. Type a title for your pie chart, something like "December Toy Category Sales." Drag the left and right control handles in order both to center the title and to extend it onto one line.

2. You may have also decided to spice up the chart with a decorative background shape. Click the Backgrounds stencil title bar in order to view its contents. Drop a background shape onto the page. The Background Cosmic shape works well in this instance. Click Yes on the Make Background dialog box. The new background is automatically inserted behind your pie chart and title.

Creating a Map with International Shipping Routes

Suppose that you're an executive at a software development and production house. Your company's preparing to enter the international market, starting with a few points of interest in the Far East. As part of your presentation at the corporate board meeting, you need to illustrate that initial software shipments will be relayed from your company's distribution center in San Diego to three Asian countries: Japan, Taiwan, and Australia (see Figure C-3).

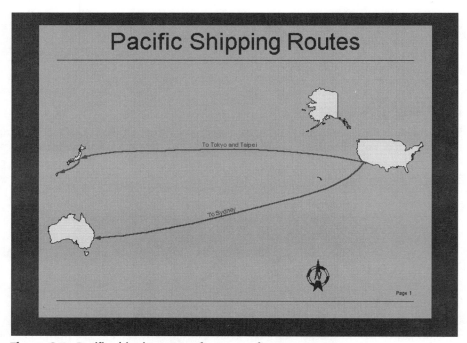

Figure C-3: Pacific shipping routes for your software company

Setting up the page

Begin your project by choosing the Geographic Maps template and then set the page's orientation. Follow these steps:

1. Open the Visio 2000 Standard program.

2. Select File ⇨ New ⇨ Map ⇨ Geographic Maps.

3. Because the Pacific spans quite some distance, you will need to change the orientation of the page. Choose File ⇨ Page Setup to access the Page Setup dialog box.

4. Look for the Paper Orientation section on the Print Setup tab. Select the Landscape radio button. (The Print Setup tab on the Page Setup dialog box should automatically reflect the change in orientation without you having to change the orientation setting there.) Click the OK button on the Page Setup dialog box.

Arranging map shapes on the page

Find the shapes that you need from the Geographic Maps template. Using the following instructions, arrange the shapes so that they are sized and placed appropriately, fitting the page.

1. Click the North and South America stencil title bar in order to view its contents. Drag the United States shape from the stencil onto the drawing page.

2. Click the Asia stencil title bar in order to view its contents. Drag the Australia, Japan, and Taiwan shapes from the stencil onto the drawing page.

3. Select the Australia, Japan, and Taiwan shapes. Simply click the first shape and then hold down the <Shift> key while clicking the other shapes. Right-click and then choose Arrange to Shape from the pop-up menu. Double-click the United States shape and then click the Arrange to Shape dialog box's OK button.

4. Although the distance and shape sizes are now arranged proportionately, some of the shapes probably are not on the page. You can solve this by using the Arrange to Page command. Select all four shapes and then right-click. Select Arrange to Page from the pop-up menu. Click the OK button on the Arrange to Page dialog box.

Rearranging map shapes on the page

You wanted the United States on the right side of the page and Australia, Japan, and Taiwan on the left. However, the Visio program places these shapes in the opposite manner. With a few flipping functions here and there, though, everything will look as you want. Just follow these steps:

1. Select all four shapes and then choose Shape ⇨ Grouping ⇨ Group. All four objects now operate as one unit.

2. Select the group and then choose Shape ⇨ Flip Horizontal. The shapes invert, becoming a mirror image of their former image from step one.

3. Select the group and then choose Shape ⇨ Grouping ⇨ Ungroup.

4. Select the United States shape and then choose Shape ⇨ Flip Horizontal. The shape appears in the correct orientation.

5. To save time, regroup Japan, Australia, and Taiwan. Select the three shapes and then choose Shape ⇨ Grouping ⇨ Group.

6. Select the Japan-Australia-Taiwan group and then choose Shape ⇨ Flip Horizontal. All three countries now appear in the correct orientation; they are on the left of the page and the United States is on the page's right.

Drawing shipping routes

You have the countries on the page but no routes. Follow these steps to run the shipping lines so that Japan and Taiwan are part of one major route while another major route runs to Australia:

1. Click the Freeform Tool button. Draw a line from the Southern California area to Tokyo, Japan. Draw another line from Southern California to Sydney, Australia. Draw one last line from Tokyo, Japan to Taipei, Taiwan. Add smooth curvature to the routes by dragging the freeform line nodes.

2. Select each line and then click the arrow next to the Line Ends button. Choose the arrows that illustrate the San Diego-Tokyo, Tokyo-Taipei, and San Diego-Sydney shipping routes.

3. Customize the thickness of the routes by selecting the lines and then clicking the arrow button next to the Line Weight button. Choose from the options on the button's drop-down menu.

4. Add text identifying each route, by using the Text Tool button or by double-clicking each line and then entering the information. For instance, for the San Diego-Japan-Taiwan route, type "To Tokyo and Taipei."

Adding color to the map

Spice up the map with a little color. Follow these steps in order to paint the ocean blue and also get rid of that drab map-shape color:

1. Select Tools ⇨ Options in order to access the Option dialog box.

2. Look for the Color Settings section on the General tab. To access the Edit Color dialog box, click the color block labeled Page. Select a blue color from the Edit Color dialog box and then click the OK button. Click the OK button on the Options dialog box to finalize your decision.

3. Select the United States, Japan, Australia, and Taiwan shapes and then click the arrow button next to the Fill button. Choose a color that you like. Yellow-colored countries, I've found, work well with the blue ocean.

Adding some finishing touches

You're almost finished. Add a title and perhaps a little clip art in order to improve the map's aesthetic appeal. After all, both the CEO and Chairperson are supposed to be at the presentation. Follow these steps:

1. Click the Text Tool button and then click your cursor near the top of the page. Type in the title: "Pacific Shipping Routes." Highlight the text and then adjust the font size (48 points works well). Stretch the left and right control handles so that the title is centered on one line. Use the horizontal ruler for assistance.

2. If you would like, add a compass shape (either North or Direction) to the drawing from the Landmark Shapes stencil. A Background shape from the Backgrounds stencil would look nice, too.

Designing an Organization Chart with Hyperlinks

Your supervisor at Techno Savvy Systems was so impressed with the business card that you designed in the "Designing a Business Card" section of this appendix that she now wants you to create an organization chart detailing the members in your engineering team. She also wants each member to insert hyperlinks to their business-card files. Therefore, you need to create a chart of your entire team (see Figure C-4), but only insert a hyperlink for yourself. The others will have to do their own — boss's orders!

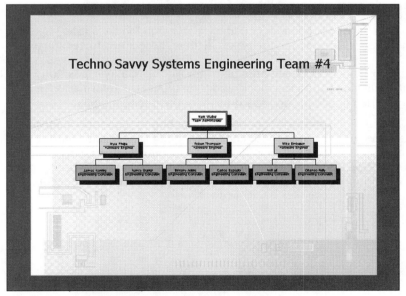

Figure C-4: A Techno Savvy Systems organization chart

Setting up the page

The Organization Chart template is located in the Organization Chart solutions folder. Locate and open the file, using these simple steps:

1. Open the Visio 2000 Standard program if you do not already have it open.

2. Select File ➪ New ➪ Organization Chart ➪ Organization Chart to open the Organization Chart template.

Putting together the chart

Organization-chart shapes require that you place all subordinate positions onto their immediate supervisor. In this case, you'll have three employees under your direct supervision, and each of those three will be directly responsible for two more employees. The following walkthrough guides you through the process:

1. Drop the Manager shape from the Organization Chart Shapes stencil onto the drawing page. Click OK in the dialog box that immediately emerges on the screen.

2. Drop the Three Positions shape on the Manager shape.

3. Drop two Position shapes on each of the previous three shapes.

4. Select all of the shapes and then choose Tools ➪ Center Drawing. The organization chart is now centered upon the page.

Adding names and titles to position blocks

Currently, you have only a bunch of nameless position blocks on the page. Insert names and titles within each of the boxes. Follow these steps to get started:

1. Add your name and "Team Administrator" in the Manager position block by double-clicking within the block, and then typing the information in the text block. When finished, just click outside of the position block.

2. Add more names to the rest of the position blocks. Use titles such as "Hardware Engineer" for the second row of blocks and "Engineering Consultant" for the third row. To fit all of the information neatly within the position blocks, you may have to resize the information. Use the Center Drawing command again if you feel the connectors are not lining up.

Color coding position blocks

Although not necessary, color coding position blocks in an organization chart makes the diagram more colorful and easier to read. For example, choose a base color and make each row of position blocks a lighter or darker shade of that color (as shown in Figure C-4). Remember that shadows help bring out organization-chart shapes. Use them, along with several hues, in order to make the diagram more aesthetically pleasing. Here's how to get started:

1. Click the Fill Color button arrow in order to choose a color and then apply the color to each row of blocks. Use the More Fill Colors button, located on the Fill Color drop-down menu, in order to view additional colors in the Fill dialog box.

2. Use the Fill dialog box in order to add fill and shadows to the blocks. The preview window, located on the dialog box's right, shows how the shapes will look if you click the Apply button.

Placing a background and title on the page

You're just several clicks from creating a wonderful looking organization chart. The shadows and color-coded blocks look nice, but you still need a title and a background shape. These steps instruct you on how to quickly add these two features:

1. Select the Text Tool button. Drag a rectangular-like text block near the top of the page. Type "Techno Savvy Systems Engineering Team #4." A 30-point font size works well here. Pull on the text bock's left and right control handles in order to extend the title across the page. Make sure that the title is centered by checking that the same amount of space is situated to the left and right of the text block

2. Click the Backgrounds stencil's title bar in order to view its contents. Choose a background from the stencil to place on the drawing page. Because Techno Savvy Systems is a technology company, you may want to use the Background High-Tech shape. Drag the background onto the page and then click the OK button in the Make Background dialog box.

Inserting a hyperlink into your position block

Your supervisor wants every position block to link to each employee's business-card file; thus, the company's administration assistant can simply click a specific coworker's block in order to access and print that employee's business card. I bet you're wondering how one can tell if a shape contains a hyperlink. The answer is simple. A globe and chain-link icon (shown in Figure C-5) appears when you place your cursor over shapes linked to other files or to web addresses. Follow these instructions to insert a hyperlink:

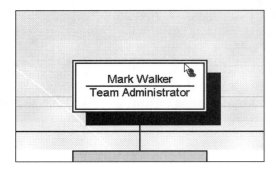

Figure C-5: If a cursor passes over a hyperlinked object, a globe and chain-link icon appears.

1. Select the Manager position block bearing your name.

2. Choose Insert ⇨ Hyperlinks.

3. The Hyperlinks dialog box enables you to insert both URLs and files as hyperlinks. Click the Browse button next to the Address edit box. In this case, select Local File.

4. Select the file that you wish to insert as a hyperlink in the Link to File dialog box. In this case, you're looking for the document that contains the Techno Savvy business cards. Click the Open button once you've found the file.

5. The file's directory is now located in the Address edit box. Click OK to connect the file to your position box.

6. Move your cursor over your position block. A small globe and a chain link appear next to your arrow cursor, indicating that the shape contains a hyperlink. Right-click the shape and on the pop-up menu select the file next to the globe and chain-link icon. This action takes you to your business cards.

Creating an Office Map

Visio 2000 enables users to add the names and owners of office furniture into the Office Layout template. Aware of the program's capabilities, your supervisor wants you to create an office map along with the inventory information about each office PC. She expects the document to be in her e-mail box by 5 o'clock sharp. So, let's get started.

Setting up the page

You can only create office layouts in Visio 2000 Standard with the Office Layout template. Follow these steps in order to access the Office Layout template:

1. Open the Visio 2000 Standard program.

2. Select File ➪ New ➪ Office Layout ➪ Office Layout to open the Office Layout template.

Creating office space

Before adding any furniture, begin your project by laying out the office space. Several room and wall shapes are included in the template. Apply the Room shape and modify it on your drawing page by following these steps:

1. Drop the Room shape from the stencil onto the drawing page.

2. The Room shape is only 100 square feet; however, your public relations office is square shaped and contains 289 square feet. Drag one of the vertical guides and one of the horizontal guides to size the walls. Next, drag one of the Space shape's corner handles and stretch it to the walls. Continue this process until the space totals 289 square feet and the walls touch the space.

3. Select all of the shapes and then choose Tools ➪ Center Drawing.

Adding furnishings

Once the walls and floors are in place, you can haul furniture and PCs into the office. Arranging items in an orderly manner is not difficult with the Distribute Shapes and Align Shapes features. Just follow these steps:

1. Drop four Desks into the room. Arrange them along the top wall. Use Guides if you like.

2. Select the four Desks, clicking from left to right. Choose Tools ➪ Distribute Shapes. Select the first Left/Right distribution button and then click the OK button.

3. Drop a Desk Chair into the room. Use the Rotation Tool to turn the chair so that it's facing the left side of your screen. Right-click the shape and then choose Duplicate. This action makes duplicates of the chair that you've already rotated. Place these chairs on each Desk.

4. Select all four Desk Chairs and then choose Shape ➪ Send Backward in order to place the chairs behind the desks.

5. Select the four Desk Chairs, clicking from left to right. Choose Tools ⇨ Distribute Shapes. Select the first Left/Right distribution button and then click the OK button.

6. Drop a PC shape on each of the Desks.

7. Add fill colors to the PCs, Desks, and Desk Chairs.

8. Select the four Desk Chairs, PCs, and Desks. Choose Tools ⇨ Align Shapes. Select the middle button on the Up/Down alignment section and then click OK.

9. Select the Desk Chairs, PCs, and Desks and then choose Shape ⇨ Grouping ⇨ Group.

10. Right-click the group and then choose Duplicate from the pop-up menu. Drag the duplicated group to the bottom wall (as shown in Figure C-6).

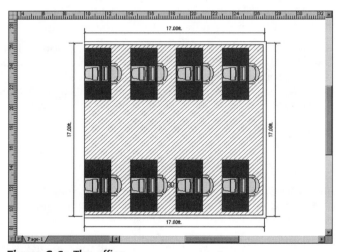

Figure C-6: The office

Inserting shape properties for inventory purposes

Good work on the layout thus far. However, your supervisor not only needs a map of the office but also inventory information about the PCs. This is not too much to ask. In fact, with these instructions, you should be able to beat the 5 o'clock deadline with ease:

1. Select both groups and then choose Shape ⇨ Grouping ⇨ Ungroup.

2. Right-click a computer and then choose Properties from the pop-up menu. Type in an inventory number and list yourself as the owner on the Custom Properties dialog box (see Figure C-7). Click OK. Insert various inventory numbers and owners for each PC.

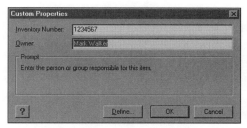

Figure C-7: Viewing a PC's inventory data

3. To view each computer's owner and inventory number, right-click the PC shape and then choose Properties from the pop-up menu. The information that you inserted appears in each PC's Custom Properties dialog box.

4. Add a title to the drawing page if necessary. Save the document and then attach it to an e-mail file. Once you send it to your supervisor, the project is completed.

✦ ✦ ✦

Index

Continued